COVENTRY CITY

A Complete Record
1883-1991

COVENTRY
CITY

A Complete Record 1883-1991

ROD DEAN
WITH DAVID
BRASSINGTON,
JIM BROWN
AND
DON CHALK

BREEDON
BOOKS
SPORT

First published in Great Britain by
The Breedon Books Publishing Company Limited
44 Friar Gate, Derby DE1 1DA
1991

ISBN 0 907969 88 7

Printed and bound in Great Britain by Bath Press, Bath and London.
Jacket printed by The Nuffield Press, Cowley, Oxford.

Contents

The Coventry City Story 8
The Grounds 44
International Matches at Highfield Road 50
The Bury Scandal 54
The Little Blackbirds 57
The FA Cup Disasters 59
The Aston Villa Matches of 1936-1938 62
Coventry City's Managers 66
City Stars A-Z 86
Matches to Remember 145
Coventry City in the Football League 1919-1991 182
City Against Other League Clubs 184
Coventry City Season-by-Season 186
Coventry in Other Competitions 370
Third Division South v Third Division North 374
Coventry City in Europe 375
Overseas Matches 376
Coventry City Reserves 380
FA Youth Cup 381
Abandoned & Void Games 386
Leagues and Games Played 388
Coventry City Testimonial Matches at Highfield Road 389
Coventry City Internationals 391
Coventry City Awards 397
Players Sent Off 1967-1991 398
Coventry's Footballing Cricketers 399
Coventry City Career Records 1908-1915 400
Coventry City Career Records 1919-1991 402
Subscribers 412

Acknowledgements

THIS book has taken shape over the past 12 years, much of the earlier work going into our previous publication *From Singers to Sky Blues* published in 1986 with a reprint in 1989. There has been dramatic progress in the last year or so since we added Jim Brown in our team. Books of this nature are very much a team effort and without the assistance of a large number of people are impossible to complete.

Members of the Association of Football Statisticians have kindly responded to many queries and their assistance is noted, their names too many to list here. A lot of the early biographical entries would have been impossible without the help of Paul and Martin O'Connor, the 'Who's Who specialists'. The staff at the National Newspaper Library, Colindale, the Coventry Record Library and the *Coventry Evening Telegraph* have all been patient with what must seem to them strange and obscure requests. Frank Hopkins, the veteran City fan and statistician, has spent many hours checking our season-by-season grids, filling in a lot of the irritating gaps and loaning many splendid photographs. The doyen of directors from the mid-1930s to late-1950s, W.Erle Shanks, has passed on his reminiscences of the club and its many characters with many hitherto unknown facts. Tony Stanford, the premier Coventry City programme collector, has lent us many of his programmes, books and photographs. Graham Hover and his team at Highfield Road have helped us considerably with post-1968 information. Many other supporters, both young and old, have passed on information and artefacts, some of which have been used in this publication. Our colleagues in the London Supporters' Club have given much support and encouragement during the past year or so and specific thanks are given to Richard Woodfield, Jon Strange, Colin Heys, Mark Georgevic, Geoff Moore, Mark Styles, Sam and Joshua Barton. Some photographs have been supplied by Colorsport of London.

Introduction and Notes On The Text

AS all the official club records from 1883 to 1968 were destroyed in the Main Stand fire of March 1968, it has been doubly difficult to retrace the records of Coventry City FC from those early days. The authors have therefore been involved in painstaking research, using the facilities at the National Newspaper Library at Colindale, the Coventry Record Library and the offices of the *Coventry Evening Telegraph*. It was sometimes difficult to obtain correct goalscorers for the early days, as often it was the view of the local journalist, who on away grounds was not always familiar with the visiting players. Even through to the end of the 1938-9 season, there are many discrepancies concerning goalscorers, attendances and sometimes even line-ups. We believe we have eliminated many of these discrepancies but certainly there may be the occasional error which are a constant thorn in the side of any historian. Pre-war attendances are mainly those reported in the national Press with the exception of official attendances reported in the 'Pink', those obtained from other club statisticians or estimated by local journalists. Post-war attendances are official club attendances given at the end of each season. Where there is a known dispute concerning goalscorers (*eg* own-goals), this is noted at the bottom of the grid concerned.

Rod Dean
June 1991

The Coventry City Story

SINGERS FC was founded in October 1883, by William Stanley at the Aylesford Inn, Hillfields. Prominent in the formation of the new club were Andrew Poole, Harry Hathaway, Frank Moseley, 'Cock' Heath, Shiner Turner, Harry Banks and Joe Collins. George Singer became the first president of the club, although more active interest was manifested by his brother-in-law, J.C.Stringer.

The club's first headquarters were at the White Lion and their pitch was on Dowells Field, off the Binley Road. Between 1883 and 1887 they played about 40 games, although many of these were of a very rudimentary nature. Thanks to the occasional publication of the halfpenny *Athletic Reporter* we have some insight into these early games. The reports were under headings such as 'Club v Shop' or 'Joe Collin's XI v Rotherham's XI' and contained such details as how many were missing and who possessed boots. Anyone who has taken part in Sunday morning parks football will be familiar with the scene.

All that changed in 1887 when J.G.Morgan became secretary and under his guidance the first great transformation of the club began.

A plot of land, on a site approximately beside the present stadium, was acquired and became the Stoke Road ground, a genuine enclosure with a small grandstand and a twopenny admission fee which was collected at the two entrances, one at the White Lion on the Walsgrave Road and the other at the Binley Oak, Paynes Lane.

In 1887, for the first time, a fixture list was arranged in advance of the season and it also marked the club's entry into the Birmingham & District Junior Cup, the very pinnacle of Singers' ambitions at the time.

Judged by modern standards there were still aspects of the club which had a somewhat primitive air. It was not unusual before an away game for the secretary to make a last-minute dash to the home of a committee member who was asked to make up a shortfall in the train fare; at the other end of the line it was often necessary to go in search of coach and horses to convey the players to a pitch which, as in the case of the ground of great rivals, the Unity Gas Works, earned the description a 'quagmire among quagmires'.

Notwithstanding, Singers were developing all the time. The club were able to put together strong sides and retain their amateur status because the Singers cycle works gave priority to keeping its footballers in employment. Even at this stage its more astute directors recognized the value of a successful football club, which by the end of the decade was able to attract crowds of 4,000 for clashes with their rivals from Rudge Whitworth.

By 1890 the 'team of teams', the great 'Little Blackbirds', was taking shape. They were already a formidable outfit in Midlands junior football and with the arrival of a new centre-forward, the sublime Frank Mobley, the final part of the jigsaw was in place.

In April 1891, Singers beat Willenhall Pickwicks 1-0 in the Birmingham Cup Final at Villa's Perry Barr ground and the scenes which accompanied their victory

Singers FC in 1885-6. Back row (left to right): H.Hathaway (secretary), Andrew Poole, H.Barnacle, W.Hardy, Joe Collins, Mr Smith. Middle row: Dowell, 'Cock' Heath. Front row: Harry Banks, George Bowers, J.Grady, Frank Moseley, 'Shiner' Turner.

— and those celebrations which took place in Coventry that evening — convinced any remaining doubters that 'King Football' had come to stay.

The following year Singers achieved their own treble, retaining the Birmingham Cup by beating Willenhall, beating Bloxwich Strollers in the Walsall Cup and winning the Wednesday Cup on protest after a drawn game with Wednesbury Old Athletic.

The period from 1887 to 1892 was one of unparalleled growth and success still talked about 15 years later as the town's 'golden age'; subsequent players must have groaned at hearing unfavourable comparisons with Mobley, Banks and Dorrell.

For a variety of reasons, though, it was not to be a step up to bigger and better things, for the successes of this period were not built upon and the club slipped into the doldrums. Indeed, 15 years would pass before the city again experienced such excitement.

In August 1892 four first-team players left Singers: Edwards and Mobley went to Small Heath, Sheldon to West Brom, Dorrell to Leicester Fosse. All were destined to play League football and Mobley was to enjoy a career in the First Division.

In 1893 it was decided to go professional, which in reality simply meant a few players received expenses and appearance money. But Singers still maintained the 'shop club system' which effectively prevented anyone not employed at the cycle works from representing the football club.

In 1894, Singers joined the Birmingham League. The introduction of league football

The Binley Oak in Paynes Lane. Pictured around 1913, the pub advertises that it is 'the late headquarters of Coventry City Football Club'.

with games against the strong reserve sides of Aston Villa, Wolves, West Brom and Small Heath was an important step, but Singers, haphazardly managed by a committee of well-meaning amateurs and unable to hang on to their best players, were destined to struggle. To compound their problems they received little support with attendances of 1,500 regarded as quite normal.

There was an inability to come to terms with their own potential and the demands of an ever-growing urban population who wanted their city to have a truly representative football team, not just a works side to follow.

The next major step came in May 1898 when, after five years of interminable debate, it was finally agreed to change the club's name to Coventry City. However, the change did not reap immediate rewards and it was six games before the 'City' managed a win.

An equally important move took place a year later when, in 1899, building development necessitated a move from Stoke Road to the adjoining land still with us at Highfield Road.

The first season at their new home was truly dismal. Coventry City finished last and suffered a number of heavy defeats. There were also a series of acrimonious disputes between players, former players and the committee over 'unfulfilled contracts'. Finances hit rock-bottom and for the first time there was a serious threat of the club closing down.

They struggled on but the following season of 1900-01 was even worse and included their heaviest defeat — 14-0 to Aston Villa Reserves and a record 102 goals conceded. The 1901-02 campaign ended with City again at the bottom of the Birmingham League and having to make another application for re-election. They also suffered their heaviest defeat in the FA Cup — 11-2 against Berwick Rangers, (later Worcester City).

For all the struggles, though, this period still produced its crop of crowd favourites and loyal stalwarts. At the top of this list was goalkeeper Nat Robinson, who made his debut in 1895. In 1897, a formidable trio of half-backs — Whitehouse, Roberts and Lomas — was brought together. The veteran Charlie Roberts was regarded as the 'uncle' of the side; Charlie Lomas, was a robust, 'roughhouse' and a thorn in the side of any winger; and Joe Whitehouse, was to captain the side for six seasons and become the first Coventry player to be given a testimonial after ten years' service. For five years from 1897, the chief supplier of goals was Harry Walker.

In 1902-03, City enjoyed one of their better seasons; they finished seventh and scored 75 goals, 21 of them coming from Johnny Porter. He was partnered on the left wing by one of the most remarkable players of the era — Ben Craythorne, who was destined to join Notts County in the First Division and represent the Football League.

In the close season of 1905 the club once again stirred itself and made changes of organization when the old board of directors was taken over by a 'syndicate' headed by Fred Lee and with former player Joe Beaman appointed as full-time coach.

There were also some notable additions to the team: Harry Whitehouse was the goalkeeper and captain, Fred Edwards and Bert Gilbert were two local players who came into the defence, and James McIntyre (who later managed the club), an inside-left from Notts County. McIntyre was a great favourite, scoring 23 goals in an exciting season with still better things to come in 1906.

McIntyre moved on after a season but new quality men arrived: John Tooth from Villa, Will Layton from Wolves and Albert Lewis, a sensational 19-year-old from West Brom.

On 24 July 1907, City registered as a limited liability company, announcing capital of £2,000 divided into five-shilling shares. The first board of directors was Fred Lee (secretary), Harry Whitehouse (assistant secretary), Sam Rowllason (treasurer), Thomas Owen (chairman), A.G.Sage, John Tipping, J.Sydney Clarke and T.Stone.

Whatever re-organization took place off the field, without team success it would all amount to nothing, but this time the signs were unmistakable that, at last, a team was emerging worthy of the burgeoning town of Coventry. At the heart of the side was Albert Lewis, regarded by the *Telegraph* as the finest player of the Birmingham League era. Around him City had a team able to challenge for the championship.

In 1907, local man Fred Chaplin joined the club along with two goalscorers, 'Tubby' Warren from Nuneaton and teenager Billy Smith from West Brom. Thus, City embarked on their best-ever season so far. They finished fourth and scored 97 goals, including a record 11-2 win over West Brom Reserves. Billy Smith scored over 40 goals in all competitions.

Of even more significance was City's FA Cup run which brought success in that competition for the first time. The last of six qualifying ties paired them with the famous amateurs Bishop Auckland and a record attendance of nearly 8,000 saw City win 7-1.

A month later, City lost 4-2 to Crystal Palace, but the team's performance and the behaviour of their 10,000 supporters made a lasting impression on Palace officials, who later gave invaluable support to Coventry City's next move — an application to join the Southern League.

In 1908, the Football League was regarded as being somewhat conservative with

Coventry City in 1907-08. Back row (left to right): Bullivant (trainer), Juggins, Jones, Gilbert, Whitehouse, Kifford, Chaplin, Parkes. Front row: Layton, Smith, Warren, Lewis, Tooth.

regard to considering new applicants, whilst the Southern League had slightly higher average attendances than the Second Division. It was also believed that the Southern League would eventually merge with the Football League.

At the Southern League's annual meeting on 27 May 1908, the voting was announced: Exeter City 33 votes; Leyton FC 32; New Brompton (later Gillingham) 32; Southend United 26; Coventry City 25. Polling only ten votes, Croydon Common failed to gain election.

As was the fashion in those days, the Birmingham League were indignant and removed Coventry City's name from their list of members, leaving the club without a home for their reserve side. During the close season of 1908, City suffered two serious set-backs when they lost stars Billy Smith (who returned in 1909) and Albert Lewis. Smith headed for Small Heath whilst Lewis was lured to Northampton Town by the great Herbert Chapman.

Without doubt, City's election to the Southern League was one of the most important steps in the club's history, not least because it provided a better class of football. The Southern League, which had been formed in 1894, was recognized as the strongest competition outside the Football League and Southern League clubs regularly fought their way to the later stages of the FA Cup. Indeed, Tottenham Hotspur, then a Southern League club, won the Cup in 1901. An important factor was that the transfer laws, as applied to League clubs, were not in operation in the Southern League and many former Football League players found their way to Southern League clubs.

However, before the season started, City had signed only two prominent Football League players, both wingers: Charlie Tickle from Birmingham, who had played in an inter-League match the previous season; and Harry Buckle, an Irish international who had played for Sunderland. City subsequently signed another two ex-League players, Dodd and Dougherty, but they relied heavily upon the Birmingham League side of 1907-08. The main reason for this sad state of affairs was that City were not elected to the Southern League until late May and, by that time, the experienced players they desperately needed had signed for other clubs.

Improvements to the ground were carried out in the close season and the board of directors was strengthened with the election of three new members including Charles Charsley, chief constable of Coventry and a former amateur international goalkeeper, who had successfully presented City's case for election to the Southern League the previous May. A full-time trainer, Ted Kinnear, was appointed in June.

Unfortunately, City were unable to find a satisfactory league for their newly-formed reserve side, failing to gain election to the Birmingham League and eventually settling for the United League, which provided only a dozen fixtures.

The season started with a home game against Crystal Palce, who had knocked Coventry out of the FA Cup the previous season but had been instrumental in gaining City's election to the Southern League. The crowd, some 5,000, was well up on Birmingham League levels but despite having most of the play, City could only manage a 1-1 draw.

They went on to lose their next four matches and by the end of September were bottom of the League. Coventry supporters rapidly became disenchanted, players were jeered at home matches and letters published regularly in the *Midland Daily Telegraph* criticizing team selection.

The directors, sensitive to criticism, made four changes for the home game against Plymouth and, although it did not produce a win, there was a considerable improvement in City's form. The following week City gained their first victory at Bristol Rovers.

Following their Cup exploits the previous season, City were exempt until the final qualifying round of the FA Cup, when they were drawn at home against Lancashire Combination side, Carlisle. Despite special training which included long walks and Turkish baths, City could only draw 1-1 and were eliminated after a second replay.

Although their League form had improved in October and November, another bad run of results in December saw City placed firmly at the bottom of the table by the end of 1908. Their form for the remainder of the season was decidedly erratic and they eventually finished one place off the bottom. Fortunately the Southern League was increased to 22 clubs, so City avoided the ignominy of relegation in their first season.

Clearly the team needed strengthening and immediately the season ended a number of signings were made, including arguably the two outstanding players of the club's Southern League era, R.O.(Bob) Evans, the Welsh international goalkeeper, and the hard-tackling former West Brom half-back, Eli Bradley. The board of directors was also strengthened with the election of David Cooke, who was to play a prominent part in City's affairs in future years.

Despite this transfer activity, City made an indifferent start to the 1909-10 season, although home attendances improved by nearly 50 per cent. The main problem was the failure to turn chances into goals but this was to change with the signing of the future England cricketer Elias (Patsy) Hendren, who made an immediate impact with two goals on his debut. City went on to win seven out of the next eight matches and by the end of the year were well placed to make a bid for the championship.

Meanwhile, City were embarking on their best Cup run so far, indeed better than any for the next 60 years. It started quietly with comfortable wins against Wrexham and Kettering, but when Coventry beat First Division Preston in the first round, Cup fever really began to grip the city. It was not until the quarter-finals that City finally succumbed, to mighty Everton, having beaten Nottingham Forest, another First Division side, in the previous round.

Distracted by the Cup run, City's form in the New Year was fairly mediocre and once they had been knocked out of the Cup, attendances slumped. Although there was an improvement towards the end of the season, they finished a disappointing seventh.

A 5-0 defeat at Queen's Park Rangers in the opening game of the 1910-11 season showed that there were defensive deficiencies, although the attack, with Parkes and Buckle on the wings, Tickle, who had switched to inside-right, and Smith at centre-forward, scored freely.

By Christmas, City were comfortably placed in the middle of the table but clearly any glory that season could only come through another Cup run.

After their success in the previous season, City were exempted from the preliminary rounds and were drawn away to First Division Sheffield Wednesday. Some 2,000 travelling supporters were rewarded wth a magnificent 2-1 victory in a hard-fought game. The star of the match was Billy Smith, who scored the winner in the second half.

City beat Brighton in the next round, after a replay, but then succumbed 5-1 to Second Division Burnley in a dull game. Coventry battled hard in the wind and the rain on a sloping pitch affected by mining subsidence, but their forwards never really got going.

The close season saw a big exodus of players, including old favourites Buckle and Tickle, and Hendren, who had not lived up to his early promise. But the defence was strengthened considerably with the signings of Thomson and Yates from Portsmouth. There were also new forwards Turnbull, Jones, Holmes and Brown, all of whom were to become first-team regulars. Thus, the team had been completely remodelled with younger and — belying the club's nickname of the Bantams — heavier players.

The new players settled in quickly, with Brown and Jones scoring freely, and by Christmas the side was lying seventh in the table. More consistent form led to an improvement in attendances, which now averaged 7,500. Their biggest win in the Southern League First Division came on 27 December, when Brentford were beaten 9-0. The game was a personal triumph for Smith, who scored five goals.

City started their Cup campaign with a 2-0 win at Southampton, but came down to earth in the next round when they lost 5-1 to Manchester United. The Manchester club were too clever for City, scoring twice in the first five minutes, and by common consent gave one of the best displays of football ever seen at Highfield Road. The disappointment of Cup defeat did not affect City's League form, however, and they eventually finished sixth, which was to be their highest final position in the Southern League.

The 1912-13 season was to be something of an anticlimax. Most of the previous season's players had re-signed, the notable exception being Fred Jones, who accepted a tempting offer from his old club, Notts County. But in October, Eli Bradley asked to be placed on the transfer list and subsequently signed for Hearts. His drive and the goalscoring ability of Jones were sorely missed.

There was not even the consolation of a good Cup run as City fell again to Manchester United, this time at the first hurdle. City had played well, particularly their defence, to draw 1-1 at Old Trafford, but before a record 20,000 crowd they lost the replay 2-1. The Bantams were 1-0 down at half-time but they dominated the second half and Harry Parkes equalized with six minutes left, only for United to score the winner three minutes later.

There was considerable dissatisfaction in Coventry over the team's mediocre performances. Certainly, attendances had declined — only 3,000 watched the last match of the 1912-13 season — and it was announced that due to the poor financial state of the club, the professional staff for the following season would be reduced from 24 to 18.

Fred Jones re-signed and City also acquired George Davison, a prolific goalscorer

Coventry City, 1912-13. Back row (left to right): J.Smith, S.Jackson, A.Feebury, W.Kimberley. Third row: T.Arnold (trainer), Groundsman, F.Collingbourne (director), M.McDougal, G.Dexter, A.Marr, L.Styles, R.Barnacle, R.Wakinshaw, W.M.Turrell (director), E.Juggins (trainer). Seated: H.Parkes, F.Turnbull, J.Thompson, W.Yates, D.Cooke (chairman), E.Bradley, R.Wallace (secretary), R.Evans, E.Boston, H.Poole, G.Harris. On ground: H.Gretton, J.Parton, W.Jacques, H.Welch, I.Brown, A.Holmes.

with Blyth Spartans. But, ominously, two of City's most experienced players, Thomson and Evans, left the club. Although City won the first two games of the new season, they then went ten games without a win and by the end of 1913 were in 18th position with a meagre 22 goals scored and 45 conceded.

There was to be no revival in the New Year. Indeed, City did not win another game until 10 April. Although they gained eight points from their last five matches, it was not enough to save them from finishing bottom and being relegated to the Second Division of the Southern League.

Surprisingly, attendances had held up reasonably well, averaging about 7,000, but the income from reserve-team matches had dropped alarmingly. Often there were fewer than 1,000 spectators to see Birmingham League games, compared to 3,000 the previous season when the team finished second.

There was a big exodus of players in the close season, including the trainer Eleander Juggins, who severed a long association with the club when he moved to Southampton, and Jones and Davison.

Manager-secretary Frank Scott-Walford scoured the country for new players and acquired almost a completely new team. The most notable capture was the Irish international Joe Enright, although he never lived up to his reputation in City's colours.

The discrepancies in the standards of the teams in the Second Division of the Southern League were soon apparent. Although they lost their first two games, they ran up big scores against Mardy, Ebbw Vale and Abertillery and scored ten goals against Newport County, Jack Allan, City's new centre-forward from Rochdale, scoring a hat-trick, one of the four he was to score that season.

But the goal bonanza did not attract bigger attendances and gates were some 2,500 down on the previous season. Attendances for away games, many of which were played in Wales, were even worse. In January, the club announced that good attendances for reserve-team matches was the only hope for survival, but the takings for the game against Shrewsbury were only £30, which only just covered the wages bill.

As the season progressed, City had to rely increasingly on grants from the Southern League and, sometimes, even on money from Scott-Walford's own pocket, to complete first-team fixtures; and when both teams were playing, City had great difficulty in fielding a reserve side. On two occasions the reserve team played with only ten men.

The players did all they could to help by accepting cuts in wages on two occasions, but the final indignity came in March 1915, when the club was summonsed for non-payment of rates. The season finished with a 5-2 win against Pontypridd, in front of 1,000 spectators, to put City in fifth place.

In a desperate gamble to improve its sagging fortunes, the club applied for membership of the Central League but this, and a subsequent application to the Second Division of the Football League, were unsuccessful.

The annual report for 1914-15 showed a loss of £1,500; nearly £1,000 was owed to David Cooke and another £100 to Frank Scott-Walford. As the club was unable to fulfil its obligations to the latter, he was released to take up a Government appointment.

Coventry City now had no officials, no money and very few players. There had been much criticism that professional football continued to be played after the outbreak of World War One, and in view of City's parlous financial state it was perhaps fortunate that in the summer of 1915 it was decided to abandon both the FA Cup and Southern League competitions and to cancel professional players' contracts.

There was no regular football played at Highfield Road between 1915 and 1918, although some charity matches were staged at the ground. Although no income was forthcoming, there were still such heavy items of expenditure as rent, rates, interest on mortgage and bank charges. Heavy financial losses of £500 in 1916 and £564 in 1917 were recorded.

It would have been an easy matter to have closed the club down altogether, but this would have been a serious set-back to football in Coventry and left little chance of re-establishing the club. However, not for the first time David Cooke came to the rescue in 1917, paying off all City's debts, and happily the club survived.

With the appointment of William Clayton, City now had paid officials again. Clayton, who had been associated with Birmingham, was appointed manager, albeit on a part-time basis, and Harry Harbourne was now the secretary.

Coventry's objective was League football and they started playing friendly matches on a regular basis in 1918, beating such distinguished sides as Aston Villa, Leicester Fosse and Birmingham. These results stood City in good stead for their next venture, entry to the Midland Section of the Football League.

After months of hard work and careful negotiation it was announced in August 1918 that City had been elected to the competition. It was a turning point in the club's fortunes, as they were in effect on trial for a place in the Football League when the war ended.

Coventry were soon at home amongst some of the country's élite teams and the prospect of seeing such prominent sides as the two Sheffield clubs, Bradford City and Nottingham Forest brought crowds of 10,000 to Highfield Road to watch Midland Section games. A number of former City players had signed for the new season, including Jack Allan, Harry Dobson, Sid Blake and Tommy Lowes.

The team was supplemented by guest players, which was allowed under wartime rules. Many professional footballers were engaged in munitions work in Coventry and so it was that famous players such as 'Peerless' Jesse Pennington, West Brom's England international, and George Chaplin, the Scottish international, turned out on occasions for City.

Although City's form was not consistent enough to suggest they were going to win the Midland Section, the club felt sufficiently confident in January 1919 to

The first Football League goal ever to be scored at Highfield Road, netted by Tottenham's Bert Bliss in August 1919. Cantrell (Spurs) and Lindon and Roberts (Coventry) are also seen.

resign from the Southern League and devote all its energies to seeking election to the Football League.

The campaign to gain entry culminated in March 1919 with an appeal to all League clubs. The substance of the appeal was that Coventry City had a 'fine, well-equipped' ground holding 24,000 spectators; attendances were good; the team was a big draw at away grounds; the financial position of the club was sound; Coventry had good railway facilities and the population had doubled in the last 20 years to 200,000.

All the hard work was not in vain and the late edition of the *Midland Daily Telegraph* of 10 March reported that City had been successful in their application with 25 votes, along with West Ham United (32 votes), Rotherham County (29), South Shields (28) and Burslem Port Vale (27). The *Telegraph* also reported that 'in consequence of the important issues at stake', David Cooke had resumed the chairmanship.

City attained a healthy mid-table position in the Midland Section and once the season was over the club was able to concentrate on preparations for League football. The first priority was to gain the support of the Coventry people and in early May, the mayor of the city presided over a large and enthusiastic meeting of citizens held at St Mary's Hall. Local employers were asked to assist the club financially and this met with an immediate response when Mr Harry Smith of Rovers agreed to pay the rent for Highfield Road for the next five years.

It was recognized that all the effort put in would come to nought unless sufficient money was spent on players. Strenuous efforts were made to build a strong side and amongst the first signings were Albert Lindon, the former Birmingham goalkeeper, and George Chaplin, both of whom had played regularly in the Midland Section side. Later, City signed Fred Halley from Sheffield United but perhaps the best capture of all was Alec Mercer, a goalscoring inside-forward from Bury.

Improvements were made to the ground, increasing the capacity to 40,000. The club seemed well prepared for the big day when League football at last came to Coventry. Certainly, nobody could have envisaged that City were about to enter the stormiest period in their 40-year history.

The period from 1919 to 1931 was one of protracted difficulty for Coventry City. Indeed, the club ran into trouble immediately and remained there more or less until 1928, when the gloom began to clear under the management of James McIntyre.

The first season of League football was an epic in its own bizarre fashion. City lost the opening game 5-0 to Spurs and it was ten games before they took a point;

Coventry City, 1921-2. Back row (left to right): J.Mackay, G.Chaplin, S.Blake, J.Best, J.Lawrence, C.Smith, G.Cross. Middle row: J.Dougall, A.McCaig, S.Stevens, R.Lindley, W.Morgan. Front row: B.Robinson, B.Millard, G.Hadley.

it took 20 games before they recorded their first victory, over Stoke on Christmas Day. By then manager William Clayton had resigned, Harry Pollitt taking over from November.

Transfer activity during this season, whilst never lacking an element of desperation, brought a degree of success. Particularly noteworthy were the signings of Ted Hannay, Jimmy Dougall, Alec Mercer and Dick Parker.

After looking doomed for at least half the season, City staged what became a traditional New Year recovery and avoided having to apply for re-election by winning their last game against Bury. The events of this game are covered in detail elsewhere, for this was the occasion of the 'Bury Affair' and the scandal obtaining to it cast a shadow over City throughout the 1920s.

Literally by hook or by crook, City had managed to survive in 1920, but they had to spend a massive £7,000 in transfer dealings.

In the close season of 1920, the former Aston Villa stalwart Albert Evans took over as manager and under him there was a semblance of continuity and also the introduction of some excellent players: goalkeeper Jerry Best; elegant centre-forward Sam Stevens, the first City player to score 20 League goals in a season; 'Mollie' Morgan; and, briefly, Austin Fenwick. There was also support on a scale previously unknown with attendances sustained at around 17,500 for City's first three seasons

Coventry City, 1923-4. Back row (left to right): Finlay, Allon, Jones, Best, Foster, Richmond, H.Lake (assistant trainer), Dougall. Front row: Randle, MacLachlan, Shea, Winship, Herbert, Wood, Storey, Rowley.

in the Football League. But their position did not improve and in 1921 City again avoided relegation (this time to the newly-formed Third Division) thanks to a draw in their last game; in 1922 they escaped again, by a margin of only one point.

From 1923 to 1925, City played in green and red shirts, Coventry's civic colours, which also sported an outsize coat of arms. But a change of colours did not bring the desired change of fortune.

In their first five seasons of League football, City had finished 20th, 21st, 20th, 18th and 19th. Thus, something had to give and in 1925 the club finished in bottom place and were relegated to the Third Division North. Not surprisingly, they abandoned their green and red and reverted to the good old blue and white. In the close season of 1925, James Kerr was appointed manager, Evans having been sacked in November 1924.

Before moving on to City's Third Division days, a number of players warrant an honourable mention from the era. From 1923, Frank 'Cute' Herbert was a consistent scorer — indeed, the most prolific of the decade. Two more local products were full-backs Jackie Randle and Teddy Winship. Then there was Danny Shea, a well-known, former England international from Fulham, Tom Jones, a fine centre-half from Crystal Palace, and Albert Pynegar, another high scorer from Leicester.

After what they'd been through in the previous six seasons, it seemed barely

Coventry City in 1926. Back row (left to right): Turner, Pritchett, Poole, H.Miller (trainer), Maskill, MacLachlan, Sharpe. Middle row: J.Nelson (trainer), Bellas, Brown, Campling, Best, Rowley, Findlay, McIlvanney. Front row: Randle, Watson, Paterson, Walker, Herbert, Breslin, Ball. On ground: Parkin, Jones, McGregor.

credible that City were about to hit a new low, but the three seasons from 1925 to 1928 probably represent the nadir of Coventry City's history.

James Kerr set about his task by recruiting practically an entirely new playing staff. However, with attendances declining, the 1925-6 season was disastrous, both from a playing and a financial point of view. High amongst the disasters was the 1-0 FA Cup defeat by tiny Midland Leaguers Worksop Town; and towards the end of the season, the Highfield Road attendance dropped below 1,000 for the only time since City entered the League.

In 1926, because Stoke City and Stockport County were relegated from Division Two, Coventry City were able to switch to the Third Division South, a geographical quirk which, 41 years later, enabled them to become the only club to take part in all six divisions of the Football League.

The switch to the Southern section did little to improve results, however. After finishing 16th and 15th, City dropped to 20th in 1928, avoiding an application for re-election by only one point, but by this time James Kerr had been sacked.

In the close season of 1928, former player James McIntyre became manager and at last it was possible to say the 'storm clouds' were clearing over Highfield Road.

Kerr had been sacked in February and for the remainder of that season, team affairs had been conducted by club director, Albert Saunders. It proved, in retrospect, to be an important few months, for Saunders introduced two young players, Ernie Toseland and Peter Ramage, two of the best of the decade, and in March the

Coventry City, 1928-9. Back row (left to right): Toseland, Bowen, Dinsdale, Allen, Newton, Plunkett, Herbert, Henderson. Middle row: Kimpton (trainer), Kirton, Higham, Bell, J.McIntyre (manager), Crown, Maskill, Waters. Front row: Johnstone, Raynor, Starsmore, W.Brandish (chairman), Barnes, Widdowson, Townsend.

board bought experienced defenders Norman Dinsdale and Alf Widdowson from Notts County.

McIntyre added his own men, Laurie Crown, an elegant defender, Frank 'Shadow' Allen, a spectacular goalkeeper, Billy Lake, Jimmy Loughlin, from West Ham, and the former England forward Billy Kirton from Aston Villa, who joined City for a record £1,700.

The new combination quickly warmed to their task, the crowds flocked back and the *Telegraph* was moved to proclaim them 'the best eleven Bantams since the war'.

In 1928, City finished 11th and the following season made a serious tilt at the title, beating League leaders Plymouth on Christmas Day before a record attendance 26,500. That record was broken a month later when they played Sunderland in the FA Cup in front of 31,673 spectators.

At long last the bitters of the 'Stormy Period' were being put to rest, the endless relegation battles had become a thing of the past. But whilst the team were getting it right on the park, there was still a struggle going on at board level. In 1928 Walter Brandish became chairman and he had a long-running battle with W.Carpenter for control of the club. McIntrye, who had a reputation for intolerance towards meddlesome directors, was also at loggerheads. And still hovering over everyone was the colossal debt accumulated over the decade, now standing at over £10,000.

There was a slight decline in form in 1930-31, probably the result of off-field

Jimmy Loughlin scores against Fulham at Highfield Road in January 1929.

Clarrie Bourton scores one of his two goals against Exeter City in September 1931.

Coventry City, 1931-2. Back row (left to right): Bull, Tilford, Johnson, Hackett, Bass, Boileau, J.Bennett (assistant trainer), Corbett, Baker, Underwood. Second row: Lauderdale, O'Brien, Lake, Sheppard, Allen, Simpson, Bowden, Heinemann, Bourton, Watson, Plummer. Front row: J.Collingham (secretary), Slade (director), Young (director), Stringer (director), Brandish (chairman), Jones (vice chairman), Oliver (director), H.Storer (manager), W.Kimpton (trainer). On ground: Robinson, White, Lee, Locke. The trophy is the Mayor of Coventry's Hospital Cup.

dramas. On 13 February, a majority on the board voted for the resignation of McIntyre. On 8 April, Harry Storer was appointed manager. Brandish was now in control of the board and Storer would soon take command of the team. The two dominant figures of the pre-war period had come together and for City fans a new era was about to dawn.

The 1930s were the most successful years for Coventry City until the Sky Blue era. Against the backdrop of a prosperous and expanding city — Coventry remained relatively untouched by the economic depression of the 1930s — the football club finally put the frustrations of the previous decade behind them.

Storer appointed his old colleague Dick Bayliss as chief scout but he acted as the manager's assistant in all but name and it was Bayliss who discovered many of the players who would become household names over the next 20 years.

The master-stroke was the signing of Clarrie Bourton and Jock Lauderdale from Blackburn and Blackpool respectively, for a combined fee of £1,000. And by the end of the 1931-2 season this famous Coventry double act had become the idols of the terraces.

Bourton was the Football League's top scorer with a remarkable 49 goals and the nickname 'the Old Five' was revived as City crashed home 108 goals.

Later in the season, George Mason and Harry Boileau joined the club as juniors and although promotion was never really on, better things were certainly just around the corner.

Coventry City, 1933-4. Back row (left to right): Davison, Morgan, Brown, W.Kimpton (trainer), Boileau, Pearson, Mason. Middle row: Bacon, Blytheway, Wilmot, H.Storer (manager), Bisby, Baker, Lax. Front row: White, Lauderdale, Bourton, Lake, Richards.

By 1933-4, City's great team was taking shape and the first real promotion thrust was mounted. Over 100 goals were scored for the third successive season, the first time this had been achieved in the Football League, and with average attendances back up to 15,000, Storer was able to strengthen the squad with the signing of Welsh international Leslie Jones from Cardiff City.

After going close to promotion in 1933-4 and 1934-5, the side was further strengthened with the addition of George McNestry, Arthur Fitton and, during the season, Jack Astley. All were quality players and with Bill Morgan, George Mason and Billy Frith now established, City were able to see off the challenge of Reading and Luton Town. They clinched promotion amidst great excitement, beating Torquay United on the final day of the season.

The overdraft, although gradually being reduced, still meant that Harry Storer had to operate on a tight budget and during the promotion season the *Telegraph* had loaned the club £3,000 interest free, most of which had been spent on Jack Astley and Tommy Crawley from Preston North End.

Interest in the football club had never been more intense than in the close season of 1936 and with attendances confidently expected to be higher than ever, it was decided to build a new main stand to replace the crumbling 38-year-old structure on the King Richard Street side of the ground. An appeal was launched to raise

Bourton's winning goal against Torquay United in May 1936, which clinched the Third Division South championship.

Coventry City, 1936-7. Back row (left to right): Mason, McCaughey, Pearson, Archer, R.Hill (trainer), Brown, Morgan, Smith, Astley. Middle row: Boileau, Lager, Lauderdale, H.Storer (manager), Jones, Frith, McNestry. On ground: McDonald, Bourton, Liddle, Fitton.

the £14,000 required and by August it was ready to house the hundreds of new season-ticket holders thirsting for a taste of Second Division football.

A further significant step was taken in October when it was announced that the club had purchased the freehold of Highfield Road from the Mercers Company, by way of a £20,000 loan from Sir John Siddeley, repayable by 1968.

A new team was also taking shape with the signings of Jack Archer, Billy

Coventry City, 1937-8. Back row (left to right): Lager, McPhee, Smith, Morgan, Metcalf, Crawley, Mason. Middle row: R.Hill (trainer), Frith, Brown, Jones, McDonald, Fitton, H.Storer (manager). On ground: Archer, Bourton, Roberts, Astley.

McDonald and Jackie Brown. By the end of November, promotion seemed a real possibility as crowds pushed towards the 30,000 mark with the team nicely poised in third place.

But City in the Second Division were a different type of team with the emphasis much more on a strong defence. The glory days of the 'Old Five' were now over.

A successful FA Cup run followed in 1937, with a record Highfield Road crowd of 44,492 for the fifth-round tie against West Brom, but the League challenge ran out of steam. The club still finished a creditable eighth and the general feeling was that the foundations had been laid and that Coventry were heading for the First Division.

There is little doubt that City should have won promotion in 1937-8 and it was a tragedy that they never made it. Unbeaten for the first 15 games of the season, never out of the top four, with crowds at their highest, the team was a fearsome defensive prospect with the giant Walter Metcalf adding further resiliance.

But the attack never really got going as an ageing Clarrie Bourton slipped out of the limelight after scoring a record 161 League goals, moving to Plymouth for a record fee. His replacement, Magnus McPhee, never solved the problem but the real controversy centred on the exchange deal taking Leslie Jones to Arsenal and bringing ball-playing Scot, Bobby Davidson, to Highfield Road. It was a bold move by Storer, who pinned great hopes on Davidson, but whilst Jones assisted Arsenal to the First Division title, Davidson performed fitfully for City. Another big signing had been George Taylor from Bolton Wanderers for £2,750.

As the season moved into the final stages, the club looked poised for promotion but injuries to Davidson and McDonald should have led Storer to the transfer market. Alas, the anticipated signings did not come and for the first time — but certainly not the last — the suspicion arose that City did not really want promotion.

They finished fourth, missing a place in Division One by one point. It was a bitter pill for supporters and players alike, many of whom thought it a temporary delay to City's elevation.

Although they again finished fourth in 1939, it was a fitful season and supporters deserted the club with attendances down by an average of 6,000 per match; by the end of the season they had slumped to 13,000.

Record signing George Ashall, a £3,500 buy from Wolves, had not been a success and it was likely that the best chance of promotion had gone.

It had been a decade of great achievement which had transformed Coventry City's financial position, but whether it would have been 'third time lucky' was unlikely and, anyway, it all became academic when, three games into the 1939-40 season, the Football League was suspended after the declaration of another world war.

With the uncertainty of the international situation there was very little activity in the close season of 1939. Most clubs adopted 'a wait and see' policy and City's approach was no different in those troubled times. Transfer activity was restricted to the acquisition of George Lowrie, from Preston, for a fee of £1,750, and Billy McDonald moved to Plymouth, albeit against his will, for a fee of £800, joining his old teammate Jack Archer. With the outbreak of war the season was aborted and on 6 September, all contracts were cancelled and the players paid off. Following a relatively short interlude, friendly matches began and soon afterwards regional leagues got underway. As early as 1938-9, quite a few of the Coventry team had joined the Territorial Army or other National Service organizations, and those that had not been involved found work in the city's wartime factories. The Football League sanctioned payouts of £1.50 per match. This was eventually increased to £2 in 1943-4 and up to £4 by 1945-6.

By the time the club's annual meeting was held in January 1940, the bank balance had shrunk to less than £1,000 and Harry Storer had taken a 50 per cent salary cut. The club struggled on into the 1940-41 season and it was still possible to see the fine team from the late 1930s in action during the autumn of that year. However, the season came to an abrupt halt after heavy bombing on the evening of 14 November 1940, when Highfield Road was severely damaged. All football activity there had to cease. By August 1942 the ground had been patched up sufficiently to allow football to get underway again and City rejoined the Midland Regional League. They played out the rest of the war years in a fairly unspectacular fashion with teams made up of guests, local amateurs and pre-war professionals, when available. Attendances were generally in the range of 5,000 to 10,000 and the club was able to keep its head above water.

The war saw the retirement of Morgan, Astley, Lake, Taylor and Armeson but, thankfully, no lives were lost with the exception of former player Arthur Bacon, who was killed during an air raid on Derby.

As hostilities drew to a close, Storer moved on to Birmingham City, to be replaced by his trusted assistant Dick Bayliss, and, with some of the players returning from the Forces, a near normal season got underway in August 1945. The club finished a creditable 13th in this transitional season and by the following summer were preparing to return to peacetime soccer with Highfield Road in need of repair and maintenance. Funds would not be available because of post-war restrictions which were in force

Coventry City, 1946-7. Back row (left to right): Dobbs, Cox, Tooze, Mr Hitchener (secretary), Wood, Mason, Wykes, Crawley. Middle row: R.Hill (trainer), Warner, Roberts, R.Bayliss (manager), N.Smith, Setchell, Morgan (assistant trainer). Front row: Bett, Aldecoa, Barrett, Young, S.Smith.

until the end of the decade, but the club had the £5,000 deposited in the bank from the sale of the 'A' team ground to the Lockhead Company in Leamington.

Any illusions that City were going to carry on the first post-war season where they had left off in 1939 were soon shattered. Under new manager Dick Bayliss the team, containing seasoned pre-war favourites George Mason, Alf Wood, 'Plum' Warner and Harry Barratt, and promising newcomers Peter Murphy and George Lowrie, never seemed to have the right blend, despite constant chopping and changing. Indeed, they had won only five games by the end of 1946.

Early in 1947, the club lost their manager when Dick Bayliss became seriously ill and later died. Bayliss' last signing had been Birmingham City's Welsh international utility player Dan Dearson for a record £6,000. He added stability to the side and with new manager Billy Frith — who had played for the City in the 1930s — at the helm, Coventry won eight of their last 12 games.

The 1947-8 season was not dissimilar. The pack was constantly shuffled to find a consistent winning combination, but to little effect, and City had to be content with another mid-table position. Frith did solve one long-standing problem, however, when he signed left winger Norman Lockhart. Frith was forced to recoup the money by selling George Lowrie but in August he made another excellent signing in wing-half Noel Simpson.

Billy Frith's first reign at Highfield Road came to an end after only 18 months. City lost ten of their first 16 matches in the 1948-9 season and after a week of speculation, Frith was sacked. On 16 November, Harry Storer returned to the club

Coventry City, 1948-9. Back row (left to right): Snape, Cox, Barratt, W.Frith (manager), Wood, G.Mason, R.Mason, A.McIntosh. Front row: Warner, Bett, Roberts, Murphy, Lockhart.

and pulled City around with five wins in December. Although results in the New Year were less spectacular, the threat of relegation was averted. Storer's first important signing, in January, was Ian Jamieson, who was later to play a prominent part in City's history, first as a director and later, when Jimmy Hill left the club for the second time, as chairman.

If City supporters thought that Storer was going to achieve an instant miracle they soon came face to face with reality when the Bantams won only one of their first 12 games in the 1949-50 season. Martin McDonnell was signed to strengthen a defence which had conceded 26 goals and, for a time, results improved, but after another bad run between December and February relegation began to look a distinct possibility. The club again dug deep into the coffers to sign forwards Bryn Allen and Ken Chisholm and this did the trick. City were unbeaten in their last eight games, Allen scoring seven goals.

Although Peter Murphy was sold in the close season, the side now had a more settled look and this paid dividends. The first half of the 1950-51 season was a re-run of the mid-1930s. The team played exciting football, scored goals galore, the crowds flocked back to Highfield Road and at the end of the year City were top of the table, seemingly poised for promotion. Then it all went wrong. Storer swooped to sign Grimsby Town's free-scoring centre-forward Tommy Briggs and that paid instant dividends when Briggs scored on his debut, in the 5-2 win over Bury on 30 December.

However, the man Briggs displaced was Ted Roberts, who was idolized by his

Coventry City goalkeeper Alf Wood turns away a shot from Brentford's Bill Pointon at Griffin Park in October 1950.

teammates. The spirit that had carried City to the top of the table seemed to evaporate, City won only one of their next six games and Briggs was dropped. To add to City's woes, Harry Barratt joined Noel Simpson — who had not played in the side since late October — on the injury list and the heart of the side was ripped out. Although there was a brief flurry of wins over Easter, by then promotion had become a distant dream.

The Bantams kicked off the 1951-2 season with their oldest side ever — average age 31. However, the season started reasonably well with Briggs, restored to the side on 1 September, in good form. He never really settled at Highfield Road, however, and moved to Birmingham City later in the month, in part-exchange for Don Dorman. Meanwhile, the season began to develop into a nightmare. City did not win a game between 8 September and 24 November and, although there was a brief revival in December, by February they looked certain to be relegated. George Lowrie was re-signed from Bristol City but by now he was well past his best.

Storer did make two excellent signings the following month, however, in centre-forward Eddie Brown and defender Roy Kirk. When City beat Luton Town 5-2 at Highfield Road on Easter Tuesday, there still seemed a faint chance of avoiding relegation but in the following game they were at home to top-of-the-table Sheffield Wednesday, who needed a win to ensure promotion. The Bantams were forced to play third-choice goalkeeper Derek Spencer and with goalscoring phenomenon Derek Dooley in devastating form, City were simply outclassed and lost 2-0. The attendance was over 36,000, a figure that would not be topped for the next 11 years. City lost their final game, at Leeds, 3-1 and that was that. They had lost the Second Division place that Storer himself had fought so hard to achieve.

QPR's Johnny Poppitt heads clear from a Coventry attack at Loftus Road in January 1951.

City started their first season back in the Third Division South, in which they finished sixth, with a playing staff of 39. Unfortunately, average attendances dropped from 22,000 to 13,000 and, early in the season, to balance the books, Norman Lockhart was sold to Aston Villa. The side now had a younger look. Peter Hill had become a regular and Reg Matthews, Gordon Nutt and Ronnie Waldock had made their debuts in 1952-3; the following season Frank Austin was introduced to the side.

The 1953-4 season got off to a bad start and City were soon in the lower half of the table. This was not good enough for ambitious Coventry and on 4 November it was announced that Harry Storer had resigned. The board, under George Jones, took control of team affairs until the arrival of new manager Jack Fairbrother in January. The club were then 15th in the table and before the season was over an attendance of 4,785 had been recorded, the lowest for 30 years.

A new board was elected in April, with Erle Shanks as chairman and Derrick Robins one of the two new directors. The new board paid off a large slice of the club's debt, the scouting and coaching systems were reshaped and money was pledged for new players. Fairbrother immediately set to work to revamp the side and bought the Nottingham Forest pair, Capel and Collindridge, for a five-figure fee. The season got off to a golden start but the dream soon began to fade; City lost at Gillingham in their first defeat of the season; in October, Eddie Brown was sold and a transfer request from Gordon Nutt, one of City's promising youngsters, was turned down.

The next twist in the tale came when Fairbrother resigned 'through health reasons'. Charlie Elliott took over as caretaker manager and he soon entered the transfer market to buy 34-year-old Jack Lee from Derby and Alan Moore from Forest. But in line with the club's policy in the 1950s, of buying older players and selling promising youngsters, Nutt went to Cardiff. Meanwhile, on 21 January it had been announced that Jesse Carver would take over as manager in June; and to complete the all-star managerial line-up, George Raynor was appointed as Carver's deputy.

Over 24,000 turned up to see City's 3-1 victory over Bournemouth in the opening game of the 1955-6 season and although the wins came only in fits and starts, the crowds continued to flock in to see the Third Division's glamour side. City's away form was poor, however, and for all their attractive soccer the team looked anything but promotion candidates. Carver now began to reshape his plans and bought bustling centre-forward Ken McPherson.

City's form improved immediately and after five successive wins in December, including 'the old five' in successive home games against Norwich and Millwall at Christmas, there was promotion talk in the air again. Behind the scenes, alas, all was not well and Carver announced his resignation on 30 December. Raynor took over and, although early results were promising, City's form slumped in February and they eventually finished in eighth place. Not all was gloom, however. Reg Matthews had made his international debut and, at the same time, the 17-year-old George Curtis was making his first impression in Coventry's senior side.

Harry Warren became City's sixth manager in five years in June 1956, yet despite this there was a familiar pattern to the opening of the 1956-7 season — good early results and 20,000 attendances at Highfield Road followed by a slump. A mammoth injury list did not help, but not only did the club's traditionally abysmal away form get progressively worse, City also began to lose at home. One bright spot had been the continuing brilliance of Reg Matthews, but to the despair of City's fans he was sold to Chelsea. Although Warren used some of the money to buy Bristol City forwards Jack Boxley and Jimmy Rogers, City's troubles continued and at one time five players were on the transfer list. By March, City were third from bottom with crowds down to 8,000 and, although they won their last four games, they still finished 16th. So ended one of City's most disastrous seasons.

The 1957-8 season was of vital importance as the regionalized Third Division was being reorganized and only the top 12 sides in the Northern and Southern sections would form the new Division Three. Injuries and loss of form unsettled the side at the beginning of the season and only five points were gained from the first eight games: exit Harry Warren, enter Billy Frith for the second time. The season then proceeded relatively uneventfully, at least for the remainder of 1957.

Frith made his first signing in Derby's Ray Straw, but, shortly after, Ray Sambrook, an exciting young winger, was sold. After Christmas, City's form slumped dramatically: they failed to win between 28 December and 17 March and team spirit reached rock-bottom. Frith did what he could, signing wing-half Brian Nicholas, and City won at last, 6-0 over Aldershot, but it was all too late and Coventry eventually finished 19th.

The club that had virtually given an unwritten guarantee to its supporters that they would do everything possible to get back to Division Two were now in the bottom division. Ironically it had been Coventry City who had proposed the reorganization.

Billy Frith took a long hard look at the situation and decided that his team would try to play its way out of Division Four. City started the season badly but, undeterred, Frith made his first foray into the transfer market in September, signing Reg Ryan, the veteran Irish international inside-forward and a former teammate of Straw's at Derby. The small fee wiped out Coventry's bank balance. Perhaps Ryan would not have been the first name to spring to mind if one was considering the type of player needed in the hurly burly of the bottom division, but Frith's judgement was vindicated when City started to win.

Many City fans had given up on the team in their lean years but they started coming back to Highfield Road in their thousands, delighting in the goalscoring feats of Rogers and Straw, who by October had notched 18 goals between them. Veteran goalkeeper Alf Wood returned to the side on 1 October. He went on to play in the next nine games and was only on the losing side once; by that time the Bantams were top of the Fourth Division and attendances were now regularly topping the 20,000 mark.

Frith continued to show what a shrewd negotiator in the transfer market he was, and on a shoestring budget too. After signing Ryan he waited two months, carefully assessing which positions needed strengthening, before signing winger Alan 'Digger' Daley from Crewe, proven goalscorer George Stewart from Accrington Stanley and one of the best double signings in City's history, goalkeeper Arthur Lightening and wing-half Ron Farmer for a joint fee of £6,000 from Forest. Coventry's excellent form continued: from 29 November to 2 January they secured 13 points and scored 24 goals. But perhaps the outstanding performance was the 6-1 thrashing of Carlisle United at Brunton Park in February, Stewart scoring four goals. The run of only four defeats in 32 matches, stretching back to 1 September, climaxed on 17 March in a magnificent win over the League leaders, Port Vale, at Highfield Road in front of a 28,000 crowd. There was then an inexplicable slump in form: City failed to score in five consecutive matches. But two away wins followed and promotion was finally secured with a 1-1 draw at Millwall on 21 April. The success-starved City supporters at last had something to cheer about.

City looked like going straight through to Division Two, losing only one of their first 11 games. In four games from Christmas Day they scored 14 goals in four games, with nine from former local works player Ken Satchwell.

After a run of nine matches with only one defeat, City faltered. Jack Boxley, who still lived and trained in Bristol, failed to turn up at Highfield Road for the match against Bury on 27 February and there was no ready-made replacement, so third-team full-back Brian Shepherd was rushed in to wear the number-ten shirt. Playing like a team with a vital part missing, City lost 1-0.

The following week the club made a new signing — Welsh international inside-forward Ron Hewitt for £4,000. Frith had bought modestly earlier in the season, snapping up defender Don Bennett and winger Johnny Stephens, but the club could not afford the fee for Hewitt so the directors clubbed together to provide the cash. Hewitt was a good investment as results began to improve almost immediately and City still had a slim chance of promotion when they met second-placed Norwich City at Highfield Road on 9 April. City won 2-1 in a thrilling game before a frenzied crowd of nearly 28,000 and the City Council got so carried away that they organized a civic reception in the team's honour. Then came the slump: three successive defeats. The last at home to Grimsby was accompanied by boos and the slow handclap. The general view was that money should have been made available to strengthen the side. The fact of the matter was that, as the Hewitt episode showed, the club was practically bankrupt.

Promotion, then a near-miss. Clearly there was only one way to go and that was down. City won only four of their first 16 games in the 1960-61 season and crowds slumped to the 12,000 mark. Derrick Robins became chairman in October and immediately made the money available for Frith to buy Scottish international Stewart Imlach from Luton Town. City then went through a 17-match spell with only one defeat. Their finest hour came at Liverpool in the third round of the FA Cup. After being two goals down, City battled back to 2-2, only to have a replay snatched from them in the closing stages. The Anfield fans, sporting as ever, paid their own tribute by staying to cheer the Coventry team coach on its way. But a winter of promise turned into a spring of discontent and the final 14 games yielded only nine points.

Predictably, the 1961-2 season also started badly and after the first 12 matches City were struggling, only six places from the bottom. Frith was a worried man; the side badly needed strengthening, not least in the centre-forward position. Frith had bought Myerscough in the 1960 close season but he had failed to deliver the goods, as had the other players — Satchwell, Grice, Brian Hill and Dixon — who had donned the number-nine shirt. It was immediately made clear to Frith that in view of falling attendances — they had dropped to around 7,000 — no money would be made available to buy players. The FA Cup seemed to provide some light relief. City beat Gillingham in the first round but then lost 2-1 to Southern League Kings Lynn. Only four days later, Frith was sacked, along with trainers Alf Wood and Ted Roberts and chief scout Arthur Jepson, and Jimmy Hill was appointed manager.

For a time the winds of change swept Highfield Road but when the talking stopped, much seemed the same as before. The season petered out with City winning only two out of their final eight matches and attendances sliding down to the 6,000 mark. However, behind the scenes Hill was busy working out his plans for success which were to catapault City from the Third to the First Division in only five years.

No one could have blamed the fans for being cynical, for they had seen it all before — new management, new players, new colours and, as before, desperate for success, they would turn out in large numbers to witness what they hoped would be a miracle. For once they were not let down and, although in the first half of the 1962-3 season City occupied only a mid-table position, a useful Cup run was in the making and the promise of better times was certainly in the air.

The £30,000 gift from Derrick Robins to purchase new players had been the springboard and, with Terry Bly scoring regularly, the promotion push began to take shape, only to be interrupted by the worst winter weather for nearly 20 years. Luckily for City, Jimmy Hill had arranged some innovative friendly matches in Ireland and they were able to get back into their stride much quicker than most teams. Coupled with their best-ever FA Cup run — they went out unluckily to Manchester United after a titanic clash with Sunderland — their League position improved considerably and after an unbeaten run of 23 games, promotion beckoned. The Cup run had taken a lot out of the team, however, and a tiring squad playing twice, sometimes three times a week, finally finished in fourth place.

City's 1963-4 promotion-winning squad. Back row (left to right): Hudson, Wesson, Sillett, Jimmy Hill (manager), Meeson, Kearns. Middle row: Humphries, Newton, Curtis, Kirby, Mitten, Rees. Front row: Farmer, Smith, Barr, Hill, Machin, Bruck.

The final few weeks had been dominated by the Hudson/Bly affair. Terry Bly had scored over 25 goals but one felt he lacked the craft that Hill was looking for and when a record fee was splashed out to secure Peterborough's stylish centre-forward George Hudson, the fans were split into one or other of the factions. Not for the first time Jimmy Hill was to prove the master of such situations, Bly faded into obscurity after being transferred to Notts County for a hefty £13,000 fee but Hudson went on to to become the idol of the fans and the icon of the Sky Blue era.

Although promotion was narrowly missed, nobody was down-hearted as season-ticket sales boomed and the first sections of the Sky Blue Stand were constructed, along with the much-needed pitch levelling.

The fans were not to be disappointed as the Sky Blues swept all before them in a feast of attacking football. By the turn of the year they were nine points ahead of the next club and it seemed that promotion would be clinched by the middle of March. But, as has been the case on numerous occasions, the team's form suddenly slumped and what had seemed to be a formality turned into a desperate scrimmage for every available League point. Hill fell out with Hudson, signed quality players such as Smith and Kirby at the 11th hour, and then, like the magician he was, returned Hudson to team for the final match, at home to Colchester, and clinched the championship.

All was forgotten as Coventry City returned to the Second Division after a break of 12 years. Average home attendances had returned to levels achieved only on a couple of occasions in the past, and with improvements planned both on and off the pitch, all the seats in the stadium were snapped up before the season got under way.

The season began in dramatic fashion and after six matches the Sky Blues led the Second Division and crowds were nudging the 40,000 mark. Of course, it couldn't last — and it didn't as the team finally found its level around mid-table. In many ways comparisons could be made with 1936-7. And the following season was very similar to 1937-8 as City should have gone up but missed out by one point and an inferior goal-average. Instead of Leslie Jones, this time it was George Hudson who was sold. The fans were mortified and, although Hudson never again achieved the same levels with Northampton Town, many never really forgave Jimmy Hill for their favourite's departure. Whether promotion would have been won in 1965-6 will never be known, but a general view was that, in his heyday, Hudson would have graced the First Division with his mixture of delicate touches and powerhouse play.

The fans needed another hero and as the home-grown player would never do it, so a big purchase was essential. This came in the form of Ian Gibson and, although neither he nor the club set football on fire in the first half of 1966-7, he would eventually come good after problems both on and off the pitch. Suddenly the team ran into some form and, with local boy Bobby Gould leading the line in his own inimitable style, a record unbeaten run of 25 games was achieved, culminating in the Second Division title after unforgettable matches against Wolves and Millwall.

The team had a very solid foundation with Glazier, Curtis, Clements and old faithfuls — Hill, Bruck, Farmer, Kearns and Machin — combining with the silky skills of Gibson to give them an almost unbeatable look after the New Year. In only five years the club had risen from the ashes and the fans were able to look forward to their first-ever season in the First Division. Many had dismissed a lot of the new ideas as cheap gimmickery, but the club had never been out of news and the partnership of Jimmy Hill and Derrick Robins had achieved more than anyone else in Coventry City's history. The talk was now of Europe and the League Championship. Little did the fans realize that big trouble was already brewing as the last drop of champagne was draining away.

The first of Bobby Gould's hat-trick goals against Burnley in December 1967. Gould felt that it was the best goal he had ever scored.

Coventry City in 1968-9. Back row (left to right): Clements, Martin, Bruck, Setters, Tudor, Coop. Middle row: Shepherd, Hill, Curtis, Glazier, Cattlin, Blockley, Kearns. Front row: Hannigan, Gibson, Carr, Noel Cantwell (manager), Baker, Hunt, Machin.

On 18 August 1967, only two days before the start of City's first season in Division One, chairman Derrick Robins announced that Jimmy Hill was leaving the club to take up a position with London Weekend Television. The fans, previously excited at the prospect of trips to Anfield, Highbury and Old Trafford, were stunned.

Some 7,000 Coventry supporters went to City's First Division baptism at Turf Moor and saw an ominous 2-1 defeat. Indeed, the season was long and hard, and

Maurice Setters, a £25,000 signing whose influence on Coventry City was enormous.

in what was a precursor for the future, the outcome went to the final game at The Dell, where a goalless draw kept City up as Sheffield United lost at home to Chelsea and went down.

Noel Cantwell had arrived in October and he spent over £300,000 to keep City in the top flight. His best buy was the £25,000 he spent on Maurice Setters, whose influence was enormous.

An embarrassing FA Cup defeat at Tranmere was forgotten as City chased valuable League points and injuries to key players, such as Curtis and Gibson, made Cantwell's task all the harder. Despite the paucity of results, however, City's crowds averaged over 34,500, a record never topped.

The following season was almost a carbon copy, apart from the ending when City finished their games leaving FA Cup Finalists Leicester City still to play five matches and needing seven points to send Coventry down. Rumours of favours for old friends circulated as Cantwell's former team, Manchester United, beat Leicester in their final game to save the Highfield Road club.

Yet no one could have predicted the outcome of the following season as Coventry achieved Robins' dream by 'rocketing into Europe'. They finished sixth in Division One after an excellent start to the season with the inspired purchase of Roy Barry and a club record ten away wins. A place in Europe was clinched on a passionate night at Molineux, when the old enemy were beaten by a Brian Joicey goal.

Alas, the European experience was disappointing. After convincingly beating the Bulgarians, Trakia Plovdiv, City, without the injured Glazier, slumped to a 6-1 defeat to Bayern Munich and, despite regaining some pride in the return, the European dream was over.

League form was patchy and only 37 goals were scored, the worst for 51 years. There was also another embarrassing FA Cup defeat, this time at Rochdale, to put pressure on Cantwell. He survived for another 12 months but yet another FA Cup disaster, at home to Hull, sealed his fate with City in 18th place.

The defensive emphasis of the Cantwell era was swept away by the Mercer-Milne regime and their signings of Stein and Hutchison brought two of the most exciting players of the era to the club.

Whoops! Stuart Pearson of Manchester United appears to be on the receiving end of a rather painful experience as John Craven of Coventry tries to win the ball.

Ian Wallace has just rifled home a goal to give Coventry a 1-1 draw against Spurs at Highfield Road in April 1977. Goalkeeper Barry Daines appears to be making his feelings known.

A good League run, three FA Cup wins and a high level of entertainment, raised hopes but after a sixth-round Cup defeat at Wolves, City's League form slumped and they finished 19th.

The mid-1970s were a difficult financial period for City. In the summer of 1974, Milne believed he was one player short of a Championship side — a centre-half. Deals were lined up to fund the purchase of Larry Lloyd for £240,000, but fell through *after* Lloyd signed.

Suddenly, City were desperate for cash and with Robins and his money withdrawing from the board there was panic in the air. Over the next 18 months many top players were sold to balance the books and for many fans the last straw came at Christmas 1975, when Dennis Mortimer was sold to arch rivals Aston Villa. Jimmy Hill had returned as a director in 1975 and was going to play a key role in the club's finances over the next eight years.

After the relative safety of mid-table in the mid-1970s, the 1976-7 campaign provided another nail-biting relegation battle. City ultimately needed to win their final game against Bristol City and, after taking a 2-0 lead, they were pegged back to 2-2 before reprieve came with Sunderland's defeat at Everton.

Despite the final position there were signs that a good side was in the making, with Milne's shrewd purchases of Yorath, Wallace and McDonald, together with home-grown players like Ferguson, Oakey and Blyth and old favourites like Hutchison and Coop.

The 1977-8 season was City's most exciting in the First Division with 75 goals scored, They missed a place in Europe by a whisker, despite some outstanding home performances. The promise, however, did not materialize the following season, when injuries kept out key players and, despite some great goals from Wallace, City slipped to tenth place.

Another crop of outstanding youngsters were emerging and this probably saved the club through another difficult financial period.

In 1979-80, the side finished 15th and pressure mounted on the long-serving Milne after an ignominious FA Cup defeat at Third Division Blackburn.

In the summer of 1980, Wallace was sold to Nottingham Forest for £1.25 million to help fund the new Sky Blue Connexion at Ryton, followed early the next season by the sales of Hutchison and McDonald. The only money spent was £300,000 on Gerry Daly.

However, these controversial sales were forgotten as City's youngsters reached the club's first-ever senior semi final when they got into the last four of the Football League Cup.

A stirring first-leg recovery brought a 3-2 victory and City were unlucky to lose on aggregate to a debatable last-minute goal in the second leg at West Ham.

The potential had not been fulfilled and Milne was not to get another chance, for he was moved 'sideways' to general manager as Dave Sexton became team manager. Sexton's arrival coincided with the transformation of Highfield Road into an all-seater stadium with a capacity of only 20,500.

Attendances had fallen progressivley since 1967, to an average of under 17,000 the previous season, but the problems associated with the all-seater ground and the mediocre performances of the team caused the average to fall to 13,000.

Safety was achieved in 1981-2 with a good end-of-season run, but with no new signings, matters did not improve in the following campaign. Attendances fell to 8,000 and the club was losing money.

Thus, Garry Thompson became the latest sacrifice when he was sold to West Brom in February. This sale by Jimmy Hill, against the will of Sexton, sparked off a chain of events which saw City go 13 games without a win, yet avoid relegation by the skin of their teeth. Hill was forced off the board, Sexton was sacked on the last day of the season, and eight first-team players, including Thomas, Hateley and Gillespie, rejected new contracts and left Highfield Road.

New manager Bobby Gould had the onerous task of putting together a side almost from scratch for the 1983-4 season. Gould's experience of the lower divisions enabled him to obtain some excellent bargains, many of whom were still at Highfield Road four years later, when City reached Wembley.

By Christmas the gamble appeared to have paid off: Liverpool, the champions, had just been hammered 4-0 and City were fourth in the table. Things went drastically wrong in 1984, however, and the side won only nine League games out of 42, having to win the final match of Gould's first season to survive. They were lying 21st on 28 December the following season, when he was sacked.

John Poynton had taken over as chairman in the summer of 1984 and he appointed Don Mackay as caretaker manager. The team achieved safety by virtue of winning three successive games for the first time in 18 months, including the final game against Champions Everton in an atmosphere defying description.

Once again City were in deep financial trouble and believed to be £1 million overdrawn at the bank. The following season started full of promise but, for the third successive campaign, City were left needing to win their final game to stay up. Mackay resigned in April, after eight games without a win, and with the trapdoor gaping, George Curtis was asked to look after team matters with John Sillett promoted to coach. The new duo clinched safety with two wins in the final three games and promised a new approach.

Many fans were cynical and few would have guessed that the new approach would result in Coventry City winning the FA Cup just 12 months later. City started

Above: Trevor Peake runs out, followed by Steve Ogrizovic. Opposite: Jubilation at Wembley. City have just won the FA Cup.

the new season with only two new signings — but a more attractive style — and they were rarely out of the top eight.

The real excitement, however, came in a thrilling FA Cup run which culminated in one of the finest post-war Cup Finals with City deservedly beating Spurs 3-2 after extra-time.

City always looked more relaxed than the heavily-backed Tottenham side and inflicted a first-ever Wembley FA Cup defeat on the Londoners.

Greg Downs holds aloft the FA Cup, with Phillips (left), Gynn and Pickering alongside him.

The 1987 FA Cup winners pose for an informal team group.

The scenes in Coventry the following day will never be forgotten by the estimated throng of 250,000 who lined the route, cheering their heroes home.

A summer of activity saw Sillett promoted to team manager and Curtis made managing director; some £780,000 was paid for David Speedie; and 50,000 City fans returned to Wembley for the FA Charity Shield game against Everton.

After the Cup triumph almost anything was going to be an anticlimax and the next season was certainly disappointing, despite City finishing tenth in the League. The Sky Blues' Cup luck ran out when Watford, bottom of the First Division, won at Highfield Road.

This, however, was nothing compared to the shock the following season when Sutton United took City's scalp in one of the biggest FA Cup shocks of all time.

City were in the top six at the time and finally finished seventh, a creditable performance, but many Coventry fans thought that the writing was on the wall for Sillett's ageing team. They were not scoring enough goals, still lacked a playmaker in midfield and had developed a habit of rising to the big occasions but being too casual in the potentially easier games.

The 1989-90 season was an historic one as City reached the top spot in Division One for the first time, albeit after four games of the season, but two weeks later they slumped to a Littlewoods Cup defeat at Fourth Division Grimsby Town. The Mariners were beaten on aggregate in the two-legged tie, but it was another in a long Coventry tradition of Cup disasters.

However, the shock motivated the team into an excellent run in the Littlewoods Cup which culminated in an aggregate semi-final defeat against Nottingham Forest; and in November, City won at Anfield for the first time in 25 visits. But yet again they slumped to a shock FA Cup defeat, this time at Northampton.

In an effort to achieve more consistency, Sillett broke the club transfer record twice, signing Drinkell for £800,000 and Gallacher for £900,000, and four wins out of six took City to fourth place in March. Only one win in the last ten games, though, meant that City finished 12th and were humiliated 6-1 by Champions Liverpool in the final game.

Twelve games into the 1990-91 season, Sillett was finally sacked, to be replaced by Terry Butcher, for whom City had to pay Glasgow Rangers a £400,000 transfer fee as he was classified as a player-manager.

Butcher soon realized the size of his task but still gave the fans some thrills with an outstanding 5-4 Rumbelows Cup win over Nottingham Forest, in one of the best games staged at Highfield Road in years. Gallacher scored a hat-trick in that game and ended the season with 16 goals, the most by a City player since Gibson in 1984-5.

Relegation looked a distinct possibility at one stage but some good signings and only two defeats in the last nine games made them safe. As Coventry City approached their 25th year in the First Division, the fans were confident that Terry Butcher knew what he had to do, but needed patience to achieve it.

The Grounds

SINGERS' first pitch was on Dowells Field just off the Binley Road, between St George's Road and the railway line. Further details are supplied by an early player, George Bowers, who recalled: "The pitch was reached by passing through the gate alongside Robinson's Pit, near Hilly Hollow Fields, later the site of the Gosford Park Hotel."

In 1887, Singers moved to Stoke Road where their pitch lay between Britannia Street, Wren Street, Mowbray Street and Swan Lane. The committee and supporters erected a grandstand and in the following year, 'stout fences' around the pitch and a covered press-box. In 1894 goal-nets were introduced to soccer.

Extensive house building took place in Hillfields in the 1890s and in 1897, Mr G.Storer purchased the land close to the Stoke Road pitch and this necessitated moving the goal-posts some 50 yards east of Wren Street, a move which fortunately coincided with an alteration in the law governing the minimum pitch length, which

Top: Part of the crowd for the visit of Grimsby Town in April 1919. Bottom: Buckley takes a penalty for City but the ball struck the crossbar.

Highfield Road as it would have looked at the beginning of the century. The 'John Bull' stand was built in 1899 and demolished in 1936. To the right of the picture the new houses in King Richard Street can be seen.

reduced from 200 yards to 150 yards. This now left enough room to build a stand accommodating 500 spectators.

Singers remained at this venue for another two years before the ground was acquired for building, by which time the club (now called Coventry City) had acquired a six-and-a-half-acre site from the Craven Cricket Club. A row of elm trees was removed, the pitch was levelled and a 12-row stand was built on the King Richard Street side and City kicked-off the 1899-1900 season at Highfield Road.

The correspondent of the *Coventry Reporter* described the scene in September: 'As one enters the ground from Highfield Road, the eye encounters the grand new stand on the opposite side of the enclosure. It is a gigantic wooden structure, roofed with corrugated iron, and is coloured chocolate and light blue. Indeed it presents a fine picture and is an ornament of which the committee might well be proud.'

In 1910, following a most successful season, a new barrel-roofed main stand was built on the north side at a cost of £1,200. In 1920 there was an attempt to build-up the Spion Kop and again in 1922, when waste concrete from the relaying of the city's tram track was used. Notwithstanding, by 1927 it was still described as 'a steep, scarred and totally shapeless mess'.

Also in August 1927, the terrace stand was purchased from Twickenham for £2,200. It provided cover for 11,000 spectators. During construction it was found that the pitch fell seven feet from corner to corner, a fault not rectified until 1963.

In 1936, following City's promotion to Division Two, the 'rotting planks' of the original 1899 stand were demolished to make way for a new main stand at a cost of £14,000. In November of that year the club purchased the freehold of the ground from the Mercers' Company for £20,000, thanks to a loan from Sir John Siddeley. Highfield Road could now accommodate over 40,000 spectators as was demonstrated on a number of occasions before the outbreak of war.

The additional lattice-board standing extension to the Kop, known as the 'Crows Nest', was added in 1938, and in 1939 a canopy extension was built on to the main stand.

During the air-raids of November 1940, the ground was hit three times but most of the damage was confined to the pitch area and by 1942 things had been sufficiently patched up to stage matches again.

View of the Spion Kop in April 1936 for the Southern Section Cup Final against Swindon Town. Note the rudimentary terraces, crash barriers and retaining wall.

A private practice match under the new Highfield Road floodlights in October 1957, shortly before the visit of Third Lanark.

In 1953, floodlights were installed and were first used for a friendly game against Queen of the South. In 1957 an improved set of lights made their debut for a game against Third Lanark. These were paid for by the Supporters' Club at a cost of £15,000, the original pylons still being in use in 1991.

In the summer of 1964, the old 1910-vintage stand was demolished to be replaced by the Sky Blue Stand at a cost of £120,000; and following promotion to Division One in 1967, the double-decker West Stand was erected for £85,000.

On 16 March 1968, the Main Stand was gutted by fire and the present Main Stand completed — at a cost of £150,000 — with astonishing speed in time for the start of the new season, although the first two home games were postponed.

In 1973, defects were discovered in the roof of the Sky Blue Stand and the vaulted section was replaced by a flat roof; early in 1983, part of the roof collapsed in gales but the damage was quickly patched up.

In 1981, the controversial decision was taken to convert Highfield Road to an all-seater stadium and 8,000 extra seats were installed at a cost of £400,000, thus reducing the capacity, at a stroke, from 36,500 to 20,600.

This unanimously unpopular decision was intended, amongst other things, to deter hooliganism, but the game against Leeds United in 1981 saw a major disturbance when some visiting supporters dismantled the seats in their section and used them as missiles against the police.

In 1983 the Kop above the seating area was reopened as a standing terrace. Two years later, the seats were removed and the end partially rebuilt to allow a better view.

Following the Taylor Report it is now planned to build a stand at the Kop end

The old Main Stand is gutted by fire in March 1968.

Highfield Road in the summer of 1963, apart from the floodlights unchanged since 1936.

Above and opposite: Seats on the former terrace at Highfield Road in 1981, when the club made the controversial switch to an all-seater stadium.

and extend the roof of the new stand over the Sky Blue Stand, thus creating a 25,000 all-seater stadium with covered accommodation for 95 per cent of the crowd at a cost of £6 million. This development has received a £2 million grant from the Football Trust and construction is planned to take place during the period May 1992-August 1993.

International Matches at Highfield Road

Full Internationals

1973
March 28 World Cup
Northern Ireland 1 Portugal 1
Northern Ireland: Jennings; O'Kane, Nelson, Neill, Hunter, Clements, Hamilton, Coyle, Morgan, Dickson, O'Neill.
Goalscorer: O'Neill
Portugal: Jose Henrique; Artur, Alhinho, Freitas, Adolfo, Matine, Nene, Eusébio, Pavao(Dinis), Abel, Simoẽs.
Goalscorer: Eusébio (pen)
Attendance: 11,273

Under-23 Internationals

1964
November 25
England 5 Romania 0
England: Glazier; Badger, Thomson, H.Newton, Mobley, Hunter, Murray, Tambling(Chivers), M.Jones, Ball, Hinton.
Goalscorers: Jones, Murray, Ball, Hinton, Chivers
Romania: Hajdu; Lupescu, Petescu, Dinu, Halmageanu, Matei, Iancu, Naftonaia, Pavolovici, Coe, Avram. Subs: Andrei, Adam.
Attendance: 27,476

1969
April 16
England 3 Portugal 0
England: Shilton; W.Smith, Pardoe, Doyle, Booth, Sadler, Coates, Robson, Clarke, Evans, Sissons.
Goalscorers: Clarke 2, Robson
Portugal: Fonseca; Barros, Carlo, Adriano, Murca, Pavao, Toni, Campos, Camolas, Nelson, Nere.
Attendance: 13,631

Under-21 Internationals

1980
February 12
England 2 Scotland 1
England: Bailey; Wright, Sansom, Robson, Osman, Butcher, Hilaire, Hoddle, Crooks, Owen, Rix.
Goalscorers: Owen, Robson
Scotland: Thomson; Stewart, Dawson, Orr, McLeish, Gillespie, Wark, Blair, Archibald, Aitken, Brazil.
Goalscorer: Archibald
Attendance: 15,426

1988
October 18
England 1 Sweden 1
England: Martyn; B.Statham(Burrows), Cooper, Sedgley, Redmond, Chettle, White, Ripley, Dozell(Oldfield), Samways, D.Smith.
Goalscorer: White
Sweden: L.Eriksson; Nilsson, J.Eriksson, Aattovaara, Kamark, Karlsson, Ingesson, Schwartz, J.Jansson, Dahlin(Eklund), Andersson.
Goalscorer: Ingesson
Attendance: 3,988

Inter-League Games

1970
March 18
Football League 2 Scottish League 2
Football League: Stepney(Glazier); W.Smith, Hughes: Newton, McFarland, Todd, Coates, Kidd(Peters), Astle, Harvey, Rogers.
Goalscorers: Astle 2, Rogers
Scottish League: McRae; Callaghan, Dickson, Smith, McKinnon, Stanton, Mclean, Greig, Hall(Graham), Cormack, Johnston.
Goalscorers: Cormack, Graham
Attendance: 26,693

Youth Internationals

1962
November 22
England 1 Switzerland 0
(Abandoned after nine minutes)
England: Cowan; Badger, Shaw, Beal, Chatterly, R.Harris, Pleat, Bloomfield, G.Jones, Sissons, Thwaites.
Goalscorer: G.Jones
Switzerland: Demonterjaund; Thoma, Ramseier, Lehmann, Bucher, Schmid, Althaus, Schmeid, Meier, Bosset, Tribollet.
Attendance: 3,200

1980
March 26 European Youth Tournmament – Qualifying game
England 4 Denmark 0
England: Kendall(Horn); Bennett, Barnes, Peake, Mabbutt, Pates, Gibson(Barham), Allen, Hateley, English, MacKenzie.
Goalscorer: Hateley 4
Denmark: Team unknown
Attendance: 2,425

1982
March 23 European Youth Tournament
England 2 Scotland 2
England: Francis; Parker, Pickering, Duffield, Elliott, Robson, Singleton, Steven(Bell), Pearson, Walters, Childs.
Goalscorers: Pearson, Walters.
Scotland: Team unknown
Goalscorers: McStay, Dobbin
Attendance: 2,295

Schoolboy Internationals

1948
April 10
England 2 Wales 1
England: Atherton; Barnard, Jones, Malcolm, Nicholas, Deeley, Birkett, Quixall, Brennan, Spencer, Green.
Goalscorers: Birkett 2
Wales: King; Cross, Presdee, Jones, Pycroft, Pritchard, Corten, Daniels, Davies, Harris, Griffins.
Goalscorer: Harris
Attendance: 25,199

1961
April 8
England 8 Republic of Ireland 0
England: Ogley; Harcombe, Wright, Parker, Storey, Walker, Figgin, Prosser, Pardoe, Sissons, Dawkins.
Goalscorers: Prosser 4, Dawkins, Sissons, Pardoe, Parker
Republic of Ireland: King; Dowling, Murphy, Farrington, Dooley, Sullivan, Maguire, Rodgers, Treacy, Bates, Conway.
Attendance: 9,108

1967
April 22 Under-18
England 3 Wales 0
England: Rudd; Fuschillo, Matthams, Barry, Sadler, Hardcastle, Clements, Gowling, Lappage, Armstrong, Partridge.
Goalscorers: Lappage 2, Partridge
Wales: Tootey; Davies, Wright, S.Williams, Jones, Peers, Rooney, Nancurvis, Wilson, B.Williams, Lewis.
Attendance: 8,465

1969
April 5
England 5 Holland 2
England: Team unknown
Goalscorers: Guthrie 2, Spinner 2, Goodlass
Holland: Team unknown
Goalscorer: Bourne 2

1978
April 29
England 1 Scotland 1
England: Team unknown
Goalscorer: Tate
Scotland: Team unknown
Goalscorer: Sheran

Amateur Internationals

1951
February 3
England 6 Republic of Ireland 3
England: Jarvis; Adams, Farrer, Topp, Fuller, Fright, Potts, Walton, Lewis, Noble, Robb.
Goalscorers: Lewis 4, Potts 2
Republic of Ireland: Watt; Montgomery, Moore, Wilson, Andrews, Weir, Cunningham, McGarry, McLaughlan,

Dobbin, McVeigh.
Goalscorers: McGarry 2, Cunningham
Attendance: 8,067

1974
April 5
England 1 Scotland 1
England: Smith; Deadman, Powell, Preston, Eaton, Reardon, Day, Haider, Smith, Pritchard, Bass.
Goalscorer: Preston
Scotland: Wilson; Finlayson, MacFarlane, Bowie, Thomson, Forrest, McLaren (O'Neill), Borland, Fallis, Inglis, Costello (Smith).
Goalscorer: Fallis
Attendance: 1,221

Other Representative Matches

1912
March 23
Birmingham Juniors 2 Scottish Juniors 2
Attendance: 1,500

1914
April 4
Birmingham Juniors 1 Scottish Juniors 0
Attendance: 1,000

1929
April 20
Birmingham Juniors 0 Scottish Juniors 1
Attendance: 3,696

1945
January 20
FA XI 4 RAF 6
Attendance: 12,750

Other Cup Ties at Highfield Road

1946-47
FA Cup
Second Round (2nd replay)
Northampton Town 8 Peterborough United 1
Northampton Town: Jones; Smalley, Barron, Lowrey, Dennison, Sankey, Morrall, Smith, Garrett, Thompson, Roberts.
Goalscorers: Garrett 4, Roberts 2, Morrall 2
Peterborough United: Silcocks; Bryan, Parrott, Richards, Warner, Wilson, Scobie, Brooksbank, Bramham, Padgett, Rudkin.
Goalscorer: Bramham
Attendance: 2,000

1966-67
FA Cup
Fourth Round (2nd Replay)
February 6
Hull City 1 Portsmouth 3
Hull City: Swan; Davidson, D.Butler, Jarvis, Corner, Simpkin, Henderson, Wagstaffe, Chilton, Henderson, I.Butler.
Goalscorer: Chilton
Portsmouth: Milkins; Pack, Tindall, Gordon, Haydock, Harris, McCann, Hiron, Edwards, Kellard, Jennings.
Goalscorers: McCann 2, Edwards.
Attendance: 18,448

1969-70
FA Cup
Second Round (3rd Replay)
December 17
Brighton & Hove Albion 1 Walsall 2
Brighton & Hove Albion: Powney; Henderson, Bell, Spearitt, J.Napier, Gall, Lawton, Gilliver, Dawson, Templeman, K.Napier.
Goalscorer: Lawton
Walsall: Parkes; Gregg, Evans, Trevis, Jones, Atthey, Watson(Morris), Baker, Woodward, Bennett, Taylor.
Goalscorer: Taylor 2
Attendance: 2,241

1975-76
FA Cup
First Round
November 22
Coventry Sporting 2 Tranmere Rovers 0
Coventry Sporting: Jeavons; Sorbie, Mundy, Dunk, Jones, Skelcey, Randle, Starkey, Gallagher, Gore, Manning.
Goalscorer: Gallagher 2
Tranmere Rovers: Johnson; Mathias, Griffiths, Parry, Philpotts, Young, Peplow, Mitchell (Kenny), Moore, B.Tynan, James
Attendance: 4,565
Second Round
December 13
Coventry Sporting 0 Peterborough United 4
Coventry Sporting: Jeavons; Mundy, Skelcey, Jones, Sorbie, Dunk, Starkey, Gore, Gallagher, Muir, Brassington.

Peterborough United: Steele; Murray, Lee, Eustace, Turner, Carmichael, Nixon, Gregory(Bradley), Jones, Hughes, Robson.
Goalscorers: Hughes, M.Jones, D.Jones (og), Nixon
Attendance: 8,556

1978-79
League Cup
Third Round (2nd Replay)
October 16
Aston Villa 3 Crystal Palace 0
Aston Villa: Rimmer; Gidman, Williams, Phillips, McNaught, Mortimer, Craig, Little, Gray, Gregory, Carrodus.
Goalscorers: Gray 2, Gregory
Crystal Palace: Burridge; Hinshelwood, Sansom, Chatterton, Cannon(Fenwick), Gilbert, Nicholas, Murphy, Walsh, Elwiss, Hilaire.
Attendance: 25,445

1979-80
FA Cup
Semi-final (3rd Replay)
May 1
Arsenal 1 Liverpool 0
Arsenal: Jennings; Rice, Devine, Talbot, O'Leary, Young, Brady, Sunderland, Stapleton, Price, Rix.
Goalscorer: Talbot
Liverpool: Clemence; Neal, Cohen, Thompson, R.Kennedy, Hansen, Dalglish, Lee, Johnson (Fairclough), McDermott, Souness.
Attendance: 35,335

1984-85
FA Cup
Third Round (replayed game behind closed doors)
Burton Albion 0 Leicester City 1
Burton Albion: Evans; McJannet, Blair, Dolby, Vaughan, Simms, Harrison, Newton, Mell, Kabia, Froggatt.
Leicester City: Andrews; Feeley, Wilson, R.Smith, Williams, O'Neill, Lynex, Lineker, A.Smith, Ramsey, Banks.
Goalscorer: Ramsey

Coventry City at the start of the 1919-20 season. Back row (left to right): Hillins, D.Cooke, H.Pollitt, H.Harbourne, W.Fulljames, T.Groves. Middle row: H.Taylor, B.Robinson, T.Hannay, R.Roberts, A.Lindon, A.Fenwick, G.Chaplin, S.Blake. Front row: J.Dougall, G.Wynn, W.Walker, T.Jones, A.Sheldon.

The Bury Scandal

IN 1920, Coventry City were involved in what may be considered the worst scandal in Football League history. Before detailing the events of May that year, it is worth looking into the background of the City club at that time. When the football programme was suspended in 1915, City's affairs were at their lowest ebb and only with the aid of grants had they had managed to struggle through a dire season in the Second Division of the Southern League.

Indeed, so miserable were the financial prospects in this League that City applied for a place in the Central League for the 1916-17 season. It had come to that: Coventry City wished to play in what was then, as now, a competition for reserve teams of mostly Northern clubs. And to add insult to injury, they failed in their application — an irrelevance because all peacetime football was suspended shortly afterwards.

The status of Coventry, the club and the city, was transformed during World War One, when it became a centre for munitions work. Amongst the thousands who came to work in Coventry were some prominent footballers including Chris Buckley of Aston Villa, Bert Middlemiss of Spurs and the great Jesse Pennington of West Bromwich Albion.

In 1918, with the war ended and football trying to reorganize itself ready for the resumption of the Football and Southern Leagues proper the following year, Coventry City negotiated themselves into the hastily-constructed Midland League and many players temporarily stationed in the city were recruited.

The Midland League contained five First Division clubs and City acquitted themselves very well. But their efforts were not confined to the field, for the club were also waging a campaign for support up and down the country, for their application to the Second Division of the Football League.

The turnabout from a club on the verge of folding to one being elected to Division Two was effected at some considerable expense, but getting into the Football League was to prove the easier part.

It was as odious then as it is now, to speak of an individual 'owning' a football club but if ever there was such a figure at Highfield Road it was David Cooke. And it was Cooke who had covered all expenses from 1915 onwards and who was unwilling to see his investment go up in smoke.

But that is precisely what threatened in 1919-20, as Coventry City, without their wartime 'guests', lurched from one disaster to another. It was 11 games before they gained a point and they had to wait until Christmas Day for their first win.

About this time, Harry Pollitt was appointed manager and was allowed to spend freely in an effort to keep the club in the League. The two bottom clubs had to apply for re-election and it was widely believed that City would not be voted back in.

However, after the arrival of Pollitt, things began to change for the better and by March they had lifted themselves off the bottom for the first time.

With only two matches remaining, City were one place off the bottom of the table, a point behind Lincoln City but with a game in hand. The final games were home and away to Bury, a strong side lying fifth but with nothing to play for. City drew 2-2 at Gigg Lane, so before the final game on 1 May 1920, Coventry and Lincoln were level on points.

Before a record attendance of 23,506 at Highfield Road, City came back from being 1-0 down at half-time to win 2-1, enabling them to avoid applying for re-election, whilst Lincoln lost their League place after 28 years.

One might have expected that to be the end of the affair but the 'Bury game', as it became known, refused to go away. Instead it became the subject of rumours; what the local *Telegraph* called a 'whispering campaign'.

The 'whispers' persisted but, incredibly, it took three years before things finally began to break. On 5 March 1923, the *Telegraph* reported briefly: 'A statement has been made to the Management Committee of the Football League concerning a match between Bury and Coventry. It is alleged that the result was arranged.'

A League Commission met on four separate occasions, always in camera, and finally made a statement on 29 May 1923.

It read: 'The Commission is satisified that an arrangement was made between Bury and Coventry City allowing the latter to win.'

In all, ten officials and players were suspended from football for life and the clubs were each fined £100; five of the players and three of the directors were from Bury, whilst for City, directors Jack Marshall and David Cooke and club captain George Chaplin all received life bans. Even then, the affair was not over. Two years later, in 1925, manager Harry Pollitt was also banned.

The Commission's own statement admitted to them 'not being in possession of all the facts'. This was certainly the case as their investigations concerned only the away game, which Bury were accused of allowing City to win, when it was in fact a 2-2 draw.

For many years afterwards the 'Bury game' was spoken of only in a hushed whisper, all references to it avoided in the local Press beyond official statements.

Other journals were not so reticent, amongst them the *Birmingham Argus*, which commented: 'Coventry City, to avert the penalty of their shortcomings on the field of play, resorted to dishonest methods. They have proved a danger to the game which will be better for their ostracism.'

David Cooke, the 'owner' of Coventry City who was unwilling to see his investment go up in smoke. Along with skipper George Chaplin and fellow director Jack Marshall, he was banned from football for life, a sentence later also passed on manager Harry Pollitt.

The spectre of the Bury game haunted City throughout the 1920s and when, in 1928, they avoided re-election, this time to the Third Division South, by goal-average, it was felt they would have been voted out had they needed to go cap in hand.

Eighteen years passed, David Cooke and Jack Marshall were dead, and finally it was considered appropriate for the full story to come out. Former Coventry City skipper George Chaplin detailed events to the weekly *Coventry Herald* and logic dictates that this is as close as one can ever get to the complete truth.

Chaplin told the newspaper: 'With a couple of matches left things looked so bad that I had a talk with the chairman, David Cooke. We decided that something must be done. The outcome of it all was that I went to Bury with £200 in my pocket and when I left, I had the feeling that City's prospects of gaining three points from the two games with Bury were not such a remote possibility.

'In the match at Bury we drew. On the following Saturday they came to Highfield Road and, in view of the arrangements that had been made, I was confident of gaining the vital points. None of the City players or officials, apart from Mr Cooke and myself, knew what arrangements had been made.

'Then things began to go wrong, Bury were leading 1-0 at half-time and I was in despair when one of the Bury players came into the dressing-room and told me that City were so poor, Bury couldn't lose no matter how badly they played. But things came right in the second half with Mercer's two goals.

'While the City supporters were celebrating the club's escape that night, I kept an appointment in the cloakroom of the King's Head Hotel, where I handed over the final instalment of the sum agreed without a word being spoken.'

The Little Blackbirds

The Birmingham Cup of 1891 & the Three Cups of 1892

IT TOOK Coventry City 104 years to win their first major honour, when they lifted the FA Cup in 1987, but 100 years ago Coventry possessed a Cup-winning side which caused a similar stirring of passion in the hearts of locals.

Since their entry into the Birmingham & District Junior Cup in 1887, Singers improvement had continued apace. In 1899 they reached the quarter-finals, going out to Unity Gas. The following year they went a step further, going out in the semi-finals to Packington after two replays.

Singers FC in 1891. Back row (left to right): T.Cashmore, W.Hughes, W.Glew, E.Kirk, W.Edmonds, W.Howell, T.Cannings. Front row: H.Banks, C.Pretty, F.Mobley, T.Bird, W.Dorrell.

Before the start of the 1890-91 season, Singers acquired the services of Frank Mobley, one of the greatest players to appear for the club. He played at centre-forward, which meant Harry Banks moved to the right-wing to partner Charlie Pretty with captain Tom Bird and Billy Dorrell on the left. It was the finest football team Coventry had in its first 25 years of existence.

Singers powered to the Final with victories over Kings Heath (10-1), Cannock (6-2), Brierley Hill Alliance (6-0) and, in the semi-finals, Packington (5-0).

In the Final they met the powerful Willenhall Pickwicks at Villa's Perry Barr ground. On the day of the big match, some 2,500 Coventrians made their way there by train and bicycle. By kick-off time, a crowd of 6,000 was present and the *Coventry Mercury* reported: 'The Pickwicks took the field to a hearty welcome but it was nothing to the roar which greeted Singers.' Local reporters emphasized the difference in statures: 'It was very plain if weight was to score, Singers would not have a ghost of change.'

The newspaper went on: 'Coventrians soon fell silent as the Pickwicks took up the attack, using their weight to advantage.

'Midway through the first half, Singers launched the crucial attack. The ball was kept bobbing about near the Pickwicks' goal. Then Harry Banks found Frank Mobley, and with a fair daisy-cutter he beat the Pickwick 'keeper and Singers had scored the first goal amid a scene which baffles description. Hats were thrown in the air by the hundreds and the Coventry supporters simply shouted themselves hoarse.' In the second half, Singers treated the crowd to 'such a display no other row of junior forwards in the country could give'.

By the time the team arrived back in the city, excitement was running at fever pitch and most of the population of the old town were in the streets to welcome their heroes home.

'Their triumphal path was lit by a series of coloured fires and when the coach reached the narrow Hertford Street, the crowd was so dense it bought the procession to a halt. Women screamed and children cried to be delivered from the horse hooves and coach wheels.'

In the same year, the Coventry Rugby Club and their juniors had won their respective cups, so the *Telegraph* dubbed 1891 'The Year of Coventry's Three Cups'.

To commemorate this notion, a local tobacco importer, David Cooke, introduced his own brand of 'Three Cups Tobacco'. He, of course, was destined to play a significant role in later years as director of Coventry City.

The following season, Singers football scaled yet new heights. They entered, not only the Birmingham Cup, but also the Walsall Cup and the Wednesbury Cup and won all three, thus making 1892 Singers' own 'Year of the Three Cups'.

In the Birmingham Cup they once again met Willenhall in the Final but this time achieved an easier victory by a 2-0 margin.

In their six Birmingham Cup games, Singers scored a record 37 goals, 15 of them coming from Frank Mobley. In the Final of the Walsall Cup, they beat Bloxwich Strollers 3-1 after a replay and again set a competition record with 38 goals.

In the Wednesbury Charity Cup, Singers found themselves up against full-time professionals, but that made little difference to the outcome of the games. They met Walsall Town Swifts in the second round, shortly before they were elected to the Second Division of the Football League. The cycle-shop team were unimpressed, winning 5-2.

Singers did not take part in the Final of this competition. Having drawn with Wednesbury Old Athletic in the semi-final, they saw the Wednesbury team contest the Final by a technical sleight of hand. But under threat from the FA, that decision was overruled with the outcome that the trophy was shared and the Athletic were ordered to hand over half the prize money.

The FA Cup Disasters

TODAY, thankfully, the enduring image of Coventry City and the FA Cup remains Brian Kilcline holding the trophy aloft after one of Wembley's finest occasions.

However, that 1987 success aside, City's FA Cup history has been one of enduring calamity and humiliation. Those who reeled with disbelief at the scoreline, Sutton United 2 Coventry City 1, should have checked the record books. Far from being a one-off aberration, it was wholly in keeping with tradition.

The story begins back in 1897. It was one of Singers best seasons in the Birmingham League, but the first preliminary round of the Cup paired them with the village amateurs of Wrockwardine Wood. It should have been a formality but the 'Rocks', cheered on by a crowd of 700, won 1-0.

A few years later, in 1901, came the Cup tie that found its way into all the record books: Berwick Rangers 11, Coventry City 2, the club's heaviest Cup defeat.

However, on this occasion there were extenuating circumstances. These were not the Rangers of Tweed but of Worcester, who later changed their name to Worcester City. On the day in question, Coventry were scheduled to play a League game against Ironbridge and the Birmingham League would not allow a postponement.

This was at a time when City had no reserve team, so a side was hastily recruited from local league players to represent them at Worcester, whilst the first team played out a goalless draw at Ironbridge.

When City entered the Southern League, the flow of mishaps was temporarily staunched but it was business as usual in 1914-15. War raged across Europe as City travelled to the tiny North Derbyshire town of Glossop. Excitement was hardly unconfined: there was a gate of 539 to see the home side win 3-1. City's share of the gate was £1 4s, which helped a little towards their train fares which totalled of £13 15s.

It should be said, of course, that Glossop were then in the Second Division of the Football League — albeit they would end the season bottom of the table and resign after the war — so it was not perhaps such a giantkilling act.

By the 1920s, City were members of the Football League themselves, but some things just did not change. In 1922, it was the turn of the Lancashire Combination side New Brighton. A few hours before kick-off, the City players held an emergency strike meeting, the issue being their win bonus.

It proved academic, the hero of the day was John Lyon, whose hat-trick sank the City 3-0 in front of 10,000 fans. Again, though, was this a real giantkilling feat? After all, this was still the qualifying competition of the Cup and New Brighton were to be elected to the Third Division North for the following season.

Two years later, the show moved to Worksop, where 4,410 spectators packed their tiny ground. When the Midland Leaguers took the lead, their chairman, beside himself with glee, invaded the pitch. The Bantams, meanwhile, were left to 'concentrate on the League'. At the time it was considered City's most inglorious defeat, particularly when it became known that most of the Worksop team had spent the morning of the match working down the local coalmine.

By contrast, the 1935-6 season was City's finest hour since entering the League, the year they won the Third Division South championship with Harry Storer at the helm. But they still found time to go out of the Cup, this time to Scunthorpe & Lindsey United, then in the Midland League. City lost 4-2 in a replay, despite the presence of Jock Lauderdale and Clarrie Bourton.

The date 25 November 1961, is one that has found a permanent place in City's

George Hudson, a great Highfield Road favourite who returned to inflict FA Cup humiliation upon the Sky Blues when he helped Tranmere to victory after a replay.

history. That was when some 12,080 spectators watched expectantly as City took on part-timers Kings Lynn, second from the bottom of the Southern League.

Coventry took a first-half lead, but within eight minutes they were 2-1 down. The *Telegraph* reported: 'In probably the most grim page in City's modern history, a team of part-timers inscribed their indelible mark by sweeping their Third Division opponents out of the FA Cup and leaving shocked and stunned City fans to wonder how a League side gave such puny and deplorably inept resistance.'

By 1968, City were a First Division team at last and had never been better placed to suffer serious humiliation. Trouble began immediately when they were drawn at home to Tranmere Rovers in the third round. The Sky Blues should have feared the worst when they saw the great George Hudson appearing for the opposition. Rovers drew 1-1 and in the replay, Hudson cooly dispatched the goal that began the collapse. Final score: 2-0.

Noel Cantwell failed to learn from this experience: three years later it was the turn of even lowlier Rochdale. "Rochdale, where's that?" asked Cantwell. He was about to find out.

"Seriously, this is a game we will win and we shall just hope for a home draw in the fourth round." Cantwell even objected to playing under the Spotland lights and had the match switched to Monday afternoon — 11 January, another black day in Coventry City's FA Cup history.

A crowd of 13,000 paid record receipts of £4,000 and goals from David Cross and Dennis Butler carried Rochdale to a 2-1 win.

The following season the writing was on the wall for Cantwell. Having just bought Hull City's most famous player, Chris Chilton, he might have expected to beat the Tigers at Highfield Road, but Coventry lost 1-0 and Cantwell said goodbye.

In 1980, the fans were once again contemplating a decent Cup run and some 5,000 travelled to Blackburn for the fourth round. But Gordon Milne's team of juniors gave a feeble display, the young centre-forward Mark Hateley being particularly inept.

Toward the end of the first half, an Andy Crawford header put the home side ahead and City were robbed of what would have been a dream fifth-round tie, at home to Aston Villa.

And so to the most sensational of them all. Not only in the top six in Division One, but also FA Cup winners just 18 months earlier — surely nothing could rock Coventry City's Cup boat?

But the drama moves to the most unlikely of all settings. Who could have foreseen what would happen as they strolled along Gander Green Lane, past the neatly manicured lawns, the Volvos in the drive, through a suburban nightmare designed for executives' wives to have nervous breakdowns.

In this most incongruous of football settings, City were about to experience their own personal Hades. The Coventry players clowned and laughed their way through the warm-up, but when play got underway Sutton United were taking things ominously seriously.

After 42 minutes, Rains put the home side ahead. Phillips pulled one back, but by then Sutton had the scent of victory in their nostrils and after 58 minutes, Hanlan gave the Vauxhall Conference side a quite remarkable win.

A year later John Sillett believed the 'Sutton experience' had done his players good. The venue was the County Ground, Northampton. The rain lashed down and the Cobblers hit a post after ten minutes, so it did not come as that much of a surprise when Barnes crossed and Berry converted to make it 1-0 to the home side. And 1-0 it stayed.

It would be another ten months before the Coventry board withdrew their backing for John Sillett, but many City fans took their leave at Northampton 1990.

Above and opposite page: How a newspaper cartoonist saw the Villa-Coventry tussles.

The Aston Villa Matches of 1936-1938

LOOKING back over half a century, it is difficult to place these four matches into perspective (especially as Coventry City have now been part of football's 'establishment' for 25 years).

Over 50 years ago, the situation was far different: Aston Villa were about to spend their first-ever season out of the First Division; and Coventry City were riding on the crest of a wave after finally regaining their Second Division status the previous season.

From the final match of 1935-6, local coach firms were putting up signs like, 'Watch out Villa, we're on our way,' and 'Sign up here and book your seat for the Villa'. And when the fixture list was announced, all roads led to Villa Park on 3 October 1936.

It was described as the most amazing mass departure in the city's history as over 15,000 fans packed trains and coaches (even carrying pigeons to send details of the score back to Coventry). The team was involved in a crash, even before they left Coventry, luckily without injury, and the players were able to transfer to another coach.

The game itself lived up to all expectations with City's fitness and team spirit being more than a match for Villa's superior class. Great performances were seen from Frith, Mason, McDonald, whilst Bourton was back to his best. The crowd of nearly 64,000 was the highest ever to see Coventry City play and their cheque for £494 represented a record share of gate receipts.

When the two sides met again the following February, they were both just outside the promotion area but nevertheless the second-highest ever attendance — almost 40,000 — assembled for a League match at Highfield Road. The game was described as a classic with a feast of end-to-end football.

The only goal came after five minutes play, when Jackie Brown headed home an Arthur Fitton cross. The excitement was endless as Morgan made many fine saves and Bourton almost broke the bar with Morton well beaten.

City had the satisfaction of finishing one place ahead of Villa at the end of the season and it was felt that both teams would challenge strongly for promotion the following year.

IN HIS REPERTORY

Don't despair, fellow playgoers — Little Vince, the Invincible, gets out of these situations every week!

Coventry City's Roberts gets in a header against the Villa at Highfield Road in March 1938.

Indeed, by the time the teams squared-up again the following October, City were unbeaten leaders of the Second Division with Villa not far behind. The Coventry following this time was even higher, estimated at 20,000, and the Villa Park attendance of 68,029 set a new record for the Second Division.

Both teams had lost players due to international calls and although the Villa squad was more or less unchanged from the previous season, City had added Metcalf and Taylor, although Bourton had finally bowed out, finding it much harder to hit the back of the net in the Second Division.

The 'Old Five' days were now passed, to be replaced by a defence that many fans will hold up as the finest ever to represent Coventry City. The game was as tight and thrilling as the previous two, although this time City were the favourites.

They took the lead after 24 minutes, when McDonald almost broke the net with a stinging shot from the edge of the box. And Coventry should have had a penalty when Allen pushed Lager in the back. After having most of the play, City allowed Villa a softish goal when Houghton scored with a long-range free-kick after 53 minutes.

Honours were even for the rest of the match, although it must be said that City's overall teamwork was of a superior nature.

The final great occasion in this series took place on 12 March 1938, when Villa visited Highfield Road, one point and one place behind third-placed Coventry.

The city streets had never seen such amazing scenes of mass activity. By 2.30pm, most of the gates at Highfield Road had been closed, with W.A.Camkin in charge of packing (by use of an amplifier he was able to address all sides of the ground). A new ground record of 44,930 was set, a figure which would stand for almost 30 years.

Villa were outplayed for long periods but got the goal that mattered late on in the game, Starling's shot eluding Morgan and bouncing in off the post to stun City's fans.

City had most of the chances, but threw them away in a most wasteful fashion. With so much at stake, the game was played at a frantic pace, although Villa's defensive tactics were deserving of far more vigorous action than the referee was prepared to apply.

Brown missed an easy chance early on, there was no doubt that Pritty handled on the line, and Biddlestone made many fine saves. Despite brilliant displays from McDonald and Roberts, Villa held on for a narrow victory.

That was the end of the series as Villa went on to win the Second Division championship with City narrowly missing out in fourth place. The teams would not meet again in a League match for over 37 years and many saw this game as the one which marked the beginning of City's decline. Certainly it would be many years before they were as close to promotion again.

McDonald tries a shot at the Villa goal during the same match but Villa triumphed with a goal from Ronnie Starling.

1936-37
Oct 3
Aston Villa 0 Coventry 0.
Coventry City: Morgan; Astley, Smith, Frith, Mason, Archer, Pritchard, Jones, Bourton, McDonald, Fitton.
Aston Villa: Biddlestone; Griffiths, Cobley, Massie, Allen, Hardy, Kew, Martin, Broome, Dix, Houghton.
Att: 63,686.
Feb 6
Coventry City 1 *(Brown)* **Aston Villa 0**
Coventry City: Morgan; Astley, Elliott, Frith, Mason, Archer, Brown, McDonald, Bourton, Jones, Fitton.
Aston Villa: Morton; Griffiths, Cobley, Massie, Allen, Hardy, Maund, Haycock, Starling, Broome, Houghton.
Att: 39,808

1937-38
Oct 30
Aston Villa 1 *(Houghton)* **Coventry City 1** *(McDonald)*
Coventry City: Morgan, Astley, Metcalf, Frith, Mason, Archer, Taylor, McDonald, Lager, Roberts, Brown.
Aston Villa: Biddlestone; Callaghan, Cobley, Gardner, Allen, Iverson, Broome, Haycock, Clayton, Starling, Houghton.
Att: 68,029.
Mar 12
Coventry City 0 Aston Villa 1*(Starling)*
Coventry City: Morgan; Astley, Metcalf, Frith, Mason, Archer, Taylor, Roberts, Lake, McDonald, Brown.
Aston Villa: Biddlestone; Callaghan, Cobley, Massie, Pritty, Iverson, Broome, Haycock, Shell, Starling, Houghton.
Att: 44,930.

Coventry City's Managers

WHEN compiling a list of Coventry City managers in chronological order, one faces the problem of trying to distinguish between the roles of secretary, manager and coaches, all of which, at various times, have been occupied separately or combined into one job.

From 1883 to 1887, the first two secretaries were both players. From 1887, J.G.Morgan, the first non-playing official, was responsible for all levels of development including team selection and he dominated the club for nearly six years. After Morgan, the job was less clearly defined and more responsibility fell to the committee, including that of team selection.

Towards the end of the Birmingham League period, the role of coach and secretary have become separated. This continued into the Southern League, when Harry Buckle (see *City Stars A-Z*) became manager in 1909-10 and Walter Harris acted as secretary.

In 1911, Robert Wallace was appointed with the title secretary-manager, a position which remained, in name at least, until the 1950s. It appears, though, that Wallace was never involved in team selection and although he held the title of secretary-manager until the arrival of Frank Scott-Walford in 1914, it must be said that he had no real influence on team affairs, which remained in the hands of the committee. Wallace is not, therefore, included in the biographical section which follows.

It is difficult to say at what stage the manager gained a degree of autonomy over team affairs and the recruitment of new players — accusations of boardroom interference were made well into the 1950s. Indeed, the relative independence of the manager was probably not clearly defined before the arrival of Jimmy Hill in 1961.

Attempting to assess the managers also presents a problem: so many factors beyond their immediate control are liable to consign the most talented man to abject failure. However, by the most realistic of criteria City have had two truly great managers: Harry Storer and Jimmy Hill, with perhaps a special mention for J.G.Morgan, often referred to as 'the Father of the Club'.

Outside this select trio, honours go to Bobby Gould, who did so much to revive flagging spirits and brought so many great players to the club, and John Sillett for leading City to their finest hour in 1987.

The first secretary, William Stanley, warrants a special item as founder of the club. He was succeeded in 1885 by another 'original' and fellow team member, centre-half Harry Hathaway.

J.G.Morgan then took over in 1887 and retired in December 1892. His successor, appointed on 1 January 1893, was the popular goalkeeper Teddy Kirk. He was succeeded in the close season by George Maley; and in 1894 by another ex-player, full-back Joe Collins.

In 1896, another member of the all-conquering 'Little Blackbirds' side of 1891, Tommy Cashmore, was appointed. Cashmore was a prime mover in the change of name in 1898 and the move to Highfield Road a year later. B.Newhall held office from 1900 to 1902. M.O'Shea from 1902 to 1905.

After Newhall left the club in 1905, Joe Beaman was put in control of team affairs by a committee headed by Thomas Owen.

Following the club's registration as a limited company in July 1907, Fred Lee became secretary, Thomas Owen chairman and Joe Beaman continued as coach until the appointment of Harry Buckle as player-manager in 1908.

William Stanley
1883-1885

LITTLE is known of Coventry City's first 'manager', William Stanley, yet various eye-witness accounts place him at the centre of that momentous meeting at the Aylesford Inn, Aylesford Street, back in October 1883 and credit him with being the true founder of the club.

Queen Victoria was on the throne and Gladstone was her Prime Minister, but for the little group of cycle machinists from Singers' Canterbury Street works there was only one pressing issue. They cast envious eyes toward the Birmingham area, at Small Heath, Aston Villa and West Bromwich Albion, and decided it was time that Coventry had a soccer team of its own.

Stanley's ancestors are buried in St Peter's Churchyard, next door to the original Singers works, so we can assume that he was a local man. We also know that he played at centre-forward and acted as secretary for two years, arranged the fixture lists and successfully applied for membership of the Warwickshire Football Association. After 1885, his name dissappears and vice-captain Harry Hathaway takes over, possibly on a prior agreement of rotation.

J.G.Morgan
1887-1893

A CENTURY ago in Coventry, J.G.Morgan was an instantly recognizable local celebrity. He became club secretary in 1887, the first non-player in the role, and the first figure from this time who most closely resembled the modern notion of a manager.

He was a director of the Singers Cycle works and kept a tobacconists on the opposite side of Canterbury Street, where a crowd would gather once a week to see J.G's team selection for the following Saturday. He was prominent in local sports and became a noted figure in County Association meetings in Birmingham.

Under Morgan, the club was totally transformed. From an insignificant works side, playing on an open field in front of a handful of friends, it became one of the most famous junior sides in the Midlands, playing in their Stoke Road enclosure before crowds of several thousand.

J.G. retired in 1892, by which time Singers had achieved everything possible at their level. Well into his 80s, J.G. died in 1935. The *Telegraph* paid their own tribute: 'The early seeds of our great club were sown and matured under the guidance and foresight of our departed friend'.

Frank Scott-Walford
1914-1915

FRANK Scott-Walford was manager of Coventry City for only one season, the 1914-15 campaign. A native of Perry Barr, Birmingham, Scott-Walford was an amateur goalkeeper on Tottenham Hotspur's book before he joined the Isthmian League club, London Caledonians.

However, his playing ability never matched his administrative skills and he went on to form the Enfield and District League and became a Southern League referee. He was also a keen cricketer and cyclist.

His first managerial post was with Brighton, whom he joined in March 1905, but there he faced the unenviable task of getting together almost an entirely new team. An FA Council meeting in April 1906 reported that he had achieved this by approaching players from other clubs before their contracts had expired and the FA suspended him from 16 April to 1 August that year.

He moved to Leeds City in 1908 but met with little success in the four seasons he was in charge there. He did bring Joe Enright (who would later join Coventry City) and Billy Gillespie over from Ireland but most of his imports failed to impress.

With Leeds City applying for re-election in 1912 he resigned, to be replaced by the legendary Herbert Chapman.

Two years later, with the world now at war and football destined soon to take a back seat, Scott-Walford was appointed manager of Coventry City, who had just dropped into the Second Division of the Southern League, which meant that they had to play half their away games in South Wales.

In these inauspicious circumstances, Scott-Walford was mainly involved in simply finding 11 players and just keeping the club going.

Needless to say, the season was a financial disaster and when business was finally wound up, the club's accounts revealed that Frank Scott-Walford was still owed £100 in unpaid wages.

William Clayton
January 1917-October 1919

LITTLE is known of William Clayton, except that he had previously held a part-time appointment with Birmingham and came to Highfield Road with excellent references.

During the war he worked for City only on a part-time basis, finding employment in the burgeoning armaments industry in the city to supplement his income. He was an influential figure in getting City into the Midland Section of the Football League in 1918 and became full-time manager during that season.

Both Clayton and the club were out of their depth in the first season of League football and after the club picked up only two points out of the first 22, he resigned.

Harry Pollitt
November 1919-May 1920

WITH Coventry City firmly anchored at the foot of the table, David Cooke issued a clarion call to the supporters. They would stop at nothing to retain their hard-won League status. The new manager, the hitherto unknown Harry Pollitt, was given the then astronomical sum of £5,000 to spend on new players.

Pollitt was certainly no slouch when it came to signing new players and, little by little, City inched their way to safety. Unfortunately, Pollitt's efforts were not rewarded and he was sacked in May 1920.

Five years later he was implicated in the 'Bury scandal' and suspended *sine die*. After this he disappeared once more into obscurity.

Albert Evans
June 1920-November 1924

BORN in Coventry in 1874, Albert Evans was the City manager from 1920 until his 'resignation' in November 1924.

It was not an easy time for anyone to make his managerial debut — City were staggering beneath the crippling effects of mounting debts and simmering resentment surrounding the 'Bury Affair'.

Evans also inherited an inadequate squad of players. He set about establishing continuity and built a team around regulars like Jerry Best, Jackie Randle, Teddy Winship, Jimmy Dougall and Cute Herbert. Despite his efforts, the Bantams never finished higher than 18th but his teams were well supported and many regard it a miracle he kept them up at all.

He was very loyal to his players who, in turn, made their disappointment known following his 'resignation'.

Before entering the mire that was then Highfield Road, Evans had enjoyed a distinguished playing career. He was Aston Villa's right-back for 11 years, at a time when Villa could justly claim to be the best team in the land. He won three League Championship medals and was in the double-winning side of 1896-7. He also represented the Football League.

In 1907, Evans joined West Bromwich Albion and then moved to County Durham before returning to The Hawthorns as trainer. In his playing career he suffered a broken leg four times which limited his total appearances.

After leaving football, he lead an adventurous life which included a spell of gold prospecting in the Yukon. He died in 1966, aged 92, the longest surviving member of the Villa double-winning side.

James Kerr
July 1925-February 1928

JAMES Kerr, who was manager from July 1925 until February 1928, presided over three of the most dismal seasons in Coventry City's history. Indeed, he arrived at a bad time, with City just relegated to the Third Division North.

The old players were known to be upset at the sacking of Albert Evans and this may help to explain why Kerr felt it necessary to dispense with so many of them.

Unfortunately, they were often replaced by players of inferior ability, men usually recruited from Kerr's native Scotland where he had spent his early career with Bathgate FC.

Kerr certainly worked overtime in the transfer market but as the *Telegraph* commented against a background of dwindling attendances: 'City fans have little desire to watch Coventry Celtic'.

Things went from bad to worse. After finishing 16th in 1926, City faired little better in the Southern Section, finishing 15th and then 20th in 1928, by which time Kerr had been dismissed.

In his time, James Kerr had endured some blistering attacks from the *Telegraph* who, on one famous occasion, compared the City club to a mule, being 'without pride of ancestry or hope of posterity'. How much of this could be blamed on Kerr is debatable.

Kerr moved the short distance to Fellows Park in the close season of 1928, to take over as manager of Walsall, but he met with little success in his only season in charge of the Saddlers.

He did, however, arrange the transfer of Billy Lake to Highfield Road and began a close association between the two clubs. Apart from players moving between the clubs, Walsall borrowed a set of City's shirts when they beat Arsenal in the FA Cup in 1933.

In 1929 he became manager of Norwich City, who had just finished bottom of the Third Division South. In 1934 they were champions, although, sadly, Kerr did not live to enjoy his triumph. He died of bronchial pneumonia in February of that year.

James McIntyre
June 1928-February 1931

JAMES McIntyre, who was born in Walsall in 1881, first came to Coventry City as a player in 1905 and his impact was immediate, for he scored hat-tricks in his second and third games.

He had a fine season with a record total of 23 goals and, although he left after that one campaign, he appears to have retained an interest in the club, buying shares in 1907 and acting as trainer. He later refereed in the

Coventry & North Warwickshire League.

He went on to play for Walsall, Notts County and Northampton Town, where he was a playing colleague of Herbert Chapman, and Reading and then became trainer at Southampton before returning to Coventry for munitions work during World War One.

In 1919, he became manager of Southampton and took the Saints into the new Third Division of the Football League and then to promotion to Division Two in 1922. After spending two more seasons at The Dell he retired and in 1924 went to run a hotel in Edinburgh.

In 1928, he was tempted back to football and became manager of Coventry City. Once again his impact was quickly felt. The fitness and discipline of the players had long been the subject of criticism and this he combated with 'McIntyre's Ticket', a set of rules for the players which forbade, among other things 'attendance at whist drives'.

It seemed to do the trick and the 1928-9 season was the club's best since entering the Football League. But Coventry City were still deep in debt and their two star players, Ernie Toseland and Peter Ramage, were sold. Both went on to enjoy prominent careers in the First Division, with Manchester City and Derby County respectively.

In 1930, City finished sixth and at last promotion talk was in the air. Alas, behind the scenes another crisis was brewing, McIntyre resented the interference of the board and a power struggle was underway between F.W.Kimberley and Walter Brandish.

Brandish proved the stronger and from the close season of 1930 he designed to remove McIntyre. Under such circumstances it was hardly surprising that a poor season ensued and, following a disastrous FA Cup defeat at the hands of Exeter City, Brandish took over team selection and in February 1931, McIntyre was sacked.

The following season he took over at Fulham and, as if to prove his point, guided the Cottagers to the Third Division South title, whilst City trailed in 12th position.

Yet again, however, McIntyre was not altogether popular with his directors. The club endured a run of poor results and an entry in the Fulham board minutes of February 1934 reads: 'James McIntyre was dismissed due to his unprecedented action in transferring, entirely on his own initiative, F.Newton to Reading for the impossible price of £650'.

James McIntyre left football again, this time for good, and returned to Southampton where he took employment with a company called Follands.

Harry Storer
June 1931-June 1945 and November 1948-November 1953

WHEN the Coventry City manager's job became vacant in early 1931, Harry Storer was still a regular in Burnley's First Division team, but at the age of 33 his long playing career was drawing to a close.

He was only one of 'hundreds' of applicants for the City job but impressed Walter Brandish so much at the interview that he was immediately offered the post.

Born in Liverpool in 1898, Storer was the son of a famous England and Liverpool goalkeeper and nephew of a Derbyshire and England cricketer. The family moved to the Midlands during the war and after a spell with Grimsby Town, Harry Storer moved to Derby County in 1921, for £4,500. He was also a talented opening batsman who played in Derbyshire's 1936 County Championship-winning team.

At the Baseball Ground he was described thus: 'A tower of strength whether at inside-left or left-half. In attack he is brainy, unselfish and possesses a hard shot. He is thoughtful and employs a hard and decisive tackle.'

A couple of England caps followed and in February 1929 he was on his way to Turf Moor for a large fee. Nothing more needs to be said about City's achievements in the 1930s, as Storer took them into the Second Division, but most of the players who served under him had nothing but respect for his style of management.

Stories of his antics are legion in the game and for Storer the dressing-room was essentially a 'barracks' where a constant vigil had to be kept for 'skivers' and 'cissies'. Although he was very well versed in football tactics, he was not a technocrat but basically a sergeant-major figure.

His stock in trade was fire and brimstone and he had an almost mystical concern for hardness in the working-class male. Storer's capacity to abuse his teams, and individual members of these teams, is legendary. Although he was responsible for the fabulous years of the 'Old Five', from 1936 to his retirement from the game in 1962 he was noted for the defensive qualities of his team.

Former Coventry City goalkeeper Peter Taylor, who was Brian Clough's assistant at Derby County and Nottingham Forest, paid fulsome tribute to Storer: "A manager whose soul marches on as long as Brian and myself remain in football."

Storer surprisingly left Highfield Road in June 1945, but the move was probably based on the premise that he had achieved as much as he could at Highfield Road. He took Birmingham City back to the First Division, but the lure of Highfield Road was too strong and by November 1948, he was back there.

Upon his return he said, "Coventry is my club. I made a mistake of leaving once and have regretted it ever since."

The old magic worked in the short term but, overall, things were never the same again. Maybe the war had changed too many things, or possibly Storer's judgement was waning. This time he spent heavily, in both 1950-51 and 1951-2, but ultimately he failed and when he resigned (or was he sacked?), there was much acrimony.

This time there was to be no return. It was a sad parting for a manager who had spent the best part of 20 years with the club. His relationship with Erle Shanks was always a close one; in fact, Storer had been instrumental in Shanks joining the board in 1936.

Harry Storer remained a Coventry shareholder but moved to Derby County in 1955 and stayed in charge at the Baseball Ground until his retirement in 1962. He came to take the Rams out of the Third Division North and succeeded, lifting them back with a mixture of cold steel in signings like former Coventry defender Martin McDonnell, and supreme skill in the likes of the former West Brom and Irish international inside-forward, Reg Ryan.

Storer continued to undertake scouting duties until his death at his Derby home in May 1967, having lived to see the Coventry club that was his first love finally achieve the First Division status that eluded him. He will always be referred as one of the three great managers of the club.

Dick Bayliss
June 1945-April 1947

DICK Bayliss, Harry Storer's chief scout and right-hand man at Highfield Road since 1931, was the unanimous choice to take over when Storer left to join Birmingham City in June 1945.

A native of Alfreton in Derbyshire, Bayliss had a fairly undistinguished career as a player, making a handful of appearances for Luton Town, Mansfield Town and Southend United in the 1920s.

As a scout, though, he was considered an excellent judge of a player and was known in every boardroom in the country. He was responsible for bringing to Highfield Road a constant supply of players during the period between 1931 and 1939.

Never one to believe in inflated transfer fees, he was always looking to construct a team based on a steady flow of young players from the Colts and Reserves. He was appointed manager in June 1945, a very difficult time for football with large numbers of players still in the armed forces and many clubs relying on guests from other teams.

Things gradually got back to normal in the transitional season of 1945-6 and City were ready to resume in the Football League in August 1946 with a sound if ageing squad of players. Bayliss had made few changes, acquiring Aldecoa and Bett, but it was really the 1939-40 squad minus three players who had retired.

For Bayliss it was a difficult season and by the turn of the year, his health, which had never been robust, began to deteriorate, much aggravated by a nightmare drive back from a scouting mission in Scotland during the big freeze of 1947. He caught a chill and collapsed soon afterwards. An incurable kidney complaint was diagnosed and after a spell in a Kenilworth nursing home, he died at his home in Coventry on 5 April 1947, at the early age of 47.

Universally popular with the playing staff, a number of whom maintained a vigil at his bedside during the last weeks of his life, Bayliss never really had time to develop his own team. We must assume the development of the youth squad would have laid the foundations of a successful post-war period.

Billy Frith
June 1947-November 1948 and September 1957-December 1961

WHEN Billy Frith returned to Highfield Road in 1946-7, in time to play a few games in that first post-war season, he had endured a rough introduction to management as player-boss of Port Vale (see *City Stars A-Z*).

He came back as assistant to Dick Bayliss and when Bayliss died in April 1947, Frith was the obvious choice to take over from him. He quickly got into his stride and after he signed Noel Simpson and Norman Lockhart, City had a fairly useful side which finished halfway up the Second Division.

But then things began to go downhill with the sale of George Lowrie to Newcastle United and by November 1948, with Coventry 19th in the table and with only four wins in 19 games, Frith was sacked, to be replaced by his old mentor, Harry Storer.

A bitter Frith left Highfield Road to become a full-time teacher and part-time manager of Rugby Town and then Stafford Rangers. But the lure of League football in general and Coventry City in particular was too great and in 1955 he was back at the club as coach to the juniors.

It was a period of tremendous turbulence at the club and after more managerial upheavals he was recalled to the hot seat in the hour of need, in September 1957.

Frith was unable to get Coventry into the newly-formed Third Division — the decline was too far advanced for that — but with a few astute signings, financed once again by directors' loans, and a number of promising youngsters, he was able to construct a team that climbed out of Division Four at the first attempt and almost made it straight through to the Second Division until they ran out of steam in the last few matches.

Alas, thereafter it was downhill for a club with an ageing team and mounting debts. After the FA Cup humiliation at the hands of King's Lynn, the inevitable happened as chairman Derrick Robins removed Frith and his entire management team.

Billy Frith left his beloved club with dignity and returned to teaching, in which profession he remained until his retirement in 1977. His association with Coventry City had extended to almost 30 years, with many spent as an important player and then two spells as manager.

He still kept in touch with the game, with weekly scouting missions, and in 1980 he was still scouting for Chesterfield, from his home in Kenilworth.

Jack Fairbrother
January 1954-October 1954

JACK Fairbrother's was another short-lived appointment of the stormy post-war era at Highfield Road.

As a Preston North End goalkeeper he lost a large part of his career to the war but moved to Newcastle United in July 1947 and was part of their glittering team of the late 1940s. Fairbrother was an outstanding goalkeeper at this time and very unlucky not to win full England cap, although he had appeared for the Football League during the war.

A broken collarbone ended his career with Newcastle and he moved to Peterborough United, the outstanding non-League team of the period, as manager.

As a young manager he seemed to have the

right credentials for Coventry City but his stay there was dogged with ill fortune. Within six weeks of arriving at Highfield Road, he had become a widower with two young children, after his wife died as a result of an accident sustained in their home.

On the football field there was little to be done during the latter part of 1953-4, but in the close season he had picked up the Nottingham Forest veterans, Capel and Collindridge, and with quite a strong squad of players available had moulded them into an effective unit.

The 'team that Jack built' went to the top of the table and, for a few short weeks, the Second Division beckoned. Things started to go wrong, though, and with injuries, enforced sales and general acrimony in the air, Fairbrother resigned for 'personal reasons'. It appears that the sale of Eddie Brown was the final straw.

After a spell out of the game, Fairbrother did some coaching in Israel, managed Consett, Gateshead and finally Peterborough United between 1962 and 1964. After leaving the game he retired to Lincolnshire.

Charlie Elliott
October 1954-April 1955

CHARLIE Elliott, who was born at Bolsover on 24 April 1912, was a Derbyshire cricketing teammate of Harry Storer when Storer took over at Highfield Road in the close season of 1931 and it seemed that Elliott, a versatile 19-year-old soccer player as well, would join him.

Elliott had previously been on the books of Sheffield Wednesday but had failed to make a single first-team appearance for the Owls. Over the next 16 seasons it was to be a similar story at Highfield Road, with Elliott's appearances mainly depending on injuries to other players.

One such opportunity came at the end of 1935-6, when George Mann was injured. Elliott came in at centre-half and played a couple of 'blinders' as City won the Third Division South championship.

After a spell in the Navy, Elliott returned to Coventry in 1945 and continued to play until his retirement in 1948, by which time he had totalled 101 League and Cup appearances, scoring two goals. Ironically, his most appearances came in his penultimate season as a City player, when he played in 28 League games in 1946-7.

After a spell out of the game he returned to Highfield Road as chief scout in the early 1950s and when Jack Fairbrother resigned in 1954, the Coventry board appointed Elliott as the club's caretaker manager until Jesse Carver arrived the following June. He reverted to the position of chief scout but resigned in October 1955.

Those were not happy times for Coventry City and Elliott eventually took over a hotel in West Bridgford, near the Trent Bridge cricket ground. As a first-class umpire, Elliott stood in 46 Test matches. For some years he was chairman of Derbyshire CCC's cricket committee.

Jesse Carver
June 1955-December 1955

COVENTRY City surprised the football world in January 1955, when they announced that they had secured the services of Jesse Carver as team manager. A couple of months later there was a further announcement that the renowned coach, George Raynor, would be his assistant. It appeared that Erle Shanks, who was a personal friend of Carver, had masterminded this coup.

Jesse Carver was born in Liverpool in 1911 and during the 1930s had played as a forceful wing-half for Blackburn Rovers, Newcastle United and Bury. After a spell as coach to Huddersfield Town, he moved to Holland and then to the hothouse atmosphere of Italian soccer with Roma, Lazio, Juventus and Torino.

Carver, tightly and almost symbolically belted into his fawn raincoat, was becoming an old Italian hand, highly respected and able to more or less choose his jobs.

Why he picked out Coventry City remains a mystery to this day but, like a lot of ex-patriots, he felt a desire to succeed in his native land. It was certainly headline stuff 'as mystery moves took place behind closed doors' and caught the public's imagination.

Whilst Continental-style football was certainly eye-catching, it cut no ice in the Third Division and a change of style was introduced by November. It now transpires that, almost as soon as he arrived, Carver realized he had made a mistake and was pestering Shanks to release him from his contract, even before the season had started.

Shanks finally gave way on 31 December 1955 and by the New Year, Carver was installed as manager of Lazio, having agreed not to take another job in the United Kingdom before July 1958.

He did return to England towards the end of 1958, taking up a coaching appointment with Tottenham Hotspur, but once again he failed to settle and moved on again, this time to the USA and Portugal before returning to the UK to retire in the late 1960s.

George Raynor
January 1956-June 1956

GEORGE Raynor was one of the most successful coaches in Europe in the two decades after World War Two. Like Jimmy Hogan, who had masterminded the rise of Austrian football before the war, Raynor craved success in his home country, but this was to elude him.

Born in Doncaster in 1908, he had moved around the lower reaches of the League in the 1930s, from Mansfield Town to Aldershot via Bury, Rotherham United and Sheffield United, in a playing career that never reached any great heights.

During the war he had held high-level physical-training appointments in the Army, both in the UK and overseas, and after the end of hostilities he moved to Sweden, where, after a spell in charge of AIK, he took over the national squad which won the Olympic Games in London in 1948 and reached the semi-finals of the 1950 World Cup in Rio.

From Sweden he moved to the cauldron of Italian football, holding coaching appointments with both Roma and Lazio. It was from Lazio that Jesse Carver persuaded Raynor to join Coventry City in June 1955.

In retrospect, it seems the most amazing coup for the club, but with both men there was a nagging desire to achieve something in England. And maybe Coventry City appeared to have a large amount of unfulfilled potential.

During Carver's reign, it was Raynor who was in charge of team training and match preparation and one suspects that the Continental-style game was very much his idea.

When Carver returned to Italy in January 1956, Raynor was the obvious choice to take over and when appointed he pledged himself to the club for some considerable time.

However, the Swedish FA were always hovering in the background and when City appointed Harry Warren as manager in June 1956, demoting Raynor to chief coach, his future was always in doubt.

He hung on at the club through the close season and into 1956-7, but it was obvious that the 'hurly burly' style the team were now playing was not at all to his liking and he resigned in November 1956.

Raynor rejoined the Swedish FA and coached the national team to the runners-up spot in the 1958 World Cup. At the same time, Coventry City were preparing for their first season in the Fourth Division and after three games would be placed 91st out of the 92 League clubs.

Harry Warren
June 1956-September 1957

AFTER the heady days of Jesse Carver and George Raynor, Harry Warren was perhaps a strange choice as manager. However, the one-touch, Continental-style football had failed to cut any ice in the no-nonsense Third Division, so perhaps the Coventry board thought that someone who understood the lower reaches of the Football League and who had managed a moderately successful team was the man to take City back to the Second Division.

Harry Warren, a former Exeter City, Sheffield United and Merthyr Town player who was born in the North Midlands in 1903, had been manager at Southend United since 1940 and at the age of 53 had spent 16 happy years in the Essex seaside resort. When asked why he left Southend, he gave the perfectly frank answer: "I accepted the job because Coventry offered me more money than I could ever have earned with Southend." It was perhaps the worst decision he ever made in his life.

Warren moved into Highfield Road in June and, with little money to spend, it was very much make-do-and-mend. Out went the Continental patterns and back came the hustle and bustle. it worked for a week or two, as the team made a fine start, but goals were scarce and the usual slump soon set in.

Warren was certainly no disciplinarian and his gentlemanly style did not earn him too much respect from some of the players. Morale sagged, form plummeted and there was a constant undercurrent of interference at board level.

Warren seemed impatient and after Reg Matthews was sold to balance the books, the manager was given less than half the fee received to spend on players.

After the New Year, the situation deteriorated even more as attendances dropped and the club's critics became increasingly vociferous, both in the Press and from the ranks of shareholders.

Inevitably, Warren was sacked in September 1957, after another poor start to the season. He disappeared from view soon afterwards, no doubt ruing the day he had moved into Highfield Road 15 months earlier.

Jimmy Hill
December 1961-May 1967

THE five and a half years from December 1961 until May 1967 remains the most spectacular and momentous period in the history of Coventry City. Nothing before or since, with the brief exception of the two-month period in April-May 1987, can compare to those breathtaking days which came to be known as the 'Sky Blue Era'.

Jimmy Hill's enthusiasm for the game has spread over the past half century and has taken many forms. From being an average player with Brentford and Fulham, he shot to national prominence as chairman of the PFA and for his work in ending the maximum wage for footballers.

And apart from being manager, director and chairman at Highfield Road, he has spread his interests into Saudi Arabia and the soccer boom in the USA in the late 1970s and has been the resident soccer pundit and presenter for both BBC and ITV during this period.

It was a chance meeting with Derrick Robins at the 1961 Lord's Taverners' Ball in London which opened up the management opportunity for Hill at Highfield Road. He was actually offered the position before the King's Lynn FA Cup débâcle and, when he finally agreed to join City, he insisted on complete control. This was a major departure from previous appointments and no manager could ask for more than that.

Changes came thick and fast, from new kit to new attitudes to local organizations. Hill's most positive traits were his ability to deal in the transfer market and the strength of his convictions, for he was never afraid to make what were, at the time, unpopular decisions and see them through.

The club was never out of the limelight in his period as manager and he was able to carry the fans with him like a modern-day Pied Piper.

In those five years, Hill transformed Coventry City from a middling Third Division team, going nowhere, into a First Division club; and he developed the Highfield Road ground from a pre-war antique into a modern, well-appointed stadium which still holds its own with the best some 25 years later.

When he resigned at the peak of his managerial career in August 1967, it was a bombshell to both players and supporters alike and it made national news. His mind was made up, though, and, looking back, who can argue that it was the wrong decision?

After the way he had transformed the club, many feel that it was a tragedy that Hill never took the opportunity to test his abilities at the highest level. He stayed on until Noel Cantwell took over in October 1967, then took up a position with London Weekend Television.

When he returned to the club in April 1975, as managing director, the old order had changed and First Division football was no longer a novelty. The club was ailing financially and although he managed to turn this around in time, his 'new ideas' did not go down so well with a new generation of fans.

In fact, some of them turned into disasters: the investment in the NASL club, Washington Diplomats, lost £700,000; the all-seater stadium was a public relations disaster and was partially reversed three years later; and finally the Sky Blue Connexion training and leisure complex proved to be a £1.2 million 'white elephant' and, after substantial losses, was sold for only £400,000.

On top of this the team was playing dreary football and in the final week of 1982-3 season, Hill resigned. It was sad that it had to end this way but, despite this, no one can take away the memory of the Sky Blue era.

Jimmy Hill continues his interest in the game and has once again been involved in controversy, this time at Craven Cottage, the home of his other great love, Fulham Football Club, where a number of his ideas, notably the sale of the ground, have gone down badly with the supporters.

Noel Cantwell
October 1967-March 1972

THE speculation surrounding Jimmy Hill's successor hogged the headlines in August and September 1967. The two most commonly mentioned names were Malcolm Allison and Brian Clough. Allison opened his mouth before things had been finalized and City chairman Derrick Robins changed his mind. Clough was offered the job but decided to stay at Derby. Finally, the Manchester United and Republic of Ireland international, Noel Cantwell, accepted the post.

Cantwell was born in Cork on 28 February 1932 and as a teenager he played for Cork Athletic before coming to England to try his luck in 1952. West Ham signed him and between 1952 and 1960, he made 245 League appearances for the Hammers, appearing alongside many future top managers including Allison, Dave Sexton, John Bond, Frank O'Farrell and Ken Brown.

A stylish full-back, who also played the occasional game at centre-forward, Cantwell was soon recognized as a natural leader and captained West Ham into Division One in 1958. Matt Busby was rebuilding the Manchester United team after Munich and wanted a captain. He bought Cantwell for £30,000 in November 1960 and the Irishman played a major part in the Reds' resurgence in the following decade.

He captained United in their 1963 FA Cup triumph but played only twice when they won the League Championship two years later. Towards the end of his days at Old Trafford, Cantwell concentrated on coaching and many thought that he would eventually succeed Busby as manager. He also captained the Republic of Ireland, winning a record 36 caps, and also played cricket for All-Ireland.

A charming, articulate man, Cantwell put his skills to good effect by becoming Jimmy Hill's successor as the chairman of the Professional Footballers' Association.

His achievements in his first season at Highfield Road were nothing less than miraculous. The purchase of his old teammate Maurice Setters was an inspired one and although Coventry looked doomed in January, he saved them from relegation, although the issue was not settled until the final game of the season.

After another relegation struggle the following season, the 1969-70 campaign was the zenith of Cantwell's career at Coventry. City developed a meaner streak, won ten away games and a place in Europe with a best-ever finish of sixth in the First Division. The following season, though, the goals dried up and Cup defeats in Munich and Rochdale put him under pressure. In March 1972, shortly after a Cup defeat by Hull, he was sacked: Robins was hungry for success and Noel Cantwell was not delivering any more. Who knows what would have happened if Robins had been as patient as Hill was to be with Gordon Milne.

Cantwell took the manager's job at Peterborough United and, in his first full season at London Road, the Posh won promotion from Division Four. He resigned in 1977 and for a number of years managed in the North American Soccer League with New England Tea Men and Jacksonville Tea Men. In the late 1980s he had a further spell with Peterborough and was general manager there for a time before parting company with the club in April 1989.

Bob Dennison
March 1972-May 1972

BOB Dennison was handed the caretaker manager role in March 1972, when Noel Cantwell was relieved of his duties. Dennison was chief scout at the time and for two months he relished the role of manager, although he clearly stated he was not interested in making the position permanent.

Coventry lost three of his first four games in charge but then won seven points out of ten to achieve First Division safety. Upon the arrival of Joe Mercer and Gordon Milne, he was appointed assistant manager but retained his involvement in scouting activities.

It was as a spotter of talent that he excelled and amongst the players he brought to Coventry were Danny Thomas, Mark Hateley, Andy Blair and Garry Thompson.

Dennison had an older brother, Jack, who played three games for City in 1922. Bob was born in Ambleside on 6 March 1912 and his own playing career began in 1929, when Newcastle United signed him from Radcliffe United as an inside-forward. In five years at St James' Park, however, he managed only 11 appearances before moving to Nottingham Forest in 1934. A year later he was transferred to Fulham, where he stayed until World War Two, converting to centre-half and playing 34 games in their Second Division side.

During the war he worked in the timber trade in Northampton and played as a guest for the Cobblers, becoming their manager in 1948. In July 1954, he became manager of newly-relegated Middlesbrough and, whilst he was unable to help them win promotion back to Division One, he discovered some outstanding players including Brian Clough, Alan Peacock and Mick McNeill.

In January 1963, with 19 months of his contract still to run, Dennison was told to leave. 'Boro issued a statement saying that his parting was by mutual consent but Dennison later won £3,200 damages for 'unfair dismissal'.

He joined Southern League Hereford United in December 1963 and in four years at Edgar Street he laid the foundations for their entry in the Football League before being lured to Highfield Road in December 1967. He retired from Coventry in 1978 but still scouts for the club from his Kent home.

Joe Mercer OBE
June 1972-June 1975

GENIAL Joe Mercer became general manager of Coventry City in June 1972, as the senior figure in the Mercer-Milne partnership.

Joe Mercer was one of soccer's most popular personalities and had an illustrious playing and managing career. He was born at Ellesmere Port on 9 August 1914 and before World War Two he played over 150 games for Everton, won a League Championship medal and five England caps at wing-half. During the war he was a star, winning 26 unofficial caps and being part of the famous half-back line of Britton, Cullis and Mercer.

In 1947, Mercer was allowed to leave Goodison Park and moved to Highbury for £7,000. He helped Arsenal to two League Championships and two FA Cup Finals, captaining the winning team in 1950. He was voted Footballer of the Year in 1950 but never played for England again, for he was now well into the veteran stage. His playing career ended with a broken leg in April 1954 and he eventually moved into management.

He began with Sheffield United, then moved to Aston Villa, helping them win promotion to Division One, triumph in the Football League Cup Final and twice reach the FA Cup semi-finals before his health gave way and he was forced to resign.

In 1965 he was well enough to return to football as manager of Manchester City and in harness with Malcolm Allison he achieved his greatest managerial triumphs at Maine Road. Within four years, Manchester City won the Second and First Division titles, the FA Cup, League Cup and European Cup-winners' Cup.

His team had style, with names like Bell, Summerbee and Lee, and it was a sad day when Joe Mercer was pushed 'upstairs' with a cut in salary. Within days of his 'demotion' he was on his way to Highfield Road, where he acted as a father-figure to Gordon Milne and encouraged an attacking style.

In 1974, after the sacking of Sir Alf Ramsey, Joe Mercer was asked to be England's caretaker manager and he won a lot of admirers with a brand of his own type of football. He said he wanted to 'put a smile back on the face of English football'.

He was made a director of Coventry City in 1975 and remained in that position until 1981, when he retired. He was still a familiar figure and well-loved on the Merseyside football scene, watching Tranmere Rovers regularly almost up to his death in 1990.

Gordon Milne
June 1972-May 1981

BORN in Preston on 29 March 1937, Gordon Milne was the son of the famous Preston North End player and manager, Jimmy Milne, and played for North End before transferring to Liverpool in September 1960, Bill Shankly paying £16,000 for his signature.

Milne was a regular in the Anfield side for seven seasons, playing over 250 games and winning two League Championship medals (1964 and 1966) but missing the 1965 FA Cup Final and European Cup semi-finals through injury. A polished wing-half, who would be called a midfield dynamo these days, he won the first of 14 England caps in 1963, against Brazil, and was a member of the England squad for the 1966 World Cup.

In May 1967 he was released by Liverpool and spent two years at Blackpool before becoming player-manager at non-League Wigan Athletic. Milne guided them to the Northern Premier League title and an FA Cup run that ended with a narrow defeat at Maine Road. He became part-time manager of the England Youth team in 1972, helping to win the European Youth Tournament that year.

Milne was appointed team manager at Coventry under Joe Mercer and remained in charge of playing matters until May 1981, when he reluctantly moved aside to deal with contracts and transfers. In 1982 he was released to become manager of Leicester City, who won promotion to Division One the following year. In 1986 he moved 'upstairs' at Leicester but left a year later after relegation. Since then Gordon Milne has had a successful career with Turkish Club,

Beşiktaş who won a League and Cup double in 1990.

Whilst at Coventry, he showed great skill in the transfer market in a generally difficult financial period. The purchases of Stein, Hutchison, Craven, Powell, Yorath, Wallace, McDonald, Hunt, Gillespie and Daly were shrewd and simultaneously he produced youth players of the highest calibre. The 1977-8 team was one of the best City have ever had but, like so many of Milne's sides, they failed to fulfil their potential.

This apparent under-achievment caused regular disquiet on the terraces but he could perhaps complain that he never had much money to spend. Unlike almost every other City manager, however, he couldn't say that he wasn't given time.

Dave Sexton
May 1981-May 1983

IN THE summer of 1981, when Gordon Milne was relieved of responsibility for playing matters, the role of Coventry City manager was ironically given to a man seven years his senior.

Dave Sexton, who was born in London on 6 April 1930, had just been sacked by Manchester United, despite the Reds winning their last seven games of the season.

Sexton came with an outstanding pedigree and in two seasons helped develop City's talented youngsters, but ultimately he was against the sale of Garry Thompson and football matters began to slip out of his control. He was sacked by the new chairman, Ian Jamieson, on the last day of the 1982-3 season, much to the disgust of the players.

In his time at City, the team's style became more cultured but it rarely set the First Division alight, although in Sexton's defence he was never given the freedom to spend like other City managers. The highlight of his stay at Coventry was the excellent run of 14 games with only two defeats at the end of his first season, which included a 6-1 win over Sunderland and a 5-5 draw with Southampton. The low points were two 5-1 defeats at the hands of Notts County and the dreadful run of 13 games without a win which took Coventry to the brink of relegation in his second season.

Dave Sexton was the son of Archie Sexton, a middleweight boxer of the 1930s. His career began at Chelmsford City in the late 1940s and progressed via Luton Town, West Ham United, Leyton Orient and Brighton to Crystal Palace, where a serious knee injury ended his playing days. He was a good lower division inside-forward, whose only honour as a player was a Third Division championship medal with Brighton in 1958.

Upon his retirement he switched to coaching and earned a good reputation at Chelsea, Fulham and Arsenal before taking his first manager's job at Leyton Orient in 1965.

In 1967 he succeeded Tommy Docherty at Chelsea and inherited a very talented squad which included Osgood, Hollins, Cooke and McCreadie. In 1970, Sexton's outstanding Chelsea team beat Leeds United to win the FA Cup with some champagne soccer; the following year they defeated Real Madrid to win the European Cup-winners' Cup.

He lost his job at Stamford Bridge after a couple of mediocre seasons, albeit when Chelsea were getting into dire financial straits with a new stand, but within two weeks he was appointed manager of Queen's Park Rangers and was unlucky not to win the League Championship in 1976 with an outstanding team built around Gerry Francis, Don Masson and Stan Bowles.

In 1977 he resigned from QPR and was about to become coach at Arsenal when Manchester United persuaded him to succeed Tommy

Docherty again. He accepted the challenge but always lacked the charisma needed for the Old Trafford job and, despite an FA Cup Final appearance in 1979 and League runners-up spot in 1980 (with the help of record signing Ray Wilkins from Chelsea), he was sacked on 30 April 1981 after United found themselves back in mid-table, despite Sexton spending £1 million on Gary Birtles.

If Sexton found it difficult to get close to his players at club level, his coaching ability was never in question and he was excellent with the younger players. Whilst at Coventry he managed the England Under-21 side to victory in the European Championship. He was a modest, unassuming man who always let his team do the talking on the pitch and would have probably been happier being left to play a track-suited role rather than be a front man.

Bobby Gould
May 1983-December 1984

BOBBY Gould was a much-travelled player (see *Coventry Stars A-Z*) and as a manager and coach he led a similar life with eight jobs in ten years. There were coaching posts at Aldershot and Chelsea before managerial positions at Bristol Rovers, Bristol City, Bristol Rovers again and Wimbledon before a short coaching stint at Queen's Park Rangers and, from February 1991, as West Brom manager.

He returned to Highfield Road as manager of Coventry City in May 1983, and inherited the disaster of eight first-teamers with contracts ending and with no desire to play for the club.

Gould tried hard to persuade the majority to re-sign, especially Gillespie, but soon had the job of rebuilding a team. Some of his signings were naïve, others of a short-term nature, but most were inspired and in total he bought 25 players in 18 months. Peake, Gibson, Gynn, Pearce, Bennett and Adams were all bargains and the following season he followed them with Ogrizovic, Kilcline and Regis.

The majority came from lower divisions, where Gould was an expert, and by early December they were fourth in the table. A disastrous run in the New Year left City needing to win their final game to stay up.

The following season, despite the new signings, started badly too. A 3-0 League Cup defeat by Walsall and some dreadful League results left City in 21st place at Christmas. Gould was sacked and replaced by his assistant, Don

Mackay. His talent-spotting ability was ultimately not good enough and his fan-like devotion to the club was probably a disadvantage in the end, but he left the majority of players who went on to win the FA Cup in 1987.

His experience at Highfield Road did him no harm, for he went back to Bristol Rovers in May 1985 and returned to Division One with Wimbledon in 1987, with whom he won the FA Cup the following year. Two more successful years at Plough Lane were followed by a period advising old friend Don Howe at Queen's Park Rangers until he joined West Bromwich Albion. Alas, he was unable to stop their relegation to Division Three in 1991.

Donald Mackay
December 1984-April 1986

IN SEPTEMBER 1984, Bobby Gould recruited as his assistant manager the former Forfar, Dundee United and Southend goalkeeper, Donald Mackay. Three months later, Gould was sacked and Mackay was given the manager's job on a caretaker basis.

City were in desperate trouble at the foot of the table and Mackay had little to lose. In his first two weeks in the job, he won two vital League games and a tough third round FA Cup tie. The rest of the season, though, was an uphill struggle but Mackay inspired the team to win its last three games to stay up and was rewarded with a three-year contract.

High hopes were held for the following season but Mackay's tactics were never clear, Regis was forced to be the target man and City struggled from the outset. The club's finances were in a poor state, Gibson was sold in January and the proceeds bought Pickering, Brazil and McInally. But they were not the players to keep a desperate Coventry City in Division One.

On 12 April, City lost at Anfield to go eight games without a win and Mackay resigned the following day. In hindsight he was probably not a big enough name for City but his outspoken views and dislike of what he saw as interfering directors did not help his cause.

His high principles and strong character did win him many friends and he was never one to shirk a challenge. After leaving Highfield Road he assisted in coaching at Ibrox and then became manager at Blackburn Rovers in February 1987, taking them to the Second Division play-offs three times and winning the Full Members' Cup in 1987.

Mackay was born in Partick on 19 March 1940 and prior to joining City he had coaching experience at Bristol City and in Denmark before managing at Dundee from 1980-83. In his time at Dens Park he won the Bells League Cup and promotion to the Premier Division in 1981 but left in protest at the sale of McKimmie to Aberdeen.

George Curtis
April 1986-May 1987

GEORGE Curtis had made his name as a Coventry City stalwart through the later 1950s and the 1960s (see *City Stars A-Z*) and was warmly welcomed back to Highfield Road after a short spell with Aston Villa.

Curtis returned to Coventry to work in the club's commercial department and he has remained with City for the past 20 years, becoming commerical manager and finally managing director.

When Don Mackay left the club in April 1986, Curtis was once more called upon to fill the

breach and in tandem with John Sillett managed to stave off relegation once again.

The following season was perhaps the most successful in the club's history, when the FA Cup was won for the only time, and an enthusiasm rarely witnessed before returned to the city of Coventry. Curtis eventually stepped back upstairs when Sillett was appointed team manager.

John Sillett
May 1987-November 1990

BORN at Normansland, Hampshire, on 20 July 1936, John Sillett had two careers at Coventry City. As a player he was one of Jimmy Hill's earliest signings in April 1962 and he played a key part in the Sky Blue revolution, being an almost ever-present in the 1962-3 FA Cup run and the 1963-4 Third Division championship season. He was never a regular in Division Two after suffering with a slipped disc and in 1966 he was sold to Plymouth Argyle, where he had one season before moving into coaching. His father, Charles, played for Southampton before World War Two and John joined City from Chelsea for £3,000. At Stamford Bridge he had played alongside his elder brother, Peter, who was capped for England in the 1950s. 'Snozz', as he was nicknamed, was an experienced full-back who had seen better days but nevertheless was a steadying influence in Coventry's defence. His only representative honour was an appearance for the Football League in the early 1960s.

He coached for six years at Bristol City before becoming manager of Hereford United in 1974 and won promotion to Division Two in 1975-6, lifting the Third Division Manager of the Year award.

His old teammate, Bobby Gould, brought him back to Highfield Road in 1983 as coach but he lost his job just over a year later as City struggled. Don Mackay re-employed him and Sillett became chief coach in May 1986, when Mackay resigned.

The Curtis-Sillett partnership was immediately successful, bringing a breath of fresh air after several years of struggling, with their fun-loving attitude and expressive style of football. Sillett got the best out of Bennett and Regis and with a side largely inherited from Mackay and Gould, but inspired by Curtis and Sillett, the Sky Blues roared to the FA Cup Final.

On that momentous day in May 1987 they put the smiles back on the faces of not only Coventry City but also football in general in one of the most attractive Finals for years. John Sillett was rewarded with promotion to team manager, an honour he richly deserved.

Three years later he was relieved of duties after indicating that he did not want to renew his contract at the end of the season. In those three years, Coventry suffered two catastrophic Cup defeats, at Sutton United and Northampton Town, and many fans thought he should have gone after the latter.

On the credit side the team were rarely out of the top half of the First Division and the fact that there were no relegation battles was an achievement by City's standards. Unfortunately, in winning the FA Cup he had set high standards and expectations which were rarely lived up to. His transfer dealings were hardly inspiring and many of his critics thought he should have spent the Cup winnings on a class midfielder. His cheery style, though, always shone through and 'Snozz' will forever be remembered for that day in May when City won the Cup. In June 1991, it was announced that he was returning to Hereford United as manager.

Terry Butcher
November 1990-

TERRY Butcher became the youngest manager in Coventry City's history when he was appointed in November 1990 to succeed John Sillett.

Butcher, who was born in Singapore on 28 December 1958 (his father was in the Royal Navy), had an illustrious career, playing over 300 games for Ipswich Town between 1978 and 1986 and then spending four years at Glasgow Rangers, where he was a major influence in the resurgence of the Ibrox club.

He was spotted by Ipswich Town whilst playing in local football at Lowestoft. He made his League debut at Everton in April 1978, displacing the injury-prone Kevin Beattie, and after less than 30 games he was chosen for England 'B' and Under-21 games.

Ipswich were a major force in English football at this time and Butcher got a lot of exposure and a lot of experience. He became a regular in 1979-80 and won his first full cap in Australia. The following season he was in the Ipswich side that won the UEFA Cup and finished second in Division One.

The quietly-spoken and unassuming Butcher was an excellent ambassador off the pitch but on it he was an extremely competitive central defender who led by example. His style brought with it injuries, including a serious nose injury at Luton in January 1982 when he needed two blood transfusions and was sidelined for three months. He returned to play a key role in the 1982 World Cup in Spain.

Ipswich went into decline after Bobby Robson's departure in 1982 but Butcher remained a solid rock in their defence. In 1986, however, he could not save them from relegation but his team's form did not stop him playing in his second World Cup finals.

On returning from Mexico he was on the verge of joining Spurs when Graeme Souness swooped to pay £750,000 and he quickly became a hero with the Ibrox fans. In the highly-charged Scottish soccer scene his temper sometimes got the better of him and he was in trouble for kicking dressing-room doors and was involved in the infamous assault case with McAvennie and Woods. He was one of the first of Souness' English buys and his arrival coincided with the club's most successful period for many years with three League Championships and three Skol Cup wins and total domination over the old enemy, Celtic.

Butcher had the misfortune to break a leg in November 1987 and missed the European Championships in 1988. But he played in his third World Cup finals in 1990 and had the honour of captaining England in the semi-final against West Germany. On returning to Rangers, he and Souness fell out and the only solution was for Butcher to move on.

Negotiations with City were discreetly handled by John Poynton. The story is that the only way he could get his man in the face of stiff competition from Leeds United was to offer him the player-manager's job; a transfer fee of £300,000 was also involved.

There was a lot of criticism of the City chairman over the whole deal, particularly as John Sillett was on his sick bed at the time.

It was certainly a gamble for City to take on an inexperienced manager and only time will tell whether it was a good move. Butcher inherited an ageing team and had to balance the drastic changes he wanted to make for long-term success with the immediate priority of First Division survival.

At one stage he looked in danger of failing but the inspired signings of Sansom and Woods, the promotion of Pearce and the switch of Gallacher to central striker enabled City to pull away from the relegation zone. Butcher also started to make the hard decisions: he sold Speedie and Livingstone and released the ever-popular, but ageing, Regis.

City Stars A-Z

BRIAN ALDERSON

Brian Alderson, who was born in Dundee on 5 May 1950, joined City from Scottish junior club, Lochie Harp, in 1968 as a fast winger with a powerful shot. He came into the first team early in 1970-71 and made a big impression on the left wing. After a home game against Everton (the 'donkey-kick' match), Alf Ramsey said he might call up Alderson for England Under-23s, but was informed of the player's Scottish nationality. Alderson's promise evaporated, though, and he spent two years largely in the Reserves. The purchase of Colin Stein saw him back as a striker and, feeding off Stein's knock-downs, he scored 17 goals in 1972-3, his deadly finishing earning him an Under-23 cap that February. The following season, however, he had scored only two League goals by mid-November. David Cross was purchased and that sparked Alderson into some form and he ended the season as top scorer again with 15 goals, although only nine came in the League. In the League Cup quarter-final against Manchester City he scored all four Coventry goals, two of them in the classic replay at Maine Road. In 1974-5, his scoring rate dropped again and, with Ferguson and Green emerging, he was sold to Leicester City for £105,000. He struggled at Filbert Street, scoring only nine goals in 90 games before moving to the NASL club, New England Teamen, in 1978.
Football League debut for Coventry City v Huddersfield Town (substitute) (h) 5 September 1970.

	LEAGUE		*FA CUP*		*FL CUP*		*OTHERS*		*TOTAL*	
	App	*Gls*	*App*	*Gls*	*App*	*Gls*	*App*	*Gls*	*App*	*Gls*
1970-71	12/3	1	1	0	3	0	1	0	17/3	1
1971-72	5/3	0	0	0	0	0	0	0	5/3	0
1972-73	32/1	13	4	3	1	1	1/1	0	38/2	17
1973-74	40	9	6	0	6	6	210	0	54	16
1974-75	27/4	6	3	2	1	0	0	0	31/4	8
	116/11	29	14	5	11	7	4/1	1	145/12	42

TOMMY ALLEN

Due to an administrative oversight by Sunderland in 1920, goalkeeper Tommy Allen was given a free transfer and allowed to join Southampton. In eight seasons with the Saints he made 330 appearances and was ever-present in their 1921-2 Third Division South championship-winning side. A model of consistency, he was one of James McIntyre's first signings for Coventry in the close season of 1928, featuring in an exchange deal with reserve centre-half Bill Stoddart. Although he was approaching the veteran stage he was well known to McIntyre, who had been Southampton's manager between 1921 and 1924. Allen went on to make over 100 consecutive appearances, acquiring his nickname of 'Shadow' because of his gangling fame. A dashing and spectacular 'keeper, he managed to survive the defensive nightmare of Harry Storer's first season, when over 100 League goals were conceded, but moved on soon afterwards to Accrington Stanley (with whom he made his 500th League appearance) and then to Northampton Town, where he made his final League appearance in 1934 before joining Kidderminster Harriers that August. He was born in Moxley on 1 May 1897 and died in Solihull in 1968
Football League debut for Coventry City v Norwich City (h) 25 August 1928.

	LEAGUE		*FA CUP*		*TOTAL*	
	App	*Gls*	*App*	*Gls*	*App*	*Gls*
1928-29	42	0	1	0	43	0
1929-30	42	0	4	0	46	0
1930-31	37	0	3	0	40	0
1931-32	34	0	1	0	35	0
	155	0	9	0	164	0

Jack Astley was the cultured half of City's full-back partnership of the late 1930s. Both Astley and Walter Metcalf had been signed from Brentford and, whilst Metcalf was the physical 6ft exponent of the sliding tackle, Astley was a slightly built, constructive type of player, always using the ball carefully and building attacks in a patient manner. He began his career at Southport in 1931 and, after a spell out of the League with Shelbourne, he joined Brentford in the close season of 1933. After three successful seasons with the Bees, making over 50 appearances, he became one of Harry Storer's best signings when he came to cement the promotion run in the spring of 1936. He did not miss a match until after the outbreak of war and was a model of consistency. A cultured person both on and off the field, he was a lay preacher and both he and Metcalf were often to be seen sporting 'plus fours' as *de rigeur* for away games. After the outbreak of war, he stayed at Highfield Road for a season, then joined the Army and in 1944 was an artillery officer. This marked his retirement from the game. When he came out of the Army, he returned to Coventry and was employed at the GEC as a nightshift manager for a number of years. He was born in Warrington in 1910.
Football League debut for Coventry City v Cardiff City (h) 22 February 1936.

	LEAGUE		*FA CUP*		*TOTAL*	
	App	*Gls*	*App*	*Gls*	*App*	*Gls*
1935-36	14	0	0	0	14	0
1936-37	42	0	3	0	45	0
1937-38	42	0	1	0	43	0
1938-39	42	0	1	0	43	0
	140	0	5	0	145	0

JACK ASTLEY

There are few players who have spent a longer period at Highfield Road than former England Schoolboy international Frank Austin. When he arrived at the club from Toton FC in 1950, Harry Storer was manager; when he left 13 years later, Jimmy Hill had already taken over as manager. During his career at the club, Austin survived seven managers. He was born at Stoke-on-Trent on 6 July 1933 and was a stylish and composed performer who could well have graced the First Division, given the opportunity. In his early years with City, Austin wore the number-six shirt, but his lack of height was a disadvantage and in 1956 he was converted to full-back, where he played consistently for a number of seasons. He was still a relatively young player when Jimmy Hill allowed him to move to Torquay United for a small fee in January 1963, but with Mick Kearns, Frank Kletzenbauer and Dietmar Bruck in the squad, City were well served for left-backs. He made 24 League appearances for Torquay before leaving the League scene.
Football League debut for Coventry City v Newport County (h) 11 April 1953.

	LEAGUE		*FA CUP*		*FL CUP*		*TOTAL*	
	App	*Gls*	*App*	*Gls*	*App*	*Gls*	*App*	*Gls*
1952-53	2	0	0	0	-	-	2	0
1953-54	37	1	1	0	-	-	38	1
1954-55	30	0	0	0	-	-	30	0
1955-56	40	0	1	0	-	-	41	0
1956-57	31	0	0	0	-	-	31	0
1957-58	33	1	1	0	-	-	34	1
1958-59	14	0	0	0	-	-	14	0
1959-60	41	0	2	0	-	-	43	0
1960-61	29	0	3	0	0	0	32	0
1961-62	37	0	2	0	1	0	40	0
1962-63	8	0	0	0	0	0	8	0
	302	2	10	0	1	0	313	2

FRANK AUSTIN

Arthur Bacon was not the most skilful player ever seen in a Coventry shirt, but he had a powerful shot in both feet. Once he sent a shot out of the ground which shattered a window and smashed a gas bracket in a nearby house. His surname gave rise to many witty remarks including a shout from the sparse crowd at a reserve match of: 'You and two eggs would make a fine breakfast'. John Arlott was a great admirer of Bacon, describing him thus: "A tall man with a shaving-brush tuft of hair growing out from a shallow forehead above a mighty jaw. His chest was like a drum, his thighs hugely tapering and he had two shooting feet which he threw at footballs as if with intent to burst them." He had a habit of hitting the ball well forward on his instep — a point of impact possible only to a man of immensely strong legs and ankles. He had one glorious period for City, in 15 days and five matches at the end of 1933, when he replaced the injured Bourton and scored 14 goals (including five at Gillingham which equalled the club record and four in the home match against Crystal Palace.) He scored twice more in January but returned to the obscurity of London Combination Football when Bourton returned from injury in February 1934. He was born at Birdholme in 1905 and, prior to signing for City, had spells with Chesterfield (30 apps, 6 goals), Derby County (25 apps, 7 goals), Manchester City (5 apps, 1 goal) and Reading (69 apps, 44 goals). He scored six goals for Reading against Stoke City on 3 April 1931, setting a club record which still stands. He had played in the same Derby side as Harry Storer in the 1920s and was signed from Chesterfield at a time when Bourton's scoring feats linked him with many First Division clubs. Bacon's fee was based on the number of games played (£125 plus £75 if 50 games were played). Bacon left City with an eye injury but signed for Burton Town in March 1937. He was killed in an air raid on Derby in January 1941, when he fell off his bicycle whilst serving as a special constable.

Football League debut for Coventry City v Norwich City (h) 14 December 1934.

ARTHUR BACON

	LEAGUE		*FA CUP*		*Div 3S Cup*		*TOTAL*	
	App	*Gls*	*App*	*Gls*	*App*	*Gls*	*App*	*Gls*
1933-34	14	16	0	0	3	2	17	18
1934-35	1	0	0	0	0	0	1	0
1935-36	1	1	0	0	1	0	2	1
	16	17	0	0	4	2	20	19

JIMMY BAKER

Born in the Rhondda in 1905, Jimmy Baker signed for Coventry from Wolves in the close season of 1929, after three seasons at Molineux where he made a handful of appearances, mainly as a defensive wing-half. He was a regular at either centre-half or wing-half for the next three seasons and was appointed captain when Harry Storer joined the club in 1931. On the arrival of Tom Davison in the close season of 1932, Baker surprisingly moved into non-League football with Lovells Athletic, but he was back at Highfield Road the following spring. An inspiring figure, his red mop of hair always visible in the thick of play, he returned at right-half and was a regular in the 1933-4 team which finished runners-up in the Third Division South. Although he was still an able performer the following season, the emergence of Billy Frith and the consistency of Harry Boileau led to Storer allowing him to move to Bristol City in 1935. After a couple of seasons at Ashton Gate he left League football for good in 1937.

Football League debut for Coventry City v Merthyr Town (h) 31 August 1929.

	LEAGUE		*FA CUP*		*TOTAL*	
	App	*Gls*	*App*	*Gls*	*App*	*Gls*
1929-30	29	3	0	0	0	0
1930-31	42	4	3	0	0	0
1931-32	39	1	2	0	0	0
1932-33	8	1	0	0	0	0
1933-34	40	2	2	2	0	0
1934-35	27	0	0	0	0	0
	185	11	7	2	0	0

The life of 'Little Harry' Banks is interwoven with the early years of the club — a story of heroic struggle against the odds. He came to Coventry in the early 1880s from his native Birmingham and played some football for the Coventry Association. One of hundreds seeking employment in the burgeoning cycle industry, he eventually found work at Singers and was involved in their earliest games at Binley Road. Banks played in every position in the forward line and following Singers' entry to the Birmingham Junior Cup in 1887, he took part in the first four years of that competition enjoying his best season in 1889-90 when he scored six goals in the eight Cup-ties from centre-forward. In the close season of 1890, the great Frank Mobley arrived to complete the 'team of teams' and the veteran Banks moved back to the right wing. Singers won the Cup in April 1891 at Villa's ground and it was Banks who set up Mobley for the winning goal. This was also his last competitive game, for he was already in the early stages of consumption. On New Year's Day 1895, the local newspaper announced that 'Little Harry' had died after a long and painful illness.
Birmingham Junior Cup debut for Singers v Bourneville Villa (h) 26 November 1887.

HARRY BANKS

'Get up sonny, if you want to continue playing for me.' That was Harry Barratt's early introduction to Harry Storer's unique style of management. Barratt, barely out of his teens, knew that the tackle which put him across the cinder-track and over the wall on to the terracing beneath West Ham's famous 'chicken run' stand was nothing compared with the tongue-lashing he could expect from Storer. He got up and went on to become one of City's best-ever captains. Son of a Southampton full-back, he was born at Headington on Christmas Day 1919 and signed for City in 1935, from Alfred Herbert's, a Coventry works side. Loaned to Cheltenham Town, he returned as a regular in the Reserves in 1937-8 and made a handful of League appearances before war. He joined the Royal Warwickshire Regiment and scored over 40 goals for City's wartime side, also guesting for Leicester City. Barratt was the first player to be taken back as a professional and, in his last four years, was captain. A versatile player, he even had a 20-minute spell in goal when Alf Wood was injured. In the autumn of 1950, he skippered City to the top of the Second Division, but injuries to Noel Simpson and Barratt ended promotion hopes. The following season, City were relegated and Barratt played in only the first game, when he was injured and was forced to retire. He managed Rugby Town and Snowdown Colliery (Kent), where he discovered George Curtis, Alf Bentley, and Eric Jones. Jesse Carver engaged him as chief scout at the end of 1955 but a few months after Carver left, he quit football. In the late 1950s he was Gillingham manager for two years. He died in Coventry in 1990.
Football League debut for Coventry City v Blackburn Rovers (h) 9 April 1938.

	LEAGUE		*FA CUP*		*TOTAL*	
	App	*Gls*	*App*	*Gls*	*App*	*Gls*
1937-38	1	0	0	0	1	0
1938-39	4	1	0	0	4	1
1945-46	0	0	2	1	2	1
1946-47	33	7	2	0	35	7
1947-48	38	0	2	0	40	0
1948-49	37	0	1	0	38	0
1949-50	26	2	0	0	26	2
1950-51	30	2	1	0	31	2
1951-52	1	0	0	0	1	0
	170	12	8	1	178	13

HARRY BARRATT

ROY BARRY

Roy Barry arrived at Coventry with a reputation for disciplinary problems, having been sent off several times playing for Hearts and Dunfermline. Yet, whilst Barry was undoubtedly one of the hardest men around at the time, he was never in trouble with referees in England. He was born in Edinburgh on 19 September 1942 and Coventry bought him for £40,000 from Dunfermline to replace George Curtis. He belied his 5ft 9in height with superb timing in the air and in the tackle. He suffered a broken nose in his first game, after a tussle with 'Chopper' Harris, but then embarked on a run of 14 games, only two of which were lost as he went on to captain City to fourth place with some outstanding performances. Tragedy struck in the home game against Sheffield Wednesday, when he fractured his right leg in a shuddering tackle with Tommy Craig. It was a bad break and kept him out for 14 months. He never reproduced the same form but was still a good defender, playing for two more seasons before moving to Crystal Palace in 1973. He returned to Scotland in 1975, playing for Hibs and East Fife and managing the latter. He was last heard of driving a minicab in South London. In a different era, Roy Barry would surely have won caps for Scotland.
Football League debut for Coventry City v Chelsea (substitute) (a) 1 November 1969.

	LEAGUE		*FA CUP*		*FL CUP*		*OTHERS*		*TOTAL*	
	App	*Gls*	*App*	*Gls*	*App*	*Gls*	*App*	*Gls*	*App*	*Gls*
1969-70	14/1	0	2	0	0	0	0	0	16/1	0
1970-71	1	0	0	0	0	0	0	0	1	0
1971-72	27	1	1	0	0	0	2/1	0	30/1	1
1972-73	40	1	4	0	2	0	2	0	48	1
	82/1	2	7	0	2	0	4/1	0	95/2	2

DAVID BENNETT

Born in Manchester on 11 July 1959, Dave Bennett joined Manchester City as an apprentice in 1978 and took part in the 1981 FA Cup Final against Spurs, along with Tommy Hutchison. He moved to Cardiff City in 1981 and then to Highfield Road in the close season of 1983, for £100,000 — one of Gould's 'squad of strangers' recruited at high speed. When Bennett arrived, Gould described him as a player who would 'set the crowd alight' and his delightful dribbling skills and unexpected acceleration were there for all to see. However, in the early days, a feeling prevailed that City were not getting the best out of him. When Sillett took over in 1986 that changed and Bennett began to fully express himself; liberated from his orthodox wing role, his combination with Regis was a key factor in the success of 1987. Bennett played a major part in every round of the Cup campaign, memorably rallying a harrassed midfield against Stoke, setting up the Regis goal against Sheffield Wednesday, recovering a seemingly lost ball from Ormsby to cross for Gynn's equalizer in the semi-final, and in the Final, scoring after eight minutes and then crossing for Houchen's headed equalizer. In 1989 he moved to Sheffield Wednesday for £210,000. Toward the end of 1989-90, well into the second half of Coventry's game against Wednesday, Bennett came on a substitute, the first of the 1987 Final side to return to Highfield Road in opposition colours. The crowd gave a thunderous ovation to the player who, perhaps more than any, was the architect of Coventry's Cup triumph.
Football League debut for Coventry City v Leicester City (h) 17 September 1983.

	LEAGUE		*FA CUP*		*FL CUP*		*OTHERS*		*TOTAL*	
	App	*Gls*	*App*	*Gls*	*App*	*Gls*	*App*	*Gls*	*App*	*Gls*
1983-84	32/2	6	3	0	3	1	0	0	38/2	7
1984-85	29/5	2	0	0	2	0	0	0	31/5	2
1985-86	33/5	6	1	0	4	2	2	0	40/5	8
1986-87	31	7	5	3	5	2	1	0	42	12
1987-88	27/1	4	2	0	3	0	3	0	35/1	4
1988-89	5/2	0	1	0	0	0	1	0	7/2	0
	157/15	25	12	3	17	5	7	0	193/15	33

Since entering the Football League, Coventry City had struggled for survival using a succession of goalkeepers in the process. In 1920, at least that problem was solved when Albert Evans signed Jerry Best. The young Geordie, who was born in Newcastle in 1897, was an unlikely looking 'keeper, a mere 5ft 6in tall and carrying a wartime injury after being shot in the arm. But he more than compensated with a combination of agility and courage. Two days after his debut, against Cardiff, Coventry travelled to Ninian Park for the return. Cardiff were heading for the First Division and enjoying huge support. There was an expectant crowd of 42,000 (then the biggest to watch a match involving Coventry), who saw the home side lay siege to the visitors' goal, but Jerry Best turned in a dream performance, stopping everything. In the closing stages, Mollie Morgan broke away and scored to give Coventry a shock 1-0 win. Best's future was assured. He was an ever-present for three consecutive seasons and his total appearances was a club record 236. In November 1925 he became the first of Coventry's League players to be given a testimonial. In the close season of 1926 he was sold by James Kerr to Halifax Town in an exchange deal which brought Jack Newton to City. It was a deal which mystified the *Telegraph* and angered the fans. He moved to Rotherham shortly afterwards and then out of the League with Worksop Town. After a business failure he found work with Pilkington's, the glass manufacturers, in Doncaster.
Football League debut for Coventry City v Cardiff City (h) 25 December 1920.

	LEAGUE		*FA CUP*		*TOTAL*	
	App	*Gls*	*App*	*Gls*	*App*	*Gls*
1920-21	23	0	2	0	25	0
1921-22	40	0	3	0	43	0
1922-23	42	0	1	0	43	0
1923-24	42	0	2	0	44	0
1924-25	42	0	3	0	45	0
1925-26	35	0	1	0	36	0
	224	0	12	0	236	0

JERRY BEST

Jeff Blockley was born in Leicester on 12 September 1949 and played in the same Blaby school team as Peter Shilton. Blockley had a rapid rise to fame at Highfield Road. Captain of Coventry City's Youth Cup Final team in 1968, within 12 months he was a first-team regular. A tall, uncompromising central defender, Blockley, in partnership with Roy Barry, played a major part in the successful 1969-70 season. His potential at this stage was enormous and over the next two seasons he played six times for England Under-23s and once for the Football League. He would certainly have been City's first full England international since Reg Matthews if he hadn't been sold to Arsenal soon after Mercer and Milne took over in 1972. City needed goalpower and Blockley, the club's top asset, was sold for £200,000 to help fund the purchase of Stein and Hutchison. Two days later, he was called up for England and made his only appearance, at Wembley against Yugoslavia. In his final game for City, against Chelsea, he scored a spectacular chipped own-goal. His career went into decline from the point of his move, for he was never a regular at Highbury. In January 1975 he moved to Leicester City and after 75 games at Filbert Street, and a brief loan spell to Derby County, he was transferred to Notts County for two seasons until he lost his place to a 19-year-old called Brian Kilcline. Blockley later played for Gloucester City and managed Leicester United.
Football League debut for Coventry City v Southampton (substitute) (a) 11 January 1969.

	LEAGUE		*FA CUP*		*FL CUP*		*OTHERS*		*TOTAL*	
	App	*Gls*	*App*	*Gls*	*App*	*Gls*	*App*	*Gls*	*App*	*Gls*
1968-69	10/2	0	0	0	0	0	0	0	10/2	0
1969-70	39	3	1	0	1	0	0	0	41	3
1970-71	42	1	1	0	5	1	4	1	52	3
1971-72	42	2	1	0	1	0	4	2	48	4
1972-73	11	0	0	0	1	0	2	0	14	0
	144/2	6	3	0	8	1	10	3	165/2	10

JEFF BLOCKLEY

In October 1972, Coventry City bought goalkeeper Jim Blyth from Preston North End for £20,000 plus an extra £10,000 when he played in the first team and won international honours. Blyth, who was born in Perth on 2 February 1955, had not played for Preston's first team and was not to play for City's for over three years. In the meantime, the 6ft 1in 'keeper served his apprenticeship under Bill Glazier but had the misfortune to break a leg. When Bryan King suffered a serious injury, Blyth took his chance and played in over 50 successive games before suffering a knee injury himself. He recovered to play a key part in the successful 1977-8 season, missing only three games, saving three penalties and winning full Scotland caps. Disaster struck in his second international, against Wales at Hampden, when a mix-up with Willie Donachie led to an own-goal. This incident probably cost Blyth an appearance in the World Cup finals in Argentina, although he was a squad member. Early the following season, warming up for the home game against Norwich, he injured his back and Youth team 'keeper, Steve Murcott, deputized for his only game. In November 1978, despite being out of the first team, Blyth was the subject of a £440,000 bid from Manchester United but he failed the medical because of the back injury. City had the luxury of two goalkeepers of First Division calibre in Blyth and Les Sealey and over the next three and a half years, the two shared the duties until Sealey took over permanently near the end of 1981-2, after the sixth round FA Cup defeat at West Brom. During that close season, Blyth moved to St Andrew's on a free transfer but made only 14 appearances before becoming understudy to, first Tony Coton, then David Seaman. In 1985 he moved to Nuneaton Borough.

Football League debut for Coventry City v Everton (h) 19 December 1975.

JIM BLYTH

	LEAGUE		*FA CUP*		*FL CUP*		*TOTAL*	
	App	*Gls*	*App*	*Gls*	*App*	*Gls*	*App*	*Gls*
1975-76	19	0	1	0	0	0	20	0
1976-77	31	0	2	0	3	0	36	0
1977-78	40	0	0	0	4	0	44	0
1978-79	6	0	2	0	0	0	8	0
1979-80	21	0	1	0	1	0	23	0
1980-81	7	0	0	0	3	0	10	0
1981-82	27	0	4	0	2	0	33	0
	151	0	10	0	13	0	174	0

Brian Borrows was born in Liverpool on 20 December 1960 and signed for Coventry City from Bolton Wanderers, for £80,000, in the summer of 1985. He had made 95 appearances for Bolton, following his 27 for Everton before they let him go in 1983. He plugged the gap that had not been effectively filled since Danny Thomas' move to Tottenham in 1983. Apart from the rare injury and a brief loss of form in August 1987, Borrows was a regular, missing less than a dozen games in six seasons. Luck was against him, though, when he twisted a knee seven days before the 1987 FA Cup Final and he watched the match from a hospital bed. A stylish full-back with a good turn of speed, he was one of the most skilful player on the club's books in his heyday. Although he was voted Player of the Year by the fans in 1990, he was never fully appreciated by England's managers, his only representative honour being a 'B' cap against Czechoslovakia in 1990. 'Bugsy', as he is affectionately known, scored very rarely but converted the occasional penalty in Kilcline's absence; and he did score an excellent goal from open play at Villa Park in 1990.

Football League debut for Coventry City v Manchester City (h) 17 August 1985.

BRIAN BORROWS

	LEAGUE		*FA CUP*		*FL CUP*		*OTHERS*		*TOTAL*	
	App	*Gls*	*App*	*Gls*	*App*	*Gls*	*App*	*Gls*	*App*	*Gls*
1985-86	41	0	1	0	4	0	2	0	48	0
1986-87	41	1	5	0	5	0	1	0	52	1
1987-88	32/1	0	2	0	3	0	3	0	40/1	0
1988-89	38	1	1	0	3	0	1	0	43	1
1989-90	37	1	1	0	8	0	1	0	47	1
1990-91	38	6	4	0	5	0	1	0	48	6
	227/1	9	14	0	28	0	9	0	278/1	9

Ernie Boston was born in Coventry around 1890 and started as a rugby player but then joined a local junior soccer side, Victoria Swifts. When he was selected for his first match he was so eager that he forgot his boots, delaying his debut until the following week. Boston later played for Lord Street Juniors and Clifton Vics. Whilst he was with Clifton Vics, he attracted the attention of West Bromwich Albion but City stepped in to sign him in 1907, at the age of 17. Boston played centre-half for City, although he stood only 5ft 9in tall and weighed 11st. However, what he lacked in height he made up for in his wonderful heading ability. No one could beat him in the air and he was affectionately christened 'Konk' by his teammates. Boston played over 50 games for City between 1908 and 1914, when he retired at the early age of 23, although he was effectively Eli Bradley's and later Albert Feebury's deputy. He captained Birmingham Juniors against Scotland Juniors in 1912. In an interview published in the *Coventry Herald* in 1938, Boston recalled the abandoned game at Northampton in October 1910. The train carrying the City players to the match was delayed. When it arrived at Northampton Station, three players — Boston, Lee and Saul — jumped out and got a taxi to the ground. The game started with just that trio: Lee stationed himself near the centre, Boston near him and Saul in the goalmouth. Naturally, the ball was booted out of play at every opportunity. At the time the article was published, Boston was working at the Humber-Hillman factory in Coventry.

Southern League debut for Coventry City v Southend United (h) 26 September 1908.

	LEAGUE		*FA CUP*		*TOTAL*	
	App	*Gls*	*App*	*Gls*	*App*	*Gls*
1908-09	10	0	0	0	10	0
1909-10	5	0	0	0	5	0
1910-11	9	0	0	0	9	0
1911-12	11	0	0	0	11	0
1912-13	5	2	0	0	5	2
1913-14	14	1	0	0	14	1
	54	3	0	0	54	3

ERNEST BOSTON

Clarrie Bourton was a Bristolian for most of his life. He was born in that city on 30 September 1908 and died there on 24 April 1981. He also served Bristol City as player, manager and general backroom boy for over 40 years. However, it was for his goalscoring feats at Highfield Road that he will be remembered both at local and national level. After a short spell with his local club he moved to Blackburn Rovers in 1928 and scored 37 goals in 63 games for the Ewood Park club. It was here that Harry Storer spotted him from nearby Burnley and when he took over at Highfield Road, he asked City chairman Walter Brandish to sign him as soon as possible. For a fee of £750 City got one of their biggest bargains and by the end of that first season stories of Bourton the 'goal-machine' were legion in the game. He led the Football League scorers with 49 goals, still a City record and unlikely to be beaten. He immediately established a seemingly 'telepathic' understanding with Jock Lauderdale and the following season scored 40 goals (second to Bill McNaughton of Hull City). In Bourton's six seasons at Highfield Road, Coventry scored 577 goals and he weighed in with 171 of them. A bustling, old-style centre-forward, his style was much-suited to the rough and tumble of the Third Division but found it more difficult in the higher division. He moved to Plymouth Argyle in October 1937, for a record fee received, but did not settle and was soon back with Bristol City. During 1938-9 he was appointed caretaker manager when Bob Hewison was suspended by the FA. Bourton played on and was still scoring goals when he retired in 1944. He remained in Bristol and was employed in the Ashton Gate pools office until shortly before his death.

Football League debut for Coventry City v Fulham (a) 29 August 1931.

	LEAGUE		*FA CUP*		*TOTAL*	
	App	*Gls*	*App*	*Gls*	*App*	*Gls*
1931-32	40	49	2	1	42	50
1932-33	39	40	4	3	43	43
1933-34	30	25	2	0	32	25
1934-35	39	26	3	3	42	29
1935-36	39	22	2	2	41	24
1936-37	36	9	0	0	36	9
1937-38	5	0	0	0	5	0
	228	171	13	9	241	180

CLARRIE BOURTON

Born at Dudley in 1882, Eli Bradley started his career with Bilston United, as a 16-year-old outside-right, before moving to Dudley, where he operated at either centre-half or centre-forward. At 17, he was already a well-built player when selected for Birmingham Juniors against Scotland Juniors at Celtic Park. Bradley signed for West Brom in 1905 and made his first-team debut in February 1906 at outside-right.

ELI BRADLEY

Whilst with Albion he also played at centre-half, centre-forward and inside-right but, not keen to be regarded as a utility player, he moved to Luton Town in 1908. He continued to operate in a variety of roles at Kenilworth Road. Bradley was at centre-forward against Coventry in the final game of 1908-09 and City liked what they saw, signing him soon afterwards. He proved the outstanding City player of the Southern League era. Operating at centre-half, the position he favoured, he was a robust defender who could back up the attack with fierce long-range shots. 'Eli's pile drivers' became a byword with City's supporters. At his best in a hard-fought game when his influence was often the decisive factor, he was regularly picked for the Southern League's representative team, captaining the side on a number of occasions. City turned down a substantial offer from Oldham Athletic in November 1911, when Bradley indicated that he wanted to stay at Highfield Road. The following season, however, he asked for a transfer, claiming that he had been barracked when City lost 3-2 at home to Merthyr, while he was carrying a leg injury sustained in the previous match. He never played for City again and was transferred to Hearts, on 16 October 1912 for £500. At the end of that season he was forced to retire because of a knee injury. He became a commission agent in Dudley and died in the early 1960s.

Southern League debut for Coventry City v Swindon Town (a) 1 September 1909.

	LEAGUE		*FA CUP*		*TOTAL*	
	App	*Gls*	*App*	*Gls*	*App*	*Gls*
1909-10	37	4	6	1	43	5
1910-11	33	10	4	0	37	10
1911-12	27	4	2	0	29	4
1912-13	7	1	0	0	7	1
	104	19	12	1	116	20

'Well, it's the chop for Brown.' These were the words of Eddie Brown as he climbed into the coach on 30 September 1954 after an evening game at Leyton Orient, where City had lost a scrappy affair by a single goal scored 30 seconds from time. He was right; two weeks later he was sold to Birmingham City

EDDIE BROWN

for about £10,000. Brown, who was born in Preston on 28 February 1928, started his career with his home-town club in 1948 and moved to Southampton two years later. City bought him for £7,000 in March 1952, along with Roy Kirk. Clearly both players had class but it was a case of too little too late and although Brown managed three goals in nine games, City were relegated. Over the next two seasons, Brown endeared himself to the Highfield Road faithful with his devastating speed, his brilliant anticipation and his sheer opportunism, scoring 40 goals in 70 games during that period. The 1954-5 season started with Brown at his irrepressible best, with City winning six out of their first seven games, but then things started to go wrong. The game at Orient was the sixth City had failed to win and they were slipping towards the middle of the table. In the programme for the Exeter City game three days after Brown had been sold, the board, no doubt anticipating the wrath of supporters, tried to justify their decision. They claimed that drastic changes were needed; Brown had 'a certain amount of ability' but his style of play did not fit in with the club's plans; most extraordinary of all, they claimed that he was not giving 100 per cent effort. This about a player who had scored eight goals in 12 games. Like Peter Murphy, Brown flourished at St Andrew's appearing in their FA Cup Final side of 1956. After leaving the Blues in 1959, he played for Leyton Orient for two years, was then player-coach at Scarborough and ended his career at Stourbridge. On retirement he moved back to his home town to become a teacher.

Football League debut for Coventry City v Nottingham Forest (a) 15 March 1952.

	LEAGUE		*FA CUP*		*TOTAL*	
	App	*Gls*	*App*	*Gls*	*App*	*Gls*
1951-52	9	3	0	0	9	3
1952-53	31	18	3	1	34	19
1953-54	33	20	1	0	34	20
1954-55	12	9	0	0	12	9
	85	50	4	1	89	51

Jackie Brown, who was born in Belfast on 8 November 1914, was one of Major Buckley's famous 'minors' at Wolverhampton Wanderers. He had been picked up cheaply from Belfast Celtic as a 20-year-old winger in 1934 and went on to play 27 League matches, scoring six goals, over the next two seasons. Buckley's skill was in developing young talent and then selling on to other clubs, and during the 1930s he realized Wolves profits of £100,000 through these astute deals. Ironically Brown shared the wing positions with George Ashall, who would eventually replace him at Highfield Road. When George McNestry suffered a very serious ankle injury after the first few games of 1936-7 it was quickly evident that a quality replacement would be required and it was considered a a coup on Storer's part when he acquired Brown for £3,000. An established Irish international, he was only 21 and for the next two seasons was City's leading scorer, acquitting himself well in either wing position. He became a great favourite and added to his collection of caps, becoming Coventry's first Republic of Ireland international in 1937. He seemed set for a successful career with City but Storer was never happy with his attack in the late 1930s and when he signed George Ashall from Wolves in the summer of 1938, for £3,500, someone had to make room. He was involved in an unsavoury incident at a Coventry ballroom in 1938 and with George Taylor and Leslie Warner available, Storer decided to cut his losses. In September 1938 First Division Birmingham paid £3,000 for him. He was a regular for the Blues and played in a few wartime games until a fire at St Andrew's halted football there. After the war he played for Barry Town and Bristol Rovers and between 1948 and 1951 made over 100 appearances for Ipswich Town, scoring 27 goals. He retired in the close season of 1951 and is now deceased.

Football League debut for Coventry City v West Ham United (h) 24 October 1936.

	LEAGUE		*FA CUP*		*TOTAL*	
	App	*Gls*	*App*	*Gls*	*App*	*Gls*
1936-37	29	13	3	1	32	14
1937-38	40	13	1	2	41	15
	69	26	4	3	73	29

JACKIE BROWN

Born in Danzig (later Gdańsk) on 19 April 1944, Dietmar Bruck was the first of three German-born players to appear for City, the others being Wilf Smith and David Phillips. Bruck, though, was a 'Coventry kid' through and through. After a debut at the age of 17, he returned to the Reserves to complete his apprenticeship, his big breakthrough coming in 1962-3 when, as a raw, attacking wing-half, he scored the equalizer in the epic FA Cup tie against Sunderland. It was hard going for Bruck over the next three seasons, with Farmer, Hill and Kearns contesting the half-back positions. His comeback came as a result of the sale of Allan Harris to Chelsea in the close season of 1966, leaving a vacancy at left-back. The following season proved to be his best and, after scoring in the first match of the season, he held down the position for the next 18 months. A strong, rumbustious defender, he never gave less than 100 per cent and although he initially found First Division football difficult, he eventually settled down. The signing of Chris Cattlin saw him move to right-back, but with Mick Coop fast emerging, Bruck's appearances became less frequent. After the signing of Wilf Smith, he moved to Charlton in October 1970. He took a further step down the ladder when he returned to the Midlands with Northampton Town in 1972 and then went out of the League as player-manager at Weymouth in 1974. Since then he has managed a number of non-League clubs in the Midlands.

Football League debut for Coventry City v Swindon Town (a) 28 April 1961.

	LEAGUE		*FA CUP*		*FL CUP*		*OTHERS*		*TOTAL*	
	App	*Gls*	*App*	*Gls*	*App*	*Gls*	*App*	*Gls*	*App*	*Gls*
1960-61	1	0	0	0	0	0	0	0	1	0
1961-62	6	0	0	0	0	0	0	0	6	0
1962-63	24	1	4	1	2	0	0	0	30	2
1963-64	10	0	0	0	2	0	0	0	12	0
1964-65	18	1	1	0	2	0	0	0	21	1
1965-66	22/1	2	4	0	0	0	0	0	26/1	2
1966-67	38	2	1	0	2	0	0	0	41	2
1967-68	33/1	1	3	0	1	0	0	0	37/1	1
1968-69	12/1	0	0	0	2/1	0	0	0	14/2	0
1969-70	14/3	0	0	0	0	0	0	0	14/3	0
1970-71	3/2	0	0	0	2	0	1	0	6/2	0
	181/8	7	13	1	13/1	0	1	0	208/9	8

DIETMAR BRUCK

HARRY BUCKLE

Belfast-born Harry Redmond Buckle came to Highfield Road before the start of the 1908-09 season with a big reputation, having gained Irish international caps whilst with Sunderland and Bristol Rovers. He immediately made the left-wing position his own and went on to play more than 120 games for City over the next three seasons. Buckle was speedy and clever and scored more than his fair share of goals, being the leading scorer in his first two seasons with the club. The directors thought highly of him and he was appointed team manager for the 1909-10 season. He left Highfield Road at the end of the 1910-11 season, to join Belfast Celtic. Whilst playing for the Belfast club, he was employed at the Harland & Wolff shipyard, one of only 17 Roman Catholics working there: the story goes that one day he was thrown into Belfast Lough. Unusually for a player born in the 1880s, he continued his playing career after World War One, turning out for Fordsons, Ford's League of Ireland team based in Cork, where he won Cup medals in 1924 and 1926.
Southern League debut for Coventry City v Crystal Palace (h) 1 September 1908.

	LEAGUE		*FA CUP*		*TOTAL*	
	App	*Gls*	*App*	*Gls*	*App*	*Gls*
1908-09	38	17	3	0	41	17
1909-10	38	17	6	2	44	19
1910-11	36	9	4	1	40	10
	112	43	13	3	125	46

WILLIE CARR

Willie Carr was a great prospect, a star of Coventry's 1968 youth team who eventually established himself as a key midfield player in the late 1960s and early '70s. He never quite realized this early promise and was never the same after he severely injured a knee against Liverpool in April 1973, when only 23. Brought into the first team gradually as a wide left-sided midfielder, his slight stature was always a disadvantage in the early days but he stuck to his guns and finally came through the pack, taking advantage of his pace and ability to split defences with that final pass. A number of Scotland caps followed and he seemed a certainty for the 1974 World Cup squad until the knee injury. He returned the following season but was obviously struggling and it came as a surprise when Wolves offered £240,000 for him. Unfortunately, Carr failed a medical and 12 months later was sold to the same club for a knock-down £100,000, at a time when City's financial position was very precarious. Carr went on to make well over 200 appearances for Wolves before moving to Millwall in August 1982. However, his short time at The Den was not a happy period and by the following February he had joined non-League Worcester City. A succession of moves around the West Midlands culminated in him being appointed player-manager of Willenhall Town in 1986. Carr, who was born in Glasgow on 6 January 1950, will always be remembered for his contribution to the famous 'donkey-kick' goal in 1970 (see *Ernie Hunt*).
Football League debut for Coventry City v Arsenal (a) 2 September 1967.

	LEAGUE		*FA CUP*		*FL CUP*		*OTHERS*		*TOTAL*	
	App	*Gls*	*App*	*Gls*	*App*	*Gls*	*App*	*Gls*	*App*	*Gls*
1967-68	20/3	1	3	1	/1	0	0	0	23/4	2
1968-69	33/3	3	2	0	3	0	0	0	38/3	3
1969-70	38	4	2	0	1	0	0	0	41	4
1970-71	41	5	1	0	5	1	4	0	51	6
1971-72	42	8	2	0	1	0	4	0	49	8
1972-73	36	8	3	1	2	1	2	0	43	10
1973-74	12/1	1	5	0	1	0	0	0	18/1	1
1974-75	23	3	3	0	1	0	0	0	27	3
	245/7	33	21	2	14/1	2	10	0	290/8	37

In eight years at Highfield Road, Chris Cattlin became one of the most popular players ever to don a Sky Blues' shirt, although ultimately he was poorly treated by the club. He was signed by Noel Cantwell from Huddersfield Town for £70,000 on the transfer deadline in 1968 and made his debut the next day, marking George Best. Cattlin performed the task with all the skill of a seasoned First Division full-back and never looked back. He repeated the job on Best several times and relished games against United. After less than 20 games he was picked for England Under-23s but he was never likely to make the full squad with left-backs of the quality of Cooper, McNab and Hughes around. Nicknamed 'Spider' by the fans because of his long legs and swarthy features, he was a stylish full-back in the 'Huddersfield mould'. He was twice sent off playing for City. The first time was in error at Goodison in 1971, when he was mistaken for Jeff Blockley; the second occasion was at Upton Park in 1975, after a scuffle with Bobby Gould. He never scored for City, although he went close a few times, but his cult following was undoubted. When he was freed in 1976, his fan club collected a petition for his reprieve, all to no avail. Cattlin signed for Brighton and City sent a team for his testimonial a year later. On retiring he ran a rock shop on the front at Brighton but answered an SOS call to become manager at the Goldstone in 1983. Alas, after three fairly successful seasons, he was sacked. Cattlin was born at Milnrow on 25 June 1946.

Football League debut for Coventry City v Manchester United (h) 16 March 1968.

	LEAGUE		*FA CUP*		*FL CUP*		*OTHERS*		*TOTAL*	
	App	*Gls*	*App*	*Gls*	*App*	*Gls*	*App*	*Gls*	*App*	*Gls*
1967-68	11	0	0	0	0	0	0	0	11	0
1968-69	32/1	0	2	0	3	0	0	0	37/1	0
1969-70	32/1	0	1	0	1	0	0	0	34/1	0
1970-71	14/1	0	0	0	0	0	1	0	15/1	0
1971-72	29	0	2	0	0	0	1	0	32	0
1972-73	36	0	2	0	2	0	1	0	41	0
1973-74	5/1	0	1	0	0/1	0	0	0	6/2	0
1974-75	40	0	3	0	1	0	0	0	44	0
1975-76	14	0	0	0	0	0	0	0	14	0
	213/4	0	11	0	7/1	0	3	0	234/5	0

CHRIS CATTLIN

Foleshill-born Fred Chaplin started his career with local junior team St Paul's Bible Class (a future Coventry City chairman, Walter Brandish, played in the same side) before joining Foleshill Great Heath. His normal position was wing-half but one Saturday he turned out at centre-half, was spotted by the Birmingham Juniors selectors and picked for a trial. Chaplin played for Birmingham Juniors against Scotland Juniors in 1903, in the same side as Billy Smith. He was on City's books for a short time but eventually signed for Small Heath. After two years, Chaplin moved to Woolwich Arsenal but he was glad to return to Highfield Road, in 1906. He was a model of consistency over the next six seasons, playing usually at left-half and making over 140 appearances in the Southern League side and 43 appearances in the Birmingham League side. He was noted for his steady, persistent worrying play and was always worth his place in the side. He was granted a testimonial in 1911-12, his last season at Highfield Road before he retired. The match was against Chelsea in the South-Eastern League and the attendance of 4,324 was well above average for a reserve-team fixture. In 1938, when he was interviewed for an article in the *Coventry Herald*, Chaplin was working at Humber in Coventry, having previously been employed by Courtaulds.

Birmingham League debut for Coventry City v Kidderminster Harriers (h) 17 January 1903.

	LEAGUE		*FA CUP*		*TOTAL*	
	App	*Gls*	*App*	*Gls*	*App*	*Gls*
1902-03	5	1	0	0	5	1
1906-07	6	1	0	0	6	1
1907-08	32	4	9	0	41	4
1908-09	35	0	3	0	38	0
1909-10	38	0	5	1	43	1
1910-11	24	0	4	0	28	0
1911-12	30	1	2	0	32	1
	170	7	23	1	193	8

ALFRED CHAPLIN

GEORGE CHAPLIN

One of six footballing brothers, George Chaplin began his career with his local team, Dundee Arnott, and won his only Scotland cap in 1908 (v Wales) whilst on Dundee's books. He moved to Bradford City in 1909 for £600. Despite the intervention of war, he was still highly regarded when he came to Coventry in 1918 and when City entered the Football League the following year, he was appointed captain. Following his retirement he remained in the area and became landlord of the Black Horse pub in Marton during the 1930s. He was regarded as the best full-back of his era, but his career was peppered with bad luck. He was forced to withdraw from the Scotland team to play England in 1909 and a year later had to withdraw from Bradford City's team on the eve of the 1911 FA Cup Final, through an illness which kept him out of the game for two years. In 1920 he was the central figure in the 'Bury Scandal' (dealt with in detail elsewhere in this book) and was banned for life by the FA in 1923. Despite remaining in the area, he vowed never to set foot in Highfield Road again. He was born in Dundee on 26 September 1888 and died in Coventry on 14 May 1963.
Football League debut for Coventry City v Tottenham Hotspur (h) 30 August 1919.

	LEAGUE		*FA CUP*		*TOTAL*	
	App	*Gls*	*App*	*Gls*	*App*	*Gls*
1919-20	22	0	2	0	24	0
1920-21	32	0	2	0	34	0
1921-22	42	0	3	0	45	0
1922-23	10	0	0	0	10	0
	106	0	7	0	113	0

Born in Glasgow on 12 April 1925, Ken Chisholm was one of soccer's original happy wanderers. Whenever a team needed a boost, Chisholm was usually one of the first names to come to mind. So it was that Harry Storer took out the cheque book in March 1950 and paid Leicester City £9,250 plus Jack Marsh in what turned out to be a successful attempt to save Coventry from relegation. Chisholm was a fighter pilot during the war. He joined Queen's Park in 1945 and the following year turned out for Scotland in a Victory international against Northern Ireland. He left Hampden Park in 1946, for Partick Thistle, and the legendary Major Frank Buckley, manager of Leeds United, signed him from Partick in January 1948. Chisholm stayed at Leeds for less than a year before moving to Leicester, with whom he won his only honour, an FA Cup runners-up medal in 1949. He became a great favourite at Highfield Road. By his own admission, he was not the fastest or the most skilful player but he was strong and above all brave. Heading was his great strength, although he also had a pretty good left foot. He was a terrific trainer but it was a constant struggle to keep his weight down to his ideal of 12st. At Highfield Road he would cut up tyres, then bind them around his waist to make him sweat more. His only complete season with City was 1950-51, when he scored 24 goals, most of them before Christmas. He managed ten the following season but by March, City were again struggling to avoid relegation. In a desperate attempt to revive his ailing side, Harry Storer decided to sell Chisholm, probably his only saleable player, to provide the cash to buy Eddie Brown and Roy Kirk. So Chisholm was on his travels again, this time to help Cardiff in their successful push to Division One. He left them in 1954 and played for Sunderland, Workington Town, Glentoran, where he was player-manager, Spennymoor and finally Los Angeles, none of them for more than two years. He moved to the North-East, where he worked in an insurance broker's firm. He tried to get a book of his memoirs published but without success.
Football League debut for Coventry City v Blackburn Rovers (h) 18 March 1950.

KEN CHISHOLM

	LEAGUE		*FA CUP*		*TOTAL*	
	App	*Gls*	*App*	*Gls*	*App*	*Gls*
1949-50	5	0	0	0	5	0
1950-51	38	24	1	0	39	24
1951-52	25	10	2	1	27	11
	68	34	3	1	71	35

Born at Larne on 15 September 1945, David Clements joined Wolves as a 17-year-old in 1963 and first came to notice when he appeared in the Little World Cup at Wembley in 1963, playing for the Northern Ireland youth team. He was unable to make the breakthrough at Molineux and signed for City in the close season of 1964, for a give-away fee of £1,500. His signing proved to be another of Jimmy Hill's astute deals and after a spell 'bedding-in' in the Reserves, he burst on to the scene, scoring in eight of his first ten first-team games on the left wing. Full international honours soon followed and Clements became an integral part of the City set-up, appearing in any of the left-sided positions. He never lived up to his earlier scoring feats but packed a tremendous shot in his left foot and was difficult to shake off the ball when in full flight. It came as a surprise when he was sold to Sheffield Wednesday in August 1971, for £55,000, but behind his sale was the ill-fated signing of Chris Chilton who joined City shortly afterwards. After leaving Coventry, Clements enjoyed a number of successful seasons at Sheffield Wednesday and Everton before signing for NASL giants New York Cosmos in 1976. His 21 full caps with City remain a record, equalled only by Ronnie Rees, and there can be no doubt that both players would have added to their caps had they remained at Highfield Road.

Football League debut for Coventry City v Northampton Town (a) 23 January 1965.

	LEAGUE		*FA CUP*		*FL CUP*		*OTHERS*		*TOTAL*	
	App	*Gls*	*App*	*Gls*	*App*	*Gls*	*App*	*Gls*	*App*	*Gls*
1964-65	15	9	0	0	0	0	0	0	15	9
1965-66	22/1	3	2	1	1	1	0	0	25/1	5
1966-67	40	4	1	0	3	1	0	0	44	5
1967-68	40/1	1	0	0	1	0	0	0	41/1	1
1968-69	37	3	2	0	4	1	0	0	43	4
1969-70	33	3	2	0	1	0	0	0	36	3
1970-71	40	3	1	0	5	0	4	0	50	3
1971-72	1	0	0	0	0	0	0	0	1	0
	228/2	26	8	1	15	3	4	0	255/2	30

DAVID CLEMENTS

Mick Coop was born in Grimsby on 10 July 1948 but brought up in Leamington Spa, signing professional forms for City in January 1966, after a three-year apprenticeship. For the next 15 seasons he served the club both at full-back and as a central defender and, but for poor spell in 1974 and 1975, could have run George Curtis very close in the all-time appearances charts. In his early days he was very much an attacking full-back, always looking for the overlapping opportunity. He was appointed the club's penalty-taker in 1973 and most of his goals came from the spot. With Graham Oakey breaking into the first team, Coop joined York City on loan for six months in November 1974, but returned to Highfield Road and established himself as a central defensive sweeper. It was about this time that he brought into play the famous 'Coop Scoop', a long diagonal punt from the right side of his penalty box, high into the opponents' penalty area. He went on loan to NASL club Detroit Express in 1979 but was still good enough to make over 30 appearances for Coventry in Gordon Milne's final season in 1980-81. When Dave Sexton took over in the summer, Coop decided to join Derby County in a £20,000 deal but it was a move he always regretted and his contract was cancelled in January 1982. After a few games for AP Leamington, he had retired from the game and opened an antiques shop in Leamington Spa. The lure of Highfield Road once again proved too strong and Coop returned as youth-team coach in 1985. His side won the FA Youth Cup in 1987, for the only time in City's history, but the glory days were short-lived and after a row with John Sillett he left the club in 1989.

Football League debut for Coventry City v Brighton & Hove Albion (h) 11 September 1966.

	LEAGUE		*FA CUP*		*FL CUP*		*OTHERS*		*TOTAL*	
	App	*Gls*	*App*	*Gls*	*App*	*Gls*	*App*	*Gls*	*App*	*Gls*
1966-67	2/2	0	0	0	1	0	0	0	3/2	0
1967-68	13/2	0	0/1	0	1	0	0	0	14/3	0
1968-69	36/1	0	2	0	4	0	0	0	42/1	0
1969-70	41	0	2	0	1	0	0	0	44	0
1970-71	25	0	0	0	5	0	4	0	34	0
1971-72	13/2	0	1	0	1	0	4	0	19/2	0
1972-73	42	0	4	1	2	0	2	0	50	1
1973-74	30	5	4	1	6	1	1	0	41	7
1974-75	2/4	0	0	0	0	0	0	0	2/4	0
1975-76	42	4	3	0	2	0	0	0	47	4
1976-77	39	2	2	0	3	1	0	0	44	3
1977-78	34/1	6	1	0	4	0	0	0	39/1	6
1978-79	36	0	2	0	0	0	0	0	38	0
1979-80	31	1	2	0	1/1	0	0	0	34/1	1
1980-81	27	0	2	0	5	0	0	0	34	0
	413/12	18	25/1	2	36/1	2	11	0	485/14	22

MICK COOP

JOHN CRAVEN

John Craven was bought to replace the ageing Roy Barry in the summer of 1973. Born at St Annes on 15 May 1947, he had played over 200 games, mainly as a striker, for Blackpool and Crystal Palace, but Gordon Milne obviously recognized other talents in his old Blackpool chum. After less than a season as a pivot, alongside Alan Dugdale, Craven assumed a midfield role, becoming a regular after the sale of Dennis Mortimer. At £42,500 he was a reasonable purchase and kept City's midfield afloat during the austere period in the mid-1970s, when many outstanding midfield players had to be sold. Whilst always giving 100 per cent, he lacked midfield vision and leadership qualities and the signing of Terry Yorath signalled the end of his career at City. He moved to Plymouth in January 1977, for £20,000, but could not help the Pilgrims avoid relegation to the Third Division. After 45 games, Craven went to play in the North American Soccer League, for Vancouver Whitecaps and then California Surf.
Football League debut for Coventry City v Tottenham Hotspur (h) 25 August 1973.

	LEAGUE		*FA CUP*		*FL CUP*		*TOTAL*	
	App	*Gls*	*App*	*Gls*	*App*	*Gls*	*App*	*Gls*
1973-74	30	3	6	0	2	0	38	3
1974-75	25/1	2	3	0	0/1	0	28/2	2
1975-76	27/1	3	2	0	2	0	31/1	3
1976-77	4/1	0	1	0	2	0	7/1	0
	86/3	8	12	0	6/1	0	104/4	8

Affectionately known as 'The Ironman', George Curtis ranks alongside George Mason as the greatest centre-half and captain in Coventry City's history. He was born at Dover on 5 May 1939 and signed for City from Snowdown Colliery in October 1955, on the recommendation of former skipper Harry Barratt. Curtis was an immediate success and by August 1958, at the age of 19, he had established himself as the regular centre-half and was to miss only six League games in the next nine seasons. During this period he became one of the most feared defenders in the Football League. Considered by many opposition fans to be over-physical, he always maintained he played the game in a fair but hard manner. He turned out for Coventry on many occasions when lesser mortals would have gone sick and his style epitomized the spirit of the club during this period. A lot of pundits expressed doubts as to whether Curtis the stopper would be up to the refinements of First Division football. Alas, we shall never know because in his second match, against Nottingham Forest, he broke a leg. He came back six months later but was never quite the same and, with Maurice Setters and then Roy Barry joining Coventry and with Jeff Blockley emerging, Curtis seemed the odd man out. After 50 First Division matches he moved to Villa Park in December 1969 for a fee of £25,000 (see *Coventry City's Managers).*
Football League debut for Coventry City v Newport County (a) 21 April 1956.

GEORGE CURTIS

	LEAGUE		*FA CUP*		*FL CUP*		*TOTAL*	
	App	*Gls*	*App*	*Gls*	*App*	*Gls*	*App*	*Gls*
1955-56	3	0	0	0	-	-	3	0
1956-57	19	0	0	0	-	-	19	0
1957-58	15	0	1	0	-	-	16	0
1958-59	43	0	2	0	-	-	45	0
1959-60	45	0	2	0	-	-	47	0
1960-61	46	1	3	0	2	0	51	1
1961-62	46	0	2	0	1	0	49	0
1962-63	45	0	9	1	2	0	56	1
1963-64	46	0	2	0	2	0	50	0
1964-65	41	1	1	0	4	0	46	1
1965-66	42	5	4	0	4	0	50	5
1966-67	42	2	1	0	3	0	46	2
1967-68	3/1	0	0	0	0	0	3/1	0
1968-69	28/2	2	2	1	3	0	33/2	3
1969-70	19/1	0	0	0	1	0	20/1	0
	483/4	11	29	2	22	0	534/4	13

Gerry Daly's name was linked to Coventry City several times before Gordon Milne paid Derby County £300,000 for the Republic of Ireland international and former Manchester United player in August 1980. Milne's young team were lacking direction in midfield and Daly's experience proved vital. He had an immediate effect and was very influential in the Sky Blues' League Cup run in his first season. In the semi-final first leg, with City 2-0 down, it was Daly who kept their heads up and scored a vital goal to keep Coventry in with a chance. When Dave Sexton took over the following season, he and Daly did not see eye to eye and Daly played in only 21 games. He was replaced by Gerry Francis and went on loan to Leicester City in 1982-3, when he helped them win promotion. Bobby Gould brought Daly back into the Coventry fold on his arrival and he obliged with seven goals in 27 games without ever being the influence that Gould expected. In August 1984, Daly moved to Birmingham City and subsequently to Shrewsbury Town, Stoke City and Doncaster Rovers. In 1990-91 he was player-manager at Telford United and appeared on BBC TV's *Match of the Day*. He always looked a fragile player but his natural skills and regular goals were sadly missed after his departure from Coventry. He won 44 caps for the Republic of Ireland, 16 whilst at City, and was a member of Manchester United's outstanding promotion team in 1975 and their losing FA Cup Final side the following season. He was born in Dublin on 30 April 1954.
Football League debut for Coventry City v Liverpool (h) 19 August 1980.

	LEAGUE		*FA CUP*		*FL CUP*		*TOTAL*	
	App	*Gls*	*App*	*Gls*	*App*	*Gls*	*App*	*Gls*
1980-81	34/1	8	4	2	7	1	45/1	11
1981-82	19	4	2	0	0	0	21	4
1982-83	2	0	0	0	0	0	2	0
1983-84	27/1	7	3/1	0	0	0	30/2	7
	82/2	19	9/1	2	7	1	98/3	22

GERRY DALY

Born in Sheffield on 20 June 1898, Norman Dinsdale spent seven seasons with Notts County, making over 270 appearances before joining Coventry City in a double signing with Alf Widdowson in 1928. Kerr had left the club in February and with City in danger of having to apply for re-election the directors thought these two veterans would give the team some stability. They made their double debut against Bournemouth and both were successful. Dinsdale was a very solid centre-half and was appointed captain before the 1928-9 season. The transfer precipitated yet another Highfield Road crisis when the £500 cheque to Notts County was returned by the bank, unpaid. Dinsdale was an inspiring skipper and led the side through the best two seasons for some time, scoring a number of valuable goals. In 1930, he moved to Bristol Rovers for £425 but only stayed a couple of seasons before retiring from the game. He died in Nottingham in September 1970.
Football League debut for Coventry City v Bournemouth & BA (h) 10 March 1928.

	LEAGUE		*FA CUP*		*TOTAL*	
	App	*Gls*	*App*	*Gls*	*App*	*Gls*
1927-28	12	5	0	0	12	5
1928-29	42	1	1	0	43	1
1929-30	34	4	4	1	38	5
	88	10	5	1	93	11

NORMAN DINSDALE

JIMMY DOUGALL

During a period when players arrived and left Coventry City with unseemly haste, Jimmy Dougall was one of the few permanent fixtures at Highfield Road. He was born in Scotland in 1900 and began playing with Cleland Juniors with whom he won two Scottish Junior caps. At this time he was spotted by the Bradford City player Jock Ewart, who recommended Dougall to his old friend Harry Pollitt. And so the 19-year-old winger was brought to Coventry, where he became a regular for the next seven years. He was not a prolific scorer but his accurate crosses resulted in many goals and he became the envy of many clubs, with City receiving a number of bids for him. Indeed, on one occasion they rejected an offer of £2,000 from Manchester United. He was eventually transferred to Reading for £555 in the close season of 1926 but broke his leg after only 12 games, effectively ending his League career. He returned to work in Coventry, finding employment at Morris Engines, Courthouse Green, where Albert Evans was secretary of the Sports and Social Club. In 1945, Jimmy junior, one of his six sons, also a right winger, was briefly on City's books.

Football League debut for Coventry City v Rotherham County (a) 17 January 1920.

	LEAGUE		*FA CUP*		*TOTAL*	
	App	*Gls*	*App*	*Gls*	*App*	*Gls*
1919-20	11	1	2	0	13	1
1920-21	37	2	2	0	39	2
1921-22	32	1	2	0	34	1
1922-23	34	3	1	0	35	3
1923-24	33	3	0	0	33	3
1924-25	41	2	3	0	44	2
1925-26	38	2	1	0	39	2
	226	14	11	0	237	14

GREG DOWNS

Greg Downs, who was born at Carlton, Nottingham, on 13 December 1958, was an exceptionally popular player at Highfield Road, despite having to replace Stuart Pearce, who had moved to Forest. Downs had to endure a lot of criticism in his first season but, after many steady if unspectacular performances, he won the fans over. A natural left-footer with the ability to overlap, his wholehearted approach to the game was pleasing. His rapport with the fans grew, aided by a self-deprecating attitude to his baldness. He joined Coventry from Norwich City, for £40,000 in the summer of 1985 after being left out of the Canaries' League Cup Final team. In 1979 he scored the winning goal — a rasping 25-yarder — in Norwich's first victory at Highfield Road since 1933. In all he made 169 appearances at Carrow Road. His shooting ability was not over-used at Coventry but he scored some notable long-range efforts, against Bolton and Charlton in 1986-7, Tottenham in 1987-8 and QPR in 1989-90. His contribution to the FA Cup winning side was vital and despite being 'skinned' by Chris Waddle for Allen's early goal, he recovered to mark the England star out of the Final. On several occasions in his City career he was dropped and was supposedly on the verge of leaving, but he always bounced back. He finally lost his place after a game at Luton, when two late goals cost City a game they had as good as won. He moved on a free transfer to Birmingham City, where he replaced another former Coventry City hero, Harry Roberts. In June 1991, Downs moved to Hereford United as player-coach.

Football League debut for Coventry City v Manchester City (h) 17 August 1985.

	LEAGUE		*FA CUP*		*FL CUP*		*OTHERS*		*TOTAL*	
	App	*Gls*	*App*	*Gls*	*App*	*Gls*	*App*	*Gls*	*App*	*Gls*
1985-86	40/1	0	0	0	4	0	1	0	45/1	0
1986-87	39	2	6	1	5	0	1	0	51	3
1987-88	27	2	2	0	2/1	0	3	0	34/1	2
1988-89	20/2	0	0	0	3	1	0	0	23/2	0
1989-90	16/1	0	1	0	5	1	1	0	23/1	2
	142/4	4	9	1	19/1	2	6	0	176/5	7

Robert Owen Evans was born at Wrexham around 1882 and began his career in his home town as a full-back before being persuaded to keep goal for a junior side, Stansty Villa. He signed for Wrexham when he was only 15 and was transferred to Blackburn Rovers after five years, for £150. In 1902, whilst with Wrexham, he won his first cap, against Ireland, sustaining a severe leg injury after only 15 minutes but continued to keep goal with a heavily bandaged limb. He captained Blackburn from 1905 to 1907 and became the idol of the Ewood Park. After a game against Villa, the *Athletic News* said of him: 'He twisted and turned with an agility which seemed to suggest that he is india-rubber-jointed.' Surprisingly, he was allowed to join Croydon Common and it was from that club that City signed him in May 1909. He was one of a long line of outstanding Coventry goalkeepers and a mainstay for most of the Southern League era. Perhaps his finest game was in the FA Cup tie at Preston, when he performed magnificently in torrential conditions. Evans won five of his 11 Welsh caps whilst he was at Highfield Road. He was injured towards the end of 1912-13 and never regained his place, joining Birmingham for £50 at the end of that season. Eventually he returned to the Coventry area to work in the motor industry. When he was interviewed by the *Coventry Herald* in 1938, he had just retired from refereeing but was still devoting much of his time to helping junior players. He was a regular visitor to Highfield Road until the early 1960s.
Southern League debut for Coventry City v Swindon Town (a) 1 September 1909.

	LEAGUE		*FA CUP*		*TOTAL*	
	App	*Gls*	*App*	*Gls*	*App*	*Gls*
1909-10	34	0	6	0	40	0
1910-11	37	0	3	0	40	0
1911-12	34	0	2	0	36	0
1912-13	21	0	2	0	23	0
	126	0	13	0	139	0

BOB EVANS

Ronnie Farmer is a Channel Islander, born in Guernsey on 6 March 1936. He joined City as part of the £6,000 double-signing with goalkeeper Arthur Lightening from Nottingham Forest in November 1958 and settled down immediately, with Curtis and Kearns founding the successful half-back line that was to carry the club from the Fourth to the First Division. Farmer was a constructive, wing-half with a penchant for scoring long-range goals. He was also an immaculate penalty-taker, missing only once from the spot, when his shot rapped a Millwall post in the torrid promotion battle of April 1964. He was still a regular during the three seasons in the Second Division, but the arrival of Brian Lewis in March 1967 signalled that his days were numbered. Now past his peak, he found life in Division One much tougher and was granted a free transfer in lieu of a testimonial, receiving a £10,000 payment when signing for Notts County in October 1967. After a couple of seasons at Meadow Lane, he joined Grantham Town. Returning to Coventry to find employment, he eventually rejoined City as youth-team coach but after a couple of seasons joined Massey Ferguson. His brother, Bill, was a goalkeeper with Nottingham Forest and had a trial at Highfield Road in the late 1950s.
Football League debut for Coventry City v Chester (h) 20 November 1958.

	LEAGUE		*FA CUP*		*FL CUP*		*TOTAL*	
	App	*Gls*	*App*	*Gls*	*App*	*Gls*	*App*	*Gls*
1958-59	26	1	0	0	-	-	26	1
1959-60	33	6	2	0	-	-	35	6
1960-61	36	3	3	2	2	0	41	5
1961-62	26	7	1	0	1	0	28	7
1962-63	22	6	5	1	1	0	28	7
1963-64	44	11	2	0	1	0	47	11
1964-65	25	3	0	0	1	0	26	3
1965-66	34/1	9	4	1	4	0	42/1	10
1966-67	32/2	2	1	0	2	1	35/2	3
1967-68	3/1	0	0	0	0	0	3/1	0
	281/4	48	18	4	12	1	311/4	53

RONNIE FARMER

'Fergie' was a product of City's successful youth policy of the early 1970s. He was born at Newcastle upon Tyne on 3 October 1954 but slipped through the Magpies' scouting net to join Coventry. He made his debut soon after the sale of Colin Stein, playing 12 games and scoring twice that season. The following season he was briefly overtaken by Green and Murphy, but at the start of 1976-7 he scored six goals in his first nine games and was a regular thereafter. It was not until the emergence of Ian Wallace that he won the fans over and scored regularly. In 1977-8, despite two periods of injury, he scored 17 League goals, including three hat-tricks, and the partnership was one of the most lethal in Division One. Injury and loss of form affected him over the following two season and in 1979-80 he and Wallace played together only ten times; in four of those, at the end of November, Ferguson scored eight goals including four against Ipswich. Ipswich, Forest and Villa were all supposedly keen to sign him, with Brian Clough apparently agreeing a £500,000 deal, then pulling out. In the summer of 1981, Everton paid £280,000 for a player past his best and troubled with injuries. Despite scoring a League Cup winner against City, he never overcame injury problems and drifted to St Andrew's just over a year later. He returned to City, on loan, at the end of 1983-4 and scored three goals in seven games including one in the final crucial game against Norwich, to save City and send his own club down. He wanted to return permanently but Gould would not meet his pay demands and Ferguson went to play for Chris Cattlin at Brighton and latterly Colchester and Wealdstone. Now he is back in the North-East as Football in the Community Officer at Sunderland.

Football League debut for Coventry City v Leeds United (a) 1 February 1975.

MICK FERGUSON

	LEAGUE		FA CUP		FL CUP		TOTAL	
	App	Gls	App	Gls	App	Gls	App	Gls
1974-75	12	2	0	0	0	0	12	2
1975-76	11/4	3	0	0	0/2	1	11/6	4
1976-77	32	13	0	0	3	2	35	15
1977-78	30	17	1	0	4	0	35	17
1978-79	16/2	6	0	0	1	0	17/2	6
1979-80	17	10	1	0	2	0	20	10
1980-81	3	0	1	0	0	0	4	0
1983-84	7	3	0	0	0	0	7	3
	128/6	54	3	0	10/2	3	141/8	57

Billy Frith, who was born in Sheffield on 9 June 1912, was a cultured wing-half, one of the vital cogs in Harry Storer's team of the mid- to late-1930s. He began his career as a part-time professional with Mansfield Town in 1929, moving to Chesterfield a year later. After a handful of games he was injured and was eventually given a free transfer. Storer snapped him up in the close season of 1932 and after a few games at inside-left he settled down as an attacking wing-half, a position he held until the outbreak of war. He was often the subject of bigger clubs' interest but was a big favourite of Storer's and decided to stay with City. After a home game against Bradford in 1937-8, Storer described Frith's display as: "the best exhibition of right-half play I have seen." He played for Coventry and guested for Leicester City during the war but an ankle injury cost him an unofficial England cap and in 1945 he decided to try his hand at management. Frith became player-manager of Port Vale but it was a shattering experience and he returned to Highfield Road in time to make seven appearances in 1946-7 (see *Coventry City's Managers*).

Football League debut for Coventry City v Newport County (h) 17 September 1932.

BILLY FRITH

	LEAGUE		FA CUP		TOTAL	
	App	Gls	App	Gls	App	Gls
1932-33	3	1	0	0	3	1
1933-34	8	0	0	0	8	0
1934-35	22	0	1	0	23	0
1935-36	29	2	2	0	31	2
1936-37	29	2	2	0	32	1
1937-38	32	0	0	0	32	0
1938-39	39	0	1	0	40	0
1946-47	7	0	1	0	8	0
	169	4	8	0	177	4

In January 1990, John Sillett made one of his last signings as manager when he paid Dundee United £900,000 for winger Kevin Gallacher. The 23-year-old, who was born in Clydebank on 23 November 1966, was slow to adapt to the English game and was not helped by a bone-crunching challenge from Stuart Pearce in his second game, the Littlewoods Cup semi-final first leg. Soon after Sillett's departure, however, he was successfully switched to a central striking role and ended the 1990-91 season with 16 goals, including a hat-trick in the 5-4 Rumbelows Cup victory over Forest. His importance to City was underlined by the fact that whilst he was out for two months after a knee operation, the team went out of both major Cups and slipped into the relegation zone. His performances earned him a recall to the Scottish international team — he won his fifth cap in San Marino — and both City Player of the Year awards. His speed and agility were never in doubt but his finishing power had never been seen before the switch of positions. With Dundee United he played on the losing side in the 1987 UEFA Cup Final, the 1987 and 1988 Scottish Cup Finals and won seven Under-21 caps.
Football League debut for Coventry City v Chelsea (h) 3 February 1990.

	LEAGUE		FA CUP		FL CUP		OTHERS		TOTAL	
	App	Gls	App	Gls	App	Gls	App	Gls	App	Gls
1989-90	15	3	0	0	2	0	0	0	17	3
1990-91	32	11	2	0	3	5	1	0	38	16
	47	14	2	0	5	5	1	0	55	19

KEVIN GALLACHER

Ian Gibson was a great hero of City supporters in the four seasons he spent with the club, although he was frequently injured and often fell out with the management. A skilful, ball-playing Scot — he was born at Newton Stewart on 30 March 1943 — Gibson learned his trade at those traditional English homes for Scottish players, Peel Park and Park Avenue, before moving up the League with Middlesbrough in 1962. Jimmy Hill had spotted his talents in 1965-6, in matches between the two clubs, and with 'Boro relegated to Division Three, Gibson became available. Had Hill managed to sign Barry Bridges, it is unlikely that he could have afforded Gibson but, as it was, the player moved to Highfield Road for a record £57,500 and made his debut on a sultry day in August 1966. His early matches were disappointing and by October he had fallen out with Hill over his role in the team and demanded a transfer. But with City's promotion chance waning, Gibson returned to the side in a more free-flowing role, scored twice, and the side remained unbeaten for the rest of the season, his scheming play being the main reason for the revival. Knee injuries severely restricted his appearances during the next two seasons, but enough was seen of him to realize that, had he been fully fit, the club may not have struggled so badly. Despite another knee problem in mid-season, he managed 30 appearances as City finished sixth in 1969-70. In the 1970 close season he was surprisingly sold to Cardiff City for £35,000, rejoining his old mentor, Jimmy Scouler. After a successful spell with Bournemouth, he signed for non-League Gateshead in 1974. In 1983 he was reported to be working on the new Port Stanley airport in the Falklands and not long afterwards was operating as a talent scout for City in the North-East of England.
Football League debut for Coventry City v Hull City (h) 20 August 1966.

	LEAGUE		FA CUP		FL CUP		TOTAL	
	App	Gls	App	Gls	App	Gls	App	Gls
1966-67	31	8	1	0	2	0	34	8
1967-68	14/1	0	2	0	1	0	17/1	0
1968-69	17/1	3	0	0	4	1	21/1	4
1969-70	28/1	2	0	0	1	0	29/1	2
	90/3	13	3	0	8	1	101/3	14

IAN GIBSON

TERRY GIBSON

Terry Gibson's scoring record stands comparison with any striker in Coventry City's First Division history. Born in Walthamstow on 23 December 1962, he was a classic example of outstanding Spurs home-grown players making their names elsewhere and Bobby Gould signed him for £100,000 in the summer of 1983. The 5ft 4in tall goal poacher had won many Youth caps whilst with Tottenham but made only 22 appearances for Spurs' first team. At City, his 51 goals in two and a half seasons were one reason why the club stayed up in those desperate years 1983-86. Gibson had to play alongside a succession of centre-forwards in his first season and a half, but he just kept on scoring. His hat-trick against Liverpool in December 1983 was the first scored against the Reds for over 11 years and that day his love affair with City fans was consummated. At the start of 1985-6 he scored in seven consecutive games, a club record, and his value on the transfer market was rising. After rumours that Gibson (or his wife) was unsettled in the Midlands, Ron Atkinson signed him for Manchester United in January 1986, with Alan Brazil joining City in a deal valuing Gibson at £650,000. The move was something of a disaster for Gibson and after scoring once in 29 appearances for United he joined Bobby Gould's Wimbledon in the summer of 1987, playing his part in their FA Cup triumph the following year. One is left to speculate on how successful he would have been in a team playing football to suit his style.

Football League debut for Coventry City v Watford (a) 27 August 1983.

	LEAGUE		*FA CUP*		*FL CUP*		*OTHERS*		*TOTAL*	
	App	*Gls*	*App*	*Gls*	*App*	*Gls*	*App*	*Gls*	*App*	*Gls*
1983-84	35/1	17	3	2	2	0	0	0	40/1	19
1984-85	38	15	2	3	2	1	0	0	42	19
1985-86	24	11	1	0	3	2	2	1	30	14
	97/1	43	6	5	7	3	2	1	112/1	52

GARY GILLESPIE

Gary Gillespie was born in Stirling on 5 July 1960 and arrived at Highfield Road as a fresh-faced 17-year-old in March 1978. Gordon Milne spent £75,000 on the Falkirk skipper and he turned out to be one of the manager's most inspiring signings. From Gillespie's first appearance five months later, it was obvious that he was an outstanding talent and in his time at Highfield Road he developed into one of the most accomplished defenders in the country. In the crazy events of 1983, the fans hoped that Gillespie would be one player who would stay, but his talent had attracted the big clubs and, although the player procrastinated, he finally signed for Liverpool for £325,000. Coventry fans did not begrudge him his move and he handled it with much more decorum than some of his teammates. He won eight Scotland Under-21 caps whilst with Coventry and looked set for a long international career at Anfield but injuries, club calls and stiff competition from the likes of Miller and McLeish restricted him to a paltry 13 full caps. Honours have come his way — three League Championship medals and a European Cup runners-up medal, but no Wembley winners' medals. He has losers' medals in both FA and League Cups and cruelly missed Liverpool's two FA Cup Final wins through injury.

Football League debut for Coventry City v Middlesbrough (a) 19 August 1978.

	LEAGUE		*FA CUP*		*FL CUP*		*TOTAL*	
	App	*Gls*	*App*	*Gls*	*App*	*Gls*	*App*	*Gls*
1978-79	14/1	0	0	0	1	0	15/1	0
1979-80	38	1	2	0	3	0	43	1
1980-81	37	1	4	0	7	0	48	1
1981-82	40	2	4	0	2	0	46	2
1982-83	42	2	3	0	3	0	48	2
	171/1	6	13	0	16	0	200/1	6

Jimmy Hill astonished the football world when he paid a world record fee of £35,000 for a goalkeeper and signed Bill Glazier from Crystal Palace in October 1964. It proved to be money well spent as Glazier went on to serve City for over ten years and, but for a broken leg in April 1965, he would surely have stood a good chance of making the England World Cup squad in 1966. Glazier, who was born in Nottingham on 2 August 1943, was already well known to City fans after his consistent displays for Palace in the promotion battles of 1963-4. However, had Hill successfully completed the signing of David Best from Bournemouth, Glazier would not have joined Coventry. He quickly established himself in the England Under-23 team, following in the footsteps of Reg Matthews. A key member of the 1966-7 Second Division championship side, he saved his best form for the early part of City's first season in Division One, when, with Coventry struggling, he was called upon to save the day, time and time again. He remained the regular 'keeper until the end of 1973-4, when, after a few injuries, he was succeeded by Neil Ramsbottom, who had been signed as his understudy in March 1972. It was clear that his first-team days were numbered but there was one more highlight in his testimonial year, with the England World Cup-winning squad paying tribute in November 1974. It came as no surprise when he moved to Brentford in July 1975, but his stay there was short as another injury hastened his retirement from the game. He went into the hotel business in Brighton and then Gloucestershire and is still an occasional visitor to Highfield Road. His 402 appearances place him third in City's all-time career records.

Football League debut for Coventry City v Portsmouth (a) 17 October 1964.

	LEAGUE		*FA CUP*		*FL CUP*		*OTHERS*		*TOTAL*	
	App	*Gls*	*App*	*Gls*	*App*	*Gls*	*App*	*Gls*	*App*	*Gls*
1964-65	24	0	1	0	0	0	0	0	25	0
1965-66	7	0	0	0	0	0	0	0	7	0
1966-67	41	0	1	0	3	0	0	0	45	0
1967-68	40	0	2	0	1	0	0	0	43	0
1968-69	42	0	2	0	5	0	0	0	49	0
1969-70	40	0	2	0	1	0	0	0	43	0
1970-71	40	0	1	0	5	0	3	0	49	0
1971-72	37	0	2	0	1	0	4	0	44	0
1972-73	28	0	4	0	2	0	2	0	36	0
1973-74	40	0	6	0	6	0	1	0	53	0
1974-75	7	0	0	0	1	0	0	0	8	0
	346	0	21	0	25	0	10	0	402	0

BILL GLAZIER

If heart and soul were the main criteria for football success, then Bobby Gould would have played for his country many times. What he lacked in finesse and style he made up for with his bustling, gutsy performances as one of the bravest of all Coventry City centre-forwards. He made his debut as a 17-year-old in October 1963, but over the next three seasons he made less than 30 appearances, not becoming a regular until the fans' hero, George Hudson, was sold in 1966. Many supporters made the mistake of comparing him to their hero and Gould took some severe barracking from the crowd. In 1966-7, however, he confounded his critics by topping the Second Division goalscorers with 24 goals, the highlight being a hat-trick in the 5-0 drubbing of leaders Ipswich Town. He was the 'villain' of the piece in the home game against Carlisle United when Alan Ross, the Cumbrians' goalkeeper, was sent off for retaliating after Gould clattered into him. His First Division debut was unforgettable: left out of the opening game at Burnley, he came on as substitute for George Curtis after four minutes of the game at Forest and helped City to a battling 3-3 result with two typical goals. Few of his goals were spectacular, but in his comeback game after injury in December, against Burnley, he scored with a thunderous 25-yard shot, then followed up with two more for a hat-trick. He was born in Coventry on 12 June 1946 and after leaving his home-town club in February 1968 he never spent more than two seasons with any of his ten further clubs. He was sold to Arsenal for £90,000 and later played for Wolves (two spells), West Brom, Bristol City, West Ham, Bristol Rovers, Hereford, Wimbledon and Aldershot (see *Coventry City's Managers*).

Football League debut for Coventry City v Shrewsbury Town (a) 30 October 1963.

	LEAGUE		*FA CUP*		*FL CUP*		*TOTAL*	
	App	*Gls*	*App*	*Gls*	*App*	*Gls*	*App*	*Gls*
1963-64	2	0	0	0	0	0	2	0
1964-65	8	3	0	0	1	1	9	4
1965-66	17/2	5	1	0	0	0	18/2	5
1966-67	38/1	24	1	0	3	1	42/1	25
1967-68	13/1	8	0	0	1	0	14/1	8
	78/4	40	2	0	5	2	85/4	42

BOBBY GOULD

MICHAEL GYNN

Michael Gynn was one of Bobby Gould's first buys for Coventry City and at £60,000 proved a tremendous bargain, making almost 200 League appearances (31 as a substitute) in his first eight seasons at Highfield Road. He was born at Peterborough on 19 August 1961 and was a star with Peterborough United, for whom he had a good scoring record, before becoming a valuable squad member at Highfield Road. In his early days there was a question mark about his stamina but that was laid to rest after his non-stop running in the 1987 FA Cup Final. His impact in the Cup campaign was vital. At Stoke, deputizing for the suspended Emerson, he won the game with a typical Gynn goal. In the semi-final he came on as substitute and scored the equalizer. In the Final he was called in for the injured Borrows and ran his heart out. He was almost rewarded with a goal in injury time when, clean through, he had his shot blocked by Clemence. After 1987, Gynn had injury problems but in 1989-90 enjoyed his best season, playing in a less wide role and proving adept at marking tightly. This was personified in his tussle with Steve Hodge in the Littlewoods Cup semi-final. In 1991 he scored one of his best goals for City, a 25-yard winner at home to Chelsea. At 5ft 3in he is one of the smallest players in the League.

Football League debut for Coventry City v Watford (a) 27 August 1983.

	LEAGUE		*FA CUP*		*FL CUP*		*OTHERS*		*TOTAL*	
	App	*Gls*	*App*	*Gls*	*App*	*Gls*	*App*	*Gls*	*App*	*Gls*
1983-84	20/3	2	2/1	0	2	0	0	0	24/4	2
1984-85	32/7	4	2	0	2	0	0	0	36/7	4
1985-86	6/6	1	0	0	1/1	0	1	0	8/7	1
1986-87	16/6	5	3/1	2	0/3	0	1	0	20/10	7
1987-88	19/6	3	2	0	3	2	2	1	26/6	6
1988-89	8	1	0	0	2	3	0	0	10	4
1989-90	31/3	3	1	0	6	1	1	1	39/3	5
1990-91	35	8	4	2	5	1	0	0	44	11
	167/31	27	14/2	4	21/4	7	5	2	207/37	40

LOL HARVEY

Born at Heanor, Derbyshire, on 25 July 1934, Lol Harvey was signed from City's nursery side, Modern Machine Tools FC, in July 1951. He was a solid, no-nonsense defender who could always be relied upon despite being plagued by injuries which severely limited his appearances at first-team level. In the early 1950s he wore either the number-four or number-six shirt but in 1955 switched to full-back, where he appeared for the remainder of his playing days at Highfield Road. His best season was the promotion one of 1958-9, when he was the regular left-back. He stayed at Highfield Road for two seasons after that, but made only six more appearances before retiring at the early age of 27, after another serious knee injury. Harvey renewed his association with the club in the 1980s, when he was involved in part-time scouting locally.

Football League debut for Coventry City v Brentford (a) 3 November 1951.

	LEAGUE		*FA CUP*		*TOTAL*	
	App	*Gls*	*App*	*Gls*	*App*	*Gls*
1951-52	3	0	0	0	3	0
1952-53	20	0	0	0	20	0
1953-54	3	0	0	0	3	0
1954-55	20	0	4	1	24	1
1955-56	24	1	1	0	25	1
1957-58	26	0	1	0	27	0
1958-59	41	0	2	0	43	0
1959-60	2	0	0	0	2	0
1960-61	1	0	0	0	1	0
	140	1	8	1	148	2

Tony and Mark Hateley have more in common than being father and son; they both played for Coventry City and both had their biggest successes with other clubs. Mark, who was born in Liverpool on 17 March 1961, was a prolific scorer in the Youth team and Reserves and got his first-team chance at the age of 17. However, in the following two seasons he made only six appearances, including the ill-fated trip to Blackburn. Mark made a name for himself during the League Cup run in 1981 and scored twice in the Watford replay — his first goals in his 22nd appearance. He became a regular in 1982-3 and was top scorer, earning selection for England Under-21s. On his international debut he scored twice and the season ended on high note with a hat-trick in the 5-5 game at The Dell. In his final season at City, he played three more times for the Under-21's but his scoring rate diminished and it was no secret that the ambitious Hateley wanted away. His departure was acrimonious. Pompey, then in Division Two, offered a derisory £50,000 and the £190,000 set by the tribunal was still low for a player on the verge of the full England squad. He later made disparaging remarks about City's lack of ambition and has never returned to Coventry to face the fans' wrath. Within 12 months he won the first of his 31 full caps and in his second game scored against Brazil in the Maracana. He spent only one season at Fratton Park, his goal in Rio elevating him to superstar status and earning him a £1 million transfer to AC Milan. After three years at San Siro, he moved to Monaco and in 1990 to Glasgow Rangers for another £1 million fee. Many older fans argue that his overall scoring record was poor compared to that of his father, yet Tony never played for England.

Football League debut for Coventry City v Wolverhampton Wanderers (h) 5 May 1979.

	LEAGUE		*FA CUP*		*FL CUP*		*TOTAL*	
	App	*Gls*	*App*	*Gls*	*App*	*Gls*	*App*	*Gls*
1978-79	1	0	0	0	0	0	1	0
1979-80	2/2	0	1	0	0	0	3/2	0
1980-81	17/2	3	2/1	0	6	2	25/3	5
1981-82	31/2	13	4	4	2	1	37/2	18
1982-83	35	9	3	2	0	0	38	11
	86/6	25	10/1	6	8	3	104/7	34

MARK HATELEY

Frank 'Cute' Herbert was one of Highfield Road's most popular performers throughout the 1920s. Herbert began his football with Foxford United in the Coventry and Warwickshire League, where he spent three seasons and he enjoyed local fame when he scored over 100 goals in one campaign alone. He then moved to Bedworth United and, later, Exhall Colliery, joining up with Teddy Winship and Jackie Randle, also destined for the City. Following a tremendous display for Exhall in the Birmingham Junior Cup semi-final at the Butts, Herbert was spotted by Coventry manager Albert Evans who waited at the pithead for him to emerge before signing him up. He made his debut at centre-forward in 1922 and soon established himself as a regular, operating at inside-left or on the left wing. Indeed, wherever he played, the goals kept coming with his best season of 26 in 1926-7; his career total of over 89 was the club's best of the decade. Herbert retired in 1929 and became manager of the Beehive Inn in Bedworth.

Football League debut for Coventry City v Stockport County (a) 18 November 1922.

	LEAGUE		*FA CUP*		*TOTAL*	
	App	*Gls*	*App*	*Gls*	*App*	*Gls*
1922-23	11	2	0	0	11	2
1923-24	34	12	2	0	36	12
1924-25	31	6	3	2	34	8
1925-26	38	22	1	0	39	22
1926-27	38	24	3	2	41	26
1927-28	31	14	2	0	33	14
1928-29	5	4	1	0	6	4
	188	84	12	4	200	88

FRANK HERBERT

Born at Bedworth on 23 July 1941, Brian Hill became City's youngest-ever debutant and goalscorer, at 16 years 273 days in the final match in Division Three South. There were another two Hills in the side that day, but it took the arrival of yet another Hill, namely Jimmy, for Brian's career to take off. For the next four seasons he struggled on as an 'out of sorts' inside- or outside-left and it took a move to half-back for him to blossom into one of the best man-to-man markers in League football. Equally at home at either full-back or wing-half, his best seasons were in the Third Division between 1962 and 1964. Injuries began to take their toll after that, although he was only 23, and his best years seemed to be still in front of him. He was still capable of some consistent performances and was touted as a potential England player in 1965. As time wore on, Hill became the vital utility player and could fill any position in the back-four or defensive midfield. After 1969 his appearances became infrequent but he was still able to undertake the role he knew so well — like bottling up the opposition star performer as at Liverpool in November 1970. Like his contemporary and close friend, Mick Kearns, he made his final appearance at Highfield Road on a Boxing Day against West Brom. After a spell on loan to Bristol City, he moved to Torquay in 1971 but was soon back in the West Midlands at Bedworth United.

Football League debut for Coventry City v Gillingham (a) 30 April 1958.

BRIAN HILL

	LEAGUE		*FA CUP*		*FL CUP*		*OTHERS*		*TOTAL*	
	App	*Gls*	*App*	*Gls*	*App*	*Gls*	*App*	*Gls*	*App*	*Gls*
1957-58	1	1	0	0	-	-	0	0	1	1
1958-59	10	0	0	0	-	-	0	0	10	0
1959-60	8	1	1	0	-	-	0	0	9	1
1960-61	10	1	0	0	1	0	0	0	11	1
1961-62	9	0	2	0	1	0	0	0	12	0
1962-63	37	1	9	0	1	0	0	0	47	1
1963-64	40	2	2	0	1	1	0	0	43	3
1964-65	28	0	1	0	1	0	0	0	30	0
1965-66	22	0	3	0	4	0	0	0	29	0
1966-67	15/1	0	0	0	1	0	0	0	16/1	0
1967-68	16/2	1	2/1	0	0	0	0	0	18/3	1
1968-69	31	0	2	0	5	0	0	0	38	0
1969-70	8/1	0	0	0	0	0	0	0	8/1	0
1970-71	5	0	0	0	1	0	1	0	7	0
	240/4	7	22/1	0	16	1	1	0	279/5	8

Born at Heanor, Derbyshire, on 8 August 1931, Peter Hill's playing career at Highfield Road started in 1946, when he joined City from Modern Machine Tools FC. It lasted until March 1962, when he made his final appearance in a home game against Queen's Park Rangers. There have been few players in City's history who have given such long and loyal service. Although Hill played a handful of games in the Second Division, operating as a scheming inside-forward, it was not until the 1952-3 season, the first after relegation to Division Three South, that Hill established himself in the side. He filled either the inside-right or inside-left positions in the mainly dark days of the mid-1950s, but in 1958-9 was successfully switched to outside-right, a position that had been filled by five different players, including Hill himself, the previous season. He continued to play on the wing for the remainder of his career. Many fans will remember his sensational goal from the right wing in the promotion battle against Norwich in April 1960. Hill was a wholehearted player who always gave his best. Although he was never a prolific goalscorer, he managed one in every four games, 77 in all, which has been bettered by only five City players. After he retired, Hill became trainer, a position he held until 1967. He then spent 20 years working in local industry, returning to the club in 1988 as kit manager, a position he still holds.

Football League debut for Coventry City v Sheffield Wednesday (a) 5 February 1949.

PETER HILL

	LEAGUE		*FA CUP*		*TOTAL*	
	App	*Gls*	*App*	*Gls*	*App*	*Gls*
1948-49	3	0	0	0	3	0
1949-50	5	2	0	0	5	2
1950-51	1	0	0	0	1	0
1951-52	5	0	1	0	6	0
1952-53	34	12	2	1	36	13
1953-54	17	0	0	0	17	0
1954-55	35	8	4	0	39	8
1955-56	31	6	0	0	31	6
1956-57	24	10	1	0	25	10
1957-58	38	10	2	1	40	11
1958-59	25	6	2	2	27	8
1959-60	25	6	2	0	27	6
1960-61	33	12	3	0	36	12
1961-62	9	1	1	0	10	1
	285	73	16	4	303	77

'Six foot two, eyes of blue, big Jim Holton's after you,' was the popular chant at Old Trafford and Highfield Road in the 1970s when Jim Holton was playing. A 'man mountain' who earned his reputation in Tommy Docherty's United side which bounced back to Division One in 1974-5, Holton was the one bright star in United's black days of 1973-4. He won 15 Scottish caps, including a trip to the 1974 World Cup finals, but twice suffered a broken leg and in September 1976 was transferred to Sunderland. Within six months he was on his way to Coventry for £50,000. When he arrived, City were in dire straits, without a win in 11 games and lacking credibility in the centre of defence. Despite not being totally fit, Holton pulled them together on and off the pitch and City stayed up. He spent two and half seasons with Coventry but was deposed by Paul Dyson in early 1980. Born at Lesmahagow on 11 April 1951, he started his career at Celtic but moved to West Brom in 1968, playing in their FA Youth Cup Final side in 1969. He moved to Shrewsbury Town before Tommy Docherty paid £80,000 for him in January 1973 and he was an immediate success with United's fans. A fearsome tackler and outstanding in the air, he was once described as a 'one-man grappling iron'. He finished his League career with Sheffield Wednesday in 1982 and later became publican at the Rising Sun in Coventry.
Football League debut for Coventry City v West Bromwich Albion. (h) 19 April 1977.

	LEAGUE		*FA CUP*		*FL CUP*		*TOTAL*	
	App	*Gls*	*App*	*Gls*	*App*	*Gls*	*App*	*Gls*
1976-77	8	0	0	0	0	0	8	0
1977-78	25	0	0	0	3	1	28	1
1978-79	34	0	2	0	1	0	37	0
1979-80	24	0	0	0	3	0	27	0
	91	0	2	0	7	1	100	1

JIM HOLTON

Born in Middlesbrough on 25 July 1960, Keith Houchen was the journeyman who became 'Roy of the Rovers' in the 1987 FA Cup run. After ten years travelling around the lower divisions he joined City from Scunthorpe United for £60,000 in the summer of 1986, his only claim to fame being that he scored the goal when York City knocked Arsenal out of the FA Cup. In his first season at Highfield Road his scoring rate in League games was poor, but in the FA Cup he came good, netting five in five games: the winner at Old Trafford, two marvellous individual efforts against Sheffield Wednesday, the second in the semi-final and the glorious header at Wembley. His Cup Final goal was rated one of the finest in the history of the stadium. The arrival of Speedie was a hard blow and Houchen was never first-choice again. He scored goals infrequently in 1987-8 and in March 1989 moved to Hibernian for £300,000. Houchen was a lanky, ungainly centre-forward with deceptive skills. Despite his height, he rarely scored headed goals, relying on good close control and shooting ability. At Hibs, he had similar scoring problems but in 1989-90 played in European competition. His earlier clubs included Hartlepool, Orient and York City.
Football League debut for Coventry City v West Ham United (a) 23 August 1986.

	LEAGUE		*FA CUP*		*FL CUP*		*OTHERS*		*TOTAL*	
	App	*Gls*	*App*	*Gls*	*App*	*Gls*	*App*	*Gls*	*App*	*Gls*
1986-87	20	2	5	5	0	0	0/1	0	25/1	7
1987-88	13/8	3	0	0	2	0	0	0	15/8	3
1988-89	10/3	2	0/1	0	0/1	0	1	0	11/5	2
	43/11	7	5/1	5	2/1	0	1/1	0	51/14	12

KEITH HOUCHEN

In April 1963, Jimmy Hill created a sensation when he signed George Hudson and dropped Cup hero Terry Bly. Signed from Peterborough (Bly's former club) for a record £21,000, Hudson scored a hat-trick on his debut against Halifax Town and although the protests rumbled on, it was quite obvious that Hudson was the superior player. Bly was sold to Notts County in the close season and Hudson embarked upon his phenomenal goalscoring exploits which were to elevate him into a cult figure in Coventry. In 1963-4 he scored hat-tricks in three consecutive games and his final total was a sensational 28 goals from 36 games. The most memorable came in the last game, against Colchester United, which confirmed City as Third Division champions. Hudson thrived in the Second Division, with 25 goals in 1964-5. One match is still recalled as the finest individual performance for Coventry since the war; in the 3-0 home win over Preston on a frozen, snow-covered pitch in December, Hudson put in a performance which the *Telegraph* was to describe as 'almost beyond belief'. Then one balmy September evening in 1965, against Southampton, came possibly the most memorable goal: with his back to the goal he flicked the ball over Tony Knapp's head, turned, then casually headed past the startled 'keeper. On the eve of the Everton Cup-tie in March 1966, Hudson was sold to Northampton Town, then in the First Division, for £22,000. It is part of City folklore that hundreds travelled from Coventry to watch Hudson at Northampton rather than go to Merseyside to see a 'Hudsonless' Sky Blues. Within a year, Hudson had moved to Tranmere Rovers and the apparantly rapid decline was used to justify Hill's decision; but many believe that Hudson would have thrived in the First Division with City and still rate the sale as Hill's biggest mistake. It also exposed a flaw in Hill's management style, namely an apparent inability to handle the flamboyant star (he later had bigger problems with Ian Gibson). The wholehearted artisan was always more to Hill's liking and this may have served him ill in the First Division. For those still convinced the 1960s were the golden age for just about everything, the memory of George Hudson still holds sway and few of them could be easily persuaded that 'The Hud' was not the greatest of them all.

Football League debut for Coventry City v Halifax Town (h) 6 April 1963.

GEORGE HUDSON

	LEAGUE		*FA CUP*		*FL CUP*		*TOTAL*	
	App	*Gls*	*App*	*Gls*	*App*	*Gls*	*App*	*Gls*
1962-63	15	6	0	0	0	0	15	6
1963-64	32	24	2	3	2	1	36	28
1964-65	38	19	1	0	4	5	43	24
1965-66	28	13	3	2	4	2	35	17
	113	62	6	5	10	8	129	75

Willie Humphries was Jimmy Hill's first major signing, a £5,000 fee securing his services from Irish League club, Ards. Humphries, who was born in Belfast on 8 June 1936, had already had one unsuccessful spell in the Football League, with Leeds United in 1958-9, and it took all of Hill's persuasion to tempt him back for another attempt. For both player and club it was an inspired move, for Humphries settled in immediately and had a couple of sparkling seasons on the right wing, both scoring and making goals regularly. There is no doubt he was the most popular player on the books in 1962-3 and his quiet unassuming manner both on and off the pitch endeared him to the fans. He also regained his place in the Northern Ireland team and won a further ten caps whilst at Highfield Road. After promotion to the Second Division, he continued to be a regular performer but with John Mitten and Dave Clements appearing as potential left wingers, Jimmy Hill was able to switch Ronnie Rees to the right flank and sell Humphries to Swansea Town for £14,000, good business for a 28-year-old winger and further proof of Hill's golden touch in the transfer market. Although he was unable to keep Swansea in the Second Division, Humphries had three good seasons at the Vetch Field before returning to Ards, which he later managed.

Football League debut for Coventry City v Hull City (h) 28 April 1962.

WILLIE HUMPHRIES

	LEAGUE		*FA CUP*		*FL CUP*		*TOTAL*	
	App	*Gls*	*App*	*Gls*	*App*	*Gls*	*App*	*Gls*
1961-62	1	0	0	0	0	0	1	0
1962-63	41	10	9	0	1	0	51	10
1963-64	40	10	2	0	2	1	44	11
1964-65	27	3	1	0	2	0	30	3
	109	23	12	0	5	1	126	24

Ernie Hunt was one of the true Sky Blue greats — a player whose game was full of skill, character and humour. He was born in Swindon on 17 March 1943 and started out with his home-town team, becoming a major figure in the great Swindon side which included Summerbee, Smart, and Rogers. Hunt moved to Wolves in 1965 and scored 20 goals in their promotion year. Then followed six unhappy months at Everton before Noel Cantwell brought him to Coventry City in March 1968 for a bargain £65,000. This curious transfer merry-go-round meant that he appeared for three different clubs against Fulham at Craven Cottage in the same season. In what were essentially defensive-minded teams under Cantwell, Hunt could be relied on to supply the attacking flair. He scored 45 League goals for City but none were more indelibly stamped on the memory, or at the time more hotly debated, than the 'donkey-kick' contrived with Willie Carr against champions Everton in October 1970. In 1989, Hunt came briefly into the news when he revealed a number of games in this period had been 'fixed' by City. Many dismissed these claims on the grounds that Hunt had been paid for his revelations by a Sunday tabloid. In fact these games, with their tawdry echoes of the 'Bury Affair' had long been the subject of rumour and Hunt had been telling his version of events for many years.
Football League debut for Coventry City v Manchester United (h) 16 March 1968.

	LEAGUE		*FA CUP*		*FL CUP*		*OTHERS*		*TOTAL*	
	App	*Gls*	*App*	*Gls*	*App*	*Gls*	*App*	*Gls*	*App*	*Gls*
1967-68	6/1	1	0	0	0	0	0	0	6/1	1
1968-69	39	11	2	0	5	2	0	0	46	13
1969-70	30/1	9	2	0	1	0	0	0	33/1	9
1970-71	29/2	10	1	1	4	1	4	1	38/2	13
1971-72	26/1	12	1/1	0	1	0	4	1	32/2	13
1972-73	7	2	0	0	0	0	0	0	7	2
1973-74	3/1	0	0	0	0	0	1	0	4/1	0
	140/6	45	6/1	1	11	3	9	2	166/7	51

ERNIE HUNT

Born in Birmingham on 4 August 1956, Steve Hunt came to Coventry City from Aston Villa via New York Cosmos. He was released by Villa in 1976 and allowed to go to USA, where he played alongside Pelé and Beckenbauer, helping the Cosmos win the North American Soccer League title in 1977 and being voted the NASL's Most Valuable Player. The Sky Blues offered him the opportunity to play in the First Division in the summer of 1978 and he jumped at the chance. At £40,000 he was a bargain buy and made more than 200 appearances for City over a six-year period. During that time he had a series of disagreements with the management but at his best he was one of the most accomplished midfield players City ever had. He was on the verge of the England squad for a long time and was finally rewarded with one cap after he had joined West Brom. Hunt struggled at first, despite scoring on his debut, and it was not until 1980 that he blossomed into a playmaker with a penchant for goals. He wanted a transfer in early 1982 but Sexton and Hill persuaded him to stay and he was one of the few players whose contract did not end in 1983. Subsequently he stayed at Coventry under Gould but injury restricted his appearances and in March 1984 he was sold to West Brom for £100,000, returning to Villa in 1986. He was in a relegation team in two consecutive years — West Brom (1985-6) and Villa — and had to retire prematurely with a knee injury. There is no doubt that if this talent had been better harnessed at Highfield Road, he could have become a legend.
Football League debut for Coventry City v Derby County (a) 2 September 1978.

	LEAGUE		*FA CUP*		*FL CUP*		*TOTAL*	
	App	*Gls*	*App*	*Gls*	*App*	*Gls*	*App*	*Gls*
1978-79	20/4	6	0	0	0	0	20/4	6
1979-80	34/1	1	0	0	3	0	37/1	1
1980-81	40	6	3	0	9	2	52	8
1981-82	36	9	4	3	1	0	41	12
1982-83	35	4	3	0	3	1	41	5
1983-84	13/2	1	4	1	1	0	18/2	2
	178/7	27	14	4	17	3	209/7	34

STEVE HUNT

Tommy Hutchison was probably the most popular City player of the First Division era, for he possessed breathtaking ball-control and quite dazzling dribbling skills. What were, in retrospect, often quite dull seasons were consistently enlivened and made worth watching, if only for the contribution of Hutchison. Born in Cardenden on 22 September 1947, he left Alloa for Blackpool in 1968 and joined City in October 1972 for £140,000 (including part-exchange for Billy Rafferty). He arrived at the same time as Colin Stein and together they did much to transform a previously struggling side into one of the most attractive Coventry teams since the Sky Blues entered the First Division. For all Hutchison's array of skills, he was no wayward genius, rather a dedicated, consistent, super-fit professional, as his appearances for Swansea at the age of 43 testify. Hutchison did not score too often, but those he did put away were often memorable, like the two against Bristol City in May 1977, in a 2-2 end-of-season draw which preserved Coventry's First Division status; or the 25-yard winner against Liverpool in 1973; and, unforgettably, the goal at Highbury in November 1972, when he picked up the ball in his own half and embarked on a run which took him past half the Arsenal team before he side-stepped the 'keeper and scored into an empty net. He won 17 Scotland caps, played in the 1981 FA Cup Final for Manchester City (where he scored for Manchester and deflected the equalizer for Spurs). After leaving Manchester he had spells with Bulova (Hong Kong), Burnley, Swansea City and Merthyr Tydfil.

Football League debut for Coventry City v Manchester City (a) 14 October 1972.

TOMMY HUTCHISON

	LEAGUE		*FA CUP*		*FL CUP*		*TOTAL*	
	App	*Gls*	*App*	*Gls*	*App*	*Gls*	*App*	*Gls*
1972-73	30	2	4	1	0	0	34	3
1973-74	41	3	6	1	6	0	53	4
1974-75	42	4	3	0	1	0	46	4
1975-76	42	1	3	0	2	0	47	1
1976-77	31/2	3	2	1	0	0	33/2	4
1977-78	40	3	1	0	4	1	45	4
1978-79	42	6	2	0	1	0	45	6
1979-80	40	1	2	1	3	0	45	2
1980-81	4	1	0	0	1	1	5	2
	312/2	24	23	4	18	2	353/2	30

Although Ian Jamieson was chairman of Coventry City for only 15 months from May 1973, his links with the club stretched back to January 1949, as a player and later a director. Born in Dumbarton in 1928, Jamieson was a part-time professional with Aberdeen when he was spotted by Harry Storer whilst playing for the Army. He soon signed for City, for £6,250, and stayed at Highfield Road for ten seasons. Although not a regular until 1953, he managed over 180 appearances and was also captain for a spell. Latterly he became a part-timer, enabling him to combine football with a job at Courtaulds. When he left City in 1958, he became player-manager of Rugby Town. After 15 years away from Highfield Road he returned as a director in May 1973, becoming chairman when Jimmy Hill left ten years later. Although he did not have large sums of money to put into the club, he achieved much in his time as chairman. When he handed over to John Poynton in August 1984, the *Telegraph* paid tribute: 'Most of all, Jamieson's one-year reign will be remembered for bringing the club back to the supporters.' Gone was the arrogance that had distanced it from the people of the city, in its place all the efforts of the new management team could muster to seek better relations with the local community. What was missing was the risk capital to invest in new players.

Football League debut for Coventry City v Leeds United (h) 15 January 1949.

IAN JAMIESON

	LEAGUE		*FA CUP*		*TOTAL*	
	App	*Gls*	*App*	*Gls*	*App*	*Gls*
1948-49	9	1	0	0	9	1
1949-50	9	2	0	0	9	2
1950-51	2	0	0	0	2	0
1951-52	14	2	0	0	14	2
1952-53	3	0	0	0	3	0
1953-54	38	1	1	0	39	1
1954-55	28	0	0	0	28	0
1955-56	17	0	0	0	17	0
1956-57	25	0	1	0	26	0
1957-58	36	0	1	0	37	0
	181	6	3	0	184	6

Many older City fans say that Harry Storer threw away the Bantams' chances of promotion to Division One on a foggy Thursday evening in late October 1937, when he accepted George Allison's offer of £2,000 plus Scottish schemer Bobby Davidson (originally signed from St Johnstone as the replacement for Alex James) for 26-year-old Welsh international Leslie Jones. At the time, City were top of Division Two and looking unbeatable but Arsenal went on to win the League title with considerable help from Leslie Jones as City stuttered to fourth place in Division Two as Davidson suffered loss of form and a couple of injuries. He was a gamble that failed but the financial position at Highfield Road was desperate, with large fees having been paid for McPhee and Taylor. Jones was born in Aberdare on 1 July 1911 and played for Aberdare Athletic and then Cardiff City. They were in decline but Jones scored 30 goals in 140 appearances and was capped for Wales against France in 1933. His all-action displays against Coventry in the Christmas matches that year persuaded Storer to pay £2,000 for him and with Jock Lauderdale and Clarrie Bourton he formed the perfect inside trio who scored 160 goals between them in two and a half seasons. Coventry resisted a £7,000 bid from Spurs in 1936 but could not refuse Arsenal the following year. He played for Arsenal during the war (when he won five unofficial caps) and made his final appearance for Coventry as a guest in 1945-6. He became player-coach at Swansea Town, then player-manager of Barry Town before returning to League soccer with Brighton and then managing Scunthorpe United. He died in South Wales in 1981.

Football League debut for Coventry City v Bristol Rovers (a) 20 January 1934.

	LEAGUE		*FA CUP*		*TOTAL*	
	App	*Gls*	*App*	*Gls*	*App*	*Gls*
1933-34	16	10	0	0	16	10
1934-35	41	27	3	3	44	30
1935-36	32	20	0	0	32	20
1936-37	37	9	3	1	40	10
1937-38	12	4	0	0	12	4
	138	70	6	4	144	74

LESLIE JONES

Darlaston-born Eleander Juggins played for Willenhall Swifts when he was only 17. He then turned out in the Walsall and Wolverhampton junior leagues for three seasons before turning professional for Darlaston. Juggins was with Darlaston for only seven weeks before transferring to Wolves for a sizeable fee. He had started off as an outside-right but Wolves decided that with his sturdy physique he was best suited to defensive duties. After five seasons he fell out with Wolves over a benefit he felt was due, was not retained and moved to Highfield Road in 1907. In his early days, Juggins was a tower of strength in the City side, with his hardy tackling and the coolness with which he met forward rushes. He was a sturdy man, weighing 14st and standing 5ft 9in tall, and he played a vigorous game, although he never met with a serious accident. Juggins was a regular in the Birmingham League side of 1907-08 and in City's first season in the Southern League, usually at full-back, although occasionally at centre-forward in an emergency. But his first-team appearances became fewer and fewer and by 1910 he was mainly a reserve player. He was assistant trainer in 1911 as well as being captain of the Reserves and in 1912, when James McIntyre left the club to become trainer at Southampton, he was appointed trainer. Juggins was well qualified, having learnt training duties at Wolves, and he had a wide knowledge of Midlands players. He severed his connections with City at the end of 1913-14 and moved to Southampton but returned in April 1919, as ground superintendent.

Birmingham League debut for Coventry City v Halesowen (h) 7 September 1907.

	LEAGUE		*FA CUP*		*TOTAL*	
	App	*Gls*	*App*	*Gls*	*App*	*Gls*
1907-08	30	1	9	4	39	5
1908-09	28	2	1	0	29	2
1909-10	20	0	1	0	21	0
1910-11	16	0	1	0	17	0
1911-12	2	0	0	0	2	0
1913-14	2	0	1	0	3	0
	98	3	13	4	111	7

ELEANDER JUGGINS

Mick Kearns was one of the trio of players who saw City go from the depths of the old Third Division South into the Fourth and then right up to the glory of promotion to the First Division. A local lad, born in Nuneaton on 10 March 1938, he was equally at home at either full-back or wing-half and, although playing in a poor side in the early 1960s, he was very close to an England Under-23 cap. Throughout his career he was plagued with knee injuries and was often given painkilling injections, but he missed relatively few matches. Indeed, only Curtis, Coop and Glazier have appeared in more first-team matches for City. Totally dedicated to the club, his performances were very consistent over the years and he earned a well-merited joint testimonial with George Curtis in 1967. Although he played regularly in the first half of 1967-8, injuries began to take their toll and he made his final appearance at Highfield Road on Boxing Day, against Liverpool. retiring in the close season of 1968 at the early age of 30. He went on to run his father's bingo hall in Bedworth but after 18 years out of the game returned to Highfield Road as part of the new-look 'Old Sky Blue' coaching staff. He later moved to the post of chief scout.

Football League debut for Coventry City v Bournemouth & BA (h) 9 September 1957.

MICK KEARNS

	LEAGUE		*FA CUP*		*FL CUP*		*TOTAL*	
	App	*Gls*	*App*	*Gls*	*App*	*Gls*	*App*	*Gls*
1957-58	3	0	0	0	-	-	3	0
1958-59	32	2	2	0	-	-	34	2
1959-60	31	3	0	0	-	-	31	3
1960-61	40	2	3	0	1	1	44	3
1961-62	26	2	0	0	0	0	26	2
1962-63	36	2	9	0	1	0	46	2
1963-64	42	0	2	1	1	0	45	1
1964-65	36	0	1	0	4	0	41	0
1965-66	40	2	4	0	4	0	48	2
1966-67	41	1	1	0	3	0	45	1
1967-68	17	0	2	0	0	0	19	0
	344	14	24	1	14	1	382	16

Brian Kilcline was the first Coventry City captain to hold aloft the FA Cup but his 'Viking' looks will be remembered by City fans for much more. He joined Coventry in the summer of 1984, for £60,000 from Notts County. 'Killer' was an England Under-21 international with a reputation for being hard and perhaps lacking the finer skills, but he became an outstanding skipper, developing a talent for set-piece goals. His goals direct from free-kicks against Crystal Palace in 1991 and Southampton in 1987 are particularly well remembered, not to mention his goal in 1985, in the vital home game against Luton. His penalty record was excellent, until 1989-90 when he missed several; his most vital such success was the last-minute winner against Arsenal in their Championship season of 1988-9, after he had missed one earlier in the game. A superb header of the ball with a streak of skill, Kilcline seemed to pick up niggling injuries almost every season and but for these he would have made over 300 appearances as he was always the first choice. His partnership with Trevor Peake was the corner-stone of the defence for several seasons and City never found an adequate stand-in for him. He had some problems off the pitch, but on it his inspirational ability made him a big City favourite. In July 1991 he moved to Oldham for £400,000. He was born in Nottingham on 7 May 1962.

Football League debut for Coventry City v Aston Villa (a) 25 August 1984.

BRIAN KILCLINE

	LEAGUE		*FA CUP*		*FL CUP*		*OTHERS*		*TOTAL*	
	App	*Gls*	*App*	*Gls*	*App*	*Gls*	*App*	*Gls*	*App*	*Gls*
1984-85	26	2	2	0	1/1	0	0	0	29/1	2
1985-86	32	7	1	1	4	1	2	0	39	9
1986-87	29	3	6	0	2	1	0	0	37	4
1987-88	28	8	2	1	0	0	3	0	33	9
1988-89	33	4	1	0	3	1	1	0	38	5
1989-90	11	1	0	0	4	0	1	0	16	1
1990-91	14	3	3	1	2	0	0	0	19	4
	173	28	15	3	16/1	4	7	0	211	35

Teddy Kirk, known as 'Little Teddy', was one of Coventry's early sporting heroes, excelling in cycling, cricket and rugby, but primarily as Singers' goalkeeper. He made his debut in 1888 and his final appearance eight years and some 200 games later. Kirk can justly be called the first in the club's long line of outstanding 'keepers. He played in all the great Midlands Cup ties of 1891-2 and 1892-3, 31 games in all and not a single defeat. Many times the local newspaper would report: 'Kirk and Kirk alone stood between Singers and defeat.' In those days a goalkeeper needed more than speed and agility, he also needed to withstand a tremendous buffeting and hacking from opposing forwards. Through all of this, Teddy Kirk was commended for his 'gentlemanly demeanor'. However, two famous incidents suggest 'Little Teddy' had a breaking point. In one ferocious game against Small Heath he knocked a Birmingham forward unconscious with an uppercut and was duly sent-off. He was also at the centre of a bizarre incident at the Trafalgar Arms in 1889. This was in the heyday of the great local derbies between Singers and Rudge. A group of Singers' players had been drinking in the Trafalgar — a known 'Rudge pub' — and found themselves the object of 'taunts' from some Rudge supporters. A 'skirmish' broke out, in the course of which Kirk was accused of 'stabbing a Rudge supporter in the buttocks with a dagger'. He had to appear before the magistrates but after several 'eye-witness' accounts the case was dismissed. Kirk retired in 1893 but a succession of 'keepers proved equally incompetent so following a dire first season in the Birmingham League, in which nearly 100 goals were conceded, 'Little Teddy' made his comeback by public demand in 1895. He made his final appearance against Shrewsbury in April 1896.
Birmingham Junior Cup debut for Coventry City (Singers) v Unity Gas (h) 29 December 1888.

TEDDY KIRK

	LEAGUE		*FA CUP*		*TOTAL*	
	App	*Gls*	*App*	*Gls*	*App*	*Gls*
1895-96	25	0	4	0	29	0
	25	0	4	0	29	0

The period from 1952 to 1960 was one of unceasing change at Highfield Road but the one constant factor during that time was Roy Kirk. Born at Bolsover, Derbyshire, on 11 June 1929, he began his playing career at Bolsover Colliery. After a spell at Luton Town, he joined Leeds United in August 1948 as an understudy to John Charles, and Harry Storer signed Kirk for £10,000 in March 1952. It would be tempting to say that Kirk and Eddie Brown, who was signed at the same time, were panic buys, but this was not strictly true. The post-war City side had grown old together and needed fresh blood. In any event, both players were very good purchases. Kirk was bought to replace the veteran George Mason and immediately slotted in at centre half. For the next seven seasons he was the dominant figure in City's defence, whether at left-back or at centre-half, and, from 1958-9 when George Curtis took over the number-five shirt, at right-back in which position he played his final game for City in January 1960. He missed very few games and his play always had a certain amount of arrogance about it. He was skilful but tough and was dismissed a number of times. Kirk did not score many goals but one at Northampton in November 1954 was truly memorable. Standing on the edge of his own penalty area, he looped a clearance fully 80 yards over an amazed Alf Wood's head. Two months earlier he had scored two own-goals in a home League match against Leyton Orient. Kirk moved to Cambridge United in 1960, first as player-manager, later as manager. His future within soccer management seemed assured but he resigned over a policy matter in 1962 and left the game.
Football League debut for Coventry City v Nottingham Forest (a) 15 March 1952.

ROY KIRK

	LEAGUE		*FA CUP*		*TOTAL*	
	App	*Gls*	*App*	*Gls*	*App*	*Gls*
1951-52	9	0	0	0	9	0
1952-53	40	1	3	0	43	1
1953-54	46	2	1	0	47	2
1954-55	46	0	4	1	50	1
1955-56	45	0	1	0	46	0
1956-57	39	0	0	0	39	0
1957-58	33	0	2	0	35	0
1958-59	46	3	2	0	48	3
1959-60	26	0	2	0	28	0
	330	6	15	1	345	7

Billy Lake was one of the unsung heroes of the 1930s. Always overshadowed by Clarrie Bourton, he nevertheless boasted a very high scoring rate in the 11 seasons he was with City. He was the longest-serving player of the inter-war era and, although he was never a regular after 1934, he still managed to average over a goal in every other game up to the outbreak of war. Born in the Birmingham area in 1908, the son of a Walsall FC director, he signed for the Saddlers in 1927 and managed eight goals in 25 games in the year he played at Fellows Park. He was part of the regular trade that developed between the two clubs and signed for Coventry on 1 November 1928, for a small fee. He established himself as a regular in 1929-30 and had a highly-successful spell during the next five seasons, first partnering Loughlin and then Bourton. He lost his regular place when Storer signed Leslie Jones in early 1934 but could still be relied upon to pull the rabbit out of the hat, scoring all four goals in a match at Luton in February 1938 and going on to score seven goals in three matches. Always recognizable on the field with his jet black hair and darting style of play, he remains the second-highest goalscorer in the club's history, by some distance from Ted Roberts. Lake decided to retire after the outbreak of war and never appeared again at Highfield Road after a couple of reserve matches at the beginning of the ill-fated 1939-40 season.

Football League debut for Coventry City v Queen's Park Rangers (a) 15 December 1928.

BILLY LAKE

	LEAGUE		*FA CUP*		*TOTAL*	
	App	*Gls*	*App*	*Gls*	*App*	*Gls*
1928-29	7	2	0	0	7	2
1929-30	36	15	4	2	40	17
1930-31	41	23	3	1	44	24
1931-32	28	14	2	1	30	15
1932-33	35	18	4	2	39	20
1933-34	31	16	2	1	33	17
1934-35	12	9	0	0	12	9
1935-36	18	4	1	1	19	5
1936-37	2	2	3	2	5	4
1937-38	7	7	0	0	7	7
1938-39	9	3	0	0	9	3
	226	113	19	10	245	123

JOCK LAUDERDALE

Jock Lauderdale had established himself as a regular member of Blackpool's squad when Harry Storer snapped him up for the bargain fee of £270 in the close season of 1931. Lauderdale will always be remembered as the man who made the City attack tick in that era but he was no slouch in front of goal, netting over 60 goals in five seasons. He was born in Scotland in 1907 and was a classic old-style schemer who had seen service with Third Lanark and Queen of the South before joining Blackpool. He was held in affection by City fans for his elegant performances both on and off the field. City received numerous offers for his services during this period, once turning down a bid of over £2,000 from Liverpool in 1934. There can be no doubt that without his artistry, Clarrie Bourton would have not scored as many goals. Lauderdale lost his place in the team at the beginning of 1936-7 and, although many clubs came in for him, he decided he still wanted to live in the City and signed for Northampton Town for £1,700. His best days were behind him and as injuries took their toll, he joined Nuneaton Borough in the close season of 1939. He occasionally assisted City during the war and took up employment locally with Armstrong Siddeley. He died in Coventry in 1965 at the age of 58.

Football League debut for Coventry City v Fulham (a) 29 August 1931.

	LEAGUE		*FA CUP*		*TOTAL*	
	App	*Gls*	*App*	*Gls*	*App*	*Gls*
1931-32	42	19	2	0	44	19
1932-33	41	15	4	0	45	15
1933-34	40	11	2	1	42	12
1934-35	21	4	1	2	22	6
1935-36	23	11	2	0	25	11
1936-37	4	0	0	0	4	0
	171	60	11	3	182	63

As Billy Frith watched a Football Combination game at St Andrew's between Birmingham City and Nottingham Forest in December 1958, he made up his mind to sign the Forest pair, goalkeeper Arthur Lightening and wing-half Ronnie Farmer. Frith clinched the details after the final whistle, signing the duo for £6,000. It proved to be one of City's most inspired double signings, for they were exactly the sort of players to strengthen City's bid for promotion from Division Four, which was by then gathering momentum. Lightening, who was born in Durban on 1 August 1936, had been brought over from South Africa by Forest in December 1956, but surprisingly had played few games for them before he signed for City. He proved to be one of the most popular players at Highfield Road during the late 1950s and early 1960s. Indeed, such was his brilliance that comparisons were even made with the great Reg Matthews. Lightening was a regular for three and a half seasons but then came Jimmy Hill. For some inexplicable reason, Hill decided that he did not want Lightening and the 'keeper was sold to Middlesbrough for £11,000 (a few weeks later he was fined in a Coventry court for receiving stolen property). As an immediate replacement, City paid £4,000 for Reading goalkeeper Dave Meeson. He did not succeed and City fans were left wondering what had been wrong with the goalkeeper who had been sold. Lightening stayed only one season at 'Boro before returning to South Africa to attend his brother's funeral, never to return.

Football League debut for Coventry City v Hartlepools United (h) 3 December 1958.

	LEAGUE		*FA CUP*		*FL CUP*		*TOTAL*	
	App	*Gls*	*App*	*Gls*	*App*	*Gls*	*App*	*Gls*
1958-59	25	0	0	0	-	-	25	0
1959-60	46	0	2	0	-	-	48	0
1960-61	33	0	3	0	2	0	38	0
1961-62	42	0	2	0	1	0	45	0
1962-63	4	0	0	0	0	0	4	0
	150	0	7	0	3	0	160	0

ARTHUR LIGHTENING

The wider historical implications of Larry Lloyd's transfer from Liverpool in 1974, for a record of £240,000, was that it precipitated a financial crisis at Coventry City which had dire and far-reaching consequences for years to come. It effectively marked the end of the free-spending days launched in 1963 with Derrick Robbins' 'gift' to Jimmy Hill. Manager Milne agreed a deal which would have taken McGuire and Holmes to Spurs, but then Tottenham manager Bill Nicholson left White Hart Lane and the transfers fell through. To make matters worse, Lloyd was something of a disaster, for he appeared slow and cumbersome, and when he was sold to Nottingham Forest, then in the Second Division, it was widely felt to signal the end of his career at the highest level. How wrong we were. Revitalized by Brian Clough, Lloyd became a key member at the heart of Forest's defence during five fabulous years at the City Ground which included Forest winning the European Cup. He was even recalled for the last of his four England caps. After leaving Forest he became player-manager of Wigan and manager of Notts County. He was born in Bristol on 6 October 1948 and joined Liverpool from Bristol Rovers, making his Reds' debut in 1969-70 and sharing in several glories at Anfield before he joined Coventry. Lloyd's career may tell us much about the variable managerial influences with which it came into contact.

Football League debut for Coventry City v Derby County (a) 21 August 1974.

	LEAGUE		*FA CUP*		*FL CUP*		*TOTAL*	
	App	*Gls*	*App*	*Gls*	*App*	*Gls*	*App*	*Gls*
1974-75	34	5	3	1	1	0	38	6
1975-76	11	0	0	0	0	0	11	0
1976-77	5	0	0	0	0	0	5	0
	50	5	3	1	1	0	54	6

LARRY LLOYD

NORMAN LOCKHART

Born in Belfast on 4 March 1924, Norman Lockhart started his playing career with junior club, Windsor Star, and then moved on to Irish League club, Distillery, in 1940, and to Linfield in 1942 for a fee of £225. Whilst at Linfield, he won two Irish Cup winners' medals (in 1945 and 1946) and an Irish Cup runners-up medal (in 1944). His first English club was Swansea Town, whom he joined in October 1946. He signed for Coventry City in October 1947, for a fee of £7,000, and gained a first-team place straightaway. Lockhart was a very good signing, a superb left winger who had the ability to cross on the run with great accuracy. He was not a prolific scorer, although in 1951-2 he did manage 17 League and Cup goals, more than any other City player in that non-vintage season. Lockhart had his injury problems, breaking his ankle once, but nevertheless made over 150 appearances in his six seasons with the club. During his time with City he gained three of his eight Northern Ireland caps. Unfortunately he did not last long at Highfield Road once City had been relegated to Division Three South and was transferred to Aston Villa for £15,500 in September 1952. It was the old, old story of the club needing to balance its books. After a fairly successful spell in a poor Villa side, he moved to Bury in 1956 where he finished his League career.
Football League debut for Coventry City v Bury (h) 11 October 1947.

	LEAGUE		*FA CUP*		*TOTAL*	
	App	*Gls*	*App*	*Gls*	*App*	*Gls*
1947-48	31	6	2	1	33	7
1948-49	31	5	1	0	32	5
1949-50	32	7	0	0	32	7
1950-51	38	7	1	0	39	7
1951-52	42	15	3	2	45	17
1952-53	8	1	0	0	8	1
	182	41	7	3	189	44

JIMMY LOUGHLIN

In 1928 there appeared the first faint signs that Coventry City were beginning to put the grim struggles of the decade behind them and that, at last, an attractive, winning side was emerging. One vital component of this change was centre-forward Jimmy Loughlin. Loughlin was born in Darlington in 1905 and spent three seasons with Newcastle United, including a number of appearances in their Championship side, before moving to West Ham United in 1927. He signed for City in December 1928, for £1,300 (£500 of which was provided by chairman Walter Brandish). Loughlin was an instant success, briefly forming an exciting combination with the great Ernie Toseland. The following season he formed another good attacking partnership with teenage Billy Lake and his season's total of 30 goals was a pre-Bourton club record. His exploits in the FA Cup were instrumental in taking the City through to the historic tie against Sunderland. Loughlin was injured early the following season and, although still only 25, his League career was over and he joined the Dublin club, Dolphin, in the close season of 1931 for a small fee.
Football League debut for Coventry City v Brighton & Hove Albion (h) 5 January 1929.

	LEAGUE		*FA CUP*		*TOTAL*	
	App	*Gls*	*App*	*Gls*	*App*	*Gls*
1928-29	19	8	0	0	19	8
1929-30	31	24	4	6	35	30
1930-31	11	1	0	0	11	1
	61	33	4	6	65	39

After Clarrie Bourton's departure, City lacked a consistent scorer, which probably cost them promotion to Division One in 1938 and 1939. George Lowrie was bought to correct this deficiency but, like so many players, lost seven years to the war. Lowrie was born at Tonypandy on 19 December 1919 and started with his local club before moving to Swansea Town in 1935. After three seasons of reserve-team football he joined Preston but chances there were limited and after only four first-team appearances, Harry Storer signed him for £1,750 in June 1939. He scored on his debut, on the last Saturday of peacetime soccer. Lowrie was a prolific scorer in regional matches but after City suspended operations it was as a Northampton 'guest' that he won his first Welsh wartime cap. He returned to City in September 1942 and scored 43 goals in 52 games including a hat-trick for Wales at Wembley. Army call-up restricted his appearances in the latter part of the war. Lowrie reached his peak in 1946-7 when, although still in the Army and not training with the club, he managed 29 goals in 38 games. He stood over 6ft and with slicked jet-black hair resembled that other great centre-forward of the day, Tommy Lawton. He had a terrific shot and against Bury one of his efforts hit the back of the net with the ball burst. The referee refused to allow a goal and the game finished 0-0. The attentions of First Division clubs seemed to unsettle him and he was rested twice in 1947-8. But City were going through one of their financial crises and it was obvious that the prize asset would have to be sold. Surprisingly, it was Second Division promotion contenders Newcastle United who got him for a record £18,500, but after 18 months and 12 games he moved to Bristol City for £10,000. There he recaptured his scoring touch but he was now on the wrong side of 30. Coventry, in desperate trouble in Division Two, re-signed him in February 1952 but he had lost much pace and scored only three goals in 12 games, not enough to stave off relegation. He found it easier in the Third Division but he fell out with the club and was freed at the end of the season, moving to Lovells Athletic of the Southern League, where he played for two seasons. He died in South Wales on 4 May 1989 at the age of 69.

Football League debut for Coventry City v Barnsley (h) 2 September 1939.

	LEAGUE		*FA CUP*		*TOTAL*	
	App	*Gls*	*App*	*Gls*	*App*	*Gls*
1946-47	34	26	2	3	26	29
1947-48	22	18	0	0	22	18
1951-52	12	3	0	0	12	3
1952-53	15	9	0	0	15	9
	83	56	2	3	85	59

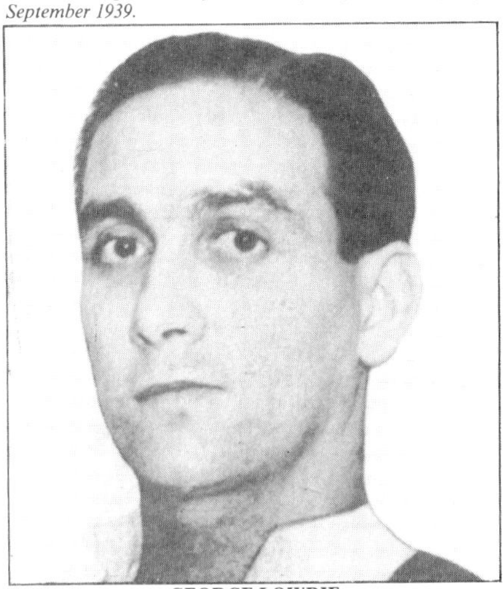

GEORGE LOWRIE

Bobby McDonald was one of Gordon Milne's shrewdest buys: for a £40,000 fee, Coventry got four years of unbroken appearances — 178 successive League and Cup games — and then sold the player for £250,000. McDonald more than adequately replaced Cattlin at left-back and was unlucky not be picked for Scotland, particularly at his peak in 1977-8. He was born in Aberdeen on 13 April 1955 and joined City from Villa, where he had been a member of the FA Youth Cup-winning side in 1973 and the League Cup-winning side in 1975 but where, by 1976, he could not be guaranteed a first-team place. His partnership with Tommy Hutchison was so good that John Bond of Manchester City bought them both in 1980 and they helped City reach the FA Cup Final in 1981. McDonald had a superb left foot and scored some great goals with feet and head. He spent three years at Maine Road before leaving under a cloud, then had three and a half years at Oxford United, where he won more honours in Oxford's rise to the First Division. From the Manor Ground, McDonald drifted to Leeds United, then Wolves, before joining the Midlands non-League circuit appearing for Rugby Town, Burton Albion and, latterly, Nuneaton Borough.

Debut for Coventry City v Bristol City (a) League Cup 31 August 1976.

	LEAGUE		*FA CUP*		*FL CUP*		*TOTAL*	
	App	*Gls*	*App*	*Gls*	*App*	*Gls*	*App*	*Gls*
1976-77	39	1	2	1	3	0	44	2
1977-78	42	5	1	0	4	0	47	5
1978-79	42	4	2	0	1	0	45	4
1979-80	37	4	2	0	3	0	42	4
1980-81	1	0	0	0	0/1	0	1/1	0
	161	14	7	1	11/1	0	179/1	15

BOBBY McDONALD

Martin McDonnell was born in Newton-le-Willows on 27 April 1924 and was on Everton's books when he was called up for the Army. After active service in Normandy and North-West Europe, he returned to England and Everton gave him a free transfer to Southport. McDonnell spent a year at Haig Avenue before being snapped up by Harry Storer, Birmingham City's manager. He played 13 times in Birmingham's Second Division championship-winning side of 1947-8 but made only the occasional First Division appearance. It came as no surprise when Storer, who had by then returned to Highfield Road, signed him for £10,000 in October 1949. McDonnell was Storer's kind of player, tough, defensive and always giving 100 per cent effort. Ostensibly he was signed to replace the ageing George Mason, but his first few games were at right-back and it was not until the following February that he took over the centre-half spot. Over the next six seasons he missed only 18 League matches and was captain for periods of 1951-2, 1953-4 and 1954-5. He was eventually replaced by Roy Kirk, towards the end of 1954-5 and in the close season was signed, yet again, by Harry Storer, this time for Derby County, who had plunged down the League. After 100 games and a Third Division North championship medal with the Rams, he moved to Crewe Alexandra where he finished his League career. He once played for some weeks for the Gresty Road club before discovering that he had broken a bone in his foot — he was that sort of man, a courageous battler. McDonnell returned to Coventry to take up a position as an insurance broker. In April 1988 he died, of a heart attack, in Coventry at the relatively early age of 63.

Football League debut for Coventry City v Cardiff City (h) 22 October 1949.

MARTIN McDONNELL

	LEAGUE		*FA CUP*		*TOTAL*	
	App	*Gls*	*App*	*Gls*	*App*	*Gls*
1949-50	28	0	1	0	29	0
1950-51	42	0	1	0	43	0
1951-52	39	0	3	0	42	0
1952-53	42	0	3	0	45	0
1953-54	44	0	1	0	45	0
1954-55	37	0	4	0	41	0
	232	0	13	0	245	0

LLOYD McGRATH

Lloyd McGrath overcame enormous adversity to celebrate his 100th first-team appearance by crossing the ball which Gary Mabbutt deflected into his own net for City's Wembley winner in the 1987 FA Cup Final. McGrath's catalogue of injuries would have ended many careers and included a broken leg, a hairline fracture, three dislocated shoulders, fractured cheekbones and eye and knee problems. He was born in Birmingham on 24 February 1965 and was an England Youth international at right-back. His full debut for Coventry, at centre-half, coincided with City's biggest League defeat since the war, 8-2. In his third appearance, again at centre-half, City lost 6-2 at Chelsea and since then Lloyd has stuck to midfield. He played once for England Under-21s in 1986 and made an outstanding contribution to Coventry's 1986-7 season. He even scored three goals, but it was his marking job on Hoddle at Wembley that was his peak. Injuries restricted the hardman's appearances after Wembley but he relished the big challenge and sent Paul Gascoigne packing with a self-inflicted broken elbow on New Year's Day 1990.

Football League debut for Coventry City v Southampton (a) 28 April 1984.

	LEAGUE		*FA CUP*		*FL CUP*		*OTHERS*		*TOTAL*	
	App	*Gls*	*App*	*Gls*	*App*	*Gls*	*App*	*Gls*	*App*	*Gls*
1983-84	1	0	0	0	0	0	0	0	1	0
1984-85	22/1	0	2	0	0	0	0	0	24/1	0
1985-86	32	0	1	0	4	0	0	0	37	0
1986-87	30	3	4	0	5	0	0	0	39	3
1987-88	17	0	2	0	3	0	2	0	24	0
1988-89	6/2	0	1	0	0	0	1	0	8/2	0
1989-90	12/1	0	1	0	2	0	0	0	15/1	0
1990-91	12/2	0	2	0	1	0	0	0	15/2	0
	132/6	3	13	0	15	0	3	0	163/6	3

On a cold, crisp morning in March 1962, Jimmy Hill nipped across the Pennines to Nelson before an away match at Barnsley and returned with the signature of a blond-haired lad for a fee of £50. "I liked the colour of his eyes," he said. It was a remark that was to rebound on him later, when he persevered with Machin through thick and thin, in the face of adverse criticism and jibes about his 'blue-eyed boy'. But they both won through in the end. Machin, who was born at Little Hulton on 26 April 1944, was an enthusiastic inside-forward with a gift for scoring vital goals. He came into the side after the 1963 Cup run and his form at the start of 1963-4 was a revelation as City went to the top of the table and an England Under-23 honour for him seemed a certainty. Alas, in the home game against Watford he severely injured his knee. He came back too soon, in January, was injured again and did not reappear that season. Dogged by a recurrence of the knee injury, it was 1965-6 before he finally established himself. He then had his best spell, being a key member of the promotion team and playing a major part in the side that fought so well to retain First Division status. His run was ended by a car accident in January 1970 and further knee trouble in 1971-2 pointed towards the end of his career with City. He moved to Plymouth in December 1972, for £35,000, and then to Brighton under Peter Taylor. His return to Highfield Road as youth-team coach was short-lived and he left the game soon afterwards. Machin scored many goals in his career, none more valuable than the late spectaculars in the second half of 1966-7, to help City win the Second Division title.

Football League debut for Coventry City v Millwall (h) 8 April 1963.

	LEAGUE		*FA CUP*		*FL CUP*		*OTHERS*		*TOTAL*	
	App	*Gls*	*App*	*Gls*	*App*	*Gls*	*App*	*Gls*	*App*	*Gls*
1962-63	6	0	0	0	0	0	0	0	6	0
1963-64	17	3	0	0	1	1	0	0	18	4
1964-65	14	4	1	0	2	0	0	0	17	4
1965-66	37/1	4	2	0	3	2	0	0	43/1	6
1966-67	34	11	1	0	1	0	0	0	36	11
1967-68	40	4	3	0	1	1	0	0	44	5
1968-69	41	5	2	1	4	0	0	0	47	6
1969-70	15/1	1	2	0	1	0	0	0	18/1	1
1970-71	24	0	1	0	1	1	2	0	28	1
1971-72	15	1	1	0	0	0	0	0	16	1
1972-73	11	0	0	0	2	0	1	0	14	0
	255/2	33	13	1	16	5	3	0	287/2	39

ERNIE MACHIN

City were one of the glamour sides of the Football League at the beginning of the 1955-6 season, drawing large crowds wherever they played. The intricate pattern of play developed by their new manager, Jesse Carver, even had away crowds roaring their appreciation. Unfortunately, it was not the sort of football that produced results in the hard school of the Third Division South, at least not in away matches. Gradually, Carver discarded push-and-run soccer and looked for a big centre-forward who would add some punch to the attack. Enter Ken McPherson. He was born at West Hartlepool on 25 March 1927 and started his career with Notts County in 1950, playing alongside the legendary Tommy Lawton for a time. McPherson was transferred to Middlesbrough in 1953, for £15,000, a large fee in those days, and moved to Coventry City for £8,000 two years later. The signing of McPherson, a bustling, no-nonsense player, whose great strength was his aerial power, had an immediate impact and he scored on his debut. There was talk of promotion as City won five games in a row, scoring 16 goals in the process. McPherson played a prominent part in these successes but shortly after, Carver resigned, and the season collapsed. McPherson scored regularly in that season and the following season, many with his head, averaging a goal every other game. The goal supply dried up in 1957-8 and City, in their unsuccessful attempt to avoid being founder-members of the Fourth Division, looked for fresh blood. It arrived in the shape of Ray Straw and, at the end of the season, McPherson was unloaded to Newport County. There he was converted to centre-half and enjoyed three good seasons before moving to Swindon Town in August 1961. McPherson retired from League football in 1964, at the age of 37.

Football League debut for Coventry City v Newport County (h) 10 December 1955.

	LEAGUE		*FA CUP*		*TOTAL*	
	App	*Gls*	*App*	*Gls*	*App*	*Gls*
1955-56	25	13	0	0	25	13
1956-57	40	22	1	1	41	23
1957-58	24	3	1	1	25	4
	89	38	2	2	91	40

KEN McPHERSON

Neil Martin was the man to whom Noel Cantwell turned for the goals that were to keep the Sky Blues in Division One in 1967-8. With the proceeds from the sale of Bobby Gould, City spent £90,000 on the 27-year-old Scot from Sunderland. Coventry then proceeded to lose only five out of 15 games and reached safety as Martin scored eight goals including a hat-trick against Sheffield Wednesday. His form earned him a recall to the Scotland international squad but a back injury forced him to pull out and also to miss almost half of 1968-9. On his recovery, Cantwell paired him with another six-footer, Tony Hateley, but the much-vaunted partnership hit it off only once, in a 3-0 win at Stoke. With Coventry bottom of the table in February, Hateley was axed but Martin hit form, scoring eight goals in the last 17 games to save City again. His most important goal was the last-minute winner against fellow strugglers, Leicester City, which kept Coventry up. He struggled in the early part of the following season, but the purchase of John O'Rourke sparked him to score 15 goals as City finished sixth. In February 1971, he was surprisingly sold to Nottingham Forest, for £70,000. It was, however, an astute sale as he was on the wane and soon drifted to Brighton and then Crystal Palace. He became manager of Walsall, then coached in the Middle East. Martin was born at Tranent on 20 October 1940 and his early career was spent with Alloa, Queen of the South and Hibernian before the rangy, skilful centre-forward signed for Sunderland for £50,000 in October 1965, where he won his three Scotland caps.

Football League debut for Coventry City v Chelsea (h) 10 February 1968.

NEIL MARTIN

	LEAGUE		*FA CUP*		*FL CUP*		*OTHERS*		*TOTAL*	
	App	*Gls*	*App*	*Gls*	*App*	*Gls*	*App*	*Gls*	*App*	*Gls*
1967-68	15	8	0	0	0	0	0	0	15	8
1968-69	25	9	2	0	2	0	0	0	29	9
1969-70	40	14	2	1	1	0	0	0	43	15
1970-71	26	9	1	0	5	2	3	2	35	13
	106	40	5	1	8	2	3	2	122	45

Perhaps the best move Harry Storer ever made was the signing of a raw 18-year-old centre-half from Redhill Amateurs. Mason was born in Birmingham on 5 September 1913 and just how Birmingham and Aston Villa missed this opportunity is a mystery, but their loss was City's gain. For three years Mason learned his trade in the reserve team and then, within 12 months, two unrelated disciplinary incidents handed him the centre-half position and then the captaincy. Both Tom Davison and Charlie Bisby were involved in off-the-field incidents and left the club soon afterwards. Mason grew in stature and by the end of 1935-6 he was established as skipper, linchpin and Storer's representative on the pitch as City won the Third Division South championship by a narrow margin. The next three years were Mason's best as City chased that elusive place in Division One. They refused many large offers for his services but Storer, basing his team on defensive strength, kept an unchanged line-up at the back, and if players were sold they tended to be forwards. The war cut across the best years of Mason's career, although he became City's first England international, albeit unofficially in two wartime matches. But for those seven lost years his appearances would have exceeded 600. After the war he was still a regular for three and a half seasons but time eventually caught up and he was freed at the end of 1951-2, after 21 years' service. After a spell at Nuneaton Borough, he became a publican and then worked at Jaguar, from where he retired in 1978. His two sons, Peter and John, were well-known local sportsmen. A giant of his times he stands alongside George Curtis as one of City's all-time greats.

Football League debut for Coventry City v Bristol Rovers (a) 12 March 1932.

GEORGE MASON

	LEAGUE		*FA CUP*		*TOTAL*	
	App	*Gls*	*App*	*Gls*	*App*	*Gls*
1931-32	3	0	0	0	3	0
1932-33	6	0	0	0	6	0
1933-34	2	0	0	0	2	0
1934-35	24	0	3	0	27	0
1935-36	40	0	2	0	42	0
1936-37	42	3	3	2	45	3
1937-38	38	1	1	0	39	1
1938-39	42	1	1	0	43	1
1945-46	0	0	2	0	0	2
1946-47	28	0	2	0	30	0
1947-48	34	0	2	0	36	0
1948-49	35	0	1	0	36	0
1949-50	28	1	1	0	29	1
1950-51	0	0	0	0	0	0
1951-52	8	0	2	0	10	0
	330	6	20	2	350	8

Dick Mason was born in Arley, Warwickshire, on 2 April 1918 and played for Arley Miners' Welfare before joining Nuneaton Borough. City signed him in May 1946 and, at the age of 28, he won a first-team place at left-half in the torrid atmosphere of St James' Park, Newcastle, in front of 55,000 fans. He was converted to left-back later in the season and played regularly in that position for the next six seasons. Mason was a consistent performer, a strong tackler and, although he was not very tall, a good header of the ball. In 1953-4, Roy Kirk took over at left-back and in February 1955, Mason left the club to take over as player-manager of Bedworth Town. His memory lived on at Highfield Road every other Saturday for some years after he left the club, for a photograph of him carrying a ball was featured on the front of the match-day programme, until the end of 1956-7 for League matches and for much longer for friendlies and reserve games.

Football League debut for Coventry City v Newcastle United (a) 11 September 1946.

RICHARD MASON

	LEAGUE		*FA CUP*		*TOTAL*	
	App	*Gls*	*App*	*Gls*	*App*	*Gls*
1946-47	24	0	2	0	26	0
1947-48	36	0	2	0	38	0
1948-49	39	0	1	0	40	0
1949-50	37	0	1	0	38	0
1950-51	36	0	0	0	36	0
1951-52	36	1	1	0	37	1
1952-53	39	1	3	0	42	1
1953-54	6	0	0	0	6	0
	253	2	10	0	263	2

Coventry City, 1947-8. Back row (left to right): Toose, R.Mason, Snape, Wood, H.Hill (trainer), Dearson, Barrett. Front row: Warner, Simpson, Billy Frith (manager), Davidson, Setchell, Ashall. On ground: Lawrie.

"I didn't feel any different being in the First Division, and I certainly didn't play any better. Of course, I was proud to be at the highest level at a time when the English game offered such a galaxy of stars. But looking back, I don't think I should have left Coventry City, that was where my heart lay." These were the words of Reg Matthews, the first Coventry player to appear in a full international for England and also the first Third Division goalkeeper to play for England. They were spoken some 27 years after he had left his home-town club for Chelsea. Matthews played rugby at Barker's Butts School and was spotted by a Highfield Road scout only when he turned out in a soccer trial after another player failed to show up. He went straight into Coventry's nursery side, Modern Machine Tools FC, who only lost one game in four years, and made rapid strides under the tuition of Alf Wood. But so consistent was Wood and his successor, Peter Taylor, that it was not until 1953, at the age of 21, that Matthews made his League debut. Even then he played in only a handful of games that season and in 1953-4. Matthews finally established himself as City's number-one goalkeeper in September 1954 and he rapidly endeared himself to the Highfield Road faithful, saving a poor City side from defeat on many occasions with his daring displays. He was very agile, boasting a lithe grace unusual in 'keepers of that period. Matthews was not so popular on away grounds; after a game at Millwall, in which he gave a particularly memorable performance, the crowd threatened him. His skill was not lost on other managers, however, and after playing a 'blinder' against Southampton at The Dell, Ted Drake, the Saints manager, told him he would play for England one day. Indeed, Matthews did make his Under-23 debut that season, after only 30 Division Three games. Later that season he won another Under-23 cap and played for England 'B' and the Football League. He gained his first full cap in 1956, against Scotland, in a side containing Finney, Wright, Lofthouse and the young Duncan Edwards. Within a fortnight Coventry rejected a record offer from a First Division club. Matthews went on to win four more caps that season. The 1956-7 campaign started with a new manager, Harry Warren, and — a recurring theme at Highfield Road in the 1950s — new enthusiasm. But after a good start, things started to go wrong; the one bright spot was the consistently brilliant form of Reg Matthews. At the beginning of the season he had lost his England place to Ted Ditchburn. Walter Winterbottom, then England's manager, found fault with his performance in the 1-1 draw against Northern Ireland in October. The newspapers were quick to advise Matthews to move to a First Division club but Matthews said no, Warren said no, the directors said no and the fans prayed that nobody would weaken. But weaken they did: on a drab November afternoon, Warren, Erle Shanks (then chairman) and the player kept a secret apppointment with Chelsea's manager Ted Drake at the Leofric Hotel and the unthinkable happened: Reg Matthews left the club for £22,500, a record fee for a goalkeeper. Shanks claimed that Matthews had wanted a move, Coventry needed the money — end of story. In retrospect, it was not a good move for Matthews. It did not make him richer — the Chelsea offer was £15 per week, top line — and it did not bring additional fame, for despite of playing in the First Division for 12 years he never appeared for England again. After five years at Chelsea he moved to Derby County for £12,000 and made 247 appearances for the Rams, including some memorable ones against the Sky Blues. After leaving Derby in 1968, he became player-manager of the now defunct Rugby Town. Reg Matthews now lives in Coventry, retaining an inbred passion for his home-town club but no doubt reflecting from time to time on life's ironies.

Football League debut for Coventry City v Southend United (a) 21 March 1953.

	LEAGUE		*FA CUP*		*TOTAL*	
	App	*Gls*	*App*	*Gls*	*App*	*Gls*
1952-53	10	0	0	0	10	0
1953-54	5	0	0	0	5	0
1954-55	36	0	4	0	40	0
1955-56	43	0	1	0	44	0
1956-57	17	0	0	0	17	0
	111	0	5	0	116	0

REG MATTHEWS

In 1891, after Singers had won the Birmingham Junior Cup by beating Willenhall Pickwicks 1-0, Frank Mobley, who scored the only goal, was described by the local correspondent as 'the most celebrated sportsman in Coventry's history'. It is sad to reflect how such heroes could be forgotten in the upheavals of a time unique to Coventry in the 20th century, and it is unlikely that many knew his name before the publication of *Singers to Sky Blues* in 1986. In 1890, Mobley became the final piece of the jigsaw in the brilliant 'Little Blackbirds' side. He scored over 20 goals in his first season and his combination with Will Dorrell and Harry Banks confounded defences throughout the Midlands. The following season (1891-2) his scoring reached new heights; this was the season that Singers won three competitions, the Birmingham & District again, the Walsall Cup and the Wednesbury Cup. In so doing they took part in 16 cup ties, in which Mobley scored a total of 26 goals. In three consecutive ties in December, Singers beat Small Heath United 12-1 (Mobley five goals), Burlington EMS 11-0 (Mobley five again) and Soho Villa 12-2 (Mobley six). Inevitably, he came to the attention of the Midland giants and a week before the start of the 1892-3 season signed professional forms for Small Heath. He established himself in their first team and then moved to Bury and played in the First Division. In 1900, by which time Singers had become Coventry City, turned professional and moved to Highfield Road, Mobley kept a promise and returned to Coventry for one season. He made his last appearance against Aston Villa Reserves in April 1901.
Birmingham League debut for Coventry City v Stoke Reserves (a) 13 October 1900.

FRANK MOBLEY

	S LEAGUE		*FA CUP*		*TOTAL*	
	App	*Gls*	*App*	*Gls*	*App*	*Gls*
1900-01	21	7	0	0	21	7
	21	7	0	0	21	7

Born in Newcastle upon Tyne in 1914, Bill Morgan had just kept goal for his local club, Mickley Colliery, against Blyth Spartans in an FA Cup qualifying round in 1931-2 when Harry Storer knocked on the door of his parents' house and announced: "I'm taking your son to Coventry." Morgan packed his bags and by the beginning of the next week had signed on and was sharing digs with Clarrie Bourton. His appearances were limited until the spring of 1936, when he established himself as the number-one 'keeper ahead of Horace Pearson. In the final three seasons of peacetime soccer, he missed only two League matches (both through injury), keeping nearly 50 clean sheets in the process. Coventry received several large offers for his services, but with the coming of war, nothing materialized. He joined the local fire brigade at the outbreak of war and played for City in regional league games. A severe shoulder dislocation at Leicester effectively ended his career and a local specialist advised him to retire from the game in January 1944. He stayed on at the club, assisting with coaching, looking after Modern Machines FC and became assistant trainer in 1946, then head trainer in 1951, but his final appointment was not a success and he left the club in 1953 to work for Standard Motors for over 20 years. He retired in the late-1970s and is now deceased.
Football League debut for Coventry City v Cardiff City (a) 6 April 1933.

BILL MORGAN

	LEAGUE		*FA CUP*		*TOTAL*	
	App	*Gls*	*App*	*Gls*	*App*	*Gls*
1932-33	8	0	0	0	8	0
1933-34	4	0	0	0	4	0
1934-35	2	0	1	0	3	0
1935-36	12	0	0	0	12	0
1936-37	42	0	3	0	45	0
1937--38	41	0	1	0	42	0
1938-39	41	0	1	0	42	0
	150	0	6	0	156	0

If you ask any City fan which, of all the sales of the austere period of the late-1970s and early '80s, hurt the most, they will answer: Dennis Mortimer. Not only was Mortimer blossoming into an outstanding midfield player, but he was also sold to arch rivals, Aston Villa — evidence to many City fans that their club would never compete at the highest level. At Villa Park, Mortimer won the honours for which he had thirsted: League Cup winners in 1977, League Champions in 1981 and European Cup winners in 1982, the latter two successes coming when he was skipper. He developed, as all City fans knew he would, but sadly he never won full England recognition. When one considers the midfield players capped in his era, it is a travesty that he went uncapped. He came into the first-team squad as a 17-year-old and within a year was a regular. He never looked ill at ease on the ball and his kind of silky skills have rarely been seen in a City shirt since his departure in 1975. His captaincy of the 1970 Youth team was a revelation and, despite outclassing Perryman and Souness of Spurs, he ended on the losing side in the classic four-match FA Youth Cup Final. He played six times for England Under-23s whilst at City and made three 'B' appearances at Villa. He had one outstanding Under-23 international, against Holland at Highbury in January 1973, when his two goals inspired England to a 3-1 victory. After almost ten years at Villa he was freed and went to Brighton but after a short time returned to the Midlands to play for Birmingham City and later Redditch, where he was player-manager.

DENNIS MORTIMER

Football League debut for Coventry City v West Ham United (substitute) (h) 11 October 1969.

	LEAGUE		FA CUP		FL CUP		OTHERS		TOTAL	
	App	Gls	App	Gls	App	Gls	App	Gls	App	Gls
1969-70	6/3	0	1	0	0	0	0	0	7/3	0
1970-71	24/3	0	0	0	2	0	1	0	27/3	0
1971-72	26/8	4	1/1	0	1	0	2/1	1	30/10	5
1972-73	39	1	4	0	2	0	2	1	47	2
1973-74	33	1	3	0	3	0	2	0	41	1
1974-75	29	3	0	0	1	0	0	0	30	3
1975-76	22	1	0	0	2	0	0	0	24	1
	179/14	10	9/1	0	11	0	7	2	206/16	12

The day before World War Two broke out, Peter Murphy, then a lanky 17-year-old, had a trial for Southbank St Peter's, the nursery side of Middlesbrough. "I had a pretty good game, was paid two shillings expenses, and was told they would be getting in contact with me later," he recalled. "But I never heard any more and I suppose I must have been forgotten with all the hubbub that was going on at the time." Murphy then moved to Coventry and was working in the local war industry when he was signed as an amateur by City. Harry Storer had spotted him playing for the works team of Dunlop, where he was employed. He joined the Armed Forces shortly afterwards, however, and did not play regularly for City until 1946-7. The late-1940s was a mediocre period for City, Murphy's performances as an inside- or outside-left providing some of the few bright moments. His best season both as goalmaker and as goaltaker was 1949-50, when City, halfway up the table. Murphy had played particularly well in both games against Spurs that season and it was no surprise when they put in a bid of £20,000 during the close season. It was even less of a surprise when the City club, in their never-ending quest to balance the books, accepted the bid. Murphy played 22 games in Arthur Rowe's famous push-and-run side of 1950-51, thus receiving a League Championship medal. But he never really settled in London and by early 1952 was heading back for the Midlands to join Birmingham City. The eight years he spent with Blues were the best of his career. He gained a Second Division championship medal in 1954 and an FA Cup runners-up medal in 1956. After leaving the Blues in 1960, Murphy had one season with Southern League Rugby Town, helping them to win promotion to the Premier Division, before retiring from the game. He returned to Highfield Road in the late-1960s to manage the 'A' team and regularly attended City's home matches until his death at the early age of 53 on 7 April 1975. He was born in West Hartlepool on 7 March 1922.

Football League debut for Coventry City v Fulham (h) 7 December 1946.

PETER MURPHY

	LEAGUE		FA CUP		TOTAL	
	App	Gls	App	Gls	App	Gls
1946-47	11	2	1	0	12	2
1947-48	28	7	2	0	30	7
1948-49	36	13	1	0	37	13
1949-50	39	15	1	0	40	15
	114	37	5	0	119	37

Born at Aberdare on 20 April 1933, Brian Nicholas was only 16 when he made his debut for Queen's Park Rangers in 1949. He played well enough to attract the attention of First Division Chelsea and signed for them in July 1955. However, Chelsea had a large squad and Nicholas made only a few first-team appearances. Billy Frith snapped him up for Coventry early in 1958, soon after signing Ray Straw, to add pep to a side which was slipping alarmingly down the Third Division South table. The 'medicine' did not work immediately; in fact, City went from 26 December to 17 March without winning a game. Nevertheless, Nicholas was a good buy, slotting into the right-half position which had been filled by three different players earlier in the season. He was a popular player at Highfield Road, instantly recognizable because of his bald pate which made him look much older than he was. He continued to wear the number-four shirt until halfway through 1958-9, when Mick Kearns took over, and then for most of 1959-60. Nicholas made a only few appearances in 1960-61 but made a comeback the following season, still at right-half. However, at the end of the season, Jimmy Hill decided to release him and he signed for Rugby Town in July 1962, at 29 still a relatively young player. He settled in the area after retiring, finding employment at Massey Ferguson, and is still a regular visitor to Highfield Road.
Football League debut for Coventry City v Torquay United (a) 1 February 1958.

	LEAGUE		FA CUP		FL CUP		TOTAL	
	App	Gls	App	Gls	App	Gls	App	Gls
1957-58	20	0	0	0	-	-	20	0
1958-59	26	0	2	0	-	-	28	0
1959-60	35	0	2	0	-	-	37	0
1960-61	8	0	0	0	1	0	9	0
1961-62	24	0	2	0	1	0	27	0
	113	0	6	0	2	0	121	0

BRIAN NICHOLAS

When Steve Ogrizovic was injured at Millwall in October 1989 and forced to miss the following game, against Luton, it brought to an end his run of 241 consecutive appearances for Coventry City — surpassing Alf Wood's 40-year-old record for the club — and a sequence of over 320 games in all. Ogrizovic, who was born at Mansfield on 12 September 1957, started his career with Chesterfield in 1977. After 16 games for the Derbyshire club he was snapped up by Liverpool, for £75,000, as cover for Ray Clemence. In five seasons at Anfield he made only four first-team appearances and yet gained European Cup winners' medals as a substitute who was never used. When Clemence left, Ogrizovic was superceded by Bruce Grobbelaar and left to join Shrewsbury Town. Two years later came his £72,500 move to Highfield Road, where he quickly impressed with his confident handling and good positioning. Like all good 'keepers he is sometimes taken for granted but has had few bad games in his City career. His first-half performance in the 1987 FA Cup semi-final was superb and kept City in the game. He was rewarded with an appearance in the Football League side against the Rest of the World in the League's centenary game in 1987. In 1986, at Hillsborough, he became the first City goalkeeper to score a goal. He signed a further three-year contract in 1991 which, if he retains his form and fitness, will surely enable him to overtake Bill Glazier's record of 402 goalkeeping appearances for the club.
Football League debut for Coventry City v Aston Villa (a) 25 August 1984.

	LEAGUE		FA CUP		FL CUP		OTHERS		TOTAL	
	App	Gls	App	Gls	App	Gls	App	Gls	App	Gls
1984-85	42	0	2	0	2	0	0	0	46	0
1985-86	42	0	1	0	4	0	2	0	49	0
1986-87	42	1	6	0	5	0	1	0	53	1
1987-88	40	0	2	0	3	0	3	0	48	0
1988-89	38	0	1	0	3	0	1	0	43	0
1989-90	37	0	1	0	7	0	1	0	46	0
1990-91	37	0	4	0	5	0	1	0	47	0
	278	1	17	0	29	0	9	0	333	1

STEVE OGRIZOVIC

Born at Gorsty Hill, Halesowen, in 1888, Harry Parkes was both cricket and football captain at Halesowen Grammar School. After leaving school he played for Halesowen Amateurs as an outside-left, Coombs Wood in the Birmingham Junior League as an outside-right, and for Halesowen before joining West Bromwich Albion in 1906. He was at The Hawthorns for three years and played in an FA Cup semi-final, against Everton, at the age of 17, coming through with flying colours. However, Parkes fell out with Albion over the question of terms and joined City on 21 December 1908. He made his debut only four days later but due to the consistency of Charlie Tickle, was not able to claim a regular place in the side at outside-right until 1910-11, when Tickle switched to inside-right. He was a dashing winger, quick on the ball, who had the happy knack of being able screw the ball back accurately from the by-line. Parkes was by no means a heavyweight (he stood 5ft 8in and weighed only 11st 4lbs) but he was able to look after himself. He was popular with his teammates, being noted for his dry wit. On being asked for his opinion of a referee whose decisions had been somewhat dubious, Parkes remarked, "He wore very pretty stockings". He gave loyal service to the club for six seasons, in 1913-14, his last at Highfield Road, he played mainly at wing-half. He rejoined Albion on leaving City and stayed at The Hawthorns until 1919, when he became Newport County's secretary-manager. Parkes subsequently managed Chesterfield (1922-27), Lincoln City (1927-36), Mansfield Town (1936-38) and Notts County (1938-39). He died at Basford, Nottinghamshire, in March 1947.
Southern League debut for Coventry City v Swindon Town (h) 25 December 1908.

HARRY PARKES

	S LEAGUE		*FA CUP*		*TOTAL*	
	App	*Gls*	*App*	*Gls*	*App*	*Gls*
1908-09	11	2	0	0	11	2
1909-10	11	1	0	0	11	1
1910-11	33	11	4	1	37	12
1911-12	36	7	2	1	38	8
1912-13	38	12	2	1	40	13
1913-14	32	2	1	0	33	2
	161	35	9	3	170	38

Born at Nuneaton on 10 February 1957, Trevor Peake was one of football's late developers, not joining a League club until he moved to Lincoln City from Nuneaton Borough at the age of 22. Peake had been an outstanding player in non-League football, playing for England at semi-professional level. After four good years at Sincil Bank, which culminated in selection for the PFA's Third Division team, he was bought by Bobby Gould in the traumatic summer of 1983. He settled into the top flight with ease having excellent timing, a superb temperament and classy skill. After a season playing alongside Sam Allardyce, Peake teamed up with Brian Kilcline to form the defensive partnership that was to serve City so well for the best part of seven seasons. Peake skippered the side during his first two seasons but lost the captaincy after a disagreement with Don Mackay in the summer of 1985. He gave an outstanding display in the 1987 FA Cup Final when, after allowing the prolific Clive Allen to score in the early minutes, he recovered to mark the Spurs star out of the game. The following season Peake was selected for the England 'B' team but injury kept him out and his international chance never came again. An infrequent goalscorer, his effort against Crystal Palace in February 1991 was his first since September 1985. Peake was promoted to a coaching position by Sillett in 1988, as a possible prelude to a career in management, and in 1990 was rewarded with a three-year contract with City.
Football League debut for Coventry City v Tottenham Hotspur (a) 29 August 1983.

TREVOR PEAKE

	LEAGUE		*FA CUP*		*FL CUP*		*OTHERS*		*TOTAL*	
	App	*Gls*	*App*	*Gls*	*App*	*Gls*	*App*	*Gls*	*App*	*Gls*
1983-84	33	3	4	1	3	0	0	0	40	4
1984-85	33/1	1	1	0	2	0	0	0	36/1	1
1985-86	37	1	1	0	4	0	2	0	44	1
1986-87	39	0	6	0	4	0	1	0	50	0
1987-88	31	0	1	0	2	0	3	0	37	0
1988-89	32	0	1	0	2	0	1	0	36	0
1989-90	33	0	1	0	8	0	1	0	43	0
1990-91	36	1	2	0	5	0	1	0	44	1
	274/1	6	17	1	30	0	9	0	330/1	7

Born at Kenilworth on 29 January 1954, Barry Powell played for City for four seasons in the late-1970s and these were his best years in the game. Despite winning four Under-23 caps and a League Cup winners' medal with Wolves, he found it hard to keep his place at Molineux and joined his local club for £75,000. Powell initially played alongside Dennis Mortimer but the following season formed an excellent partnership with Terry Yorath and it was their partnership which was the linchpin of success in 1977-8. During that season, Powell was an ever-present and, whilst not possessing the same vision as Mortimer, certainly had bags of skill and a lot of heart and stamina. He could always be relied upon to score goals and in his latter days at the club became the regular penalty-taker. His sale to Derby, only weeks after Yorath's departure, was a shock to the fans but young Andy Blair filled the gap adequately and City were £350,000 better off. Powell was never as influential at the Baseball Ground and the Rams were relegated in his first season. After leaving them in 1982, he played alongside Tommy Hutchison in Hong Kong, for Bulova, and then returned to England with first Burnley, then Swansea City. After a further spell in Hong Kong, he became coach at Molineux. He is the son of Ivor Powell, the former Aston Villa and Wales wing-half.

Debut for Coventry City v Bolton Wanderers (a) League Cup, 10 September 1975.

	LEAGUE		*FA CUP*		*FL CUP*		*TOTAL*	
	App	*Gls*	*App*	*Gls*	*App*	*Gls*	*App*	*Gls*
1975-76	32/2	7	1/1	0	1	0	34/3	7
1976-77	40	4	2	0	1	0	43	4
1977-78	42	3	1	0	4	2	47	5
1978-79	38	9	2	0	1	0	41	9
1979-80	10	4	0	0	2	0	12	4
	162/2	27	6/1	0	9	2	177/3	29

BARRY POWELL

Back in the 1920s it was a rare City side which did not include at least one player from Bedworth and none came better than full-back Jackie Randle. Like many of his generation, Randle left school at 14 to work down the mine, playing his football with Bedworth Juniors before joining the Exhall Colliery team, renowned for producing a steady supply of future Coventry City stars. Towards the end of the 1921-2 season, Randle was signed up for City by Albert Evans. Although he made a number of appearances at left-back as an amateur in the Reserves, he had to wait until 1923 before making his first-team debut. Then, he went on to make over 150 appearances for City. Although only 5ft 7in tall, he was very powerfully built and a fearless tackler, possessing a tremendous kick much valued in the days of heavy pitches and sodden footballs. It was on just such a pitch that Randle had one of his most memorable games, in a Cup tie at Kettering. City led 3-0 at half-time but in the second half, Kettering kicked down their slope with the wind behind them and quickly pulled two goals back. At this stage, Randle's mighty clearances came to the rescue, earning the wrath of the crowd for the long delays whilst the ball was retrieved. City held on to win 3-2. By contrast, one record he would have preferred to forget came in September 1926, when City lost 3-0 to Bristol City. Randle had the unenviable record of scoring all the goals at the wrong end! In 1927, Randle was transferred to Birmingham for a club record fee of over £1,000, good news for the bank but bad for the side. He quickly established himself as a First Division player but suffered a disappointment when he was dropped before the 1931 FA Cup Final. Nevertheless, the Blues still valued him sufficiently to reject a £5,000 offer from Arsenal the same year. Randle moved to Bournemouth in 1933 but retired after one season, returning to his beloved Bedworth where he continued to turn out for Newdigate in the Coventry and Warwickshire League. He died in Bournemouth in 1990 at the ripe old age of 88.

Football League debut for Coventry City v Bradford City (a) 27 August 1923.

	LEAGUE		*FA CUP*		*TOTAL*	
	App	*Gls*	*App*	*Gls*	*App*	*Gls*
1923-24	38	0	2	0	40	0
1924-25	28	0	1	0	29	0
1925-26	42	0	1	0	43	0
1926-27	29	0	3	0	32	0
1927-28	12	0	0	0	12	0
	149	0	7	0	156	0

JACKIE RANDLE

It was perhaps inevitable that one of Jimmy Hill's brand-new forward line would fail to make the grade and after Bobby Laverick's poor performances in the first four matches of the season, he was dropped, never to return, and marked down as one of Hill's few failures. Roy Dwight came in, but was obviously never going to regain his pace, so Hill was left with the gamble of playing an almost unknown ex-youth team player from South Wales. Ronnie Rees took his chance brilliantly and from that sunny debut day in September 1962, he became a fixture in the first team. Equally at home on either flank, he was never seriously threatened in his six seasons of unbroken first-team football. International honours followed quickly and after a spell in the Under-23s, a full cap came his way, the first of 21 in City's colours and a total to be equalled only by David Clements. Apart from the Third Division championship season, Rees always weighed-in with a number of useful and sometimes spectacular goals especially in 1963-4. He seemed set for a long career at Highfield Road but with Coventry struggling against relegation, changes were necessary and after the signing of Neil Martin, Ernie Hunt and Chris Cattlin, the books had to be balanced. Rees was easily the most saleable asset, although his game was beginning to suffer, and moved to West Brom for £65,000. He stayed only a season and, after a short spell with a declining Nottingham Forest side, moved down the League to Swansea City. It was his final stopping place in League football but he was still good enough to add a few more caps to a final total of 39. Rees was born at Ystradgynlais on 4 April 1944.

Football League debut for Coventry City v Shrewsbury Town (h) 15 September 1962.

RONNIE REES

	LEAGUE		FA CUP		FL CUP		TOTAL	
	App	Gls	App	Gls	App	Gls	App	Gls
1962-63	33	4	8	0	1	1	42	5
1963-64	46	13	2	1	2	1	50	15
1964-65	41	7	1	0	4	2	46	9
1965-66	41	7	3	2	4	0	48	9
1966-67	39	3	1	1	3	1	43	5
1967-68	30	8	2	1	1	0	33	9
	230	42	17	5	15	5	262	52

Cyrille Regis came to City from West Bromwich Albion in October 1984 for £300,000. It was Bobby Gould's last major signing for Coventry and many expressed surprise that Regis chose City in the face of much competition, notably from Manchester United. His first two seasons were not a great success but in 1985 he made a dramatic and crucial contribution in scoring two goals against Everton to prevent relegation. Yet Coventry fans still had to see the best of Regis, mainly because he had been used as a conventional target man — in what was a struggling side — and it was never a role he ideally suited. He equalled the club scoring record when he netted five times in a League Cup match at home to Chester in 1985. Under John Sillett a more thoughtful style was introduced (partly at Regis's own instigation) and the successful partnership with Dave Bennett was born. He played a lion's part in City's FA Cup campaign, so much so that he returned to the England side to gain the last of his five caps. His commanding physical appearance and devastating forays into the penalty box tend to raise expectations too high, although his 60-odd goals place him high in the list of Coventry City's First Division scorers. He experienced something of an 'Indian Summer' in 1990-91, when as a 'born-again Christian', he regained a lot of zest. It came as a surprise, then, when he was given a free transfer by Terry Butcher. In a decade which has not produced a terrace icon comparable with Hutchison in the 1970s or Hudson in the 1960s, Regis probably comes closest to being Coventry's man of the 1980s. No City fan will ever forget the opening goal of the FA Cup tie at Hillsborough. Powering through from the halfway line to pick up Bennett's through-ball, Regis trailed the Owls' back-four in his wake before driving the ball home from the edge of the area. It was quintessential Cyrille Regis. He signed for old rivals Aston Villa in June 1991.

Football League debut for Coventry City v Newcastle United (h) 13 October 1984.

CYRILLE REGIS

	LEAGUE		FACUP		FLCUP		OTHERS		TOTAL	
	App	Gls	App	Gls	App	Gls	App	Gls	App	Gls
1984-85	30/1	5	1	0	0	0	0	0	31/1	5
1985-86	34	5	1	0	2	5	0	0	37	10
1986-87	40	12	6	2	5	2	0	0	51	16
1987-88	30/1	10	2	1	2	1	2	0	36/1	12
1988-89	34	7	1	0	3	0	0	0	38	7
1989-90	32/2	4	0/1	0	7	1	1	0	40/3	5
1990-91	31/3	4	4	0	5	3	1	0	41/3	7
	231/7	47	15/1	3	24	12	4	0	274/8	62

Born in Manchester on 6 November 1955, Harry Roberts was christened Brian but, from his early days at Coventry, was given the nickname Harry after a notorious gangster from the late-1960s. In his early career at City, he was 'Mr Dependable' and played in several positions. Strangely, his first ten games for the club were all away from home. Roberts did not gain a regular place until August 1980, when McDonald left, but then he barely missed a game until his departure to Birmingham City for a paltry £10,000 in March 1984. Initially he played at left-back, but after Thomas' departure reverted to right-back. A frustrating player, who often did not look good enough for First Division football, he nevertheless possessed a big heart, a good turn of speed and was a big crowd favourite. He got his first goal after 160 games in 1982, with an effort he talked about for weeks afterwards. In the summer of 1983 he was one of the few players to remain at Highfield Road and was an ever-present the following season until his move to St Andrew's. After six traumatic years with the Blues he moved on a free transfer to Wolves, with his sense of humour intact. Roberts was a great servant to Coventry City and was deservedly awarded a testimonial by the club in September 1984.

Football League debut for Coventry City v Tottenham Hotspur (a) 19 April 1976.

	LEAGUE		*FA CUP*		*FL CUP*		*TOTAL*	
	App	*Gls*	*App*	*Gls*	*App*	*Gls*	*App*	*Gls*
1975-76	2	0	0	0	0	0	2	0
1976-77	12	0	1	0	0	0	13	0
1977-78	26	0	1	0	1/1	0	28/1	0
1978-79	17	0	0	0	0	0	17	0
1979-80	10/4	0	0	0	2/1	0	12/5	0
1980-81	41/1	0	4	0	9	0	54/1	0
1981-82	33/1	0	1	0	2	0	36/1	0
1982-83	38	1	2	1	2	0	42	2
1983-84	30	0	4	0	3	0	37	0
	209/6	1	13	1	19/2	0	241/8	2

BRIAN ROBERTS

'But for the war . . .' applied to Ted Roberts perhaps more than any other Coventry City player. Born in Chesterfield on 2 November 1916, Roberts started his career with local side Glapwell Colliery, moved to Derby County in 1934 and signed for City in 1937. Roberts had already made over 40 first-team appearances by the time World War Two had broken out, but by then he was nearly 23. By the time Football League matches resumed in 1946, he was nearly 30 and his best footballing years had been wasted. Roberts played for six consecutive seasons after the war, averaging a goal every other game. His great strength was his heading ability and if he was not so good on the ground, he was still revered by his teammates for being the best 'team man' in the side. This may be why Tommy Briggs, who was bought in December 1950 to replace Roberts, and who had been a prolific goalscorer for every club he had played for, could never settle down at Highfield Road. There is a strong suspicion that he was literally frozen out by his teammates and he played only six times before Roberts was restored to centre-forward. Roberts' last season was 1951-2, then he moved into non-League football with Kings Lynn and was still playing regularly for Banbury Spencer at the age of 38.

	LEAGUE		*FA CUP*		*TOTAL*	
	App	*Gls*	*App*	*Gls*	*App*	*Gls*
1936-37	5	3	0	0	5	3
1937-38	23	6	1	0	24	6
1938-39	14	3	1	0	15	3
1946-47	29	9	2	1	31	10
1947-48	26	10	1	0	27	10
1948-49	34	19	1	0	35	19
1949-50	25	8	1	0	26	8
1950-51	31	15	1	0	32	15
1951-52	25	12	3	1	28	13
	212	85	11	2	223	87

He returned to Highfield Road in the late-1950s and, after a spell as assistant coach became trainer-coach under Billy Frith. He was swept away in December 1961, along with the rest of the staff, to make way for the Sky Blue revolution and moved into local industry with Rolls-Royce. His son, Dudley, had a few seasons with the club in the mid-1960s, scoring some vital goals in 1965-6.

Football League debut for Coventry City v Burnley (a) 26 March 1937.

TED ROBERTS

NAT ROBINSON

Eighteen years separate Nat Robinson's City debut from his final game — a claim only George Mason and Alf Wood can equal in City's history. The goalkeeping position had been a problem ever since Coventry entered the Birmingham League, so much so that veteran Teddy Kirk had to be lured out of retirement for a year. His eventual successor was found towards the end of the 1895-6 season. Nat Robinson, whose real first names were Arthur Charles, was a truly great custodian and missed only one game over the next three seasons. Such was his reputation, it was accepted as inevitable that City would lose his services and in 1899 he moved 'up the road' to Small Heath. He was a regular in their 1901 Second Division championship side which conceded a record low of 24 goals, much of the credit for which lay with Robinson. He continued in the First Division with Chelsea and then returned to City in the close season of 1910. He made two appearances in 1911, one in the Cup tie at Burnley, and then a further five in 1914-15 when deputizing for Sid Blake. He retired from the game in May 1915.

Birmingham League debut for Coventry City v West Bromwich Albion Reserves (a) 1 February 1896.

	LEAGUE		*FA CUP*		*TOTAL*	
	App	*Gls*	*App*	*Gls*	*App*	*Gls*
1895-96	4	0	0	0	4	0
1896-97	30	0	1	0	31	0
1897-98	29	0	1	0	30	0
1898-99	33	0	2	0	35	0
1910-11	1	0	1	0	2	0
1914-15	5	0	0	0	5	0
	102	0	5	0	107	0

RAY SAMBROOK

The sale of Ray Sambrook to Manchester City was a typical example of Coventry City's short-sighted policies in the late-1950s. Sambrook, a product of Coventry's nursery team, was very skilful, an exciting left winger who could play havoc with defences; in other words the type of player to attract the crowds to Highfield Road and to build a side around. But Coventry looked only for short-term success, so young, promising players of Sambrook's ilk never lasted very long. A combination of the need to balance the books and the perceived necessity to buy older, more experienced players in order to win instant promotion ensured his early departure. Sambrook was born in Wolverhampton on 31 May 1933 and signed for Coventry City in September 1953. By the end of 1954-5 he had established himself in the first team. When Jesse Carver took over as manager at the beginning of the following season, it seemed that Sambrook might become a long-term fixture at Highfield Road. His style seemed highly suited to the push-and-run brand of soccer which Carver had introduced. But the manager left and Sambrook's performances began to attract attention from First Division managers. Numerous offers were rejected but Coventry's financial position worsened and the inevitable happened in November 1957, when he was sold for £15,000. After some initial success at Maine Road, he faded and by 1959 was playing in Manchester City's Central League side. He was 'freed' in 1962 and after short spells with Doncaster Rovers and Crewe Alexandra, he retired from League football.

Football League debut for Coventry City v Newport County (a) 9 October 1954.

	LEAGUE		*FA CUP*		*TOTAL*	
	App	*Gls*	*App*	*Gls*	*App*	*Gls*
1954-55	11	1	0	0	11	1
1955-56	35	9	1	0	36	9
1956-57	41	14	0	0	41	14
1957-58	9	1	2	0	11	1
	96	25	3	0	99	25

Born at Rotherham in 1881, right-back Percy Saul started his career with Gainsborough Trinity in the early 1900s. He then moved to Southern League Plymouth Argyle before signing for Liverpool, where he made 83 appearances in three seasons. Saul joined City in July 1909 and was an instant success at Highfield Road. He was just the sort of experienced player City needed. Although he was never capped, Saul was regarded as one of the best players in his position in the country; indeed, Bob Evans said that he would as soon play behind him as any player he knew. Saul was a very conscientious man: as City were about to take the field for a Southern League match in January 1910, the trainer reminded them that they were due to meet Preston in the FA Cup the following week. Hardly had he said the words than Saul gave vent to his feelings. As far as he was concerned, City were going out to win. Not until the trainer had apologized was Saul persuaded to take the field. But he could also be over-enthusiastic. In the Cup match against Preston, so intent was he on stopping one of the opposing players scoring that he pulled the shirt form his back, an unusual occurrence in those days. Saul had two excellent seasons at Highfield Road before joining his home-town team, Rotherham County, in 1911.
Southern League debut for Coventry City v Swindon Town (a) 1 September 1909.

	S LEAGUE		*FA CUP*		*TOTAL*	
	App	*Gls*	*App*	*Gls*	*App*	*Gls*
1909-10	30	0	6	0	36	0
1910-11	29	0	1	0	30	0
	59	0	7	0	66	0

PERCY SAUL

In 1923, Coventry City changed their colours to civic green and red. That year they tried to change their fortunes, too, and a key to this was the signing of the now rotund, wily veteran Danny Shea from Fulham. At the time, Shea was the most famous player to appear for City, which is why they paid him a record £7 a week. Although 36 years old, he was still a delicate dribbler, able to unleash a thunderbolt shot. He spent two seasons with City, making 66 appearances and scoring 12 goals, before moving to Clapton Orient in February 1925. Born in Wapping on 6 November 1887, he began his career with West Ham United, where he was the leading Southern League scorer for two seasons, then moved to Blackburn Rovers in 1912 for a British record fee of £2,000. Shea gained his two England caps whilst at Ewood Park, in 1914, and also won a League Championship medal that year. During World War One he guested for West Ham, Fulham, Birmingham and Nottingham Forest and played in two Victory internationals in 1919. By then he was 33 and Blackburn allowed him to return to West Ham, but he struggled to maintain a first-team place at Upton Park and joined Fulham in December 1920, going on to make 100 appearances for the Cottagers before signing for Coventry. After Orient he played for Sheppey United and worked in the East London Docks. He died in East London on Christmas Day 1960, aged 73.
Football League debut for Coventry City v Barnsley (h) 25 August 1923.

	LEAGUE		*FA CUP*		*TOTAL*	
	App	*Gls*	*App*	*Gls*	*App*	*Gls*
1923-24	39	6	2	1	41	7
1924-25	23	5	2	0	25	5
	62	11	4	1	66	12

DANNY SHEA

NOEL SIMPSON

Born at Mansfield on 23 December 1922, Noel Simpson began his playing career in the Nottingham area and appeared for both Nottingham clubs in wartime league matches. After two seasons in Forest's first team, Billy Frith signed him for £8,000 in August 1948. Simpson quickly established himself and, apart from the 1950-51 and 1953-4 seasons, when he suffered serious knee injuries, he was the regular left-half for eight seasons. Simpson was a cultured player, although more of a ball-winner than a playmaker. In a period of great upheaval he was one of the few players to perform with any great consistency. Ian Jamieson took over at left-half in the 1956-7 season and manager Harry Warren decided that there was no place for Simpson in the side, even though he had been club captain for the previous two seasons. He moved to Exeter City towards the end of that season, at the age of 34, and it was there that he ended his career. When he retired from football, Simpson returned to his native Nottinghamshire where he died, after suffering a heart attack whilst playing golf, on 21 November 1987.

Football League debut for Coventry City v Brentford (a) 21 August 1948.

	LEAGUE		*FA CUP*		*TOTAL*	
	App	*Gls*	*App*	*Gls*	*App*	*Gls*
1948-49	33	1	0	0	33	1
1949-50	38	1	1	0	39	1
1950-51	16	2	0	0	16	2
1951-52	35	1	3	0	38	1
1952-53	33	1	3	0	36	1
1953-54	18	0	0	0	18	0
1954-55	25	0	4	0	29	0
1955-56	37	1	1	0	38	1
1956-57	23	0	0	0	23	0
	258	7	12	0	270	7

Born at Brierley Hill in the 1888s, Billy Smith started his career as a raw youngster with West Bromwich Baptists just after the turn of the century. He was a phenomenal marksman there and in one match, against Handsworth, he scored six times. Smith also had a very hard shot and was reputed to have broken the crossbar in one match. Apparently the ball came over from the right wing, he volleyed it against the bar and amidst a cracking of wood, the goalkeeper jumped for safety before it could crash down on his head. It is little wonder that Smith started to attract the attention of the bigger clubs. He joined Worcester City and then, in 1902, signed for West Brom. Smith was only 18 when he made his Second Division debut at outside-right. Alderman Fred Lee signed him on amateur terms for City in 1907. In his one Birmingham League season at Highfield Road, he scored 43 goals including five hat-tricks. Unfortunately at the end of the season, due to administrative incompetence, City failed to re-sign him and he joined Small Heath. He returned to Highfield Road in 1909-10 and was a great success, becoming a firm favourite with supporters and teammates alike. He was an unselfish player who would take the ball out to the wing before releasing it to a colleague in a better position. Perhaps his finest game was in the FA Cup at Sheffield Wednesday when he scored the winning goal. Smith had three good seasons before drifting away from Highfield Road for a year. He returned for 1913-14 but never recaptured his old form and retired from football at the end of that season. In an interview published in the *Coventry Herald* in 1938, Smith said that he was a foreman in an aircraft factory and rarely missed a match at Highfield Road. He was asked to name his all-time best City side and, interestingly, nominated five of his old colleagues, Bob Evans, Eli Bradley, Albert Lewis, Percy Saul and Harry Buckle.

BILLY SMITH

Birmingham League debut for Coventry City v Halesowen (h) 7 September 1907.

	LEAGUE		*FA CUP*		*TOTAL*	
	App	*Gls*	*App*	*Gls*	*App*	*Gls*
1907-08	33	33	9	5	42	38
1909-10	22	8	4	1	26	9
1910-11	23	7	4	1	27	8
1911-12	18	9	2	0	20	9
1913-14	15	0	0	0	15	0
	111	57	19	7	130	64

David Speedie, who was born at Glenrothes on 20 February 1960, began his career in the lower divisions of the Football League. After failing to win a first-team place at Barnsley he was signed by Darlington, for whom he scored 17 goals in 1981-2. This attracted Chelsea and Speedie moved to Stamford Bridge in 1982. After enjoying five very successful seasons in London, Coventry bought him for a club record £780,000, financed largely by the profits from their FA Cup success. For the next three and a half years, Speedie was a major figure at Highfield Road. Scoring on his League debut, he instantly became a great terrace favourite. He had a remarkable ability to alter the course of a game with a moment's inspiration and he possessed a perfect chip-shot, witness such goals against QPR, Norwich City and Wimbledon. Despite his lack of inches, he was a lethal marksman, using a combination of timing and athleticism to outleap defences. Injuries made it expedient to switch him to a midfield role in 1989 and, although he performed well, it was a pity to see him used in this way. In 1990 he was involved in an 'incident' with one of the club's vice-presidents and in December was sent off at Crystal Palace after verbally abusing a linesman. This, together with the arrival of a new manager, signalled the end for Speedie but it was still a surprise when, at 31, he moved to Liverpool for £700,000. A brilliant player on his day, he also had a well-formed sense of injustice and a penchant for exacting random revenge. This restricted his international appearances and probably cost him a place in the 1986 and 1990 World Cup finals.

Football League debut for Coventry City v Tottenham Hotspur (h) 15 August 1987.

	LEAGUE		*FA CUP*		*FL CUP*		*OTHERS*		*TOTAL*	
	App	*Gls*	*App*	*Gls*	*App*	*Gls*	*App*	*Gls*	*App*	*Gls*
1987-88	35/1	6	1/1	0	2	0	2	1	40/2	7
1988-89	36	14	1	0	3	1	1	0	41	15
1989-90	32	8	1	0	7	1	0	0	40	9
1990-91	18	3	0	0	3	1	0	0	21	4
	121/1	31	3/1	0	15	3	3	1	142/2	35

DAVID SPEEDIE

Colin Stein, who was born at Philipstown, Scotland, on 10 May 1947, was one of the most popular centre-forwards ever to play for Coventry City. With his all-action style and high work-rate the fans forgave his relatively low scoring ratio. It was a major sensation in Glasgow when the former Hibernian striker left Rangers in October 1972, for £100,000 plus winger Quinton Young. He was a hero at Ibrox, a current Scottish international and only five months earlier had scored one of the goals that won the European Cup-winners' Cup Final in Barcelona. When he joined City they were one place off the bottom of the League and, along with Hutchison, he played an influential role in their rise to a mid-table position after eight unbeaten games, and a run to the sixth round of the FA Cup. He won four full caps at the end of 1972-3, adding to the 17 he won with Rangers. In 1973-4, Stein found goals harder to come by, scoring only ten in 36 games including a hat-trick against Darlington in the League Cup. The following season he managed seven in 27 games before Gordon Milne transferred him back to Rangers for £80,000, as City sold their best assets to stay solvent. He doubled the attendance on his return to Ibrox but his career was in decline and he faded into early retirement in 1978. Stein's heading ability belied his 5ft 9in height and one of the comments used to describe him by a Scottish journalist was 'he would run through a brick wall for you'. He had excellent ball control and always led the line well. He played in the 1973 Common Market match at Wembley, for The Three versus The Six and scored a goal; he also scored the goal which inadvertently caused the Ibrox disaster in 1971, when hundreds pouring out of the ground turned back upon hearing the cheers.

Football League debut for Coventry City v Crystal Palace (a) 7 October 1972.

	LEAGUE		*FA CUP*		*FL CUP*		*TOTAL*	
	App	*Gls*	*App*	*Gls*	*App*	*Gls*	*App*	*Gls*
1972-73	31	10	4	2	0	0	35	12
1973-74	28	6	2	0	6	4	36	10
1974-75	24	6	2	0	1	1	27	7
	83	22	8	2	7	5	98	29

COLIN STEIN

Ray Straw was bought by Billy Frith in November 1957 to inject some life into a City side that seemed destined to become one of the founder members of Division Four. Unfortunately, Straw did not provide an immediate boost, City lost their next four games and eventually finished 19th in Division Three South. But his 27 League goals the following season helped City bounce back to Division Three. He was born at Ilkeston on 22 May 1933 and started his career with Ilkeston Town whilst working down the pit. He signed for First Division Derby County in October 1951 but it was not until 1955-6, when the Rams were in Division Three North, that he appeared regularly. The following season, Derby were champions and Straw equalled the club record with 37 goals in 44 League games. But after only five appearances in Division Two, he joined Coventry. Although City's form for the remainder of that season was poor, Straw scored 14 goals in 22 matches including two hat-tricks. Since Clarrie Bourton left the club, some 20 years earlier, Coventry fans had yearned for a goalscoring hero. Some, like Lowrie, Brown and Chisholm, had come close but it was left to Ray Straw to don the mantle. Some critics did not like his ungainly style, whilst others said he was too slow, but he had a fine shot in either foot and his heading ability was superb. In 1958-9 he was in devastating form. In one spell, after George Stewart had joined the club from Accrington Stanley in November, Straw scored in eight successive League and Cup games. Two matches were especially memorable for Straw that season: against Aldershot in September, when he scored a hat-trick in a 7-1 win; and against League leaders Port Vale in March, when he lashed home a rocket for the only goal of the game. He created history in the first match of the following season, against Mansfield Town in Division Three, when he became the first player to have appeared in all six divisions of the Football League. Fittingly, he scored in a 2-0 win and went on to average a goal every other game as City came close to instant promotion. The 1960-61 season was an anticlimax as City's form slumped, although Straw still managed 20 League and Cup goals, including one at Anfield. Surprisingly, he was allowed to join Mansfield Town at the end of the season. He stayed at Field Mill for two years, enjoying a third promotion, before finishing his career at non-League Lockheed-Leamington. There can be few less complicated characters to have played League soccer than Ray Straw, who was known to his Derby teammates as 'Toffee' because of his passion for sweets. He still lives at Ilkeston and works at a local power-station.

RAY STRAW

Football League debut for Coventry City v Millwall (h) 23 November 1957.

	LEAGUE		*FA CUP*		*FL CUP*		*TOTAL*	
	App	*Gls*	*App*	*Gls*	*App*	*Gls*	*App*	*Gls*
1957-58	22	14	1	0	-	-	23	14
1958-59	44	27	2	3	-	-	46	30
1959-60	43	20	2	1	-	-	45	21
1960-61	33	18	3	2	1	0	37	20
	142	79	8	6	1	0	151	85

Danny Thomas was born at Worksop on 12 November 1961 and of all the good youngsters to emerge from the youth team in the late-1970s, he was the outstanding figure. His elder brother, Val, had not been quite good enough for the first team but it was obvious from Danny's first game that he had the talent to become City's first full England international for over 25 years. Originally he was a midfielder, fast and skilful with vision and a freedom of movement and elasticity that reminded one of the Brazilians. He settled at full-back by chance, forced to play there as substitute at Villa Park in August 1980. Thomas took his chance and played a key role in the latter stages of the League Cup run that season, winning Under-21 honours after less than 20 League appearances and being voted City's player of the year. Under Dave Sexton he blossomed further, winning four more Under-21 caps and being selected for the full England squad in November 1982. One of his finest performances was at Maine Road in 1982, in City's FA Cup victory there. He was switched to midfield to mark Asa Hartford and did his job so well that the fiery Scot, in frustration, got himself sent off. Thomas' performances that season won him the Midland Player of the Year award and, for the second time, the City player's award. When Sexton was dismissed, Thomas was determined to go too and after winning his two full caps in Australia, he moved to Spurs for £300,000 in July 1983. He took time to settle, but after David Pleat arrived he began to blossom until suffering a serious knee injury after a brutal tackle by a QPR defender in March 1987. Alas, he never fully recovered and was forced to retire at the age of 26.

DANNY THOMAS

Debut for Coventry City v West Bromwich Albion (a) League Cup, 26 September 1979.

	LEAGUE		*FA CUP*		*FL CUP*		*TOTAL*	
	App	*Gls*	*App*	*Gls*	*App*	*Gls*	*App*	*Gls*
1979-80	0/3	0	0	0	1	0	1/3	0
1980-81	23/2	1	2/1	1	5/1	0	30/4	2
1981-82	39	1	4	0	2	0	45	1
1982-83	41	3	3	0	3	0	47	3
	103/5	5	9/1	1	11/1	0	123/7	6

Garry Thompson made his debut late in 1977-8 and appeared four more times before the end of the season. Thompson had all the qualities needed in a top-class striker — strength, aerial power, pace and exceptional courage. During the following season he vied with Ferguson for the central striking role, the highlight being the 4-3 home win over Manchester United when his domination of Gordon McQueen was almost embarrassing. Tragically, two weeks later Thompson broke a leg in training and was out of action for almost a year. Competition for the striking places had hotted up in his absence with the emergence of English and Hateley, but with Wallace sold and Ferguson injured, Thompson became a regular in 1980-81 and played a major role in the Sky Blues' success in the League Cup, scoring six goals. The semi-final first leg, at home to West Ham, enshrined him in City folklore when, after scoring an own-goal in the first half, he led an outstanding revival. He scored two goals including a memorable winner in the dying seconds. Thompson won six Under-21 caps in the period 1980-82 and scored three goals. He always looked more likely to succeed than Mark Hateley and under Dave Sexton his partnership with Hateley stuttered along; it was always tempting to pump the long balls in, but in February 1983, his sale to West Bromwich Albion for £225,000 sparked off the 1983 'Coventry revolution'. At West Brom, Thompson teamed up with Cyrille Regis but they never really hit it off and after only one full season, Regis made the reverse trip to Coventry. Thompson's scoring record improved and overall he netted 39 goals in 91 games for the Baggies before moving to Sheffield Wednesday in August 1985. For the Owls he scored six goals in 36 games and played in their losing FA Cup semi-final side in 1986. That summer he moved to Villa Park, where in a poor side he scored six goals in 31 games as Villa were relegated. Villa bounced back at the first attempt under Graham Taylor and Thompson helped them with 11 goals in 24 games. He moved to Watford in December 1988 and to Crystal Palace in March 1990, where his first-team opportunities have been limited. His brother, Keith, has also played in Coventry City's colours in two separate spells. Garry Thompson was born in Birmingham on 7 October 1959.
Football League debut for Coventry City v Aston Villa (h) 21 March 1978.

GARRY THOMPSON

	LEAGUE		*FA CUP*		*FL CUP*		*TOTAL*	
	App	*Gls*	*App*	*Gls*	*App*	*Gls*	*App*	*Gls*
1977-78	5/1	2	0	0	0	0	5/1	2
1978-79	19/1	8	2	0	0/1	1	21/2	9
1979-80	16/1	6	0	0	0	0	16/1	6
1980-81	34/1	8	4	1	7	6	45/1	15
1981-82	35/1	10	3	2	2	0	40/1	12
1982-83	18/2	4	2	1	3	0	23/2	5
	127/7	38	11	4	12/1	7	150/8	49

Charlie Tickle was born in Birmingham in 1884 and his first club was Selly Oak St Mary. He also played for another junior club before being snapped up by Small Heath in 1902. Tickle gained a big reputation as an outside-right at Small Heath and soon won a Junior international cap against Scotland. He played for the Football League in 1905-06. After six good seasons at the Birmingham club, he was given a benefit and placed on the transfer list. Trainer Ted Kinnear signed him for City in on 17 July 1908. To a large extent, Tickle carried Coventry's 1908-09 team. It was a weak side, although Tickle was adamant that they were all triers. He was soon made captain and after a series of bad results was even asked to select the team for the next match, which was won at New Brompton. Tickle was a skilful player who drove more than one defender to desperation with his speed and trickery. However, despite the rough treatment he received, he was rarely injured, playing in over 120 games for City, either as an outside-right or inside-right, before his retirement from professional football in 1911. After leaving City he played for Bournbrook again. He subsequently served in World War One.
Southern League debut for Coventry City v Crystal Palace (h) 1 September 1908.

	LEAGUE		*FA CUP*		*TOTAL*	
	App	*Gls*	*App*	*Gls*	*App*	*Gls*
1908-09	40	4	3	1	43	5
1909-10	37	4	6	0	43	4
1910-11	35	10	4	1	39	11
	112	18	13	2	125	20

CHARLIE TICKLE

CHARLIE TIMMINS

Born at Birmingham on 29 May 1922, right-back Charlie Timmins began his career with Jack Moulds Athletic, a Birmingham junior club, and signed for City in 1946. The right-back position was always a problem for City in the late-1940s and between 1946 and 1949, no less than eight different players filled the number-two slot but nobody was really able to establish himself. It was surprising, in the circumstances, that Timmins had to wait until August 1949 before he made his League debut at the age of 27. Even after that he never played more than 34 games in a season. He suffered quite a number of injuries and in the early 1950s vied with Ken Jones and Martin McDonnell, and in the mid-1950s with Frank Austin, for the number-two shirt. In 1956-7 he switched to left-back and played 20 times in that position the following season, his final one at Highfield Road. Thus, although he was at Highfield Road for 13 seasons, he played in only some 160 games. Nevertheless, he was a dependable player and very loyal to the club. Towards the end of his career he was appointed captain for a spell. In 1958, he moved to non-League Lockhead-Leamington, where he finished his career.

Football League debut for Coventry City v Luton Town (a) 24 August 1949.

	LEAGUE		*FA CUP*		*TOTAL*	
	App	*Gls*	*App*	*Gls*	*App*	*Gls*
1949-50	23	0	0	0	23	0
1950-51	33	0	1	0	34	0
1951-52	7	0	0	0	7	0
1952-53	11	0	0	0	11	0
1953-54	16	0	0	0	16	0
1954-55	9	1	0	0	9	1
1955-56	19	2	1	0	20	2
1956-57	23	1	1	0	24	1
1957-58	20	1	1	0	21	1
	161	5	4	0	165	5

ERNIE TOSELAND

Occasionally a player comes along, who, with just a few appearances to his name, finds a way into any club's history. In 1928-9, Ernie 'Twinkletoes' Toseland played only 23 games and scored 11 goals, and yet many contemporary reports describe him as City's most gifted player of the decade. Toseland joined City from Higham Ferrers for £50, after being spotted in a reserve game against City. In his first game, for the Reserves against Southampton, he suffered a badly broken collarbone and did not play for about a year. His sensational speed and dribbling skills became a legend in a Coventry side that was at last beginning to thrill its followers under James McIntyre's management. Veteran England international Billy Kirton was signed from Villa, for a record £1,700, to partner Toseland on the right wing, and City went briefly to the top of the League. First Division scouts were soon alerted to Toseland's skills and in March he was sold to Manchester City for a club record £3,000. He spent ten years with the Manchester club, making 368 appearances (61 goals) and representing the Football League. With Manchester City he won FA Cup winners' and League Championship medals before joining Sheffield Wednesday. War curtailed his Football League career but he was still playing Cheshire League football in 1945-6. He was born at Kettering in 1905 and died in Northampton in 1982.

Football League debut for Coventry City v Watford (a) 5 September 1928.

	LEAGUE		*FA CUP*		*TOTAL*	
	App	*Gls*	*App*	*Gls*	*App*	*Gls*
1928-29	22	11	1	0	23	11
	22	11	1	0	23	11

Born at Wallsend about 1888, 'Boxer' Turnbull, a blacksmith by trade, served his apprenticeship with the less important sides of the North-East. His first club was Carvelle, a village near Newcastle. Turnbull subsequently played for Wallsend Park Villa and Newcastle City in the Northern Alliance. Coventry City signed him from Ashington United in 1911 after he had scored 21 goals for Ashington the previous season. Turnbull became a firm favourite at Highfield Road. He was a bustling inside-forward, quick and clever with the ball, a player who bored through opposing defences and who was able to score goals, given half a chance. Although not tall, he was strongly built and able to take his share of knocks. He played 40 games for City before moving to Southampton in October 1912, for £55.
Southern League debut for Coventry City v Stoke (h) 16 September 1911.

	LEAGUE		FA CUP		TOTAL	
	App	Gls	App	Gls	App	Gls
1911-12	34	12	2	1	36	13
1912-13	4	0	0	0	4	0
	38	12	2	1	40	13

FRED 'BOXER' TURNBULL

Ian Wallace is the most recent City player to make his first-team debut after having already caused a stir of expectation by his form in the Reserves. When he burst on the scene in October 1976, his brave, aggressive and slightly reckless style, made him an instant hero with the fans. He was a born goalscorer and he remains the only City player to score over 20 in a First Division season. Wallace was born in Glasgow on 23 May 1956 and joined City as a 20-year-old from Dumbarton for £40,000, spending just under four years at Highfield Road. His first season was quite traumatic: just before Christmas he was involved in a road accident and was hurled through the windscreen, suffering severe cuts around an eye. He was out of action for two months, then, on his comeback, he was struck in the eye and had to be rushed to hospital. He bounced back again and, a few weeks later, celebrated his first season in Division One with a hat-trick against Peter Shilton, then with Stoke. His best season was 1977-8, when his striking partnership with Mick Ferguson was forged and they scored 40 goals between them. By 1979-80, things were beginning to go off the boil for Wallace and transfer talk was afoot. A general impression was that he was ill-equipped to cope with media attention and, towards the end, he appeared to be 'going through the motions' as he determined to move on. He joined Nottingham Forest for a club record £1,250,000, at a time when the transfer market was seriously overheated, but Forest were themselves going through a period of readjustment and Wallace's career took a downward turn. He joined Brest in 1984, Sunderland in 1985 and then moved to Australia in 1987 after a spell with CS Marítimo of Madeira. His international career also petered out after initial success. He scored on his debut for Scotland but won only three caps and was very unlucky not to go to Argentina for the 1978 World Cup finals.
Football League debut for Coventry City v Sunderland (substitute) (h) 3 October 1976.

	LEAGUE		FA CUP		FL CUP		TOTAL	
	App	Gls	App	Gls	App	Gls	App	Gls
1976-77	24/2	9	0	0	0	0	24/2	9
1977-78	41	21	1	0	4	2	46	23
1978-79	38	15	2	0	1	0	41	15
1979-80	25	13	1	0	1	0	27	13
	128/2	58	4	0	6	2	138/2	60

IAN WALLACE

LESLIE WARNER

Born in Birmingham on 19 December 1918, Leslie Warner — known as 'Plum' after the famous Middlesex and England cricketer Sir Pelham Warner — signed for City in the close season of 1937, from Birmingham junior club Jack Moulds Athletic, having previously played for Shirley Juniors. He quickly settled into the outside-right position in the London Combination side, but after an injury to George Taylor, was pitched into the first team at the age of only 19. Warner made a sensational debut, destroying the left flank of the Swansea defence and creating all the goals in Coventry's 5-0 victory. At the end of the match the crowd invaded the pitch and chaired him all the way to the dressing-room. However, Taylor quickly regained his place in the team and Warner played only a few more games before war broke out. He served in the Royal Warwickshire Regiment and spent most of the war in Northern Ireland. Warner returned to the club in Christmas 1945, taking over the number-seven shirt, but in the following two seasons he had competition from Dennis Simpson and his appearances were limited. Warner had great dribbling skills and was a good crosser of the ball, although subjected to some heavy tackling. However, he was inclined to over-elaborate; he would take on the whole of the opposing defence and then infuriate everyone by turning round and trying to beat them all again. This may have been why the more mundane Simpson was preferred on occasions. Warner's best season was 1950-51, when he and Norman Lockhart provided the ammunition in a free-scoring forward line spearheaded by Ted Roberts. He was still making regular appearances in 1952-3, but at the end of the following season he decided to call it a day and went into the bookmaking business in Coventry. 'Plum' was still living in Coventry at the time of his death in 1982.
Football League debut for Coventry City v Swansea Town (h) 26 February 1938.

	LEAGUE		*FA CUP*		*TOTAL*	
	App	*Gls*	*App*	*Gls*	*App*	*Gls*
1937-38	2	0	0	0	2	0
1938-39	4	0	0	0	4	0
1945-46	-	-	2	0	2	0
1946-47	16	0	0	0	16	0
1947-48	7	3	2	2	9	5
1948-49	29	3	1	0	30	3
1949-50	31	3	1	0	32	3
1950-51	41	4	1	0	42	4
1951-52	30	1	0	0	30	1
1952-53	34	5	3	1	37	6
1953-54	3	0	0	0	3	0
	197	19	10	3	207	22

ALF WOOD

Few players can say they made their final appearance for a club some 20 years after their debut, but such is the boast of goalkeeper Alf Wood. He appeared in City's promotion-chasing side of 1937-8 and in the promotion-winning side of 1958-9, becoming the third oldest player to play in League football since the war. He said of his recall to the first team, "I was really 43 when I came out of retirement to play for Coventry City after Jim Sanders had broken his leg. Everyone thought I was younger and I let them go on thinking that I was. They might not have played me if they had known. As I was feeling fit and well I didn't let on." Wood was born at Aldridge in Staffordshire on 14 May 1915 and signed for Coventry City in 1935, after playing for Nuneaton Town and Sutton Town. He made only two appearances in the first team before the outbreak of World War Two, both when regular goalkeeper Bill Morgan was injured. He was then called up into the Army and guested for Northampton Town, in the same side as Bob Dennison and Bill Shankly. Wood also played for the Army, when Frank Swift was unavailable. Towards the end of the war he contracted spinal meningitis and doctors told him he would never play again. Happily he recovered, re-signed for City in 1945 and went on to make 260 consecutive appearances (218 of them in the Football League) over the next six seasons. The story goes (and it is probably not apocryphal) that when asked for the team sheet by reporters, Harry Storer would say: "Wood and ten others." Alf Wood, in his heyday, was considered one of the finest uncapped goalkeepers. He was consistent and brave, giving many memorable performances. Perhaps his greatest game was the third round FA Cup tie at Sunderland in 1951, which, despite Wood making a number of courageous saves, City lost 2-0. In the days when centre-forwards took great delight in bundling goalkeepers into the net, Wood failed to complete a match only once, when he dislocated a finger stopping a shot from Grimsby Town's Tommy Briggs. Wood lost his place to Peter Taylor in September 1951 and in December was transferred to Northampton Town for £2,100. He dislocated his shoulder shortly after joining the Cobblers but he came back to make 98 consecutive appearances. He returned to Highfield Road in 1955, as assistant trainer, then came his 'Indian Summer' when he played 12 consecutive games between October and December 1958. He did not concede a goal in his first four games and brought the house down at Highfield Road on 1 November when he saved a Colin Addison penalty in a 2-0 win over York City. He finally hung up his boots after the 3-1 home FA Cup defeat by Plymouth Argyle and continued as the club's trainer. Sadly, Alf Wood was a victim of the revolution at Highfield Road in November 1961, following the FA Cup defeat by non-League King's Lynn. The club's statement, following the sacking, spoke of 'loyal and conscientious service', but nothing could compensate him for being shown the door after spending over half his life at Highfield Road. He took over as manager of Walsall in 1963-4 season and whilst there 'discovered' Allan Clarke. When he was given the sack — he was the 500th Football League manager to be dismissed since the end of the war — he got out of football for good. He moved back to Coventry in the mid-1960s, to work at Massey-Ferguson, and managed their football side whose players included former City favourites Lol Harvey, Brian Nicholas and Ron Farmer.

Football League debut for Coventry City v Swansea Town (a) 26 February 1938.

	LEAGUE		*FA CUP*		*TOTAL*	
	App	*Gls*	*App*	*Gls*	*App*	*Gls*
1937-38	1	0	0	0	1	0
1938-39	1	0	0	0	1	0
1945-46	-	-	2	0	2	0
1946-47	42	0	2	0	44	0
1947-48	42	0	2	0	44	0
1948-49	42	0	1	0	43	0
1949-50	42	0	1	0	43	0
1950-51	41	0	1	0	42	0
1951-52	10	0	0	0	10	0
1955-56	1	0	0	0	1	0
1956-57	2	0	1	0	3	0
1958-59	10	0	2	0	12	0
	234	0	12	0	246	0

Born in Birmingham around 1884, William Yates was spotted by Aston Villa whilst playing in junior football. He spent two seasons at Villa Park as an inside-forward, although he did not make their League side, and subsequently served Brighton, Manchester United, Hearts and Portsmouth, for whom he played from 1907 to 1911. Whilst he was with Hearts, Yates played in a Scottish Cup Final, the first Englishman to do so. He converted to half-back in his second season at Portsmouth. Yates joined City in May 1911 and rapidly made an impression as a sound, consistent footballer. He was a quick tackler, his footwork was above average and he had sound positional sense and a good shot. Yates was appointed captain in the 1912-13 season. He made over 100 appearances for the club before retiring at the end of 1913-14.

Southern League debut for Coventry City v Northampton Town (h) 2 September 1911.

WILLIAM YATES

	S LEAGUE		*FA CUP*		*TOTAL*	
	App	*Gls*	*App*	*Gls*	*App*	*Gls*
1911-12	38	0	2	0	40	0
1912-13	38	1	2	0	40	1
1913-14	30	0	1	0	31	0
	106	1	5	0	111	1

TERRY YORATH

Terry Yorath spent nine seasons at Leeds United, perennially consigned to the fringes of Don Revie's team of stars and using his occasional opportunities to catch the manager's eye with an array of wincing tackles. Indeed, his contribution did little to soften public attitudes to what was, at one and the same time, the most envied and most reviled side in the Football League. All this changed with his move to Highfield Road in August 1976, for £125,000. Yorath was immediately made captain and given a pivotal role in the centre of midfield. His qualities of leadership did much to steer City clear of relegation in 1977 and the following season he partnered Barry Powell when City adopted their attacking 4-2-4 formation; despite being outnumbered they often dominated the midfield in one of City's best First Division sides. Yorath was plagued by injury the following season and moved to Spurs for £275,000 in August 1979. Terry Yorath's time with City has tended to be mythologicized — the ferocious tackle sometimes obscuring the fact that his first touch and passing were never much to write home about — but he was a player who inspired those around him and was probably the finest First Division captain City have had. In 1986 he was offered the position of assistant to Don Mackay, which he eventually turned down. A few weeks later, Mackay was sacked and Curtis and Sillett took over, but who knows what might have been. Yorath has pursued a mangerial career that has taken him to Bradford City and Swansea City. Throughout his career he was a regular fixture in the Welsh team, winning 59 caps, and is currently the Wales national manager.
Football League debut for Coventry City v Liverpool (a) 4 September 1976.

	LEAGUE		*FA CUP*		*FL CUP*		*TOTAL*	
	App	*Gls*	*App*	*Gls*	*App*	*Gls*	*App*	*Gls*
1976-77	38	1	1	0	3	0	42	1
1977-78	40	2	1	0	3	0	44	2
1978-79	21	0	0	0	0	0	21	0
	99	3	2	0	6	0	107	3

An unusual training stint for Coventry City in 1947 at Warwick racecourse. Going through their paces are (left to right): Roberts, Smith, Dick Mason, Warner, Murphy, Lockhart, Lovering, Wood, Davidson, Barratt and George Mason.

Coventry City 3 Nottingham Forest 1

COVENTRY City went into this third round FA Cup game against First Division Nottingham Forest with one leading scalp already under their belts.

After wins at Wrexham and Kettering in the preliminary rounds, City had scored a sensational victory at Preston in the first-round proper. Few people had given them a chance at Deepdale, but City had won six of their previous seven Southern League games and had trained hard all week, the last two days in Blackpool.

In appalling conditions accurate football was impossible and Preston took the lead from a controversial penalty. Buckle equalized early in the second half and then Hendren grabbed the winner, slamming home a rebound after Tickle's drive from near the corner-flag was parried away by the goalkeeper.

Evans gave a brave display as Preston laid siege to the Coventry goal in the last 20 minutes and a little bit of history was made. City had triumphed in the first-ever meeting with First Division opposition.

City beat fellow Southern League side, Portsmouth, in the second round, again away from home, with a third-minute goal from Fred Chaplin.

Now, in the third round, City were at last drawn at home, against First Division Forest. Supporters from as far afield as Watford flocked to Highfield Road and special arrangements were made to accommodate what was expected to be a record crowd.

Forest, confident of victory, brought 2,000 fans with them. City had trained all week at Droitwich with a strict regime of walks and brine baths, whilst Forest had trained at Sutton-on-Sea.

City kept the side that had won at Preston and Portsmouth, with Warren retaining his place at inside-right in place of Arnold; Forest were at full strength with their captain, Welsh international Grenville Morris, returning to the side after a bout of flu.

The ground was on the soft side, after overnight rain, when Forest kicked off. The game started in lively fashion and City took the lead after only five minutes. Smith, receiving the ball from Warren, took advantage of hesitation in the Forest defence to shoot home.

Forest equalized after 20 minutes when a long cross from Hooper went to Morris, who found the back of the net.

Although City took the lead again before half-time, when a collision between Smith and Hasell left Warren with an open goal, it was still anybody's game.

However, in the second half City gradually took command. Their long-ball game was much more suited to the conditions than Forest's more elaborate style of play and it was no surprise when Smith, receiving a pass from the unselfish Warren, scored their third. Forest missed a penalty near the end of the game, but by then it was too late anyway and City ran out deserved winners.

Their reward for beating Forest was another home tie, this time against what was reputedly the richest club in the country, Everton, who had seven internationals on their books.

Everton wanted the tie switched to Goodison Park, but City refused and the match went ahead at Highfield Road in front of a record attendance of 19,095.

City were well beaten and a glorious Cup run came to an end. It would be over 60 years before City again reached the last eight of the competition.

Coventry City: Evans; Saul, Hanson, Hickleton, Bradley, Chaplin, Tickle, Warren, W.Smith, Hendren, Buckle.
Nottingham Forest: Hasell; Dudley, Maltby, Hughes, Wolfe, Needham, Hooper, Marrison, West, Morris, Palmer.
Referee: A.E.Farrant (Bristol) *Attendance: 12,500*

Coventry City in 1910. Back row (left to right): R.Kinnear (trainer), W.Hickleton, P.Saul, R.Evans, E.Bradley, W.Hanson, A.Chaplin. Front row: C.Tickle, G.Warren, W.Smith, E.Hendren, H.Buckle.

Match to Remember 2 — 14 January 1911

Sheffield Wednesday 1 Coventry City 2

SHEFFIELD Wednesday, with four internationals in their side, lying 12th in the First Division and with three successive wins behind them, did not carry out any special training for this first round FA Cup match.

However, as in the games against Preston and Forest the previous season, City found the heavy pitch to their liking and delighted their 2,000 travelling supporters by taking an early lead.

After a four-man move involving Bradley, Tickle, Smith and Welch, the ball went out to Buckle on the left. He gathered the ball on the run and, coming in from the wing, drove the ball past Davison in the Wednesday goal.

Sheffield appeared nervous after this early shock but managed to equalize with a scrambled goal from Wilson. Now City had to fight hard but they kept their nerve and gave as good as they got for the remainder of the half.

For the first 25 minutes of the second half, the Coventry goal was under constant siege, but Wednesday's shooting was poor and City's defence, with Saul, Evans and Bradley in excellent form, stood firm.

Sheffield had now shot their bolt and City carried the game to them. The winner came 12 minutes from time. Buckle won the ball from Spoors on the left-hand touch-line and passed to Smith in the middle. The Coventry centre-forward was off like a shot, as both backs desperately tried to close in, and with only a split-second to take aim, he slammed the ball wide of Davison and into the net to seal another glorious Coventry victory.

Sheffield Wednesday: Davison; Spoors, Holbem, Lloyd, O'Connell, Weir, Kirkman, Stringfellow, Glennon, Wilson, Robertson.
Coventry City: Evans; Saul, Barnacle, Johnson, Bradley, Chaplin, Parkes, Tickle, Smith, Welch, Buckle.
Referee: A.Baker (Nantwich) *Attendance: 19,603*

Match to Remember 3 11 January 1930

Coventry City 1 Sunderland 2

'FOOTBALL is booming in Coventry', wrote a well-known London daily newspaper correspondent early in 1930. City had just established a record League attendance, on Christmas Day against Plymouth Argyle, and were anticipating an all-time record 'gate' for this FA Cup third-round tie against the North-East giants from Roker Park.

Although their bank overdraft remained, City's financial position was slowly improving. The build-up to this match was recorded daily in the local newspapers, with visits to Droitwich brine baths, charabanc rides and a theatre visit all being on the team's agenda in the week before the match.

It was also suggested that Coventry supporters should wear caps (instead of trilbys or bowlers) and that wounded soldiers in wheelchairs should get to the ground by noon.

By two o'clock, Highfield Road was full with the ground a mass of blue and white favours — although City played in black and white stripes for the only time in their history — as home supporters created a terrific din.

The struggle that ensued on the pitch was worth going a long way to see. The game was hard-fought, intense, fast, energetic and, above all, so very even, for the contestants were fairly matched.

Sunderland opened in spirited fashion and scored a beauty after 19 minutes, when Gallacher got a rebound from Watson and sent an unstoppable shot past Allen.

City fought back strongly and both Lake and Pick went close as Coventry placed the Sunderland goal under siege.

The pressure continued after the break, as attack after attack was launched. The equalizer duly came on the hour, when Pick, who was finally getting past his full-back, centred for Loughlin to head down. Robinson, the Sunderland 'keeper, appeared to scoop the ball clear but it was adjudged to have crossed the line.

That goal set the home crowd seething with excitement and, time and again, good fortune came to Sunderland's aid. Then, ten minutes from the end and right out of the blue, came a gift goal for the visitors.

The ball was put tamely across the City goalmouth, three yards past the far upright. There appeared no danger as Allen, Bell and Watson were all there, but no one appeared to be sure whose ball it was.

Allen and Bell both went for it and the ball rolled across the empty goalmouth to Sunderland's Gurney, who was in like a flash. And that was that.

The local newspaper stated that the Bantams' performance had done more to recuperate them in their supporters' good books than a succession of League wins would have done. 'They are not a great side yet, their day is surely coming,' said the paper.

Coventry City: Allen; Crown, Watson, Stokes, Dinsdale, Bell, Richards, Widdowson, Loughlin, Lake, Pick.
Sunderland: Robinson; Oakley, England, Clunas, McDougall, Andrews, McLean, McKay, Gurney, Gallacher, Gunson.
Referee: W. Cousins (Sheffield) *Attendance: 31,673*

Match to Remember 4 — 28 April 1934

Coventry City 9 Bristol City 0

COVENTRY City's record victory came with the penultimate match of the 1933-4 season. Although there was little at stake in this encounter, City never let up from start to finish, peppering the unfortunate Ken Scattergood from the first minute.

Yet Scattergood, despite conceding nine goals, had a splended match, saving many more shots than he let in.

It was the sort of game where Clarrie Bourton could be seen at his vintage best, in the role of provider and scorer. As the Bristol City centre-half, Parker, allowed him too much room, Bourton constantly picked the ball up on the halfway line, sent sweeping passes to either White or Lake on the wings, and was ready to pick up the return in the penalty area.

It was 'Old Five' football at its flowing, brilliant best, the style of play that captivated the Highfield Road audience between 1931 and 1936.

The goals came at regular intervals and Bristol only made a fight of it in the final 30 minutes of the first half, when they played spirited football, with Loftus particularly prominent.

Jones opened the account for Coventry after five minutes, when he finished off clever approach work from close range. Lauderdale dribbled through the Bristol defence to slot home the second after seven minutes, and Bourton crashed in the third after a quarter of an hour.

The match virtually ended as a contest at the end of the first half, when White ran through to slide the ball home in the 43rd minute and Bourton scored with a simple close-range effort on the whistle.

The rout continued after the break, with a beauty from Jones on 50 minutes and further goals from Bourton (72 and 86 minutes) and White (83 minutes) completed the scoreline. Bristol's cup of woe was complete when, with a couple of minutes remaining, Riley blasted wide from the penalty-spot.

It was a pity the match was watched by a crowd of only 7,035, the lowest of the season.

Coventry City: Pearson; Brown, Bisby, Perry, Davison, Frith, White, Lauderdale, Bourton, Jones, Lake.

Bristol City: Scattergood; Roberts, Birks, Morgan, Parker, Brinton, Horner, Banfield, Riley, Loftus, Scriven.

Referee: F. Wort (London) *Attendance: 7,035*

Match to Remember 5 25 April 1936

Luton Town 1 Coventry City 1

THICK fog in December had led to the postponement of the originally scheduled fixture against Luton Town at Highfield Road. Now, after a spell of confusion when matches were announced only on the day before, to thwart the pools companies who were in dispute with the Football League, both Luton games were fixed for a three-day period at the end of April.

And fate conspired that both teams would be fighting it out for promotion at the top of the Third Division South. City went into the game level on points but with a vastly superior goal-average and today, both games would have been all-

Packing them in at Highfield Road. A crowd marshall organizes part of the huge attendance which saw the second game against Luton Town.

City goalkeeper Morgan fields the ball with Astley and Smith looking on.

ticket affairs. Indeed, even half a century ago, many complained when this was not the case and thousands were locked out with massive crushes in and around both grounds. Only the good nature of supporters and the cheery attitude of the police averted some ugly scenes.

The game at Luton was described as one of the most exciting ever to involve Coventry City. And City's achievement in fighting back for a point after being reduced to ten fit men when Mason injured a knee early in the game, was a particularly fine effort.

Luton had swarmed forward at Kenilworth Road but City had held firm, with some fine goalkeeping from Morgan, until ten-goal Joe Payne scored for the Hatters after a freak overhead kick from Martin. Then it was City's turn to hit back and only some rough play and some fine saves from Dolman kept them at bay until Bourton sent the large City contingent into raptures when he equalized after 78 minutes. Near the end, Bourton almost snatched the winner.

The scene was set for a gripping finale at Highfield Road 48 hours later but Coventry now had a psychological advantage, with their last two games at home, although they would be without the injured Mason.

The second encounter was nearly as thrilling as the first and Luton used some heavy tactics to stop Bourton. But overall it was a defender's day, with Elliott giving a superb display to check Payne, a goalless draw helped City towards Division Two, where Luton joined them 12 months later. The attendance of 42,975 was a new record, over 10,000 more than the Sunderland match in 1930.

Luton Town: Dolman; Mackay, Smith, Finlayson, Nelson, Godfrey, Hodge, Martin, Payne, Roberts, Stephenson.

Coventry City: Morgan; Astley, Smith, Frith, Mason, Curtis, McNestry, Lauderdale, Bourton, Lake, Liddle.

Referee: W. Walden (West Bridgford) *Attendance: 23,142*

Match to Remember 6 8 January 1955

Huddersfield Town 3 Coventry City 3

THERE was no indication from their form over the previous few matches to suggest that Coventry City would cause any problems for a First Division team rated second favourites for the FA Cup and containing four internationals.

However, City surprised their 500 supporters who had made the trip to Leeds Road with a remarkably couragous display in this third-round game.

They took the lead in only the fourth minute with a beautifully worked goal involving Simpson, Capel, Alan Moore (who had joined City from Nottingham Forest for £10,000 only two weeks previously) and Eric Johnson, who learned just before the match that he had become a father for the second time.

Johnson crossed the ball first time and Capel was on hand to sweep it home.

The pitch had been liberally sanded but Town, making light of the conditions, played good football and, showing greater speed and mobility in attack, put the City defence under constant pressure for the remainder of the half.

The whole City team performed heroically. Reg Matthews, in particular, was superb, diving, sprawling, twisting and leaping like a deer. However, even he could

Coventry City, 1954-5, 'the team that Jack built'. Back row (left to right): Johnson, Bradbury, Cook, Jamieson, J.Hill, Jones, Austin, Sambrook, McDonnell. Middle row: Jack Fairbrother (manager), Dutton, Hawkings, Taylor, Dorman, Simpson, Matthews, Mason, Timmins, V.Brown (trainer). Front row: Kirk, Brown, Nutt, P.Hill, Cresswell, Wassall, Harvey, Lane. On ground: Collindridge, Capel.

do nothing to prevent the two goals scored by Jimmy Glazzard in the 28th and 34th minutes.

It looked all over in the 57th minute, when Watson added a third, but only seven minutes later Lee pulled one back. Then, with seven minutes remaining, City equalized. Capel gathered the ball after Taylor miskicked, ran through the mud with two defenders at his heels and smashed the ball home with almost contemptuous ease.

It was all City in the last few minutes but they could not get the winner and the game finished all-square. Unfortunately, City were not able to continue where they left off, losing the replay at Highfield Road the following Thursday, 2-1 after extra-time.

But those supporters who travelled to Leeds Road on that cold Saturday in January, saw a City side in truly inspired form and displaying a brand of courage that was sadly lacking for the remainder of the season.

Huddersfield Town: Wheeler; Staniforth, Kelly, McGarry, Taylor, Quested, Burrell, Watson, Glazzard, Cavanagh, Metcalf.
Coventry City: Matthews; Jones, Kirk, Harvey, McDonnell, Simpson, Moore, P.Hill, Lee, Capel, Johnson.
Referee: H.J.Husband (London) *Attendance: 31,576*

Match to Remember 7 — 25 March 1963

Coventry City 2 Sunderland 1

LIKE a wild mammoth freed from years of entombment in ice, Coventry City burst out of the big freeze of 1963 and into a run that would carry them through to the quarter-finals of the FA Cup and to the brink of Second Division football.

All this was heady stuff for their loyal supporters, who had been fed on a diet of despair and failure for a quarter of a century.

There had been indications of an up-turn the previous autumn, as the new broom swept away the cobwebs both on and off the pitch. But it was the FA Cup run that really brought the momentum back to the club, as Lincoln City and then Portsmouth were eliminated, the latter after a three-match marathon.

With the competition now well behind schedule, the draws for both fifth and sixth rounds had already been made and excitement mounted as both Sunderland and Manchester United appeared as potential visitors to Highfield Road.

It would be the Sunderland match, however, that would live on as a legend in Coventry football folklore as supporters finally rid themselves of the years of frustration.

Those who were there on that clear spring evening will never forget it. In their excitement to see the game, the fans broke down three gates to gain entrance and it has always been widely believed that the final attendance was over 50,000 as against the officially reported figure of 40,487.

The match itself was worthy of the occasion as City, urged on by the fanatical crowd, stormed back from being a goal down to score twice in the last eight minutes to clinch victory.

Johnny Crossan had put Sunderland ahead after 33 minutes of what was a slightly

Above and below: Two views of Deitmar Bruck's equalizing goal against Sunderland with ten minutes to play. The City left-half deceived Jim Montgomery with a shot-cum-centre which hit the angle and fell into the net.

tentative first half. After the break, though, there was only one team in it as City hurled wave after wave of attacks at the Sunderland goal.

It seemed as if Charlie Hurley and his defenders might hold out, until a freak goal put City back on terms. A lob-cum centre from young defencer Dietmar Bruck deceived Jim Montgomery, hit the angle and fell into the net.

Pandemonium broke out as hundreds of fans ran on to the pitch, a situation to be repeated three minutes later when George Curtis rose above the Sunderland defence to powerfully head home a John Sillett centre, the same partnership that would bring even more excitement to the club 24 years later.

The abiding memory of the final five minutes is of the deafening sound of the *Sky Blue Song* reaching out all over the ground and the shell-shocked look of the Sunderland players as they went through the motions.

The following day, Jimmy Hill and his team were the toast of all football followers, outside Wearside of course. There was to be no fairy-tale ending to the Cup run, but as far as the Sky Blue revolution is concerned, it was the evening that the club and its supporters stormed the winter palace.

Coventry City: Wesson; Sillett, Kearns, Hill, Curtis, Bruck, Humphries, Barr, Bly, Whitehouse, Rees.
Sunderland: Montgomery; Nelson, Ashhurst, Anderson, Hurley, McNab, Davison, Herd, Sharkey, Crossan, Mulhall.
Referee: G.McCabe (Sheffield) *Attendance: 40,487*

Match to Remember 8 — 25 April 1964

Coventry City 1 Colchester United 0

FOR those too young to have experienced the early Sky Blue era, it is difficult to convey the level of passion and involvement surrounding it. It was surpassed only by the FA Cup run of 1987, the difference being that the 1987 glory was confined to six games, whilst in the 1960s, the fever pitch was sustained over several years.

And it was all fuelled by a conviction that victory, in the end, was the logical outcome for City, and defeat almost unthinkable.

At the centre of all this was the charismatic figure of Jimmy Hill and at the heart of the team the behemothic presence of skipper George Curtis.

Curious then perhaps, that the usual focus of attention was the centre-forward George Hudson. Statisticians will demonstrate that his goal tally cannot compare with those greats from the past, Clarrie Bourton, Billy Smith, or even Frank Mobley; similarly, the modern fan, familiar only with the First Division, will argue that strikers operating in the lower divisions cannot be compared to their more recent counterparts like Ian Wallace, Terry Gibson and Cyrille Regis.

But for those of us who remember that era, there was only one George Hudson. And the Colchester game of April 1964 was as much about Hudson as it was about Coventry City.

City began the season in blistering style, opening up a nine-point gap at the top of Division Three by the New Year, with Hudson having already amassed 26 goals in League and Cup.

Then came a collapse. From 11 January until the end of March, City failed to win a match and finally lost their top place. A hypnotist offered his services but Hill opted for the transfer market, buying George Kirby and John Smith for £24,000.

The legendary George Hudson scores the only goal of the game against Colchester United and City are on the way back to the Second Division after a 12-year absence.

Young City fans celebrate as City clinch the Third Division title.

Kirby scored a hat-trick on his home debut and the City promotion train was back on the rails, albeit totally lacking the style of the early season. And Hudson was suddenly out of favour and consigned to the Reserves, where he was attracting crowds of 4,000.

After beating Queen's Park Rangers, City went briefly, back to the top of the table with three games to go and a nervously-gained point at Millwall. Then came Peterborough and the largest pre-Hillsborough exodus of City fans, as 13,000 trekked across the Midlands. They witnessed a disaster as City went down 2-0 to leave the top of the table thus:

1. Crystal Palace	P44, Pts 59
2. Coventry City	P45, Pts 58
3. Watford	P44, Pts 57

The following day, however, the gods came to the rescue. Watford drew at home to Brentford, which meant that City would go into the final game knowing victory over Colchester would ensure promotion.

On Wednesday, the *Telegraph's* front-page headline announced that Hudson was back and the scene was set for the final act.

In front of a crowd of 36,901, City opened in style and the breakthrough came in the 24th minute. A long ball down the left had the Colchester defence back-pedalling as winger Ronnie Rees whipped over a lightning cross and there was Hudson to slam the ball home.

Moments later, Hudson nearly scored again and Colchester were lucky to get off at half-time only one goal adrift. But as news filtered through that their two rivals were losing, nerves gripped the side.

Finally, it was announced Palace had lost 4-1 at home to Oldham, and Watford had gone down at Luton Town, both games had kicked off 15 minutes earlier. So the final 15 minutes were played out in an atmosphere of mounting hysteria. At the final whistle the crowd poured on to the pitch to celebrate Coventry City's first promotion for 28 years — and as Third Division champions, too.

Coventry City: Wesson; Sillett, Kearns, Hill, Curtis, Farmer, Humphries, Hudson, Kirby, Smith, Rees.
Colchester United: Ames; Forbes, Fowler, McCrohan, Rutter, Docherty, Grice, Hill, King, Stark, Wright.
Referee: H.Richards (Oldham) *Attendance: 36,901*

Match to Remember 9 28 December 1964

Coventry City 3 Preston North End 0

CONDITIONS at Highfield Road on this freezing cold night were hardly conducive to good football. The pitch was snowbound and as the game wore on, the surface became more and more like an ice rink.

But City defied the elements in this Second Division game and in outclassing Preston, reached heights of skill and control which would have been exceptional, even under normal conditions.

The star of the show was George Hudson, who gave one of the finest individual performances ever seen at Highfield Road. His passes were accurate, he fought unstintingly, cheekily jinked his way around Preston defenders as if they didn't exist, and his ball-control had to be seen to be believed.

Poor Singleton, Preston's centre-half, who had the unenviable job of trying to mark Hudson, was driven to distraction.

City scored only three times but it should have been many more. After five minutes, Hudson moved in sharply on Glazier's long downfield punt and headed sideways to Machin, who headed past Barton.

Machin should have scored again after 20 minutes but hit the post and there were several more hair-raising escapes for Preston before City scored their second. Rees fed Hudson, who, with Barton rushing out, nonchalently chipped the ball over his head. The goalkeeper's hands touched the ball but it tucked in under the bar for a brilliantly-taken goal.

Five minutes after the interval, Hill swung a free-kick into the goalmouth and Humphries was on hand to slide the ball home.

Ten minutes from time, Hudson came desperately close to scoring a second goal when he placed the ball over Barton's head, only to see it rebound from the crossbar into the goalkeeper's hands. Preston had their moments but by the end they were a well-beaten side.

Coventry City: Glazier; Sillett, Hill, Bruck, Curtis, Kearns, Humphries, Machin, Hudson, Hale, Rees.
Preston North End: Barton; Ross, Smith, Davidson, Singleton, Cranson, Wilson, Godfrey, Dawson, Spavin, Holden.
Referee: J.Finney (Hereford) *Attendance: 22,667*

Match to Remember 10 — 29 April 1967

Coventry City 3 Wolverhampton Wanderers 1

COVENTRY City supporters who witnessed this titantic struggle will never forget it — the dramatic atmosphere and sheer electricity of the occasion giving a champagne climax to the greatest season in the club's history up to that time.

The previous week both teams had assured themselves of promotion. Now all that remained was the destiny of the Second Division championship.

Jimmy Hill labelled it the 'Midlands Match of the Century' and he was probably right as a vast throng of football fans made their way to Highfield Road that day. The gates were closed with a crowd in excess of 51,000 crammed inside, far too many for the stadium to hold in comfort as the swaying terraces and crowded touch-lines demonstrated.

For the first hour of the match, Wolves were the superior team and led through a Peter Knowles goal after 40 minutes, after Curtis had mishit a clearance to Derek Dougan's feet.

The turning point came on the hour, when Rees sped past Mike Bailey and centred to Gibson. He touched the ball on to Machin and the Coventry man levelled the scores with a drive from close range.

Now it was Gibson's turn to take the game by the scruff of the neck and within five minutes City were in front after Gibson received a pass from Tudor, flicked it over a defender's head and then ran on to lob his shot past a bemused Phil Parkes in the Wolves goal.

Both these goals triggered off pitch invasions by ecstatic Coventry fans and the referee indicated that a further instance would result in him abandoning the game.

There was still some life left in Wolves and first Knowles hit an upright and then Kearns headed off the line with Glazier beaten.

Four minutes from the end, though, it was all over after an interchange of passes between Gibson and Machin set up a chance for Rees to complete the scoring. This time not one of the thousands around the touch-line encroached upon the playing area — a remarkable feat of restraint.

When the final whistle blew, the crowd did spill on to the pitch and into the area in front of the Main Stand. After a while, the players emerged from the directors' box and the crowd, led by Jimmy Hill, sang the *Sky Blue Song* as the champagne

Ian Gibson has just put City ahead against Wolves and hundreds of fans run on to the pitch to join in the celebrations.

flowed freely amidst scenes which eclipsed even those which followed the famous Torquay United and Sunderland games in 1936 and 1963 respectively.

The championship was finally clinched two weeks later and was met with similar celebrations. It had been a dramatic end to the season and the Sky Blue express seemed to be heading ever upwards. It was, however, the zenith of the Sky Blue revolution and things would never be quite the same again,

Coventry City: Glazier; Kearns, Bruck, Lewis, Curtis, Clements, Key, Machin, Tudor, Gibson, Rees.
Wolverhampton Wanderers: Parkes; Bailey, Thomson, Hunt, Hawkins, Holsgrove, Wharton, Knowles, Dougan, Burnside, Wagstaffe.
Referee: N.Callender (Richmond, Yorkshire) *Attendance: 51,455*

Match to Remember 11 19 May 1977

Coventry City 2 Bristol City 2

AN INTRIGUING First Division relegation struggle ended in the most bizarre circumstances and Sunderland, playing at Goodison Park, were relegated, when any result, other than a draw at Highfield Road, would have given them a reprieve.

The position at the start of the evening was as follows:

	Pld	Pts	Gl-dif
18. Sunderland	41	34	-6
19. Bristol City	41	34	-10
20. Coventry City	41	34	-11
21. Stoke City	42	34	-23
22. Tottenham Hotspur	42	33	-24

The simple facts were that Coventry and Bristol had to win to stay up, unless they wanted to rely upon Sunderland losing. Coventry had recovered some form after a disastrous spring, when they went 13 games without a win and slipped from mid-table into the relegation zone. New faces had been drafted in, including a goalscorer in Wallace, whilst Holton gave some security at the back and Sealey was in for the injured Blyth.

Coventry had looked too good to go down, but they needed points for survival. A large, almost capacity crowd had assembled but the start was delayed for five minutes to allow all the Bristol fans to get into the ground.

That five minutes could have saved Coventry's First Division life. They attacked the Kop and after a ponderous start went ahead on 15 minutes, when Hutchison shot home for his second goal of the season, after Shaw palmed away a cross.

Bristol, however, were matching Coventry and McDonald cleared off the line. Sealey saved well from Tainton's 20-yard effort but just before half-time let a shot through his hands. Luckily it went past the post.

Hutchison began to weave his magic in the second half and a mazy run set up Powell, who went close. But on 52 minutes the same player put Coventry 2-0 ahead, shooting in off the bar after Powell's shot had hit a post.

Within a minute, though, Bristol pulled one back, Gerry Gow scoring with a low shot after combining neatly with Gillies.

The visitors, roared on by their travelling fans, pressed hard and with 11 minutes

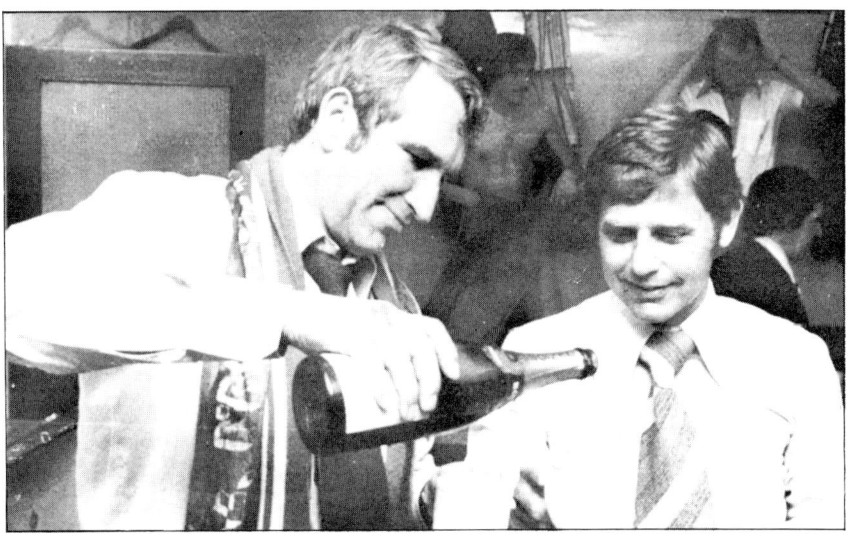

Bristol City boss Alan Dick (left) pours champagne for City manager Gordon Milne after the two sides had ensured their First Division futures with a 2-2 draw at Highfield Road.

left they got the equalizer. Gillies, overlapping on the right, squeezed a shot in at the near post.

For the next five minutes Coventry were 'dead', their composure went and they were forced to kick the ball upfield in desperation; Bristol, meanwhile, were cool and going for the kill.

Suddenly the score-board proclaimed that Sunderland had lost and, therefore, as long as the score at Highfield Road remained level, then both teams were safe.

The remaining minutes were played out in Bristol City's half of the field, their players passing between themselves, knowing that they were safe.

The scenes at the end were as though both teams had won the Cup. Rival players hugged on the pitch and fans danced with delight. Sunderland lodged a complaint and the Football League carried out an enquiry, but most fans agreed that Coventry and Bristol were too good to be relegated and that the Wearsiders deserved their fate.

Coventry City: Sealey; Oakey, McDonald, Yorath, Holton, Coop, Beck, Wallace, Ferguson, Powell, Hutchison.
Bristol City: Shaw; Gillies, Sweeney, Gow, Collier, Hunter, Tainton, Ritchie, Garland, Mann, Whitehead(Cormack).
Referee: R.Challis (Tonbridge) *Attendance: 36,903*

Match to Remember 12 — 4 October 1977

Coventry City 4 Manchester City 2

THE *Coventry Evening Telegraph* described this as one of the most gripping First Division games for years and there would have been few people present that night who would have disagreed.

Manchester City came to Highfield Road as title favourites and League leaders, having conceded only four goals in eight games. Coventry were in 11th place in the table and doubts were already being expressed about the 4-2-4 system which Gordon Milne had introduced at the beginning of the season.

Manchester City were magnificent in the first half. They took the lead after only four minutes, when Tueart swept the ball home with his right foot from Royle's headed pass. Barnes and Tueart were in devastating form and the Sky Blues might have conceded more but, surprisingly they equalized on the half-hour.

Wallace fed a perfectly weighted ball to Beck on the right and he pulled the ball back for Ferguson to shoot home. Sealey saved a Royle header spectacularly just before the interval, but he could do nothing a minute later when Barnes latched on to a long ball upfield from Clements and found the corner of the net.

The second half was a complete contrast: for the first 30 minutes the Sky Blues attacked non-stop, but they could not find a way through the City defence.

Then in the 73rd minute, Powell set Oakey free on the right, the full back's measured pass was flicked on by Beck and Ferguson came through to beat Corrigan with a lob high into the net.

Six minutes later, Yorath floated a pass into the heart of the Manchester City defence, Ferguson leapt high to glide the ball into the path of Wallace, who flicked the ball into the roof of the net.

Ian Wallace and Mike Ferguson, the goalscoring heroes of Coventry City's win over Manchester City in one of the most gripping First Division games for years.

Manchester came back after that, but in the last minute Hutchison centred from the left, Ferguson took the ball on his chest and, as it dropped, planted a shot wide of Corrigan to secure his hat-trick.

City left the field to a well-deserved standing ovation. It had been a truly magnificent match, marred only by some over-exuberant play by Manchester which resulted in five of their players being booked.

Coventry City: Sealey; Oakey, McDonald, Yorath, Holton, Coop, Beck, Wallace, Ferguson, Powell, Hutchison.
Manchester City: Corrigan; Clements, Donachie, Kidd, Watson, Booth, Barnes, Power, Royle, Hartford, Tueart.
Referee: B.Martin (Keyworth) *Attendance: 19,586*

Match to Remember 13 27 December 1977

Coventry City 5 Norwich City 4

THE build-up to this match gave no indication that the game would be a nine-goal thriller and one of the most exciting matches at Highfield Road since World War Two.

City's excellent start to the season had faded and since going third in the League on 19 November they had gone five games without a win, including a demoralizing 6-0 defeat at Everton.

Before the match they stood eighth, one place behind their visitors. A good draw the previous day in the local derby match at Villa Park had proved an unhappy encounter for an already injury hit Coventry, with Graham Oakey sustaining a serious injury that was ultimately to force his retirement.

Ray Graydon turns in delight after scoring what turned out to be the winning goal, thanks to Jim Blyth's late penalty save.

Holton and Coop were also on the injured list and Beck and Yorath were forced to play in the back four, Ray Gooding getting a rare game in midfield.

Coventry started strongly, attacking the Kop, and the Wallace-Ferguson partnership was soon in action, Wallace flicking into Ferguson's path and Keelan saving well from the big man's volley.

The home side, though, were 2-0 up after 21 minutes, thanks to a Barry Powell penalty (his first for the club and City's 500th goal in Division One) and a spectacular second from Wallace.

In a crowded penalty area, Wallace swivelled in mid-air to score with a glorious bicycle-kick which brought the whole ground to its feet, including Norwich manager, John Bond.

Wallace's 16th goal of that season must be rated one of the finest of the Division One era.

However, three Norwich goals in 13 minutes brought City down to earth: a John Ryan penalty and two goals from future million-pound striker Kevin Reeves. In addition, former England star Martin Peters had a goal disallowed for offside.

The second half continued at a hectic pace and Gooding brought Coventry level with a thunderous shot from the edge of the box for his first-ever City goal.

Ten minutes later, Bobby McDonald put them ahead with a delicate, curling shot around Keelan and the Sky Blues had two more goals disallowed before the Canaries bounced back with Peters heading an equalizer and then hitting a post with a free-kick.

The winner came after 81 minutes, when Graydon headed over Keelan. Coventry were now in rampant mood but even then the excitement was not over.

With 90 seconds remaining, Norwich were awarded the third penalty of the match, which Jim Blyth brilliantly saved to give Coventry victory and extend the visitors' dismal record at Highfield Road to 17 successive defeats and no wins since 1933.

Afterwards, John Bond described the game as one of the most exciting he had ever seen as the holiday crowd went home buzzing with excitement.

Coventry City: Blyth; Beck, McDonald, Yorath, Roberts, Gooding, Graydon, Wallace, Ferguson, Powell, Hutchison..
Norwich City: Keelan; Bond, Sullivan, Ryan, Jones, Powell, Neighbour, Suggett, Gibbins, Reeves, Peters.
Referee: L.Shapter (Newton Abbott) *Attendance: 21,578*

Match to Remember 14 27 January 1981

Coventry City 3 West Ham United 2

COVENTRY City reached their first major semi-final in 1980-81, when they reached the last four of the Football League Cup.

After winning both legs of a tough second-round tie against Manchester United, they achieved three outstanding away results to reach the semi-final stage. In round three, a good 2-1 win at First Division Brighton, in round four a 1-0 victory at Cambridge, after a draw at Coventry, and in a fifth-round replay, a 5-0 hammering of Watford at Vicarage Road.

That gave City an appointment with West Ham, top of the Second Division.

Garry Thompson scores the first of his two goals as West Ham 'keeper Phil Parkes lunges at his feet.

Both legs were marvellous entertainment and with 18 minutes left in the first game at Highfield Road, West Ham appeared to be heading for their second Wembley final in successive seasons, when they led by two soft goals given to them by City in the first half.

In those sensational last 18 minutes, though, the Sky Blues scored three goals to give themselves a chance in the second leg at Upton Park and the villain of the first half, Garry Thompson, netted twice, including the winner with the last kick of the match.

It was a triumph for the courage and persistence of City's young side, who received tremendous support from the all-ticket crowd.

Two terrible errors had put West Ham into the driving seat; first Sealey seemed to have a harmless header from Bond's covered, but it squirmed out of his grasp and rolled agonizingly over the line. Then, eight minutes later, Thompson, chasing back to dispossess Devonshire, won the ball and poked it back to Sealey, only to see that the 'keeper had come off his line and the ball had trickled past him into the net.

The big striker fell to the ground in dismay and had to be consoled and helped to his feet by Steve Hunt before he could continue. Then Hunt turned to the West

End and raised a clenched fist which implored vocal help; from then on, the fans were behind City.

Coventry tried to rescue the game with some exciting, attacking football but they were thwarted by the goalkeeping of Parkes and the efforts of Billy Bonds and his well-marshalled defence.

When it seemed as if City were to be denied, they got the breakthrough they deserved. Thompson, put clear by Blair, steered the ball past the advancing Parkes; and four minutes later, Gerry Daly scored after Parkes could only parry Danny Thomas' fierce shot.

The game had now reached a breathtaking climax. With five minutes to go former City star David Cross met a low cross from Goddard and his firm shot flew into the net past Sealey but Allen was given offside.

Then, in the 90th minute, Thompson collected a short, square pass from Hunt and fooled Alvin Martin before shooting low into the left-hand corner of the net almost in the same movement. City had a vital one-goal advantage to take to Upton Park.

Alas, the second leg never matched the first for drama. City survived for the first hour of intense West Ham pressure, when the East Enders looked far better than a Second Division team. Devonshire and Brooking were outstanding in midfield and Sealey kept City in the game with some brilliant saves.

Then Paul Goddard found space to turn on the edge of the penalty area and hit a stunning shot past Sealey to bring the Hammers level and give them the initiative.

The goal jerked City into some action and four minutes later, Cross had to clear a Thompson header off the line with a spectacular overhead kick; and with ten minutes left, Parkes spectacularly saved a Daly volley which looked like counting.

Despite the vocal support of 10,000 fans in a crowd of nearly 36,000, Coventry's luck finally ran out in the 89th minute when Thompson was penalized for an obscure offence on Bonds and the resulting free-kick was missed by City's defence. Neighbour, looking offside, was on hand to make the aggregate score 4-3.

On the night, City did not do themselves justice. They suffered from nerves and were outplayed by a more experienced side. West Ham went on to the Final at Wembley, where they lost in a replay to Liverpool.

Coventry City: Sealey; Thomas, Roberts, Blair, Dyson, Gillespie, Bodak, Daly(Jacobs), G.Thompson, Hateley, Hunt.
West Ham United: Parkes; Stewart, Brush, Bonds, Martin, Devonshire, Allen, Goddard, Cross, Brooking, Pike.
Referee: G.Courtney (Spennymoor) *Attendance: 35,468*

Match to Remember 15 4 May 1982

Southampton 5 Coventry City 5

THE superlatives rolled off the pens of the Press corps after this result at The Dell. Breathtaking, exhilarating, unbelievable, memorable, all adjectives used to describe only the second 5-5 draw in Coventry's history, the first coming in 1932 against Fulham.

Southampton were fighting hard for a UEFA Cup place and had their traditional outstanding home record, whilst City were enjoying a good end-of-season run and had beaten Sunderland 6-1 the previous week.

It was a feast of football and the goals and excitement had the crowd in almost hysterical mood and left Southampton substitute Danny Wallace believing that his side had lost 5-4 until his teammates corrected him in the dressing-room.

Apart from the number of goals, the quality of most of them was outstanding and Mark Hateley scored his first senior hat-trick.

Steve Whitton started the feast in the 11th minute, volleying in at the far post after Steve Hunt's looping cross exposed the Saints' defence.

Kevin Keegan equalized after 22 minutes, racing through to slide the ball past a hesitant Sealey. Then, amazingly, an endless stream of attacking football from both sides failed to produce another goal until the 43rd minute, when Hunt created another, this time from close-in by Hateley with a little help from the butter-fingered Katalinic.

Southampton were level again two minutes into the second half, Cassells glancing a header from a Williams free-kick past Sealey.

Then two goals in ten dramatic minutes seemed to have won the game for City. After 50 minutes, Hateley brilliantly beat Golac on the left and got the ball past Katalinic with a low left-foot shot. Then Whitton scored one of his finest goals for the club, outpacing Chris Nicholl before beating Katalinic with an explosive shot from a narrow angle, the ball hitting the net almost before the 'keeper had moved.

Fatally, City relaxed and were still celebrating when veteran Alan Ball was allowed to run through straight from the kick-off and hit a glorious shot past Sealey from 30 yards.

The Saints were buzzing now and the predictable equalizer came in the 68th minute from Cassells, a delicate chip into the top corner from the edge of the box.

Six minutes from time The Dell went wild as Keegan beat City's fragile offside trap to score his second and put Southampton ahead for the first time.

City were not beaten, though, and had more chances before Hateley squeezed in the equalizer from a narrow angle in the dying seconds.

There were some outstanding individual performances in addition to the scorers: the unselfish Garry Thompson, the playmaker Hunt and the veteran Gerry Francis. Joe Mercer said it was the best game he had seen since the 1930s and if both managers were critical of their defensive performances, the fans went home happy.

Southampton: Katalinic; Golac, Holmes, Williams, Nicholl, Whitlock, Keegan, Channon, Cassells, Armstrong, Ball(D.Wallace).
Coventry City: Sealey; Thomas, Jacobs, Butterworth, Dyson, Gillespie, Whitton, Francis, Hateley, Thompson, Hunt.
Referee: G.Bune (Cranleigh) *Attendance: 18,522*

Match to Remember 16 — 10 December 1983

Coventry City 4 Liverpool 0

THE soccer world blinked when they saw the stunning scoreline from Highfield

Bruce Grobbelaar and Alan Hansen can only watch as Nicky Platnauer scrambles the ball over the line after only 90 seconds.

Terry Gibson is in like a flash to score Coventry's second goal against the mighty Merseysiders.

Road — Liverpool's biggest defeat for seven years and a personal triumph for hat-trick hero Terry Gibson.

City dominated Liverpool from start to finish and the result must rank as Coventry's best ever in the First Division. They went into the game lying fifth in the table, unbeaten for six games and remarkably settled after Bobby Gould's rebuilding job in the summer of 1983.

Liverpool, meanwhile, had won the League Championship two years running and were top of the table once again, having lost only two out of 17 games and conceded only nine goals in the process.

The game started explosively with Nicky Platnauer bundling the ball in after Grobbelaar failed to hold Gibson's shot after 90 seconds.

Dave Bamber was causing problems for the Liverpool defence in the air and from one of his knock-downs, Gibson scored the second after 19 minutes.

On the stroke of half-time, Gibson shot through a ruck of players to make it 3-0 and end a very satisfying 45 minutes.

Grobbelaar was at fault for the first and third goals but partially atoned with super saves from Daly and Gibson. He had no chance, however, in the 84th minute when Gibson broke clear and chipped the Zimbabwean to make it 4-0 and become the first player for 11 years to score a hat-trick against Liverpool, the last being Keith Weller.

The standing ovation at the final whistle was reward for an outstanding team performance and Joe Fagan, the Liverpool boss, admitted that City had outclassed the Reds in every department and tipped them as Championship contenders.

For a couple of weeks, City were in the media spotlight but, sadly, the result was the high point in a season that went rapidly downhill and required a last-match victory to avoid relegation. Liverpool quickly got back on the winning trail, lost only three more games all season and won the Championship in a canter.

Coventry City: Avramovic; Roberts, Pearce, Platnauer, Peake, Allardyce, Bennett, Gynn, Bamber(Withey), Gibson, Daly.
Liverpool: Grobbelaar; Neal, Kennedy, Lawrenson, Nicol, Hansen, Dalglish, Lee, Rush, Whelan, Souness.
Referee: D.Letts (Basingstoke) *Attendance: 20,586*

Match to Remember 17 — 26 May 1985

Coventry City 4 Everton 1

FOR the second season running, Coventry City needed to win their final match to stay in the First Division. The major difference this time had been that City had to win three successive matches, something they had not done for almost two years, in order to overtake Norwich City.

Yet most Coventry fans travelling home from the goalless draw at Ipswich, hearing that Norwich had pulled off an unexpected win at Chelsea, were resigned to Second Division football.

The first of the three games, against Stoke who were already relegated, was played in a frenzied atmosphere and City won, thanks to a late Stuart Pearce penalty, although Ian Painter missed a spot-kick for Stoke in the final minutes.

Six days later, another 1-0 victory, this time over Luton, thanks to a Kilcline free-kick through the defensive wall six minutes from time, set up the grand finale with Everton on the last Sunday in May.

Everton were League Champions and had lost only one game since Christmas, but they were without the injured Reid, Stevens, Gray and Mountfield.

An all-ticket crowd assembled for the 11.30am kick-off and the home fans were rewarded with a City goal inside four minutes, a powerful Regis header from a Kilcline flick on.

Regis had his best game since arriving at Highfield Road the previous October and after 17 minutes he found Micky Adams with a superb pass inside the full-back. The Coventry left winger beat Southall with a good ground shot.

Nerves were dispelled and City could have scored more goals before an inexplicable 15-minute period at the end of the first half, during which the Merseysiders pulled a goal back through Wilkinson and could have had more.

The half-time period was tense for the fans as City seemed to have let the initiative slip, but their fears were unfounded and with City attacking the West End, Regis made it 3-1 after only 90 seconds of the second period.

Gibson 'turned' Hughes and fired in a shot which Southall could only parry. For what seemed an eternity, the ball bobbled in front of the big man before he prodded it home.

The fans were delirious and after 78 minutes Gibson got his reward for a superb performance when he raced clear of the defence and beat Southall, the Footballer of the Year, from the edge of the box for his 19th goal of the season.

More chances were missed as City played their best football of the campaign. At the final whistle, the jubilant crowd engulfed the pitch and manager Don Mackay and his happy players got a rousing ovation as they emerged into the directors' box.

Norwich City, naturally, were stunned by the result but made only a token protest at Everton's weakened line up.

Even Footballer of the Year Neville Southall is powerless to prevent Micky Adams scoring City's second goal.

Pearce and Butterworth never played for Coventry City again, being sold to Nottingham Forest for a joint fee of £450,000 two days later to reduce the Highfield Road club's overdraft. Pearce, of course, went on to gain a regular place in the England side.

After his disappointing season, many Coventry fans expected Cyrille Regis to move in the summer but he stayed to become one of the most popular City players of all time.

Coventry City: Ogrizovic; Butterworth, Pearce, Hibbitt, Kilcline, Peake, Bennett, McGrath, Regis, Gibson, Adams.
Everton: Southall; Harper, Van den Hauwe, Ratcliffe, Hughes, Richardson, Steven, Wilkinson, Sharp, Bracewell, Sheedy.
Referee: R.Lewis (Great Bookham) *Attendance: 21,224*

Match to Remember 18 — 14 March 1987

Sheffield Wednesday 1 Coventry City 3

THIS was only City's fifth appearance in the quarter-finals of the FA Cup, the last time being in 1982 when they were destroyed by a man called Cyrille Regis, who was then playing for West Brom.

Indeed, they had lost on each of the previous four occasions but that did not prevent some 15,000 City fans taking over the Leppings Lane end of Hillsborough to see if history could be made. Wednesday were unbeaten at home in 23 Cup-ties, their last reverse being in 1973. Coventry, meanwhile, had won there in an FA Cup tie back in 1911.

There was a fantastic atmosphere in the ground but, strangely, the early stages of the game lacked passion and even tension. If anything, Wednesday had the better of the exchanges but City gradually improved.

Regis almost latched on to the end of a long cross and shortly afterwards Coventry took the lead with a memorable goal. McGrath tackled bravely and won the ball in the centre of the field, then Regis laid it back to Bennett, who side-stepped Madden and delivered a perfectly weighted pass. Regis thundered through on the right, completely in the clear, and shot hard and low into the right-hand corner of the net after 17 minutes.

For a time it was all City. McGrath nearly got on the end of a long through ball and Houchen headed just wide. The game was now being played at a furious pace and both teams had their chances. Ogrizovic made a wonderful stop from Shelton and shortly before half-time, Chapman nearly fastened on to a bad back-pass from Downs.

The game continued to swing from end to end in the second half. Snodin committed himself, Bennett eluded his tackle but just failed to get his centre across.

At last, in the 67th minute and shortly after making a double substitution, Wednesday equalized. Hodge's long goal-kick was flicked on by Chapman, City's defence hesitated and Megson was on hand to shoot home.

For the next ten minutes it was all Wednesday, but then City delivered the counter-punch. Bennett, in his own half, delivered the ball down the right and Regis let

Big Cyrille Regis thunders through to put Coventry ahead in the 17th minute of the quarter-final against Sheffield Wednesday at Hillsborough.

it run on to Houchen, who made space for himself and shot home off the hapless Smith.

Whether Hodge would have saved but for Smith's untimely intervention is a open to debate, but it hardly mattered because only five minutes later City made the game safe.

Bennett delivered a long ball down the middle. Worthington attempted to head clear but Houchen collected the ball and shot into the far corner of the net.

Still Wednesday came back. Shelton's shot just cleared the far post and, in injury time, Megson shot over after Ogrizovic could only parry away a corner.

Shortly afterwards Allan Gunn blew his whistle, the game was over and Coventry City had reached the FA Cup semi-finals for the first time in their 103-year history.

It had been a magnificent Cup-tie. The whole team played heroically but some performances stood out: that of Greg Downs whose unrivalled commitment personified the revitalized City; the dominant Ogrizovic; and Dave Bennett, who had only played in one other game in the previous two months but who laid on all three City goals. Cyrille Regis was at his devastating best and, of course, there was Keith 'Roy of the Rovers' Houchen, whose two goals in the last 12 minutes will live longest in the memory.

Sheffield Wednesday: Hodge; Sterland(Morris), Snodin, Smith, Madden, Worthington, Marwood, Megson, Chapman, Bradshaw(Hirst), Shelton.
Coventry City: Ogrizovic; Borrows, Downs, McGrath(Sedgley), Kilcline, Peake, Bennett, Phillips, Regis, Houchen, Pickering.
Referee: A. Gunn (Burgess Hill) *Attendance: 48,005*

Coventry City 3 Leeds United 2
(after extra-time)

THIS FA Cup semi-final was rated by David Miller in *The Times* as one of the best the competition had seen for the last 20 years, a match of rare drama and excitement. It was all those things but it also, arguably, produced the most important result in Coventry City's history.

City were returning to the Sheffield Wednesday ground only four weeks after their epic sixth-round win and this time more than 27,000 City supporters made the journey to see the Sunday lunchtime confrontation with Leeds United.

Ground conditions were good on a bright, cool spring day, the pitch having been heavily watered. City were favourties to win the tie against the Second Division side, but in contrast to the game against Wednesday, when they were cool and confident, they appeared nervous and it was all Leeds in the opening stages.

Ogrizovic had already made one excellent save from Pearson before United took the lead in the 14th minute with a great header from Rennie which gave the City goalkeeper no chance.

The Sky Blues at last started to put their game together, but Regis missed three good chances. Indeed, it was one of those games where he did everything right until he got near goal.

Substitute Mickey Gynn draws City level after 68 minutes.

Keith Houchen makes it to 2-1 to Coventry with 15 minutes remaining.

Dave Bennett hits the winner after eight minutes of extra-time.

First of all he took the ball out to the right, overpowering Ashurst on the way before firing wide of the near post; then he shot over from a Bennett cross; and finally he failed to make contact with a Phillips cross. The half ended with City on top but still a goal down.

City continued where they had left off but when Leeds attacked, the defence looked as vulnerable as it had done in the first 20 minutes of the game.

On the hour, Coventry brought on Gynn for Pickering, who had been limping, and this seemed to give them an extra dimension in attack. City pressed hard and just as Leeds seemed to have quelled the storm, the equalizer came.

Bennett chased the ball down the right to the by-line, Ormsby could have put the ball anywhere but lost it, the Coventry number-seven centred, McGrath missed his kick, but Gynn, lurking on the left-hand edge of the penalty area, shot home just inside the near post after 68 minutes.

City were now well on top and Leeds were gradually worn down. It was no surprise, then, when City took the lead ten minutes later. Gynn won the ball on the edge of the penalty area, Houchen gathered a ricochet off Ormsby, calmly sidestepped Day and slotted home.

Regis could have made the game safe shortly afterwards but after getting clean through, he tried one trick too many and his shot was blocked.

Leeds brought on Edwards and Haddock for one last throw and with only seven minutes to go, the Coventry defence got into a tangle. Ritchie was allowed to cross the ball and Edwards was on hand to plant it into the far corner of the net.

Leeds looked slightly the better side at the start of extra-time but it was City who scored the vital third goal after eight minutes. Bennett was fouled on the right,

Kilcline, Houchen and Phillips in celebratory mood.

Gynn floated the ball across, Regis won it in the air at the far post, Houchen shot against Day and Bennett was there to tap in.

With only three minutes left, Aspin put the ball down the middle and Edwards got clear and shot, but Ogrizovic positioned himself well and deflected the ball to safety.

There were no more scares for City. The final whistle brought an end to a truly extraordinary match and Coventry had reached Wembley for the first time.

The win was well deserved. Although Leeds had fought hard, City had the edge in class. The Sky Blues were more imaginitive in attack, particularly when Gynn replaced Pickering, and Bennett's mastery of Adams was also important. But the crucial factor was that City did not panic when they went a goal down. Downs gradually got to grips with Ritchie, who had initially given him a roasting, and the whole team played good, incisive football throughout, the way John Sillett liked it played.

Coventry City: Ogrizovic; Borrows, Downs, McGrath, Kilcline, Peake, Bennett, Phillips, Regis, Houchen, Pickering(Gynn).
Leeds United: Day; Aspin, Adams, Stiles(Haddock), Ashurst, Ormsby, Ritchie, Sheridan, Pearson(Edwards), Baird, Rennie.
Referee: R.G. Milford (Bristol) *Attendance: 51,372*

Coventry City meet the Duchess of Kent before the 1987 FA Cup Final.

Match to Remember 20 — 16 May 1987

Coventry City 3 Tottenham Hotspur 2
(after extra-time)

THE dreams of all Coventry fans at last came true at Wembley in a fairy-tale game as City twice came from behind to win the FA Cup in their first Final.

In a classic confrontation the never-say-die attitude of City's players won the day over the superstars from Tottenham in a good humoured Final.

Yet we should have known that this would be Coventry's day. John Sillett had been saying since February that City's name was on the trophy and *Old Moore's Almanack* predicted that a team in blue stripes would win the Cup, but the bookmakers still made Tottenham odds-on favourites.

And after only two minutes it looked as though the bookies were right as Clive Allen darted in front of Trevor Peake to score with a near-post header after Waddle had 'fleeced' Downs on the right.

But City refused to lie down after this early blow and seven minutes later they were level. Downs crossed, Houchen's head flicked the ball on into space and Dave Bennett was there in a flash, guiding the ball past the hesitant 39-year-old Ray Clemence in the Tottenham goal.

Spurs had the slight edge in an outstanding and breathless first half in which Hoddle, despite the close attentions of Lloyd McGrath, was pulling the strings and Waddle was having a field day against Downs. It was City, though, who almost went ahead when Gynn was clear through but could not beat Clemence.

After 40 minutes, a glorious free-kick by Hoddle caught Ogrizovic in two minds, the ball bounced off Kilcline and Spurs were ahead again. The goal was later credited to Mabbutt by the FA.

The second half started at the same pace but City began to get the upper hand. Bennett, after a quiet first half, started to see more of the ball and it was his delicate cross in the 63rd minute that eluded Gough for Houchen to score with a beautiful diving header. 'Roy of the Rovers' had struck again with his fifth Cup goal of the season, an effort which was just reward for an outstanding performance.

Both sides had half-chances to avert extra-time and although City finished in stronger fashion, no one on the ground was willing to predict the outcome of this ding-dong battle.

Six minutes into the first period of extra-time, Rodger, who had come on as substitute for the injured Kilcline, sent McGrath clear down the right and his cross-cum-shot was deflected off Mabbutt's knee over the diving Clemence for the winning goal.

All the doubts about City's ability to last the extra half-hour were unfounded and it was Spurs who found it hard to keep up with the strong-running Sky Blues. Bennett and Gynn were everywhere and Downs and McGrath had doused the flames

Nick Pickering (far left) looks delighted. Keith Houchen (on ground) has just scored with a magnificent diving header.

It's Coventry's Cup! Brian Kilcline, sufficiently recovered from injury, lifts the trophy.

Back home. City players parade the FA Cup through the streets of Coventry.

of Waddle and Hoddle. Peake had Allen 'in his pocket' and Rodger enjoyed probably his best-ever half-hour of football.

The unsung heroes, Pickering and Phillips — the latter deputizing for the injured Borrows — tackled and harrassed and Regis and Houchen kept on causing problems for the Spurs defence.

Gynn had another chance in the dying minutes but Clemence saved well. City, though, kept the pressure on right to the final whistle. The *Sky Blue Song* echoed around Wembley and Brian Kilcline recovered sufficiently to receive the Cup.

City's fans gave a sporting ovation to Spurs and taunted TV pundit Jimmy Greaves, who had predicted Coventry's demise at every hurdle in the competition. The media all agreed that this had been one of the best FA Cup Finals since the war and the underdogs had deserved to win.

Coventry City: Ogrizovic; Phillips, Downs, McGrath, Kilcline(Rodger), Peake, Bennett, Gynn, Regis, Houchen, Pickering.
Tottenham Hotspur: Clemence; Hughton(Claessen), Thomas, Hodge, Gough, Mabbutt, C.Allen, P.Allen, Waddle, Hoddle, Ardíles(Stevens).
Referee: N.Midgley (Salford) *Attendance: 98,000*

Match to Remember 21 28 November 1990

Coventry City 5 Nottingham Forest 4

IN TERMS of 'shock factor', this result ranks alongside the 4-0 victory over Liverpool in 1983. Forest had not lost a League Cup tie for three years and had not conceded five goals in a match for two and a half years.

This was only Terry Butcher's third game in charge of Coventry and rarely in his playing career can he have experienced such emotions. He will surely remember this staggering match — his first victory as a manager — for ever.

Revenge was in the air as Forest had knocked City out of the League Cup in the previous two seasons. The hero of this match was Kevin Gallacher, who scored his first hat-trick in English football, although he could not match Nigel Clough's feat of a hat-trick in eight minutes for Forest.

Gallacher struck first in the 14th minute with a close-range shot after Speedie's header was blocked. A minute later, Regis produced a defence-splitting pass to Gallacher, who beautifully chipped the badly-positioned Crossley.

Steve Livingstone scored City's third after Gallacher attacked the Forest defence and the ball broke for the big striker. That was after 29 minutes and six minutes later, Gallacher completed his hat-trick with another close-range shot after Billing had won the ball in the air.

Their side four goals down after 35 minutes, Forest fans were pouring out of the ground, disgusted at their team's performance.

But they missed more action as City pressed the self-destruct button and let Forest back into the game, Clough scoring from the edge of the area after being given acres of space.

This helped restore the Reds' confidence and suddenly they looked a different team as Clough scored two more soft goals before half-time to make it 4-3.

City fans were shattered and, whatever Butcher said at the break did not alter things. Nine minutes into the second half, Speedie dived in on Parker on the edge of the box and the midfielder turned to shoot past Ogrizovic to make it 4-4.

Yet there was even more inexplicable drama: either Forest relaxed, having climbed their mountain, or their fight-back brought City to their senses. Whatever, from somewhere the Sky Blues dragged up more energy and spirit and after 62 minutes,

Top: Livingstone (left) has just scored City's fifth goal and Gallacher and Speedie begin to celebrate. Bottom: The electronic scoreboard tells the remarkable story.

Livingstone got what proved to be the winner after a terrific scramble in the Forest goalmouth.

Even then both sides had more chances and at the finish the teams received a standing ovation.

In the quarter-final, City were drawn at home to Second Division Sheffield Wednesday but, without the injured Gallacher, they succumbed to a powerful performance from the eventual winners of the competiton in what turned out to be David Speedie's last game for Coventry.

Coventry City: Ogrizovic; Borrows, Edwards, Gynn, Billing, Peake, Gallacher, Speedie, Regis, Livingstone, Smith.
Nottingham Forest: Crossley; Laws, Pearce, Walker, Chettle, Hodge, Crosby, Keane, Clough, Jemson, Parker.
Referee: R.Pawley (Cambridge) *Attendance: 16,304*

David Speedie who played his last game in the quarter-final.

Coventry City in the Football League 1919-1991

		HOME					AWAY						
	P	W	D	L	F	A	W	D	L	F	A	Pts	Pos
					DIVISION TWO								
1919-20	42	7	7	7	20	26	2	4	15	15	47	29	20th
1920-21	42	8	6	7	24	25	4	5	12	15	45	35	21st
1921-22	42	8	5	8	31	21	4	5	12	20	39	34	20th
1922-23	42	12	2	7	35	21	3	5	13	11	42	37	18th
1923-24	42	9	6	6	34	23	2	7	12	18	45	35	19th
1924-25	42	10	6	5	32	26	1	3	17	13	58	31	22nd
					DIVISION THREE NORTH								
1925-26	42	13	6	2	47	19	3	0	18	26	63	38	16th
					DIVISION THREE SOUTH								
1926-27	42	11	4	6	44	33	4	3	14	27	53	37	15th
1927-28	42	5	8	8	40	36	6	1	14	27	60	31	20th
1928-29	42	9	6	6	35	23	5	8	8	27	34	42	11th
1929-30	42	14	3	4	54	25	5	6	10	34	48	47	6th
1930-31	42	11	4	6	55	28	5	5	11	20	37	41	14th
1931-32	42	17	2	2	74	28	1	6	14	34	69	44	12th
1932-33	42	16	1	4	75	24	3	5	13	31	53	44	6th
1933-34	42	16	3	2	70	22	5	9	7	30	32	54	2nd
1934-35	42	14	5	2	56	14	7	4	10	30	36	51	3rd
1935-36	42	19	1	1	75	12	5	8	8	27	33	57	1st
					DIVISION TWO								
1936-37	42	11	5	5	35	19	6	6	9	31	35	45	8th
1937-38	42	12	5	4	31	15	8	7	6	35	30	52	4th
1938-39	42	13	4	4	35	13	8	4	9	27	32	50	4th
1946-47	42	12	8	1	40	17	4	5	12	26	42	45	8th
1947-48	42	10	5	6	33	16	4	8	9	26	36	41	10th
1948-49	42	12	3	6	35	20	3	4	14	20	44	37	16th
1949-50	42	8	6	7	32	24	5	7	9	23	31	39	12th
1950-51	42	15	3	3	51	25	4	4	13	24	34	45	7th
1951-52	42	9	5	7	36	33	5	1	15	23	49	34	21st
					DIVISION THREE SOUTH								
1952-53	46	15	5	3	52	22	4	7	12	25	40	50	6th
1953-54	46	14	5	4	36	15	4	4	15	25	41	45	14th
1954-55	46	15	5	3	50	26	3	6	14	17	33	47	9th
1955-56	46	16	4	3	54	20	4	5	14	19	40	49	8th
1956-57	46	12	5	6	52	36	4	7	12	22	48	44	16th
1957-58	46	10	9	4	41	24	3	4	16	20	57	39	19th
					DIVISION FOUR								
1958-59	46	18	4	1	50	11	6	8	9	34	36	60	2nd
					DIVISION THREE								
1959-60	46	14	6	3	44	22	7	4	12	34	41	52	4th
1960-61	46	14	6	3	54	25	2	6	15	26	58	44	15th
1961-62	46	11	6	6	38	26	5	5	13	26	45	43	14th
1962-63	46	14	6	3	54	28	4	11	8	29	41	53	4th
1963-64	46	14	7	2	62	32	8	9	6	36	29	60	1st

		HOME						*AWAY*					
	P	W	D	L	F	A	W	D	L	F	A	Pts	Pos
DIVISION TWO													
1964-65	42	10	5	6	41	29	7	4	10	31	41	43	10th
1965-66	42	14	5	2	54	31	6	8	7	19	22	53	3rd
1966-67	42	17	3	1	46	16	6	10	5	28	27	59	1st
DIVISION ONE													
1967-68	42	8	5	8	32	32	1	10	10	19	39	33	20th
1968-69	42	8	6	7	32	22	2	5	14	14	42	31	20th
1969-70	42	9	6	6	35	28	10	5	6	23	20	49	6th
1970-71	42	12	4	5	24	12	4	6	11	13	26	42	10th
1971-72	42	7	10	4	27	23	2	5	14	17	44	33	18th
1972-73	42	9	5	7	27	24	4	4	13	13	31	35	19th
1973-74	42	10	5	6	25	18	4	5	12	18	36	38	16th
1974-75	42	8	9	4	31	27	4	6	11	20	35	39	14th
1975-76	42	6	9	6	22	22	7	5	9	25	35	40	14th
1976-77	42	7	9	5	34	26	3	6	12	14	33	35	19th
1977-78	42	13	5	3	48	23	5	7	9	27	39	48	7th
1978-79	42	11	7	3	41	29	3	9	9	17	39	44	10th
1979-80	42	12	2	7	34	24	4	5	12	22	42	39	15th
1980-81	42	9	6	6	31	30	4	4	13	17	38	36	18th
1981-82	42	9	4	8	31	24	4	7	10	25	38	50	14th
1982-83	42	10	5	6	29	17	3	4	14	19	42	48	19th
1983-84	42	8	5	8	33	33	5	6	10	24	44	50	19th
1984-85	42	11	3	7	29	22	4	2	15	18	42	50	18th
1985-86	42	6	5	10	31	35	5	5	11	17	36	43	17th
1986-87	42	14	4	3	35	17	3	8	10	15	28	63	10th
1987-88	40	6	8	6	23	25	7	6	7	23	28	53	10th
1988-89	38	9	4	6	28	23	5	9	5	19	19	55	7th
1989-90	38	11	2	6	24	25	3	5	11	15	34	49	12th
1990-91	38	10	6	3	30	16	1	5	13	12	43	44	16th

City Against Other League Clubs

Coventry City have played 103 clubs in the Football League since 1919. Below is the Sky Blues' record against each club. Some clubs changed their names (eg Clapton Orient became Leyton Orient then Orient and then Leyton Orient again) and some clubs modified their titles (eg Swansea Town became Swansea City). In all cases the current name used by each club cover all games under previous names.

		HOME					*AWAY*				
	P	W	D	L	F	A	W	D	L	F	A
Aberdare Athletic	2	1	0	0	1	0	1	0	0	7	0
Accrington Stanley	4	2	0	0	4	2	1	0	1	3	3
AFC Bournemouth	42	13	2	6	52	28	5	7	9	25	32
Aldershot	22	8	2	1	34	7	3	5	3	17	18
Arsenal	48	6	6	12	24	32	3	7	14	17	43
Ashington	2	1	0	0	2	0	0	0	1	0	2
Aston Villa	34	4	6	7	22	26	0	7	10	9	27
Barnsley	38	12	5	2	41	19	3	5	11	19	37
Barrow	4	2	0	0	4	0	2	0	0	7	1
Birmingham City	40	8	5	7	28	27	4	7	9	20	33
Blackburn Rovers	16	3	1	4	13	9	6	0	2	13	6
Blackpool	16	3	1	4	9	9	1	0	7	3	20
Bolton Wanderers	10	1	4	0	8	6	1	3	1	7	7
Bradford	24	7	5	0	27	7	4	4	4	14	18
Bradford City	12	3	3	0	10	6	1	1	4	4	11
Brentford	40	11	6	3	31	18	6	4	10	34	41
Brighton & Hove Albion	42	9	6	6	39	29	1	7	13	16	40
Bristol City	44	11	9	2	52	28	3	8	11	17	33
Bristol Rovers	26	9	3	1	34	14	2	3	8	16	26
Burnley	22	4	3	4	17	14	1	6	4	11	16
Bury	38	11	2	6	30	18	5	5	9	18	29
Cardiff City	28	11	0	3	33	16	3	4	7	18	30
Carlisle United	10	4	0	1	11	8	2	2	1	10	5
Charlton Athletic	24	8	2	2	23	10	1	5	6	13	24
Chelsea	34	7	4	6	27	27	2	4	11	17	29
Chester City	2	1	0	0	5	1	0	1	0	1	1
Chesterfield	22	7	2	2	20	11	3	2	6	16	24
Colchester United	20	6	3	1	17	10	3	2	5	12	15
Crewe Alexandra	6	3	0	0	10	4	0	2	1	4	5
Crystal Palace	70	18	10	7	81	46	9	14	12	43	46
Darlington	2	0	1	0	0	0	1	0	0	4	1
Derby County	44	9	7	6	28	25	5	3	14	21	40
Doncaster Rovers	10	3	1	1	10	4	0	2	3	3	12
Durham City	2	1	0	0	3	1	0	0	1	1	4
Everton	50	13	4	8	45	36	3	6	16	21	50
Exeter City	34	9	7	1	35	13	5	2	10	18	39
Fulham	34	9	2	6	28	21	3	5	9	15	31
Gateshead	2	1	0	0	4	0	0	1	0	1	1
Gillingham	34	12	2	3	50	19	6	4	7	28	27
Grimsby Town	16	4	3	1	11	5	3	0	5	9	17
Halifax Town	10	4	0	1	14	7	2	2	1	10	7
Hartlepool United	4	2	0	0	9	3	0	0	2	3	5
Huddersfield Town	12	2	1	3	5	9	2	0	4	5	11
Hull City	28	6	3	5	21	17	2	4	8	14	28
Ipswich Town	50	11	7	7	43	33	3	7	15	15	43
Leeds City	2	0	0	1	0	4	0	0	1	0	3

		HOME					AWAY				
	P	W	D	L	F	A	W	D	L	F	A
Leeds United	50	10	5	10	36	30	1	6	18	14	51
Leicester City	54	12	5	10	38	34	6	7	14	25	41
Leyton Orient	38	12	6	1	47	14	5	6	8	20	32
Lincoln City	8	3	1	0	8	4	2	0	2	6	6
Liverpool	48	6	8	10	18	30	1	4	19	10	55
Luton Town	58	21	6	2	65	26	10	6	13	39	50
Manchester City	50	9	10	6	39	33	3	2	20	18	54
Manchester United	54	12	7	8	37	34	6	7	14	21	45
Mansfield Town	6	2	0	1	7	4	1	1	1	9	8
Merthyr Town	8	2	1	1	14	6	0	2	2	6	8
Middlesbrough	24	6	3	3	19	14	4	6	2	16	15
Millwall	38	12	2	5	44	21	4	5	10	26	45
Nelson	4	2	0	0	5	0	0	0	2	1	7
New Brighton	2	0	1	0	0	0	0	0	1	1	5
Newcastle United	44	10	8	4	31	28	6	4	12	29	44
Newport County	38	14	1	4	58	21	1	6	12	25	46
Northampton Town	42	9	6	6	31	21	4	6	11	28	47
Norwich City	74	30	5	2	78	28	7	14	16	40	62
Nottingham Forest	58	6	13	10	36	41	3	7	19	26	65
Notts County	28	6	3	5	25	22	2	3	9	14	27
Oldham Athletic	8	4	0	0	15	4	0	1	3	1	10
Oxford United	6	3	0	0	9	2	1	0	2	1	3
Peterborough	6	1	1	1	7	8	2	0	1	6	4
Plymouth Argyle	32	8	5	3	28	17	5	2	9	17	34
Portsmouth	12	5	0	1	14	6	2	1	3	6	6
Port Vale	24	3	5	4	11	11	4	3	5	9	17
Preston North End	10	4	1	0	11	2	0	3	2	6	8
Queen's Park Rangers	80	23	12	5	89	34	12	8	20	60	70
Reading	32	9	5	2	26	11	0	4	12	16	38
Rochdale	2	0	1	0	2	2	0	0	1	1	4
Rotherham United	18	5	2	2	25	13	3	3	3	12	12
Sheffield United	26	5	5	3	23	20	4	3	6	11	17
Sheffield Wednesday	42	11	4	6	44	23	3	6	12	21	41
Shrewsbury Town	24	8	4	0	34	12	1	3	8	10	24
Southampton	80	26	10	4	74	29	5	11	24	48	97
Southend United	42	11	5	5	46	29	4	5	12	19	39
Southport	4	1	1	0	1	0	2	0	0	4	2
South Shields	12	2	1	3	3	5	0	1	5	5	15
Stockport County	12	3	3	0	8	4	0	4	2	4	11
Stoke City	42	12	3	6	38	25	5	3	13	26	45
Sunderland	20	5	3	2	18	10	1	5	4	3	10
Swansea City	20	8	1	1	26	9	3	3	4	16	22
Swindon Town	42	15	2	4	52	19	6	8	7	27	43
Thames	4	2	0	0	9	1	1	0	1	4	6
Torquay United	36	15	1	2	63	18	5	7	6	26	27
Tottenham Hotspur	62	11	11	9	42	40	4	8	19	32	64
Tranmere Rovers	8	3	0	1	8	3	1	0	3	4	8
Walsall	28	9	3	2	28	12	2	5	7	13	29
Watford	54	14	5	8	46	29	7	4	16	30	57
West Bromwich Albion	40	9	4	7	30	25	3	7	10	18	41
West Ham United	64	10	10	12	38	34	7	6	19	32	68
Wigan Borough	2	0	1	0	0	0	0	0	1	1	5
Wimbledon	10	3	2	0	8	5	2	1	2	4	4
Wolverhampton W	44	14	5	3	42	19	8	6	8	20	22
Workington	2	1	0	0	4	0	0	1	0	2	2
Wrexham	8	4	0	0	13	3	1	1	2	6	10
York City	4	2	0	0	7	2	0	2	0	1	1

1894-95

Manager: J.Collins

1	Sep	1	(h)	Kidderminster H	D	4-4	Lucas, Cotterill, Hubberd, Chatland	
2		8	(h)	Berwick R	L	0-2		
3		15	(h)	Worcester R	L	1-3	Opp own-goal	
4		22	(a)	Oldbury T	L	2-4	Hubberd 2	
5		29	(h)	Small Heath Res	W	2-0	Holloway, Bird	
6	Oct	6	(h)	Smethwick CW	L	2-3	Cotterill 2	
7		27	(a)	Smethwick CW	W	4-1	Holloway, Cotterill, Bird, Shaw	
8	Nov	3	(a)	Wolves Res	L	0-8		
9		10	(h)	Redditch T	W	3-1	Holloway, Shaw, Opp own-goal	
10		17	(a)	Worcester R	D	3-3	Holloway, Bird, Shaw	
11		24	(a)	Small Heath Res	L	0-3		
12	Dec	8	(h)	Old Hill W	D	0-0		1,000
13		15	(a)	Stourbridge	L	2-5	Newhall, Bird	
14		22	(a)	Redditch T	L	1-5	Scorer unknown	
15		26	(a)	Old Hill W	L	2-5	Scorers unknown	200
16		27	(h)	West Brom A Res	L	2-3	Cotterill, Newhall	
17		29	(a)	Kidderminster H	L	1-0	Scorer unknown	
18	Jan	5	(h)	Oldbury T	L	2-3	Cotterill, Roberts	
19		12	(a)	Aston Villa Res	L	1-4	Bird	
20		26	(h)	Halesowen	W	3-0	Newhall 2, Cotterill	
21	Feb	2	(a)	West Brom A Res	L	0-8		
22		23	(h)	Wolves Res	L	1-6	Roberts	
23	Mar	2	(h)	Stafford R	W	4-1	Roberts, Bird, Newhall, Law	
24		9	(a)	Brierley Hill All	L	0-3		
25		30	(h)	Brierley Hill All	D	1-1	Newhall	
26	Apr	6	(h)	Aston Villa Res	L	0-4		
27		13	(a)	Berwick R	D	1-1	Opp own-goal	4,000
28		16	(a)	Stafford R	W	2-1	Scorers unknown	
29		20	(h)	Stourbridge	L	1-2	Chatland	
30		27	(a)	Halesowen	L	1-2	Scorer unknown	

FINAL LEAGUE POSITION: 13th in Birmingham & District League

Appearances

Goals

Flavell	Cashmore	Alldrick	Bagnall	Roberts	Edmunds	Lucas	Cotterill	Yorke	Hubberd	Chatland	Bond	Bird	Gallier	Holloway	Wilson	Shaw	Hollins	Law	Newhall	Neeve	Edge	Fletcher	Day	Briggs	Hinds	
1	2	3	4	5	6	7	8	9	10	11																1
1	2	3	6	5	4	8	9	7	11	10																2
1	2	3	6	5	4	8	7	11			9	10														3
1	2	3	6	5	4			11	7		9	8	10													4
1	2	3	6	5	4		9			11	10	8		7												5
1	2	3		5	4		9		8	11		10		7	6											6
1	2	3	6	5	4		9		8			10		7		11										7
1	2	3	6	5	4		9		8			10		7		11										8
		3	6	5	4		9		8			10		7	2	11	1									9
		3	4	5					8	6		10		9	2	11	1	7								10
		3	4	5			9		8	6		10		7	2	11	1									11
1	2	3		5	6				8	4		10		7					9	11						12
	2	3	4	5	6				8	7		10						11	9		1					13
	2	3		5	6				8	4		10		7				11	9		1					14
	2	3		5	6				8	4		10		7				11	9		1					15
	2	3		5	6		7		8	4		10						11	9		1					16
	2	3		5	6		7		8	4		10						11	9		1					17
	2	3		5					8	4		10		7				11	9		1	6				18
	2			5	4		10		7			8						11	9		1	3	6			19
	2	3		5	6		10		7	4		8							9		1			11		20
	2	3		5	6		10		7	4		8						11	9		1					21
	2	3		5	6		10		7	4		8							9		1				11	22
	2	3		5	6		10		7	4		8						11	9		1					23
	2	3		5	6		10		7	4		8						11	9		1					24
	2	3		5	6		10		7	4		8						11	9		1					25
	2	3		5	6		10		7	4		8						11	9		1					26
	2	3		5	6		10		7	4		8						11	9		1					27
	2	3		5	6		10		7	4		8						11	9		1					28
	2	3		5	6		10		7	8								11	9		1	4				29
	2	3		5	6		10		7	8								11	9		1	4				30
9	27	29	11	30	27	3	23	4	28	24	3	26	1	11	4	5	3	17	19	1	18	4	1	1	1	
				3		1	7		3	2		6		4		3		1	6							

Scorers unknown: 7. 3 own-goals

1895-96

Manager: T Cashmore

1	Sep	7	(h)	West Brom A Res	L	2-6	Bird 2	
2		14	(h)	Berwick R	L	0-1		
3		21	(h)	Aston Villa Res	L	2-4	Bird, Austin	
4		28	(a)	Brierley Hill All	D	1-1	Austin	
5	Oct	19	(a)	Small Heath Res	L	0-4		
6	Nov	9	(h)	Small Heath Res	L	1-6	Taylor	
7		16	(h)	Wolves Res	L	2-3	Roberts, Slater	
8		30	(h)	Hereford Thistle	W	3-2	Bird, Tasker 2	
9	Dec	14	(a)	Berwick R	D	2-2	Roberts, Tasker	
10		26	(a)	Stafford R	L	0-4		
11		28	(a)	Halesowen	L	2-3	Scorers unknown	
12	Jan	4	(a)	Oldbury	W	2-0	Scorers unknown	
13		11	(a)	Wolves Res	L	0-8		
14		18	(h)	Worcester R	W	2-1	Lowe, Bird	
15		25	(a)	Hereford Thistle	L	1-2	Tasker	
16	Feb	1	(a)	West Brom A Res	L	1-4	Scorer unknown	
17		8	(h)	Stafford R	W	2-0	Weston 2	
18		15	(a)	Redditch T	L	0-1		
19		22	(h)	Oldbury T	W	3-0	Hemmersley, Taylor, Bird	
20		27	(a)	Stourbridge	W	1-0	Scorer unknown	
21		29	(a)	Kidderminster H	L	0-1		
22	Mar	14	(h)	Brierley Hill All	W	2-0	Bird, Hemmersley	
23		21	(h)	Kidderminster H	L	0-1		
24		28	(a)	Shrewsbury T	L	0-3		
25	Apr	4	(h)	Halesowen	W	2-1	Weston, Bird	
26		6	(a)	Worcester R	L	1-2	Lowe	
27		7	(h)	Shrewsbury T	L	1-3	Lowe	
28		11	(a*)	Aston Villa Res	L	1-2	Taylor	1,000
29		18	(h)	Reddith T	W	1-0	Newhall	2,000
30		25	(h)	Stourbridge	L	0-1		

FINAL LEAGUE POSITION: 14th in Birmingham & District League

*Played at Warwick

Appearances
Goals

FA Cup

Q1	Oct	12	(h)	Hereford Thistle	W	6-1	Roberts, Bird, Tasker 2, Austin 2
Q2	Nov	2	(a)	Kidderminster H	D	0-0	
R		6	(h)	Kidderminster H	W	2-1	Tasker, Opp own-goal
Q3		23	(h)	Burton Swifts	L	0-2	

Appearances
Goals

Allsop	Alldrick	Fletcher	Windridge	Whitehouse	Roberts	Flessey	Law	Bird	Slater	Austin	Kirk	Cashmore	Lowe	Newhall	Tasker	Chatland	Holmes	Taylor	Godsell	Edwards	Hemmersley	Robinson	Foley	Weston	Watts	Wright	Price	Hinds		
1	2	3	4	5	6	7	8	9	10	11																				1
	3	6		4	5	11		8	7	10	1	2	9																	2
	3	6		4	5	11		8	7	10	1	2	9																	3
	3	6		4	5	11			7	10	1	2	9	8																4
	3	6		4	5	11		8	7	10	1	2			9															5
	3			4	5			8	7	10	1	2				6	9	11												6
	3			4	5				7	10	1	2			8	6	9	11												7
	3			4	5			8	10		1				9	6		7	2	11										8
	3			4	5			9	7		1	2			8	6		11			10									9
	3			4	5			9	7		1	2			8	6		11			10									10
	2			4	5			10	11		1	3			9	6		7			8									11
	2	3		4	5			10	11		1				9	6		7			8									12
	3			4	5			10	11		1	2			9	6		7			8									13
	3	2		4	5			10	11		1		7		9	6					8									14
	2			4	5			8	7		1	3	11		9	6					10									15
	2			4	5			10	11			3			9	6		7			8	1								16
		4		3	5			10	11		1	2						9			8		6	7						17
		2		4	5			10	11		1	3	7					9			8		6							18
	3			4	5			10	11		1	2						9			8		6	7						19
	3			4	5			10	11		1	2						9			8		6	7						20
	3			4	5			9	10		1	2	11								8		6	7						21
	2	3		4	5			8			1					6		9			10			11	7					22
	2	3		4	5			8			1					6		9			10			11	7					23
	3			4	5			10			1	2				6		9			8			7		11				24
	3	11		4	5			10			1	2				6		9			8			7						25
	3			4	5			10			1	2	7			6		9			8					11				26
	3	11		4	5			10			1		7			6		9			8							2		27
	3	11		4	5			10				2	7			6		9			8	1								28
	3			4	5			10				2	7	9		6					8	1							11	29
	3			4	5			10				2	8			6		9				1		7		11				30
1	28	14	1	30	30	5	1	28	21	7	25	23	12	2	10	20	2	22	1	1	21	4	5	9	2	3		1	1	
					2			8	1	2			3	1	4			3			2			3						

Scorers unknown: 6

Allsop	Alldrick	Fletcher	Windridge	Whitehouse	Roberts	Flessey	Law	Bird	Slater	Austin	Kirk	Cashmore	Lowe	Newhall	Tasker	Chatland	Holmes	Taylor	
	3	4		5	6	7		8	11	10	1	2			9				Q1
	3			6	5				11	8	1	2			9	4		7	Q2
	3			6	5				11	8	1	2			9	4		7	R
	3			6	5				11	8	1	2	9		10	4		7	Q3
	4	1		4	4	1		1	4	4	4	4	1		4	3		3	
					1			1		2					3				

1 own-goal

1896-97

Manager: T Cashmore

1	Sep	12	(h)	Hereford Town	L	2-3	Roberts, Slater	
2		26	(h)	Brierley Hill All	L	0-2		
3	Oct	10	(a)	Stourbridge	L	0-5		
4		17	(a)	Wolves Res	L	0-4		1,500
5	Nov	7	(h)	Oldbury T	W	2-0	Wright, Taylor	
6		14	(a)	Aston Villa Res	D	2-2	Wright, Rowe	
7		21	(a)	Brierley Hill All	L	1-4	Scorer unknown	
8		28	(h)	Shrewsbury T	W	3-1	Wright, Taylor, Hemmersley	750
9	Dec	5	(a)	West Brom A Res	L	0-3		
10		12	(h)	Berwick R	D	0-0		
11		26	(a)	Oldbury T	W	6-0	Taylor 2, Hemmersley, Bird, Slater, Scorer unknown	
12		28	(h)	Redditch T	W	5-0	Lomas, Wright, Bird, Slater 2	
13		29	(a)	Redditch T	L	3-7	Scorers unknown	
14	Jan	2	(h)	Worcester R	L	1-2	Bird	
15		9	(a)	Small Heath Res	L	0-7		
16		16	(a)	Berwick R	W	2-0	Scorers unknown	
17		23	(h)	West Brom A Res	W	3-2	Chatland, Wright, Taylor	
18		30	(a)	Worcester R	D	3-3	Scorers unknown	
19	Feb	6	(a)	Hereford Thistle	L	1-2	Taylor	
20		13	(a)	Hereford Town	L	0-3		
21		27	(h)	Kidderminster H	D	1-1	Whitehouse	
22	Mar	6	(a)	Kidderminster H	W	2-1	Scorer unknown	
23		13	(a)	Halesowen	L	0-2		
24		20	(a)	Shrewsbury T	W	1-0	Hemmersley	
25		27	(h)	Wolves Res	W	1-0	Taylor	
26	Apr	3	(h)	Hereford Thistle	L	1-3	Scorer unknown	3,000
27		10	(h)	Small Heath Res	L	1-2	Hemmersley	
28		17	(h)	Aston Villa Res	D	1-1	Scorer unknown	
29		19	(h)	Stourbridge	L	0-2		
30		20	(h)	Halesowen	W	4-0	Scorers unknown	

FINAL LEAGUE POSITION: 13th in Birmingham & District League

Appearances
Goals

FA Cup

Q	Oct	31	(a)	Stourbridge	L	2-4	Taylor, Hemmersley	

Appearances
Goals

Robinson	Harris	Carpenter	Lomas	Roberts	Whitehouse J	Slater	Buckley	Haywood	Taylor	Lowe	Hemmersley	Bird	Whitehoue H	Bentley	Gordon	Carter	Wright	Dunsbee	Rowe	Alldrick	Chatland	Cashmore	Bottrill	
1	2	3	4	5	6	7	8	9	10	11														1
1	2	3	4	5	6	7		8			9	10	11											2
1	2		6	5		11		10			8		7	4	9							3		3
1	3		6	5		11		4	8							2	7	9	10					4
1	3		6	5	4			11	8		9						7		10	2				5
1	3		6	5	4			11	8		9						7		10	2				6
1	3		6	5	4			11	8		9						7		10	2				7
1	3		10	5	4	11	6		8		9						7			2				8
1	3		10	5	4	11	6		8		9						7			2				9
1	3		10	5	4	11	6		8		9						7			2				10
1	3			5	4	11	6		8		9	10					7			2				11
1	3		6	5	4	11			8		9	10					7			2				12
1	3		6	5	4	11			8		9	10					7			2				13
1	3		6	5	4	11			8		9	10					7			2				14
1	3		6	5	4	11			8		9	10					7			2				15
1	3		6	5	4	11			8		9	10					7			2				16
1	3		8		4	11			9			10		5			7			2	6			17
1	3		8		4	11			9			10		5			7			2	6			18
1	6		5		4	11			8		9	10					7			2		3		19
1	3		5		4	11			8		9	10					7				6	2		20
1	3		6	5	4	11			8		9	10					7			2				21
1	3		6	5	4	11			8		9	10					7			2				22
1	3		6	5	4	11			8		9	10					7			2				23
1	3		6	5	4	11			8		9	10					7			2				24
1	3		6	5	4	11			8		9	10					7			2				25
1	3		6	5	4	11			8		9	10					7			2				26
1	3		6		4	11			8		9	10					7			2			5	27
1	3		6	5	4	11			8		9	10					7			2				28
1	3		6	5	4	11			8		9	10					7			2				29
1	3		6	5	4	11			8		9	10					7			2				30
30	30	2	29	25	28	27	5	7	28	1	26	21	2	3	1	1	27	1	4	25	3	3	1	
			1	1	1	4			7		4	3					5		1		1			

Scorers unknown: 18

1	3		6	5	4			11	8		9						7		10	2				Q
1	1		1	1	1			1	1		1						1		1	1				
									1		1													

1897-98

Manager: T.Cashmore

1	Sep	4	(h)	Bristol Eastville R	L	1-2	Davis	
2		11	(a)	Wolves Res	D	0-0		
3		18	(h)	Hereford Town	W	1-0	Davis	
4	Oct	9	(h)	Small Heath Res	W	3-1	Roberts, Davis, Newhall	
5		16	(h)	Kidderminster H	W	4-0	Davis, Taylor, Newhall 2	
6		23	(a)	Aston Villa Res	L	0-3		
7		30	(a)	Shrewsbury T	L	1-4	Davis	
8	Nov	6	(h)	Bristol St George	W	1-0	Taylor	
9		13	(h)	Shrewsbury T	W	4-0	Davis 2, Haywood, Newhall	
10		20	(a)	Bristol St George	L	3-4	Davis, Haywood, Newhall	
11		27	(a)	Stourbridge	L	1-2	Newhall	
12	Dec	4	(a)	Bristol Eastville R	L	3-11	Taylor, Davis, Newhall	
13		11	(h)	Wolves Res	W	2-1	Woodfield, Newhall	
14		28	(a)	Brierley Hill All	W	3-2	Scorers unknown	
15	Jan	1	(h)	Hereford Thistle	D	2-2	Lowe, Taylor	
16		8	(a)	Worcester R	L	0-3		
17		15	(h)	Stourbridge	W	4-1	Taylor, Davis, Newhall 2	800
18		22	(h)	Brierley Hill All	L	2-3	Taylor 2	1,100
19		29	(h)	West Brom A Res	W	3-0	Taylor, Haywood, Newhall	1,200
20	Feb	5	(a)	Small Heath Res	L	0-2		
21		12	(h)	Halesowen	W	2-1	Wright, Newhall	
22		19	(a)	Hereford Thistle	W	3-0	Bentley, Davis, Scorer unknown	
23		26	(h)	Worcester R	W	1-0	Taylor	
24	Mar	5	(h)	Kidderminster H	L	0-4		
25		12	(a)	Hereford Town	L	0-1		
26		19	(h)	Aston Villa Res	L	0-3		
27	Apr	4	(h)	Berwick R	W	2-1	Taylor, Newhall	
28		9	(a)	West Brom A Res	L	0-3		
29		12	(a)	Halesowen	L	3-4	Scorers unknown	
30		23	(a)	Berwick R	D	1-1	Scorer unknown	

FINAL LEAGUE POSITION: 7th in Birmingham & District League

Appearances
Goals

FA Cup

Q1	Oct	2	(a)	Wrockwardine Wood	L	0-1	700

Appearances
Goals

Robinson	Alldrick	Harris	Whitehouse	Roberts	Lomas	Wright	Taylor	Davis	Haywood	Spicer	Newhall	Hemmersley	Lowe	Woodfield	Bentley	Fletcher	Craddock	Cashmore	Gallier	Potter	
1	2	3	4	5	6	7	8	9	10	11											1
1	2	3	4	5	6	7	8	9	11		10										2
1	2	3	4	5	6	7	8	9	10		11										3
1	2	3	4	5	6	7	8	9	10		11										4
1	2	3	4	5	6	7	8	9	10		11										5
1	2	3	4	5	6			9	10		11	7	8								6
1	2	3	4	5	6	7	8	9	10		11										7
1	2	3	4	5	6	7	8	9	10		11										8
1	2	3	4	5	6	7	8	9	10		11										9
1	2	3	4	5	6	7	8	9	10		11										10
1	2	3	4	5	6	7	8	9	10		11										11
1	2	3	4	5	6		7	9	10		11			8							12
1		3	4	5	6	8		9	10		11			7	2						13
1		3	4	5	6		8	9	10		11			7	2						14
1		3	4	5			8	9	10		11	6	7		2						15
1		3	2	5	4	7	8	9	10		11	6									16
1		3	4	5	6	7	8	9	10		11					2					17
		3	4	5	6	7	8	9	10		11					2	1				18
1		3	4	5	6	7	8	9	10		11							2			19
1		3	4	5	6	7	8	9	10		11							2			20
1		3	4	5	6	7	8	9			10				11			2			21
1		3	4	5	6		8	9			10				7			2	11		22
1		3	4	5	6		8	9	10		11				7			2			23
1		3	4	5	6	2	8	9	10		11				7						24
1		3	4	5	6	2	8	9	10		11				7						25
1		3	4	5	6	2	8	9	10		11				7						26
1		3	4	5	6	2	8	9	10		11				7						27
1		3	4	5	6	2	8	9	10		11				7						28
1		3	4	5	6	2	8	9	10		11				7						29
1		3	4	5	6	2	8	9	10		11				7						30
29	12	30	30	30	29	24	28	30	28	1	29	3	2	3	13	2	1	5	1		
				1		1	10	11	3		13		1	1	1						

Scorers unknown: 8

1	2	3	4	5	6	7	8	9	10	11	Q1
1	1	1	1	1	1	1	1	1	1	1	

1898-99

Manager: T.Cashmore

1	Sep	3	(a)	Wellington T	L 0-5		
2		10	(h)	Berwick R	L 0-3		
3		17	(a)	Bristol R	L 1-5	Hayward	
4		24	(h)	Aston Villa Res	L 0-2		2,000
5	Oct	8	(a)	Stourbridge	W 3-2	Taylor, Davis, Edwards	
6		15	(h)	Dudley	D 1-1	Edwards	
7		22	(a)	Halesowen	W 3-2	Wright, Charley, Scorer unknown	
8		29	(h)	Hereford Town	L 0-1		
9	Nov	5	(a)	Shrewsbury T	L 2-3	Lomas, Wright	
10		12	(h)	Bristol St George	D 2-2	Wright, Hayward	
11		19	(a)	West Brom A Res	L 1-3	Charley	1,000
12		26	(h)	Small Heath Res	D 2-2	Lomas, Hayward	
13	Dec	3	(a)	Brierley Hill All	L 1-2	Whitehouse	
14		10	(h)	Kidderminster H	W 2-1	Lomas 2	
15		17	(a)	Wolves Res	L 0-3		
16		24	(h)	Hereford Thistle	D 1-1	Lomas	
17		31	(h)	Wellington T	W 4-1	Lomas, Chatland 2, Charley	
18	Jan	7	(a)	Berwick R	W 3-1	Charley 2, Opp own-goal	
19		14	(h)	Bristol R	L 1-3	Walker	1,000
20		21	(a)	Aston Villa Res	L 2-3	Wright, Charley	1,500
21		28	(h)	Worcester R	W 6-1	Lomas 2, Chatland, Charley 3	1,000
22	Feb	4	(h)	Stourbridge	D 1-1	Charley	1,200
23		11	(a)	Dudley	D 1-1	Chatland	
24		18	(h)	Halesowen	W 2-1	Walker 2	1,200
25		25	(a)	Hereford Town	W 1-0	Walker	
26	Mar	4	(h)	Shrewsbury T	W 3-1	Lomas, Chatland, Charley	800
27		11	(a)	Bristol St George	W 3-2	Chatland, Taylor 2	
28		18	(h)	West Brom A Res	D 1-1	Wright	1,500
29		25	(a)	Small Heath Res	W 2-1	Taylor, Edwards	
30	Apr	1	(h)	Brierley Hill All	W 4-2	Taylor, Chatland 2, Charley	
31		3	(a)	Worcester R	W 3-1	Walker, Chatland, Charley	
32		8	(h)	Kidderminster H	L 0-1		
33		15	(h)	Wolves Res	L 0-2		2,000
34		22	(a)	Hereford Thistle	L 1-3	Robinson	

FINAL LEAGUE POSITION: 7th in Birmingham & District League

Appearances
Goals

FA Cup

P	Oct	1	(h)	Hereford Town	D 0-0	1,200
R			(a)	Hereford Town	L 0-1	

Appearances
Goals

Robinson	Whitehouse	Harris	Wareham	Roberts	Lomas	Edwards	Taylor	Bodley	Hayward	Newhall	Wright	Alldrick	Turner	Davis	Charley	Clithero	Walker	Brame	Chatland	Allsop	Robertson	Rowley	Cashmore	Jackson	Sheldon	Robinson	
1	2	3	4	5	6	7	8	9	10	11																	1
1	4	3	9	5	6	7	8		10	11	2																2
1	4	3	9	5	6	7	8		10	11	2																3
1	4	3	7	5	6	9	8		10	11	2																4
1	4	3		5	6	10	8					2	7	9	11												5
1	4	3		5	6	10	8					2	7	9	11												6
1	4	3		5	6	10				7	8	2			11	9											7
1	4	3		5	6	10					8	2			11	9	7										8
1	4	3		5	6	11			10	9	8	2					7										9
1	4	3		5	6				10	9	8	2			11		7										10
1	4	3		5	6				10	9	8	2			11		7										11
1	4	3		5	6				10	9	8	2			11		7										12
1	4	3		5	6				10	9	8	2			11		7										13
1	4	3	6	5	9						8	2			11		7	10									14
1	4	3	6	5	9				10		8	2			11		7										15
1	4	3		5	6		9		10		8	2			11		7										16
1	4	3		5	6		10				8	2			11		7		9								17
1	4	3		5	6		10				8	2			11		7		9								18
1	4	3		5	6		10				8	2			11		7		9								19
1	4	3		5	6		10				8	2			11		7		9								20
1	4	3		5	6		10				8	2			11		7		9								21
1	4	3		5	6		10				8	2			11		7		9								22
1	4	3		5	6		10				8	2			11		7		9								23
1	4	3		5	6	10					8	2			11		7		9								24
1	4	3		5	6	10					8	2			11		7		9								25
1	4	3		5	6	10					8	2			11		7		9								26
1	4	3		5	6		10				8	2			11		7		9								27
1	4	3		5	6		10				8	2			11		7		9								28
1	4	3		5	6	9	10				8	2			11		7										29
1	4	3		5	6	9	8					2			11		7		10								30
1	4	3		5	6	9	8					2			11		7		10								31
1	4	3		5	6	9	8					2			11		7		10								32
1	4	3		5	6		9				8	2			11		7		10								33
					6		10					11						7		1	2	3	4	5	8	9	34
33	33	33	6	33	34	16	22	1	11	10	27	30	2	2	28	2	26	2	16	1	1	1	1	1	1	1	
	1				9	3	5		3		5			1	13		5		9								

Scorer unknown: 1. 1 own-goal

1	4	3	7	5	6	9	8		11	10		2	P
1	4	3	7	5	6	9	8		11	10		2	R
2	2	2	2	2	2	2	2		2	2		2	

1899-1900

Manager: T.Cashmore

1		9	(h)	Shrewsbury T	W	1-0	Ridout	3,000
2		16	(a)	Wolves Res	L	0-3		
3	Oct	7	(h)	Dudley	L	2-5	Ridout 2	1,200
4		14	(h)	Kidderminster H	W	4-2	Walker, Porter, Crofts 2	1,000
5		21	(a)	Small Heath Res	L	3-6	Ridout, Porter, Crofts	2,000
6		28	(h)	West Brom A Res	L	2-3	Holmes, Opp own-goal	1,100
7	Nov	4	(a)	Wellington T	L	0-3		
8		17	(h)	Halesowen	W	2-0	Ridout 2	
9		25	(h)	Brierley Hill All	D	4-4	Walker 2, Ridout, Crofts	500
10	Dec	2	(a)	Bristol R	L	6-7	Walker, Holmes, Porter 2, Crofts 2	
11		9	(h)	Hereford Town	L	1-3	Walker	
12		16	(a)	Walsall	L	0-2		300
13		23	(h)	Aston Villa Res	W	3-0	Walker 3	800
14		26	(a)	Stourbridge	L	1-4	Wareham	1,800
15	Jan	6	(a)	Shrewsbury T	L	0-2		
16		13	(h)	Wolves Res	D	4-4	Walker, Chatland, Porter, Crofts	
17		27	(a)	Aston Villa Res	L	1-9	Porter	
18	Feb	3	(h)	Stourbridge	W	4-2	Walker 2, Chatland, Scorer unknown	
19		10	(a)	Dudley	L	0-7		
20		17	(a)	Kidderminster H	L	1-4	Porter	
21		24	(h)	Small Heath Res	L	2-3	Walker, Chatland	700
22	Mar	3	(a)	West Brom A Res	L	0-2		
23		10	(h)	Wellington T	D	1-1	Chatland	
24		17	(a)	Halesowen	L	0-8		
25		24	(h)	Berwick R	L	1-3	Lomas	300
26		31	(a)	Brierley Hill All	L	0-6		
27	Apr	7	(h)	Bristol R	L	1-2	Robinson	200
28		14	(a)	Hereford Town	L	0-3		
29		16	(a)	Berwick R	L	0-1		
30		21	(h)	Walsall	W	3-1	Jones 2, Robson	

FINAL LEAGUE POSITION: 16th in Birmingham & District League

*Results of the fixtures against Wellington St George and Worcester Rovers were later expunged from League records

Appearances

Goals

FA Cup

P	Sep	30	(a)	Stourbridge	L	0-5	

Appearances

Goals

Harris A	Wareham	Harris J	Whitehouse	Brampton	Lomas	Holmes	Walker	Ridout	Porter	Crofts	Partridge	Roberts	Robertson	Jones	Hantin	Hogan	Pickering	Chatland	Wright	Cashmore	Whalton	McPherson	Robinson	Newey	Nadin	Robson	Rock	
1	2	3	4	5	6	7	8	9	10	11																		1
1	2	3	4	5	6	7	8	9	10	11																		2
	2	3	4	7	6	8		9	10	11	1	5																3
	2	3	4		6	8	7	9	10	11	1	5																4
	2	3	4	6		8	7	9	10	11	1	5																5
	2		4		6	8	7	9	10	11		5	1						3									6
1	2	3	4		6	8	7	9	10	11		5																7
1	2		4		6	8	7	9	10	11		5		3														8
1	2		4		6	8	7	9	10	11		5		3														9
1	2		4	5	6	8	7	9	10	11		3																10
1	2		4	5	6	8	7	9	10	11		3																11
1	2		4	8	6		7	9	10	11		5			3													12
1	2	3	4		6	8	7	9	10	11		5																13
1	2	3	4		6	8	7	9	10	11		5																14
1	2		4		6	8	7	9	10	11		5				3												15
1	2		4		6	8	7		10	11		5				3		9										16
	2		4		6	8	7		10	11		5				3	1	9										17
	2	3	4		6	8	7		10	11		5					1	9										18
	2	3	4		6	8			10	11		5					1	9	7									19
	2		4			8	7		10	11		5					1	9	6	3								20
		3	4			8	7		10	11		5		2			1	9	6									21
		3	4		6	8	7		10	11		5		2			1	9										22
		3	4		6	8	7		10	11		5		2			1	9										23
	2	3	4		6	8	7		10	11		5					1	9										24
	6	3	4		7	8	7		10	11				2			1	9										25
	5	3	4		6	7			10					2			1	11	8		9							26
		3	4						10			5		11			1					2	6	7	8	9		27
		3	4						10			5		11			1						6	7	8	9	2	28
		3	4				9		10			5		11	6		1							7	8		2	29
		3	4						10			5		11	6		1							7	8	9	2	30
12	23	20	30	7	23	25	24	15	30	25	3	26	1	11	3	3	14	11	5	1	1	1	2	4	4	3	3	
	1				1	4	13	9	7	11				2				4					1			1		

Scorer unknown: 1. 1 own-goal

1	2	3	4	5	6	8	7	9	10	11	P
1	1	1	1	1	1	1	1	1	1	1	

1900-01

Manager: B.Newhall

1	Sep	1	(h)	Ruabon Druids	D	1-1	Lee	600
2		8	(a)	Hereford Town	L	0-1		
3		15	(h)	Ironbridge	W	3-0	Crofts 2, Charley	500
4		22	(a)	Wellington St George	L	2-5	Crofts, Charley	
5	Oct	13	(a)	Stoke Res	L	2-6	Walker, Nadin	1,500
6		20	(h)	West Brom A Res	W	3-2	Nadin, Mobley, Porter	
7		27	(a)	Small Heath Res	L	0-10		
8	Nov	3	(h)	Kidderminster H	W	4-1	Walker 2, Mobley, Crofts	
9		10	(a)	Berwick R	D	1-1	Porter	
10		17	(h)	Halesowen	L	2-3	Walker, Nadin	
11		24	(a)	Shrewsbury T	D	1-1	Charley	
12	Dec	1	(h)	Stourbridge	W	5-1	Wareham, Walker 3, Charley	
13		18	(a)	Dudley	L	2-3	Charley, Porter	
14		15	(h)	Wolves Res	L	0-8		
15		22	(a)	Aston Villa Res	L	1-14	Scorer unknown	3,500
16		29	(a)	Ruabon Druids	L	4-6	Whitehouse, Mobley 2, Charley	
17	Jan	5	(h)	Hereford Town	W	3-1	Charley 2, Mobley	
18		19	(h)	Wellington St George	W	4-0	Lomas, Walker 2, Charley	
19	Feb	9	(a)	Stafford R	L	0-2		
20		16	(h)	Stoke Res	L	2-3	Walker, Crofts	
21		23	(a)	West Brom A Res	L	1-7	Hannibat	
22	Mar	2	(h)	Small Heath Res	W	2-1	Chatland, Crofts	
23		9	(a)	Kidderminster H	L	0-6		
24		16	(h)	Berwick R	L	0-1		
25		23	(a)	Halesowen	L	1-2	Walker	
26		30	(h)	Shrewsbury T	W	5-2	Chatland, Hannibat, Mobley, Gilchrist, Crofts	
27	Apr	5	(h)	Brierley Hill All	W	4-1	Roberts, Mobley, Porter, Crofts	
28		6	(a)	Stourbridge	L	1-2	Crofts	
29		8	(a)	Ironbridge	D	1-1	Robson	
30		9	(h)	Stafford R	L	1-2	Robson	
31		13	(h)	Dudley	L	1-2	Gilchrist	
32		20	(a)	Wolves Res	L	0-2		
33		22	(a)	Brierley Hill All	D	1-1	Robson	
34		27	(h)	Aston Villa Res	D	2-2	Robson 2	

FINAL LEAGUE POSITION: 14th in Birmingham & District League

Appearances

Goals

In the FA Cup Coventry City were drawn against Oswestry Town but withdrew to fulfill a League fixture.

Pickering	Wareham	Harris	Whitehouse	Roberts	Eburne	Walker	Williams	Lee	Porter	Charley	Galma	Nadin	Crofts	Lomas	Mobley	Jarvis	Rock	Porter	Chatland	Sharp	Mealing	Hannibat	Gilchrist	Harbridge	Bradley	Shaw	Robson	Peers	
1	2	3	4	5	6	7	8	9	10	11																			1
1	2	3	4	5		7			10	11	6	8	9																2
1	2	3	4	5		7			10	11		8	9	6															3
1	2	3	4	5		7			10	11		8	9	6															4
1	2	3	4	5		7			10	11		8		6	9														5
1	2	3	4	5		7			10	11		8		6	9														6
	2	3	4	5		7			10	11		8	6		9	1													7
	2	3	4	5		7			10	11		8		6	9	1													8
	2	3	4	5		7			10	11		8		6	9	1													9
	2	3	4	5		7			10	11		8		6	9	1													10
		3	4	5		7			10	9		8		6		1	2	11											11
	5	3	4			7			10	9		8		6		1	2	11											12
	5	3	4			7			10	9		8		6		1	2	11											13
	5	3	4			7			10	11		8	9	6		1	2												14
	5	3	4			7			10	11			8	6	9	1	2												15
	5	3	4			7			10	11			8	6	9	1			5										16
	5	3	4	5		7			10	9				6	11	1				8									17
	2	3	4			7			10	11			8	6	9	1					5								18
	2	3	4			7			10	9			11	6		1					5	8							19
	2	3	4			7			10				11	6	9	1					5	8							20
	2	3	4			7			10				11	6	9	1					5	8							21
	2	3	4						10				11	6	9	1			5	8		7							22
	2	3	4						10	9			11	6		1			5	7		8							23
	2	3	5			7				9			11	6		1	4					8	10						24
	2	3	5			7				9			11			1						4	10	6	8				25
	3		4			7				6			11		9		2		5			8	10			1			26
	3		4	5		7			10	6			11		9		2						8			1			27
	3		4	5		7			10	6			11		9		2									1	8		28
	3			5		7				6			4		9		2			10			11			1	8		29
	3		4	5		7			10	6			11		9		2									1	8		30
	3		4	5		7			10				10		9		2						11			1	8		31
	3		4	5		7			10	6			11		9		2									1	8		32
	3		4	5		7			10	6			11		9		2									1	8		33
	3		4	5		7			10				11		9		2									1	8	6	34
6	33	25	33	20	1	32	1	1	30	29	1	13	24	22	21	19	15	3	4	4	4	8	6	1	1	9	7	1	
	1		1	1		11		1	4	9		3	9	1	7			3	2			2	2				5		

Scorer unknown: 1

1901-02

Manager: B.Newhall

1	Sep	7	(a)	Crewe A	L 0-4	
2		14	(h)	Aston Villa Res	D 1-1	Walker
3		21	(a)	Hereford Town	L 1-4	Hannibat
4		28	(h)	Ruabon Druids	W 4-1	Robson 2, Beardsworth 2
5	Oct	5	(a)	Kidderminster H	W 2-0	Beardsworth 2
6		12	(h)	Brierley Hill All	L 1-3	Whitehouse
7		26	(a)	Stoke Res	L 0-3	
8	Nov	2	(h)	Ironbridge	D 0-0	
9		9	(a)	Berwick R	L 2-4	Davis, Walker
10		23	(a)	Halesowen	D 1-1	Davis
11		30	(h)	Dudley	W 3-1	Walker, Fern, Porter
12	Dec	7	(a)	Stourbridge	L 0-4	
13		14	(h)	Stafford R	L 3-4	J.Seddons, Fern, Peers
14		21	(a)	Wolves Res	L 1-3	S.Seddons
15		26	(a)	Ironbridge	L 0-10	
16		28	(h)	Shrewsbury T	L 3-4	Fern, Porter, Lee
17	Jan	4	(a)	Crewe A	L 0-3	
18		11	(a)	Aston Villa Res	L 0-6	
19		18	(h)	Hereford Town	D 0-0	
20		25	(a)	Ruabon Druids	L 1-4	Lee
21	Feb	1	(h)	Kidderminster H	W 1-0	Walker
22		8	(a)	Brierley Hill All	D 3-3	Walker, Fern, Lee
23		15	(a)	West Brom A Res	L 1-3	Harris
24		22	(h)	Stoke Res	W 4-2	Walker, Harris, Porter 2
25	Mar	8	(h)	Berwick R	L 0-1	
26		15	(a)	Small Heath Res	L 1-6	Fern
27		22	(h)	Halesowen	W 2-0	Harris, Porter
28		29	(a)	Dudley	L 0-2	
29	Apr	1	(h)	West Brom A Res	L 0-3	
30		2	(h)	Small Heath Res	D 2-2	Walker, S.Seddons
31		5	(h)	Stourbridge	L 0-2	
32		12	(a)	Stafford R	L 2-5	Whitehouse, Walker
33		19	(h)	Wolves Res	L 2-5	Fern 2
34		26	(a)	Shrewsbury T	L 0-2	

FINAL LEAGUE POSITION: 16th in Birmingham & District League

Appearances

Goals

FA Cup

Q	Nov	2	(a)	Berwick R	L 2-11	Gold, Opp own-goal	1,000

Appearances

Goals

Shaw	Wareham	Seddons J	Whitehouse	Buckingham	Peers	Walker	Downing	Devine	Beardsworth	Crofts	Davis	Robson	Gilchrist	Griffin	Hannibat	Gold	Porter	Harris	Saunders	Fern	Seddons S	Sutthery	Buckingham	Redman	Lee	Andrews	Charley	Dipple	Griffon	Gillingham	Paulson	
1	2	3	4	5	6	7	8	9	10	11																						1
1	2	3	4		6	7		9	11		5	8	10																			2
1		3	4		6	7		9	10		5			2	8	11																3
1	2	3	4		5	7		9	10		6	8					11															4
1	2	3	4		5	7		9	10		6	8					11															5
1	2	3	4		5	7		9	10		6	8					11															6
1	2	3	4		5	7		9	10		6	8					11															7
1	2		4		5	7			9		6	8					11	3	10													8
1	2	3	4	9	5	7			10		6	8					11															9
1	2	3	4		5	7			8		6						10			9	11											10
	2	3	4		5	7			8		6						10			9	11	1										11
	2	3	4		5	7			8		6						10			9	11		1									12
	2	3	4	5	9	7					6						10			8	11	1										13
	2	3	4		5	7			8		6						10			9	11	1										14
	2	3	4		5	7			8		6	9					10				11			1								15
	2	3	4			7					6	9					10			8	11		1		5							16
1	2	3	4	5	6	7				8		10					11			9												17
	2	3	4		5	7				8	6						10			9	11	1										18
	2		4		5	7			11		3	9								8	10	1			6							19
1	2	3	4		5	7					6	10					11			8					9							20
1	2	3	4		5	7					6						10			8	11				9							21
1	2	3	4		5	7					6	10					11			8					9							22
1	2	3	4		5	7					6						10	9		8	11											23
1	2	3	4		5	7					6						10	9		8	11											24
1	2	3	4		5	7					6						10	9		8	11											25
1	2	3	4		5	7					6						10	9		8	11											26
1	2	3	4		5	7					6						10	9		8	11											27
1		3	4		5	7	9				6						10	2		8	11											28
1		3	4		5	7	9				6						10	2		8	11											29
1	2	3	4			7	9		8		6						10				11				5							30
1	2	3	4			7	9		8		6						10				11				5							31
1		3	4		6	7					2	9					10			8					5	11						32
1		3	4		2	7					6	9					10			8					5		11					33
1		3	4			7					6	9					10	2		8	11				5							34
26	28	32	34	4	30	34	5	7	17	3	32	16	1	1	1	1	30	9	1	22	20	5	2	1	10	1	1					
		1	2		1	8			4		2	2			1		5	3		7	2				3							

		3					8			6			9		7	11							5					1	2	4	10	Q
		1					1			1			1		1	1							1					1	1	1	1	
																1																

1 own-goal

1902-03

Manager: B.Newhall

1	Sep	6	(h)	Aston Villa Res	L	2-6	Lee, Taplin	
2		13	(a)	Ruabon Druids	L	2-5	Craythorne, Porter	
3		20	(a)	Kidderminster H	L	1-2	Whitmore	
4		27	(h)	Brierley Hill All	L	2-3	Craythorne, Taplin	
5	Oct	4	(h)	Crewe A	L	1-4	Porter	
6		11	(h)	Stoke Res	W	2-1	Sawyer, Craythorne	
7		18	(a)	Dudley	L	2-3	Porter, Scorer unknown	
8		25	(h)	Worcester C	D	2-2	Sawyer, Scorer unknown	
9	Nov	8	(h)	West Brom A Res	L	1-3	Opp own-goal	
10		22	(h)	Dudley	W	3-0	Craythorne 2, Porter	
11	Dec	6	(h)	Stafford R	W	4-1	Sawyer 2, Craythorne, Porter	
12		13	(a)	Wolves Res	W	5-4	Walker 2, Taplin, Sawyer, Craythorne	
13		20	(h)	Ironbridge	W	9-0	Porter 4, Sawyer 3, Taplin 2	
14		25	(a)	Small Heath Res	L	0-1		
15		26	(h)	Small Heath Res	L	2-3	Taplin, Porter	
16		27	(a)	Shrewsbury T	D	0-0		
17	Jan	3	(a)	Aston Villa Res	D	1-1	Taplin	8,000
18		10	(h)	Ruabon Druids	W	2-0	Taplin, Sawyer	3,840
19		17	(h)	Kidderminster H	W	2-0	Lee, Porter	
20		24	(a)	Brierley Hill All	W	5-3	Chaplin, Walker, Sawyer, Porter 2	
21		31	(a)	Crewe A	W	6-1	Lee, Walker, Taplin, Sawyer, Porter 2	
22	Feb	7	(a)	Stoke Res	D	0-0		
23		14	(h)	Wellington T	D	0-0		
24		21	(a)	Worcester C	L	1-2	Craythorne	
25	Mar	2	(a)	Stourbridge	W	3-2	Craythorne 2, Porter	
26		7	(a)	West Brom A Res	L	0-1		
27		14	(h)	Halesowen	W	4-3	Taplin 2, Porter, Whitehouse	
28		23	(a)	Wellington T	L	1-5	Walker	
29		28	(h)	Stourbridge	W	3-2	Mundy, Porter 2	
30	Apr	4	(a)	Stafford R	L	0-4		
31		6	(a)	Halesowen	W	3-1	Taplin, Porter, Craythorne	
32		11	(h)	Wolves Res	W	2-1	Craythorne 2	
33		18	(a)	Ironbridge	D	1-1	Walker	
34		24	(h)	Shrewsbury T	W	3-2	Taplin 2, Craythorne	

FINAL LEAGUE POSITION: 7th in Birmingham & District League

Appearances
Goals

FA Cup

Q1	Nov	1	(h)	Aberaman	W	3-1	Fern, Taplin 2
Q2		15	(h)	Stafford R	W	5-2	Lea, Taplin 2, Sawyer, Craythorne
Q3		29	(h)	Kidderminster H	D	2-2	Davis, Taplin
R	Dec	1	(a)	Kidderminster H	L	2-4	Sawyer, Porter

Appearances
Goals

Thompson	Wareham	Woodward	Davis	Lee	Ellard	Whitmore G	Fern	Taplin	Craythorne	Porter	Shaw	Whitehouse J	Whitmore J	Walker	Savage	Morrey	Sawyer	Fetcher	Whitehouse H	Hewitt	Jenkyns	Chapplin	Ray	Smith	Mundy	
1	2	3	4	5	6	7	8	9	10	11																1
	2	3	6	5		7	8	9	10	11	1	4														2
	2		6	5		7		9	10	11	1	4	3	8												3
	2		6	5			8	9	10	11	1	4		7	3											4
	2		6			8		9	10	11	1	4	5			3	7									5
	2		6	5		8		9	10	11	1	4				3	7									6
	2		6	5		8		9	10	11	1	4				3	7									7
	2		6	5				9	10	11	1	4				3	7	8								8
	2		6	5				9	10	11	1	4				3	7	8								9
	2		6	5				8	10	11		4		7		3	9		1							10
	2		6					8	10	11		4		7			9		1	3	5					11
			6					8	10	11		4		7		2	9		1		5					12
			2	5				8	10	11		4		7			9		1	3	5					13
			2	5				8	10	11		4		7			9		1	3	5					14
			2	5				8	10	11		4		7			9		1	3	5					15
			2	5				8	10	11		4		7			9		1	3	5					16
	2		6	4				8	10	11		4		7			9		1	3						17
	2		6	4				8	10	11		4		7			9		1	3						18
			2	5				8	10	11		4		7			9		1	3		5				19
			2	5				8	10	11		4		7			9		1	3		5				20
			2	5				8	10	11		4		7			9		1	3		5				21
			6					8	10	11		4		7			9		1	3		5	2			22
			6					8	10	11		4		7			9		1	3		5	2			23
	5		6	9				8	10	11		4		7					1	3			2			24
	5		6	9				8	10	11		4		7					1	3			2			25
	9		6	5		8			10	11		4		7					1	3			2			26
	2		6	5		8		9	10	11		4		7					1	3						27
			2	6		8		9	10	11		4		7					1	3				5		28
			6	5				9	10	11		4		7					1	3			2			29
			6	5				9	10	11		4		7					1	3			2		8	30
			6	5		8		9	10	11		4		7					1	3			2			31
			6	5				8	10	11		4		7					1	3			2	9		32
			6	5				8	10	11		4		7					1	3			2	9		33
			6	5				8	10	11		4		7					1	3			2	9		34
1	17	2	34	29	1	11	3	33	34	34	8	33	2	27	1	7	19	2	25	24	6	5	11	4	1	
				3		1		14	14	20		1	1	6			11					1			1	

Scorers unknown: 2. 1 own-goal

	2		6	5			8	9	10	11	1	4				3	7									Q1
	2		6	5				8	10	11	1	4		7		3	9									Q2
	2		6	5				8	10	11		4		7		3	9		1							Q3
	2		6	5				8	10	11		4		7		3	9		1							R
	4		4	4			1	4	4	4	2	4		3		4	4		2							
			1	1			1	5	1	1							2									

1903-04

Manager: M.O'Shea

1	Sep	5	(a)	Wolves Res	W	2-0	Craythorne, Porter	
2		12	(h)	Ruabon Druids	W	3-1	Walker, Sawyer, Craythorne	4,000
3		19	(h)	Stoke Res	L	2-3	Tovey, Porter	
4		26	(a)	Brierley Hill All	L	1-2	Porter	
5	Oct	3	(h)	Kidderminster H	L	1-3	Walker	3,000
6		10	(a)	Wellington T	D	0-0		
7		17	(h)	West Brom A Res	L	0-1		5,000
8		24	(a)	Small Heath Res	W	3-2	Walker 2, Craythorne	
9	Nov	7	(a)	Worcester C	W	7-2	Walker 2, Bartram, Taplin, Craythorne 3	
10		14	(h)	Dudley	W	3-0	Bartram, Walker, Porter	4,000
11		21	(a)	Stourbridge	L	1-2	Smith	
12	Dec	5	(a)	Shrewsbury T	W	2-0	Hadley, Scorer unknown	
13		12	(h)	Aston Villa Res	L	0-5		
14		19	(a)	Stafford R	L	1-2	Walker	1,500
15		25	(a)	Aston Villa Res	L	0-5		
16		26	(h)	Walsall R	W	2-0	Craythorne 2	
17		28	(h)	Crewe A	L	1-2	Craythorne	
18	Jan	2	(h)	Wolves Res	D	1-1	Craythorne	
19		16	(a)	Stoke Res	D	3-3	Taplin, Craythorne, Scorer unknown	
20		23	(h)	Brierley Hill All	D	1-1	Griffiths	3,000
21		30	(a)	Kidderminster H	W	1-0	Walker	
22	Feb	6	(h)	Wellington T	L	0-3		
23		20	(h)	Small Heath Res	L	1-3	Opp own-goal	
24		27	(a)	Crewe A	L	1-3	Walker	
25	Mar	2	(a)	Ruabon Druids	W	2-1	Taplin, Craythorne	
26		5	(h)	Worcester C	W	1-0	Robinson	
27		12	(a)	Dudley	L	4-6	Hadley, Lee, Griffiths 2	
28		19	(h)	Stourbridge	D	1-1	Taplin	
29		21	(h)	West Brom A Res	D	2-2	Taplin, Opp own-goal	
30		26	(a)	Halesowen	W	3-2	Clive, Taplin, Craythorne	
31	Apr	2	(h)	Shrewsbury T	W	2-1	Griffiths, Craythorne	
32		4	(h)	Halesowen	D	0-0		
33		16	(h)	Stafford R	L	1-2	Craythorne	
34		23	(a)	Walsall	L	0-1		

FINAL LEAGUE POSITION: 11th in Birmingham & District League — Appearances / Goals

FA Cup

Q1	Oct	31	(h)	Walsall	L	2-4	Walker, Opp own-goal	5,000

Appearances

Goals

Whitehouse H	Parish	Hewitt	Whitehouse J	Smith	Davis	Walker	Taplin	Sawyer	Craythorne R	Porter	Tovey	Wareham	Taylor	Hadley	Whitmore	Phillip	Macalea	Lea	Bartram	Pugh	Spence	Dexter	Jones H	Robinson	Griffiths	Small	Kearns	Clive	McDonald	
1	2	3	4	5	6	7	8	9	10	11																				1
1	2	3	4	5	6	7	8	9	10	11																				2
1	2	3	4	5	6	7	8		10	11	9																			3
1	2	3	4	5	6	7	8		10	11		9																		4
1	2	3	4	5		7	8	9	10	11		6																		5
		3	4	5	2	7	9		10	11			1	6	9															6
		3		5	2	7	8		10	11			1	4		6	9													7
		3	4	5	2	7	9		10	11			1					6	8											8
	2	3		5		7	9		10	11			1	4					8	6										9
	2	3		5		9	7		10	11			1	4					8	6										10
	2	3		5		9	7		10	11			1	4					8	6										11
	2	3		5		9	7		10	11			1	4						6	8									12
	2	3		5		9	7		10	11			1	4						6	8									13
	2	3		5		9	7		10	11			1	4					8	6										14
	2	3		5		7	8		10	11			1	4				6				9								15
	2	3	8	5		9	7		10	11			1	4				6												16
	2	3	8	5		9	7		10	11			1	4				6												17
	2		4	5	3	7	9		10	11			1	6					8											18
	2	3		5		7	8		10				1	6								11	4	9						19
	2	3		5		7	8		10	11			1	6									4		9					20
	2	3				7	8		10	11			1							6			4		9					21
		3		2		7	8		10	11			1							6			4		9	5				22
	2	3					7		10	11			1	6				5					4		9	8				23
	3			5		7	8		10	11			1					6					4		9		2			24
	3			5		7	8		10	11			1					6					4		9		2			25
	3			5		7	8		10	11			1					6					4	9			2			26
	2	3		5			7			11			1	6				9					4	10	8					27
	2	3					9			11			1	6				5					4		7			8	10	28
	2	3				11	9		10				1	6				5					4		7			8		29
	2	3				11	9		10				1	4				5		6					7			8		30
	2	3					9		10	11			1	6				5					4		7			8		31
	2	3		5			9		10	11			1	4						6					7			8		32
	3						9		10	11			1	6				5					4		7		2	8		33
1	3			5					10	11				6						9			4		7		2	8		34
6	30	28	10	27	8	28	33	3	32	31	1	2	28	23	1	1	1	14	6	11	2	2	14	3	14	2	5	7	1	
				1		10	6	1	15	4	1			2				1	2					1	4			1		

Scorers unknown: 2. 2 own-goals

		3	4	5	2	7	9		10	11			1					6	8	Q1
		1	1	1	1	1	1		1	1			1					1	1	
						1														

1 own-goal

1904-05

Manager: M.O'Shea

1	Sep	3	(h)	Wolves Res	D	2-2	Clive, Banks	3,000
2		10	(a)	Aston Villa Res	L	1-7	Edwards	5,000
3		17	(h)	Walsall	W	2-0	Belton, Banks	
4		24	(a)	Burslem P Vale Res	D	2-2	Edwards, Banks	1,000
5	Oct	8	(h)	Worcester C	L	1-2	Belton	2,500
6		22	(h)	Kidderminster H	L	2-3	Arnold, Belton	3,000
7	Nov	5	(h)	Stoke Res	W	2-1	Edwards, Arnold	2,000
8		12	(a)	Small Heath Res	L	1-4	Belton	4,000
9		19	(h)	West Brom A Res	L	2-3	Beaman, Porter	
10		26	(a)	Halesowen	L	3-5	Mundy 2, Belton	
11	Dec	3	(h)	Stourbridge	W	2-0	Belton, Banks	
12		10	(a)	Dudley	L	2-5	Banks 2	
13		17	(h)	Shrewsbury T	W	4-0	Mundy 2, Belton, Banks	
14		24	(a)	Stafford R	D	1-1	Banks	
15		26	(h)	Halesowen	W	2-1	Banks, Cart	
16		31	(a)	Wolves Res	L	2-3	Arnold 2	
17	Jan	7	(h)	Aston Villa Res	L	0-2		
18		14	(a)	Walsall	W	3-1	Banks 2, Wright	
19		21	(h)	Burslem P Vale Res	W	2-0	Arnold, Wright	
20		23	(a)	Brierley Hill All	L	0-1		
21		28	(h)	Brierley Hill All	L	1-5	Banks	
22	Feb	4	(a)	Worcester C	L	1-3	Kearns	
23		11	(h)	Wellington T	L	1-2	Arnold	
24		18	(a)	Kidderminster H	L	0-2		1,000
25		25	(h)	Crewe A	D	2-2	Mundy, Cart	
26		27	(a)	Wellington T	L	0-5		
27	Mar	4	(a)	Stoke Res	L	0-5		
28		11	(h)	Small Heath Res	L	1-2	Arnold	
29		18	(a)	West Brom A Res	L	1-2	Arnold	
30	Apr	1	(a)	Stourbridge	L	1-2	Bryant	
31		8	(h)	Dudley	W	2-1	Arnold 2	300
32		15	(a)	Shrewsbury T	L	1-3	King	
33		22	(h)	Stafford R	W	4-2	Arnold 2, Bryant, Wright	
34		24	(a)	Crewe A	L	0-3		

FINAL LEAGUE POSITION: 17th in Birmingham & District League

Appearances
Goals

FA Cup

Q1	Oct	1	(h*)	Halesowen	D	2-2	Belton 2	
R		6	(h*)	Halesowen	W	3-2	Edwards, Banks 2	
Q2		15	(h)	Walsall	W	2-0	Beaman, Arnold	2,000
Q3		29	(a)	Stafford R	L	2-3	Banks, Arnold	2,000

*Both matches played at Coventry

Appearances
Goals

Taylor	Kearns	Spittle	Jones H	Pears	Court	Edwards	Clive	Belton	Banks	Archer	Whitehouse H	King	Arnold	Beaman	Peers	Porter	Morris	Mundy	Cart	Parish	Camwell	Penn	Wright	Hewitt	Hickman	Hadley	Peacock	Pearson	Williams	Sawyer	Harris	Wale	Parkes	Bryant	
1	2	3	4	5	6	7	8	9	10	11																									1
1	2	3	4	5	6	7	8	9	10	11																									2
	2	3	4		6	7	8	9	10	11	1	5																							3
1	2	3	4		6	7	8	9	10	11		5																							4
	2	3	4		6	7	8	9	10		1	5	11																						5
1	2	3	4		6	7	10	9					8	5	11																				6
1	2	3	4		6	7		9				10	8	5		11																			7
1	2	3	4		6	7		9				10	8	5			11																		8
1	2	3	4		6		10			7		5	8	9		11																			9
1	2	3	4		6		10					5	7	9		11		8																	10
1	2		4		6			9	10			5	7			11		8		3															11
1	2		4					9	10			6	7			11		8		3	5														12
	2	3	4					9	10			6	7					8	11		5	1													13
	2	3	4					9	10			6	7					8	11		5	1													14
	2	3	4					9	10			6	7					8	11		5	1													15
	2	3	4					9	10			6	7					8	11		5	1													16
	2	3	4					9	10			6	7					8	11		5	1													17
	2	3	4						9			6	7					8	11		5	1	10												18
	2	3	4		6				9				7					8	11		5	1	10												19
	2	3	4		6				9				7					8	11		5	1	10												20
	2	3							9			6	7	4				8				1	10	5	11										21
	2	3			6				9			5	7					8	11			1	10			4									22
	2	3							9			5	7					8	11			1	10				4	6							23
	2	3										5	7	9				8	11			1	10			4		6							24
	2	3										5	7	9				8	11			1	10			4		6							25
	2	3										5	7	9				8	11			1	10			4		6							26
	2	3				7						5	9					8	11			1	10			4		6							27
	2	3				7						5	8								4		10					6	1	9	11				28
	2	3				7						9	8										10			4		6	1		11	5			29
	2	3				7						9	8								4		10						1			5	6	11	30
	2	3				7						9	8								4		11						1			5	6	10	31
	2	3				7						9	8								4		11						1			5	6	10	32
	2	3				7						9	8								5		11					4	1				6	10	33
	2	3				7						9	8								5		11					4	1				6	10	34
10	34	32	20	2	14	16	8	15	18	5	2	29	30	9	1	5	1	18	14	2	15	15	17	1	1	6	1	9	7	1	2	4	5	5	
	1					3	1	7	12			1	12	1		1		5	2				3											2	

	2	3	4		6	7	8	9	10	11	1	5					Q1
	2	3	4		6	7	8	9	10		1	5	11				R
	2	3	4		6	7	10	9			1		8	5	11		Q2
	2	3	4		6	7	8		10		1	5	9			11	Q3
	4	4	4		4	4	4	3	3	1	4	3	3	1	1	1	
						1		2	3				2	1			

1905-06

Manager: Joe Beaman

1	Sep	2	(a)	Brierley Hill All	L	1-5	Such	
2		9	(h)	Burslem P Vale Res	W	6-1	King, McIntyre 3, Pember, Elliott (og)	2,000
3		16	(a)	Stoke Res	L	1-2	McIntyre	2,000
4		23	(h)	Wrexham	D	1-1	McIntyre	
5		30	(a)	Worcester C	D	2-2	Arrowsmith, Cramp	1,500
6	Oct	9	(a)	Stourbridge	L	0-2		
7		14	(a)	Crewe A	L	1-3	Arrowsmith	
8		21	(h)	Shrewsbury T	W	5-1	E.Smith 2, Edwards, McIntyre 2	
9		28	(a)	Wellington T	W	3-1	Such, McIntyre 2	
10	Nov	4	(h)	Walsall	W	5-1	C.Smith, McIntyre 4	2,000
11		11	(a)	West Brom A Res	L	0-3		2,000
12		18	(h)	Aston Villa Res	L	1-3	Cramp	
13		25	(a)	Birmingham Res	L	1-4	McIntyre	2,000
14	Dec	9	(h)	Kidderminster H	D	0-0		1,000
15		16	(a)	Wolves Res	L	1-3	Such	1,000
16		23	(h)	Stourbridge	W	1-0	Cramp	1,500
17		25	(h)	Dudley	W	3-0	E.Smith 2, Brown (og)	3,000
18		26	(a)	Dudley	W	3-2	Such, McIntyre	
19		27	(h)	Stafford R	W	3-0	E.Smith, Arrowsmith, Cramp	2,000
20		30	(h)	Brierley Hill All	W	4-1	Such, King, Boardman 2	1,000
21	Jan	13	(a)	Wrexham	L	1-5	Gilbert	
22		20	(h)	Stoke Res	W	3-2	Arrowsmith 2, Cramp	1,500
23	Feb	10	(h)	Worcester C	D	2-2	Arrowsmith 2	2,500
24		17	(h)	Crewe A	D	1-1	McIntyre	3,000
25		24	(a)	Shrewsbury T	L	0-1		2,000
26	Mar	3	(h)	Wellington T	W	7-2	Arrowsmith, Cramp 2, McIntyre 2, Pember 2	2,000
27		10	(a)	Walsall	L	1-2	King	1,000
28		17	(h)	West Brom A Res	L	0-2		3,000
29		24	(a)	Aston Villa Res	D	2-2	Cramp, Hartopp	5,000
30		31	(h)	Birmingham Res	W	1-0	Such	4,000
31	Apr	7	(a)	Stafford R	L	0-2		
32		14	(h)	Kidderminster H	W	2-1	Hartopp, Boardman	2,000
33		16	(a)	Burslem P Vale Res	L	1-2	McIntyre	
34		21	(h)	Wolves Res	L	1-2	Arrowsmith	

FINAL LEAGUE POSITION: 11th in Birmingham & District League

Appearances
Goals

FA Cup

Q1	Oct	7	(h)	Worcester C	L	0-3	

Appearances
Goals

Whitehouse H	Kearns	Smith C	Smith E	Edwards	King	Such	Arrowsmith	Cramp	McIntyre	Pember	Parkes	Walker	Wright	Jones H	Gilbert	Boardman	Wright S	Young	Hartopp	Wright A	
1	2	3	4	5	6	7	8	9	10	11											1
1	2	4	3		5	7	8	9	10	11	6										2
1	2	4	3		5	7	8	9	10	11	6										3
1	2	3		4	5	7	8	9	10	11		6									4
1	2	3	7	4	5		8	9	10	11		6									5
1	2	3	7	4	5		8	9	10	11		6									6
1	2	4		3	5	7	8	9		11		6	10								7
1	2	4	3	5	9	7		8	10	11		6									8
1	2	4	3	5	8	7		9	10	11	6										9
1	2	4	3	5	8	7		9	10	11		6									10
1	2	4	3	5	8	7		9	10	11	6										11
1	2	4	3	5	8	7		9	10	11	6										12
1	2	4	3	5	8	7		9	10	11	6										13
1	2	4	3	5	10	7	8	9			6		11								14
1	2	4	3		5	7	8	9	10	11	6										15
1	2	4	3		5	7	8	9	10	11	6										16
1	2		3		9	7	8		10	11	6			4	5						17
1	2		3			7	8	9	10	11	6			4	5						18
1	2	4	3			7	8	9		10	6				5	11					19
1	2		3		10	7	8	9			6			4	5	11					20
	2	4	3			7	8	9	10		6				5	11				1	21
1	2		3			7	8	9			6		10	4	5	11					22
1	2		3			7	8	9	10			6		4	5	11					23
1	2		3			7	8	9	10			6		4	5	11					24
1	2		3		10	7	8		9		6			4	5	11					25
1			3		5	7	8	9	10	11	6			4	5						26
1			3	2	8	7		9	10		6			4	5	11					27
1			3	2	8	7	10	9		11	6			4	5						28
1			3	2		11	10	9			4				5		7	6	8		29
1			3	2		7	8	9			6			4	5		11		10		30
1			3	2	5	11		9	10	7	6			4					8		31
1			3	2	5	7	8	9			6			4		11			10		32
1			3	2	5	7	8	9	10		6			4		11					33
1			3	2	5	7	8	9				6				11			10		34
33	25	18	32	20	26	32	26	32	24	21	24	9	3	14	14	11	2	1	5	1	
		1	5	1	3	6	9	8	19	3					1	3			2		

2 own-goals

1	2	4	3		5	7	8	9	10	11		6	Q1
1	1	1	1		1	1	1	1	1	1		1	

1906-07

Manager: Joe Beaman

1	Sep	1	(h)	Stafford R	D 2-2	Cramp 2	
2		8	(a)	Wolves Res	W 2-1	Lewis, Downing	3,000
3		15	(a)	Worcester C	W 4-3	Cramp, Lewis 2, Opp own-goal	1,500
4		22	(h)	Stoke Res	W 4-1	Cramp, Lewis 3	
5		29	(a)	Brierley Hill All	L 0-1		
6	Oct	6	(h)	Crewe A	L 1-3	Cramp	
7		13	(a)	West Brom A Res	L 0-3		2,000
8		20	(h)	Birmingham Res	L 1-3	Cramp	3,000
9		27	(a)	Halesowen	W 2-1	Layton, Cramp	
10	Nov	10	(h)	Wrexham	W 2-0	Lewis, Tooth	2,000
11		17	(h)	Shrewsbury	W 5-1	Cramp 3, Arnold, Lewis	2,500
12		24	(a)	Burslem P Vale Res	L 1-2	Tooth	
13	Dec	1	(h)	Stourbridge	W 5-1	Layton 2, Arnold, Kinsey, Lewis	2,000
14		8	(a)	Dudley	L 0-3		
15		15	(h)	Aston Villa Res	L 1-3	Lewis	3,000
16		22	(a)	Walsall	L 1-3	Cramp	800
17		25	(h)	Dudley	W 4-0	Such 2, Kinsey, Tooth	2,000
18		27	(h)	Kidderminster H	W 2-0	Scorers unknown	
19	Jan	5	(h)	Wolves Res	D 1-1	Tooth	2,500
20		12	(a)	Stourbridge	D 0-0		
21		19	(h)	Worcester C	W 3-0	Arnold 2, Lewis	3,000
22		26	(a)	Stoke Res	D 1-1	Haddon	
23	Feb	2	(h)	Brierley Hill All	W 3-1	Such, Arnold, Lewis	4,000
24		9	(a)	Crewe A	L 1-5	Tooth	
25		16	(h)	West Brom A Res	L 2-5	Chaplin, Lewis	4,000
26		23	(a)	Birmingham Res	L 0-1		5,000
27	Mar	2	(h)	Halesowen	W 2-1	Kinsey 2	3,000
28		9	(a)	Kidderminster H	L 0-3		1,000
29		16	(h)	Wrexham	W 6-2	Edwards, Layton, Arnold, Kinsey, Lewis, Tooth	
30		23	(a)	Shrewsbury T	W 2-1	Kinsey 2	
31		30	(h)	Burslem P Vale Res	W 5-0	Layton 2, Arnold, Kinsey, Lewis	2,000
32	Apr	1	(a)	Stafford R	L 1-2	Kinsey	
33		20	(a)	Aston Villa Res	L 2-4	Layton, Tooth	8,000
34		27	(h)	Walsall	W 4-2	Layton, Kinsey, Lewis, Tooth	1,500

FINAL LEAGUE POSITION: 7th in Birmingham & District League

Appearances

Goals

Coventry City did not enter the FA Cup.

Whitehouse	Edwards	Smith E	Jones H	Gilbert	Parkes	Layton	Downing	Cramp	Lewis	Tooth	Such	Chaplin	Arnold	Kinsey	Davis	Wright	Haddon	Cotterill	Laughland	Talbot	Match
1	2	3	4	5	6	7	8	9	10	11											1
1	2	3	4	5	6	7	8	9	10	11											2
1	2	3	4	5	6	7	8	9	10	11											3
1	2	3	4	5	6	7	8	9	10	11											4
1	2	3	4	5	6	7	8	9	10	11											5
1	2	3	4	5	6	7		9	10	11	8										6
1	2	3		5	6	7	8	9	10	11		4									7
1	2		4	5	6	7	8	9	10	11		3									8
1	2	3	4	5	6	7	8	9	10	11											9
1	2	3	4	5	6	7		9	10	11			8								10
1	2	3	4	5	6	7		9	10	11			8								11
1	2	3	4	5	6	7		9	10	11			8	9							12
1	2	3	4	5	6	7		9	10	11			8	9							13
1	2	3	4	5	6	7		9	10	11			8								14
1	2	3	4	5	6	7		9	10	11			8								15
1	2	3	4	5	6	7		9	10	11			8								16
1	2	3	4	5		10				11	7		8	9	6						17
1	2	3	4	5	6	10				11	7		8	9							18
1	2	3	4	5	6					11	7		8	9		10					19
1	2	3	4	5	6			9	10	11	7		8								20
1	2	3	4	5	6				10	11			8	9			7				21
1	2	3	4	5	6				10	11			8	9			7				22
1	2	3	4	5	6				10	11	7		8	9							23
1	2	3	4	5	6				10	11	7		8	9							24
1	2	3	4	5	6				10	11		9	7					8			25
1	2	3	4	5	6	7			10	11			8	9							26
1	2	3	4	5	6	7			10	11			8	9							27
1	2	3	4	5	6	7			10	11			8						9		28
1	2	3	4	5		7							8	9						6	29
1	2	3	4	5	6	7			10	11			8	9							30
1	2	3	4	5	6	7			10	11			8	9							31
1		3	4	5	6	7			10	11		2	8	9							32
1		3	4	5	6	7			10	11		2	8	9							33
1		3	4	5	6	7			10	11		2	8	9							34
34	31	33	33	34	32	27	8	17	30	33	7	6	25	17	1	1	2	1	1	1	
	1					8	1	11	16	8	3	1	7	10			1				

Scorers unknown: 2. 1 own-goal

1907-08

Manager: Joe Beaman

1	Sep	7	(h)	Halesowen	W 4-2	Layton, Warren, Lewis, Tooth	
2		14	(a)	Dudley	L 1-2	Warren	
3		28	(h)	Wrexham	D 1-1	Lewis	3,500
4	Oct	12	(h)	Shrewsbury T	W 3-1	Smith 2, Warren	3,000
5		14	(a)	Stourbridge	W 9-1	Layton, Smith 3, Warren 2, Lewis 2, Tooth	1,000
6	Nov	9	(h)	Wolves Res	W 4-1	Layton, Smith 2, Tooth	2,000
7		16	(a)	Kidderminster H	D 2-2	Lewis, Tooth	1,500
8	Dec	14	(a)	Stoke Res	L 1-2	Layton	
9		21	(h)	Birmingham Res	L 2-3	Lewis 2	5,500
10		24	(a)	Crewe A	L 1-5	Lewis	
11		25	(h)	Kidderminster H	W 2-0	Smith 2	3,000
12		28	(a)	West Brom A Res	L 1-4	Warren	3,000
13	Jan	4	(h)	Halesowen	W 3-1	Smith, Parkes, Tooth	
14		18	(a)	Stafford R	L 1-5	Lewis	
15		25	(a)	Wrexham	L 1-2	Chaplin	
16	Feb	1	(h)	Stourbridge	W 9-0	Gilbert, Chaplin, Smith 2, Warren 3, Lewis 2	2,000
17		8	(a)	Shrewsbury T	L 1-4	Lewis	
18		15	(h)	Aston Villa Res	W 4-2	Warren 2, Lewis 2	4,000
19		22	(a)	Walsall	L 1-2	Smith	
20		29	(h)	Burton U	W 2-0	Warren, Lewis	2,000
21	Mar	2	(h)	Dudley	W 1-0	Lewis	1,000
22		7	(a)	Wolves Res	L 0-2		
23		21	(h)	Worcester C	W 4-2	Chaplin, Smith 2, Tooth	3,000
24		23	(h)	Walsall	W 3-0	Smith, Lewis, Tooth	
25		28	(h)	Crewe A	W 4-3	Smith 2, Lewis 2	5,000
26	Apr	4	(a)	Brierley Hill	W 3-1	Dunn, Smith, Lewis	
27		6	(h)	Brierley Hill	W 6-0	Jones, Layton, Smith 4	
28		11	(h)	Stoke Res	W 5-0	Smith 3, Lewis 2	2,000
29		17	(a)	Burton U	L 0-4		
30		18	(a)	Birmingham Res	D 2-2	Warren, Smith	3,000
31		20	(a)	Worcester C	L 1-5	Lewis	2,000
32		21	(h)	Stafford R	W 4-0	Juggins, Chaplin, Warren, Smith	2,000
33		22	(a)	Aston Villa Res	L 0-3		3,000
34		29	(h)	West Brom A Res	W 11-2	Warren 2, Smith 5, Lewis 2, Tooth 2	3,000

FINAL LEAGUE POSITION: 4th in Birmingham & District League

Appearances
Goals

FA Cup

Q1	Sep	21	(a)	Brierley Hill	W 6-2	Juggins, Layton, Warren, Lewis 3	2,000
Q2	Oct	5	(h)	Darlaston	W 7-1	Juggins, Jones, Layton, Smith, Warren 2, Tooth	4,000
Q3*		19	(a)	Bilston	W 2-1	Smith, Lewis	4,000
Q3		26	(h)	Bilston	W 2-1	Gilbert, Warren	3,000
Q4	Nov	2	(h)	Worcester C	W 2-0	Smith, Warren	4,259
Q5		23	(a)	Oswestry U	D 2-2	Juggins, Gilbert	2,000
Q5R		28	(h)	Oswestry U	W 2-0	Lewis, Tooth	
Q6	Dec	7	(h)	Bishop Auckland	W 7-1	Juggins, Smith 2, Lewis 3, Tooth	7,820
1	Jan	11	(h)	Crystal P	L 2-4	Warren, Lewis	9,884

Appearances
Goals

*Match abandoned

Whitehouse	Juggins	Kifford	Jones	Gilbert	Chaplin	Layton	Smith	Warren	Lewis	Tooth	Barnes	Whitfield	Talbot	Parkes	Grimley	Gallier	Bivins	Ravenscroft	Moult	Dunn	Troop	Fisher	Read	
1	2	3	4	5	6	7	8	9	10	11														1
	2	3	4	5	6	7	8	9	10	11	1													2
1	2	3	4	5	6	7	8		10	11		9												3
1	2	3	4	5	6	7	8	9	10	11														4
1	2	3	4	5	6	7	8	9	10	11														5
1	2	3	4	5	6	7	8	9	10	11														6
1	2	3	4	5	6	7	8	9	10	11														7
	2	1	4	5	6	7	8		10	11			3	9										8
1	2	3	4	5	6	7	8		10	11				9										9
1	2	3	4	5	6		8		10					9	7	11								10
1	2	3	4	5	6	7	8		10	11				9										11
1	2	3	4	5	6	7	8		10	11				9										12
1		3	4		5		8	9		11			6	10		7	2							13
1	2	3	4		5	7	8	9	10	11				6										14
	2		4	5	6	7	8	9	10	11							3	1						15
	2		4	5	6	7	8	9	10	11							3	1						16
	2		4	5	6	7	8	9	10	11							3	1						17
		2	4	5	6	7	8	9	10	11							3		1					18
	2		4	5	6	7	8	9	10	11			3						1					19
	2		4	5	6		7	9	10	11				8			3		1					20
	2		4	5	6		8	9	10	11				7			3		1					21
	2	3	4	5		7	8		10	11			6	9					1					22
	2		4	5	6	7	9		10	11							3		1	8				23
	2		4	5	6	7	9		10	11							3		1	8				24
	2	3	4	5	6	7	9		10	11									1	8				25
	2	3	4	5	6	7	9		10	11									1	8				26
	2	3	4	5	6	7	9		10	11									1	8				27
	2		4	5	6	7	9	8	10	11			3						1					28
	2		4	5	6	7	9	8	10	11			3						1					29
			4	5	6	7	9	8	10	11							3		1		2			30
		2	4	5		7		9	10				6	11			3		1			8		31
	2		4	5	6	7	9	8	10	11							3		1					32
	2		4	5	6	7	9	8	10	11							3		1					33
	2		4	5	6	7	9	8	10	11							3		1					34
12	30	20	34	32	32	30	33	22	33	32	1	1	7	11	1	2	14	3	17	5	1	1		
	1		1	1	4	5	33	16	25	9				1						1				

Whitehouse	Juggins	Kifford	Jones	Gilbert	Chaplin	Layton	Smith	Warren	Lewis	Tooth	Barnes	Whitfield	Talbot	Parkes	Grimley	Gallier	Bivins	Ravenscroft	Moult	Dunn	Troop	Fisher	Read	
1	2	3	4	5	6	7	8	9	10	11														Q1
1	2	3	4	5	6	7	8	9	10	11														Q2
1	2	3	4	5	6	7	8	9	10	11														Q3
1	2	3	4	5	6	7	8	9	10	11														Q3
1	2	3	4	5	6	7	8	9	10	11														Q4
1	2	3	4	5	6	7	8	9	10	11														Q5
1	2	3	4	5	6	7	8		10	11													9	Q5R
1	2	3	4	5	6	7	8		10	11				9										Q6
1	2	3	4	5	6	7	8	9	10	11														1
9	9	9	9	9	9	9	9	7	9	9				1									1	
	4		1	2		2	5	6	9	3														

1908-09

Manager: W.J.Harris

1	Sep	1	(h)	Crystal P	D	1-1	Marvin	5,000
2		5	(a)	Northampton T	L	1-3	Farrant	10,000
3		12	(h)	New Brompton	L	3-4	Turner, Farrant, Buckle	5,000
4		19	(a)	Millwall	L	0-3		8,000
5		26	(h)	Southend U	L	2-5	Buckle 2	4,000
6	Oct	3	(h)	Plymouth A	L	1-2	Arnold	7,000
7		10	(a)	Bristol R	W	3-1	Drennan (pen), Warren, Buckle	7,500
8		12	(a)	Queen's Park R	L	2-4	Buckle 2	7,000
9		17	(h)	Watford	W	3-2	Tickle, Warren, Turner	6,105
10		24	(a)	Norwich C	L	0-2		5,000
11		31	(h)	Reading	D	2-2	Farrant, Buckle	
12	Nov	7	(a)	Southampton	L	1-2	Arnold	
13		14	(h)	Leyton	W	2-1	Buckle 2	
14		21	(a)	West Ham U	L	0-2		5,000
15		28	(h)	Brighton & HA	W	2-1	Arnold (pen), Buckle	3,000
16	Dec	12	(h)	Brentford	L	1-2	Arnold	6,047
17		19	(a)	Luton T	L	1-6	Warren	4,000
18		25	(h)	Swindon T	D	1-1	Hickman	7,000
19		26	(a)	Portsmouth	L	0-3		14,000
20	Jan	2	(h)	Northampton T	L	1-4	Hickman	7,524
21		9	(a)	New Brompton	W	1-0	Tickle	4,000
22		23	(h)	Millwall	W	4-2	Arnold, Turner, Warren 2	5,377
23		30	(a)	Southend U	L	0-4		
24	Feb	6	(h)	Queen's Park R	W	2-1	Tickle, Warren	5,000
25		8	(a)	Exeter C	W	3-0	Arnold, Turner, Warren	2,500
26		10	(a)	Plymouth A	L	1-4	Juggins (pen)	11,642
27		13	(h)	Bristol R	D	2-2	Arnold, Warren	5,000
28		20	(a)	Watford	L	1-3	Warren	3,000
29		27	(h)	Norwich C	W	2-0	Arnold, Buckle	5,000
30	Mar	13	(h)	Southampton	W	2-0	Warren, Buckle	7,300
31		20	(a)	Leyton	L	0-5		5,000
32		22	(h)	Exeter C	L	0-1		2,500
33		27	(h)	West Ham U	W	3-1	Parkes, Warren, Arnold	6,000
34	Apr	3	(a)	Brighton & HA	L	1-5	Warren	5,000
35		10	(a)	Crystal P	W	1-0	Turner	6,000
36		12	(a)	Swindon T	L	1-2	Buckle	10,000
37		13	(h)	Portsmouth	W	5-3	Turner, Warren, Buckle 3	4,000
38		17	(a)	Brentford	L	2-5	Warren, Buckle	5,000
39		21	(a)	Reading	W	1-0	Turner	
40		24	(h)	Luton T	W	5-2	Juggins (pen), Tickle, Parkes, Turner, Warren	7,069

FINAL LEAGUE POSITION: 20th in Southern League, Division One.

Appearances
Goals

FA Cup

P	Dec	5	(h)	Carlisle U	D	1-1	Tickle	6,215
R		10	(a)	Carlisle U	D	1-1	Warren	5,000
2R		14	(n*)	Carlisle U	L	1-3	Fisher	2,000

*Played at Hyde Road, Manchester.

Appearances
Goals

Moult	Juggins	Bivins	Jones	Marvin	Chaplin	Tickle	Farrant	Turner	Fisher	Buckle	Warren	Sparkes	Talbot	Hodges	Dodd	Dougherty	Drennan	Boston	Archer	Barnacle	Gilbert	Hopkins	Camwell	Hickman	Parkes	Hanson	Arnold	
1	2	3	4	5	6	7	8	9	10	11																		1
1	2	3	4	5	6	7	8	9		11	10																	2
1		2		5		7	9	8	10	11		3	4	6														3
1	2	3		4		7	9	8	10	11					5	6												4
1	2			4	6	7	8		10	11				9			3	5										5
				4	6	7	10			11	9						3		1	2	5						8	6
			5	4	6	7	10			11	9						3		1	2							8	7
			4	5	6	7	10			11	9						3		1	2							8	8
			4	5	6	7	10	9		11	8						3		1	2								9
				4	5	7	10			11	8					6	3	9	1	2								10
				4	5	7	10	9		11						6	3		1	2							8	11
			4		5	7	10	9		11						6	3		1	2							8	12
	9				4	7				11					5	6	3		1	2		10					8	13
					4	7	10			11	8				5	6	3		1	2							9	14
					4	7			10	11					5	6	3		1	2			9				8	15
	2				6	7	10			11					5		3	4	1					9			8	16
	2				4	7			10		9				5	6	3		1			11					8	17
1	2			4		8				11	10				5	6	3							9	7			18
1	2			4		8		9		11	10				5	6	3								7			19
1				4		8				11	10				5	6	3			2				9	7			20
1	2			4	6	7		9		11	10							5								3	8	21
1	2			4	6	7		9		11	10							5								3	8	22
1	2			4	6	7		9		11	10							5								3	8	23
1	2			4	6	7		9		11	10							5								3	8	24
1	2			4	6	7		9		11	10							5								3	8	25
1	2			4	6	7		9		11	10							5								3	8	26
1	2			4	6	7		9		11	10				5											3	8	27
1	2			4	6	7		9		11	10				5											3	8	28
1	2			4	6	7		9		11	10										5					3	8	29
1	2			4	6	7		9		11	10										5					3	8	30
1	2			4	6	7		9		11	10										5					3	8	31
1				4	6	7		9		11	10									2	5					3	8	32
1	2				4	7				11	9					6					5				8	3	10	33
1	2				4	7		9		11	10					6		5							8	3		34
1	2			4	6	7		9		11	10										5				8	3		35
1	2			4	5	7		9		11	10					6									8	3		36
1	2			4	6	7		9		11	10										5				8	3		37
1	2			4	6	7		9		11	10										5				8	3		38
	2			4	6	7		9		11	10								1	3	5				8			39
	2			4	6	7		9		11	10								1		5				8	3		40
26	28	4	6	32	35	40	14	27	6	39	31	1	1	2	11	14	16	10	14	13	11	2	1	3	11	19	23	
	2			1		4	3	8		17	15						1							2	2		9	
					4	7			10	11					5	6	3		1	2			9				8	P
					4	7			10	11	9				5	6	3		1	2							8	R
	2				4	7			10	11	9				5	6	3		1								8	2R
	1				3	3			3	3	2				3	3	3		3	2			1				3	
						1			1		1																	

1909-10

Manager: H.Buckle

1	Sep	1	(a)	Swindon T	L 1-2	Smith	8,000
2		2	(h)	Northampton T	W 1-0	Warren	7,000
3		4	(h)	Crystal P	D 1-1	Smith	7,000
4		11	(a)	Brighton & HA	L 1-4	Buckle	7,500
5		18	(h)	West Ham U	D 2-2	Legge, Buckle	3,000
6		22	(h)	Leyton	D 1-1	Buckle	7,000
7		25	(a)	Portsmouth	D 0-0		8,000
8	Oct	2	(h)	Bristol R	L 1-3	Buckle	6,199
9		9	(a)	Norwich C	W 1-0	Powell	7,500
10		16	(h)	Brentford	W 3-0	Tickle, Powell, Buckle	6,000
11		18	(a)	Queen's Park R	L 0-4		5,000
12		23	(a)	Exeter C	L 0-3		4,000
13		30	(a)	Watford	W 3-0	Hendren 2, Powell	8,000
14	Nov	11	(h)	Reading	W 3-0	Powell 2, Arnold	3,000
15		13	(a)	Southend U	W 1-0	Tickle	8,000
16		27	(a)	Plymouth A	L 0-6		3,000
17	Dec	11	(a)	Croydon Com	W 3-1	Warren, Hendren, Buckle	7,000
18		18	(h)	Millwall	W 1-0	Buckle	5,000
19		24	(h)	Luton T	W 6-2	Arnold 2, Bradley, Tickle, Smith, Buckle	8,000
20		27	(h)	New Brompton	W 2-1	Smith, Hendren	12,000
21		28	(h)	Queen's Park R	W 4-0	Arnold 2, Hendren, Buckle	12,000
22	Jan	1	(h)	Swindon T	L 0-2		5,000
23		8	(a)	Crystal P	W 2-1	Warren, Opp own-goal	7,000
24		22	(h)	Brighton & HA	D 1-1	Warren	8,000
25		29	(a)	West Ham U	L 2-3	Hendren, Buckle	4,000
26	Feb	12	(a)	Bristol R	W 1-0	Buckle	7,000
27		26	(a)	Brentford	L 1-3	Hendren	5,000
28	Mar	12	(h)	Watford	W 5-0	Warren 2, Bradley, Hendren, Buckle	3,000
29		14	(h)	Southampton	D 2-2	Smith, Hendren	3,000
30		19	(a)	Reading	L 0-1		4,000
31		25	(a)	Luton T	L 1-4	Powell	5,000
32		26	(h)	Southend U	L 0-2		5,000
33		28	(a)	New Brompton	W 1-0	Hendren	10,000
34		29	(a)	Northampton T	W 1-0	Powell	3,000
35	Apr	2	(a)	Leyton	D 0-0		6,000
36		9	(h)	Plymouth A	D 2-2	Powell, Buckle	3,000
37		11	(h)	Norwich C	W 2-1	Parkes, Powell	2,000
38		16	(a)	Southampton	L 2-3	Warren, Smith	1,500
39		18	(h)	Portsmouth	L 1-3	Bradley (pen)	3,000
40		23	(h)	Croydon Com	W 6-1	Smith 2, Buckle 2, Tickle, Warren	3,000
41		25	(h)	Exeter C	W 6-0	Powell 2, Buckle 2, Warren, Bradley	3,000
42		30	(a)	Millwall	L 0-1		1,000

FINAL LEAGUE POSITION: 8th in Southern League, Division One

Appearances

Goals

FA Cup

Q4	Nov	20	(h)	Wrexham	W 3-0	Arnold 2, Opp own-goal	7,000
Q5	Dec	4	(a)	Kettering T	W 5-0	Hendren 2, Bradley, Arnold, Buckle	3,000
1	Jan	15	(a)	Preston NE	W 2-1	Hendren, Buckle	8,000
2	Feb	5	(a)	Portsmouth	W 1-0	Chaplin	11,631
3		19	(h)	Nottingham F	W 3-1	Warren 2, Smith	12,500
4	Mar	3	(h)	Everton	L 0-2		19,095

Appearances

Goals

Evans	Juggins	Saul	Hickleton	Bradley	Chaplin	Tickle	Parkes	Smith W	Warren	Buckle	Wilson	Newbigging	Turner	Legge	Arnold	Hanson	Powell	Lee	Bourne	Boston	Hendren	Johnson	Barnacle	
1	2	3	4	5	6	7	8	9	10	11														1
1	2		4	5	6	7	8	9	10	11	3													2
	2		4	5	6	7	8	9	10	11	3	1												3
1	2		4	5	6	7	8	9	10	11	3													4
1	2		4	5	6	7	8			11	3		9	10										5
1	2	3	4	5	6		8	9		11				10	7									6
1		2	4	5	6	7	8						9			3	10	11						7
1		2	4	5	6		8			11			9		7	3	10							8
1		2	4	5	6	7				11			10		8	3	9							9
1		2	4	5	6	7				10					8	3	9	11						10
1		2		5	6	7				10					8	3	9	11	4					11
1		2	4		6	7				11			10		8	3	9			5				12
1	2		4		6	7				11					8	3	9			5	10			13
1	2	3	4	5	6	7				11					8		9				10			14
1	2	3	4	5	6	7				11					8		9				10			15
1	2		4	5	6	7				11					8	3	9				10			16
1		2	4	5	6	7			8	11						3	9				10			17
1		2	4	5	6	7				11					8	3	9				10			18
		2	4	5	6	7		9		11		1			8	3					10			19
1		2	4	5	6	7		9		11					8	3					10			20
1		2	4	5	6	7		9		11					8	3					10			21
1	2		4	5	6	7		9	8	11						3					10			22
1	2		4		6	7		9	8							3		11		5	10			23
1	2		4	5	6	7		9	8	11						3					10			24
1	2		4	5	6	7		9		11					8	3					10			25
1		3	4			7		9	8	11										5	10	6	2	26
1		2	4	5	6	7		9	8	11						3					10			27
1		2	4	5	6	7		9	8	11						3					10			28
1		2	4	5	6	7		9	8	11						3					10			29
1		2	4	5	6	7		9		11					8	3					10			30
1		2	4	5	6	7				11					8	3	9				10			31
1		2	4	5	6	7		9		11					8	3					10			32
	2			5	6	7				11		1			8	3	9				10	4		33
	2	3		5	6		7			11		1		10	8		9					4		34
	2	3		5	6		7			11		1		10	8		9					4		35
	2	3		5	6	7				11		1		10	8		9					4		36
		2	4				7	8				1				3	9	11		5	10	6		37
1	2	3	4	5		7		9	8					10				11				6		38
	2		4	5		7		9	8	11		1				3					10	6		39
1		2		5	6	7		9	8	11				10		3						4		40
1		2		5	6	7			8	11				10		3	9					4		41
1		2		5	6	7			8	11				10		3	9					4		42
34	20	30	34	37	38	37	11	22	17	38	4	8	5	9	22	29	20	6	1	5	23	11	1	
				4		4	1	8	9	17				1	5		11				10			

1 own-goal

1	2	3	4	5	6	7				11					8		9				10			Q4
1		2	4	5		7			9	11					8	3					10	6		Q5
1		2	4	5	6	7		9	8	11						3					10			1
1		2	4	5	6	7		9	8	11						3					10			2
1		2	4	5	6	7		9	8	11						3					10			3
1		2	4	5	6	7		9	8	11						3					10			4
6	1	6	6	6	5	6		4	5	6					2	5	1				6	1		
				1	1			1	2	2					3						3			

1 own-goal

1910-11

Manager: R.Wallace

1	Sep	3	(a)	Queen's Park R	L 0-5		15,000
2		10	(h)	West Ham U	W 3-0	Bradley, Arnold, Powell	8,000
3		17	(a)	Luton T	L 2-4	Bradley, Warren	8,000
4		24	(h)	Portsmouth	W 1-0	Hendren	8,000
5	Oct	8	(h)	Brighton & HA	L 0-2		8,000
6		15	(a)	Exeter C	W 3-2	Parkes, Tickle 2	3,000
7		22	(h)	Swindon T	D 2-2	Tickle, Bradley	9,500
8		29	(a)	Bristol R	D 1-1	Opp own-goal	4,000
9	Nov	5	(h)	Crystal P	L 0-2		8,000
10		12	(a)	Brentford	L 0-1		5,000
11		19	(h)	Leyton	W 3-1	Barnacle, Warren, Buckle	6,000
12		26	(a)	Watford	W 2-0	Bradley, Powell	4,000
13	Dec	1	(a)	Northampton T	L 1-4	Bradley	
14		3	(h)	Plymouth A	W 6-1	Parkes, Tickle, Smith 2, Warren, Buckle	4,000
15		10	(a)	Southampton	L 1-2	Tickle	5,000
16		17	(h)	Southend U	W 5-1	Tickle, Warren, Buckle 3	3,300
17		214	(a)	Norwich C	L 2-5	Parkes, Opp own-goal	3,261
18		26	(a)	New Brompton	L 1-2	Bradley	7,000
19		27	(h)	New Brompton	W 5-2	Parkes, Tickle, Smith, Welch, Buckle	6,000
20		31	(h)	Queen's Park R	W 3-2	Parkes, Welch, Buckle	7,000
21	Jan	7	(a)	West Ham U	D 1-1	Parkes	10,000
22		21	(h)	Luton T	D 1-1	Buckle	7,000
23		28	(a)	Portsmouth	L 0-3		4,000
24	Feb	11	(a)	Brighton & HA	L 1-2	Parkes	5,000
25		18	(h)	Exeter C	L 1-3	Welch	5,000
26	Mar	4	(h)	Bristol R	W 4-0	Bradley, Parkes, Tickle, Smith	4,000
27		11	(a)	Crystal P	L 0-2		6,000
28		18	(h)	Brentford	W 2-0	Parkes, Tickle	4,000
29		25	(a)	Leyton	W 1-0	Smith	4,000
30		30	(h)	Northampton T	D 1-1	Tickle	2,000
31	Apr	1	(h)	Watford	W 4-1	Bradley, Parkes, Warren 2	5,000
32		8	(a)	Plymouth A	L 0-6		7,000
33		14	(a)	Millwall	W 1-0	Smith	12,000
34		15	(h)	Southampton	W 2-0	Warren, Smith	6,000
35		17	(h)	Millwall	D 1-1	Bradley	6,000
36		22	(a)	Southend U	L 1-4	Bradley	
37		26	(a)	Swindon T	L 0-3		
38		29	(h)	Norwich C	W 3-1	Parkes, Welch, Buckle	

FINAL LEAGUE POSITION: 10th in Southern League, Division One

Appearances
Goals

FA Cup

1	Jan	14	(a)	Sheffield W	W 2-1	Smith, Buckle	19,603
2	Feb	4	(a)	Brighton & HA	D 0-0		13,000
R		9	(h)	Brighton & HA	W 2-0	Parkes, Tickle	15,711
3	Feb	25	(a)	Burnley	L 0-5		11,714

Appearances
Goals

Evans	Saul	Gordon	Hickleton	Bradley	Chaplin	Tickle	Smith W	Warren	Buckle	Arnold	Powell	Johnson	Boston	Hendren	Juggins	Davies	Barnacle	Welch	Fisher	Hill	Robinson	Parkes	
1	2	3	4	5	6	7	9	10	11											8			1
1	2	3	4	5	6	7		10	11	8	9												2
1	2	3	4	5		7		10	11	8	9	6											3
1	2	3	4			7			11	8	9	6	5	10									4
1	2		4					10		8	9	6	5		3	11						7	5
1	2	3	4	9		8		10	11			6	5									7	6
1		3	4	9		8		10	11			6	5				2					7	7
1	2	3	4	9		8		10	11			6	5									7	8
1	2	3	4	9		8		10	11			6	5									7	9
1	2	3	4	5		9		8	11			6		10								7	10
1	2		4	5		9		8	11			6		10			3					7	11
1	2		4	5		8		10	11		9	6					3					7	12
1	2		4	5		8		10	11		9	6					3					7	13
1	2			5	6	8	9	10	11			4					3					7	14
1	2				6	8	9	10	11			4	5				3					7	15
1	2				6	8	9	10	11			4	5				3					7	16
1		3		5	6	8	9	10	11			4			2							7	17
1		3		5	6	8	9	10	11			4			2							7	18
1			4	5	6	8	9		11			3			2			10				7	19
1			4	5	6	8	9		11			2					3	10				7	20
1	2			5	6	8	9		11			4					3	10				7	21
1	2			5	6	8	9		11			4					3	10				7	22
	2			5	6	8	9		11			4					3	10			1	7	23
1			4	5	6	8	9	10				3			2	11						7	24
1			4		6	8	9		11			3	5		2			10				7	25
1				5	6	8	9		11			4			2		3	10				7	26
1				5	6	8	9		11			4			2		3	10				7	27
1	2			5	6	8	9		11			4					3	10				7	28
1	2			5	6	8	9	10	11			4					3					7	29
1	3		4	5		8	9	10	11			6			2							7	30
1	3		4	5		8	9	10	11			6			2							7	31
1	3		4	5		8	9		11			6		10					2	7			32
1	3			5	6	8	9		11			4			2			10				7	33
1	3			5	6		9	8	11			4			2			10				7	34
1	3			5	6		9		11			4			2			10		8		7	35
1	3			5	6	8		9	11			4			2			10				7	36
1	3			5	6	8		9	11			4			2			10				7	37
1	3			5	6	8		9	11			4			2			10				7	38
37	29	11	20	33	24	35	23	25	36	4	6	36	9	4	16	2	15	15	1	3	1	33	
				10		10	7	7	9	1	2			1			1	4				11	

2 own-goals

1	2			5	6	8	9		11			4					3	10				7	1
1			4	5	6	8	9		11			2					3	10				7	2
1			4	5	6	8	9		11			3			2			10				7	R
			4	5	6	8	9		11			2					3	10			1	7	3
3	1		3	4	4	4	4		4			4			1		3	4			1	4	
						1	1		1													1	

1911-12

Manager: R.Wallace

1	Sep	2	(h)	Northampton T	L 1-2	Parkes	10,000
2		9	(a)	Brighton & HA	L 1-3	Brown	5,000
3		16	(h)	Stoke	W 3-2	Turnbull, Jones 2	7,855
4		23	(a)	Luton T	W 4-2	Parkes 2, Brown 2	7,000
5		30	(a)	Leyton	L 0-1		3,000
6	Oct	7	(h)	Norwich C	W 3-0	Brown, Jones 2	7,046
7		14	(a)	Crystal P	L 0-3		10,000
8		21	(h)	Southampton	W 2-1	Bradley, Jones	5,256
9		28	(a)	Plymouth A	L 1-4	Jones	8,043
10	Nov	4	(h)	Reading	W 3-0	Turnbull, Brown, Jones	5,375
11		11	(a)	Watford	L 2-6	Bradley, Brown	4,000
12		25	(a)	Exeter C	D 0-0		3,000
13	Dec	2	(a)	Southampton	W 2-1	Turnbull, Smith	6,000
14		9	(a)	Queen's Park R	D 0-0		5,000
15		16	(h)	Millwall	W 2-0	Turnbull, Jones	6,086
16		23	(a)	West Ham U	W 1-0	Turnbull	4,000
17		25	(h)	Bristol R	L 1-2	Turnbull	10,016
18		26	(a)	Bristol R	L 0-1		3,000
19		27	(h)	Brentford	W 9-0	Turnbull, Smith 5, Jones 2, Holmes	7,000
20		30	(a)	Northampton T	L 1-2	Jones	12,000
21	Jan	6	(h)	Brighton & HA	W 2-0	Turnbull, Holmes	3,000
22		20	(a)	Stoke	L 1-3	Smith	7,000
23		27	(h)	Luton T	W 1-0	Smith	5,000
24	Feb	10	(a)	Norwich C	D 1-1	Brown	5,261
25		17	(h)	Crystal P	W 3-2	Turnbull 2, Jones	5,000
26		24	(h)	New Brompton	W 3-2	Turnbull, Jones, Holmes	5,000
27	Mar	2	(h)	Plymouth A	W 4-1	Parkes, Jones 3	7,000
28		9	(a)	Reading	L 0-2		4,000
29		16	(h)	Watford	W 3-1	Parkes, Brown, Turnbull	4,000
30		21	(h)	Leyton	W 2-0	Parkes, Jones	500
31		23	(a)	New Brompton	D 3-3	Bradley, Jones 2	2,000
32		30	(h)	Exeter C	D 1-1	Bradley (pen)	5,000
33	Apr	5	(a)	Swindon T	D 2-2	Jones, Opp own-goal	
34		6	(a)	Brentford	L 0-3		5,453
35		8	(h)	Swindon T	D 1-1	Parkes	8,200
36		13	(h)	Queen's Park R	D 0-0		8,000
37		20	(a)	Millwall	L 1-2	Jones	8,000
38		27	(h)	West Ham U	W 2-0	Chaplin, Smith	6,000

FINAL LEAGUE POSITION: 6th in Southern League, Division One — Appearances

Goals

FA Cup

1	Jan	13	(a)	Southampton	W 2-0	Turnbull, Parkes	12,649
2	Feb	3	(h)	Manchester U	L 1-5	Jones	17,251

Appearances

Goals

Evans	Thomson	Barnacle	Yates	Bradley	Feebury	Parkes	Brown	Smith W	Welch	Holmes	Juggins	Jones	Parton	Chaplin	Alden	Jackson	Jacques	Boston	Turnbull	
1	2	3	4	5	6	7	8	9	10	11										1
1		3	4	5	6	7	8	9	11		2	10								2
1		3	4	5		7	9				2	10		6	11				8	3
1		3	4	5		7	9					10	2	6	11				8	4
1		3	4			7				9		10	2	6	11			5	8	5
1		3	4	5		7	9					10	2	6	11				8	6
1			4	5	6	7	9					10	2		11	3			8	7
1	2		4	5		7	9					10	3	6	11				8	8
1	2		4	5		7	9			8		10	3	6	11					9
1	2	3	4	5	6	7	9			11		10							8	10
	2	3	4	5		7	9			11		10		6			1		8	11
1	2	3	4	5		7		9		11		10		6					8	12
1	2	3	4	5		7		9		11		10		6					8	13
1	2	3	4	5		7		9		11		10		6					8	14
1	2	3	4	5		7		9	11			10		6					8	15
1	2	3	4	5		7		9		11		10		6					8	16
1	2	3	4	5		7		9		11		10		6					8	17
1	2	3	4			7		9		11		10		6				5	8	18
1	2	3	4			7		9		11		10		6				5	8	19
	2	3	4	5		7		9		11		10		6			1		8	20
1	2		4	5		7		9		11		10	3	6					8	21
1	2		4				7	9		11		10	3	6				5	8	22
1	2		4	5				9		11		10	3	6	7				8	23
1	2	3	4			7	8	9	11			10		6				5		24
1	2	3	4	5		7	8			11		10		6					9	25
1	2	3	4	5	6	7	8			11		10							9	26
	2	3	4		6	7	8			11		10					1	5	9	27
1	2	3	4		6	7	8			11		10						5	9	28
1	2	3	4		6	7	8			11		10						5	9	29
1	2	3	4	5		7	8			11		10		6					9	30
1	2		4	5		7	8			11		10	3	6					9	31
1	2		4	5		7	8			11		10	3	6					9	32
1	2	3	4	5		7	8			11		10		6					9	33
1	2	3	4	5		7	8			11		10		6					9	34
1		2	4	5		7	8			11		10	3	6					9	35
	2	3	4			7		9		11		10		6			1	5	8	36
1	2	3	4			7		9		11		10		6				5	8	37
1	2	3	4			7		9		11		10		6				5	8	38
34	31	30	38	27	8	36	23	18	4	30	2	37	12	30	8	1	4	11	34	
				4		7	8	9		3		21		1					12	

1 own-goal

1	2	3	4	5		7		9		11		10		6					8	1
1	2	3	4	5		7		9		11		10		6					8	2
2	2	2	2	2		2		2		2		2		2					2	
						1						1							1	

1912-13

Manager: R.Wallace

1	Sep	5	(h)	Swindon T	W 2-1	J.Smith 2	6,500
2		7	(a)	West Ham U	W 2-1	Bradley (pen), Parkes	10,000
3		11	(a)	Swindon T	L 0-1		
4		14	(h)	Brighton & HA	D 1-1	Brown	8,200
5		21	(h)	Stoke	W 5-2	Yates, Parkes, Brown 2, Kimberley	7,000
6		28	(a)	Watford	D 1-1	Holmes	4,000
7	Oct	5	(h)	Merthyr T	L 2-3	Parkes, Brown	7,000
8		12	(a)	Crystal P	L 0-3		9,000
9		19	(h)	Plymouth A	L 2-3	Brown, J.Smith	8,000
10		26	(a)	Southampton	D 0-0		3,000
11	Nov	2	(h)	Reading	W 3-1	Brown, McCulloch, Mitchell	6,000
12		9	(a)	Norwich C	W 3-0	Parkes, Brown 2	5,000
13		16	(h)	Gillingham	L 1-2	Holmes	7,000
14		23	(a)	Northampton T	W 1-0	Brown	8,000
15		30	(h)	Queen's Park R	D 1-1	McCulloch	6,000
16	Dec	7	(a)	Brentford	L 0-2		3,000
17		14	(h)	Millwall	W 3-0	Brown 2, McCulloch	6,000
18		21	(a)	Bristol R	L 0-2		5,000
19		25	(h)	Portsmouth	W 2-0	Parkes, Mitchell	8,500
20		28	(h)	West Ham U	W 4-1	Parkes 3, Welch	7,000
21	Jan	4	(a)	Brighton & HA	D 0-0		3,000
22		18	(a)	Stoke	W 1-0	Feebury	7,000
23		25	(h)	Watford	W 2-1	Parkes, Welch	6,000
24	Feb	8	(a)	Merthyr T	D 1-1	Mitchell	3,000
25		15	(h)	Crystal P	L 1-2	Opp own-goal	4,000
26		22	(a)	Plymouth A	L 1-4	Parkes	8,104
27	Mar	1	(h)	Southampton	D 1-1	Holmes	5,000
28		8	(a)	Reading	L 0-1		4,000
29		15	(h)	Norwich C	W 3-0	Feebury (pen), Parkes, Welch	5,000
30		21	(h)	Exeter C	L 0-1		3,000
31		22	(a)	Gillingham	L 0-3		6,000
32		24	(a)	Exeter C	L 0-3		5,000
33		29	(h)	Northampton T	D 4-4	J.Smith, Holmes 3	4,000
34	Apr	5	(a)	Queen's Park R	L 0-4		6,000
35		9	(a)	Portsmouth	L 1-2	Holmes	5,000
36		12	(h)	Brentford	W 3-0	Parkes, McCulloch, Holmes	4,000
37		19	(a)	Millwall	L 0-4		6,000
38		26	(h)	Bristol R	L 2-3	Boston 2	3,000

FINAL LEAGUE POSITION: 13th in Southern League, Division One

Appearances

Goals

FA Cup

1	Jan	11	(a)	Manchester U	D 1-1	Mitchell	11,502
R		16	(h)	Manchester U	L 1-2	Parkes	20,042

Appearances

Goals

Evans	Thomson	Harris	Yates	Bradley	Feebury	Parkes	Turnbull	Smith J	Holmes	Jacques	Barnacle	Jackson	Kimberley	Boston	Styles	Welch	Marr	Brown	Jarvis	McCulloch	Mitchell	Poole	Wakinshaw	
1	2	3	4	5	6	7	9	10	11									8						1
1	2	3	4	5	6	7	9	10	11									8						2
	2	3	4	5	6	7	9	10	11	1								8						3
	2	3	4	5	6	7	9	10	11	1								8						4
	2	6	4	5		7		10	11	1	3		9					8						5
	2	3	4	5	6	7		10	11	1			9					8						6
	2	3	4	5	6	7		10	11	1			9					8						7
1	2	3	4		6	7		10	11					5				8	9					8
1	2	3	4		6	7		9	11					5				8			10			9
1	2	6	4		5	7		10	11		3							8		9				10
1	2	6	4		5	7			11		3							8		9	10			11
1	2	6	4		5	7			11		3							8		9	10			12
1	2	6	4		5	7		9	11		3							8			10			13
1	2	6	4		5	7			11		3							8		9	10			14
1	2	6	4		5	7			11		3							8		9	10			15
1	2	6	4		5	7			11			3						8		9	10			16
1	2	6	4		5	7			11			3						8		9	10			17
1	2	6	4		5	7			11		3							8		9	10			18
1	2	6	4		5	7			11		3					8				9	10			19
1	2	6	4		5	7			11		3					8				9	10			20
1	2	6	4		5	7			11		3					8				9	10			21
1	2	6	8		5	7			11		3		4							9	10			22
1	2	6	4		5	7			11			3				10		8			9			23
1	2	6	4		5	7			11		3							8		9	10			24
1	2	6	4		5	7			11		3							8		9	10			25
1	2	6	4		5	7			11		3					8		10			9			26
	2	6	4		5	7		9	11	1		3						10		8				27
	2	6	4		5	7			11	1		3				8		9		10				28
	2	6	4		5	7			11	1	3					8		9			10			29
	2	6	4		5	8			11	1	3					10	7			9				30
	2		4		5	7		9	11	1	3		6					8		10				31
	2		4			7		9	11	1	3	6	5					8		10				32
	2		4			7		9	11	1	3		6	5				8		10				33
	2		4			7		9	11	1	3		6		5			8		10				34
	2		4			7		9	11	1	3		6	5				8					10	35
	2		4		5	7			11	1	3				6			8		9			10	36
	2		4		5	7			11	1			3			6		8		10		9		37
	2		4		5	7			11	1	3			9	6			8				10		38
21	38	30	38	7	33	38	4	17	38	17	24	6	10	5	3	9	1	33	1	23	18	2	2	
			1	1	2	12		4	8				1	2		3		11		4	3			

1 own-goal

1	2	6	4		5	7			11		3					8				9	10			1
1	2	6	8		5	7			11		3		4							9	10			R
2	2	2	2		2	2			2		2		1			1				2	2			
						1															1			

1913-14

Manager: R.Wallace

1	Sep	3	(a)	Gillingham	W	2-0	Dobson, Craig	5,000
2		6	(h)	Brighton & HA	W	2-1	Parkes, Davison	8,511
3		11	(h)	Gillingham	L	2-3	Dobson, Davison	5,000
4		13	(a)	Portsmouth	D	0-0		10,000
5		20	(h)	Millwall	D	1-1	Davison	8,000
6		24	(a)	Watford	L	0-7		500
7		27	(a)	Exeter C	D	0-0		4,000
8	Oct	4	(h)	Cardiff C	D	2-2	Davison 2	8,000
9		11	(a)	Swindon T	L	1-6	Opp own-goal	4,000
10		18	(h)	Bristol R	D	2-2	Feebury (pen), Holmes	8,000
11		25	(a)	Merthyr T	L	0-3		7,000
12	Nov	1	(h)	West Ham U	L	2-4	Davison, Opp own-goal	
13		8	(a)	Plymouth A	W	3-0	Davison 2, Holmes	8,654
14		15	(h)	Southampton	D	2-2	Davison, Holmes	7,000
15		22	(a)	Reading	L	0-1		
16		27	(h)	Crystal P	W	2-0	Davison, Welch	2,000
17	Dec	6	(a)	Queen's Park R	L	0-3		5,000
18		20	(h)	Norwich C	L	1-2	Davison	5,000
19		25	(h)	Northampton T	L	0-1		8,000
20		26	(a)	Northampton T	D	0-0		9,000
21		27	(a)	Brighton & HA	D	2-2	Holmes 2	5,000
22	Jan	3	(h)	Portsmouth	D	2-2	Davison, Welch	6,000
23		17	(a)	Millwall	L	1-4	Boston	12,000
24		24	(h)	Exeter C	L	1-2	Tosswill	5,000
25	Feb	7	(a)	Cardiff C	L	1-2	Feebury (pen)	8,000
26		14	(h)	Swindon T	D	1-1	Feebury	8,700
27		21	(a)	Bristol R	L	2-3	Parkes, Davison	10,000
28		28	(h)	Merthyr T	D	0-0		5,000
29	Mar	7	(a)	West Ham U	L	0-1		10,000
30		14	(h)	Plymouth A	D	1-1	Holmes	7,000
31		21	(a)	Southampton	L	0-3		6,000
32		28	(h)	Reading	L	1-2	Jones	6,000
33	Apr	4	(a)	Crystal P	L	1-3	Jones	6,000
34		10	(h)	Southend U	W	3-0	Davison, Jones 2	2,000
35		11	(h)	Queen's Park R	L	0-1		8,500
36		13	(a)	Southend U	D	1-1	Harris	
37		18	(h)	Watford	W	3-1	Davison 3	5,000
38		25	(a)	Norwich C	D	1-1	Davison	5,000

FINAL LEAGUE POSITION: 20th in Southern League, Division One — Appearances

Goals

FA Cup

Q4	Nov	29	(a)	Port Vale	L	1-3	Davison	12,108

Appearances

Goals

Jacques	Barnacle	Lawrance	Yates	Feebury	Harris	Parkes	Dobson	Davison	Jones	Craig	Rogers	Jackson	Kimberley	Juggins	Dexter	Parton	Welch	Tosswill	Boston	Gretton	Hall	Smith W	Mitchell	Bunn	Holmes	
1	2	3	4	5	6	7	8	9	10	11																1
1	2		4	5	6	7	8	9	10	11		3														2
1	2	3	4	5	6	7	8	9	10	11																3
1	2		4		6	7	8	9		10		3							5			11				4
1	2		4		6	7	8	9		10		3							5			11				5
1	2		4		6	7	8	9		10		3							5			11				6
1	2		4	5	6	7	8	9	10	11						3										7
1	2		4	5	6	7	8	9		10						3									11	8
1	2		4	5	6			9	10							3				7		8			11	9
1			4	5		7		9	10			2	6			3						8			11	10
1		6	4	5		7		9					2			3						8	10		11	11
1	2	6	4	5		7		9								3						8	10		11	12
1	2		4	5		7		9					6			3		8					10		11	13
1	2		4	5		7		9					6			3		8					10		11	14
1			4	5		7		9					6	2		3		8						10	11	15
1			4	5		7	8	9					6	2		3	10								11	16
1	2		4			7	8	9					6			3	10	5							11	17
1	2		4		6	7		9					5			3	10	8				11				18
1	2		6		3	4		9										8	5	7		10			11	19
1	2		6		3	4		9					5					8		7		10			11	20
1	2		6		3	4		9					5					8		7		10			11	21
	2		6		3	4		9			1						10	8	5	7					11	22
	2				3	4		9			1		6				10	8	5	7					11	23
1	2			5		4		9				3					10	8	6	7					11	24
1			3	8	6	4		9	10						2				5	7		11				25
1			3	8	6	4		9	10						2				5	7		11				26
1			3	8	6	4		9	10						2				5	7		11				27
1			3	8	6	4		9	10						2				5	7		11				28
1	3			9	6	4		8	10						2				5	7					11	29
1	2		3	9	6	4		8	10										5	7					11	30
1	2		3	9	6	4		8	10										5	7					11	31
1	3		4	5				9	10						2		8	6		7					11	32
1	3		2	5				9	10	6							8	4		7					11	33
1	3			5			8	9	10	6					2			4		7					11	34
1	3			5			8	9	10	6					2			4		7					11	35
1	3				5	4	8	9	10	6					2					7					11	36
1	3				5	7	8	9		6					2		10	4							11	37
1	3				5		8	9	10	6					2			4			7				11	38
36	30	4	30	25	25	32	15	38	19	14	2	6	11	2	11	12	9	17	14	19	1	15	4	1	26	
				3	1	2	2	18	4	1							2	1	1						6	

2 own-goals

1			4	5		7	8	9					6	2		3	10								11	Q4
1			1	1		1	1	1					1	1		1	1								1	
								1																		

1914-15

Manager: F.S.Walford

1	Sep	5	(a)	Brentford	L	1-3	Lowes	3,000
2		12	(h)	Stoke	L	1-3	Allan	2,000
3		19	(a)	Pontypridd	W	3-2	Harris, Lowes, Allan	
4		26	(a)	Barry	L	0-2		2,000
5	Oct	10	(a)	Ton Pentre	L	1-2	Dobson	
6		24	(h)	Stalybridge C	W	3-0	Dobson, Allan, Enright	3,000
7	Nov	7	(h)	Merthyr T	L	1-2	Allan	5,000
8		14	(h)	Ebbw Vale	W	6-0	Morris, Dobson 2, Allan 3	
9		21	(a)	Llanelly	W	2-1	Allan, Enright	
10		28	(h)	Newport C	W	10-1	Harkins, Dobson, Allan 3, Enright 4, Turner	3,500
11	Dec	4	(a)	Mid Rhondda	L	1-2	Enright	
12	Jan	2	(h)	Brentford	W	3-2	Dobson, Allan, Opp own-goal	4,000
13		9	(h)	Barry	W	3-0	Dobson 2, Allan	3,000
14		16	(a)	Stoke	L	1-9	Allan	2,000
15	Feb	13	(h)	Ton Pentre	W	7-2	Alderson 2, Dobson, Allan 3, Enright	1,500
16		27	(a)	Stalybridge C	L	0-1		2,000
17	Mar	6	(h)	Mid Rhondda	W	3-0	Morris, Dobson, Allan	2,000
18		13	(a)	Merthyr T	L	0-3		
19		20	(a)	Ebbw Vale	W	3-1	Alderson, Doran 2	
20		27	(h)	Llanelly	W	1-0	Dobson	1,500
21	Apr	2	(a)	Swansea T	L	0-1		5,000
22		3	(a)	Newport C	W	1-0	Allan	
23		5	(h)	Swansea T	D	0-0		
24		10	(h)	Pontypridd	W	5-0	Roberts, Dobson 2, Allan 2	1,000

FINAL LEAGUE POSITION: 5th in Southern League, Division Two

Appearances

Goals

FA Cup

Q6	Dec	19	(a)	Glossop	L	1-3	Enright	539

Appearances

Goals

Blake	Barnacle	Meunier	Fulljames	Morris	Harkins	Alderson	Lowes	Allan	Welch	Turner	Enright	Holmes	CaseyJ	Crutchley	Shields	Craig	Robinson	Harris	Bennett	Roberts	Dobson	Doran	
1	2	3	4	5	6	7	8	9	10	11													1
1	2	3		5	6	7	8	9	10	11						4							2
1		3		5	6	7	8	9			10	11						4		2			3
1		3	4	5	6		8	9		7	10	11								2			4
1		3	4	5	6	7	8	9		11										2	10		5
1		3	4	5	6	7		9		11	10									2	8		6
1		3	4	5	6	7		9		11	10									2	8		7
1		3	4	5	6			9		11	10	7								2	8		8
1	2		4	5	6			9		7	10	11								3	8		9
1	3		4	5	6			9		11	10	7								2	8		10
1	3		4	5	6			9		11	10	7								2	8		11
1	3			5	6	7		9		11	10			4						2	8		12
		3		5	6	7		9		11	10			4			1	2			8		13
	3			5	6	7		9		11	10			4			1			2	8		14
	3			5		7		9	11		10			4		6	1			2	8		15
1	3			5		7	8	9	11		10			4		6				2			16
		3		5		7		9	11		10			4		6	1			2	8		17
1	3			5		7	11	9			10					6		4		2	8		18
1	3				6	7		9			11	10			2	4		5				8	19
	3					7		9	11		10			4		5	1		6	2	8		20
1	3				6			9			10		11	4	2	5				7	8		21
1	3				6			9			10		11	4	2	5				7	8		22
1	3				6			9			10		11	4	2	5				7	8		23
1	3							9	11		10			4	2	5			6	7	8		24
19	16	10	9	18	18	15	7	24	7	13	21	7	3	11	5	11	5	4	2	20	18	1	
				2	1	3	2	21		1	8							1		1	13	2	

1 own-goal

1	2	3		5	6			9		11	10	7								4	8		Q6
1	1	1		1	1			1		1	1	1								1	1		
											1												

1918-19

Manager: W.Clayton

1	Sep	7	(h)	Grimsby T	W	7-4	Bishop, Dunn, Sambrooke 3, Lowes 2	10,000
2		14	(a)	Grimsby T	D	1-1	Middlemiss	
3		21	(h)	Bradford C	L	1-2	Sambrooke	8,600
4		28	(a)	Bradford C	W	1-0	Sambrooke	
5	Oct	5	(h)	Sheffield W	W	2-0	Buckley, Craig	8,000
6		12	(a)	Sheffield W	L	0-3		
7		19	(a)	Huddersfield T	L	1-4	Howell	
8		26	(h)	Huddersfield T	W	7-1	Buckley, Howell, Sambrooke 3, Lowes, Middlemiss	6,000
9	Nov	2	(a)	Notts C	L	0-4		
10		9	(h)	Notts C	W	5-1	Richards, Sambrooke 3, Smith	8,000
11		16	(a)	Birmingham	L	1-3	Buckley (pen)	20,000
12		23	(h)	Birmingham	L	1-3	Bowser	10,000
13		30	(a)	Rotherham C	D	1-1	Lowes	
14	Dec	7	(h)	Rotherham C	W	3-2	Sambrooke, Lowes, Middlemiss	6,000
15		14	(a)	Nottingham F	W	1-0	Sambrooke	
16		21	(h)	Nottingham F	L	2-5	Sambrooke 2	8,000
17		25	(a)	Lincoln C	L	2-3	Buckley, Lowes	
18		26	(h)	Lincoln C	W	2-0	Lowes 2	
19		28	(a)	Leeds C	W	1-0	Sambrooke	7,000
20	Jan	11	(a)	Sheffield U	L	1-3	Buckley	16,000
21		18	(h)	Sheffield U	L	2-4	Buckley, Sambrooke	12,000
22		25	(a)	Hull C	L	0-2		7,000
23	Feb	1	(h)	Hull C	W	3-0	Davies, Sambrooke 2	7,000
24		8	(a)	Bradford	D	0-0		8,000
25		15	(h)	Bradford	W	2-1	Sambrooke 2	10,000
26		22	(a)	Barnsley	L	2-6	Davies, Lowes	5,800
27	Mar	1	(h)	Barnsley	W	2-1	Allan, Lowes	10,000
28		8	(a)	Leicester F	D	2-2	Johnstone, Craig	10,000
29		15	(h)	Leicester F	W	1-0	Lowes	12,000
30	Apr	22	(h)	Leeds C	L	1-3	Sambrooke	9,000

FINAL LEAGUE POSITION: 9th in English League Midland Section

Appearances

Goals

Subsidiary Competition

31	Mar	22	(a)	Grimsby T	D	1-1	Allan	4,000
32		29	(h)	Grimsby T	W	2-1	Smith, Middlemiss	8,000
33	Apr	5	(h)	Hull C	L	1-3	Andrews	10,000
34		12	(a)	Hull C	W	1-0	Sambrooke	7,000
35		18	(a)	Lincoln C	D	1-1	Davies	
36		19	(h)	Lincoln C	W	1-0	Lowes	7,000

Appearances

Goals

Blake	Roberts	Aston	Craig	Buckley	Bishop	Newman	Dunn	Sambrooke	Lowes	Middlemiss	Lindon	Chaplin	Pennington	Richardson	Allan	Wilde	Sheldon	Littlewood	Mackrill	Fulljames	Smith	Wells	Gallagher	Richards	Waterhouse	Brookes	Best	Johnstone	Savage	Bell	Howell	Osborne	Bowser	Needham	Davies	Gregory	Pate	Wootton	
1	2	3	4	5	6	7	8	9	10	11																													1
	2	3	6			7	4	9	10	11	1												5							8									2
	2	3	4	5	6	7		9	10	11	1																				8								3
	2	3	4	5	6	7		9	10	11	1																				8								4
	2		6	5	3	7		9	10		1									4											8							11	5
	2		4	5	6	7		9	10		1	3																			8							11	6
	2		6	5	3	7		9	10		1										4										8							11	7
	4		6	5	3	7		9	10	11	1	2																			8								8
	4		6	5	3	7		9	10	11	1	2									8																		9
	4			5	3	7		9		11	1	2									8			6												10			10
	4			5	3	7		9		11	1	2									6											8					10		11
	4			5	3			9	10	11	1	2													6	7							8						12
	4			5	3			9	10	11	1	2		6			7																8						13
	4			5	3	7		9	10	11	1	2		6																			8						14
	4			5	3	7		9	10	11	1	2		6			8																						15
	4			5	3	7		9	10	11	1	2		6							8																		16
	4			5	3	7		9	10	11	1	2		6							8																		17
	4			5	3	7		9	10	11	1	2		6							8																		18
	4		6	5	3	7		9	10	11	1	2									8																		19
	4		6	5	3			9	10	11	1	2					7				8																		20
	4		6	5	3			9	10	11	1	2					7				8																		21
	4		6		5	7		9	10	11	1	2						3																8					22
				5	6	7		9	10	11	1	2	3	4																					8				23
			5		6	7		9	10	11	1	2	3	4																					8				24
	2				6			9	10	11	1		3	5	4												7								8				25
	4				6				10	11	1	2	3	5	9													7							8				26
	2			5					10	11	1	3			9	6						4						7							8				27
	2		9	5					10	11	1	3			4	6												7							8				28
	2		5					9	10	11	1	3			4	6												7							8				29
				5				9	10		1	2			6	4	11		3		8								7										30
1	27	4	16	24	25	20	2	27	28	26	29	23	4	10	6	4	5	1	1	1	11	1	1	1	1	1	1	4	1	1	6	1	3	1	7	1	1	3	
			2	6	1		1	22	11	3					1						1			1				1			2		1		2				

	2		4						10		1	3		6	9					5								7							8				31
	2			5						10	1	3			4		7				8						11												32
	2		5				4		10	11	1	3					8										7												33
						7		9	10		1	2			4	3	8				5																		34
				5				9	10		1	2			6							4						3							7				35
				5				9	10		1	2			6	4	11		3																				36
	3		2	3		1	1	3	5	2	6	6		1	5	2	4		1	1	2	1					2	2							2				
								1	1	1					1						1														1				

Hennessey played number 11 in Matches 34 & 35; Andrews played number 9 in Match 33 and scored one goal; Pye played number 11 in Match 31; Pugh played number 6 in Match 32; Edwards played number 6 in Matches 33 & 34; Dalton played number 8 in Matches 35 & 36; Barrett played number 7 in Match 36; Hopkins played number 9 in Match 32.

1919-20

Manager: Will Clayton until November 1919, then Harry Pollitt.

1	Aug	30	(h)	Tottenham H	L	0-5		16,500
2	Sep	3	(a)	Leeds C	L	0-3		7,000
3		6	(a)	Tottenham H	L	1-4	Mercer	30,610
4		11	(h)	Leeds C	L	0-4		12,000
5		13	(a)	Birmingham	L	1-4	Mercer	20,000
6		20	(h)	Birmingham	L	1-3	Mercer	16,000
7		27	(a)	Leicester C	L	0-1		10,000
8	Oct	4	(h)	Leicester C	L	1-2	Lowes	17,500
9		11	(h)	Fulham	L	0-1		16,000
10		18	(a)	Fulham	D	0-0		20,000
11		25	(h)	Bristol C	D	0-0		17,500
12	Nov	1	(a)	Bristol C	L	0-1		11,000
13		8	(h)	Huddersfield T	L	0-2		15,000
14		15	(a)	Huddersfield T	L	0-5		5,000
15		22	(h)	Blackpool	D	0-0		19,000
16		29	(a)	Blackpool	L	0-2		5,000
17	Dec	6	(h)	West Ham U	D	0-0		18,000
18		13	(a)	West Ham U	L	0-2		20,000
19		20	(h)	Clapton O	D	0-0		18,000
20		25	(h)	Stoke	W	3-2	Miller, Walker, A.Sheldon	19,000
21		26	(a)	Stoke	L	1-6	Quinn	
22		27	(a)	Clapton O	D	2-2	Quinn, Walker	12,500
23	Jan	1	(a)	Grimsby T	W	1-0	Walker	4,000
24		3	(h)	Rotherham C	D	1-1	Walker	18,000
25		17	(a)	Rotherham C	L	3-4	Kemp 2, Gibson	8,000
26		24	(h)	South Shields	D	1-1	Walker	15,800
27		31	(a)	South Shields	L	0-1		12,000
28	Feb	7	(h)	Wolves	W	1-0	Parker	20,070
29		14	(a)	Wolves	L	0-2		25,000
30		21	(h)	Hull C	L	0-1		18,000
31		28	(a)	Hull C	W	1-0	Walker	7,000
32	Mar	6	(a)	Stockport C	D	1-1	Walker	3,000
33		13	(h)	Stockport C	D	1-1	Parker	10,000
34		20	(a)	Barnsley	L	0-1		10,000
35		27	(h)	Barnsley	W	1-0	Parker	18,000
36	Apr	3	(a)	Nottingham F	L	1-2	Parker	9,000
37		6	(h)	Grimsby T	W	2-0	Dougall, Parker	18,000
38		10	(h)	Nottingham F	W	4-2	Wynn, Parker, Mercer, Gibson	19,000
39		17	(a)	Lincoln C	L	1-4	Parker	8,000
40		24	(h)	Lincoln C	W	2-0	Parker 2	20,000
41		28	(a)	Bury	D	2-2	Wynn, Lowes	7,000
42	May	1	(h)	Bury	W	2-1	Mercer 2	23,506

FINAL LEAGUE POSITION: 20th in Division Two

Appearances

Goals

FA Cup

1	Jan	10	(a)	Luton T	D	2-2	Walker, Jones	13,000
R		15	(h)	Luton T	L	0-1		21,893

Appearances

Goals

Lindon	Roberts	Chaplin	Allan	Hawley	Clarke	Sheldon L	Mercer	Sambrooke	Lowes	Gibson	Sheldon A	Howe	Stone	Johnson	Mite	Copeland	Crowe	Wright	Godfrey	Cross	Kemp	Jarvis	Hanney	Wynn	Walker	Quinn	Nelson	Miller	Robinson	Fenwick	Gallacher	Dougall	Blair	Parker	Mitchell	Dalton	Stirling	Binks	
1	2	3	4	5	6	7	8	9	10	11																														1
1	2	3	4	5	6	7	9		10		11																														2
1	2	3	4	5			8	9		11	10	6	7																											3
1	2	3	4	5			8			11	10	6	7	9																										4
1	2	3	4		5	7	8		10	11		6		9																										5
1		2			5	7	8	9		11		4			6																									6
1	3				5		8	9		11		4			10	2	6	7																						7
1		3			5		8		10	11					6	2	4		9																					8
1		3		5	4		8		10		11				6	2		7	9																					9
1		3		5	4		8				11				10	2		7	9	6																				10
1		3		5	4		8				11				10	2		7	9	6																				11
1		3		5	4		8				11					2		7	9	6	10																			12
1		3		5	4					11						2		7	9	6	10						8													13
1	3			5	4		8	9	10	11						2		7		6																				14
	3			4				9		11						2		7		6		1	5	8	10																15
		3		4	6					11						2		7				1	5	8	9	10															16
	3			4	6											2		7				1	5	8	9	10	11														17
1		3		4	6		8			11						2								5		9	10		7												18
1	3									11						2								5	8	10	9		7	4	6									19
1	3										11					2								5	8	10	9		7	4	6									20
1	3										11					2								5	8	10	9		7	4	6									21
1	3										11				6	2								5	8	10	9		7		4									22
1	3										11					2								5	8	10	9		7	4	6									23
1	3										11					2								5	8	10	9		7	4	6									24
1		3					8			11						2						9				10				4	6	5	7							25
1		3			4		8			11						2								5		10	9				6		7							26
1					4		8			11						2								5		10					6		7	3	9					27
1						7	8			11						2								5		10				4	6			3	9					28
1	3					7	8			11						2								5		10				4	6				9					29
							4			11						2								5	8	10					6		7	3	9	1				30
										11						2										8	10			4	6		7	3	9	1	5			31
										11						2										8	10			4	6			3	9	1	5	7		32
										11						2										8	10			4	6			3	9	1	5	7		33
										11						2										8	10			4	6			3	9	1	5	7		34
										11						2								5	8		10			4	6			3	9	1		7		35
		3					10			11						2								5	8					4	6				9	1		7		36
		3					10			11						2								5	8					4	6		7		9	1				37
		3					10			11						2								5	8					4	6		7		9	1				38
	3						10			11						2								5	8					4	6		7		9	1				39
		3					11		10															8					4	6		7		9	1	5		2	40
		3					11		10															8					4	6		7		9	1	5		2	41
		3					11		10															8					4	6		7		9	1	5		2	42
26	17	22	5	14	17	6	27	6	9	28	12	5	2	2	7	33	2	10	6	6	3	3	20	18	20	15	2	7	20	24	1	11	8	16	13	7	5	3	
							6		2	2	1											2			2	7	2		1				1		9				

1	2	3										11												5	8	9				4	6		7							1
1	2	3										11												5	8	9				4	6		7							R
2	2	2										2												2	2	2				2	2		2							
																										1															

A.Smith played number 8 in Match 2; C.Smith played number 7 in Match 8; P.Mackrill played number 3 in Match 6; F.Jones played number 10 in Match 6, FA Cup Round 1 and in the FA Cup replay and scored one goal.

1920-21

Manager: A.J.Evans

1	Aug	28	(a)	Rotherham C	W	3-2	Mercer, Gibson, Hadley	17,000
2		30	(h)	Port Vale	D	0-0		21,533
3	Sep	4	(h)	Rotherham C	L	0-1		20,000
4		6	(a)	Port Vale	D	0-0		10,000
5		11	(a)	Blackpool	L	0-4		15,000
6		18	(h)	Blackpool	L	0-2		18,000
7		25	(a)	Sheffield W	L	0-3		20,000
8	Oct	2	(h)	Sheffield W	L	2-3	Parker, Smith	18,000
9		4	(h)	West Ham U	L	0-1		6,500
10		9	(a)	South Shields	L	1-4	Parker	18,000
11		16	(h)	South Shields	W	1-0	Dougall	18,000
12		23	(a)	Stoke	L	1-4	Fenwick	7,000
13		30	(h)	Stoke	W	1-0	Nash	20,000
14	Nov	6	(a)	Notts C	D	1-1	Leitch	14,000
15		13	(h)	Notts C	D	1-1	Nash	22,000
16		27	(h)	Leeds U	D	1-1	Millard	19,000
17	Dec	1	(a)	Leeds U	L	0-4		9,257
18		4	(a)	Birmingham	L	2-3	Nash, Morgan	30,000
19		11	(h)	Birmingham	L	0-4		22,800
20	Dec	25	(h)	Cardiff C	L	2-4	Foster, Smith	18,000
21		27	(a)	Cardiff C	W	1-0	Morgan	42,000
22	Jan	1	(a)	West Ham U	L	0-7		8,000
23		15	(a)	Hull C	D	1-1	Foster	10,000
24		22	(h)	Hull C	W	3-2	Dougall, Wynn, Gibson	17,000
25	Feb	5	(h)	Fulham	L	0-2		16,000
26		12	(a)	Wolves	L	0-1		21,485
27		24	(h)	Wolves	W	4-0	Howell, Foster, Morgan 2	6,000
28		26	(a)	Stockport C	L	0-3		10,000
29	Mar	5	(h)	Stockport C	D	1-1	Foster	17,000
30		12	(a)	Clapton O	D	0-0		15,000
31		14	(a)	Fulham	L	0-2		6,000
32		19	(h)	Clapton O	D	1-1	Morgan	16,000
33		26	(h)	Bury	W	1-0	Leitch	16,000
34		28	(a)	Leicester C	W	1-0	Millard	20,000
35		29	(h)	Leicester C	W	1-0	Mercer	20,000
36	Apr	2	(a)	Bury	L	0-2		8,000
37		9	(h)	Bristol C	W	2-1	Hadley, Morgan	12,000
38		16	(a)	Bristol C	L	0-2		30,000
39		23	(h)	Barnsley	W	3-1	Millard 2, Morgan	15,000
40		30	(a)	Barnsley	D	2-2	Stevens 2	8,000
41	May	2	(h)	Nottingham F	D	0-0		18,000
42		7	(a)	Nottingham F	W	2-0	Dalton, Stevens	6,000

FINAL LEAGUE POSITION: 21st in Division Two

Appearances
Goals

FA Cup

Q6	Dec	8	(h)	Rochdale	D	1-1	Millard	15,500
Q6R		22	(a)	Rochdale	L	1-2	Hanney	6,000

Appearances
Goals

Mitchell	Chaplin	Lawrence	Fenwick	Hanney	Hadley	Dougall	Mercer	Parker	Nash	Gibson	Binks	Hann	Pointon	Wynn	Dyke	Smith	Leitch	Robinson	Dalton	Millard	Morgan	Cross	Blair	Best	Foster	Campbell	Howell	Mackay	Stevens	Devlin	
1	2	3	4	5	6	7	8	9	10	11																					1
1	2	3	4	5	6	7	8	9	10	11																					2
1		3	4	5	6	7	8	9	10	11	2																				3
1		3	4	5	6	7	8	9			2	10	11																		4
1		3	4	5	6	7	8	9	10	11	2																				5
1	2		4	5	6	7	9		10	11	3			8																	6
1	2	3	4	5	6	7	8	9	10	11																					7
1	2		4	5	6		8	9		11	3				7	10															8
1	2	3	4	5	6		8	9					11		7		10														9
1	2	3			6		8	9	11						7		10	4	5												10
1		3	4		6	7	8	9	11		2						10		5												11
1		3	4		6	7	8		11		2			9			10		5												12
1		3	6			7	8		11		2						10	4	5	9											13
1		3	6			7			8		2						10	4	5	9	11										14
1		3	4			7			10		2						8		5	9	11	6									15
1		3	6			7	8		10		2							4	5	9	11										16
1		3	6			7			10		2						8	4	5	9	11										17
1	2		6	5		7			10								8		4	9	11		3								18
1	2		6	5		7			10								8		4	9	11		3								19
	2	3		5	6	7	4									10				8	11			1	9						20
	2	3			6	7								8		10				5	11	4		1	9						21
	2	3			4	7								8		10				5	11	6		1	9						22
	2	3	6			7				11				8					4	5	10			1	9						23
	2	3	6		4	7				11				8						5	10			1	9						24
	2	3	6		4	7				11				8						5	10			1	9						25
	2	3				7	8			11									4	5	10			1	9	6					26
	2	3	6			7				11									4	5	10			1	9		8				27
	2	3	6			7				11									4	5	10			1	9		8				28
	2	3	6			7				11						8			4	5	10			1	9						29
	2	3	6			7				11						8			4	5	10			1			9				30
	2	3	6			7				11						8			4	5	10			1			9				31
	2	3			6		8			11									4	5	10			1				7	9		32
	2	3			6	7				11							8		4	5	10			1					9		33
	2	3			6	7				11							8		4	5	10			1					9		34
	2	3			6	7	11										8		4	5	10			1					9		35
	2	3			6	7	11										8		4	5	10			1					9		36
	2	3			6	7				11							8		4	5	10			1					9		37
	2	3			6	7											8		4	5	10			1				11	9		38
	2	3			6	7											8		4	5	10			1				11	9		39
	2	3			6	7											8		4	5	10			1				11	9		40
	2	3			6	7											8		4	5	10			1				11	9		41
	2	3			6												8		4	5	10			1				7	9	11	42
19	32	38	26	12	28	37	19	10	16	20	12	1	2	7	3	7	20	5	28	30	29	3	2	23	10	1	4	6	11	1	
			1		2	2	2	2	2	3				1		2	2		1	4	7				4		1		3		

Mitchell	Chaplin	Lawrence	Fenwick	Hanney	Hadley	Dougall	Mercer	Parker	Nash	Gibson	Binks	Hann	Pointon	Wynn	Dyke	Smith	Leitch	Robinson	Dalton	Millard	Morgan	Cross	Blair	Best	Foster	Campbell	Howell	Mackay	Stevens	Devlin	
	2	3		5	6	7			10								8			9	11	4		1							Q6
	2	3	4	5	6	7			10							8				9	11			1							Q6R
	2	2	1	2	2	2			2							1	1			2	2	1		2							
				1																1											

1921-22

Manager: A.J.Evans

1	Aug	27	(a)	Fulham	L 0-5		26,000
2		29	(h)	Rotherham C	W 4-0	Dalton, Millard, McCaig, Stevens	17,000
3	Sep	3	(h)	Fulham	W 2-0	Millard, McCaig	25,000
4		5	(a)	Rotherham C	D 0-0		8,000
5		10	(h)	Nottingham F	L 0-1		25,000
6		17	(a)	Nottingham F	L 0-1		14,000
7		24	(h)	Wolves	W 3-1	Hadley, Lindley, Morgan	16,339
8	Oct	1	(a)	Wolves	L 0-1		17,482
9		3	(h)	West Ham U	W 2-0	Morgan 2	10,000
10		8	(a)	Barnsley	W 1-0	Stevens	18,912
11		15	(h)	Barnsley	L 0-1		20,000
12		22	(a)	Bury	L 2-3	Stevens, Morgan	7,000
13		29	(h)	Bury	L 1-2	Stevens	18,000
14	Nov	5	(a)	Derby C	L 0-1		8,000
15		17	(h)	Derby C	L 1-2	Stevens	9,000
16		19	(h)	Leicester C	D 0-0		18,000
17		26	(a)	Leicester C	D 1-1	Morgan	18,000
18	Dec	10	(a)	West Ham U	L 0-3		18,000
19		24	(h)	Sheffield W	D 2-2	Lawrence, Allon	16,000
20		26	(h)	South Shields	L 0-1		18,000
21		31	(h)	Port Vale	W 4-1	Dalton, Stevens 2, Gough	16,000
22	Jan	2	(a)	South Shields	L 1-2	Stevens	10,000
23		21	(a)	Blackpool	L 1-2	Stevens	5,000
24		28	(h)	Blackpool	L 0-1		15,000
25		30	(a)	Port Vale	W 2-1	Stevens 2	5,000
26	Feb	11	(h)	Bradford	D 2-2	Stevens, Mercer	11,924
27		15	(a)	Bradford	W 2-1	Stevens, Mercer	6,000
28		18	(a)	Clapton O	L 0-4		5,000
29		25	(h)	Clapton O	L 1-2	Stevens	15,000
30	Mar	4	(a)	Stoke	D 2-2	Millard, Stevens	7,000
31		11	(h)	Stoke	L 0-1		15,000
32		13	(h)	Sheffield W	L 2-3	Stevens 2	6,000
33		18	(h)	Leeds U	W 1-0	Dougall	15,000
34		25	(a)	Leeds U	L 2-5	Millard, Morgan	10,000
35	Apr	1	(h)	Hull C	W 2-0	Stevens, Mercer	13,000
36		8	(a)	Hull C	L 0-2		8,000
37		15	(a)	Notts C	D 1-1	Dalton	14,000
38		17	(a)	Bristol C	W 2-0	Stevens 2	29,000
39		18	(h)	Bristol C	D 1-1	Warren	12,000
40		22	(h)	Notts C	W 4-2	Stevens 2, Mercer, Gibson	25,000
41		29	(h)	Crystal P	D 1-1	Warren	14,000
42	May	6	(a)	Crystal P	D 1-1	Warren	10,000

FINAL LEAGUE POSITION: 20th in Division Two

Appearances
Goals

FA Cup

Q5	Dec	3	(a)	Rotherham C	D 1-1	Mercer	12,000
Q5R		8	(h)	Rotherham C	W 1-0	Gough	8,000
Q6		17	(a)	Southport Cen	L 0-1		8,000

Appearances
Goals

Best	Chaplin	Lawrence	Dalton	Millard	Hadley	Dougall	McCaig	Stevens	Lindley	Morgan	Robinson	Mackay	Allon	Mercer	Devlin	Leitch	Findlay	Swindale	Gough	Cross	Warren	Gibson	
1	2	3	4	5	6	7	8	9	10	11													1
1	2	3	4	5	6	7	8	9	10	11													2
1	2	3	4	5	6	7	8	9	10	11													3
1	2	3	4	5	6	7	8	9	10	11													4
1	2	3		5	6	7	8	9	10	11	4												5
1	2	3		5	6		8	9	10	11	4	7											6
1	2	3		5	6		8	9	10	11		7	4										7
1	2	3		5	6		8	9	10	11		7	4										8
1	2	3		5	6			9		10		7	4	8	11								9
1	2	3		5	6			9		10		7	4		11	8							10
1	2	3		5	6			9		10		7	4		11	8							11
1	2	3		5	6	7		9	8	10			4		11								12
1	2	3		5	6	7		9	8	10			4		11								13
1	2	3		5	6	7		9	8	10			4		11								14
	2	3		5	6			9	10	11			4		8		1	7					15
	2	3						9	10	11			5	4	8	6	1	7					16
1	2	3		5	6			9		11			4	8				7	10				17
1	2	3		5	6			9	10				4	8				7	11				18
1	2	3		5	6	7	8	9					4	10					11				19
1	2			5	6	7	8	9					4	10					11	3			20
1	2	3	8	5	6	7		9					4	10					11				21
1	2	3	8	5	6	7		9					4	10					11				22
1	2	3	8	5	6	7		9					4	10					11				23
1	2	3	5	8	6	7		9	10				4	11									24
1	2	3	5	8	6	7		9					4	10					11				25
1	2	3		5	6	7		9					4	10					11		8		26
1	2	3		5	6	7		9					4	10					11		8		27
1	2	3		5	6	7		9					4			10			11		8		28
1	2			5	6	7		9		10			4						11	3	8		29
1	2	3		5	6	7		9		11			4	10							8		30
1	2	3		5	6	7		9		11			4	10							8		31
1	2	3		5	6	7		9		11			4	10							8		32
1	2	3		5	6	7		9		11			4	10							8		33
1	2	3		5	6	7		9		11			4	10							8		34
1	2	3	5		6	7		9					4	10					11		8		35
1	2	3	5		6	7		9					4	10					11		8		36
1	2	3	5		6	7		9		10			4	8								11	37
1	2	3	5		6	7		9					4	10							8	11	38
1	2	3	5		6	7		9					4	10					11		8		39
1	2	3	5		6	7		9					4	10							8	11	40
1	2	3	5		6	7		9					4	10							8	11	41
1	2	3	5		6	7		9					4	10							8	11	42
40	42	40	17	33	41	32	10	42	15	24	2	6	36	26	8	4	2	4	15	2	16	5	
		1	3	4	1	1	2	22	1	6			1	4					1		3	1	

1	2	3		5	6	7		9		10			4	8					11				Q5
1	2	3		5	6	7		9		10			4	8					11				Q5R
1	2	3		5	6			9			8		4	7		10			11				Q6
3	3	3		3	3	2		3		2	1		3	3		1			3				
														1					1				

1922-23

Manager: A.J.Evans

1	Aug	26	(h)	Notts C	L 1-2	Stevens	20,000
2		30	(a)	Crystal P	D 0-0		12,000
3	Sep	2	(a)	Notts C	L 0-2		14,000
4		7	(h)	Crystal P	W 2-1	Toms 2	14,000
5		9	(h)	Port Vale	L 1-2	Toms	17,000
6		16	(a)	Port Vale	W 1-0	Toms	8,000
7		23	(h)	Manchester U	W 2-0	Mercer, Toms	17,000
8		30	(a)	Manchester U	L 1-2	Mercer	20,000
9	Oct	7	(h)	Bury	W 3-0	Mercer 3	18,000
10		14	(a)	Bury	D 1-1	Wood	12,000
11		21	(h)	Derby C	D 1-1	Toms	16,000
12		28	(a)	Derby C	L 0-4		17,000
13	Nov	4	(a)	Rotherham C	L 0-2		10,000
14		11	(h)	Rotherham C	W 2-1	Dougall, Wood	18,000
15		18	(a)	Stockport C	L 1-5	Toms	11,000
16		25	(h)	Stockport C	W 1-0	Toms	14,000
17	Dec	9	(a)	Fulham	L 0-4		15,000
18		11	(h)	Fulham	W 1-0	Toms	4,000
19		16	(h)	Leeds U	L 1-2	Toms	12,000
20		23	(a)	Leeds U	L 0-1		10,000
21		25	(h)	Wolves	W 7-1	Jones, Richmond 2, Toms 3, Wood	18,000
22		26	(a)	Wolves	W 2-1	Toms 2	21,485
23		30	(h)	West Ham U	L 1-3	Toms	15,000
24	Jan	6	(a)	West Ham U	L 0-1		15,000
25		20	(h)	South Shields	L 0-2		8,000
26		27	(a)	South Shields	D 0-0		7,000
27	Feb	10	(a)	Southampton	L 0-3		7,000
28		17	(h)	Bradford C	W 2-1	Mercer, Toms	12,000
29		24	(a)	Bradford C	L 0-4		7,000
30	Mar	3	(h)	Blackpool	L 1-2	Toms	13,312
31		10	(a)	Blackpool	W 1-0	Dougall	10,000
32		17	(a)	Leicester C	L 1-2	Herbert	20,000
33		24	(h)	Leicester C	D 1-1	Dougall	17,000
34		31	(a)	Barnsley	L 2-6	Lawrence, Wood	8,000
35	Apr	2	(a)	Clapton O	D 0-0		16,000
36		3	(h)	Clapton O	W 2-1	Rowley, Wood	16,000
37		7	(h)	Barnsley	W 3-0	Wood 3	10,000
38		14	(a)	Sheffield W	L 0-3		14,000
39		21	(h)	Sheffield W	D 1-1	Wood	12,000
40		28	(a)	Hull C	D 1-1	Wood	6,000
41		30	(h)	Southampton	W 2-0	Wood, Herbert	12,000
42	May	5	(h)	Hull C	L 0-1		8,000

FINAL LEAGUE POSITION: 17th in Division Two

Appearances
Goals

FA Cup

Q5	Dec	2	(a)	New Brighton	L 0-3	

Appearances
Goals

Best	Chaplin	Lawrence	Dalton	Jones	Allon	Storey	Davidson	Stevens	Toms	Wood	Warren	Leitch	Mercer	Dougall	Winship	Hadley	Richmond	Rowley	Herbert	Clews	Robinson	Dennison	Ormiston	Campling	
1	2	3	4	5	6	7	8	9	10	11															1
1	2	3	4	5	6	7		9	10	11	8														2
1	2	3		5	6	7		9	10	11		4	8												3
1	2	3		5	4	7		9	10	11		6	8												4
1	2	3		5	4	8		9	10	11		6		7											5
1		3		5	4	8			10	11			9	7	2	6									6
1		3		5	4	8			10	11			9	7	2	6									7
1		3		5	4	8			10	11			9	7	2	6									8
1		3		5	6	8			10	11			9	7	2		4								9
1		3		5	6	8			10	11			9	7	2		4								10
1		3		5	6	8			10	11			9	7	2		4								11
1		3		5	6	8			10	11			9	7	2		4								12
1		3		5	6	8			10	11			9	7	2		4								13
1		3		5	4				10	11	8		9	7	2			6							14
1		3		5	4				10	11			8	7	2			6	9						15
1		3		5	4				10	11			8	7	2			6	9						16
1		3		5	4	7		9	10	11			8		2			6							17
1		3		5		7	8		10	11					2		4	6		9					18
1		3		5		7	8		10	11					2		4	6		9					19
1		3		5					10	11			8	7	2		4	6		9					20
1		3		5	4				10	11			8	7	2		9	6							21
1		3		5	4				10	11			8	7	2		9	6							22
1		3		5	4				10	11			8	7	2		9	6							23
1		3		5	4		8		10	11				7	2		9	6							24
1		3		5	4				10	9				7	2		8	6			11				25
1		3		5	4	9			10	11			8	7	2			6							26
1		3		5	4	8			10	11			9	7	2			6							27
1		3			5	8			10	11			9	7	2			6				4			28
1		3			5	8			10	11			9	7	2			6				4			29
1		3		5	4	8			10	11			9	7	2			6							30
1		3			4	8				11			9	7	2		5	6	10						31
1		3			4	7				11			8		2		5	6	10				9		32
1		3			4	8				11				7	2		5	6	10				9		33
1		3			4	8				11				7	2		5	6	10				9		34
1	2	3		4		8				11			9	7			5	6	10						35
1	2	3		4		8				11			9	7			5	6	10						36
1	3			4		8				9				7	2		5	6	10		11				37
1	3			4		8				9				7	2		5	6	10		11				38
1				4		8				9				7	3		5	6	10		11			2	39
1	3			4		8				9			10	7	2		5	6			11				40
1				4		8				9			10	7	3		5	6			11			2	41
1				4		8				9			10	7	3		5	6			11			2	42
42	10	36	2	36	31	33	4	6	30	42	2	3	30	34	35	3	25	29	11	3	7	2	3	3	
		1		1		1		1	18	9			6	3			4		2						

1		3		5	4	8			10	11			9	7	2							6			Q5
1		1		1	1	1			1	1			1	1	1							1			

1923-24

Manager: A.J.Evans

1	Aug	25	(h)	Barnsley	L	2-3	Gittos, Wolfe	20,000
2		27	(a)	Bradford C	D	0-0		10,000
3	Sep	1	(a)	Barnsley	D	1-1	Wood	12,000
4		3	(h)	Bradford C	W	1-0	Shea	14,500
5		8	(h)	Bristol C	D	1-1	Wood	16,000
6		15	(a)	Bristol C	D	2-2	Wood 2	18,000
7		22	(h)	Southampton	D	0-0		10,000
8		29	(a)	Southampton	W	3-1	Richmond, Herbert, Wood	12,000
9	Oct	6	(h)	Fulham	W	3-0	Herbert 2, Wood	15,117
10		13	(a)	Fulham	D	1-1	Herbert	10,000
11		20	(a)	Blackpool	L	0-5		12,000
12		27	(h)	Blackpool	W	3-1	Richmond 2, Herbert	13,517
13	Nov	3	(a)	Nelson	L	0-3		5,000
14		10	(h)	Nelson	W	4-0	Storey, Richmond 3	10,000
15		17	(h)	Manchester U	D	1-1	Richmond	16,100
16	Dec	8	(a)	Hull C	L	2-3	Richmond 2	8,000
17		15	(h)	Stoke	L	1-2	Shea	11,290
18		17	(h)	Hull C	L	0-2		13,000
19		22	(a)	Stoke	L	1-2	Herbert	11,000
20		25	(h)	Sheffield W	W	5-1	Dougall, Storey, Richmond 2, Herbert	16,000
21		26	(a)	Sheffield W	L	0-2		
22		29	(h)	Crystal P	D	0-0		13,000
23	Jan	2	(a)	Manchester U	W	2-1	Dougall, Shea	
24		5	(a)	Crystal P	L	1-3	Herbert	15,000
25		19	(h)	Port Vale	L	1-3	Shea	8,000
26		26	(a)	Port Vale	D	1-1	Pynegar	
27	Feb	2	(h)	Bury	W	1-0	Herbert	12,000
28		9	(a)	Leeds U	L	1-3	Pynegar	11,239
29		16	(h)	Leicester C	L	2-4	Shea, Wood	12,000
30		23	(a)	Leicester C	L	0-2		18,000
31	Mar	1	(h)	Clapton O	D	1-1	Pynegar	10,000
32		8	(a)	Clapton O	L	0-4		16,000
33		10	(h)	Leeds U	W	2-1	Pynegar 2	6,000
34		15	(a)	Stockport C	D	0-0		10,000
35		22	(h)	Stockport C	D	0-0		
36		29	(a)	Oldham A	D	1-1	Herbert	11,082
37	Apr	5	(h)	Oldham A	W	5-2	Shea, Pynegar 3, Herbert	14,000
38		12	(a)	South Shields	L	2-4	Dougall, Pynegar	
39		19	(h)	South Shields	W	1-0	Herbert	14,766
40		21	(a)	Derby C	L	0-1		17,000
41		22	(h)	Derby C	L	0-1		16,000
42		26	(a)	Bury	L	0-5		8,000

FINAL LEAGUE POSITION: 19th in Division Two

Appearances

Goals

FA Cup

Q5	Dec	1	(h)	Tranmere R	D	2-2	Richmond 2	9,000
Q5R			(a)	Tranmere R	L	2-3	Shea, Richmond	8,000

Appearances

Goals

Best	Winship	Yorke	Allon	MacLachlan	Rowley	Dougall	Shea	Gittos	Wolfe	Wood	Randle	Jones	Herbert	Storey	Richmond	Maskill	Thompson	Campling	Pynegar	Lawrence	Cook	
1	2	3	4	5	6	7	8	9	10	11												1
1	2		4	5	6	7	8	9	10	11	3											2
1	2			5	6	7	8	9	10	11	3	4										3
1	2			5	6	7	8	9	10	11	3	4										4
1	2			5	6	7	8	9	10	11	3	4										5
1	2			5	6	7	8		11	9	3	4	10									6
1	2			5	6		8		11	9	3	4	10	7								7
1	2			5	6		8			11	3	4	10	7	9							8
1	2			5	6		8			11	3	4	10	7	9							9
1	2			5	6		8			11	3	4	10	7	9							10
1	2			5	6		8			11	3	4	10	7	9							11
1	2			5	6		8			11	3	4	10	7	9							12
1	2			5	6		8			11	3	4	10	7	9							13
1	2			5	6		8			11	3	4	10	7	9							14
1	2			5	6		8			11	3	4	10	7	9							15
1	2			5	6	7	8			11	3		10		9	4						16
1	2			5	6	7	8			11	3		10		9	4						17
1	2			5	6	7	8			11	3	4	10		9							18
1	2			5	6	7	8		11		3		10			4	9					19
1	2			5	6	7			11		3		10	8	9	4						20
1	2			5	6	7			11		3		10	8	9	4						21
1	2			5	6	7				11	3		10	8	9	4						22
1	2			5	6	7	8				3		10	11	9	4						23
1	2			5	6	7	8				3		10	11	9	4						24
1	2			5	6	7	8			11	3		10			4	9					25
1				5	6	7	8			11	3		10			4		2	9			26
1				5	6	7	8			11	3		10			4		2	9			27
1			4	5	6	7	8			11	3		10					2	9			28
1	2		6	5		7	8			11	3		10			4			9			29
1	2			5		7	8			11	3		10		6	4			9			30
1	2			5	6	7	8			11			10			4			9	3		31
1	2			5	6	7	8			11			10			4			9	3		32
1				5	6	7	8			10	2				4				9	3	11	33
1				5	6	7	8			10	2				4				9	3	11	34
1				5	6	7	8			10	2				4				9	3	11	35
1				5	6	7	8				2		11	10	4				9	3		36
1				5	6	7	8				2		11	10	4				9	3		37
1				5	6	7	8				2		11	10	4				9	3		38
1				5	6	7	8				2		11	10	4				9	3		39
1				5	6	7	8				2		11	10	4				9	3		40
1				5	6	7	8				2		11	10	4				9	3		41
1		2		5	6	7	8						11	10	4				9	3		42
42	29	2	4	42	40	33	39	5	10	30	38	14	34	21	27	15	2	3	17	12	3	
						3	6	1	1	7			12	2	11				9			

Best	Winship	Yorke	Allon	MacLachlan	Rowley	Dougall	Shea	Gittos	Wolfe	Wood	Randle	Jones	Herbert	Storey	Richmond	Maskill	Thompson	Campling	Pynegar	Lawrence	Cook	
1	2			5	6		8			11	3	4	10	7	9							Q5
1	2			5	6		8			11	3	4	10	7	9							Q5R
2	2			2	2		2			2	2	2	2	2	2							
							1								3							

1924-25

Manager: A.J.Evans

1	Aug	30	(a)	Chelsea	L 0-1		20,000
2	Sep	1	(h)	Crystal P	L 1-4	Pynegar	16,000
3		6	(h)	Stockport C	W 4-2	Shea, Pynegar, Morris 2	12,759
4		13	(a)	Manchester U	L 1-5	Morris	10,000
5		15	(h)	Southampton	W 1-0	Pynegar	13,000
6		20	(h)	Leicester C	W 4-2	Shea 2, Morris, Herbert	18,000
7		27	(a)	Stoke	L 1-4	Morris	7,000
8	Oct	1	(a)	Crystal P	D 0-0		8,000
9		4	(h)	Bradford C	D 0-0		11,000
10		11	(h)	Oldham A	W 5-1	Dougall, Shea, Pynegar 2, Morris	14,397
11		18	(a)	Sheffield W	L 0-2		15,000
12		25	(a)	Port Vale	L 0-4		
13	Nov	1	(h)	Middlesbrough	D 2-2	Allon, Pynegar	8,839
14		8	(a)	Barnsley	L 1-3	Herbert	6,000
15		15	(h)	Wolves	L 2-4	Shea, Pynegar	15,546
16		22	(a)	Fulham	L 0-2		10,000
17	Dec	6	(a)	Hull C	L 1-4	Pearson	9,000
18		20	(a)	Derby C	L 1-5	Pynegar	10,000
19		25	(h)	South Shields	L 0-1		
20		27	(h)	Chelsea	L 0-3		8,000
21	Jan	1	(a)	South Shields	L 1-4	Morris	9,000
22		3	(a)	Stockport C	D 1-1	Herbert	10,000
23		17	(h)	Manchester U	W 1-0	Morris	12,000
24		24	(a)	Leicester C	L 1-5	Richmond	17,000
25		31	(h)	Stoke	W 3-1	Pynegar 3	12,000
26	Feb	7	(a)	Bradford C	L 0-1		12,000
27		12	(h)	Portsmouth	W 2-1	Herbert 2	3,000
28		14	(a)	Oldham A	L 0-5		8,482
29		21	(h)	Sheffield W	D 1-1	Pynegar	14,242
30		28	(h)	Port Vale	D 0-0		10,168
31	Mar	7	(a)	Middlesbrough	D 1-1	Parkin	9,800
32		9	(h)	Blackpool	W 2-1	Maskill, Pynegar	
33		14	(h)	Barnsley	W 3-2	Parkin, Pynegar 2	12,263
34		21	(a)	Wolves	L 1-3	Pynegar	12,000
35		28	(h)	Fulham	L 0-1		10,000
36	Apr	4	(a)	Portsmouth	L 0-1		11,000
37		10	(a)	Clapton O	W 2-1	Turner, Wood	14,000
38		11	(h)	Hull C	D 0-0		12,914
39		14	(h)	Clapton O	W 1-0	Pynegar	
40		18	(a)	Blackpool	L 1-3	Dougall	
41		25	(h)	Derby C	D 0-0		10,000
42	May	2	(a)	Southampton	L 0-3		5,000

FINAL LEAGUE POSITION: 22nd in Division Two

Appearances
Goals

FA Cup

Q5	Nov	8	(a)	Walsall	W 2-1	Morris, Herbert	10,000
Q6	Dec	13	(a)	Nelson	W 1-0	Herbert	
1	Jan	10	(h)	Notts C	L 0-2		21,736

Appearances
Goals

Best	Randle	Lawrence	MacLachlan	Thompson	Rowley	Dougall	Shea	Pynegar	Morris	Herbert	Richmond	Maskill	Ross	Yorke	Winship	Allon	Clark	Campling	Storey	Pearson	Parkin	Bellas	Wood	Turner	Deeming	
1	2	3	4	5	6	7	8	9	10	11																1
1	2	3		5	6	7	8	9	10	11	4															2
1	2	3			6	7	8	9	10	11		4	5													3
1	2				6	7	8	9	10	11		4	5	3												4
1	2		4		6	7	8	9	10	11			5	3												5
1	2		4		6	7	8	9	10	11			5	3												6
1	2		4		6	7	8	9	10	11			5	3												7
1			4		6	7	8	9	10	11			5	3	2											8
1			4		6	7	8	9	10	11			5	3	2											9
1			4		6	7	8	9	10	11			5	3	2											10
1			4		6	7	8	9	10	11			5	3	2											11
1			4		6	7	8	9	10	11			5	3	2											12
1					6	7	8	9	10				5	3	2	4	11									13
1					6	7	8	9		10			5	3	2	4	11									14
1	3		4		6	7	8	9	10				5		2		11									15
1			5		6	7	8	9	10	11					3			2	4							16
1					6	7		9	10	11		4	5		3			2		8						17
1			4		6	7	8	9		10			5	3	2		11									18
1			4		6	7	8	9		11			5	3	2						10					19
1			5		6	7	8		10	11		4		3	2						9					20
1	2	3	5		6	7	8		10	11		4								9						21
1	3		5		6	7	8		10	11		4			2					9						22
1	3		5		6	7	8		10	11	9	4			2											23
1	3		5		6	7	8		10	11	9	4										2				24
1	3				6	7		9		10		4	5								8	2	11			25
1	3				6	7		9		11		4	5				10				8	2				26
1			4			7		9	10	11		6	5					2			8	3				27
1						7		9	10	11		6	5			4		2			8	3				28
1	3					7		9		11	5	4					10		6		8	2				29
1	3				6	7		9	10		5	4									8	2	11			30
1	3				6	7		9			5	4							10		8	2	11			31
1	3				6	7		9			5	4							8		10	2	11			32
1	3				6	7		9		11	5	4							10		8	2				33
1	3				6	7		9		11	5	4							8		10	2				34
1	3				6	7		9		10	5	4									11	2		8		35
1	3				6	7		9			5	4									11	2	10	8		36
1	3				6	7		9			5	4									11	2	10	8		37
1	3		5		6	7		9				4									11	2	10	8		38
1	3		5		6	7		9				4									11	2	10	8		39
1	3		5		6	7		9				4									11	2	10	8		40
1	3		5		6	7		9				4									11	2	10	8		41
1	3		5		6			9		10		4									11	2		8	7	42
42	28	4	24	2	39	41	23	37	24	31	12	26	20	14	15	3	6	4	6	3	20	19	10	8	1	
						2	5	16	8	6	1	1				1				1	2		1	1		

1			5		6	7	8	9	10	11					3			2	4							Q5
1			4		6	7		9		10			5	3	2		11				8					Q6
1	2		5		6	7	8	9	10	11		4			3											1
3	1		3		3	3	2	3	2	3		1	1	1	3		1	1	1		1					
									1	2																

1925-26

Manager: James Kerr

1	Aug	29	(h)	Lincoln C	W 3-2	Paterson, Herbert, Walker	15,054
2		31	(a)	Wigan B	L 1-5	Turner	13,000
3	Sep	5	(a)	Southport	W 2-1	Herbert 2	
4		7	(h)	Wigan B	D 0-0		
5		9	(a)	Ashington	L 0-2		4,000
6		12	(h)	Doncaster R	W 4-0	Paterson 4	10,000
7		19	(a)	Wrexham	L 1-2	Herbert	4,500
8		26	(h)	Halifax T	W 4-1	Poole, Paterson, Herbert 2	8,000
9	Oct	3	(h)	Nelson	W 1-0	Herbert	12,000
10		10	(a)	Barrow	W 4-1	Poole, Paterson, Herbert 2	6,000
11		17	(a)	Accrington S	L 1-3	Paterson	3,500
12		24	(h)	Durham C	W 3-1	Turner, Herbert 2	
13		31	(a)	Grimsby T	L 0-2		9,500
14	Nov	7	(h)	Rotherham U	W 7-1	Dougal, Poole, Paterson 2, Herbert 3	8,000
15		14	(a)	Tranmere R	L 1-2	Paterson	6,000
16		21	(h)	Walsall	W 2-0	Paterson, Herbert	14,500
17	Dec	5	(h)	Bradford	D 2-2	Poole, Paterson	10,000
18		12	(a)	Hartlepools U	L 2-3	Paterson 2	2,000
19		19	(h)	Rochdale	D 2-2	Houldey, Herbert	7,000
20		25	(h)	Crewe A	W 2-1	Paterson 2	8,000
21		26	(a)	Crewe A	L 1-2	Houldey	5,000
22	Jan	2	(a)	Lincoln C	W 3-0	Paterson 2, Dougall	4,000
23		9	(h)	Barrow	W 2-0	Paterson, Herbert	8,000
24		16	(h)	Southport	D 0-0		8,000
25		23	(a)	Doncaster R	L 1-8	Paterson	6,000
26		30	(h)	Wrexham	W 2-0	Watson, Paterson	5,430
27	Feb	6	(a)	Halifax T	L 0-1		
28		13	(a)	Nelson	L 1-4	Rowley	6,000
29		27	(h)	Accrington S	W 2-1	Poole, Herbert	9,181
30	Mar	6	(a)	Durham C	L 1-4	Shankley	2,500
31		13	(h)	Grimsby T	D 1-1	Herbert	12,000
32		17	(a)	Chesterfield	L 3-4	McIlvaney, Paterson 2	
33		20	(a)	Rotherham U	L 1-2	Poole	6,000
34		27	(h)	Tranmere R	L 1-2	Herbert	5,000
35	Apr	2	(a)	New Brighton	L 1-5	Turner	5,720
36		3	(a)	Walsall	L 1-4	Herbert	
37		5	(h)	Ashington	W 2-0	McGregor, Paterson	
38		6	(h)	New Brighton	D 0-0		5,479
39		10	(h)	Chesterfield	L 2-4	Turner, Herbert	5,000
40		17	(a)	Bradford	L 0-3		8,000
41		24	(h)	Hartlepools U	W 5-2	Rowley, Turner 2, Shankley, Breslin	1,660
42	May	1	(a)	Rochdale	L 1-4	Breslin	

FINAL LEAGUE POSITION: 6th in Division Three North

Appearances

Goals

FA Cup

1	Nov	28	(a)	Worksop	L 0-1		4,410

Appearances

Goals

Best	Bellas	Randle	Maskill	Jones	Rowley	Dougall	Turner	Paterson	Herbert	Walker	Houldey	Watson	MacLachlan	Poole	McIlvaney	Richards	Findlay	Brown	Breslin	Shankley	Wood	McGregor	Tinning	Campling	Roberts	
1	2	3	4	5	6	7	8	9	10	11																1
1	2	3	4	5	6	7	8	9	10	11																2
1		3	4		6	7	8	9	10	11	2	5														3
1		3	4		6	7	8	9	10	11	2	5														4
1	2	3	4		6	7	8	9	10	11			5													5
1		3	4		6	7	8	9	10	11	2	5														6
1		3	4		6	7		9	10	11	2	5		8												7
1	2	3	4		6	7		9	10	11		5		8												8
1		3	4		6	7		9	10	11	2	5		8												9
1		3			6	7		9	10	11	2	5		8	4											10
1		3			6	7	8	9	10	11	2	5			4											11
1		3			6	7	8	9	10	11	2	5			4											12
1		3			6	7		9	10	11	2	5		8	4											13
1		3			6	7		9	10	11	2	5		8	4											14
1		3			6	7		9	10	11	2	5		8	4											15
1		3			6	7	8	9	10	11	2	5			4											16
1		3			6	7	10	9			2	5		8	4	11										17
1	2	3			6	7		9	10			5		8	4	11										18
	2	3			6	7		9	10		8	5			4	11	1									19
	2	3			6	7		9	10		8	5			4	11	1									20
	2	3			6	7		9	10		8	5			4	11	1									21
	2	3	4		6	7		9	10			5		8		11	1									22
	2	3	4		6	7		9	10			5		8		11	1									23
	2	3			6	7		9	10			5				11	1	4	8							24
	2	3		5	6	7		9	10							11	1	4	8							25
1	2	3			6	7	8	9	11			5			4				10							26
1		3			6	7	8	9	11		2	5			4				10							27
1		3			6	7	8	9	11		2	5		8	4				10							28
1		3			6	7		10	11		2	5		8	4					9						29
1		3			6	7		10	11		2	5		8	4					9						30
1		3			6	7		10	11		2	5		8	4					9						31
1		3			6	7		10	11		2	5		8	4					9						32
1	2	3				7		9	10		5			8				4			6	11				33
1	5	3	6			7		10	11		2							4		9						34
1		3	4		6		8	7	10		5									9		11	2			35
1		3	4		6		8	7	10		5									9		11		2		36
1		3	4		6		8	9	11			5							10			7			2	37
1		3	4		6	7	8	9	11		2	5							10							38
1		3			6		8	9	11		4	5							10			7	2			39
1		3	4	5	6	7	8				2								10	9		11				40
1		3	4	5	6	7	8												10	9		11	2			41
1		3		5	6	7	8	9										4	10			11	2			42
35	15	42	18	6	40	38	21	40	38	16	29	31	1	17	19	9	7	5	11	9	1	8	4	1	1	
					2	2	6	25	22	1	2	1		6	1				2	2		1				

Best	Bellas	Randle	Maskill	Jones	Rowley	Dougall	Turner	Paterson	Herbert	Walker	Houldey	Watson	MacLachlan	Poole	McIlvaney	Richards	Findlay	Brown	Breslin	Shankley	Wood	McGregor	Tinning	Campling	Roberts	
1		3			6	7	8	9	10	11	2	5			4											1
1		1			1	1	1	1	1	1	1	1			1											

1926-27

Manager: James Kerr

1	Aug	28	(h)	Northampton T	L 0-3		16,000
2	Sep	1	(a)	Watford	L 0-1		12,000
3		4	(a)	Queen's Park R	D 1-1	Herbert	14,000
4		6	(h)	Gillingham	L 0-2		12,000
5		19	(h)	Charlton A	W 1-0	Herbert	10,000
6		15	(a)	Gillingham	L 0-2		4,000
7		18	(a)	Bristol C	L 0-3		12,000
8		25	(h)	Bournemouth	W 6-2	Hopper, Daily, Heathcote 3, Ferguson	6,000
9	Oct	2	(a)	Plymouth A	L 0-3		11,000
10		9	(h)	Newport C	W 3-1	Dunne, Heathcote, Herbert	6,000
11		16	(h)	Millwall	L 1-4	Heathcote	12,000
12		23	(a)	Brentford	L 3-7	McClure, Heathcote, Herbert	10,000
13		30	(h)	Brighton & HA	L 1-2	Bird	6,000
14	Nov	6	(a)	Norwich C	L 0-3		9,000
15		13	(h)	Luton T	W 4-1	J.Ramage, Heathcote, Herbert 2	5,000
16		20	(a)	Southend U	L 1-3	Herbert	4,000
17	Dec	4	(a)	Exeter C	L 1-8	Heathcote	5,000
18		18	(a)	Bristol R	W 2-1	Heathcote 2	5,000
19		25	(h)	Crystal P	W 3-1	Heathcote, Herbert, Ferguson	12,507
20		27	(a)	Crystal P	W 2-1	Heathcote, Fergus	18,220
21		28	(h)	Swindon T	L 1-3	McClure	17,600
22	Jan	1	(h)	Watford	W 5-1	Heathcote, Herbert 4	12,000
23		8	(h)	Merthyr T	W 5-1	McClure 2, Heathcote, Herbert 2	10,000
24		15	(a)	Northampton T	L 1-2	Herbert	8,880
25		22	(h)	Queen's Park R	W 1-0	Dunne	8,000
26		29	(a)	Charlton A	L 2-4	Herbert 2	6,000
27	Feb	5	(h)	Bristol C	L 2-5	McClure, McIlvanney	12,000
28		12	(a)	Bournemouth	W 2-1	Bird, Herbert	8,000
29		19	(h)	Plymouth A	D 3-3	Crisp, Bird, Herbert	15,500
30		26	(a)	Newport C	l 1-4	Heathcote	5,000
31	Mar	12	(h)	Brentford	W 3-1	Heathcote	13,000
32		14	(a)	Millwall	L 0-1		4,000
33		19	(a)	Brighton & HA	D 1-1	Heathcote	7,318
34		26	(h)	Norwich C	W 1-0	Herbert	8,000
35	Apr	2	(a)	Luton T	L 1-4	Dunne	6,900
36		9	(h)	Southend U	D 1-1	Dunne	10,000
37		16	(a)	Merthyr T	L 0-1		2,000
38		18	(a)	Aberdare A	W 7-0	McClure, Crisp, Heathcote 2, Bird, Herbert, Ferguson	3,797
39		19	(h)	Aberdare A	W 1-0	Bird	10,896
40		23	(h)	Exeter C	D 0-0		10,000
41		30	(a)	Swindon T	D 2-2	Lavender, Herbert	4,000
42	May	7	(h)	Bristol R	D 2-2	Herbert 2	8,000

FINAL LEAGUE POSITION: 15th in Division Three South

Appearances
Goals

FA Cup

1	Nov	27	(a)	Kettering T	W 3-2	Dunne, Herbert 2	8,603
2	Dec	11	(h)	Lincoln C	D 1-1	J.Ramage	14,047
R		15	(a)	Lincoln C	L 1-2	Gaffney	

Appearances
Goals

Newton	Houldey	Gay	Daily	Gaffney	Gardiner	Hopper	Dunne	Raynor	Heathcote	Ferguson	McClure	Heigh	Smith	Herbert	Randle	Brown	Bird	Shanks	Ramage J	Breslin	Tinning	McIlvanney	Crisp	Fergus	Lavender	Askew	
1	2	3	4	5	6	7	8	9	10	11																	1
1	2	3	4		6	7	8		10	11	5	9															2
1	2	3			6	7		9	8	11	5		4	10													3
1	2	3			6	7			8	11	5	9	4	10													4
1	2	3			6	7		9	8	11	5		4	10													5
1	2	3			6	7		9	8	11	5		4	10													6
1	2		8		6	7			9	11	5		4	10	3												7
1	2		8		6	7			9	11	5			10	3	4											8
1	2	3			6	7	8		9	11	5			10		4											9
1	2	3				7	8		9	11	5			10		4	6										10
1	2	3				7	8		9	11	5	10				4	6										11
1	2	3			4	7	8		9	11	5			10			6										12
1	2	3			6		8		9	11				10		4	5	7									13
1	2	3			6	7	8		9	11				10		4			5								14
1	2	3			6	7	8		9	11				10		4			5								15
1		3			6	7	8		9	11				10	2	4			5								16
1		3	7		6		8		9	11				10	2	4			5								17
1					6		8		9	11	5			10	3	4			2	7							18
1					6		8		9	11	5			10	3	4			2	7							19
1				5	6		8		9	11				10	3	4			2	7							20
1					6		8		9	11	5			10	3	4			2	7							21
1					6		8		9	11	5			10	3	4				7	2						22
1					6		8		9	11	5			10	3	4				7	2						23
1					6		8		9	11	5			10	3	4				7	2						24
1					6		8		9	11	5			10	3	4				7	2						25
1					6		8		9	11	5			10	3	4				7	2						26
1							8		9	11	5			10	3	4				7	2	6					27
1							8			11	5			10	3	4	9				2	6	7				28
1							8			11	5			10	3	4	9				2	6	7				29
1		3							8	11	5			10	2	4	9					6	7				30
1					6		8		9	11	5			10	3	4							7	2			31
1					6		8		9	11	5			10	3	4							7	2			32
1					6		8		9	11	5			10	3	4							7	2			33
1					6		8			11	5			10	3	4	9						7	2			34
1					6		8			11	5			10	3	4	9						7	2			35
1					6		8			11	5			10	3	4	9						7	2			36
1					6				8	11	5			10	3	4	9						7	2			37
1					6				8	11	5			10	3	4	9						7	2			38
1					6				8		5			10	3	4	9						7	2	11		39
1					6				8		5				3	4	9			10			7	2	11		40
1					6				8	11	5			10	3		9							2	7	4	41
1					6				8	11	5	9		10	3							4	7	2			42
42	15	16	5	2	36	15	29	4	37	40	35	4	5	38	29	32	15	1	8	11	8	5	14	12	3	1	
			1			1	4		22	3	6			24			5		1			1	2		1		

1					6	7	8		9	11				10	3	4	5		2								1
1					6	7	8		9	11				10	3	4	5		2								2
1				8	6		7		9	11	5			10	3	4			2								R
3				1	3	2	3		3	3	1			3	3	3	2		3								
				1			1							2					1								

1927-28

Manager: James Kerr

1	Aug	27	(a)	Watford	L	1-3	Stoddart	10,000
2		29	(a)	Swindon T	L	0-1		5,000
3	Sep	3	(h)	Charlton A	D	3-3	Heathcote 2, Herbert	15,000
4		5	(h)	Swindon T	W	4-0	Hickman, Heathcote, Johnstone, P.Ramage	9,300
5		10	(a)	Bristol R	D	1-1	Heathcote	6,000
6		17	(h)	Plymouth A	D	1-1	Heathcote	15,000
7		24	(a)	Merthyr T	L	2-3	Hickman, Johnstone	2,500
8	Oct	1	(h)	Walsall	L	0-1		15,000
9		8	(a)	Gillingham	W	2-1	Bird, Herbert	5,000
10		15	(h)	Southend U	W	6-1	Heathcote 2, Johnstone 2, P.Ramage 2	11,000
11		22	(a)	Brentford	L	1-4	Heathcote	5,000
12		29	(h)	Bournemouth	W	3-2	Heathcote 2, Johnstone	15,000
13	Nov	5	(a)	Brighton & HA	L	0-3		8,000
14		12	(h)	Luton T	W	4-2	Heathcote 2, Johnstone 2	10,000
15		19	(a)	Millwall	L	1-9	P.Ramage	10,000
16	Dec	3	(a)	Exeter C	W	1-0	Heathcote	5,000
17		10	(h)	Watford	L	2-3	McClure, Heathcote	7,200
18		17	(a)	Norwich C	W	2-0	Bird 2	6,000
19		24	(h)	Northampton T	L	2-4	Heathcote, Townsend	7,000
20		27	(h)	Queen's Park R	D	0-0		5,000
21	Jan	7	(a)	Charlton A	L	1-2	Herbert	8,000
22		14	(h)	Torquay U	W	5-1	Bird 2, Crisp, Galloway, Herbert	8,000
23		21	(h)	Bristol R	L	2-3	Herbert 2	9,388
24		28	(a)	Plymouth A	L	0-4		6,000
25	Feb	4	(h)	Merthyr T	L	1-2	Herbert	7,000
26		11	(a)	Walsall	L	0-7		5,000
27		13	(h)	Crystal P	D	2-2	Herbert 2	2,059
28		18	(h)	Gillingham	L	1-2	Hunter	10,000
29		25	(a)	Southend U	L	2-3	Bird, Herbert	8,000
30	Mar	3	(h)	Brentford	D	0-0		11,000
31		10	(h)	Bournemouth	W	3-2	Johnstone 2, Herbert	5,000
32		17	(h)	Brighton & HA	D	2-2	Dinsdale, Widdowson	12,000
33		24	(a)	Luton T	L	1-3	Ward	8,000
34		31	(h)	Millwall	L	0-3		11,000
35	Apr	7	(a)	Torquay U	W	3-2	Herbert 2, Ward	3,500
36		9	(a)	Newport C	D	0-0		6,325
37		10	(h)	Newport C	L	0-2		7,000
38		14	(h)	Exeter C	D	0-0		6,000
39		21	(a)	Crystal P	L	0-1		5,908
40		26	(a)	Queen's Park R	W	5-1	Dinsdale 3, P.Ramage 2	5,000
41		28	(h)	Norwich C	D	2-2	Herbert, Opp own-goal	12,000
42	May	5	(a)	Northampton T	L	1-2	Dinsdale	8,000

FINAL LEAGUE POSITION: 20th in Division Three South

Appearances

Goals

FA Cup

1	Nov	26	(h)	Bournemouth	D	2-2	Bird, P.Ramage	13,627
R		30	(a)	Bournemouth	L	0-2		7,000

Appearances

Goals

Newton	Fergus	Randle	Ramage J	McClure	Bird	Johnson	Heathcote	Stoddart	Herbert	Lavender	Askew	Heigh	Hickman	Clarke	Johnstone	Townsend	Stanford	Ramage P	Reeve	Gardiner	Hunter	Gay	Brown	Tinning	Bell	Crisp	Galloway	Thompson	Ward	Barnes	Houldey	Dinsdale	Widdowson	Ball	Raynor	
1	2	3	4	5	6	7	8	9	10	11																										1
1	2	3	5		6	7		9	10	11	4	8																								2
1	2	3			6	7	8		10		4		5		9	11																				3
	2	3			4		8			7			5	6	9	11	1	10																		4
	2	3			4		8			7			5	6	9	11	1	10																		5
	2	3			4		8			7			5	6	9	11	1	10																		6
1	2	3			4		8						5	6	9	11		7	10																	7
	2	3			4		8		11				5	6	9		1	10	7																	8
	2	3			4	7	8		11				5		9		1	10		6																9
	2	3			4	7	8		11						9		1	10		6	5															10
	2	3			4	7	8		11						9		1	10		6	5															11
	2	3			4		8		11	7					9		1	10		6	5															12
	2				4		8		11			7			9		1	10		6	5	3														13
					4	7	8		11				5		9		1	10		6	2	3														14
	2		3		6	7	8		11				5		9		1	10					4													15
1				5	7		8				4				9			10			6	3		2	11											16
1				5	7		8				4				9	11		10			6	3		2												17
1				5	7		8				4				9	11					6	3		2		10										18
1				5	7		8				4				9	11					6	3		2		10										19
1				5			8					7			9	11					6	3	4	2		10										20
1				5	7				10						9	11					6	3	4	2		8										21
1				5	7				10							11					6	3	4	2		8	9									22
1				5	7				10							11					6	3	4	2		8	9									23
1				5	7				10							11					6	3	4	2		8	9									24
1	2			5		7			10						9	11				6		3	4			8										25
	2			5		7	9		10							11		8			6	3	4					1								26
	3							9	10						7			8		6	5		4	2				1		11						27
	3								10						7			8		6	5		4	2				1	9	11						28
1				5	7				10							11		8			3		4		6				9		2					29
1				5	7				10							11		8			3		4		6				9		2					30
1									10						7	11					3		4		6				9		2	5	8			31
1						7			10							11					3		4		6				9		2	5	8			32
1						7										11		10		6	3		4						9		2	5	8			33
1						7										11		10		6	3		4						9		2	5	8			34
1							8		11											6	3		4						9		2	5	10	7		35
1							8		11											6	3		4						9		2	5	10	7		36
1							8		11											6	3								9		2	5	10	7	4	37
1									11									10		6	3						9				2	5	8	7	4	38
1									11						9			10			3				6						2	5	8	7	4	39
1								5	11									10			3				6						2	9	8	7	4	40
1								5	11									10			3				6						2	9	8	7	4	41
1								5	11									10			3				6						2	9	8	7	4	42
28	18	12	3	14	25	13	23	6	31	6	6	3	9	5	24	21	11	26	2	15	31	13	18	11	9	8	4	3	10	2	14	12	12	8	6	
				1	6		15	1	14				2		9	1		6			1					1	1		2			5	1			

1 own-goal

1	2		5		7		8		11						9			10			4	3			6	1
1				5	7		8		11						9			10			4	3		2	6	R
2	1		1	1	2		2		2						2			2			2	2		1	2	
					1													1								

1928-29

Manager: James McIntyre

1	Aug	25	(h)	Norwich C	W	3-0	Bowen 2, Widdowson	18,000
2		27	(h)	Watford	D	1-1	Higham	12,000
3	Sep	1	(a)	Brighton & HA	W	1-0	Johnstone	8,500
4		5	(a)	Watford	L	2-4	Toseland, Johnstone	8,000
5		8	(h)	Exeter C	D	1-1	Townsend	18,000
6		15	(a)	Southend U	D	0-0		9,000
7		22	(h)	Merthyr T	W	6-1	Higham, Johnstone 3, Widdowson, Townsend	18,000
8		29	(a)	Bournemouth	L	1-2	Widdowson	7,000
9	Oct	6	(h)	Brentford	W	1-0	Starsmore	16,000
10		13	(a)	Luton T	D	1-1	Townsend	9,000
11		20	(a)	Walsall	D	0-0		14,000
12		27	(h)	Newport C	W	3-1	Toseland 2, Starsmore	12,000
13	Nov	3	(a)	Crystal P	W	3-0	Herbert 2, Townsend	12,470
14		10	(h)	Swindon T	W	4-1	Toseland, Starsmore 2, Herbert	16,706
15		17	(a)	Torquay U	W	2-0	Starsmore, Herbert	7,000
16	Dec	1	(a)	Plymouth A	L	0-3		11,000
17		8	(h)	Gillingham	W	2-0	Toseland, Pick	16,000
18		15	(a)	Queen's Park R	L	1-3	Toseland	10,000
19		22	(h)	Bristol R	W	2-0	Toseland, Lake	13,000
20		25	(h)	Charlton A	L	0-1		22,000
21		26	(a)	Charlton A	L	1-3	Pick	5,000
22		29	(a)	Norwich C	L	0-3		8,000
23	Jan	5	(h)	Brighton & HA	W	3-0	Toseland 2, Shone	15,000
24		12	(h)	Fulham	L	1-2	Loughlin	18,088
25		19	(a)	Exeter C	W	3-2	Toseland, Loughlin 2	6,000
26		28	(h)	Southend U	D	1-1	Loughlin	18,000
27	Feb	2	(a)	Merthyr T	D	2-2	Toseland, Starsmore	3,000
28		9	(h)	Bournemouth	L	1-2	Dinsdale	12,000
29		16	(a)	Brentford	L	0-1		4,000
30		23	(h)	Luton T	D	1-1	Pick	14,000
31	Mar	2	(h)	Walsall	D	1-1	Pick	14,000
32		9	(a)	Newport C	L	1-2	Starsmore	7,000
33		16	(h)	Crystal P	L	1-3	Henderson	12,289
34		23	(a)	Swindon T	W	2-1	Starsmore 2	4,518
35		30	(h)	Torquay U	W	2-1	Loughlin 2	16,000
36	Apr	1	(h)	Northampton T	L	0-2		20,000
37		2	(a)	Northampton T	D	3-3	Richards, Loughlin 2	10,000
38		6	(a)	Gillingham	D	1-1	Richards	4,000
39		13	(h)	Plymouth A	L	1-4	Bell	10,738
40		20	(a)	Fulham	D	2-2	Bowen, Lake	18,000
41		27	(h)	Queen's Park R	D	0-0		16,000
42	May	4	(a)	Bristol R	D	1-1	Pick	5,000

FINAL LEAGUE POSITION: 11th in Division Three South

Appearances
Goals

FA Cup

1	Nov	24	(h)	Fulham	L	1-4	Starsmore	26,000

Appearances
Goals

Allen	Crown	Plunkett	Higham	Dinsdale	Bell	Henderson	Bowen	Widdowson	Herbert	Townsend	Ball	Ward	Toseland	Kirton	Houldey	Johnstone	Starsmore	Maskill	Jenkins	Pick	Lake	Loughlin	Shone	Tinning	Watson	Raynor	Richards	Robbins	
1	2	3	4	5	6	7	8	9	10	11																			1
1	2	3	4	5	6	7		10		11	8	9																	2
1	2	3	4	5	6	7	8	10		11						9													3
1	2	3	4	5	6			10		11	8		7			9													4
1	2	3	4	5	6			10		11			7	8		9													5
1	2	3	4	5	6			10		11			7	8		9													6
1	2		4	5	6	7		10		11				8	3	9													7
1	2		4	5	6	7		10		11				8	3	9													8
1	2		4	5	6	7		10		11				8	3		9												9
1	2	3	4	5	6	7		10		11				8			9	4											10
1	2	3	4	5	6	7		10		11				8			9												11
1	2	3	4	5	6			10		11			7	8			9												12
1	2	3	4	5	6				10	11			7	8			9												13
1	2	3	4	5	6				10	11			7	8			9												14
1	2	3	4	5	6				10	11			7	8			9												15
1	2			5	6			8		10			7				9	4	3	11									16
1	2	3	4	5	6			8	10				7				9			11									17
1	2	3	4	5	6			8					7				9			11	10								18
1	2	3		5	6	8							7				9	4		11	10								19
1	2	3		5	6	8							7				9	4		11	10								20
1	2			5	6	9		8					7					4	3	11	10								21
1	2			5	6	7		10					8				9	4	3	11									22
1	2			5	6								7				8	4	3	11		9	10						23
1				5	6								7				8	4	3	11		9	10	2					24
1	2			5	6								7				8		3	11		9	10						25
1	2	3	4	5	6								7				8			11		9	10						26
1	2	3	4	5	6								7				8			11		9	10						27
1		3	4	5	6								7	10			8			11		9		2					28
1	2	3	4	5	6								7				8			11		9	10						29
1	2	3	4	5	6								7	8			9			11			10						30
1	2	3		5	6	7											8	4		11		9	10						31
1	2	3	4	5	6	7											8			11		9	10						32
1	2		4	5	6	7	10										8			11		9			3				33
1	2			5	6		10										8			11		9			3	4	7		34
1	2			5	6		10										8			11		9			3	4	7		35
1	2		4	5			10										8			11		9			3	6	7		36
1	2		4	5			10										8			11		9			3	6	7		37
1	2		4	5	6												8			11		9			3		7	10	38
1	2		4	5	6												8			11		9			3		7	10	39
1	2		4	5	6		8													11	10	9			3		7		40
1	2		4	5	6		8													11	10	9			3		7		41
1	2		4	5	6												8			11	10	9			3		7		42
42	40	23	31	42	40	15	9	17	5	16	2	1	22	13	3	6	31	9	6	27	7	19	9	2	10	4	9	2	
			2	1	1	1	3	3	4	4			11			5	9			5	2	8	1				2		

1	2	3	4	5	6				10	11			7	8			9												1
1	1	1	1	1	1				1	1			1	1			1												
																	1												

1929-30

Manager: James McIntyre

1	Aug	31	(h)	Merthyr T	D 2-2	Lake, Pick	13,235
2	Sep	2	(a)	Bristol R	W 3-1	Starsmore, Lake, Pick	5,000
3		7	(a)	Torquay U	W 3-1	Baker, Starsmore, Pick	5,000
4		9	(h)	Bristol R	W 1-0	Widdowson	13,750
5		14	(h)	Newport C	W 2-0	Starsmore, Lake	17,000
6		16	(a)	Swindon T	D 1-1	Richards	5,592
7		21	(a)	Watford	W 3-1	Bell, Starsmore, Loughlin	10,000
8		28	(h)	Bournemouth	L 0-2		18,750
9	Oct	5	(h)	Clapton O	W 5-2	Dinsdale, Richards, Loughlin, Lake, Bowden	12,220
10		12	(a)	Brentford	L 1-3	Loughlin	18,000
11		19	(a)	Walsall	L 2-3	Loughlin 2	15,000
12		26	(h)	Queen's Park R	L 2-3	Loughlin, Dinsdale	12,000
13	Nov	2	(a)	Fulham	L 0-2		15,000
14		9	(h)	Norwich C	W 3-1	Lake 3	11,000
15		16	(a)	Crystal P	L 3-4	Richards, Widdowson, Pick	2,862
16		23	(h)	Gillingham	W 5-0	Loughlin 2, Widdowson 2, Dinsdale	9,000
17	Dec	7	(h)	Exeter C	D 3-3	Loughlin 2, Dinsdale	8,000
18		21	(h)	Luton T	W 5-1	Loughlin, Lake 2, Pick, Widdowson	13,000
19		25	(h)	Plymouth A	W 1-0	Loughlin	26,500
20		26	(a)	Plymouth A	L 0-3		28,572
21	Jan	4	(h)	Torquay U	W 4-1	Lake 2, Pick, Widdowson	14,000
22		18	(a)	Newport C	L 2-4	Loughlin, Pick	4,500
23		25	(h)	Watford	W 3-1	Loughlin, Richards, Bell	13,000
24	Feb	1	(a)	Bournemouth	L 0-1		6,000
25		8	(a)	Clapton O	L 1-3	Baker	9,003
26		15	(h)	Brentford	W 2-1	Pick 2	11,000
27		22	(h)	Walsall	W 4-0	Loughlin 2, Lake, Widdowson	17,000
28	Mar	1	(a)	Queen's Park R	L 1-3	Starsmore	17,000
29		8	(h)	Fulham	W 3-1	Loughlin, Pick, Widdowson	12,000
30		15	(a)	Norwich C	L 2-10	Pick 2	8,230
31		22	(h)	Crystal P	W 1-0	Loughlin	10,360
32		29	(a)	Gillingham	W 3-0	Loughlin 2, Starsmore	6,000
33	Apr	5	(h)	Northampton T	D 2-2	Pick 2	14,000
34		7	(a)	Northampton T	D 2-2	Loughlin, Pick	5,000
35		12	(a)	Exeter C	D 1-1	Lake	6,000
36		14	(a)	Merthyr T	D 2-2	Loughlin, Baker	683
37		18	(a)	Brighton & HA	D 1-1	Pick	8,330
38		19	(h)	Southend U	W 5-1	Loughlin 2, Widdowson 2, Lake	8,000
39		22	(h)	Brighton & HA	L 0-2		16,000
40		26	(a)	Luton T	D 1-1	Widdowson	7,000
41		30	(a)	Southend U	W 2-1	Pick, Starsmore	4,000
42	May	3	(h)	Swindon T	L 1-2	Lake	12,000

FINAL LEAGUE POSITION: 6th in Division Three South

Appearances
Goals

FA Cup

1	Nov	30	(a)	Norwich C	D 3-3	Loughlin 2, Richards	12,469
R	Dec	4	(h)	Norwich C	W 2-0	Loughlin, Widdowson	7,702
2		14	(h)	Bath C	W 7-1	Loughlin 2, Lake 2, Widdowson, Pick, Dinsdale	18,248
3	Jan	11	(h)	Sunderland	L 1-2	Loughlin	31,673

Appearances
Goals

Allen	Crown	Watson	Baker	Dinsdale	Bell	Richards	Bowen	Loughlin	Lake	Pick	Widdowson	Starsmore	Stokes	Kirton	Higham	Robson	Tilford	Alsop	
1	2	3	4	5	6	7	8	9	10	11									1
1	2	3	4	5	6	7			10	11	8	9							2
1	2	3	4	5		7			10	11	8	9	6						3
1	2	3	4	5		7			10	11	8	9	6						4
1	2	3	4	5		7			10	11	8	9	6						5
1	2	3	4	5	6	7	8		10	11		9							6
1	2	3	4	5	6	7		10		11		9		8					7
1	2	3	4	5	6	7		10		11		9		8					8
1	2	3	4	5		7	11	9	10			8	6						9
1	2	3	4	5		7	11	9	10			8	6						10
1	2	3		5	6	7		9		11		8			4	10			11
1	2		4	5	6	7		9		11		8				10	3		12
1	2	3		5	6	7			10	11		9	4			8			13
1	2	3		5	6	7			10	11		9	4			8			14
1	2	3		5	6	7			10	11	8	9	4						15
1	2	3		5	6	7		9	10	11	8		4						16
1	2	3		5	6	7		9	10	11		8	4						17
1	2	3		5	6	7		9	10	11	8		4						18
1	2	3		5	6	7		9	10	11	8		4						19
1	2	3		5	6	7		9	10	11	8		4						20
1	2	3		5	6	7		9	10	11	8		4						21
1	2	3		5	6	7		9	10	11	8		4						22
1	2	3		5	6	7	11	9	10		8		4						23
1	2	3		5	6	7	11	9	10		8		4						24
1	2	3	5		6	7	11	9	10		8		4						25
1	2	3	5		6	7		9	10	11	8		4						26
1	2	3	5		6	7		9	10	11	8		4						27
1	2	3	6	5		7			10	11	8	9	4						28
1	2	3	6	5		7		9	10	11	8		4						29
1	2	3	6	5		7		9	10	11	8		4						30
1	2	3	4	5	6	7		9	10	11								8	31
1	2	3	4	5	6	7		9	10	11		8							32
1	2	3	4	5	6	7		9	10	11		8							33
1	2	3	4		6	7		9		11	10			8	5				34
1	2	3	4		6	7		9	10	11	8				5				35
1	2	3	4		6	7		9	10	11	8				5				36
1	2	3	4	5	6	7		9	10	11	8								37
1	2	3	4	5	6			9	10	11	8							7	38
1	2	3	4	5	6			9	10	11	8							7	39
1	2	3	5		6			9	10	11	8		4					7	40
1	2	3	4		6		10			11	8	9			5			7	41
1	2	3	4	5	6				10	11	8	9						7	42
42	42	41	29	34	34	37	8	31	36	37	28	20	24	3	5	4	1	6	
			3	4	2	4	1	24	15	17	11	7							

1	2	3		5	6	7		9	10	11	8		4	1
1	2	3		5	6	7		9	10	11	8		4	R
1	2	3		5	6	7		9	10	11	8		4	2
1	2	3		5	6	7		9	10	11	8		4	3
4	4	4		4	4	4		4	4	4	4		4	
				1		1		6	2	1	2			

1930-31

Manager: James McIntyre until 13 February 1931, Harry Storer from 11 April 1931.

1	Aug	30	(h)	Notts C	L	1-2	Lake	17,915
2	Sep	1	(a)	Fulham	D	0-0		10,000
3		6	(a)	Clapton O	D	3-3	Lake, Bell, Phillips	9,030
4		8	(h)	Swindon T	W	4-0	Lake, Phillips 2, Bowden	14,000
5		13	(h)	Thames	W	7-1	Lake, Richards 2, Phillips, Ball, Heap (og), Lindsay (og)	9,000
6		17	(a)	Swindon T	L	0-4		3,500
7		20	(a)	Norwich C	D	2-2	Bell, Phillips	8,503
8		27	(h)	Queen's Park R	W	2-0	Lake, Pick	15,000
9	Oct	4	(a)	Walsall	W	2-1	Lake, Phillips	7,000
10		11	(h)	Northampton T	L	0-1		19,800
11		18	(a)	Brentford	W	2-1	Loughlin, Phillips	12,000
12		25	(h)	Crystal P	L	3-5	Phillips 2, Pick	11,460
13	Nov	1	(a)	Southend U	L	0-2		4,500
14		8	(h)	Luton T	L	1-2	Pick	11,000
15		15	(a)	Bristol R	L	0-1		5,000
16		22	(h)	Newport C	W	6-4	Lake 2, Phillips 2, Ball, Bowden	8,276
17	Dec	6	(h)	Exeter C	W	3-1	Lake, Phillips, Reay	10,000
18		20	(h)	Torquay U	W	6-1	Lake, Baker, Bowden 2, Alsop 2	7,000
19		25	(h)	Bournemouth	D	3-3	Lake 2, Alsop	18,724
20		26	(a)	Bournemouth	L	0-2		7,800
21		27	(a)	Notts C	L	1-4	Lake	16,803
22	Jan	3	(h)	Clapton O	W	4-0	Lake, Richards 2, Ball	7,013
23		10	(a)	Gillingham	L	0-2		4,000
24		17	(a)	Thames	W	2-1	Phillips, Bowden	1,058
25		24	(h)	Norwich C	W	3-0	Lake, Richards, Ball	9,019
26		31	(a)	Queen's Park R	L	0-2		8,000
27	Feb	7	(h)	Walsall	W	2-1	Lake, Baker	8,975
28		14	(a)	Northampton T	W	3-0	Lake, Bowden, Phillips	7,000
29		21	(h)	Brentford	L	0-1		9,651
30		28	(a)	Crystal P	L	0-1		10,546
31	Mar	7	(h)	Southend U	D	0-0		7,000
32		14	(a)	Luton T	L	0-2		8,000
33		21	(h)	Bristol R	W	5-1	Lake 4, Alsop	7,632
34		28	(a)	Newport C	D	1-1	Baker	2,950
35	Apr	3	(a)	Watford	L	1-4	Baker	5,500
36		4	(h)	Gillingham	L	1-2	Lake	10,000
37		7	(h)	Watford	D	2-2	Reay, Widdowson	8,000
38		11	(a)	Exeter C	W	3-2	Lake, Phillips 2	5,000
39		18	(h)	Brighton & HA	D	0-0		5,329
40		22	(a)	Brighton & HA	L	0-2		3,060
41		25	(a)	Torquay U	D	0-0		4,000
42	May	2	(h)	Fulham	W	2-1	Phillips, Reay	8,000

FINAL LEAGUE POSITION: 14th in Division Three South

Appearances
Goals

FA Cup

1	Nov	29	(a)	Northampton T	W	2-1	Lake, Bowden	8,807
2	Dec	13	(a)	Exeter C	D	1-1	Phillips	9,600
R		18	(h)	Exeter C	W	1-2	Bowden	8,633

Appearances
Goals

Allen	Crown	Watson	Baker	McNab	Bell	Richards	Ball	Loughlin	Lake	Pick	Smailes	Bowden	Phillips	Roe	Widdowson	Reay	Stokes	Tilford	Owen	Plummer	Alsop	Smith	Simpson	O'Brien	Lee	
1	2	3	4	5	6	7	8	9	10	11																1
1	2	3	4		6	7	8	9	10		5	11														2
1	2	3	4		6	7	8		10		5	11	9													3
1	2	3	4		6	7	8		10		5	11	9													4
1	2	3	4		6	7	8		10		5	11	9													5
1	2	3	4	5	6	7	8		10	11			9													6
1	2	3	4	5	6	7						11	9	8	10											7
1	2	3	5		6	7			10	11	4		9	8												8
1	2	3	5		6	7			10	11	4		9	8												9
1	2	3	5		6				10	11	4		9		8	7										10
1	2	3	5		6			8	10	11	4		9			7										11
1	2	3	5		6			8	10	11	4		9			7										12
1	2	3	5		6			8	10	11			9			7	4									13
1	2		5		6				10	11			9	8		7		3				4				14
	2		5		6	7		9	10	11	4		8					3	1							15
	2		5		6		8		10		4	11	9			7		3	1							16
1		2	5		6		8		10			11	9			7	4	3								17
1			5		6	7	8		10			11					4	3		2	9					18
1			5		6	7	8		10			11					4	3		2	9					19
1			5			7	8		10			11					4	3		2	9	6				20
1			5		6	7	8		10			11					4	3		2	9					21
1	2		5		6	7	8	9	10			11					4	3								22
1	2		5		6	7	8	9	10			11					4	3								23
1	2		5		6	7	8		10			11	9				4	3								24
1	2		9		6	7	8		10			11						3				4	5			25
1	2		5		6	7	8	9	10			11						3				4				26
1	2		5	6		7	8		10			11	9				4	3								27
1	2		5		6	7	8		10			11	9				4	3								28
1	2		5		6	7	8		10			11	9				4	3								29
1	2		5		6	7	8		10			11	9				4	3								30
1	2		5		6	7			10			11	9				4	3			8					31
1	2		5	6		7	10		9			11					4	3			8					32
	2		5	6		7			10			11			9		4	3	1		8					33
	2		5	6	11	7			10						9		4	3	1		8					34
	2		6	5		7			10			11			9		4	3	1		8					35
1			4	5	6	7		11	10						9			3		2	8					36
1			5		6			9	10						8	7	4	3		2				11		37
1			5		6				10				9		8	7	4	3		2				11		38
1			5		6				10				9		8	7	4	3		2					11	39
1			5		6				10						9	7		3		2		4		8	11	40
1			4		6	7			10				8		9			3		2			5		11	41
1			4		6				10				8		9	7		3		2			5		11	42
37	30	14	42	9	37	30	22	11	41	10	11	24	25	4	12	12	21	29	5	11	10	5	3	3	4	
			4		2	5	4	1	23	3		6	17		1	3					4					

2 own-goals

1		2	5		6		8		10			11	9			7	4	3	1
1		2	5		6		8		10			11	9			7	4	3	2
1		2	5		6		8		10			11	9			7	4	3	R
3		3	3		3		3		3			3	3			3	3	3	
									1			2	1						

1931-32

Manager: Harry Storer

1	Aug	29	(a)	Fulham	L 3-5	Lake, Lauderdale, Cull	20,000
2		31	(h)	Southend U	L 0-2		12,500
3	Sep	5	(h)	Thames	W 2-0	Bourton 2	9,250
4		7	(h)	Cardiff C	W 2-1	Lake, Johnson	11,650
5		12	(a)	Brentford	L 2-4	Bourton, Lake	8,000
6		14	(a)	Cardiff C	L 1-6	Lauderdale	8,000
7		19	(h)	Exeter C	W 4-0	Bourton 2, Lake, Bowden	10,750
8		26	(a)	Crystal P	D 2-2	Bourton, Lauderdale	16,259
9	Oct	3	(a)	Gillingham	W 3-1	Bourton, Lauderdale, White	5,000
10		10	(h)	Luton T	W 3-2	Bourton 2, Sheppard	12,271
11		17	(h)	Bournemouth	W 6-1	Bourton 5, Sheppard	14,000
12		24	(a)	Queen's Park R	D 1-1	Bourton	12,590
13		31	(h)	Bristol R	D 1-1	Bourton	15,017
14	Nov	7	(a)	Torquay U	D 3-3	Bourton 2, Baker	4,000
15		14	(h)	Clapton O	W 4-2	Bourton 3, Lauderdale	13,878
16		21	(a)	Swindon T	D 2-2	Bourton, Lake	5,000
17	Dec	5	(a)	Brighton & HA	L 1-4	Lauderdale	6,228
18		12	(h)	Mansfield T	W 5-1	Bourton 4, Cull	11,046
19		19	(a)	Watford	L 0-2		7,110
20		25	(h)	Reading	W 5-1	Bourton 3, White, Sheppard	23,271
21		26	(a)	Reading	L 1-2	Cull	10,000
22	Jan	2	(h)	Fulham	D 5-5	Lake 3, Lauderdale, Heinneman	11,000
23		9	(h)	Norwich C	W 3-0	Bourton, Lake, White	13,492
24		16	(a)	Thames	L 2-5	Lauderdale, White	1,215
25		28	(h)	Brentford	L 0-1		6,000
26		30	(a)	Exeter C	L 0-3		6,000
27	Feb	6	(h)	Crystal P	W 8-0	Bourton 3, Lauderdale 2, Lake, White, Holmes	11,459
28		13	(h)	Gillingham	W 6-4	Lake 2, Holmes 3, Bourton	10,000
29		20	(a)	Luton T	L 1-3	Lauderdale	8,000
30		27	(a)	Bournemouth	D 2-2	Bourton, Lauderdale	4,000
31	Mar	5	(h)	Queen's Park R	W 1-0	Bourton	12,800
32		12	(a)	Bristol R	L 1-3	Bourton	5,000
33		19	(h)	Torquay U	W 3-1	Lauderdale, Sheppard 2	11,000
34		26	(a)	Clapton O	L 2-5	Sheppard, Broadbent (og)	7,571
35		28	(h)	Northampton T	W 4-1	Bourton, Lake, Lauderdale 2	17,000
36		29	(a)	Northampton T	L 2-3	Bourton, Lauderdale	7,716
37	Apr	2	(h)	Swindon T	W 3-2	Bourton 2, Lauderdale	11,167
38		9	(a)	Norwich C	L 2-6	Lauderdale, Cull	5,968
39		16	(h)	Brighton & HA	W 4-3	Bourton 2, Lauderdale, Holmes	10,000
40		23	(a)	Mansfield T	D 3-3	Bourton 3	4,492
41		30	(h)	Watford	W 5-0	Bourton 3, Lake, White	15,000
42	May	7	(a)	Southend U	L 0-4		8,000

FINAL LEAGUE POSITION: 12th in Division Three South

Appearances

Goals

FA Cup

1	Nov	28	(h)	Clapton O	D 2-2	Bourton, Lake	19,127
R	Dec	2	(a)	Clapton O	L 0-2		3,500

Appearances

Goals

Allen	Plummer	Tilford	Underwood	Simpson	Heinneman	Cull	Lauderdale	Bourton	Lake	Bowden	White	Watson	O'Brien	Baker	Boileau	Johnson	Sheppard	Lee	Hackett	Corbett	Hewett	Holmes	Elliott	Mason	Hall	
1	2	3	4	5	6	7	8	9	10	11																1
1	2	3	4	5	6		8	9	10	11	7															2
1		3					8	9	10		7	2	4	5	6	11										3
1		3					8	9	10		7	2	4	5	6	11										4
1		3			6		8	9	10		7	2	4	5		11										5
1		3			6		8	9	10	11	7	2	4	5												6
1		3			6		8	9	10	11	7	2	4	5												7
1		3			6		8	9	10	11	7	2	4	5												8
1		3			6		8	9		11	7	2	4	5			10									9
1		3			6	11	8	9			7	2	4	5			10									10
1		3			6	11	8	9			7	2	4	5			10									11
1		3			6	11	8	9			7	2	4	5			10									12
1		3			6	11	8	9			7	2	4	5			10									13
1		3			6		8	9	10		7	2	4	5				11								14
		3			6		8	9	10		7	2	4	5				11	1							15
		3			6		8	9	10		7		4	5				11	1	2						16
1		3	4		6		8	9		11	7			5			10			2						17
1		3	4		6	7	8	9			11			5			10			2						18
1		3	4		6	7	8	9			11			5			10			2						19
1		3			6	7	8	9			11	2	4	5			10									20
		3	6			7	8		9		11	2	4	5			10		1							21
		3			6		8		9		7	2	4	5		11	10		1							22
		3			6		8	9	11		7	2	4	5			10				1					23
		3			6		8	9	11		7	2	4	5			10				1					24
	2	3			6		8	9			7		4	5	11		10				1					25
	2	3			6		8	9			7		4	5		11	10				1					26
1	2	3			6		8	9	10		11		4	5								7				27
1	2				6		8	9	10		11	3	4	5								7				28
1	2				6		8	9	10		11		4	5								7	3			29
1	2				6	7	8	9	10		11		4	5									3			30
1	2				6		8	9	10		11		4	5						3		7				31
1	2				6	7	8	9	10		11			4									3	5		32
1	2				6	7	8	9			11		4	5			10						3			33
1	2				6	7	8	9			11		4	5			10						3			34
1	2			4	6	7	8	9	10		11												3	5		35
1			4		6	7	8	9	10		11			5						2			3			36
1				4	6		8	9	10	11				2								7	3	5		37
1	2			4	6	7	8	9	10		11			5									3			38
1			5		6		8	9	10		11		4	2								7	3			39
1			5	4	6		8	9	10		11			2								7	3			40
1			4		6		8	9	10		11			5								7	3		2	41
1			4		6	7	8	9			11			5			10						3		2	42
34	14	27	11	6	39	17	42	40	28	8	40	19	29	39	3	5	18	3	4	6	4	8	13	3	2	Apps
					1	4	19	49	14	1	6			1		1	6					5				Goals

1 own-goal

Allen	Plummer	Tilford	Underwood	Simpson	Heinneman	Cull	Lauderdale	Bourton	Lake	Bowden	White	Watson	O'Brien	Baker	Boileau	Johnson	Sheppard	Lee	Hackett	Corbett	Hewett	Holmes	Elliott	Mason	Hall	
		3			6		8	9	10	11	7	2	4	5					1							1
1		3	4		6		8	9	10	11	7			5						2						R
1		2	1		2		2	2	2	2	2	1	1	2					1	1						Apps
								1	1																	Goals

1932-33

Manager: Harry Storer

1	Aug	27	(a)	Torquay U	D 3-3	Bourton 2, White	5,740
2		29	(h)	Brentford	L 2-3	Bourton, Davison	18,000
3	Sep	3	(h)	Exeter C	W 4-0	Bourton, Lauderdale, Holmes 2	15,000
4		8	(a)	Brentford	L 1-2	Bourton	12,000
5		10	(a)	Luton T	L 1-4	Lake	7,234
6		17	(h)	Newport C	W 3-1	Bourton, Lauderdale, Frith	14,000
7		24	(a)	Bournemouth	L 1-3	Lake	6,000
8	Oct	1	(h)	Swindon T	W 2-1	Lake, Davison	10,000
9		8	(a)	Clapton O	L 1-2	Elliott	7,073
10		15	(h)	Northampton T	W 3-1	Bourton 2, Lake	15,000
11		22	(a)	Queen's Park R	D 3-3	Bourton 2, Lauderdale	7,575
12		29	(h)	Southend U	L 2-3	White 2	7,000
13	Nov	5	(a)	Crystal P	W 3-1	White, Sheppard, Woolhouse	12,203
14		12	(h)	Gillingham	W 4-2	Lauderdale 2, Bourton, White	9,000
15		19	(a)	Watford	L 1-3	Brown (og)	5,748
16	Dec	3	(a)	Reading	D 3-3	Bourton, Lauderdale, Lake	8,000
17		17	(a)	Brighton & HA	L 0-1		5,184
18		24	(h)	Bristol R	W 2-0	Bourton, Perry	10,000
19		26	(a)	Bristol C	L 3-5	Lake, Bourton 2	11,000
20		27	(h)	Bristol C	W 6-0	Bourton 3, Lake 2, White	17,000
21		31	(h)	Torquay U	W 5-0	Bourton, Lauderdale, Holmes 3	8,000
22	Jan	7	(a)	Exeter C	L 0-5		7,000
23		14	(h)	Cardiff C	W 5-0	Bourton 2, Lake, Holmes, Perry	9,000
24		21	(h)	Luton T	W 4-0	Lake 2, Lauderdale, Perry	8,000
25		28	(a)	Newport C	L 1-2	Bourton	4,000
26	Feb	2	(h)	Norwich C	L 3-5	Bourton, Lake, White	7,000
27		4	(h)	Bournemouth	W 3-0	Bourton, Lauderdale, White	11,000
28		11	(a)	Swindon T	W 2-1	Bourton, Lauderdale	3,477
29		18	(h)	Clapton O	W 5-0	Bourton 2, Lake, Lauderdale, Holmes	10,635
30		25	(a)	Northampton T	L 1-5	Bourton	2,681
31	Mar	4	(h)	Queen's Park R	W 7-0	Bourton 2, Lake 3, Lauderdale, Richards	11,000
32		11	(a)	Southend U	W 3-1	Bourton 2, Lauderdale	6,000
33		18	(h)	Crystal P	W 6-2	Bourton 2, Lauderdale, White, Richards, Goddard (og)	14,610
34		25	(a)	Gillingham	L 0-3		6,000
35	Apr	1	(h)	Watford	L 1-3	Bourton	12,000
36		8	(a)	Cardiff C	D 2-2	Bourton, Richards	6,000
37		14	(a)	Aldershot	D 1-1	Bourton	4,000
38		15	(h)	Reading	W 3-1	Bourton, Lake, Lauderdale	14,000
39		18	(h)	Aldershot	W 3-0	Bourton 2, White	15,000
40		22	(a)	Norwich C	L 1-2	Lake	9,329
41		29	(h)	Brighton & HA	D 2-2	White, Baker	12,000
42	May	6	(a)	Bristol R	L 0-1		3,000

FINAL LEAGUE POSITION: 6th in Division Three South — Appearances / Goals

FA Cup

1	Nov	26	(a)	Guildford	W 2-1	Bourton, Woolhouse	4,741
2	Dec	10	(a)	Reading	D 2-2	Bourton, Lake	13,063
R		15	(h)	Reading	D 3-3	Bourton, Lake, Davison	11,275
2R		19	(n*)	Reading	L 0-1		6,756

*Played at Stamford Bridge, London. — Appearances / Goals

McSevich	Bennett	Bisby	O'Brien	Davison	Heinneman	White	Lauderdale	Bourton	Kilcar	Richards	Holmes	Lake	Underwood	Thompson	Elliott	Frith	Russell	Simpson	Sheppard	Woolhouse	Mason	Morgan	Perry	Boileau	Baker	Wilmot	
1	2	3	4	5	6	7	8	9	10	11																	1
1	2	3	4	5	6	7	8	9	10	11																	2
1	2	3	4	5	6	11	8	9			7	10															3
1	2	3	4	5		11	8	9			7	10	6														4
1	2	3		5	6	11		9			7	10	4	8													5
1		3	4	5		7	8	9		11			6		2	10											6
1	2	3	4	5		7	8			11		9	6			10											7
1	2		4	5		7	8		10	11		9	6		3												8
1	2		4	5		7	8		10	11		9	6		3												9
1	2		4	5		11	8	9			7	10	6		3												10
1	2		4	5		11	8	9			7	10	6		3												11
1	2		4	5		11	8	9			7	10	6		3												12
1				5	6	7	8	9							3		2	4	10	11							13
1	2			5	6	7	8	9							3			4	10	11							14
1	2			5	6	7	8	9							3			4	10	11							15
1	2				6	7	8	9				10			3			4		11	5						16
		3			6	7	8	9								10		4		11	5	1	2				17
1	2	3		5	6	11	8	9			7	10											4				18
1	2	3		5	6	11	8	9			7	10											4				19
1	3		4	5		11	8	9			7	10											2	6			20
1	3		4	5		11	8	9			7	10											2	6			21
1	3		4	5		11	8	9				10								7			2	6			22
1	2			5		11	8	9			7	10			3								4	6			23
1		3		5		11	8	9			7	10			2								4	6			24
1	2					11	8	9			7	10			3						5		4	6			25
1	2	3		5		7	8	9		11		10											4	6			26
1	3		4	5		7	8	9		11		10											2	6			27
1	3		4	5			8	9		11		10								7			2	6			28
1			4	5			8	9		11	7	10			3								2	6			29
1				5		7	8	9		11		10			3								2	6	4		30
1				5		7	8	9		11		10			2								4	6		3	31
1				5		7	8	9		11		10			2								4	6		3	32
1				5		7	8	9		11		10			2								4	6		3	33
1				5		7	8	9		11		10			2								4	6		3	34
1						7	8	9		11		10			2						5		4	6		3	35
						7	8	9		11		10									5	1	2	6	4	3	36
						7	8	9		11		10									5	1	2	6	4	3	37
				5		7	8	9		11		10										1	2	6	4	3	38
				5		7	8	9		11		10										1	2	6	4	3	39
				5		7	8	9		11		10										1	2	6	4	3	40
				5		7	8	9		11		10										1	2	6	4	3	41
				5		7	8	9		11		10										1	2	6	4	3	42
34	24	12	17	36	11	40	41	39	4	23	14	35	9	1	20	3	1	5	3	7	6	8	26	23	8	12	
				2		11	15	40		3	7	18			1	1			1	1			3		1		

2 own-goals

McSevich	Bennett	Bisby	O'Brien	Davison	Heinneman	White	Lauderdale	Bourton	Kilcar	Richards	Holmes	Lake	Underwood	Thompson	Elliott	Frith	Russell	Simpson	Sheppard	Woolhouse	Mason	Morgan	Perry	Boileau	Baker	Wilmot	
1	2			5	6	7	8	9				10			3			4		11							1
1	2			5	6	7	8	9				10			3			4		11							2
1	2			5	6	7	8	9				10			3			4		11							R
1	2	3		5	6	7	8	9				10								11			4				2R
4	4	1		4	4	4	4	4				4			3			3		4			1				
				1				3				2								1							

1933-34

Manager: Harry Storer

1	Aug	26	(h)	Gillingham	W	7-1	Bourton 2, Lake 2, Lauderdale 2, Richards	17,000
2		30	(a)	Exeter C	L	0-1		8,000
3	Sep	2	(a)	Crystal P	L	1-2	Baker	17,888
4		4	(h)	Exeter C	L	1-3	Bourton	17,000
5		9	(h)	Bristol R	W	5-3	Bourton, Lake 2, Lauderdale 2	14,000
6		16	(a)	Southend U	L	1-2	Lake	8,000
7		23	(h)	Swindon T	W	5-1	Bourton 3, Richards, Baker	15,000
8		30	(h)	Reading	D	0-0		15,000
9	Oct	7	(a)	Watford	D	3-3	Bourton, Lake 2	8,610
10		14	(h)	Charlton A	W	3-2	Bourton 2, Bytheway	16,000
11		21	(a)	Brighton & HA	D	1-1	Lake	6,642
12		28	(h)	Aldershot	W	5-1	Lake 2, White, Perry, Bytheway	12,611
13	Nov	4	(a)	Luton T	W	1-0	Lake	7,690
14		11	(h)	Northampton T	W	3-1	Bourton, Lake 2	17,976
15		18	(a)	Torquay U	W	3-1	Bourton 3	3,146
16	Dec	2	(a)	Newport C	D	0-0		4,000
17		14	(h)	Norwich C	D	0-0		7,362
18		16	(a)	Bristol C	D	0-0		6,143
19		23	(h)	Clapton O	W	3-1	Lauderdale, Bacon 2	14,164
20		25	(h)	Cardiff C	W	4-1	Lauderdale, Bacon, Richards 2	27,589
21		26	(a)	Cardiff C	D	3-3	Lake, Bacon 2	11,700
22		30	(a)	Gillingham	W	7-3	Lake, Bacon 5, White	4,882
23	Jan	6	(h)	Crystal P	W	5-1	White, Bacon 4	17,065
24		18	(h)	Queen's Park R	L	0-1		9,703
25		20	(a)	Bristol R	L	1-4	Bacon	14,000
26		27	(h)	Southend U	W	2-0	Bacon, White	13,867
27	Feb	3	(a)	Swindon T	W	1-0	Lake	7,926
28		10	(a)	Reading	L	0-1		10,000
29		17	(h)	Watford	W	2-0	Davison, Lauderdale	13,745
30		24	(a)	Charlton A	L	0-2		11,179
31	Mar	3	(h)	Brighton & HA	W	2-0	Davison, White	14,013
32		10	(a)	Aldershot	D	1-1	Lauderdale	5,000
33		17	(h)	Luton T	D	2-2	Bourton, Lauderdale	12,000
34		24	(a)	Northampton T	D	2-2	Davison, Lauderdale	6,875
35		31	(h)	Torquay U	W	3-1	Bourton 2, Lievesley (og)	12,848
36	Apr	2	(a)	Bournemouth	D	3-3	Bourton, Jones, O'Brien	7,000
37		3	(h)	Bournemouth	W	4-1	Bourton, Jones 3	14,484
38		7	(a)	Queen's Park R	W	1-0	Jones	10,000
39		14	(h)	Newport C	W	5-2	Bourton 2, Jones 2, O'Brien	10,424
40		21	(a)	Norwich C	L	1-3	Jones	16,787
41		28	(h)	Bristol C	W	9-0	Bourton 4, Jones 2, White 2, Lauderdale	7,035
42	May	5	(a)	Clapton O	D	0-0		8,894

FINAL LEAGUE POSITION: 2nd in Division Three South

Appearances
Goals

FA Cup

1	Nov	25	(h)	Crewe A	W	3-0	Baker 2, Lauderdale	21,729
2	Dec	9	(a)	Rotherham U	L	1-2	Lake	9,230

Appearances
Goals

Morgan	Brown VC	Bisby	Baker	Davison	Boileau	White	Lauderdale	Bourton	Lake	Richards	Perry	Pearson	Elliott	Bytheway	Mason	Bacon	O'Brien	Frith	Jones	Crisp	Heinneman	Match
1	2	3	4	5	6	7	8	9	10	11												1
1		3	4	5	6	7	8	9	10	11	2											2
1		3	4	5	6	7	8	9	10	11	2											3
1		3	4	5	6	7	8	9	10	11	2											4
	2	3	4	5	6	7	8	9	10	11		1										5
	2	3	4	5	6	7	8	9	10	11		1										6
	2	3	4	5	6	7	8	9	10	11		1										7
	2	3	4	5	6	7	8	9	10	11		1										8
	2	3	4	5	6	7	8	9	10	11		1										9
	2		4	5	6	7	8	9	10			1	3	11								10
	2		4	5	6	7	8	9	10		3	1		11								11
	2		4	5	6	7	8	9	10		3	1		11								12
	2		4		6	7	8	9	10		3	1		11	5							13
	2		4		6	7	8	9	10		3	1		11	5							14
	2		4	5	6	7	8	9	10		3	1		11								15
	2		4	5	6	7	8	9	10		3	1		11								16
	2	3	4	5	6	7	8		10	11		1				9						17
	2	3	4	5	6				10	11		1				9	7	8				18
	2	3	4	5	6	7	8		10	11		1				9						19
	2	3	4	5	6	7	8		10	11		1				9						20
	2	3	4	5	6	7	8		10	11		1				9						21
	2	3	4	5	6	7	8		10	11		1				9						22
	2	3	4	5	6	7	8		10	11		1				9						23
	2	3	4	5	6	7	8			11		1				9		10				24
	2	3	4	5	6	7	8					1				9			10	11		25
	2	3	4	5	6	7			10			1				9			8	11		26
	2	3		5	6	11	8		10		4	1				9			7			27
	2	3	4	5	6	7	8		10			1				9			11			28
	2	3	4	5	6	7	8	9		11		1							10			29
	2	3	4	5	6		8	9		11		1				7						30
	2	3	4	5	6	7	8	10		11		1				9						31
	2	3	4	5	6		8	9	10	11		1							7			32
		3	4	5	6		8	9	10	11	2	1							7			33
	2	3	4	5			8	9		11	6	1					7		10			34
	2	3	4	5			8	9				1					7		10	11	6	35
	2	3	4	5			8	9				1					7		10	11	6	36
	2	3	4	5			8	9				1					7	6	10	11		37
	2	3	4	5			8	9				1					7	6	10	11		38
	2	3	4	5			8	9				1					7	6	10	11		39
	2	3	4	5			8	9	11			1					7	6	10			40
	2	3		5		7	8	9	11		4	1						6	10			41
	2	3		5		7	8	9	11		4	1						6	10			42
4	38	35	40	40	33	31	40	30	31	23	14	38	1	7	2	14	8	8	16	7	2	
			2	3		7	11	25	16	4	1			2		16	2		10			

1 own-goal

	2		4	5	6	7	8	9	10		3	1		11	1
	2		4	5	6	7	8	9	10		3	1		11	2
	2		2	2	2	2	2	2	2		2	2		2	
			2				1		1						

1934-35

Manager: Harry Storer

1	Aug	25	(h)	Northampton T	W	2-0	Bourton, Birtley	20,000
2		30	(a)	Clapton O	W	1-0	Lauderdale	8,407
3	Sep	1	(a)	Bournemouth	W	2-0	Bourton 2	7,000
4		3	(h)	Clapton O	W	4-0	Jones 3, Bourton	19,000
5		8	(h)	Watford	D	1-1	Bourton	20,021
6		15	(a)	Newport C	L	1-2	Lauderdale	11,000
7		22	(h)	Exeter C	D	1-1	Bourton	12,000
8		29	(a)	Bristol C	W	2-0	Lake 2	7,200
9	Oct	6	(h)	Millwall	W	5-1	Bourton 2, Lake 2, White	18,000
10		13	(a)	Crystal P	L	1-3	Wilson	20,943
11		20	(h)	Charlton A	W	4-0	Bourton, Jones, Birtley 2	25,000
12		27	(a)	Bristol R	L	1-2	Watson	5,000
13	Nov	3	(h)	Torquay U	W	6-0	Bourton 2, Jones, Lake 2, Birtley	18,000
14		10	(a)	Queen's Park R	D	1-1	Jones	6,000
15		17	(h)	Brighton & HA	L	0-2		15,000
16	Dec	1	(h)	Aldershot	D	0-0		14,000
17		15	(h)	Southend U	W	6-3	Bourton 2, Jones 3, Liddle	10,000
18		22	(a)	Luton T	L	0-4		9,231
19		25	(h)	Gillingham	W	4-0	Jones, Liddle 2, Birtley	27,000
20		26	(a)	Gillingham	W	5-2	Jones 3, Lake, Wilson	6,000
21		29	(a)	Northampton T	W	4-3	Jones, Lake 2, Liddle	10,000
22	Jan	5	(h)	Bournemouth	W	4-1	Jones 2, Wilson 2	18,000
23		16	(a)	Cardiff C	W	4-2	Jones 2, Bourton 2	8,000
24		19	(a)	Watford	L	0-2		13,448
25		26	(h)	Newport C	W	5-0	Jones 3, Bourton, Birtley	12,000
26	Feb	2	(a)	Exeter C	L	0-2		5,000
27		9	(h)	Bristol C	D	1-1	Bourton	14,000
28		16	(a)	Millwall	W	3-1	Bourton, Jones, Liddle	12,000
29		23	(h)	Crystal P	D	1-1	Jones	15,041
30	Mar	2	(a)	Charlton A	D	3-3	Jones, Lauderdale 2	30,114
31		9	(h)	Bristol R	W	1-0	Jones	13,000
32		16	(a)	Torquay U	L	0-1		3,593
33		23	(h)	Queen's Park R	W	4-1	Jones, Bourton, Liddle 2	10,000
34		30	(a)	Brighton & HA	L	0-2		5,400
35	Apr	6	(h)	Cardiff C	W	2-0	Bourton, White	10,000
36		13	(a)	Aldershot	L	1-3	Bourton	5,000
37		19	(a)	Reading	L	0-2		12,618
38		20	(h)	Swindon T	W	3-0	Jones, Bourton 2	8,000
39		23	(h)	Reading	L	1-2	Bourton	12,000
40		27	(a)	Southend U	D	1-1	Bourton	7,000
41	May	1	(a)	Swindon T	D	0-0		3,234
42		4	(h)	Luton T	W	1-0	Bourton	10,000

FINAL LEAGUE POSITION: 3rd in Division Three South

Appearances
Goals

FA Cup

1	Nov	24	(h)	Scunthorpe U	W	7-0	Birtley 2, Lauderdale 2, Bourton, Jones, Liddle	12,939
2	Dec	8	(a)	Hartlepools U	W	4-0	Bourton 2, Jones, Birtley	13,054
3	Jan	12	(a)	Birmingham	L	1-5	Jones	40,349

Appearances
Goals

Pearson	Brown VC	Bisby	Baker	Davison	Boileau	Birtley	Lauderdale	Bourton	Jones	Liddle	Crisp	White	Lake	Wilson	Watson	Frith	Mason	Elliott	Morgan	Brook	Bacon	Curtis	Grundy	
1	2	3	4	5	6	7	8	9	10	11														1
1	2	3	4	5	6	7	8	9	10	11														2
1	2	3	4	5	6	7	8	9	10	11														3
1	2	3	4	5	6	7	8	9	10	11														4
1	2	3	4	5	6	7	8	9	10	11														5
1	2	3	4	5	6	7	8	9	10		11													6
1	2	3	4	5	6	7	8	9	10			11												7
1	2	3	4	5	6	7		9	8			11	10											8
1	2	3	4	5	6	7		9	8			11	10											9
1	2	3	4	5	6	7		9	8					10	11									10
1	2	3	4	5		7		9	8				10		11	6								11
1	2	3	4	5		7		9	8				10		11	6								12
1	2	3	4	5		7		9	8	11			10			6								13
1	2	3	4	5		7		9	8	11			10			6								14
1	2	3		5	6	7		9	8	11			10			4								15
1	2	3		5	6	7		9	8	11			10				4							16
1	2	3		5	6	7		9	10	11				8			4							17
1	2	3		5	6	7	8	9	10	11							4							18
1	2	3		5	6	7	8	9	10	11							4							19
1		3		5	6	7			9	11			10	8		4		2						20
1		3		5	6	7			9	11			10	8		4		2						21
1	2	3		5	6	7			9	11			10	8		4								22
	2	3			6	7		9	10	11				8		4	5		1					23
		3			6	7		9	10	11				8		4	5		1	2				24
1		3	4			7	8	9	10	11						6	5			2				25
1		3	4			7	8	10		11						6	5			2	9			26
1	2	3	4					9	8			7	10			6	5					11		27
1	2	3	4		6	7	8	9	10	11							5							28
1	2	3	4		6	7	8	9	10	11							5							29
1	2	3	4		6	7	8	9	10	11							5							30
1	2	3	4		6		8	9	10	11					7		5							31
1	2	3	4		6		8	9	10	11					7		5							32
1	2	3	4		6		8	9	10	11					7		5							33
1	2	3						9	10					8	7	6	5					11	4	34
1	2	3		5			8	9	10	11		7				6	4							35
1	2	3		5			8	9	10	11		7				6	4							36
1	2		4			7		9	10	11						6	5			3		8		37
1	2							9	10	11		7		4		6	5			3		8		38
1	2		4					9	10	11		7				6	5			3		8		39
1	2							9	10	11				4	7	6	5			3		8		40
1	2		4				8	9	10	11						6	5			3		7		41
1	2		4				8	9	10						11	6	5			3		7		42
40	37	36	27	24	26	30	21	39	41	32	1	8	12	10	9	22	24	2	2	9	1	8	1	
						6	4	26	27	7		2	9	4	1									

Pearson	Brown VC	Bisby	Baker	Davison	Boileau	Birtley	Lauderdale	Bourton	Jones	Liddle	Crisp	White	Lake	Wilson	Watson	Frith	Mason	Elliott	Morgan	Brook	Bacon	Curtis	Grundy	
1	2	3		5	6	7	8	9	10	11							4							1
1	2	3		5	6	7		9	10	11				8			4							2
	2	3			6	7		9	10	11				8		4	5		1					3
2	3	3		2	3	3	1	3	3	3				2		1	3		1					
						3	2	3	3	1														

1935-36

Manager: Harry Storer

1	Aug	31	(a)	Reading	L	1-2	Lake	14,000
2	Sep	2	(a)	Millwall	D	2-2	Bourton, McNestry	8,000
3		7	(h)	Newport C	W	7-1	Bourton 3, Jones 2, Lauderdale 2	17,138
4		9	(h)	Millwall	W	5-0	Jones 2, Bourton, Fitton, Turnbull (og)	17,774
5		14	(a)	Exeter C	W	3-1	Bourton, Lauderdale, Fitton	8,000
6		18	(a)	Torquay U	D	3-3	Bourton, McNestry, Fitton	4,439
7		21	(h)	Brighton & HA	W	5-0	Bourton, Jones 2, Fitton 2	18,776
8		28	(a)	Queen's Park R	D	0-0		16,000
9	Oct	5	(h)	Watford	W	2-0	Liddle, Lewis (og)	17,786
10		12	(a)	Bristol C	D	0-0		17,000
11		19	(a)	Cardiff C	L	0-1		10,000
12		26	(h)	Gillingham	W	4-0	Jones, McNestry, Fitton, Bacon	14,811
13	Nov	2	(a)	Bournemouth	D	1-1	Elliott	10,000
14		9	(h)	Crystal P	W	8-1	Bourton 3, Jones 2, McNestry 2, Lauderdale	20,818
15		16	(a)	Notts C	L	1-2	Bourton	17,902
16		23	(h)	Bristol R	W	3-1	Bourton, Lauderdale, Lake	15,644
17	Dec	7	(h)	Southend U	W	3-0	Lauderdale 2, Fitton	10,000
18		14	(a)	Northampton T	W	4-2	Bourton, Lauderdale, Fitton, Frith	5,000
19		25	(h)	Aldershot	L	0-2		24,800
20		26	(a)	Aldershot	W	2-1	Liddle, Frith	6,800
21		28	(h)	Reading	W	3-1	Bourton 2, Jones	25,000
22	Jan	4	(a)	Newport C	L	1-2	Bourton	6,500
23		16	(a)	Clapton O	W	1-0	McNestry	2,505
24		18	(h)	Exeter C	W	3-0	McNestry 2, Liddle	13,000
25		25	(a)	Brighton & HA	L	1-2	Liddle	7,369
26	Feb	1	(h)	Queen's Park R	W	6-1	Jones 3, Lake 2, Fitton	19,000
27		8	(a)	Watford	L	0-5		11,478
28		15	(h)	Bristol C	W	3-1	Bourton, Jones, McNestry	16,000
29		22	(h)	Cardiff C	W	5-1	McNestry 3, Lauderdale, Crawley	10,000
30		29	(a)	Crystal P	L	1-3	Bourton	14,638
31	Mar	7	(h)	Northampton T	W	4-0	Bourton, McNestry 2, Lauderdale	14,000
32		14	(a)	Gillingham	D	1-1	Jones	7,000
33		21	(h)	Notts C	W	5-1	Jones 2, Bourton, McNestry, Fitton	17,145
34		28	(a)	Bristol R	L	2-3	Bourton, Jones	10,000
35	Apr	4	(h)	Clapton O	W	2-0	Jones, Fitton	12,429
36		11	(a)	Southend U	D	0-0		8,000
37		13	(a)	Swindon T	W	2-1	McNestry, Lauderdale	9,710
38		14	(h)	Swindon T	W	3-1	McNestry 2, Fitton	25,894
39		18	(h)	Bournemouth	W	2-0	McNestry, Lager	20,000
40		25	(a)	Luton T	D	1-1	Bourton	23,142
41		27	(h)	Luton T	D	0-0		42,975
42	May	2	(h)	Torquay U	W	2-1	Bourton, Curtis	30,514

FINAL LEAGUE POSITION: 1st in Division Three South

Appearances

Goals

FA Cup

1	Nov	30	(h)	Scunthorpe U	D	1-1	Lake	11,591
R	Dec	9	(a)	Scunthorpe U	L	2-4	Bourton 2	7,084

Appearances

Goals

Pearson	Brown VC	Bisby	Frith	Mason	Boileau	McNestry	Jones	Bourton	Lake	Fitton	Lauderdale	Curtis	McCaughey	Liddle	Watson	Bacon	Elliott	Smith	Webb	Astley	Crawley	Morgan	Lager	
1	2	3	4	5	6	7	8	9	10	11														1
1	2	3	4	5	6	7	10	9		11	8													2
1	2	3	4	5	6	7	10	9		11	8													3
1	2	3	4	5	6	7	10	9		11	8													4
1	2	3	4	5	6	7	10	9		11	8													5
1	2	3	4	5	6	7	10	9		11	8													6
1	2	3	4	5	6	7	10	9		11		8												7
1	2	3	4	5	6	7	10	9		11		8												8
1	2	3	4	5	6	7		9	10				8	11										9
1	2	3	4	5	6	7	10	9					8	11										10
1	2	3	4	5	6	7		9	10	11			8											11
1	2	3	4	5	6	7	10			11					8	9								12
1	2	3	4	5	6	7	10			11	8						9							13
1	2	3	4	5	6	7	10	9		11	8													14
1	2	3	4	5	6	7	10	9		11	8													15
1	2	3	4	5	6	7		9	10	11	8													16
1	2	3	4	5	6	7		9		11	8	10												17
1	2		4	5	6		10	9		11	8				7		3							18
1	2		4	5	6		10	9		11	8				7		3							19
1	2		4	5			8	9	10			6		11	7		3							20
1	2		4	5		7	8	9	10			6		11			3							21
1	2		4	5		7	8	9	10			6		11			3							22
1				5	6	7	8	9	10				4	11			2	3						23
1				5	6	7	8	9	10				4	11				3	2					24
1				5	6	7	8	9	10				4	11			2	3						25
1				5	6	7	8	9	10	11			4				2	3						26
1				5	6	7	8	9	10	11			4				2	3						27
1	2			5	6	7	8	9	10				4		11			3						28
1				5	6	7		10			8		4		11			3		2	9			29
1				5	6	7	8	10				11	4					3		2	9			30
				5	6	7	10	9			8		4		11			3		2		1		31
				5	6	7	10	9		11	8		4					3		2		1		32
				5	6	7	10	9		11	8		4					3		2		1		33
				5	6	7	10	9		8			4	11				3		2		1		34
			6	5		7	8	9	10	11			4					3		2		1		35
			6	5		7	10	9			8		4	11				3		2		1		36
			6	5		7	10	9		11	8		4					3		2		1		37
				5	6	7		9		11	8	10	4						3	2		1		38
			6	5		7			10		8		4	11					3	2		1	9	39
			4	5		7		9	10		8	6		11				3		2		1		40
			4			7		9	10		8	6		11			5	3		2		1		41
			4			7		9	10		8	6		11			5	3		2		1		42
30	23	17	29	40	32	39	32	39	18	25	23	11	20	14	7	1	12	18	3	14	2	12	1	
			2			19	19	24	4	12	11	1		4		1	1				1		1	

2 own-goals

1	2	3	4	5	6	7		9	10	11	8		1
1	2	3	4	5	6	7		9		11	8	10	R
2	2	2	2	2	2	2		2	1	2	2	1	
								2	1				

1936-37

Manager: Harry Storer

1	Aug	29	(a)	Doncaster R	D	1-1	McNestry	15,495
2		31	(h)	Swansea T	W	2-1	Jones, Bourton	26,245
3	Sep	5	(h)	Bury	L	1-3	Curtis	24,693
4		7	(a)	Swansea T	L	0-2		8,596
5		12	(h)	Plymouth A	W	2-0	Bourton, Fitton	24,442
6		14	(h)	Fulham	D	1-1	Fitton	18,273
7		19	(a)	Nottingham F	D	1-1	Pritchard	20,011
8		26	(h)	Chesterfield	W	2-1	Jones, Frith	22,567
9	Oct	3	(a)	Aston Villa	D	0-0		63,686
10		10	(h)	Bradford C	W	3-1	Jones 2, Pritchard	22,407
11		17	(a)	Leicester C	L	0-1		30,000
12		24	(h)	West Ham U	W	4-0	Bourton, Jones, McDonald, Fitton	28,154
13		31	(a)	Norwich C	W	3-0	Jones, Fitton 2	12,140
14	Nov	7	(h)	Newcastle U	D	2-2	Fitton, McDonald	33,150
15		14	(a)	Bradford	W	3-1	Jones, Fitton 2	9,292
16		21	(h)	Barnsley	W	3-0	Brown 2, Bourton	25,773
17		28	(a)	Sheffield U	D	2-2	Brown, Bourton	21,463
18	Dec	5	(h)	Tottenham H	W	1-0	McDonald	27,394
19		12	(a)	Blackpool	L	0-3		15,000
20		19	(h)	Blackburn R	L	0-1		21,984
21		25	(h)	Southampton	W	2-0	McDonald 2	32,042
22		26	(h)	Doncaster R	D	1-1	Liddle	26,358
23		28	(a)	Southampton	D	1-1	Mason	9,016
24	Jan	2	(a)	Bury	W	4-0	Brown 2, Lake, Liddle	7,000
25		9	(a)	Plymouth A	L	0-1		22,290
26		23	(h)	Nottingham F	D	2-2	Mason, Lake	14,397
27	Feb	3	(a)	Chesterfield	W	3-2	Bourton, Jones, McDonald	5,000
28		6	(h)	Aston Villa	W	1-0	Brown	39,808
29		13	(a)	Bradford C	L	0-1		8,861
30		25	(h)	Leicester C	L	0-2		14,109
31		27	(a)	West Ham U	L	0-4		22,300
32	Mar	6	(h)	Norwich C	D	1-1	Bourton	15,791
33		13	(a)	Newcastle U	L	2-4	Brown 2	15,000
34		20	(h)	Bradford	W	4-0	Brown 2, Roberts, Marshall (og)	15,724
35		26	(a)	Burnley	D	3-3	Bourton, Roberts, McDonald	8,870
36		27	(a)	Barnsley	L	0-3		15,000
37		30	(h)	Burnley	L	0-1		21,000
38	Apr	3	(h)	Sheffield U	W	2-0	Jones, Bourton	19,162
39		10	(a)	Tottenham H	L	1-3	Brown	18,988
40		17	(h)	Blackpool	L	1-2	Roberts	16,725
41		24	(a)	Blackburn R	W	5-2	Brown 2, Lager 2, Mason	10,640
42	May	1	(a)	Fulham	W	2-0	McDonald, Lager	8,000

FINAL LEAGUE POSITION: 8th in Division Two

Appearances

Goals

FA Cup

3	Jan	16	(h)	Charlton A	W	2-0	Lake 2	29,118
4		30	(h)	Chester	W	2-0	Mason 2 (1 pen)	21,605
5	Feb	20	(h)	West Brom A	L	2-3	Jones, Brown	44,492

Appearances

Goals

Morgan	Astley	Smith	Frith	Mason	Archer	McNestry	Lauderdale	Bourton	Jones	Liddle	Brown VC	Curtis	McCaughey	McDonald	Boileau	Fitton	Pritchard	Lager	Brown J	Lake	Elliott	Crawley	Roberts	
1	2	3	4	5	6	7	8	9	10	11														1
1	3		4	5		7	8	9	10	11	2	6												2
1	3			5		7	8	9	10	11	2	6	4											3
1	2	3	6	5		7		9	10	11			4	8										4
1	2	3	4	5		7		9	10					8	6	11								5
1	2	3	4	5			8	9	10						6	11	7							6
1	2	3	4	5				10						8	6	11	7	9						7
1	2	3	7	5					10				4	8	6	11		9						8
1	2	3	4	5	6			9	8					10		11	7							9
1	2	3	4	5	6			9	8					10		11	7							10
1	2	3	4	5	6			9						10		11	7	8						11
1	2	3		5	6			9	8				4	10		11			7					12
1	2	3		5	6			9	8				4	10		11			7					13
1	2	3		5	6			9	8				4	10		11			7					14
1	2	3	4	5	6			9	8					10		11			7					15
1	2	3		5	6			9	10				4	8		11			7					16
1	2	3	4	5	6			9	10					8		11			7					17
1	2	3	4	5	6			9	10					8		11			7					18
1	2	3	4	5	6			9	10					8		11			7					19
1	2	3	4	5	6			9	10					8		11			7					20
1	2	3	4	5	6			9	10	11				8					7					21
1	2	3		5	6	7		9	10	11			4	8										22
1	2	3		5	6	7		10	9	11			4	8										23
1	2	3	4	5	6				10	11				8					7	9				24
1	2	3		5	6			9	10	11			4	8					7					25
1	2	3	4	5	6				10	11				8					7	9				26
1	2	3	4	5	6			9	10					8		11			7					27
1	2		4	5	6			9	10					8		11			7		3			28
1	2		4	5	6			9	10	11				8					7		3			29
1	2	3	4	5	6			10	8	11									7			9		30
1	2	3	4	5	6			10	7					8					11			9		31
1	2	3	4	5	6			9	10	11				8					7					32
1	2	3	4	5	6			9	8	10						11			7					33
1	2	3	4	5				9						8	6	11			7				10	34
1	2	3		5				9					4	8	6	11			7				10	35
1	2	3		5				9					4	8	6	11			7				10	36
1	2	3	4	5	6			9	10					8		11			7					37
1	2			3	6			9	8				4			11			7			5	10	38
1	2			3	6			10	8				4			11		9	7			5		39
1	2	3	4	5	11				8				6					9	7				10	40
1	2		4	5	6				8	11				10				9	7		3			41
1	2			5	6				8	11				10	4			9	7		3			42
42	42	34	29	42	32	7	4	36	37	16	2	2	15	33	8	25	5	7	29	2	4	4	5	
			1	3		1		9	9	2		1		8		8	2	3	13	2			3	

1 own-goal

1	2	3	4	5	6				10	11				8					7	9				3
1	2	3	4	5	6				10					8		11			7	9				4
1	2	3	4	5	6				10					8		11			7	9				5
3	3	3	3	3	3				3	1				3		2			3	3				
				2					1										1	2				

1937-38

Manager: Harry Storer

1	Aug	28	(a)	Tottenham H	D	0-0		32,974
2		30	(h)	Manchester U	W	1-0	Griffiths (og)	30,566
3	Sep	4	(h)	Burnley	W	1-0	Brown	25,592
4		8	(a)	Manchester U	D	2-2	Jones, Fitton	17,455
5		11	(a)	Bury	W	2-0	Brown, Jones	10,048
6		13	(h)	Stockport C	W	1-0	Brown	18,500
7		18	(h)	Chesterfield	D	2-2	Brown, Fitton	27,827
8		25	(h)	Nottingham F	D	1-1	Mason	24,188
9	Oct	2	(a)	Newcastle U	W	2-1	Lager 2	30,000
10		9	(h)	Luton T	W	2-1	Jones, Taylor	30,549
11		16	(a)	Swansea T	D	3-3	Brown, Lager 2	15,233
12		23	(h)	Norwich C	W	2-0	Jones, Brown	23,584
13		30	(a)	Aston Villa	D	1-1	McDonald	68,029
14	Nov	6	(h)	Bradford	D	0-0		29,593
15		13	(a)	West Ham U	D	0-0		42,300
16		20	(h)	Sheffield W	L	0-1		28,250
17		27	(a)	Blackburn R	W	3-1	McPhee, Brown, Taylor	17,870
18	Dec	11	(a)	Fulham	W	4-3	McPhee 3, McDonald	15,000
19		18	(h)	Plymouth A	W	4-0	McPhee 2, McDonald 2	21,511
20		25	(a)	Sheffield U	L	2-3	Roberts, McDonald	49,019
21		27	(h)	Sheffield U	D	2-2	Brown, McDonald	40,718
22	Jan	1	(h)	Tottenham H	W	2-1	Brown 2	24,338
23		15	(a)	Burnley	L	0-2		8,284
24		22	(h)	Southampton	W	2-0	Davidson, Taylor	20,034
25		27	(h)	Bury	L	0-2		12,000
26		29	(a)	Chesterfield	L	0-4		12,000
27	Feb	5	(a)	Nottingham F	L	1-2	Lager	20,670
28		12	(h)	Newcastle U	W	1-0	Brown	20,957
29		19	(a)	Luton T	W	4-1	Lake 4	17,188
30		26	(h)	Swansea T	W	5-0	Lake 2, Roberts 2, McDonald	20,677
31	Mar	5	(a)	Norwich C	W	2-0	McDonald, Lake	16,045
32		12	(h)	Aston Villa	L	0-1		44,930
33		19	(a)	Bradford	W	1-0	Taylor	10,675
34		26	(h)	West Ham U	D	1-1	McDonald	22,154
35	Apr	2	(a)	Sheffield W	L	1-2	McDonald	25,956
36		9	(h)	Blackburn R	W	3-2	McDonald 2, Roberts	20,007
37		16	(a)	Southampton	W	4-0	Lager 2, Roberts, Taylor	20,760
38		18	(a)	Barnsley	D	1-1	Brown	15,000
39		19	(h)	Barnsley	W	1-0	Brown	30,104
40		23	(h)	Fulham	L	0-1		28,306
41		30	(a)	Plymouth A	L	1-3	Lager	21,049
42	May	7	(a)	Stockport C	D	1-1	Roberts	11,000

FINAL LEAGUE POSITION: 4th in Division Two

Appearances

Goals

FA Cup

3	Jan	8	(a)	York C	L	2-3	Brown 2	13,917

Appearances

Goals

Morgan	Astley	Metcalf	Frith	Mason	Archer	Brown	Jones	McPhee	McDonald	Pearson	Bourton	Fitton	Lager	Snape	Taylor	Roberts	Davidson	Conwell	Crawley	Boileau	Lake	Warner	Wood	Barratt	
1	2	3	4	5	6	7	8	9	10	11															1
1	2	3	4	5	6	7	8	9	10	11															2
1	2	3	4	5	6	7	8	9	10	11															3
1	2	3	4	5	6	7	8		10		9	11													4
1	2	3	4	5	6	7	8		10		9	11													5
1	2	3	4	5	6	7	8		10		9	11													6
1	2	3	4	5	6	7	8		10		9	11													7
1	2	3	4	5	6	7	10				8	11	9												8
1	2	3	8	5	6	11	10						9	4	7										9
1	2	3		5	6	11	10		8				9	4	7										10
1	2	3		5	6	11	8		4				9		7	10									11
1	2	3		5	6	11	8		4				9		7	10									12
1	2	3	4	5	6	11			8				9		7	10									13
1	2	3	4	5	6	11							9		7	10	8								14
1	2	3	4	5	6	11			8				9		7		10								15
1	2	3	4	5	6	11		9	8						7		10								16
1	2	3	4	5	6	11		9	8						7		10								17
1	2	3	4	5	6	11		9	7							8	10								18
1	2	3		5	6	11		9	10					4	7	8									19
1	2	3		5	6	11		9	10					4	7	8									20
1	2	3		5	6	11		9	10					4	7			8							21
1	2	3		5	6	11		9	10					4	7			8							22
1	2	3		4	6	11		9	7							8	10		5						23
1	2	3			6	11		9	8					4	7		10		5						24
1	2	3	4			11			8				9		7		10		5	6					25
1	2	3	4	5	6	11			8				9		7		10								26
1	2	3	4	5	6	11			8				9		7		10								27
1	2	3	4	5	6	11			10						7	8					9				28
1	2	3	4	5	6	11			10						7	8					9				29
	2	3	4	5	6	11			10							8					9	7	1		30
1	2	3	4	5	6				10						11	8					9	7			31
1	2	3	4	5	6	11			10						7	8					9				32
1	2	3	4	5	6	11			10						7	8					9				33
1	2	3		5	6	11			9					4	7	8	10								34
1	2	3	4	5	6	11			8				10		7	9									35
1	2	3	4	5	6				10						11	9	8							7	36
1	2	3	4	5		7							10		11	9	8			6					37
1	2	3	4	5		7							10		11	9	8			6					38
1	2	3	4			7							10		11	9	8		5	6					39
1	2	3	4	5	6	7							10		11	9	8								40
1	2	3	4		6	7			8				10		11	9			5						41
1	2	3	4	5		7			8						11	10				6	9				42
41	42	42	32	38	37	40	12	12	35	3	5	5	17	8	31	23	16	2	5	5	7	2	1	1	
				1		13	4	6	12			2	8		5	6	1				7				

1 own-goal

1	2	3		5	6	11		9	4						7	8	10								3
1	1	1		1	1	1		1	1						1	1	1								
						2																			

1938-39

Manager: Harry Storer

1	Aug	27	(h)	Burnley	D 1-1	Chester (og)	25,830
2		29	(a)	Sheffield U	D 0-0		17,017
3	Sep	3	(a)	Tottenham H	L 1-2	Lager	40,535
4		5	(h)	Luton T	W 1-0	Lake	19,000
5		10	(h)	Southampton	W 3-0	Davidson, Taylor, Roberts	20,326
6		17	(a)	West Ham U	L 1-4	Coen	27,200
7		24	(a)	Nottingham F	L 0-3		19,342
8	Oct	1	(h)	Newcastle U	W 1-0	McDonald	18,774
9		8	(a)	West Brom A	L 1-3	Barratt	30,943
10		15	(h)	Bury	D 0-0		18,305
11		22	(a)	Sheffield W	D 2-2	Crawley 2	24,068
12		29	(h)	Chesterfield	W 2-0	Taylor, McDonald	18,174
13	Nov	5	(a)	Blackburn R	W 2-0	Lager, Ashall	15,787
14		12	(h)	Millwall	W 2-1	Lager, Crawley	18,502
15		19	(a)	Manchester C	L 0-3		38,712
16		26	(h)	Bradford	W 3-1	Crawley 2, Ashall	17,260
17	Dec	3	(a)	Swansea T	W 4-2	Lager 2, Ashall, Davidson	11,022
18		10	(h)	Fulham	W 3-1	Lager 2, Davidson	21,825
19		17	(a)	Tranmere R	W 2-1	Lager, Davidson	8,000
20		24	(a)	Burnley	L 0-1		10,879
21		26	(h)	Plymouth A	L 1-2	Ashall	13,428
22		27	(a)	Plymouth A	W 2-0	Taylor, Crawley	27,766
23		31	(h)	Tottenham H	W 4-0	Taylor, Crawley, Roberts, McDonald	19,499
24	Jan	14	(a)	Southampton	W 2-0	Crawley 2	11,578
25		28	(h)	Nottingham F	W 5-1	Crawley 3, Davidson 2	17,820
26	Feb	4	(a)	Newcastle U	W 4-0	Crawley 2, Davidson, Taylor	43,000
27		11	(h)	West Brom A	D 1-1	Davidson	38,163
28		18	(a)	Bury	L 0-5		9,000
29		25	(h)	Sheffield W	W 1-0	Taylor	22,786
30	Mar	4	(a)	Chesterfield	L 0-3		12,200
31		11	(h)	Blackburn R	L 0-1		24,717
32		18	(a)	Millwall	D 0-0		35,000
33		25	(h)	Manchester C	L 0-1		20,088
34	Apr	1	(a)	Bradford	W 2-0	Green, Mason	7,166
35		8	(h)	Swansea T	W 3-0	Lager, Metcalf, Green	18,207
36		10	(a)	Norwich C	D 1-1	Lake	28,865
37		11	(h)	Norwich C	W 2-0	Lager, Lake	18,707
38		15	(a)	Fulham	L 0-1		14,831
39		22	(h)	Tranmere R	W 2-0	Lager, Roberts	11,869
40		24	(h)	West Ham U	D 0-0		12,229
41		29	(h)	Sheffield U	L 0-3		13,225
42	May	6	(a)	Luton T	W 3-1	Lager 2, Coen	18,674

FINAL LEAGUE POSITION: 4th in Division Two

Appearances
Goals

FA Cup

3	Jan	7	(a)	Chester	L 0-1		11,198

Appearances
Goals

Morgan	Astley	Metcalf	Frith	Mason	Archer	Warner	Davidson	Roberts	McDonald	Ashall	Taylor	Lager	Lake	Coen	Boileau	Smith N	Barratt	Armeson	Crawley	Smith B	Wood	Lewis	Snape	Green	Elliott	
1	2	3	4	5	6	7	8	9	10	11																1
1	2	3	4	5	6			8	10	11	7	9														2
1	2	3	4	5	6			10	8	11	7	9														3
1	2	3	4	5	6		8	10		11	7		9													4
1	2	3	4	5	6		10	8		11	7		9													5
1	2	3	4	5	6		10	8			7	9		11												6
1	2	3	4	5					8	11	7		10		6	9										7
1	2	3	4	5			8	9	10	11					6		7									8
1	2	3	4	5	6		8			11		10				9	7									9
1	2	3	4	5			8		10	7	11					9		6								10
1	2	3	4	5	7		8		10		11							6	9							11
1	2	3	4	5	7		8		10		11							6	9							12
1	2	3	4	5			8			7	11	10			6				9							13
1	2	3	4	5			8			7	11	10			6				9							14
1	2	3	4	5			8			7	11	10			6				9							15
1	2	3	4	5			8			7	11	10			6				9							16
1	2	3	4	5			8		9	7	11	10			6											17
1	2	3	4	5			8		10	7	11	9			6											18
1	2	3	4	5			8		10	7	11	9			6											19
1	2	3	4	5			8		10	7	11	9			6											20
1	2	3	4	5			8		10	7	11	9			6											21
1	2	3	4	5				8	10	7	11				6				9							22
1	2	3	4	5				8	10	7	11				6				9							23
1	2	3	4	5			10	8		7	11				6				9							24
1	2	3	4	5			8	10		7	11				6				9							25
1	2		4	5			8			7	11	10			6				9	3						26
1	2	3	4	5			8			7	11	10			6				9							27
1	2	3	4	5			8			7	11	10			6				9							28
	2	3	4	5			8	10		7	11				6				9		1					29
1	2	3	4	5		7	8		10									6	9			11				30
1	2	3		5			10			11	7	8						6	9				4			31
1	2	3		5			10	8	4	11	7							6						9		32
1	2	3		5			10		4	11	7	9						6	9					8		33
1	2	3	4	5						11	7	9	10		6									8		34
1	2	3	4	5						11	7	9	10		6									8		35
1	2		4	5						11	7	9	10		6					3				8		36
1	2		4	5						11	7	9	10		6									8	3	37
1	2		4	5		7				11		9	10		6									8	3	38
1	2		4	5				10		11	7	9			6									8	3	39
1	2		4	5		7			10		11	9			6		8								3	40
1	2		4	5						11		9	10	7	6		8								3	41
1	2		4	5						11		10		7	6				9					8	3	42
41	42	34	39	42	9	4	28	14	19	37	35	26	9	3	28	3	4	7	18	2	1	1	1	9	6	
		1		1			8	3	3	4	6	13	3	2			1		14					2		

1 own-goal

1	2	3	4	5				8	10	7	11				6				9							3
1	1	1	1	1				1	1	1	1				1				3							

1939-40

Manager: Harry Storer

1	Aug	26	(a)	Burnley	D 1-1	Lager	11,661
2		28	(h)	West Brom A	D 3-3	Green 2, Lager	18,500
3	Sep	2	(h)	Barnsley	W 4-2	Crawley 2, Lowrie, Mason	11,611

FINAL LEAGUE POSITION: 3rd in Division Two (season aborted)

Appearances

Goals

1	Oct	21	(a)	Northampton T	D 1-1	Frith	3,000
2		28	(h)	West Brom A	W 6-3	Frith 3, Green 2, Lowrie	3,056
3	Nov	4	(a)	Leicester C	L 2-4	Green, Lowrie	3,000
4		11	(h)	Birmingham	W 3-1	Green, Lowrie, Frith	5,501
5		18	(a)	Wolves	L 0-4		5,210
6		25	(h)	Walsall	W 4-3	Crawley 2, Lowrie, Green	2,000
7	Dec	2	(a)	Luton T	L 0-7		4,477
8		9	(h)	Northampton T	L 1-4	Green	1,643
9		16	(a)	West Brom A	L 1-3	Lowrie	3,802
10		23	(h)	Leicester C	L 0-1		1,212
11		30	(a)	Birmingham	W 4-2	Crawley 2, Green, Taylor	2,112
12	Jan	6	(h)	Wolves	L 0-3		3,085
13		13	(a)	Walsall	W 2-0	Davidson, Taylor	1,720
14	Feb	24	(a)	Wolves	L 0-1		2,532
15	Mar	2	(h)	Walsall	W 4-1	Crawley 2, Davidson, Barratt	1,983
16		9	(a)	Luton T	W 5-1	Davidson 3, Crawley, Barratt	2,968
17		16	(h)	Northampton T	W 6-3	Taylor 3, Davidson 2, Crawley	2,950
18		23	(a)	West Brom A	L 1-3	Crawley	6,743
19		25	(h)	Luton T	W 10-2	Crawley 8, Green, Barratt	5,650
20		26	(a)	Northampton T	L 0-2		3,997
21		30	(h)	Leicester C	W 4-1	Crawley, Davidson, Green, Barratt	4,036
22	Apr	6	(a)	Birmingham	L 0-2		8,138
23		13	(h)	Wolves	D 1-1	Lauderdale	5,448
24	May	25	(a)	Walsall	L 1-2	Murray	1,552
25		29	(a)	Leicester C	W 3-1	Crawley, Lauderdale, Murray	2,000
26	Jun	1	(h)	Luton T	W 5-1	Crawley 2, Davidson 2, Lewis	1,200
27		5	(a)	Birmingham	D 0-0		600
28		8	(h)	West Brom A	W 4-0	Murray 3, Davidson	1,742

FINAL LEAGUE POSITION: 3rd in Regional League Midland Division

Appearances

Goals

League War Cup

1	Apr	20	(h)	Luton T	W 3-0	Taylor 2, Davidson	5,089
2		27	(a)	Luton T	L 1-2	Davidson	4,000
3	May	4	(a)	Wolves	W 2-0	Lowrie 2	6,035
4		11	(h)	Wolves	W 5-2	Lowrie 2, Davidson 2, Crawley	8,713
5		18	(h)	West Brom A	L 0-1		7,821

Appearances

Goals

1940-41

Manager: Harry Storer

1	Aug	31	(h)	Leicester C	D 1-1	Lowrie	2,165
2	Sep	7	(a)	Leicester C	W 2-0	Lowrie, Crawley	2,106
3		14	(h)	Reading	W 7-3	Lowrie 3, Crawley 2, Lauderdale 2	2,958
4		21	(a)	Reading	L 2-3	Frith 2	2,066
5		28	(h)	Notts C	D 1-1	Elliott	2,911
6	Oct	5	(a)	Notts C	W 3-1	Crawley 2, Taylor	2,114
7		12	(h)	Cardiff C	W 5-2	Crawley, Taylor, Davidson, Ashall, Mason	2,535
8		19	(a)	Cardiff C	D 2-2	Frith, O'Brien	5,090
9	Nov	2	(h)	Northampton T	L 1-2	Lowrie	307
10		9	(a)	West Brom A	W 4-1	Lowrie, Crawley, Ashall, O'Brien	978

FINAL LEAGUE POSITION: 3rd in South Regional League

Appearances

Goals

Wood	Astley	Metcalf	Frith	Elliott	Boileau	Smith N	Green	Crawley	Davidson	Lewis	Morgan	Snape	Warner	Lowrie	Taylor	Mason	Ashall	Armeson	Harris	Barratt	Mitchell	Smith B	Lauderdale	Murray	Coen	Lager	
	2	3	4		6			9	10		1					5	11								7	8	1
	2		4		6		10	9			1					5	11					3			7	8	2
	2		4		6			9			1			10		5	11					3			7	8	3
	3	1	3		3		1	3	1		3			1		3	3					2			3	3	
							2	2						1		1										2	

1	2	3	4	5	6	7	8	9	10	11																	1
	2	3	8		6		9	5			1	4	7	10	11												2
	2	3	8		6		9				1	4	7	10	11	5											3
1	2		8	3	6		9	5				4		10	11		7										4
	2	3	8		6		9	5			1	4		10	11		7										5
1	2	3			6		8	9		11		4	7	10		5											6
	2	3	4		6		8	9		11	1			10	7	5											7
1		3	8	2			9					4	7	10	11	5		6									8
	2	3	8	6			9	5			1	4	7	10	11												9
1	2	3	6				10	9				4	7	8	11	5											10
1	2	3	4		6		8	9					7	10	11	5											11
	2	3	4		6		8	9			1		7	10	11	5											12
1		3	4	2	6		9		10				7		11	5			8								13
	2	3	4		6			9	10		1			8	11	5				7							14
1	2	3	4		6		8	9	10						11	5				7							15
	2	3			6		8	9	10		1	4			11	5				7							16
1	2			3			8	9	10			4			11	5				7	6						17
	2			3	6		8	9	10		1	4	7		11	5											18
1	2			3			8	9	10			4			11	5		6		7							19
			2		6		8	9	10		1			7	11	5		4				3					20
1	2	3			6		8	9	10	11		4				5				7							21
	2	3			6		8	9	10	11	1	4	7			5											22
	2	3			6		10	9			1	4			11	5				7			8				23
1		2	4		6		8		10	11			7			5						3		9			24
1		2	4	5	6			8	7	11												3	10	9			25
		2	4	5				8	10	11	1		7			6						3		9			26
1		3	4	2	6			9	8	11			7			5							10				27
		3	4	2	6			8	7	11	1					5							10	9			28
14	20	23	20	12	22	1	23	24	16	10	14	15	14	13	19	22	2	3	1	7	1	4	4	4			
			5				9	21	11	1				5	5					4			2	5			

1	2		4	3	6		10	9	8				7		11	5											1
	2		10	3	6			9	8		1	4	7		11	5											2
	2	3	4		6			9	8		1		7	10	11	5											3
	2	3	4		6			9	8		1		7	10	11	5											4
	2	3	4		6			9	8		1		7	10	11	5											5
1	5	3	5	2	5		1	5	5		4	1	5	3	5	5											
								1	4					4	2												

Wood	Elliott	Metcalf	Armeson	Mason	Boileau	Davidson	Crawley	Murray	Lowrie	Taylor	Morgan	Frith	Lauderdale	O'Brien	Lewis	Ashall	Jones	
1	2	3	4	5	6	7	8	9	10	11								1
	2	3	6	5		7	9		10	11	1	4	8					2
	2	3		5	6		9		10	11	1		8	4	7			3
	2	3		5	6	10	9			11	1	7	8	4				4
1	2	3		5	6	10	9			11		8		4		7		5
1	2	3		5	6	10	9			11		4		8		7		6
	2	3		5	6	8	9		10	11	1	4				7		7
	2	3		5	6	7	9		10	11	1	8		4				8
		3		5	6	8	9		10	7	1	4		2			11	9
	2	3		5	6		9		10	11	1	4		8		7		10
3	9	10	2	10	9	8	10	1	7	10	7	8	3	7	1	4	1	
	1			1		1	7		7	2		3	2	2		2		

1942-43

Manager: Harry Storer

1	Aug	29	(a)	Walsall	L 0-1		2,000
2	Sep	5	(h)	Walsall	W 1-0	Taylor	6,356
3		12	(h)	Aston Villa	W 2-1	Crawley 2	14,720
4		19	(a)	Aston Villa	D 1-1	Crawley	13,600
5		26	(a)	Leicester C	D 0-0		6,025
6	Oct	3	(h)	Leicester C	W 5-1	Lowrie 3, Ashall, Simpson	9,575
7		10	(h)	Northampton T	W 5-0	Lowrie 4, Bolan	10,875
8		17	(a)	Northampton T	W 2-1	Murray, Young	3,076
9		24	(h)	Birmingham	D 2-2	Crawley, Mason	8,638
10		31	(a)	Birmingham	L 0-1		5,000
11	Nov	7	(h)	Wolves	W 1-0	Lowrie	10,257
12		14	(a)	Wolves	D 1-1	Armeson	4,904
13		21	(a)	Northampton T	W 2-1	Crawley, Simmons	414
14		28	(h)	Northampton T	W 2-1	Lowrie, Lee	6,936
15	Dec	5	(a)	Walsall	D 1-1	O'Brien	2,500
16		12	(h)	Walsall	W 1-0	Crawley	6,111
17		19	(h)	West Brom A	W 2-1	Crawley 2	5,043
18		25	(a)	West Brom A	L 0-3		5,199
19		26	(h)	Walsall	W 2-0	Simmons, Simpson	10,359
20	Jan	2	(a)	Walsall	W 3-1	Lowrie 2, Simmons	1,997
21		9	(a)	West Brom A	W 3-2	Coen 2, Lowrie	3,676
22		16	(h)	West Brom A	W 1-0	Simmons	8,315
23		23	(a)	Northampton T	W 2-0	Lowrie, Simmons	4,024
24		30	(h)	Northampton T	L 0-1		8,505
25	Feb	6	(a)	Leicester C	W 2-0	Lowrie, Setchell	8,187
26		13	(h)	Leicester C	L 1-3	Lowrie	9,544
27		20	(h)	Birmingham	W 1-0	Lowrie	7,578
28		27	(a)	Birmingham	L 1-3	Lager	3,000
29	Mar	6	(h)	West Brom A	D 1-1	Crawley	11,502
30		13	(a)	West Brom A	L 0-3		13,792
31		20	(a)	Birmingham	W 2-1	Lowrie, Simmons	1,000
32		27	(h)	Birmingham	W 2-1	Lowrie, Barratt	4,864
33	Apr	3	(a)	Derby C	D 1-1	Lager	6,000
34		10	(h)	Derby C	L 0-1		6,034
35		17	(a)	Leicester C	W 3-1	Lowrie 2, Simmons	3,556
36		24	(h)	Leicester C	D 0-0		4,188
37		26	(h)	Notts C	W 7-0	Lowrie 4, Crawley 2, Simmons	4,384
38	May	1	(a)	Notts C	L 1-2	Simpson	1,127
							Appearances
							Goals

FINAL LEAGUE POSITION: 7th in Football League North First Championship; 9th Football League North Second Championship; 8th in Football League Cup North Qualifying Competition.
Matches 20 to 30 were League Cup Qualifying games.

Morgan	O'Brien	Metcalf	Frith	Mason	Boileau	Barratt	Lauderdale	Crawley	Lowrie	Lewis	Elliott	Taylor	Armeson	Murray	Kelley	Chapman	Bolan	Humphries	Evans	Walker	Wood	Snape	Simpson	Ashall	Simmons	Smith S	Lee	Bond	Setchell	Bennett	Coen	Lager	Kelly	Greenway	Gardner	Ryan	Chapman	Bennett	
1	2	3	4	5	6	7	8	9	10	11																													1
1	3		4	5	6	7		9	10	8	2	11																											2
1	4	3		5		7		8	10	11	2		6	9																									3
1	2		4	6		7		10	11					9	3	5	8																						4
1	3		6	5		7		10						9			8	2	4	11																			5
	2		6	5				10	9		3						8				1	4	7	11															6
	2		4	5	6			10	9		3						8				1		7	11															7
	2		4	5	6			10	9	7	3			8							1																		8
	2		4	5		7		10			3		6	9			8				1																		9
	2		4	5	6	7		10	9		3						8				1		11																10
		3	4	5	6	7		10	9		2		11				8				1																		11
	8	3	4	5	6			9	10		2		11								1		7																12
		3	4	5				9	10		2		11				6				1		7		8														13
		3		5	6			10	8		2		11				7				1					4	9												14
	8	3		5	11			4			2										1		7				9	6											15
		3		5				9	10		2										1		7		8	4		6	11										16
			4	5	3			8	10		2										1		7					6	11	9									17
	8	3		5	6			9	10		2										1	4	7						11										18
			2		6			5	9	10	3										1	2	7		8				11										19
			4	5	6			10	9		3										1	4	7		8				11										20
	2		4		6			5	9		3										1		7		8				11		10								21
	2		6	5				10	9		3										1	4	7		8				11										22
	2		4	5	6			10	9		3										1		7		8						11								23
	7	3	4	5				10			2										1	6			8						11								24
	2		4	5	6				9		3										1		7		8				11		10								25
	2		4	5	6				9		3										1		7		8				11		10								26
	2			5				8	9		3		6								1	4	7						11		10								27
	2	3			6			10			5										1	4	7		8				11			9							28
	2	3		5	6	8		10	9												1	4	7						11										29
	2	3		5	6	7			9	11											1											10							30
	1			5	6	7			9																8	4					3		11	10					31
	2			5		7			9		3										1				8								11	10	4	6			32
	2			5	6	8			9		3											4									7	10		11					33
	2			5		8			9	11	3										1					4						10				6			34
	2			5	6				9		3										1				8									10			4	11	35
	2			3		7			9												1				8								11	10			4		36
	2			3		11		10	9														7		8	4								6					37
	2			6		11		10	9														7		8	4													38
5	31	13	21	35	23	17	1	29	33	7	29	1	7	5	1	1	9	1	1	1	29	10	21	2	17	6	2	3	12	1	8	4	3	6	1	2	2	1	
	1			1		1		11	23			1	1	1			1						3	1	8		1		1		2	2							

Grubb played number 5 in Matches 36 and 37; C.Young played number 11 in Match 8 and scored 1 goal; Lapworth played number 11 in Match 9; T.Whitcroft played number 10 in Match 15; E.Roberts played number 9 in Match 24; C.Shaw played number 4 in Match 30; C.Craven played number 8 in Match 30; Quinton played number 2 in Match 31; G.Merrick played number 1 in Match 33; A.Bainbridge played number 7 in Match 34; Hartopp played number 7 in Match 35; F.Mitchell played number 6 in Match 36; J.Thacker played number 1 in Match 37; E.Batchelor played number 3 in Match 38; J.Laurie played number 5 in Match 38.

1943-44

Manager: Harry Storer

1	Aug	28	(a)	Birmingham	D	0-0		7,000
2	Sep	4	(h)	Birmingham	W	2-1	Lowrie, Crawley	7,929
3		11	(h)	Walsall	D	3-3	Lowrie 2, Simpson	6,341
4		18	(a)	Walsall	D	1-1	Crawley	2,750
5		25	(h)	Leicester C	L	0-1		5,962
6	Oct	2	(a)	Leicester C	L	0-1		9,108
7		9	(a)	Aston Villa	D	0-0		15,000
8		16	(h)	Aston Villa	L	0-1		14,014
9		23	(a)	Northampton T	W	3-0	Vinall 2, Simpson	6,000
10		30	(h)	Northampton T	W	4-1	Crawley 2, Gardner 2	8,220
11	Nov	6	(a)	Wolves	L	1-2	Barratt	4,006
12		13	(h)	Wolves	D	1-1	Lowrie	7,168
13		20	(h)	Northampton T	L	0-1		5,320
14		27	(a)	Northampton T	L	1-4	Gardner	4,224
15	Dec	4	(h)	Walsall	L	1-3	Barratt	3,610
16		11	(a)	Walsall	D	0-0		2,957
17		18	(a)	West Brom A	L	0-3		2,647
18		25	(h)	West Brom A	W	8-0	Crawley 5, McKeown 2, Barratt	7,398
19		26	(h)	Walsall	W	3-0	Mason 2, McKeown	12,950
20	Jan	1	(a)	Walsall	L	0-3		4,000
21		8	(h)	Wolves	W	3-2	Lowrie 3	6,356
22		15	(a)	Wolves	D	2-2	Lowrie, Crawley	7,856
23		22	(a)	West Brom A	D	2-2	Crawley 2	5,577
24		29	(h)	West Brom A	D	3-3	Lowrie, Crawley, McKeown	8,542
25	Feb	5	(a)	Aston Villa	L	0-4		16,500
26		12	(h)	Aston Villa	W	2-0	Crawley, Barratt	15,770
27		19	(h)	Northampton T	W	2-0	Lowrie, Dennison (og)	5,701
28		26	(a)	Northampton T	W	2-1	Edwards 2	2,102
29	Mar	4	(a)	Derby C	L	1-2	Lowrie	12,000
30		11	(h)	Derby C	W	3-0	Lowrie, McKeown, Coen	12,172
31		18	(h)	Aston Villa	L	1-2	Lowrie	23,664
32		25	(a)	Aston Villa	L	1-2	Pritchard	30,000
33	Apr	1	(a)	Nottingham F	L	1-4	Simpson	5,073
34		8	(h)	Nottingham F *	W	3-1	Boileau, McKeown, Newbold	6,432
35		10	(h)	Birmingham	L	0-3		5,860
36		15	(a)	Leicester C	D	1-1	Edwards	4,037
37		22	(h)	Leicester C	W	6-2	Crawley 3, McKeown, Edwards, Barratt	3,420
38		29	(a)	Notts C	W	4-1	Crawley 2, Barratt, Setchell	1,540
39	May	6	(h)	Notts C	W	8-2	Barratt 4, McKeown 2, Crawley, Coen	1,775

FINAL LEAGUE POSITION: 38th in Football League North First Championship; 17th in Football League North Second Championship; 18th in Football League Cup North Qualifying Competition. Matches 19 to 28 were League Cup Qualifying games.
*After extra-time, counted as a Midland Cup game.

Appearances
Goals

Morgan	O'Brien	Metcalf	Snape	Mason	Boileau	Simpson	Simmons	Crawley	Barratt	Coen	Wright	Smith S	Bond	Lowrie	Astley	Elliott	Chapman	Cornwell	Wood	Edwards	Watkins	Gardner	Vinall	Setchell	Warner	McKeown J	Lewis	Garner	Grubb	Murphy	Dougall	Smith N	Armeson	Nash	Frith	Pritchard	Newbold	Quinney	
1	2	3	4	5	6	7	8	9	10	11																													1
1	2			5	11	7		10	8		3	4	6	9																									2
1				5		11	8	10	7					9	2	3	4	6																					3
				5		7	8	10	4	11	3			9		2		6	1																				4
1		3		5		7	8	9	4	11						2		6		10																			5
1	8	3		5	6	11		10	7					9		2					4																		6
1	10	3		5		7		9	4							2		6		11		8																	7
1	10	3		5				9	4	7						2		6		11		8																	8
1	4	3		5		7		9								2		6		10			8	11															9
1	4	3		5				9	7							2		6		11		8	10																10
1	6	3		5				9	4							2				11		8	10		7														11
1	4	3		5					7					9		2		6				8		11		10													12
1		3		5				9	4							2		6		11		8				10	7												13
1	4	3			6			5		9						2				11	7	8				10													14
	2		4		6				9	7						3				11		8				10		1	5										15
1	7	3			6			5	9	11						2						8				10				4									16
1		3			6			5	9	7						2						8				10				4									17
1	6	3		5				9	8	11						2										10				4	7								18
1	6	3		5				9	8					11		2										10				4	7								19
1	4	3		5	6	7			8					9		2				11						10													20
1	6	3		5				8	4	7				9		2				11						10													21
1	2			5				8	4	7				9		3				11						10	6												22
	6	3		5				8	4	11				9		2			1							10						7							23
1		3		5				8	4					9		2				11					7	10	6												24
1	2	3		5				8	4					9						11						10							6	7					25
	2	3		5	6			9	7					10					1	11							8								4				26
	2			5	6			10	8					9		3			1	11							7						4						27
	8	3		5	6			10		7				9		2				11								1		4									28
	4	3		5	6			10		8				9		2			1	11														7					29
		3		5	6			8	4	7				9		2			1	11						10													30
		3		5	6			8	4					9		2			1	11						10										7			31
		3		5	6			10	8					9		2				11								1								7			32
		3		5	6	7		9	4	1						2				11						10													33
				5	6				8	3						2	4			11					7	10		1									9		34
				5	6					8			4			2									7	10		1									9	3	35
				5	6			9	8	7		4				3				11						10		1											36
		3		5	6			9	8	7		4				2				11						10		1											37
	4	2		5	6			9	8	7														11		10		1											38
	4	3		5	6			9	8	7																10		1											39
22	25	30	2	35	22	10	4	34	34	22	2	3	2	19	1	33	2	9	7	25	2	10	3	3	4	23	5	9	1	5	2	1	2	2	1	2	2	1	
				2	1	3		20	10	2				13						4		3	2	1		9										1	1		

Green played number 2 in Match 36; Miles played number 11 in Match 17; Harris played number 4 in Match 32; Hale played number 8 in Match 33; Keeble played number 11 in Match 36; Cryer played number 3 in Match 38; R.Ward played number 2 in Match 39; Doyle played number 11 in Match 39.

1 own-goal

1944-45

Manager: Harry Storer

1	Aug	26	(a)	Walsall	W	3-2	Currie 2, Lowrie	4,800
2	Sep	2	(h)	Walsall	W	2-1	Barratt, O'Brien	2,900
3		9	(a)	Birmingham	W	2-1	Barratt, Currie	12,000
4		16	(h)	Birmingham	L	0-1		9,927
5		23	(h)	West Brom A	D	1-1	Edwards	8,245
6		30	(a)	West Brom A	L	1-4	Lewis	9,512
7	Oct	7	(a)	Port Vale	L	0-2		6,036
8		14	(h)	Port Vale	W	4-3	Paul 3, Edwards	4,957
9		21	(a)	Northampton T	L	1-4	Paul	3,125
10		28	(h)	Northampton T	W	3-1	Paul, Crawley, McKeown	4,816
11	Nov	4	(a)	Leicester C	L	1-2	Paul	5,989
12		11	(h)	Leicester C	W	3-1	Paul 2, Frith	4,829
13		18	(a)	Aston Villa	L	0-4		15,000
14		25	(h)	Aston Villa	L	0-6		10,450
15	Dec	2	(h)	Stoke C	L	0-1		6,405
16		9	(a)	Stoke C	L	0-5		4,020
17		16	(a)	Wolves	D	1-1	Crawley	6,148
18		23	(h)	Wolves	L	1-2	Dougall	5,044
19		30	(a)	West Brom A	D	1-1	Edwards	8,659
20	Jan	6	(a)	Birmingham	L	1-5	Edwards	12,000
21		13	(h)	Birmingham	L	1-2	Crawley	5,084
22		20	(a)	Walsall	L	5-6	Crawley 3, Dougall 2	1,095
23		27	(h)	Walsall	L	0-2		2,667
24	Feb	3	(h)	Aston Villa	L	2-3	Elliott, McKeown	7,051
25		10	(a)	Aston Villa	L	2-4	Smith, Dougall	19,000
26		17	(a)	Northampton T	L	1-8	Edwards	7,128
27		24	(h)	Northampton T	W	3-0	Crawley, Dougall, Edwards	4,959
28	Mar	3	(h)	West Brom A	L	0-3		7,048
29		10	(h)	Notts C	W	4-0	Elliott 2, Kerry, Opp own-goal	3,166
30		17	(a)	Leicester C	D	2-2	Elliott, Edwards	5,133
31		24	(h)	Notts C	W	1-0	Morby (og)	4,339
32		31	(a)	Notts C	W	2-1	Crawley, Faulkner	2,007
33	Apr	7	(h)	Nottingham F	D	1-1	Crawley	5,000
34		14	(a)	Nottingham F	D	1-1	Jarvis	3,188
35		21	(a)	Birmingham	W	2-1	Elliott 2	8,015
36		28	(h)	Birmingham	D	2-2	Elliott, Faulkner	3,867
37	May	5	(a)	Aston Villa	L	2-9	Dougall, Faulkner	8,000
38		12	(h)	Aston Villa	W	3-1	Jones, Dougall, Lewis	5,310

FINAL LEAGUE POSITION: 41st in Football League North First Championship; 41st Football League North Second Championship; 57th in Football League Cup North Qualifying. Matches 19 to 29 were League Cup Qualifying games.

Appearances
Goals

Garner	Ward	Metcalf	O'Brien	Mason	Evans	Simpson	Simmons	Lowrie	Currie	Edwards	Hall	Crawley	Barratt	Elliott	Cook	Snape	Boileau	Dougall	Copson	Ryan	Lewis	Paul	Frith	Kendall	Taylor	Morton	Bowles	McKeown J	Brown	McKeown A	Douglas	Robinson	Kerry	Armeson	Green	Kelley	Faulkner	Carey	
1	2	3	4	5	6	7	8	9	10	11																																					1
1		3	4	5	6	7	8			11	2	9	10																														2
1		3	4	5	6				10	11		8	9	2	7																												3
1		3		5					10	11		8	9	2		4	6	7																										4
1			4	5						11		8	9	3	7				2	6	10																				5
1		3	4	5						11		10	8	2						6	7	9																		6
1			2	5			8		10	11			7	3									9	4	6																7
1			2						10	11		8	7	3									9	4	6	5															8
1													10	8	3					2		11	9	4	6	5	7														9
			2						11		8	7	3									9	4	6	5		1	10													10
		3	6						11		8		2								7	9	4		5		1	10													11
		3		5		7			6	11		8		2									9	4				1	10													12
		3	6	5						11		8	7	2									9	4				1	10													13
		3	2	5						11		8									7	9	4	6			1	10													14
			4	5						11		6		3									9	8				1	10	2	7										15
			6	5		7				11		8		3										4				1					2	9	10						16
	2		3	5						11		9			7			8					4				1	10							6						17
		3		5						11	2				7	4		8									1	10							6	9				18
		3	4	5						11		9						10					2				1								7	6	8				19
			4	5						11				3				9					2				1	10							7	6	8				20
			2	5						11		9		3				9					4				1	10									6	8				21
			3	5						11		9						10					4	6			1	7										8	2			22
1		3	4	5								9		2				10					7	6				11									8				23
1	2	3		5						11		4		9				8						6				10											7		24
1	2	3	6	5						11		4		9				8										10													25
1			2	5						11		4		9				8		6															10				7		26
			2	5						11		9		3				10																				8		7	1	27
			2	5						11		9		3											6									10		8		7	1	28
			2							11		5		9			3			6													10		8		7	1	29
			2	5						11		6		9		4	3																10		8			1	30
			2	5						11		6		9			3																			8		7	1	31
			2	5						11		6		9			3	8																		4		7	1	32
	2			5						11		9		3			6	8																		4		7	1	33
	2			5						11		9		3			6	10																		4		7	1	34
	2	3	6	5								4		9				8																				7		35
1	2	3		5								4		9				8																		6		7		36
	2	3		5								4		9				8			10																		7		37
	2			5								4					6	9			10																		7		38
14	10	17	28	32	3	4	3	1	6	33	2	34	10	30	4	4	8	19	2	4	7	10	17	9	4	1	13	14	1	1	1	1	7	5	15	1	13	8	
			1			3		1	3	7		9	2	7				7			2	8	1					2					1				3		

Watkins played number 4 in Matches 27, 28, 29 and 31; Smith played number 7 in Match 25; Fitzpatrick played number 5 in Match 26; Warner played number 7 in Match 30; Jones played number 10 in Matches 31, 32, 33, 35 and 36, number 6 in Match 37 and number 8 in Match 38; Jarvis played number 8 in Match 34; King played number 1 in Matches 35, 37 and 38; Matthews played number 11 in Matches 35, 36, 37 and 38.

2 own-goals

1945-46

Manager: Dick Bayliss

1	Aug	25	(h)	Arsenal	W	2-0	Lowrie, Gardner	20,943
2	Sep	1	(a)	Arsenal	D	0-0		22,323
3		8	(a)	Charlton A	L	1-3	Lowrie	15,558
4		15	(h)	Charlton A	D	1-1	Barratt	15,520
5		17	(h)	Birmingham C	L	2-3	Barratt 2	14,416
6		22	(h)	Fulham	W	3-1	Barratt, Lowrie, Matthews	14,113
7		29	(a)	Fulham	L	0-2		17,888
8	Oct	6	(h)	Plymouth A	W	3-1	Lowrie, Small 2	12,750
9		13	(a)	Plymouth A	D	1-1	Lowrie	19,825
10		20	(h)	Portsmouth	W	3-1	Barratt, Small, Aldecoa	13,621
11		27	(a)	Portsmouth	D	1-1	Lowrie	18,554
12	Nov	3	(a)	Nottingham F	D	0-0		14,657
13		10	(h)	Nottingham F	L	1-4	Pritchard	10,920
14		15	(h)	Newport C	W	7-1	Barratt 4, Lowrie 2, Simpson	3,146
15		22	(a)	Newport C	W	3-1	Lowrie, Simpson, Small	4,300
16	Dec	1	(a)	Wolves	L	0-1		19,730
17		8	(h)	Wolves	W	1-0	Simpson	13,824
18		15	(h)	West Ham U	L	2-5	Barratt, Crawley	11,719
19		22	(a)	West Ham U	L	3-6	Lowrie, Simpson, Fenton (og)	14,128
20		24	(a)	West Brom A	D	2-2	Roberts, O'Brien	18,038
21		26	(h)	West Brom A	W	3-2	Barratt, Aldecoa 2	19,303
22		29	(a)	Birmingham C	L	0-2		24,107
23	Jan	12	(h)	Brentford	W	1-0	Warner	13,450
24		19	(a)	Brentford	W	2-1	Owens 2	10,309
25		26	(a)	Tottenham H	L	0-2		17,995
26	Feb	2	(h)	Chelsea	W	2-0	Barratt, Aldecoa	19,289
27		9	(h)	Millwall	W	7-2	Barratt 4, Aldecoa, Simpson, Bilbao	13,712
28		16	(a)	Millwall	D	1-1	Barratt	17,535
29		23	(a)	Southampton	L	3-4	Barratt 3	13,834
30	Mar	2	(h)	Southampton	L	0-1		11,811
31		14	(h)	Derby C	W	3-1	Barratt, Roberts 2	14,246
32		16	(a)	Derby C	L	0-3		19,974
33		23	(a)	Leicester C	W	3-1	Barratt 2, Crawley	13,864
34		30	(h)	Leicester C	L	0-1		14,240
35	Apr	6	(h)	Swansea T	D	2-2	Barratt, Metcalf	12,993
36		10	(a)	Chelsea	L	1-2	Barratt	10,000
37		13	(a)	Swansea T	L	2-3	Crawley 2	23,056
38		19	(a)	Luton T	W	2-1	Barratt, Roberts	16,340
39		20	(a)	Aston Villa	D	0-0		40,000
40		22	(h)	Luton T	L	0-3		14,982
41		27	(h)	Aston Villa	D	2-2	Lowrie, Aldecoa	12,968
42	May	4	(h)	Tottenham H	L	0-1		11,446

FINAL LEAGUE POSITION: 13th in Football League South

Appearances

Goals

FA Cup

3	Jan	5	(h)	Aston Villa	W	2-1	Barratt, Simpson	27,197
		8	(a)	Aston Villa	L	0-2		40,000

Appearances

Goals

Wood	O'Brien	Metcalf	Wakins	Mason G	Crawley	Pritchard	Barratt	Lowrie	Jones L	Gardner	Elliott	Lewis	Smith	Dougal	Kelley	Simpson	McKeown	Matthews	Small	Snape	Aldecoa	Kelly	Ward	Kendall	Harris	Ashall	Davidson	Warner	Lewis	Roberts	Houghton	Owens	Bilbao	Loughran	Goddard	Lyman	Eggleston	Setchell	
1	2	3	4	5	6	7	8	9	10	11																													1
1	4	3		5	6	7	8	9		11	2	10																											2
1	4	3		5	6		8	9		11	2		7	10																									3
1	10	3	4	5	6		8	9		11			7		2																								4
1		3	4	5	6		8	9	10	11					2	7																							5
1		3	4	5	6		8	9							2	7	10	11																					6
1		3		5		7	4	9		8					2		10	11	6																				7
1	2				5	7	6	9		8					3			11	10	4																			8
1		3			5	7	4	9		8					2			11	10	6																			9
1	6	3	4		5		9			8	2					7			10		11																		10
1		3		5	6	7	4	9		8	2								10		11																		11
1		3			6		4	10		8	5				2	7		11				9																	12
1		3	4			11	9			8	5					7			10				2	6															13
1		3	8	5	6		4	9		11	2					7			10																				14
1		3			5		4	9			2					7			10		11				6	8													15
1		3		5	6		4	9		10	2					7					11						8												16
1		3		5	6		4	9		10	2					7					11						8												17
1			4	5	6		9			10	2				3	7					11						8												18
1		3		5	6		4	9			2					11					8							7	10										19
1	2			5	6		9				3								10	4	11							7		8									20
1	4	3		5	6		9				2					10					11							7		8									21
1		3		5	6		9	8			2					10				4	11							7											22
1		3		5	6		9				2					8				4	8							7			11								23
1		3		5	6		8				2					10				4	11							7				9							24
1		3		5	6		4				2					10					11						8	7				9	11						25
1		3		5	6		9								2	8				4	10							7					11						26
1		3		5	6		9								2	8				4	10							7					11						27
1		3		5	6		9								2	8				4	10							7											28
1		3		5	6		9								2	8	11			4	10							7					11						29
1				5	6		9				2				3	8					10							7					11	4					30
1				5	6		9				2				3					4	10							7		8									31
1		3			6		9				5				2	11					10							7		8					4				32
1		3		5	6		9				2									4	10							7		8						11			33
1	6	3			5		9				2									4	11							7		8							10		34
1		3		5	6		9	11			2					7				4	10									8									35
1				5	6		9				2				3	7				4	10									8								11	36
1				5	10		4	9			2				3					6	11							7		8									37
1		3		5	6		9				2									4	10							7		8									38
1		3		5	6		9				2									4	10							7		8									39
1		3		5	6		9				2									4	10							7		8								11	40
1		3		5			4	9			2									6	10							7		8									41
1		3			5		4	9			2									6	10							7		8			5						42
42	9	35	8	33	39	7	42	21	2	16	31	1	2	1	17	24	3	5	9	21	30	1	1	1	1	1	4	22	1	14	1	2	1	1	1	1	1	2	
	1	1			4	1	26	11		1						5		1	4		6							1		4		2							

1 own-goal

1		3		5	6		9				2					8		10		4	11							7											3
1		3		5	6		9				2					8		11			10		4					7											
2		2		2	2		2				2					2		2		1	2		1					2											
							1									1																							

Johnson played number 11 in Matches 38 and 39; Calvelley played number 11 in Match 42.

1946-47

Manager: Dick Bayliss

1	Aug	31	(a)	Burnley	D 1-1	Bett	16,971
2	Sep	2	(h)	West Brom A	W 3-2	Bett, Barratt 2	23,816
3		7	(h)	Barnsley	D 1-1	Bett	23,409
4		11	(a)	Newcastle U	L 1-3	Ashall	55,313
5		14	(a)	Newport C	L 2-4	Bett, Roberts	13,116
6		16	(h)	Newcastle U	D 1-1	Crawley	26,024
7		21	(h)	Southampton	W 2-0	Gardner, Lowrie	19,353
8		28	(a)	Nottingham F	L 0-1		27,943
9	Oct	5	(a)	Plymouth A	D 2-2	Bett, Lowrie	27,130
10		12	(h)	Birmingham C	D 0-0		29,379
11		19	(a)	Leicester C	L 0-1		28,583
12		26	(h)	Chesterfield	D 1-1	Barratt	15,722
13	Nov	2	(a)	Millwall	W 5-3	Barratt, Roberts, Ashall 3	23,180
14		9	(h)	Bradford	D 0-0		19,164
15		16	(a)	Manchester C	L 0-1		25,569
16		23	(h)	West Ham U	W 2-1	Snape, Barratt	19,436
17		30	(a)	Sheffield W	L 2-4	Coen, Barratt	24,596
18	Dec	7	(h)	Fulham	W 1-0	Lowrie	17,011
19		14	(a)	Bury	L 0-1		9,695
20		21	(h)	Luton T	D 0-0		13,087
21		25	(h)	Tottenham H	W 3-1	Snape, Lowrie, Ashall	23,317
22		26	(a)	Tottenham H	D 0-0		44,311
23		28	(h)	Burnley	L 0-3		26,944
24	Jan	4	(a)	Barnsley	W 2-0	Barratt, Lowrie	14,000
25		18	(h)	Newport C	W 6-0	Roberts 2, Lowrie 3, Ashall	18,762
26	Feb	1	(h)	Nottingham F	D 1-1	Murphy	16,440
27		5	(a)	Southampton	L 2-5	Roberts, Bett	4,289
28		15	(a)	Birmingham C	L 0-2		44,000
29	Mar	15	(a)	Bradford	L 1-5	Lowrie	13,516
30		22	(h)	Manchester C	D 1-1	Bett	26,679
31		29	(a)	West Ham U	W 2-1	Bett, Lowrie	32,000
32	Apr	5	(h)	Sheffield W	W 5-1	Lowrie 4, Roberts	19,478
33		7	(a)	Swansea T	W 3-2	Bett 2, Roberts	26,584
34		8	(h)	Swansea T	W 3-2	Lowrie 3	16,952
35		12	(a)	Fulham	L 0-2		20,026
36		19	(h)	Bury	W 3-1	Lowrie 3	18,660
37		26	(a)	Luton T	D 1-1	Lowrie	13,686
38	May	3	(a)	West Brom A	D 1-1	Lowrie	23,807
39		10	(h)	Leicester C	W 2-1	Lowrie, Jones (og)	13,522
40		17	(h)	Plymouth A	W 1-0	Roberts (pen)	16,713
41		24	(h)	Millwall	W 4-0	Roberts, Lowrie 2, Murphy	15,400
42		26	(a)	Chesterfield	L 1-2	Lowrie	12,000

FINAL LEAGUE POSITION: 8th in Division Two

Appearances
Goals

FA Cup

3	Jan	11	(h)	Newport C	W 5-2	Lowrie 3, Roberts, Ashall	21,457
4		25	(a)	Burnley	L 0-2		39,790

Appearances
Goals

Wood	Elliott	Coen	Snape	Mason G	Crawley	Warner	Bett	Barratt	Roberts	Aldecoa	Tooze	Kelley	Cox	Mason R	Lowrie	Gardner	Dearson	Frith	Young	Murphy	Simpson	Davidson	Dobbs	Latham	Lovering	Smith N	Ashall	
1	2	3	4	5	6	7	8	9	10	11																		1
1			4		6	7	8	9		11	2	3	5		10													2
1			4		5	7	8	9		11	2	3			10										6			3
1	3		4		5	7	8	9	10		2			6													11	4
1	3		4		5	7	8	2	10					6	9												11	5
1		11	4		9	7		2		10		3	5	6		8												6
1	3		4		6			2		10			5		9	8					7						11	7
1	3		4		6			2		10			5		9	8					7						11	8
1	3		4	5	6		8	2	10						9						7						11	9
1	3		4		6		8	2	10				5		9						7						11	10
1	3		4		5		8	2	10					6	9						7						11	11
1	2		4	5			10	8		11		3		6	9												7	12
1	2	3	4	5	10			8	9	7				6													11	13
1	2	3	4	5				8	9	7				6	10												11	14
1	2	3	4	5				8	9	7				6	10												11	15
1	2	3	4	5		7	10	8		11				6	9													16
1	2	3	4	5			7	8	10	11				6	9													17
1	2	3	4	5		7		8		11				6	9					10								18
1	2	3	4	5		7		8	9	11				6						10								19
1	2	3	4	5				8		7				6		11				10						9		20
1	2	3	4	5				8						6	9					10						7	11	21
1	2	3	4	5				6							9					10		8				7	11	22
1	2	3	4	5			8	6		11					9					10						7		23
1	3		4					8					5	6	9			2		10						7	11	24
1	3		4	5					8					6	9			2		10						7	11	25
1		3		5		7			8	11			4	6	9			2		10								26
1		11	4	5		7	10	8	9		3			6				2										27
1		3	4	5		7		8	10					6	9			2									11	28
1			4	5		7		8	10		3			6	9		2		11									29
1			4	5		7	8		10		3				9		6	2									11	30
1	3			5		7	8		10	11	2				9		6	4										31
1	3		4	5			8	7	10	11	2				9		6											32
1	3		4	5			8	7	10	11	2				9		6											33
1			4	5	8	7			10	11	2				9		6						3					34
1	3		4	5			8		10	11	2				9		6				7							35
1	3		4				8	7	10	11	2		5		9		6											36
1	3						8	4	10	11	2		5		9		6				7							37
1							8	4	10	11	2			3	9		6				7			5				38
1			4				8		10	11			5	3	9		6				7		2					39
1			4	5			8		10	11	2			3			6				7					9		40
1			4	5					8	11	2			3	9		6			10	7							41
1			4	5				2	8	11	3				9		6			10	7							42
42	28	16	38	28	13	16	23	33	29	29	17	4	10	24	34	4	14	7	1	11	12	1	2	1	1	7	17	
		1	2		1		10	7	9						26	1				2							6	

1 own-goal

1		3	4	5				8	10					6	9			2								7	11	3
1	2	3		5				4	8					6	9					10						7	11	4
2	1	2	1	2				2	2					2	2			1		1						2	2	
									1						3												1	

1947-48

Manager: Billy Frith

1	Aug	23	(h)	Luton T	W 4-1	Lowrie 4	25,355
2		25	(h)	Birmingham C	L 0-1		30,465
3		30	(a)	Brentford	W 4-1	Lowrie 3, Murphy	19,087
4	Sep	3	(a)	Birmingham C	D 1-1	Roberts	36,000
5		6	(h)	Leicester C	L 0-1		28,628
6		10	(a)	West Brom A	L 1-3	Roberts	21,421
7		13	(a)	Leeds U	L 1-2	Dearson	30,462
8		15	(h)	West Brom A	W 1-0	Roberts	19,220
9		20	(h)	Fulham	W 5-2	Roberts 2, Newsome 2, Dearson	20,216
10		27	(a)	West Ham U	L 0-1		25,000
11	Oct	4	(a)	Newcastle U	D 0-0		55,569
12		11	(h)	Bury	D 0-0		25,577
13		18	(a)	Southampton	L 1-3	Roberts (pen)	21,767
14		25	(h)	Doncaster R	W 1-0	D.Simpson	26,056
15	Nov	1	(a)	Nottingham F	L 0-4		26,083
16		8	(h)	Bradford	W 5-0	Lowrie 4, Dearson	21,579
17		15	(a)	Cardiff C	D 1-1	Lockhart	38,000
18		22	(h)	Sheffield W	W 3-1	Dearson, Murphy, Lockhart	21,817
19		29	(a)	Tottenham H	L 1-2	Lockhart	41,483
20	Dec	6	(h)	Millwall	L 0-1		20,721
21		13	(a)	Chesterfield	L 3-4	Lowrie, Lockhart 2	15,888
22		20	(a)	Luton T	W 3-2	Lowrie 2, Cooke (og)	15,687
23		25	(h)	Barnsley	W 3-2	Murphy 2, Lowrie	27,613
24		26	(a)	Barnsley	W 1-0	Murphy	18,866
25	Jan	3	(h)	Brentford	W 3-0	Lowrie 2, Dearson	20,180
26		17	(a)	Leicester C	D 2-2	Warner, Dearson	27,168
27		31	(h)	Leeds U	L 1-2	Dearson	22,270
28	Feb	14	(h)	West Ham U	L 0-1		24,851
29		21	(h)	Newcastle U	D 1-1	Lowrie	22,047
30		28	(a)	Bury	D 0-0		15,475
31	Mar	6	(h)	Southampton	L 0-1		23,687
32		13	(a)	Doncaster R	D 0-0		24,060
33		20	(h)	Nottingham F	D 1-1	McIntosh	16,536
34		27	(a)	Bradford	D 2-2	Roberts, Murphy	16,700
35		29	(a)	Plymouth A	L 0 1		26,000
36		30	(h)	Plymouth A	D 0-0		19,301
37	Apr	3	(h)	Cardiff C	W 1-0	Roberts	26,175
38		10	(a)	Sheffield W	D 1-1	Murphy	38,695
39		17	(h)	Tottenham H	D 1-1	McIntosh	18,230
40		24	(a)	Millwall	L 2-6	Roberts, Lockhart	12,000
41		28	(a)	Fulham	W 2-0	Warner, McIntosh	7,000
42	May	1	(h)	Chesterfield	W 3-0	Warner, Roberts, Gardner	12,193

FINAL LEAGUE POSITION: 10th in Division Two

Appearances
Goals

FA Cup

3	Jan	10	(h)	Walsall	W 2-1	Warner 2	34,278
4		24	(a)	Luton T	L 2-3	Lockhart (pen), Dearson	23,982

Appearances
Goals

Wood	Tooze	Mason R	Snape	Mason G	Dearson	Simpson	Barratt	Lowrie	Roberts	Ashall	Murphy	Elliott	Dobbs	Smith S	Alderton	Cox	Lovering	Soden	Warner	Lockhart	Bett	Newsome	Gardner	McIntosh	Coen	Lewis	Davidson	Smith N	Betts	
1	2	3	4	5	6	7	8	9	10	11																				1
1	2	3	4	5	6	7		9	10	11	8																			2
1	2	3	4	5	6	7		9	8	11	10																			3
1	2	3	4	5	6	7		9	8	11	10																			4
1		3	4	5		7	6	9	10	11	8	2																		5
1		3			6		8	9	10	11		2		4		5						7								6
1		3			6	7	8	9	10	11		2		4		5														7
1		3			6	7	9		10	11			2	4		5						8								8
1		3		5	6	7	9		10				2	4								8							11	9
1	2	3		5	6	7	9		10					4								8			11					10
1	2	3		5	6	7	8	9	10					4								11								11
1	2	3		5	6	7	8	9	10					4						11										12
1	2	6		5		7	9		10			3		4						11		8								13
1		3		5	6	7		9			10	2			4					11		8								14
1	2	3		5		7	4	8	9		10				6					11										15
1		3	4		8	7	2	9			10	5			6					11										16
1		3	4		8	7	2				10	5			6					11								9		17
1		3	4		8	7	2				10	5			6					11								9		18
1		3	4		8	7	2				10	5			6					11								9		19
1		3	4		5	7	2	9			10				6					11							8			20
1		3	4	5	8	7	2	9			10			6						11										21
1		3	4	5	8		2	9			10			6					7	11										22
1		3	4	5	8		2	9			10			6					7	11										23
1		3	4	5	8		2	9			10			6					7	11										24
1		3	4	5	8		2	9			10			6					7	11										25
1		3		5	9		2				10				4		6		7	11							8			26
1		3	4	5	8	7	10		9				2	6						11										27
1		3	4	5	8	7	2	9			10			6						11										28
1		3		5		7	2	9			8			6	4					11				10						29
1		3		5		7	2	9			10				4		6			11				8						30
1		3		5		7	2	9			10				4		6			11				8						31
1		3		5		7	2		9		10				4		6			11				8						32
1		3		5		7	2		9		10				4		6			11				8						33
1		3		5	4	7	2		9		10			6						11				8						34
1		3		5	4	7	2		9		10			6						11				8						35
1		3		5	4		2		9		10			6						7			11	8						36
1	3			5	6		2		9		10			4						11	7			8						37
1	3			5			2		9		10			6	4					11				8		7				38
1	3			5	8		2		9					6	4					11				10		7				39
1	3			5			2		10					6	4			9		11			8			7				40
1	3			5			2		9					6		4			7	11	10			8						41
1	3			5			2		9					6		4			7	11			10	8						42
42	15	36	17	34	30	29	38	22	26	8	28	9	3	25	16	5	5	1	7	31	2	7	3	13	1	3	2	3	1	
					7	1		18	10		7								3	6		2	1	3						

1 own-goal

Wood	Tooze	Mason R	Snape	Mason G	Dearson	Simpson	Barratt	Lowrie	Roberts	Ashall	Murphy	Elliott	Dobbs	Smith S	Alderton	Cox	Lovering	Soden	Warner	Lockhart	Bett	Newsome	Gardner	McIntosh	Coen	Lewis	Davidson	Smith N	Betts	
1		3	4	5	8		2		9		10			6					7	11										3
1		3	4	5	9		2				10			6					7	11							8			4
2		2	2	2	2		2		1		2			2					2	2							1			
					1														2	1										

1948-49

Manager: Billy Frith, Harry Storer (from 29 November 1948).

1	Aug	21	(a)	Brentford	D	2-2	Warner, Roberts	26,031
2		23	(h)	Tottenham H	W	2-0	Roberts, Murphy	21,144
3		28	(h)	Leicester C	L	1-2	Roberts	32,641
4		30	(a)	Tottenham H	L	0-4		31,764
5	Sep	4	(a)	Leeds U	L	1-4	Bett	29,559
6		6	(h)	West Ham U	W	1-0	Roberts	16,494
7		11	(h)	Bradford	W	2-0	Roberts, Gardner	16,375
8		13	(a)	West Ham U	D	2-2	D.Simpson 2	18,000
9		18	(h)	Sheffield W	L	3-4	Roberts, Murphy 2	23,790
10		25	(a)	Lincoln C	L	0-1		14,821
11	Oct	2	(h)	Chesterfield	L	0-2		17,699
12		9	(a)	Southampton	L	2-5	Warner, Roberts	23,362
13		16	(h)	Barnsley	W	4-0	D.Simpson, Roberts, Murphy 2	15,709
14		23	(a)	Grimsby T	L	1-4	Murphy	15,000
15		30	(h)	Nottingham F	L	1-2	Murphy	20,369
16	Nov	6	(a)	Fulham	L	0-1		25,000
17		13	(h)	Plymouth A	D	1-1	Roberts	14,153
18		20	(a)	Blackburn R	L	0-2		22,800
19		27	(h)	Cardiff C	L	0-1		22,114
20	Dec	4	(a)	Queen's Park R	W	3-0	Roberts, Lockhart 2	16,500
21		11	(h)	Luton T	W	2-0	N.Simpson, Murphy	19,947
22		18	(h)	Brentford	W	2-1	Dearson, Roberts	21,284
23		25	(a)	Bury	W	2-0	Roberts, Murphy	15,603
24		27	(h)	Bury	W	2-1	Murphy, Lockhart	32,323
25	Jan	1	(a)	Leicester C	L	1-3	Dearson	33,230
26		15	(h)	Leeds U	W	4-1	Jamieson, Roberts 2, Lockhart	23,670
27		22	(a)	Bradford	L	1-2	Horsman (og)	17,624
28	Feb	5	(a)	Sheffield W	L	1-2	Roberts	36,171
29		19	(h)	Lincoln C	W	1-0	Murphy	23,448
30		26	(a)	Chesterfield	D	0-0		15,000
31	Mar	5	(h)	Southampton	D	2-2	Roberts, Murphy	21,920
32		12	(a)	Barnsley	D	1-1	Roberts	15,200
33		19	(h)	Grimsby T	W	4-1	Warner, Roberts 2, Murphy	22,260
34		26	(a)	Nottingham F	L	0-3		20,834
35	Apr	2	(h)	Fulham	W	1-0	Evans	26,365
36		9	(a)	Plymouth A	W	3-2	Marsh 3	17,083
37		16	(h)	Blackburn R	L	0-1		23,450
38		18	(a)	West Brom A	L	0-1		42,488
39		19	(h)	West Brom A	W	1-0	Lockhart	39,480
40		23	(a)	Cardiff C	L	0-3		27,000
41		30	(h)	Queen's Park R	D	1-1	Marsh	14,519
42	May	7	(a)	Luton T	L	0-2		13,705

FINAL LEAGUE POSITION: 16th in Division Two

Appearances

Goals

FA Cup

3	Jan	8	(a)	Torquay U	L	0-1		14,000

Appearances

Goals

Wood	Barratt	Mason R	Cox	Mason G	Simpson	Warner	Bett	Roberts	Murphy	Lockhart	Tooze	Dearson	Alderton	Smith	Snape	Simpson	McIntosh	Gardner	Marsh	Jamieson	Hill P	Evans	Shore	Soden	Bull	
1	2	3	4	5	6	7	8	9	10	11																1
1	2	3		5	6	7		9	10	11			4				8									2
1	2	3		5	6	7		9	10	11			4				8									3
1	2	3		5	6	7		9	10					4			8						11			4
1	2	3	5		6	7	8	9	10					4				11								5
1	8	3	4	5	6			9			2	10				7		11								6
1	8	3	5		6			9	10			2	4			7		11								7
1	8	3	5		6			9	10			2	4			7		11								8
1	8	3	5		6			9	10			2	4			7		11								9
1	2	3		5	6			9	10	11			4			7		8								10
1	8	3		5	6			9	10	11			4	2		7										11
1	9	3		5		7		10	11				6	2	4	8										12
1	2	3		5		7		9	11				6		4	8	10									13
1	2	3		5		7		9	11				6		4	8	10									14
1	2	3		5	6			9	10	11					4	7			8							15
1	2	3	5		6	7		9	11			10			4	8										16
1	2	3	5		6	7		9	11			10			4	8										17
1	2	3	5		6	7		9	10	11		8	4													18
1	2			5	6	7			9	11	3	10			4		8									19
1	2	3		5	6	7		9	10	11		8			4											20
1	2	3		5	6	7		9	10	11		8			4											21
1	2	3		5	6	7		9	10	11		8			4											22
1	2	3		5	6	7		9	10	11		8			4											23
1	2	3		5	6	7		9	10	11		8			4											24
1	2	3		5	6	7		9	10	11		8			4											25
1		3		5		7		9	10	11	2		6		4					8						26
1		3		5		7		9	10	11	2	6			4					8						27
1		3		5				9	10	11		2	6		4	7					8					28
1		3		5	6			9	10	11		2			4	7	8									29
1		3		5	6			9	10	11		2			4	7					8					30
1	2	3		5	6	7		9	10	11					4					8						31
1	2	3		5	6	7		9	10	11					4					8						32
1	2	3		5	6	7		9	10	11					4				8							33
1	2	3		5	6	7			10	11		8			4				9							34
1	2	3		5	6	7			10	11					4				8			9				35
1	2	3		5	6	7		9	10	11					4				8							36
1	2	3		5	6	7		9	10	11					4				8							37
1	9	3		5	6					11		2			4	7			10	8						38
1	9		2	5	6					11		3			4	7			10	8						39
1	2			5		7				11		3	6		4				10	8				9		40
1	2	3		5						11		6			4	7			9	8	10					41
1	2	3		5		7				11		6			4				10	8					9	42
42	37	39	10	35	33	29	2	34	36	31	4	24	14	4	30	18	7	6	11	9	3	1	1	1	1	
					1	3	1	19	13	5		2				3		1	4	1		1				

1 own-goal

1	2	3	6	5		7		9	10	11		8			4	3
1	1	1	1	1		1		1	1	1		1			1	

1949-50

Manager: Harry Storer

1	Aug	20	(h)	Sheffield U	L	2-4	Marsh, Murphy	26,414
2		24	(a)	Luton T	L	0-2		15,996
3		27	(a)	Grimsby T	L	2-3	Dearson, Murphy	20,000
4		29	(h)	Luton T	W	1-0	Roberts	22,641
5	Sep	3	(h)	Queen's Park R	D	0-0		22,610
6		7	(a)	Barnsley	L	3-4	Murphy, Lockhart 2	15,509
7		10	(a)	Preston NE	D	1-1	P.Hill	25,000
8		17	(h)	Swansea T	L	1-2	P.Hill	25,078
9		24	(a)	Leeds U	D	3-3	D.Simpson, Murphy, Lockhart	22,590
10	Oct	1	(h)	Southampton	L	1-2	Roberts	22,549
11		8	(h)	Bury	L	1-2	Warner	18,383
12		15	(a)	Tottenham H	L	1-3	Roberts	54,375
13		22	(h)	Cardiff C	W	2-1	Jamieson, Murphy	23,089
14		29	(a)	Blackburn R	W	1-0	Murphy	15,204
15	Nov	5	(h)	Brentford	D	1-1	Roberts	16,110
16		12	(a)	Hull C	L	1-2	Warner	40,170
17		26	(a)	Plymouth A	W	2-1	Barratt, Marsh	20,995
18	Dec	3	(h)	Chesterfield	W	3-0	Murphy 3	20,311
19		10	(a)	Bradford	D	2-2	N.Simpson, Marsh	9,928
20		17	(a)	Sheffield U	D	1-1	Murphy	21,463
21		24	(h)	Grimsby T	D	1-1	Murphy	24,058
22		26	(a)	Leicester C	L	0-1		37,903
23		27	(h)	Leicester C	L	1-2	G.Mason	36,981
24		31	(a)	Queen's Park R	L	0-2		16,768
25	Jan	14	(h)	Preston NE	D	0-0		21,046
26		21	(a)	Swansea T	W	2-1	Jamieson, Lockhart	20,320
27	Feb	4	(h)	Leeds U	L	0-4		22,990
28		11	(h)	Sheffield W	W	3-0	Allen, Roberts, Murphy	18,005
29		18	(a)	Southampton	D	1-1	Wilkins (og)	23,412
30		25	(a)	Bury	D	0-0		11,234
31	Mar	4	(h)	Tottenham H	L	0-1		36,296
32		11	(a)	Cardiff C	L	0-1		25,000
33		18	(h)	Blackburn R	D	1-1	Lockhart	21,280
34		25	(a)	Brentford	L	0-2		16,984
35	Apr	1	(h)	Plymouth A	W	3-0	Barratt, Warner, Lockhart	20,882
36		8	(a)	Chesterfield	W	1-0	Roberts	10,193
37		10	(a)	West Ham U	W	1-0	Roberts	11,000
38		11	(h)	West Ham U	W	5-1	Allen 2, Murphy 3	26,648
39		15	(h)	Hull C	W	2-0	Allen, Roberts	25,515
40		22	(a)	Sheffield W	D	1-1	Allen	44,035
41		29	(h)	Bradford	W	3-1	Allen 2, Lockhart	12,609
42	May	6	(h)	Barnsley	D	1-1	Allen	16,119

FINAL LEAGUE POSITION: 12th in Division Two

Appearances

Goals

FA Cup

3	Jan	7	(h)	Bolton W	L	1-2	Alderton	29,390

Appearances

Goals

Wood	Dearson	Mason R	Snape	Mason G	Simpson	Warner	Marsh	Roberts	Murphy	Lockhart	Timmins	Barratt	McDonnell	Bell	Cook	Alderton	Simpson	Lewis	Jamieson	Allen	Evans	Hill P	Chisholm	Hill J	Shore	Cox	
1	2	3	4	5	6		8	9	10	11							7										1
1		3	4	5	6	7	8	9	11		2				10												2
1	8	2	4	5	6	7		9	10	11				3													3
1	8	2	4	5	6	7		9	10	11				3													4
1	8	2	4	5	6	7			10	11				3							9						5
1	8	2	4	5	6	7			9	11				3								10					6
1		3		5	6	7			9	11	2				4				8			10					7
1		3		5	6	7			9	11	2				4				8			10					8
1	8			5	6			9	10	11	3	2			4		7										9
1	8			5	6			9	10	11	3	2			4		7										10
1				5		7		9	8	11	3	2			6	4						10					11
1		3		5		7		9	10	11		2			6	4			8								12
1		3		5	6	7		9	10	11			2		4				8								13
1		3		5	6	7		9	10	11			2		4				8								14
1		3		5	6			9	10	11			2		4		7		8								15
1	8	3	4	5	6	7		9	10				2											11			16
1	8	3	4	5	6	7	10		11			9	2														17
1	8	3	4	5	6	7	10		11			9	2														18
1	8	3	4	5	6	7	10		11			9	2														19
1	8	3	4	5	6	7	10		11			9	2														20
1	8	3	4	5	6	7	10		11			9	2														21
1	8	3		5	6		10		11			9	2		4			7									22
1	4	3		5	6				10	11		9	2					7	8								23
1	8	3		5	6	7	10		11			9	2		4												24
1		3		5	6	7		8	10				2								9				11	4	25
1				5	6	7			9	11	3		2						8			10				4	26
1				5	6	7			9	11	3		2						8	10						4	27
1		3			6			9	10	11	2	4	5				7			8							28
1		3			6			9	10	11	2	4	5				7			8							29
1		3			6			9	10	11	2	4	5				7			8							30
1		3			6			9	10	11	2	4	5				7			8							31
1		3							10	11	2	4	5			6		7		8	9						32
1		3							9	11	2	4	5		6			7		8			10				33
1		3			6	7			9	11	2	4	5							8			10				34
1		3			6	7		9		11	2	4	5							8			10				35
1		3			6	7		9	10	11	2	4	5							8							36
1		3			6	7		9	10	11	2	4	5							8							37
1		3			6	7		9	10	11	2	4			5					8							38
1		3		5	6	7		9	10	11	2	4								8							39
1		3			6	7		9	10	11	2	4	5							8							40
1		3			6	7		9		11	2	4	5							8			10				41
1		3			6	7		9		11	2		5		4					8			10				42
42	16	37	12	28	38	30	9	25	39	32	23	26	28	4	15	3	8	4	9	16	3	5	5	1	1	3	
	1			1	1	3	3	8	15	7		2					1		2	8		2					

1 own-goal

1	8	3		5	6	7		9	10				2			4								11			3
1	1	1		1	1	1		1	1				1			1								1			
																1											

1950-51

Manager: Harry Storer

1	Aug	19	(a)	Notts C	W 2-0	Warner, Chisholm	41,023
2		21	(h)	Leeds U	W 1-0	Roberts	30,226
3		26	(h)	Preston NE	W 1-0	Roberts	24,674
4		30	(a)	Leeds U	L 0-1		28,938
5	Sep	2	(a)	Bury	L 0-1		15,990
6		6	(a)	Birmingham C	D 1-1	Simpson	25,000
7		9	(h)	Queen's Park R	W 3-0	Chisholm 2, Lockhart	22,298
8		11	(h)	Birmingham C	W 3-1	Roberts 2, Chisholm	30,453
9		16	(a)	Chesterfield	D 1-1	Chisholm	16,035
10		23	(h)	Leicester C	W 2-1	Chisholm 2	33,240
11		30	(a)	Manchester C	L 0-1		40,839
12	Oct	7	(a)	Brentford	W 4-0	Simpson, Allen, Chisholm, Lockhart	19,731
13		14	(h)	Blackburn R	W 6-1	Allen 2, Roberts, Chisholm, Lockhart 2	34,915
14		21	(a)	Hull C	W 2-0	Warner, Roberts	33,263
15		28	(h)	Doncaster R	W 3-1	Roberts, Chisholm, Hainsworth (og)	32,713
16	Nov	4	(a)	West Ham U	L 2-3	Allen, Roberts	26,000
17		11	(h)	Swansea T	W 3-1	Roberts, Chisholm 2	29,672
18		18	(a)	Southampton	L 4-5	Allen, Roberts, Chisholm, Lockhart	22,438
19		25	(h)	Barnsley	D 3-3	Allen 2, Chisholm	28,681
20	Dec	2	(a)	Sheffield U	L 0-2		29,127
21		9	(h)	Luton T	W 4-1	Allen, Chisholm 3	22,044
22		16	(h)	Notts C	L 1-2	Allen	25,114
23		23	(a)	Preston NE	D 1-1	Chisholm	30,031
24		25	(a)	Cardiff C	L 1-2	Barratt	34,000
25		26	(h)	Cardiff C	W 2-1	Chisholm 2	33,195
26		30	(h)	Bury	W 5-2	Warner, Allen, Briggs, Chisholm 2	27,584
27	Jan	13	(a)	Queen's Park R	L 1-3	Briggs	17,279
28		20	(h)	Chesterfield	W 1-0	Warner	24,897
29	Feb	3	(a)	Leicester C	L 0-3		33,485
30		17	(h)	Manchester C	L 0-2		29,205
31		24	(h)	Brentford	D 3-3	Barratt, Allen, Briggs	22,885
32	Mar	3	(a)	Blackburn R	L 0-1		31,144
33		10	(h)	Hull C	W 4-1	Allen 2, Roberts, Chisholm	22,550
34		17	(a)	Doncaster R	L 1-2	Roberts	18,464
35		23	(a)	Grimsby T	W 2-1	Allen, Roberts	18,715
36		24	(h)	West Ham U	W 1-0	J.Hill	21,881
37		27	(h)	Grimsby T	W 1-0	Lockhart	26,442
38		31	(a)	Swansea T	L 1-2	Beech (og)	20,567
39	Apr	7	(h)	Southampton	D 2-2	Roberts, Lockhart	20,156
40		14	(a)	Barnsley	L 0-3		12,351
41		21	(h)	Sheffield U	L 2-3	Roberts, Chisholm	17,533
42		18	(a)	Luton T	D 1-1	Hart	12,060
FINAL LEAGUE POSITION: 7th in Division Two							Appearances
							Goals

FA Cup

3	Jan	6	(a)	Sunderland	L 0-2		36,988
							Appearances
							Goals

Wood	Taylor	Timmins	Springthorpe	Mason	Bell	Barratt	Alderton	McDonnell	Simpson	Cook	Warner	Allen	Hill P	Roberts	Evans	Briggs	Chisholm	Hart	Lockhart	Hill J	Jamieson	
1		2		3		4		5	6		7	8		9			10		11			1
1		2		3		4		5	6		7	8		9			10		11			2
1		2		3		4		5	6		7	8		9			10		11			3
1		2		3		4		5	6		7	8		9			10		11			4
1		2		3		4		5	6		7			9			10		11		8	5
1		2		3		4		5	6		7	8		9			10		11			6
1		2		3		4		5	6		7	8		9			10		11			7
1		2		3		4		5	6		7	8		9			10		11			8
1		2		3		4		5	6		7	8		9			10		11			9
1		2		3		4		5	6		7	8			9		10		11			10
1		2		3		4		5	6		7	8		9			10		11			11
1		2		3		4		5	6		7	8		9			10		11			12
1		2		3		4		5	6		7	8		9			10		11			13
1		2		3		4		5	6		7		8	9			10		11			14
1		2		3			4	5	6		7	8		9			10		11			15
1		2		3		4	6	5			7	8		9			10			11		16
1		2		3		4	6	5			7	8		9			10		11			17
1		2		3		4	6	5			7	8		9			10		11			18
1		2		3		4	6	5			7	8		9			10		11			19
1		2		3		4		5		6	7	8		9			10		11			20
1		2		3		4		5		6	7	8		9			10		11			21
1		2		3		4	6	5			7	8		9			10		11			22
1			2	3		4	6	5			7	8			9		10		11			23
1			2	3		4	6	5			7	8			9		10		11			24
1			2	3		4	6	5			7	8			9	9	10		11			25
1		2	3			4	6	5			7	8				9	10		11			26
1		2	3			4	6	5			7	8				9	10		11			27
1		2			3	4	6	5			7	8					10		11			28
1			2		3	4	6	5			7	8		9		9	10		11			29
1		2		3		4	6	5			7	8				9	10		11			30
1		2		3		4		5	6		7	8				9	10		11			31
1			2	3			4	5		6	7	8					10		11			32
1			2	3			4	5		6	7	8		9			10		11			33
1			2	3			4	5		6	7	8		9			10			11		34
1			2	3			4	5		6	7	8		9				10		11		35
1			2	3			4	5		6	7	8		9				10		11		36
1		2		3			4	5		6	7	8		9				10	11			37
1		2		3			4	5		6	7	8		9			10		11			38
1		2		3			4	5		6	7	8		9			10		11			39
1		2		3			4	5		6		8		9			10		11		7	40
1		2			3		4	5		6	7	8		9			10		11			41
	1	2	3				4	5		6	7	8				9		10	11			42
41	1	33	12	36	3	30	25	42	16	13	41	40	1	31	4	7	38	4	38	4	2	
						2			2		4	14		15		3	24	1	7	1		

2 own-goals

1		2	3			4	6	5			7	8		9			10		11			3
1		1	1			1	1	1			1	1		1			1		1			

1951-52

Manager: Harry Storer

1	Aug	18	(a)	Notts C	L	1-2	Roberts	34,001
2		20	(h)	Swansea T	W	3-2	Allen, Roberts, Chisholm	23,962
3		25	(h)	Queen's Park R	D	0-0		22,649
4		30	(a)	Swansea T	L	1-7	Chisholm	19,874
5	Sep	1	(a)	Blackburn R	W	1-0	Briggs	17,300
6		3	(h)	Rotherham U	W	2-1	Briggs 2	20,710
7		8	(h)	Hull C	L	1-4	Briggs	25,325
8		15	(a)	Barnsley	L	0-1		13,392
9		22	(h)	Sheffield U	D	1-1	Roberts	22,798
10		29	(a)	West Ham U	L	1-3	Allen	27,000
11	Oct	6	(a)	Cardiff C	L	1-4	N.Simpson	28,000
12		13	(h)	Birmingham C	D	1-1	Allen	23,580
13		20	(a)	Leicester C	L	1-3	Roberts	26,000
14		27	(h)	Nottingham F	D	3-3	Roberts 3	19,249
15	Nov	3	(a)	Brentford	L	0-1		23,050
16		10	(h)	Doncaster R	L	1-2	Roberts	19,375
17		17	(a)	Everton	L	1-4	Chisholm	29,945
18		24	(h)	Southampton	W	3-1	Roberts, Chisholm, Lockhart	14,540
19	Dec	1	(a)	Sheffield W	L	1-3	Lockhart	35,739
20		8	(h)	Leeds U	W	4-2	Chisholm 2, Lockhart 2	14,613
21		15	(h)	Notts C	L	0-2		20,274
22		22	(a)	Queen's Park R	W	4-1	Roberts, Chisholm 2, Lockhart	12,783
23		25	(a)	Bury	W	2-0	Allen, Lockhart	16,001
24		26	(h)	Bury	W	3-0	Roberts 2, Lockhart	26,538
25		29	(h)	Blackburn R	L	1-2	Nutt	22,409
26	Jan	5	(a)	Hull C	L	0-5		26,648
27		19	(h)	Barnsley	D	0-0		17,552
28		26	(a)	Sheffield U	W	2-1	Lockhart 2	25,464
29	Feb	9	(h)	West Ham U	L	1-2	R.Mason	19,486
30		16	(h)	Cardiff C	W	2-1	Chisholm, Lockhart	26,397
31		23	(a)	Rotherham U	W	1-0	Chisholm	17,393
32	Mar	1	(a)	Birmingham C	L	1-3	Jamieson	33,000
33		8	(h)	Leicester C	L	1-3	Lockhart	30,244
34		15	(a)	Nottingham F	L	1-3	Lowrie	31,036
35		22	(h)	Brentford	W	2-1	Brown, Lowrie	27,577
36		29	(a)	Doncaster R	L	0-1		8,575
37	Apr	5	(h)	Everton	W	2-1	Warner, Lowrie	13,489
38		12	(a)	Southampton	D	2-2	Lockhart 2	20,790
39		14	(a)	Luton T	L	1-2	Jamieson	15,216
40		15	(h)	Luton T	W	5-2	Dorman 2, Brown, Lockhart 2	26,162
41		19	(h)	Sheffield W	L	0-2		36,331
42		26	(a)	Leeds U	L	1-3	Brown	16,322

FINAL LEAGUE POSITION: 21st in Division Two

Appearances

Goals

FA Cup

3	Jan	12	(a)	Leicester C	D	1-1	Allen	36,116
R		14	(h)	Leicester C	W	4-1	Roberts, Chisholm, Lockhart 2	24,240
4	Feb	2	(a)	Burnley	L	0-2		41,056

Appearances

Goals

Wood	Taylor	Gilbert	Spencer	Timmins	Mason	Cook	McDonnell	Jones	Bell	Harrison	Barratt	Alderton	Dorman	Mason	Kirk	Simpson	Bradbury	Warner	Lewis	Jamieson	Nutt	Allen	Hart	Lowrie	Roberts	Briggs	Brown	Chisholm	Hill P	Lockhart	Gray	Cox	Harvey	
1				2	3		5				4					6		7				8			9			10		11				1
1				2	3		5					4				6		7				8			9			10		11				2
1				2	3		5					4				6		7				8			9			10		11				3
1				2	3		5					4				6		7				8			9			10		11				4
1					2	4	5		3							6		7		8			10			9				11				5
1					2	4	5		3							6		7		8			10			9				11				6
1					2	4	5		3							6		7		8			10			9				11				7
1					3	6	5	2				4							7			8				9		10		11				8
1					3	2	5						4			6			7			8			9			10		11				9
1					3	2	5						4			6			7			8			9			10		11				10
	1				3	2	5						4			6		7				8			9				10	11				11
	1				3	2	5									6		7				8			9				10	11	4			12
	1			2	3		5									6		7				8			9				10	11	4			13
	1			2	3		5										6	7				8			9			10		11		4		14
	1				3	2	5									6		7					8		9			10		11			4	15
	1				3	2	5									6		7					10		9			8		11			4	16
	1				3	2	5									6		7				8			9			10		11			4	17
	1			2	3								4	5		6		7				8			9			10		11				18
	1				3	2							4	5		6		7				8			9			10		11				19
	1				3	2	5						4			6		7				8			9			10		11				20
	1				3	2	5						4			6		7				8			9			10		11				21
	1						2			3			4	5		6		7				8			9			10		11				22
	1						2			3			4	5		6				7		8			9			10		11				23
	1						2			3			4	5		6				7		8			9			10		11				24
	1						2			3			4	5		6					7	8			9			10		11				25
	1						2			3			4	5		6					7	8			9			10		11				26
	1				2	4	5			3						6				7		8			9			10		11				27
	1				2	4	5			3						6		7				8			9				10	11				28
	1				3	4	2							5		6		7				8	9					10		11				29
	1				2		5			3			4			6		7				8		9				10		11				30
	1				2	8	5			3			4			6				7				9				10		11				31
	1				2		5			3			4			6				7		8		9				10		11				32
	1					4	5	2		3						6		7						8	9				10	11				33
	1				2	8				3			4		5	6					7			10			9			11				34
		1			3	4	2								5	6		7				8		10			9			11				35
		1			3	6	2						4		5			7				8		10			9			11				36
		1			3	6	2						4		5			7		8				10			9			11				37
		1			3	6	2						4		5			7		8				10			9			11				38
	1				3	6	2						4		5			7		8				10			9			11				39
	1				3	6	2						4		5			7		8				10			9			11				40
			1		3	6	2						4		5	10		7		8							9			11				41
		1			3		2						4		5	6		7		8				10			9			11				42
10	26	5	1	7	36	27	39	2	3	12	1	4	23	8	9	35	1	31	3	14	3	28	6	12	25	4	9	25	5	42	2	1	3	
					1								2			1		1		2	1	4		3	12	4	3	10		15				

Wood	Taylor	Gilbert	Spencer	Timmins	Mason	Cook	McDonnell	Jones	Bell	Harrison	Barratt	Alderton	Dorman	Mason	Kirk	Simpson	Bradbury	Warner	Lewis	Jamieson	Nutt	Allen	Hart	Lowrie	Roberts	Briggs	Brown	Chisholm	Hill P	Lockhart	Gray	Cox	Harvey	
	1					4	2			3				5		6					7	8			9			10		11				3
	1					4	2			3				5		6					7	8			9			10		11				R
	1				2	4	5			3						6					7	8			9				10	11				4
	3				1	3	3			3				2		3					3	3			3			2	1	3				
																						1			1			1		2				

1952-53

Manager: Harry Storer

1	Aug	23	(h)	Swindon T	L 1-2	Lockhart	18,214
2		28	(a)	Leyton O	W 2-1	Lowrie, Brown	11,797
3		30	(a)	Queen's Park R	W 4-0	Lowrie, Harrison 2, P.Hill	14,238
4	Sep	1	(h)	Leyton O	W 3-0	P.Hill 3	17,322
5		6	(h)	Shrewsbury T	D 0-0		17,233
6		11	(a)	Northampton T	L 1-3	P.Hill	13,280
7		13	(a)	Walsall	D 1-1	Lowrie	9,915
8		15	(h)	Northampton T	D 1-1	Dorman	18,204
9		20	(h)	Gillingham	W 2-1	Warner, Lowrie	12,255
10		25	(a)	Newport C	D 4-4	Dorman, Lowrie, P.Hill 2	10,928
11		27	(a)	Millwall	L 0-2		19,995
12		29	(h)	Exeter C	W 1-0	P.Hill	8,588
13	Oct	4	(h)	Bristol R	D 1-1	Warner	19,052
14		11	(a)	Ipswich T	L 0-3		13,775
15		18	(h)	Reading	W 4-0	Nutt, Brown, P.Hill, Johnson	15,450
16		25	(a)	Bournemouth	L 0-3		13,792
17	Nov	1	(h)	Southend U	W 2-1	Brown, P.Hill	12,623
18		8	(a)	Watford	D 1-1	Dorman	18,929
19		15	(h)	Brighton & HA	W 3-1	Brown, P.Hill, McCafferty (og)	11,863
20		29	(h)	Crystal P	W 4-2	Dorman 3, George (og)	11,625
21	Dec	13	(h)	Torquay U	W 7-2	Dorman 3, Brown 3, Waldock	9,901
22		20	(a)	Swindon T	W 3-2	Dorman 2, Brown	7,362
23		26	(a)	Aldershot	L 1-4	Warner	7,262
24		27	(h)	Aldershot	W 3-0	Dorman 2, Brown	16,997
25	Jan	3	(h)	Queen's Park R	W 2-0	Brown 2	15,063
26		15	(h)	Norwich C	W 2-1	Warner, Brown	6,840
27		17	(a)	Shrewsbury T	L 0-1		12,261
28		24	(h)	Walsall	W 3-1	Dorman 2, Brown	13,881
29		31	(a)	Norwich C	D 1-1	Brown	16,387
30	Feb	7	(a)	Gillingham	D 0-0		10,383
31		14	(h)	Millwall	W 4-1	Brown, Lowrie 3	14,544
32		21	(a)	Bristol R	L 2-5	Kirk, Brown	28,614
33		28	(h)	Ipswich T	W 2-0	Warner, Lowrie	14,040
34	Mar	7	(a)	Reading	L 0-1		11,697
35		14	(h)	Bournemouth	L 2-3	Brown, Waldock	13,264
36		21	(a)	Southend U	L 0-1		9,500
37		28	(h)	Watford	W 1-0	Johnson	8,059
38	Apr	3	(a)	Colchester U	W 1-0	Brown	10,618
39		4	(a)	Brighton & HA	D 1-1	J.Hill	14,771
40		6	(h)	Colchester U	D 2-2	R.Mason, Simpson	11,284
41		11	(h)	Newport C	L 0-1		11,204
42		18	(a)	Crystal P	D 2-2	Dorman, J.Hill	13,120
43		22	(a)	Exeter C	L 0-1		7,357
44		25	(h)	Bristol C	D 2-2	Thomas, P.Hill	11,011
45		28	(a)	Bristol C	L 0-1		10,404
46	May	2	(a)	Torquay U	L 1-2	Dorman	6,892

FINAL LEAGUE POSITION: 6th in Division Three South

Appearances

Goals

FA Cup

1	Nov	22	(h)	Bristol C	W 2-0	Brown, P.Hill	17,062
2	Dec	6	(a)	Bishop Auckland	W 4-1	Dorman, Waldock, Johnson, Marshall (og)	16,319
3	Jan	10	(a)	Plymouth A	L 1-4	Warner	23,799

Appearances

Goals

Gilbert	Taylor	Spencer	Matthews	McDonnell	Timmins	Jones	Quinney	Mason	Harrison	Dorman	Harvey	Cook	Kirk	Simpson	Austin	Jamieson	Warner	Lewis	Nutt	Brown	Lowrie	Allen	Thomas	Hill P	Waldock	Lockhart	Hill J	Johnson	
1				2				3		4			5	6		8	7			9		10				11			1
1				2				3			4	6	5				7			9	8			10		11			2
1				2				3	9		4	6	5				7				8			10		11			3
1				2				3	9		4	6	5				7				8			10		11			4
1				2				3	9		4	6	5				7				8			10		11			5
1				2				3	9	8	4	6	5				7							10		11			6
1				2				3				4	5	6		7					9	8		10		11			7
	1			5	2			3		8		4	9	6				7						10		11			8
		1		5	2			3		8		6	4				7				9			10			11		9
		1			2			3		8		4	5	6			7				9			10				11	10
		1			2			3		8		4	5	6			7				9			10	11				11
		1			2			3		8		4	5	6			7		11		9			10					12
		1			2			3		4			5	6			7			9		8		10				11	13
		1		5	2			3		4				6			7			9		8		10				11	14
		1		2					3			4	5	6			7		8	9				10				11	15
		1		2					3			4	5	6			7		8	9				10				11	16
1				2				3		8		4	5	6			7			9				10				11	17
		1		2				3		8		4	5	6			7			9				10				11	18
		1		2				3		8		4	5	6			7			9				10				11	19
		1		2				3		8		4	5	6			7			9					10			11	20
		1		2				3		8		4	5	6			7			9					10			11	21
		1		2				3		8		4	5	6			7			9				10				11	22
		1		2				3		8		4	5	6			7			9				10				11	23
		1		2				3		8		4	5	6			7			9					10			11	24
		1		2				3		8		4	5	6					7	9				10				11	25
	1			2				3		8		4	5	6			7			9					10			11	26
	1			2					3	8		4	5	6			7			9					10			11	27
	1			2					3	8	4		5	6			7			9				10				11	28
	1			2	3					8		4	5	6			7			9				10				11	29
	1			2	3					8		4	5	6			7			9	10							11	30
	1			2				3		8	4	6	5				7			9	10							11	31
	1			2				3		8	4	6	5				7			9	10							11	32
		1		2				3		8	4	6	5				7			9	10							11	33
		1		2				3			4	6	5				7			9	8			10				11	34
		1		2				3		8		4	5	6			7			9					10			11	35
			1	2				3				4	5	6			7			9				8	10			11	36
			1	2				3		8	4		5	6			7			9					10			11	37
			1	2			3			8	4		5	6						7			9	10			11		38
			1	2				3		8	4		5	6						7			9	10			11		39
1				2				3		8	4		5	6						7			9	10			11		40
			1	2				3		8	4		5		6				7	9				10			11		41
			1	5		2		3		8	4			6					7				9	10			11		42
			1	5	2			3		8	4			6					7				9	10			11		43
			1	5	2			3			4			6					7		8		9	10			11		44
			1	5			2	3		8	4				6				7				9	10			11		45
			1	5			2	3		8	4					6			7				9	10			11		46
9	8	19	10	42	11	1	3	39	8	36	20	32	40	33	2	3	34	1	10	31	15	4	8	34	9	8	10	26	
								1	2	17			1	1			5		1	18	9		1	12	2	1	2	2	

2 own-goals

		1		2				3		8		4	5	6			7			9				10				11	1
		1		2				3		8		4	5	6			7			9					10			11	2
		1		2				3		8		4	5	6			7			9				10				11	3
		3		3				3		3		3	3	3			3			3				2	1			3	
										1							1			1				1	1			1	

1 own-goal

1953-54

Manager: Harry Storer (resigned 4 November 1953), Jack Fairbrother (from 11 January 1954).

1	Aug	19	(a)	Aldershot	L	2-4	Nutt, J.Hill	7,487
2		22	(h)	Leyton O	W	4-0	Dorman, Brown 2, J.Hill	11,661
3		26	(a)	Gillingham	L	0-2		14,401
4		29	(a)	Reading	L	3-4	Kirk, Bradbury, Johnson	12,086
5		31	(h)	Gillingham	W	2-1	Bradbury, Brown	11,385
6	Sep	5	(h)	Southend U	W	1-0	Dorman	13,051
7		9	(a)	Bournemouth	L	0-1		11,000
8		12	(a)	Brighton & HA	L	1-3	Waldock	20,620
9		14	(h)	Bournemouth	W	2-0	Bradbury, Dutton	10,544
10		19	(h)	Watford	L	0-1		13,752
11		21	(a)	Millwall	W	2-1	Austin, Dutton	7,564
12		26	(a)	Torquay U	D	1-1	Dutton	9,000
13		28	(h)	Millwall	D	0-0		10,151
14	Oct	3	(h)	Northampton T	D	0-0		17,528
15		10	(a)	Colchester U	W	3-0	Brown 3	8,174
16		17	(h)	Crystal P	D	0-0		13,536
17		24	(a)	Bristol C	L	0-1		16,184
18		31	(h)	Aldershot	W	2-1	Brown, Waldock	8,995
19	Nov	7	(a)	Swindon T	D	1-1	Dorman	10,656
20		14	(h)	Walsall	W	2-0	Nutt, Brown	11,064
21		28	(h)	Exeter C	W	2-0	Brown, Bradbury	10,224
22	Dec	5	(a)	Newport C	L	1-2	Nutt	10,572
23		19	(a)	Leyton O	L	0-1		8,077
24		25	(h)	Ipswich T	L	1-3	Waldock	16,820
25		26	(a)	Ipswich T	L	1-4	Nutt	18,922
26	Jan	2	(h)	Reading	D	1-1	Johnson	8,110
27		9	(a)	Shrewsbury T	D	1-1	Dorman	7,000
28		16	(a)	Southend U	D	2-2	Brown, Waldock	6,700
29		23	(h)	Brighton & HA	L	1-2	Dorman	10,175
30		30	(a)	Queen's Park R	W	3-0	Brown, Bradbury, Poppitt (og)	5,247
31	Feb	6	(a)	Watford	L	0-1		9,630
32		13	(h)	Torquay U	W	4-0	Brown, Bradbury, Waldock 2	10,280
33		20	(a)	Northampton T	W	1-0	Nutt	10,539
34		27	(h)	Colchester U	W	2-1	Jamieson (pen), Bradbury	11,852
35	Mar	6	(a)	Crystal P	L	1-3	Dorman	10,453
36		13	(h)	Shrewsbury T	W	2-1	Brown 2	7,883
37		20	(a)	Exeter C	L	0-4		7,800
38		27	(h)	Swindon T	D	0-0		7,493
39	Apr	3	(a)	Walsall	L	0-1		8,728
40		10	(h)	Newport C	L	1-2	Brown	7,940
41		12	(h)	Queen's Park R	W	3-1	Brown 2, J.Hill	4,785
42		17	(a)	Norwich C	L	1-2	Brown	15,913
43		19	(a)	Southampton	L	1-2	Kirk (pen)	9,664
44		20	(h)	Southampton	W	2-1	Nutt, Dorman	9,640
45		24	(h)	Bristol C	W	3-0	Dorman, Brown 2	7,439
46		26	(h)	Norwich C	W	1-0	Nutt	6,923

FINAL LEAGUE POSITION: 14th in Division Three South

Appearances
Goals

FA Cup

1	Nov	21	(a)	Brighton & HA	L	1-5	Dorman	20,436

Appearances
Goals

Matthews	Taylor	McDonnell	Kirk	Jones	Timmins	Mason	Cook	Harvey	Jamieson	Simpson	Austin	Nutt	Warner	Brown	Dorman	Bradbury	Hawkings	Thomas	Dutton	Waldock	Hill P	Hill J	Johnson	
1		2	5			3	4			6		7		9	8	10						11		1
1		5	2			3		4		6		7		9	8	10						11		2
1		5	2			3		4		6		7		9		8					10	11		3
1		5	2			3		4		6		7		9		8					10		11	4
1			5	2		3			4	6		7		9		8					10		11	5
	1		5	2		3			4	6		7			10	8		9					11	6
	1	5	3	2					4	6		7				8		9		10		11		7
	1	5	3	2					4	6		7				8		9		10		11		8
	1	5	3	2					4		6	7				8			9	10		11		9
	1	5	3	2					4		6	7				8			9	10		11		10
	1	5	3	2					4		6	7			8				9		10	11		11
	1	5	3	2					4		6	7				8			9		10	11		12
	1	5	3	2					4	6		7				8			9		10		11	13
	1	5	3	2					4		6	7				8			9		10	11		14
	1	5	3	2					4		6	7		9	8					10			11	15
	1	5	3	2					4		6	7		9	8					10			11	16
	1	5	3	2					4		6	7		9	8						10		11	17
	1	5	3	2					4		6	7		9	8					10			11	18
	1	5	3	2					4		6	7		9	8					10			11	19
	1	5	3	2					4		6	7		9	8					10			11	20
	1	5	3	2					4		6	7		9	8	10							11	21
	1	5	3	2					4		6	7		9	8	10						11		22
	1	5	3	2					4		6	7			8	10			9			11		23
	1	5	3	2					4		6	7			8	10				9		11		24
	1	5	3		2				4		6	7			8		10			9		11		25
	1	5	3		2				4		6	7			8		10		9				11	26
	1	5	3		2				4		6		7	9	8						10		11	27
	1	5	3		2				4		6		7	9	8					10		11		28
	1	5	3		2				4		6		7	9	8					10		11		29
	1	5	3		2				4		6	7		9	8	10						11		30
	1	5	3		2				4		6	7		9	8	10						11		31
	1	5	3		2				8	4	6	7		9		10				11				32
	1	5	3		2				8	4	6	7		9		10						11		33
	1	5	3		2				8	4	6	7		9		10						11		34
	1	5	3		2					4	6	7		9	8					10		11		35
	1	5	3		2					4	6	7		9	8					10		11		36
	1	5	3		2				8	4	6	7		9						10		11		37
	1	5	3		2				8	4	6	7		9	10							11		38
	1	5	3		2					4	6			7			8	9			10	11		39
	1	5	3		2					4	6	7		9			8			11	10			40
	1	5	3	2					4		6	7		9	8						10	11		41
	1	5	3	2					4		6	7		9	8						10	11		42
	1	5	3	2					4		6	7		9	8						10	11		43
	1	5	3	2					4		6	7		9	8						10	11		44
	1	5	3	2					4		6	7		9	8						10	11		45
	1	5	3	2					4		6	7		9	8						10	11		46
5	41	44	46	26	16	6	1	3	38	18	37	42	3	33	30	22	4	4	8	18	17	31	13	
			2						1		1	7		20	8	7			3	6		3	2	

1 own-goal

	1	5	3	2					4		6	7		9	8					10			11	1
	1	1	1	1					1		1	1		1	1					1			1	
															1									

1954-55

Manager: Jack Fairbrother to 31 October 1954, Charlie Elliott (acting Manager).

1	Aug	21	(h)	Bournemouth	W	1-0	Crosland (og)	19,376
2		23	(h)	Reading	W	2-1	Brown, Capel	14,411
3		28	(a)	Brentford	W	3-2	Brown 3	13,057
4	Sep	1	(a)	Reading	D	2-2	Brown, Capel	12,046
5		4	(h)	Brighton & HA	W	2-1	Brown, Capel	20,674
6		6	(h)	Gillingham	W	4-1	P.Hill, Capel 2, Collindridge	18,228
7		11	(a)	Torquay U	W	2-1	Brown 2	9,981
8		15	(a)	Gillingham	L	1-2	Brown	10,425
9		18	(h)	Bristol C	L	1-3	Capel	29,865
10		20	(h)	Leyton O	D	2-2	Hawkings, Capel	14,841
11		25	(a)	Walsall	D	1-1	Nutt	13,909
12		30	(a)	Leyton O	L	0-1		8,843
13	Oct	3	(h)	Shrewsbury T	W	3-0	Dorman 2, Dutton	15,264
14		9	(a)	Newport C	D	1-1	Nutt	10,372
15		16	(h)	Exeter C	D	1-1	Capel	13,819
16		23	(a)	Colchester U	W	1-0	Capel	8,124
17		30	(h)	Watford	W	3-2	Nutt, P.Hill, Capel	14,143
18	Nov	6	(a)	Southend U	L	0-1		9,223
19		13	(h)	Aldershot	W	2-1	P.Hill, Capel	11,447
20		27	(h)	Crystal P	W	4-1	P.Hill, Lee 2, Capel	14,823
21	Dec	4	(a)	Northampton T	L	0-1		10,708
22		18	(a)	Bournemouth	L	1-2	Lee	8,510
23		25	(h)	Southampton	D	1-1	Moore	23,507
24		27	(a)	Southampton	L	0-1		22,528
25	Jan	1	(h)	Brentford	W	1-0	Lee	14,464
26		22	(h)	Torquay U	L	0-1		15,884
27		29	(a)	Queen's Park R	L	2-3	Capel 2	12,471
28	Feb	5	(a)	Bristol C	L	0-2		21,555
29		12	(h)	Walsall	W	5-3	Johnson, Lee 2, Capel, Collindridge	14,333
30		19	(a)	Shrewsbury T	L	0-1		6,503
31	Mar	5	(a)	Exeter C	D	0-0		7,551
32		12	(h)	Colchester U	D	0-0		10,058
33		19	(a)	Watford	L	0-1		8,956
34	Apr	2	(a)	Aldershot	D	1-1	Lee	4,883
35		4	(h)	Newport C	W	3-2	Hawkings, Lee, P.Hill	3,936
36		8	(a)	Millwall	L	1-3	P.Hill	16,276
37		9	(h)	Swindon T	W	1-0	P.Hill	9,416
38		12	(h)	Millwall	W	4-1	Timmins, P.Hill, Collindridge, Dutton	11,928
39		16	(a)	Crystal P	L	0-1		9,412
40		18	(h)	Norwich C	W	4-0	Hawkings 2, Capel, Johnson	9,110
41		23	(h)	Northampton T	D	0-0		11,610
42		27	(a)	Swindon T	L	0-3		4,293
43		30	(a)	Norwich C	D	1-1	Moore	10,251
44	May	2	(h)	Queen's Park R	W	5-1	Moore, Sambrook, Hawkings, Capel 2	7,350
45		4	(h)	Southend U	L	1-4	Hawkings	7,271
46		7	(a)	Brighton & HA	L	0-2		3,384

FINAL LEAGUE POSITION: 9th in Division Three South

Appearances

Goals

FA Cup

1	Nov	20	(a)	Northampton T	W	1-0	Kirk	14,680
2	Dec	11	(h)	Scunthorpe U	W	4-0	Harvey, Lee, Capel 2	21,333
3	Jan	8	(a)	Huddersfield T	D	3-3	Lee, Capel 2	31,576
R		13	(h)	Huddersfield T	L	1-2*	Moore	23,716

*After extra-time

Appearances

Goals

Taylor	Matthews	Jones	Timmins	Jamieson	Harvey	McDonnell	Kirk	Austin	Simpson	Nutt	Cresswell	Moore	Johnson	Hill P	Hawkings	Dorman	Sambrook	Brown	Lee	Rowley	Dutton	Capel	Bradbury	Collindridge	Hill J	
1		2		4		5	3	6		7				8				9				10		11		1
1		2		4		5	3	6		7				8				9				10		11		2
1		2		4		5	3	6		7				8				9				10		11		3
1		2		4		5	3	6		7				8				9				10		11		4
1		2		4		5	3	6		7				8				9				10		11		5
1		2		4		5	3	6		7				8				9				10		11		6
1		2		4		5	3	6		7				8				9				10		11		7
1		2		4		5	3	6		7				8				9				10			11	8
1		2		4		5	3	6		7				8				9				10		11		9
1		2		4		5	3		6	7					8			9				10		11		10
	1	2			4	5	3		6	7					8			9				10		11		11
	1	2			4	5	3		6	7					8			9					10	11		12
	1	2			4	5	3		6	7						8					9	10		11		13
	1	2		8	4	5	3		6	7							11				9	10				14
	1	2		8	4	5	3		6	7							11				9	10				15
	1	2			4	5	3		6	7				8							9	10			11	16
	1	2			4	5	3	6		7				8			11				9	10				17
	1	2			4	5	3	6		7				8			11				9	10				18
	1	2			4	5	3	6		7			11	8							9	10				19
	1	2			4	5	3		6	7			11	8					9			10				20
	1	2			4	5	3		6	7			11	8					9			10				21
	1	2			4	5	3	6			7		11	8					9	10						22
	1	2			4	5	3		6			7	11	8					9			10				23
	1	2			4	5	3		6		7		11	8					9			10				24
	1	2			4	5	3		6				7	8					9			10		11		25
	1	2			4	5	3		6			7	11	8					9			10				26
	1				4	5	2	3	6			7	11	8					9			10				27
	1	2		4		5	3		6			9	7						8			10		11		28
	1	2		4		5	3	6					7	8					9			10		11		29
	1	2		4		5	3	6					7	8					9			10		11		30
	1	2		4		5	3	6				7		10						8	9			11		31
	1	2		4		5	3	6				7								8	9	10		11		32
	1	2		4		5	3	6					7	10	8				9					11		33
	1	2		4		5	3	6				7		10	8				9					11		34
	1	2		4		5	3	6				7		10	8				9					11		35
	1	2		4		5	3	6				7		10	8				9					11		36
	1	2			4	5	3		6			7		10	8						9			11		37
	1		2		4		5	3	6				7	8			10				9			11		38
	1		2		4		5	3	6				7	8			10				9				11	39
	1		2	4			5	3	6			7	11	8	9							10				40
	1		2	4			5	3	6			7	11	8	9							10				41
	1		2	4			5	3	6			7	11	8	9		10									42
	1		2	4			5	3	6			7	11	8	9		10									43
	1		2	4			5	3	6			7	11		9		8					10				44
	1		2	4			5	3	6			7	11		9		8					10				45
	1	2	3	4			5		6			7	11		9		8					10				46
10	36	37	9	28	20	37	46	30	25	21	2	17	22	35	15	1	11	12	15	3	12	34	1	24	3	
			1							3		3	2	8	6	2	1	9	8		2	18		3		

1 own-goal

Taylor	Matthews	Jones	Timmins	Jamieson	Harvey	McDonnell	Kirk	Austin	Simpson	Nutt	Cresswell	Moore	Johnson	Hill P	Hawkings	Dorman	Sambrook	Brown	Lee	Rowley	Dutton	Capel	Bradbury	Collindridge	Hill J	
	1	2			4	5	3		6	7			11	8							9	10				1
	1	2			4	5	3		6	7			11	8					9			10				2
	1	2			4	5	3		6			7	11	8					9			10				3
	1	2			4	5	3		6			7	11	8					9			10				R
	4	4			4	4	4		4	2		2	4	4					3		1	4				
					1		1					1							2			4				

1955-56

Manager: Jesse Carver to December 1955, then George Raynor.

1	Aug	20	(h)	Bournemouth	W	3-1	Hawkings, Capel, Collindridge	24,234
2		23	(a)	Watford	L	1-2	Moore	12,996
3		27	(a)	Norwich C	L	0-1		17,281
4		29	(h)	Watford	W	3-0	Moore, Sambrook, Shipwright (og)	18,053
5	Sep	3	(h)	Colchester U	W	2-0	P.Hill, Stewart (og)	23,171
6		7	(a)	Gillingham	D	1-1	Dutton	11,458
7		10	(a)	Leyton O	L	1-3	Moore	18,935
8		12	(h)	Gillingham	W	2-0	Dutton, Sambrook	18,444
9		17	(h)	Exeter C	D	2-2	Moore, Davey (og)	20,790
10		21	(a)	Reading	L	0-1		7,244
11		24	(a)	Southend U	L	0-3		14,107
12		26	(h)	Brentford	W	2-1	P.Hill, Hawkings	12,524
13	Oct	1	(h)	Swindon T	W	6-0	Harvey, Sambrook 2, Hawkings 3	17,185
14		8	(a)	Northampton T	L	1-2	Hawkings	20,370
15		15	(h)	Aldershot	D	1-1	Dutton	17,613
16		22	(a)	Crystal P	L	0-3		7,657
17		29	(h)	Brighton & HA	W	3-2	Uphill, Moore, Collindridge	14,734
18	Nov	5	(a)	Southampton	L	0-3		13,690
19		12	(h)	Shrewsbury T	W	2-1	Uphill 2	16,252
20		26	(h)	Walsall	W	1-0	Collindridge	17,618
21	Dec	3	(a)	Torquay U	D	0-0		8,002
22		10	(h)	Newport C	W	3-0	Simpson, McPherson, P.Hill	17,325
23		17	(a)	Bournemouth	W	1-0	Moore	5,029
24		24	(h)	Norwich C	W	5-3	Timmins, Uphill 2, P.Hill, J.Hill	19,769
25		26	(a)	Millwall	W	2-0	Moore, McPherson	5,506
26		27	(h)	Millwall	W	5-1	Uphill, McPherson, P.Hill, J.Hill, Jardine (og)	29,976
27		31	(a)	Colchester U	L	0-2		8,616
28	Jan	7	(a)	Ipswich T	L	0-1		14,991
29		14	(h)	Leyton O	W	3-0	Uphill, McPherson, Sambrook	23,579
30		21	(a)	Exeter C	W	3-2	Uphill 2, McPherson	7,472
31	Feb	11	(a)	Swindon T	D	1-1	Timmins (pen)	6,414
32		18	(h)	Northampton T	L	0-1		19,511
33		25	(a)	Aldershot	D	2-2	McPherson 2	4,607
34	Mar	3	(h)	Crystal P	L	1-3	McPherson	17,033
35		10	(a)	Brighton & HA	L	1-2	Uphill	16,908
36		17	(h)	Southampton	W	2-0	Newman, McPherson	13,471
37		19	(h)	Southend U	D	0-0		12,852
38		24	(a)	Shrewsbury T	L	0-3		8,235
39		30	(a)	Queen's Park R	W	2-1	Uphill, McPherson	10,898
40		31	(h)	Ipswich T	W	3-1	McPherson 2, Sambrook	15,352
41	Apr	3	(h)	Queen's Park R	W	4-1	Uphill, Newman, McPherson, Sambrook	16,711
42		7	(a)	Walsall	L	0-2		14,750
43		14	(h)	Torquay U	L	1-2	Sambrook (pen)	9,020
44		21	(a)	Newport C	L	2-4	Uphill, Sambrook	5,874
45		23	(a)	Brentford	D	1-1	P.Hill	6,078
46		28	(h)	Reading	D	0-0		10,461

FINAL LEAGUE POSITION: 8th in Division Three South

Appearances

Goals

FA Cup

1	Nov	19	(h)	Exeter C	L	0-1		17,919

Appearances

Goals

Matthews	Bentley	Wood	Jones	Wassall	Austin	Timmins	Patrick	Curtis	Harvey	Jamieson	Regan	Kirk	Simpson	Moore	Johnson	Collindridge	Hawkings	Hill P	Sambrook	Uphill	Dutton	McPherson	Capel	Newman	Hill J	Wyer	
1			2		3				4			5	6	7		11	9	8					10				1
1			2		3				4			5	6	7		11	9	8					10				2
1			2		3				4			5	6	7			9	8	10						11		3
1			2		3				4			5	6	7	11			8	10		9						4
1			2				3		4			5	6	7	11			8	10		9						5
1			2				3		4			5	6	7	11			8	10		9						6
1			2				3		4			5	6	7		11	8		10		9						7
1			2		3				4			5	6	7			8		10		9				11		8
1			2		3				4	6		5		7			8		10		9				11		9
1			2	3	6				4			5		7			9	8	10						11		10
1				2	3		9		4			5	6	7				8	10						11		11
1				2	3				4			5	6	7			9	8	10						11		12
1				2	3				4			5	6	7			9	10	8						11		13
1				2	4		3					5	6	7			9	10	8						11		14
1			2		3				4			5	6	7		11			10	8	9						15
1			2	11	6		3		4			5		7			9			8						10	16
1					2		3		4			5	6	9	7	11	10			8							17
1					2		3		4			5	6		7	9	10		11	8							18
1					2	3			4			5	6	7	11	9			10	8							19
1					2	3				4		5	6	7		9			10	8					11		20
1					2	3				4		5	6	7				10	8	9					11		21
1					2	3				4		5	6	7				10		8		9			11		22
1					2	3			6	4		5		7				10		8		9			11		23
1					2	3			6	4		5		7				10		8		9			11		24
1					2	3			6	4		5		7				10		8		9			11		25
1					2	3			6	4		5		7				10		8		9			11		26
1					2	3			6	4		5	8				7	10				9			11		27
1					2	3			6	4		5			7			10		8		9			11		28
1					2	3				4		5	6		7			10	11	8		9					29
1					2	3				4		5	6		7			10	11	8		9					30
1					2	3				4		5	6		7			10	11	8		9					31
1					2	3				4		5	6		7			10	11	8		9					32
1					2	3				4		5	6			7	10		11	8		9					33
1					2	3					4	5	6			7		8	11	10		9					34
1				3	2		9				4	5	6		7				11	8		10					35
1				3		2					4	5	6					10	11	8		9		7			36
1				3		2					4	5	6					10	11	8		9		7			37
1				3		2				6	4	5						10	11	8		9		7			38
1			2		3						4	5	6		7			10	11	8		9					39
1			2		3						4	5	6		7			10	11	8		9					40
1			2		3						4	5	6		7				11	8		9		10			41
1			2		3						4	5	6		7				11	8		9		10			42
	1		2		3						4	5	6		7				11	8		9		10			43
1					2			3		4	10	5	6		7				11	8		9					44
	1				2			3			4	5	6		7			10	11	8		9					45
		1		5	2			3			4		6		7			10	11	8		9					46
43	2	1	17	11	40	19	9	3	24	17	13	45	37	25	20	10	15	31	35	31	7	25	2	6	17	1	
						2			1				1	7		3	6	6	9	13	3	13	1	2	2		

4 own-goals

1					2	3			4			5	6	7	11	9			10	8							1
1					1	1			1			1	1	1	1	1			1	1							

1956-57

Manager: Harry Warren

1	Aug	18	(h)	Exeter C	W 1-0	Churms	20,100
2		20	(h)	Southampton	W 2-1	P.Hill, McPherson	20,235
3		25	(a)	Crystal P	D 1-1	P.Hill	9,654
4		29	(a)	Southampton	D 1-1	McPherson	15,097
5	Sep	1	(h)	Southend U	W 2-0	Uphill, McPherson	20,365
6		5	(a)	Norwich C	L 0-3		17,344
7		8	(a)	Northampton T	L 0-4		15,491
8		10	(h)	Norwich C	W 3-2	Timmins (pen), McPherson, Sambrook	18,354
9		15	(h)	Queen's Park R	W 5-1	McPherson 2, Sambrook, Churms, Woods (og)	18,120
10		19	(a)	Ipswich T	L 0-4		9,264
11		22	(a)	Plymouth A	D 0-0		11,922
12		24	(h)	Ipswich T	D 1-1	Moore	19,225
13		29	(h)	Reading	L 0-1		16,130
14	Oct	6	(a)	Torquay U	L 1-3	Uphill	8,200
15		13	(h)	Millwall	L 1-2	Sambrook	20,227
16		20	(a)	Brighton & HA	L 1-2	Sambrook	14,274
17		27	(h)	Gillingham	W 4-1	P.Hill 2, Mokone, Uphill	16,958
18	Nov	3	(a)	Swindon T	D 2-2	Sambrook, P.Hill	11,160
19		10	(h)	Brentford	D 1-1	P.Hill	10,008
20		24	(h)	Watford	L 0-2		10,705
21	Dec	1	(a)	Shrewsbury T	L 0-5		7,969
22		8	(h)	Walsall	D 2-2	McPherson 2	10,099
23		15	(a)	Exeter C	L 2-4	Johnson, Ferrier (og)	4,119
24		29	(a)	Southend U	W 2-1	P.Hill, Boxley	9,008
25	Jan	5	(a)	Colchester U	L 2-3	Rogers, McPherson	7,302
26		12	(h)	Northampton T	W 3-1	Sambrook 2, Boxley	15,297
27		19	(a)	Queen's Park R	D 1-1	Boxley	7,832
28		26	(h)	Colchester U	L 2-4	McPherson, Boxley (pen)	14,934
29	Feb	2	(h)	Plymouth A	L 1-4	Uphill	12,668
30		9	(a)	Reading	L 0-3		8,562
31		16	(h)	Torquay U	W 3-2	P.Hill, McPherson, Sambrook	10,375
32		23	(a)	Millwall	L 2-3	Rogers, McPherson	5,019
33	Mar	2	(h)	Brighton & HA	L 1-2	Rogers	11,665
34		9	(a)	Walsall	D 1-1	P.Hill	14,758
35		16	(h)	Swindon T	W 3-0	McPherson 2, Boxley	8,752
36		21	(a)	Newport C	L 0-3		6,332
37		23	(a)	Brentford	D 1-1	Rogers	10,050
38		30	(h)	Aldershot	W 5-1	Rogers, McPherson 2, Sambrook, Wetton (og)	7,745
39	Apr	1	(h)	Crystal P	D 3-3	P.Hill, Sambrook 2	5,517
40		6	(a)	Watford	L 0-1		5,583
41		8	(h)	Newport C	W 2-0	McPherson, Sambrook	5,569
42		13	(h)	Shrewsbury T	D 3-3	Moore, McPherson, Boxley	8,299
43		19	(a)	Bournemouth	W 2-1	McPherson, Boxley	10,772
44		20	(a)	Gillingham	W 2-1	Moore, Sambrook	5,076
45		23	(h)	Bournemouth	W 4-2	McPherson 3, Hughes (og)	12,620
46		27	(a)	Aldershot	W 1-0	Sambrook	4,607

FINAL LEAGUE POSITION: 16th in Division Three South

Appearances

Goals

FA Cup

1	Nov	17	(a)	Swindon T	L 1-2	McPherson	17,097

Appearances

Goals

Matthews	Wood	Bentley	Austin	Timmins	Patrick	Curtis	Kirk	Kletzenbauer	Regan	Proverbs	Jamieson	Jones	Wassall	Simpson	Meadows	Johnson	Churms	Newman	Moore	Mokone	McPherson	Rogers	Uphill	Walton	Hill P	Sambrook	Boxley	Ferguson	
1			2			3	5		4					6		7	8				9				10	11			1
1			2			3	5		4					6		7					9		8		10	11			2
1			2			3	5		4					6		7					9		8		10	11			3
1			2			3	5			4				6		7					9		8		10	11			4
1			2			3	5			4				6		7					9		8		10	11			5
1			2			3	5		4					6			7				9		8		10	11			6
1			2			3	5		4					6			10	7			9		8			11			7
1			2	3			5			4				6	8		10	7			9					11			8
1			2	3			5			4				6	8		10	7			9					11			9
	1		2	3			5			4				6			10	8	7		9					11			10
1			2	3			5			4				6			10	8	7		9					11			11
1				2		3	5			4				6			10	8	7		9					11			12
1				2		3	5		6		4						10		7		9		8			11			13
	1			3		2	5		10		4			6					7		9		8			11			14
1				2		3	5				4			6						7	9		8			10		11	15
1				2		3	5				4			6						7	9		8	10		11			16
1				2		3	5				4			6						7			8	10	11	9			17
1				2		3	5				4			6						7				8	10	9		11	18
1				3	2					4		5		6		7								8	10	9		11	19
		1		3	2		5				4	6					10	7			9			8		11			20
		1		3	2		5				4	6									7		9	8	10	11			21
		1		3	2		5			4		6							7		9		8	10		11			22
		1		2			3			4		5			6	7					9		8	10				11	23
		1		2		3	5		4					6							9	7	8		10		11		24
		1		2		3	5		4					6							9	7	8		10		11		25
		1		2		3	5		4					6					8			7			10	9	11		26
		1	2				5	3	4					6		7			8			9			10		11		27
		1	2				5	3	4					6		7			8		10	9					11		28
		1	2				5	3	4						6						9	7	8			10	11		29
		1	2			3	5				4				6						9	7	8			10	11		30
		1	2				5	3			4				6						9	7			8	10	11		31
		1	2				5	3			4				6						9	7			8	10	11		32
		1	2				5	3			4				6						9	7			8	10	11		33
		1	4		2			3			6		5			10						7			8	9	11		34
		1	4		2			3			6		5								9	7			8	10	11		35
		1	4		2			3			6		5								9	7			8	11	10		36
		1	4		2			3			6		5								9	7			8	11	10		37
		1	4		2			3			6		5								9	7			8	11	10		38
		1	4		2			3			6		5								9	7			8	11	10		39
		1	4		2		5	3			6										9	7			8	11	10		40
		1	4		2		5	3			6								8		9	7				11	10		41
		1	4		2		5	3			6								8		9	7				11	10		42
		1	4	3	2		5				6								8		9	7				11	10		43
		1	4	3	2	8	5				6								7		9					11	10		44
		1	4	3	2		5				6								8		9	7				11	10		45
		1	4	3	2		5				6								8		9	7				11	10		46
17	2	27	31	23	17	19	39	15	13	10	25	5	6	23	8	10	10	7	15	4	40	22	18	8	24	41	23	4	
				1												1	2		3	1	22	5	4		10	14	7		

4 own-goals

Matthews	Wood	Bentley	Austin	Timmins	Patrick	Curtis	Kirk	Kletzenbauer	Regan	Proverbs	Jamieson	Jones	Wassall	Simpson	Meadows	Johnson	Churms	Newman	Moore	Mokone	McPherson	Rogers	Uphill	Walton	Hill P	Sambrook	Boxley	Ferguson	
	1			3	2					4	6	5				7					9			8	10			11	1
	1			1	1					1	1	1				1					1			1	1			1	
																					1								

1957-58

Manager: Harry Warren until September 1957, then Billy Frith.

1	Aug	24	(h)	Reading	W	1-0	McPherson	16,002
2		29	(a)	Newport C	D	2-2	Pounder, Rogers	12,100
3		31	(a)	Northampton T	L	0-4		12,037
4	Sep	2	(h)	Newport C	L	1-2	McPherson	14,759
5		7	(h)	Watford	D	2-2	Boxley 2	13,461
6		9	(h)	Bournemouth	L	0-3		10,009
7		14	(a)	Crystal P	L	0-2		11,543
8		18	(a)	Bournemouth	D	0-0		11,365
9		21	(h)	Torquay U	W	2-1	Rogers, Patrick	10,834
10		28	(a)	Brentford	W	3-1	Patrick 2, Boxley	12,090
11	Oct	5	(h)	Colchester U	W	1-0	Griffiths	14,423
12		12	(h)	Southampton	D	0-0		17,227
13		19	(a)	Brighton & HA	L	0-3		17,250
14		26	(h)	Southend U	W	1-0	P.Hill	13,371
15	Nov	2	(a)	Queen's Park R	L	0-3		9,121
16		9	(h)	Exeter C	W	6-1	Timmins, Patrick 3, McPherson, Sambrook	12,707
17		23	(h)	Millwall	L	1-4	Rogers	17,199
18		30	(a)	Swindon T	L	1-2	Straw	12,236
19	Dec	14	(a)	Plymouth A	L	0-4		14,539
20		21	(a)	Reading	L	1-3	Smith	9,878
21		25	(h)	Port Vale	W	1-0	Straw	13,847
22		26	(a)	Port Vale	W	1-0	Smith	17,310
23		28	(h)	Northampton T	D	1-1	P.Hill	20,342
24	Jan	4	(a)	Millwall	L	1-4	Boxley	7,898
25		11	(a)	Watford	L	0-1		5,958
26		18	(h)	Crystal P	D	2-2	Straw, Boxley	8,181
27	Feb	1	(a)	Torquay U	L	0-1		6,400
28		8	(h)	Brentford	D	0-0		9,361
29		15	(a)	Colchester U	L	1-4	P.Hill	8,613
30		22	(a)	Southampton	L	1-7	Straw	11,195
31	Mar	1	(h)	Brighton & HA	D	2-2	R.Hill 2	9,073
32		5	(a)	Norwich C	D	1-1	Austin	18,458
33		8	(a)	Southend U	L	1-5	Straw	9,881
34		10	(a)	Walsall	L	1-4	R.Hill	6,600
35		15	(h)	Queen's Park R	D	1-1	Rogers	7,646
36		17	(h)	Aldershot	W	6-0	Rogers 3, P.Hill 3	5,830
37		24	(h)	Walsall	W	4-1	Straw 3, McPherson (og)	8,152
38		29	(h)	Plymouth A	D	1-1	Straw	11,653
39	Apr	5	(a)	Exeter C	L	0-1		5,304
40		7	(a)	Shrewsbury T	W	3-1	Straw 2, P.Hill	8,685
41		8	(h)	Shrewsbury T	W	5-0	Straw 3, Rogers 2	12,489
42		12	(h)	Swindon T	L	0-1		11,941
43		19	(a)	Aldershot	D	1-1	P.Hill	4,221
44		21	(h)	Norwich C	W	2-1	R.Hill 2	7,532
45		26	(h)	Gillingham	D	1-1	P.Hill	6,914
46		30	(a)	Gillingham	L	2-3	B.Hill, P.Hill	4,124

FINAL LEAGUE POSITION: 19th in Division Three South

Appearances
Goals

FA Cup

1	Nov	16	(h)	Walthamstow Ave	W	1-0	McPherson	19,064
2	Dec	7	(a)	Aldershot	L	1-4	P.Hill	6,200

Appearances
Goals

Ashcroft	Spratt	Patrick	Kirk	Austin	Shepherd	Harvey	Timmins	Walters	Curtis	Jamieson	Griffiths	Nicholas	Kearns	Pounder	Rogers	Simms	Smith	Hill P	McPherson	Walton	Sambrook	Straw	Hill R	Boxley	Knox	Hill B	
1		2	5	6			3			4				7	10				9	8				11			1
1		2	5	6			3			4				7	10			8	9					11			2
1		2	5	6			3			4				7	10			8	9					11			3
1		2	5	6			3			4					7			10	9	8				11			4
	1	2	5			4	3			6					7				9	8	11			10			5
	1		2			4	3		5				6	7	8				9					11	10		6
	1		5	2		4	3			6				7	8				9	10				11			7
	1	8	5	2		4	3			6					7				9	10				11			8
	1	8	5	2		4	3			6					7			10	9					11			9
	1	8	5	2			3			6	4				7			10	9					11			10
	1	9	5	2			3				4		6		8	7		10						11			11
	1		5	2			3			6	4			7	8			10	9					11			12
	1	9		2			3		5		4		6		7			10			11			8			13
	1	8	5	2			3			6	4				7			10	9		11						14
	1		5	2			3			6	4				7			10	9		8			11			15
	1	8	5	2			3			4	6				7			10	9		11						16
	1		5	2				3		4	6				7			10			11	9			8		17
	1	8	5	2				3		6	4				7			10	9					11			18
	1		5			4		2	3		6						7	8			11	9	10				19
	1		5	2		4	3				6						7	8	10		11	9					20
	1		5	3	2	4				6					9		7	8			11	10					21
	1		5	3	2	4				6					9		7	8				10		11			22
	1		5	3	2	4				6					9		7	8				10		11			23
	1		5	3	2	4				6					9		7	8				10		11			24
	1	5	9	6	2		3			4							7	10				8		11			25
	1		5	6	2		3			4					7			10	8			9		11			26
	1		5	3	2					6		4			7			10	8			9		11			27
	1		5		2		3			6		4			7				8			9	10	11			28
	1		5	3	2	6						4			8		7	10					9	11			29
	1		5	3	2	6				8		4					7	10				9	11				30
1		2	5	6	3							4					7		8			9	10	11			31
1		2	5	6	3							4						7	8			9	10	11			32
1		2	5	6	3							4					11	7	8			9	10				33
	1		5	6	3	2						4			7			10	9				8	11			34
1					3	2			5	6		4			7			10				9	8	11			35
1					3	2			5	6		4			9		7	10				8		11			36
1					3	2			5	6		4			9		7	10				8		11			37
1					3	2			5	6		4			9		7	10				8		11			38
1					3	2			5	6		4			9		7	10				8		11			39
1					3	2			5	6		4			9		7	10				8		11			40
1					3	2			5	6		4			9		7	10				8		11			41
1		8			3	2			5	6		4			9		7	10						11			42
1					3	2			5	6		4			9		7	10	8					11			43
1				3		2			5	6	8	4			9		7						11	10			44
1				3		2			5	6	8	4			9		7	10						11			45
1				3		2			5	6		4					7	10					9	11		8	46
19	27	18	33	33	23	26	20	3	15	36	13	20	3	6	38	1	22	38	24	5	9	22	11	38	2	1	
		6		1			1				1			1	9		2	10	3		1	14	5	5		1	

1 own-goal

	1	8	5	2			3			4	6				7			10	9		11						1
	1		5			4		2	3		6				7			8			10	9		11			2
	2	1	2	1		1	1	1	1	1	2				2			2	1		2	1		1			
																		1	1								

1958-59

Manager: Billy Frith

1	Aug	23	(h)	Darlington	D 0-0		15,104
2		26	(a)	Oldham A	L 0-2		6,921
3		30	(a)	Shrewsbury T	L 1-4	Straw	9,487
4	Sep	1	(h)	Oldham A	W 1-0	Kearns	10,023
5		6	(h)	Southport	W 1-0	Kirk	10,875
6		8	(a)	Gateshead	D 1-1	Straw	4,965
7		13	(h)	Exeter C	W 2-0	P.Hill, Boxley	14,537
8		15	(h)	Gateshead	W 4-1	Straw 2, Rogers 2	16,204
9		20	(a)	Gillingham	L 0-2		8,865
10		22	(h)	Aldershot	W 7-1	Straw 3, Rogers 4	15,212
11		27	(h)	Carlisle U	L 1-2	Rogers	19,119
12	Oct	1	(a)	Aldershot	W 4-1	Kearns, Rogers 3	3,925
13		4	(a)	Barrow	W 3-0	Rogers 2, Ryan	5,228
14		6	(h)	Millwall	W 1-0	Satchwell	21,017
15		11	(a)	Crewe A	D 1-1	Straw	9,023
16		18	(h)	Northampton T	W 2-0	Straw 2	22,281
17		25	(a)	Workington	D 2-2	P.Hill, Rogers	5,500
18	Nov	1	(h)	York C	W 2-0	Straw, Boyes (og)	24,430
19		8	(a)	Bradford	L 0-2		8,619
20		22	(a)	Crystal P	D 1-1	Noakes (og)	12,319
21		29	(h)	Chester	W 5-1	P.Hill 2, Straw, Stewart, Ryan	15,791
22	Dec	13	(h)	Hartlepools U	W 4-1	P.Hill, Straw, Daley, Waugh (og)	11,104
23		20	(a)	Darlington	W 4-1	Straw 2, Stewart, Daley	6,283
24		26	(h)	Torquay U	W 3-0	Kirk, Straw 2	27,238
25		27	(a)	Torquay U	D 1-1	Straw	8,591
26	Jan	3	(h)	Shrewsbury T	W 3-2	Straw, Stewart, Ryan	18,485
27		24	(a)	Watford	W 4-1	Straw 2, Stewart 2	8,913
28		31	(a)	Exeter C	L 1-2	Daley	12,578
29	Feb	7	(h)	Gillingham	D 1-1	Ryan	13,438
30		14	(a)	Carlisle U	W 6-1	Straw, Stewart 4, Daley	5,297
31		21	(h)	Barrow	W 2-0	P.Hill, Straw	15,619
32		28	(h)	Crewe A	W 3-2	Farmer, Straw, Daley	15,428
33	Mar	7	(a)	Northampton T	L 0-4		14,365
34		14	(h)	Workington	W 4-0	Straw 2, Stewart, Ryan	12,854
35		17	(h)	Port Vale	W 1 0	Straw	28,416
36		21	(a)	York C	D 0-0		8,633
37		28	(h)	Bradford	D 0-0		16,374
38		30	(a)	Walsall	L 0-3		10,949
39	Apr	1	(h)	Walsall	D 0-0		19,523
40		4	(a)	Port Vale	L 0-3		20,920
41		11	(h)	Crystal P	W 2-0	Stewart, Boxley	12,485
42		13	(a)	Southport	W 2-1	Stewart, Boxley	2,275
43		18	(a)	Chester	D 1-1	Stewart	5,920
44		21	(a)	Millwall	D 1-1	Stewart	8,780
45		25	(h)	Watford	W 1-0	Kirk	13,434
46		27	(a)	Hartlepools U	L 1-2	Stewart	4,032

FINAL LEAGUE POSITION: 2nd in Division Four

Appearances

Goals

FA Cup

1	Nov	16	(a)	Weymouth	W 5-2	P.Hill 2, Straw 2, Boxley	10,500
2	Dec	7	(h)	Plymouth A	L 1-3	Straw	27,295

Appearances

Goals

Sanders	Spratt	Wood	Lightening	Kirk	Shepherd	Harvey	Nicholas	Kearns	Austin	Curtis	Jones	Farmer	Griffiths	Hill P	Hill B	Satchwell	Smith	Daley	Wyer	Straw	Rogers	Stewart	Hill R	Ryan	Boxley	
1				2	3		4		6		5		7	10						8	9				11	1
1				2	3		4	6			5		7	10		11				8	9					2
1				2	3		4	6			5			10	8		7			9			11			3
1				2	3		4	6		5					11		7		8	9			10			4
1				2	3		4	6		5				10	11		7			9			8			5
1				2		3	4		6	5				10	11	7				8	9					6
1				2		3	4	6		5				7						8	9			10	11	7
1				2		3	4	6		5				7						8	9			10	11	8
1				2		3	4	6		5				7						8	9			10	11	9
1				2		3	4	6		5						7				8	9			10	11	10
	1			2		3	4	6		5						7				8	9			10	11	11
		1		2		3	4	6		5					11	7				8	9			10		12
		1		2		3	4	6		5					11	7				8	9			10		13
		1		2		3	4	6		5					11	7				8	9			10		14
		1		2		3	4	6		5					11	7				8	9			10		15
		1		2		3	4	6		5				7		11				8	9			10		16
		1		2		3	4	6		5				7		11				8	9			10		17
		1		2		3	4	6		5				7	11					8	9			10		18
		1		2		3	4	6		5				7		11				8	9			10		19
		1		2		3	4	6		5				7				11		8	9			10		20
		1		2		3	4			5		6		7				11		8		9		10		21
			1	2		3	4			5		6		7				11		8		9		10		22
			1	2		3	4			5		6		7				11		8		9		10		23
			1	2		3	4			5		6		7				11		8		9		10		24
			1	2		3		4		5		6		7				11		8		9		10		25
			1	2		3		4		5		6		7				11		8		9		10		26
			1	2		3		4		5		6		7				11		8		9		10		27
			1	2		3		4		5		6		7				11		8		9		10		28
			1	2		3		4		5		6			7			11		8		9		10		29
			1	2		3		4		5		6		7				11		8		9		10		30
			1	2		3		4		5		6		7				11		8		9		10		31
			1	2		3		4		5		6				7		11		8		9		10		32
			1	2		3		4		5		6				7		11		8		9		10		33
			1	2		3		4		5		6		7				11		8		9		10		34
			1	2		3			4	5		6		7						8		9		10	11	35
			1	2		3			4	5		6					7			8		9		10	11	36
			1	2		3	4		6	5		7							8			9		10	11	37
			1	2		3	8	10	4	5		6						11	7			9				38
			1	2		3			4	5		6				9		11	7	8				10		39
			1	2		3			4	5		6				7		11		8		9		10		40
			1	2		3			4	5		6					7			8		9		10	11	41
			1	2		3			4	5		6					7			8		9		10	11	42
			1	2		3			4	5		6						7		8		9		10	11	43
			1	2		3		6	4	5		10						7		8		9			11	44
			1	2		3		6	4	5		10						7		8		9			11	45
			1	2		3		6	4	5		10						7		8		9			11	46
10	1	10	25	46	5	41	26	32	14	43	3	26	2	25	10	15	6	22	4	44	17	25	3	36	15	
				3				2				1		6		1		5		27	13	15		5	3	

3 own-goals

		1		2		3	4	6		5				7						8	9			10	11	1
		1		2		3	4	6		5				7		9		11		8				10		2
		2		2		2	2	2		2				2		1		1		2	1			2	1	
														2						3					1	

1959-60

Manager: Billy Frith

1	Aug	22	(h)	Mansfield T	W	2-0	Straw, Ryan	19,769
2		24	(h)	Halifax T	L	0-1		19,980
3		29	(a)	York C	D	1-1	Boxley	9,354
4		31	(a)	Halifax T	D	2-2	Straw, Stewart	8,868
5	Sep	5	(h)	Swindon T	W	3-1	Straw, Stewart 2	16,354
6		7	(h)	Bradford	D	2-2	Daley, Boxley	19,605
7		12	(a)	Chesterfield	W	3-0	Straw 2, Ryan	8,505
8		15	(a)	Bradford	W	3-1	Farmer, Stewart 2	10,116
9		19	(h)	Newport C	D	1-1	Straw	18,251
10		21	(h)	Queen's Park R	D	0-0		16,752
11		26	(a)	Accrington S	W	2-0	Straw 2	5,663
12		28	(a)	Queen's Park R	L	1-2	Stewart	16,037
13	Oct	3	(h)	Bournemouth	W	4-0	Kearns, Straw, Farmer 2	17,877
14		5	(h)	Tranmere R	W	1-0	Farmer	18,846
15		10	(a)	Bury	L	1-2	Straw	11,506
16		12	(a)	Tranmere R	L	1-3	Straw	9,134
17		17	(h)	Barnsley	W	2-1	Ryan, B.Hill	17,319
18		24	(a)	Southampton	L	1-5	Daley	16,613
19		31	(h)	Southend U	W	2-0	Straw, Satchwell	14,114
20	Nov	7	(a)	Shrewsbury T	L	2-3	Satchwell 2	9,822
21		21	(a)	Norwich C	W	4-1	Kearns (pen), Farmer, Stewart, Daley	20,409
22		28	(h)	Brentford	W	2-1	Stewart, P.Hill	14,959
23	Dec	12	(a)	Reading	L	2-4	P.Hill, Daley	8,316
24		25	(h)	Wrexham	W	5-3	Satchwell 4, Farmer	17,468
25		26	(a)	Wrexham	W	3-1	Straw, Satchwell 2	10,631
26	Jan	2	(h)	York C	W	5-2	P.Hill, Straw, Satchwell 2, Jackson (og)	14,374
27		23	(h)	Chesterfield	W	1-0	Satchwell	9,223
28		30	(a)	Colchester U	D	0-0		7,200
29	Feb	13	(h)	Accrington S	W	2-1	Satchwell, Daley	10,691
30		15	(a)	Newport C	L	0-2		4,764
31		20	(a)	Bournemouth	D	2-2	Straw, Satchwell	9,327
32		27	(h)	Bury	L	0-1		21,133
33	Mar	5	(a)	Barnsley	L	0-1		7,211
34		7	(h)	Port Vale	D	1-1	Simcoe	15,541
35		12	(h)	Southampton	W	4-1	P.Hill, Straw, Hewitt, Conner (og)	17,842
36		19	(a)	Brentford	L	1-3	Straw	9,938
37		26	(h)	Shrewsbury T	D	1-1	Hewitt	12,456
38	Apr	2	(a)	Port Vale	W	1-0	Poole (og)	7,686
39		4	(a)	Mansfield T	W	4-2	Straw 3, Satchwell	7,019
40		9	(h)	Norwich C	W	2-1	P.Hill, Hewitt	27,806
41		15	(a)	Grimsby T	L	0-3		11,819
42		16	(a)	Southend U	L	0-1		12,114
43		20	(h)	Grimsby T	L	0-2		16,737
44		23	(h)	Colchester U	W	3-1	Hewitt 2, P.Hill	8,382
45		30	(h)	Reading	D	1-1	Kearns	9,717
46	May	4	(a)	Swindon T	L	0-2		6,415

FINAL LEAGUE POSITION: 4th in Division Three

Appearances

Goals

FA Cup

1	Nov	14	(h)	Southampton	D	1-1	Straw	14,291
R		18	(a)	Southampton	L	1-5	Daley	18,650

Appearances

Goals

Lightening	Kirk	Bennett	Kletzenbauer	Austin	Harvey	Nicholas	Ryan	Kearns	Curtis	Farmer	Simcoe	Daley	Hill B	Satchwell	Boxley	Hill P	Stephens	Straw	Stewart	Hewitt	Jones	Shepherd	
1	2			3		4	10		5	6	7				11			8	9				1
1	2			3		4	10		5	6	7				11			8	9				2
1	2			3		4	10		5	6		7			11			8	9				3
1	2			3		4	10		5	6		7			11			8	9				4
1	2			3		4	10		5	6		7			11			8	9				5
1	2			3		4	10			6		7			11			8	9		5		6
1	2			3		4	10		5	6		7			11			8	9				7
1	2			3		4	10		5	6		7			11			8	9				8
1	2			3		4	9		5	6		7			11			8	10				9
1	2			3		4	9		5	6		7			11			8	10				10
1	2			3		4	9		5	6		7			11			8	10				11
1	2			3		4	9		5	6		7			11			8	10				12
1	2	11		3		4	9	6	5	10			7					8					13
1	2	11		3		4	9	6	5	10				7				8					14
1	2	11		3			4	6	5	10	9			7				8					15
1	2	7		3			4	6	5	10	9	11						8					16
1	2			3		4	9	6	5	10			11			7		8					17
1	2			3		4		6	5	10	7	11		9				8					18
1	2			3		4	10		5	6		11		9	7			8					19
1	2			3		4	10		5	6		11		9	7			8					20
1	2			3		4		6	5	8		11		7		10			9				21
1	2			3		4		6	5	8		11		7		10			9				22
1	2			3		4		6	5	8		11		7		10			9				23
1		2			3	4		6	5	10		11		9		7		8					24
1		2			3	4		6	5			11	10	9		7		8					25
1	2	3				4		6	5			11	10	9		7		8					26
1	2	3				4		6	5			11	10	9		7		8					27
1	2	3				4		6	5			11		9		10	7	8					28
1		2		3		4		6	5			11		9		10	7	8					29
1		2		3		4		6	5			11	10	9		7		8					30
1		2		3		4		6	5			11	10	9		7		8					31
1		2		3		4		6	5			11		9		7		8				10	32
1		2		3		4		6	5		7			9	11			8		10			33
1		2		3		4		6	5		9			7	11			8		10			34
1		2		3		4		6	5					9		7	11	8		10			35
1		2		3		4		6	5					9		7	11	8		10			36
1		2		3		4			5	6	9					7	11	8		10			37
1		2		3				4	5	6				9		7	11	8		10			38
1		2		3				4	5	6				9		7	11	8		10			39
1		2		3				4	5	6				9		7	11	8		10			40
1		2		3				4	5	6				9		7	11	8		10			41
1		2		3				4	5	6				9		7	11	8		10			42
1		2		3				4	5	6				9		7	11	8		10			43
1		2		3				4	5	6		11				10	7	9		8			44
1		2	3	6				4	5					7		10	11	9		8			45
1			2	3				4	5	6			7			10	11	9		8			46
46	26	26	2	41	2	35	19	31	45	33	8	27	8	28	16	25	14	43	15	14	1	1	
							3	3		6	1	5	1	15	2	6		20	8	5			

3 own-goals

Lightening	Kirk	Bennett	Kletzenbauer	Austin	Harvey	Nicholas	Ryan	Kearns	Curtis	Farmer	Simcoe	Daley	Hill B	Satchwell	Boxley	Hill P	Stephens	Straw	Stewart	Hewitt	Jones	Shepherd	
1	2			3		4	10		5	6		11		9		7		8					1
1	2			3		4			5	6		11	10	9		7		8					R
2	2			2		2	1		2	2		2	1	2		2		2					
												1						1					

1960-61

Manager: Billy Frith

1	Aug	20	(a)	Barnsley	L	1-4	Straw	6,037
2		22	(h)	Bradford C	D	2-2	Straw, Myerscough	18,190
3		27	(h)	Newport C	W	4-1	Myerscough 3, Peake (og)	11,819
4		30	(a)	Bradford C	L	1-4	Straw	7,636
5	Sep	3	(a)	Colchester U	L	3-4	Straw 2, Myerscough	5,431
6		5	(h)	Queen's Park R	D	4-4	Straw 2, Myerscough (pen), Farmer	15,784
7		10	(h)	Grimsby T	D	0-0		13,894
8		12	(a)	Queen's Park R	L	1-2	Stiffle	9,323
9		17	(a)	Hull C	D	1-1	Garvey (og)	10,374
10		19	(h)	Bournemouth	W	1-0	Straw	9,693
11		24	(h)	Reading	W	2-1	Curtis, Myerscough	13,180
12		28	(a)	Bournemouth	L	1-2	Satchwell	4,355
13	Oct	1	(a)	Torquay U	L	0-3		6,634
14		4	(a)	Bristol C	L	0-2		14,036
15		8	(h)	Southend U	W	3-0	Farmer, Myerscough, Costello (og)	7,412
16		15	(a)	Chesterfield	L	1-4	Ryan	4,590
17		22	(h)	Bury	L	1-2	Straw	11,302
18		28	(a)	Walsall	D	1-1	Kearns	13,053
19	Nov	12	(a)	Halifax T	D	2-2	P.Hill 2	6,805
20		19	(h)	Tranmere R	W	4-1	Farmer, Stiffle, P.Hill, Straw	9,967
21	Dec	2	(h)	Brentford	W	2-0	Myerscough 2	13,589
22		10	(a)	Swindon T	W	2-1	Straw, Myerscough	8,703
23		17	(h)	Barnsley	W	5-2	P.Hill, Straw Imlach, Hewitt,Hopkins (og)	10,246
24		26	(h)	Notts C	D	2-2	Straw, Hewitt	19,792
25		27	(a)	Notts C	L	0-3		26,759
26	Jan	14	(h)	Colchester U	W	2-0	Kletzenbauer, Straw	10,197
27		30	(h)	Shrewsbury T	W	3-2	P.Hill, Straw, Hewitt	9,579
28	Feb	4	(h)	Hull C	W	4-0	Straw, Hewitt 3	11,140
29		11	(a)	Reading	D	0-0		6,329
30		20	(h)	Torquay U	W	5-1	P.Hill, Hewitt 3, Imlach	15,437
31		25	(a)	Brentford	D	1-1	Imlach (pen)	5,500
32	Mar	3	(h)	Chesterfield	W	3-1	P.Hill, Straw, Myerscough	16,717
33		11	(a)	Bury	L	0-1		10,767
34		18	(h)	Walsall	L	1-2	Hewitt	14,389
35		20	(a)	Newport C	D	3-3	Straw, Imlach, Myerscough	3,660
36		25	(a)	Shrewsbury T	L	1-2	Holder	8,562
37		31	(a)	Port Vale	L	1-3	Poole (og)	6,491
38	Apr	1	(h)	Halifax T	W	2-0	P.Hill, Hewitt	8,756
39		4	(h)	Port Vale	D	1-1	P.Hill	8,280
40		8	(a)	Tranmere R	L	0-2		11,416
41		11	(a)	Watford	L	2-7	B.Hill, P.Hill	10,514
42		14	(h)	Watford	L	0-1		10,437
43		18	(a)	Grimsby T	W	3-2	Kearns, P.Hill, Holder	5,462
44		22	(a)	Southend U	L	1-4	Satchwell	7,748
45		24	(h)	Bristol C	W	2-1	P.Hill, Allen	8,328
46		28	(h)	Swindon T	D	1-1	Holder	7,793

FINAL LEAGUE POSITION: 15th in Division Three

Appearances
Goals

FA Cup

1	Nov	5	(a)	Worcester C	W	4-1	Farmer 2, Myerscough 2	7,751
2		26	(a)	Queen's Park R	W	2-1	Straw, Cockell (og)	8,927
3	Jan	7	(a)	Liverpool	L	2-3	Straw, Myerscough	30,909

Appearances
Goals

League Cup

1	Oct	10	(h)	Barrow	W	4-2	Kearns, Satchwell 2, Myerscough	6,643
2	Nov	2	(a)	Portsmouth	L	0-2		4,523

Appearances
Goals

Lightening	Caine	Wesson	Harvey	Kletzenbauer	Bennett	Austin	Nicholas	Ryan	Kearns	Curtis	Farmer	Jones	Stiffle	Satchwell	Hill B	Daley	Hill P	Imlach	Straw	Hewitt	Myerscough	Holder	Allen	Bruck	
1			2			3	4		6	5			7				11		8	10	9				1
1				2		3	4		6	5			7				11		8	10	9				2
1				2		3	4		6	5			7				11		8	10	9				3
1				2		3	4		6	5			7				11		8		9		10		4
1				2		3	4	6		5	10		7				11		8		9				5
	1			2		3	4	6		5	10		7				11		8		9				6
1				2		3	4		6	5	10		7		11				8		9				7
1				2	4	3			6	5	10		7	8	11						9				8
1				2	3			4	6	5	10		7	8	11						9				9
1				2	3			4	6	5	10			7		11			8		9				10
1				2	3			4		5	6		7	10		11			8		9				11
1				2	3			4		5	6			10	11	7			8		9				12
1				2	3			8	4	5		6		10	7	11					9				13
1				2	3			8	4	5	10	6	7	9	11										14
1				2	3			10	4	5	8	6		7		11					9				15
1				2	3			10	4	5	8	6		7		11					9				16
1				2	3				4	5	10	6				7		11	8		9				17
1				2	3		4		6	5	10		7	9				11	8						18
1				2		3			4	5	6		7				8	11	9		10				19
1				2		3			4	5	6		7				8	11	9		10				20
1				2		3			4	5	6		7				8	11		10	9				21
1				2		3			4	5	6						7	11	8	10	9				22
1					2	3			4	5	6						7	11	8	10	9				23
1				2		3			4	5	6						7	11	8	10	9				24
1				2		3			4	5	6						7	11	8	10	9				25
1				2		3			4	5	6						7	11	8	10	9				26
1				2		3			4	5	6						7	11	8	10	9				27
1				2	3				4	5	6						7	11	8	10	9				28
1				2	3				4	5	6						7	11	8	10	9				29
1				2	3				4	5	6				9		7	11	8	10					30
1				2	3				4	5	6						7	11	8	10	9				31
1				2	3				4	5	6						7	11	8	10	9				32
1				2	3				4	5	6						7	11	8	10	9				33
1				2	3				4	5	6						7	11	8	10	9				34
		1		2	3	6			4	5							7	11	8		9	10			35
		1		2	3	6			4	5							7	11	8		9	10			36
		1		2	3	6			4	5							7	11	8		9	10			37
		1		2	3	6			4	5							7	11	8	10	9				38
		1		2	3	6			4	5					8		7	11		10	9				39
		1		2	3	4				5	6				8		7	11		10	9				40
		1		2	3	4				5	6				7		8	11	9	10					41
		1		2		3			4	5	6			7				11	9	10	8				42
		1		2		3			4	5	6			7			8			10	11	9			43
		1		2		3			4	5	6			7			8			10	11	9			44
		1		2		3			4	5	6						10	7		8		9	11		45
		1		2		3			4	5	6						8	7				9	11	10	46
33	1	12	1	44	26	29	8	10	40	46	36	5	15	13	10	7	33	28	33	25	40	7	3	1	
				1				1	2	1	3		2	2	1		12	4	18	11	13	3	1		

5 own-goals

1				2		3			4	5	6		7				8	11	9		10				1
1				2		3			4	5	6		7				8	11	9		10				2
1				2		3			4	5	6						7	11	8	10	9				3
3				3		3			3	3	3		2				3	3	3	1	3				
											2								2		3				

1 own-goal

1				2	3			10	4	5	8	6		7		11					9				1
1				2	3		4			5	6		7	9	11				8		10				2
2				2	2		1	1	1	2	2	1	1	2	1	1			1		2				
									1					2							1				

1961-62

Manager: Billy Frith then Jimmy Hill from 29 November 1961

1	Aug	19	(a)	Reading	L 0-4		11,578
2		21	(h)	Swindon T	W 2-1	Grice, Burton (og)	13,755
3		25	(h)	Newport C	W 3-0	Grice 2, Imlach	12,675
4		29	(a)	Swindon T	D 3-3	Grice, Myerscough, Dixon	10,563
5	Sep	2	(a)	Southend U	L 0-2		9,248
6		4	(h)	Halifax T	W 3-1	Grice, Dixon, Imlach	13,137
7		9	(h)	Notts C	D 2-2	Hewitt, Dixon	13,329
8		16	(a)	Shrewsbury T	D 1-1	Farmer	7,036
9		19	(a)	Brentford	L 1-2	Imlach (pen)	6,100
10		23	(h)	Peterborough U	L 1-3	Farmer	19,913
11		25	(h)	Brentford	W 2-0	P.Hill, Imlach	10,243
12		30	(a)	Port Vale	L 0-2		9,821
13	Oct	6	(h)	Torquay U	D 2-2	Dixon 2	9,436
14		9	(h)	Bradford C	W 3-0	Hewitt, Dixon, Imlach	7,142
15		14	(a)	Lincoln C	W 2-1	Myerscough, Green (og)	4,874
16		16	(a)	Bradford C	D 0-0		8,681
17		20	(h)	Barnsley	D 1-1	Hewitt	8,173
18		28	(a)	Queen's Park R	L 1-4	Hewitt	9,881
19	Nov	11	(a)	Bournemouth	D 1-1	Hewitt	9,113
20		17	(h)	Crystal P	L 0-2		13,751
21	Dec	2	(h)	Northampton T	W 1-0	Dixon	13,668
22		9	(a)	Hull C	L 1-3	Dixon	3,817
23		16	(h)	Reading	W 1-0	Hewitt	8,091
24		23	(a)	Newport C	W 2-1	Dixon 2	3,360
25		26	(h)	Grimsby T	W 2-0	Myerscough, Dixon	11,199
26	Jan	13	(h)	Southend U	D 3-3	Dixon, Hewitt, Imlach	9,360
27		20	(a)	Notts C	L 0-2		8,827
28		27	(a)	Portsmouth	L 2-3	McCann, Imlach	13,405
29	Feb	2	(h)	Shrewsbury T	W 4-1	Kearns, Allen, Satchwell, Morrall (og)	8,822
30		10	(a)	Peterborough U	W 3-2	Satchwell 2, McCann	11,751
31		24	(a)	Torquay U	L 0-1		3,379
32	Mar	2	(h)	Lincoln C	D 2-2	Kearns, Grice	9,119
33		9	(a)	Barnsley	L 1-2	Dwight	6,008
34		12	(h)	Watford	W 1-0	Dwight	7,233
35		16	(h)	Queen's Park R	L 2-3	Kletzenbauer, McCann	8,626
36		23	(a)	Watford	W 1-0	Dwight	5,604
37		30	(h)	Bournemouth	L 0-1		8,644
38	Apr	7	(a)	Crystal P	D 2-2	Dwight 2	8,438
39		10	(a)	Grimsby T	L 0-2		12,760
40		14	(h)	Portsmouth	W 2-0	Farmer 2	9,711
41		16	(h)	Port Vale	L 0-1		5,894
42		21	(a)	Northampton T	L 1-4	Dwight	10,388
43		23	(h)	Bristol C	D 1-1	Farmer	5,965
44		24	(a)	Bristol C	L 2-3	Holder, Farmer	6,437
45		28	(h)	Hull C	L 0-2		7,573
46		30	(a)	Halifax T	W 2-0	Dwight, Farmer	2,351

FINAL LEAGUE POSITION: 14th in Division Three

Appearances
Goals

FA Cup

1	Nov	4	(h)	Gillingham	W 2-0	Hewitt, Satchwell	10,628
2		25	(h)	King's Lynn	W 1-2	Hindle (og)	12,080

Appearances
Goals

League Cup

1	Sep	13	(a)	Workington	L 0-3		4,682

Appearances
Goals

Lightening	Wesson	Kletzenbauer	Tedds	Austin	Bennett	Sillett	Nicholas	Farmer	Kearns	Bruck	Hill B	Curtis	Allen	Grice	Hill P	Dwight	Turner	McCann	Myerscough	Hewitt	Satchwell	Dixon	Holder	Imlach	Bassett	Humphries	
1		2		3			4	6				5		7	8				9	10				11			1
1		2		3			4	6				5		7	8				9	10				11			2
1		2		3			4	6				5		7					8	10		9		11			3
1		2		3			4	6			10	5		7					8			9		11			4
1		2		3			4	6			10	5		7					8			9		11			5
1		2		3			4	6			10	5		7						8		9		11			6
1		2		3			4	6			10	5		7						8		9		11			7
1			2	4	3			6				5	10	7				8				9		11			8
1			2	4	3			10				5	6	7				8				9		11			9
1			2	4	3			10				5	6	7				8				9		11			10
1			2		3			6				5	4	7	10			8			9			11			11
1				2	3			6	4		9	5		7	10			8						11			12
1				3	2			6	4			5		7					10	8		9		11			13
1				3	2		4	6				5			7				10	8		9		11			14
1				3	2		4		6			5			7				10	8		9		11			15
1		3		6	2		4					5		11	7			8	10		9						16
1				3	2		4		6			5						7	10	8	9			11			17
1				3	2		4		6		10	5						7		8	9			11			18
	1	3		6	2		4				10	5		7						8	9			11			19
1		3		6	2				4		10	5		9	7					8				11			20
1		3			2		4		6			5		7					8	10		9		11			21
1		3			2		4		6			5		7					8	10		9		11			22
1					2		4		3			5	6	7					8	10		9		11			23
1		3			2		4		6			5		7					8	10		9		11			24
1		3			2		4		6			5		7					8	10		9		11			25
	1	3			2		4		6			5		7					8	10		9		11			26
1		3			2		4		6			5		7					8	10		9		11			27
1		3			2				4			5	6	7		9		10	8					11			28
1		3		2					4			5	6	7		8		10			9			11			29
1		3		2					4			5	6	7		8		10			9			11			30
1		2		3			4		6			5		8		7				10	9			11			31
1		2		3			4		6			5	10	8		7					9			11			32
1		2		3			4		6			5	10	7		9					8			11			33
1		2		3			4	8	6			5	10	7		9								11			34
1		2		3					4			5	6	7	8	9		10						11			35
1		2		3				4		6		5	8	7		9		10						11			36
1		2		3				4		6		5	8	7		9		10						11			37
1		2		3				8		4		5	6	7		9		10						11			38
1		2		3				8	4			5	6	7		9		10						11			39
1		2		3				8	4			5	6	7		9		10						11			40
1		2		3				8	4			5	6	7		9		10						11			41
1		2		3				8	4			5	6			7		10			9			11			42
1		2		3				8	4	6		5				7		10			9			11			43
1		2		3				10		4		5	6				8						9	7	11		44
	1			3		2		8		4		5	6			9		10						11		7	45
	1			3		2		8			4	5	6			7		10					9	11			46
42	4	33	4	37	21	2	24	26	26	6	9	46	22	37	9	18	1	22	18	20	12	18	2	45	1	1	
		1						7	2				1	6	1	7		3	3	7	3	12	1	7			

3 own-goals

Lightening	Wesson	Kletzenbauer	Tedds	Austin	Bennett	Sillett	Nicholas	Farmer	Kearns	Bruck	Hill B	Curtis	Allen	Grice	Hill P	Dwight	Turner	McCann	Myerscough	Hewitt	Satchwell	Dixon	Holder	Imlach	Bassett	Humphries	
1				3	2		4	6			9	5		7						8	10			11			1
1		3		6	2		4				10	5			7					8		9		11			2
2		1		2	2		2	1			2	2		1	1					2	1	1		2			
																				1	1						

1 own-goal

Lightening	Wesson	Kletzenbauer	Tedds	Austin	Bennett	Sillett	Nicholas	Farmer	Kearns	Bruck	Hill B	Curtis	Allen	Grice	Hill P	Dwight	Turner	McCann	Myerscough	Hewitt	Satchwell	Dixon	Holder	Imlach	Bassett	Humphries	
1		2		3			4	6			10	5							7	8		9		11			1
1		1		1			1	1			1	1							1	1		1		1			

1962-63

Manager: Jimmy Hill

1	Aug	18	(h)	Notts C	W	2-0	Bly, Barr	22,832
2		21	(a)	Swindon T	L	1-4	Farmer	14,410
3		25	(a)	Colchester U	D	0-0		5,781
4		28	(h)	Swindon T	W	2-0	Barr, Whitehouse	19,386
5	Sep	1	(h)	Southend U	L	3-4	Bly 3	17,949
6		4	(h)	Watford	W	3-1	Barr, Humphries, Kearns	16,287
7		8	(a)	Millwall	D	3-3	Bly 2, Humphries	17,831
8		11	(a)	Watford	L	1-6	Barr	10,123
9		15	(h)	Shrewsbury T	D	0-0		14,122
10		18	(h)	Bradford	W	3-1	Barr 2, Bly	13,010
11		22	(a)	Port Vale	L	1-2	Barr	9,816
12		24	(a)	Bradford	D	0-0		7,664
13		29	(h)	Reading	W	2-1	Barr, Bly	13,416
14	Oct	2	(a)	Bristol C	D	1-1	Whitehouse	13,422
15		5	(a)	Barnsley	L	1-2	Barr	9,432
16		13	(h)	Northampton T	D	1-1	Bly	21,985
17		23	(h)	Bristol C	W	4-2	Bly, Barr, Whitehouse, Farmer (pen)	11,390
18		27	(h)	Hull C	D	2-2	Humphries, Dwight	11,804
19	Nov	10	(h)	Wrexham	W	3-0	Bly 2, Whitehouse	11,466
20		17	(a)	Halifax T	W	4-2	Bly, Humphries, Rees, Farmer	3,742
21	Dec	1	(a)	Brighton & HA	D	2-2	Bly, Farmer	9,296
22		8	(h)	Carlisle U	W	3-2	Bly, Humphries, Whitehouse	8,853
23		15	(a)	Notts C	D	1-1	Bly	6,793
24		26	(a)	Peterborough U	W	3-0	Bly 2, Kearns	13,112
25		29	(h)	Peterborough U	D	3-3	Bly, Humphries, Whitehouse	25,399
26	Feb	23	(h)	Barnsley	W	2-0	Hale, Whitehouse	12,654
27		26	(h)	Colchester U	D	2-2	Bly, Humphries	13,062
28	Mar	2	(a)	Northampton T	D	0-0		18,717
29		9	(h)	Queen's Park R	W	4-1	Bly 3, Barr	15,029
30		23	(h)	Crystal P	W	1-0	Bly	17,860
31	Apr	1	(a)	Wrexham	L	1-5	Bly	11,192
32		6	(h)	Halifax T	W	5-4	Hudson 3, Whitehouse, Bruck	19,632
33		8	(h)	Millwall	W	2-0	Hudson, John (og)	22,899
34		12	(a)	Bournemouth	D	1-1	Barr	15,152
35		13	(a)	Bristol R	D	2-2	Bly, Humphries	13,145
36		16	(h)	Bournemouth	L	1-2	Whitehouse	30,289
37		20	(h)	Brighton & HA	D	1-1	Hill	14,966
38		27	(a)	Carlisle U	W	1-0	Hudson	4,751
39		29	(h)	Bristol R	W	5-0	Rees 2, Humphries 2, Hudson	20,412
40	May	1	(a)	Reading	L	1-4	Farmer	9,442
41		4	(h)	Port Vale	L	0-1		18,307
42		7	(a)	Hull C	L	0-2		5,255
43		11	(a)	Southend U	D	1-1	Costello (og)	9,362
44		15	(a)	Crystal P	D	0-0		12,672
45		20	(a)	Shrewsbury T	L	1-2	Farmer (pen)	4,695
46		24	(a)	Queen's Park R	W	3-1	Rees, Hale (pen), Sillett	3,245

FINAL LEAGUE POSITION: 4th in Division Three — Appearances

In Match 7 some sources credit Wilson (og) not Bly — Goals

FA Cup

1	Nov	3	(h)	Bournemouth	W	1-0	Whitehouse	14,499
2		24	(a)	Millwall	D	0-0		14,633
R		27	(h)	Millwall	W	2-1	Barr, Whitehouse	22,434
3	Mar	7	(a)	Lincoln C	W	5-1	Jackson (og), Whitehouse, Bly, Barr, Farmer	7,440
4		13	(a)	Portsmouth	D	1-1	Hale	11,482
R		16	(h)	Portsmouth	D	2-2	Whitehouse 2	25,462
2R		19	(n*)	Portsmouth	W	2-1	Bly, Whitehouse	15,867
5		25	(h)	Sunderland	W	2-1	Bruck, Curtis	40,487
6		30	(h)	Manchester U	L	1-3	Bly†	44,000

*Played at White Hart Lane, Tottenham, London.

†Some sources credit Foulkes (og) not Bly

Appearances

Goals

League Cup

1	Sep	26	(h)	Swansea T	W	3-2	Bly, Whitehouse, Rees	10,321
2	Oct	17	(a)	Portsmouth	L	1-5	Laverick	8,685

Appearances

Goals

Lightening	Sillett	Austin	Farmer	Curtis	Kearns	Humphries	Barr	Bly	Whitehouse	Laverick	Hill B	Meeson	Kletzenbauer	Dwight	Rees	Bruck	Wesson	Hale	Hudson	Machin	Tedds	Satchwell	
1	2	3	4	5	6	7	8	9	10	11													1
1	2	3	4	5	6	7	8	9	10	11													2
1	2	3		5	6	7	8	9	10	11	4												3
1	2	3		5	6	7	8	9	10	11	4												4
		3		5	4	7	8	9	10		6	1	2	11									5
	2	3		5	6	7	8	9	10		4	1		11									6
		3		5	4	7	8	9	10		6	1	2	11									7
		3		5	6	7	8	9	10		4	1	2	11									8
			6	5	3	7	8	9	10		4	1	2		11								9
				5	3	7	8	9	10		4	1	2		11	6							10
	2			5	3		8	9	10		4	1		7	11	6							11
	2			5			8	9	10		4	1	3	7	11	6							12
	2			5		7	8	9	10		4	1	3		11	6							13
	2			5		7	8	9	10		4	1	3		11	6							14
	2			5	4	7	8	9	10			1	3		11	6							15
	2			5	4	7	8	9	10			1	3		11	6							16
	2		6	5		7	8	9	10		4	1	3	11									17
	2		6	5		7	8	9	10		4	1	3	11									18
	2		6	5	3	7	8	9	10						11	4	1						19
			6	5	3	7	8	9	10		4		2		11		1						20
	2		6	5	3	7	8	9	10		4				11		1						21
	2		6		3	7	8	9	10		5				11	4	1						22
	2		6	5	3	7		9	10		4				11		1	8					23
	2		6	5	3	7		9	10		4				11		1	8					24
	2		6	5	3	7		9	10		4				11		1	8					25
	2			5	3	7		9	10		4				11	6	1	8					26
	2		6	5	3	7		9	10		4				11		1	8					27
	2			5	3	7	8	9	10		4				11	6	1						28
	2			5	3	7	8	9	10		4				11	6	1						29
	2			5	3	7	8	9	10		4					6	1	11					30
	2		6	5	3	7		9	10		4				11		1	8					31
	2			5	3	7	8		10		4	1			11	6			9				32
	2			5	3	7	8				4				11	6	1		9	10			33
	2			5	3	7	8		10		4				11	6	1		9				34
	2			5		7		8			4		3	11		6	1		9	10			35
	2			5	3	7	8		10		4				11	6	1		9				36
	2		6	5			8		10		4		3		7		1	11	9				37
	2		6	5	3	7			10		4				11		1	8	9				38
	2		6	5	3	7									11	4	1	8	9	10			39
	2		6	5	3	7			10		4				11		1	8	9				40
	2			5		7	8				6		3		11	4	1		9	10			41
	2		6	5		7					4		3	11			1	8	9	10			42
			10	5	3		4						2	7	11	6	1	8	9				43
			10	5			3				4			7	11	6	1	8	9		2		44
	2		10	5	3	7	4							8	11	6	1		9				45
	2			5	4	7							3		11	6	1	8	9	10			46
4	38	8	22	45	36	41	34	32	37	4	37	15	19	13	33	24	27	15	15	6	1		
	1		6		2	10	12	26	9		1			1	4	1		2	6				

2 own-goals

Lightening	Sillett	Austin	Farmer	Curtis	Kearns	Humphries	Barr	Bly	Whitehouse	Laverick	Hill B	Meeson	Kletzenbauer	Dwight	Rees	Bruck	Wesson	Hale	Hudson	Machin	Tedds	Satchwell	
	2		6	5	3	7	8	9	10		4			11			1						1
	2		6	5	3	7	8	9	10		4				11		1						2
	2		6	5	3	7	8		10		4			9	11		1						R
	2		6	5	3	7	8	9	10		4				11		1						3
	2			5	3	7		9	10		4				11	6	1	8					4
	2		6	5	3	7		9	10		4				11		1	8					R
	2			5	3	7	8	9	10		4				11	6	1						2R
	2			5	3	7	8	9	10		4				11	6	1						5
	2			5	3	7	8	9	10		4				11	6	1						6
	9		5	9	9	9	7	8	9		9			2	8	4	9	2					
			1	1			2	3	6							1		1					

1 own-goal

Lightening	Sillett	Austin	Farmer	Curtis	Kearns	Humphries	Barr	Bly	Whitehouse	Laverick	Hill B	Meeson	Kletzenbauer	Dwight	Rees	Bruck	Wesson	Hale	Hudson	Machin	Tedds	Satchwell	
	2			5		7	8	9	10		4	1	3		11	6							1
	2		8	5	4			9	10	11		1	3			6						7	2
	2		1	2	1	1	1	2	2	1	1	2	2		1	2						1	
								1	1	1					1								

1963-64

Manager: Jimmy Hill

1	Aug	24	(h)	Crystal P	W 5-1	Farmer 3 (2 pens), Hudson, Machin	26,037
2		29	(a)	Notts C	W 3-0	Hudson 2, Humphries	18,669
3		31	(a)	Walsall	W 3-0	Hudson, Rees, Farmer	17,440
4	Sep	7	(h)	Reading	D 0-0		24,992
5		10	(h)	Notts C	W 2-0	Hudson, Humphries	27,796
6		14	(a)	Luton T	W 3-1	Barr, Humphries 2	14,539
7		17	(h)	Crewe A	W 5-1	Hudson 2, Hale, Machin, Keery (og)	29,572
8		21	(a)	Hull C	L 1-2	Hale	12,315
9		28	(h)	Mansfield T	L 0-3		22,903
10	Oct	2	(a)	Crewe A	D 2-2	Hudson, Hale	7,385
11		5	(a)	Brentford	W 3-2	Hudson, Rees, Farmer (pen)	15,830
12		8	(h)	Bristol C	W 2-1	Hudson, Hale	23,884
13		12	(h)	Wrexham	W 3-0	Hudson, Hale, Rees	23,682
14		15	(a)	Bristol C	W 1-0	Hale	13,582
15		19	(a)	Colchester U	L 1-2	Humphries	7,189
16		22	(h)	Shrewsbury T	W 8-1	Rees 3, Hudson 2, Barr 2, Harley (og)	27,294
17		26	(h)	Watford	D 2-2	Hudson, Machin	25,910
18		30	(a)	Shrewsbury T	D 0-0		13,669
19	Nov	2	(a)	Southend U	W 2-1	Rees, Hale	12,012
20		9	(h)	Peterborough U	W 3-2	Hale 2, Hudson	29,633
21		23	(h)	Bristol R	W 4-2	Hudson 2, Hale, Humphries	23,901
22		30	(a)	Queen's Park R	W 6-3	Hudson 3, Hale, Rees, Humphries	10,997
23	Dec	14	(a)	Crystal P	D 1-1	Humphries	18,943
24		21	(h)	Walsall	W 1-0	Hale	19,563
25		26	(a)	Barnsley	D 1-1	Whitehouse	12,308
26		28	(h)	Barnsley	W 3-1	Hudson 2, Hale	26,922
27	Jan	3	(h)	Millwall	W 3-0	Rees, Humphries, Farmer (pen)	27,437
28		11	(a)	Reading	D 2-2	Whitehouse 2	16,923
29		18	(h)	Luton T	D 3-3	Rees, Farmer, Kletzenbauer	20,921
30		22	(a)	Oldham A	L 0-2		20,008
31	Feb	1	(h)	Hull C	D 2-2	Rees, Farmer (pen)	23,476
32		8	(a)	Mansfield T	L 2-3	Farmer (pen), Hill	16,755
33		15	(h)	Brentford	D 2-2	Hale, Crowe (og)	22,775
34		22	(a)	Wrexham	D 1-1	Newton	9,677
35		29	(h)	Bournemouth	D 2-2	Newton, Hill	24,881
36	Mar	7	(a)	Watford	D 1-1	Hale	22,833
37		13	(h)	Southend U	L 2-5	Farmer (pen), Hudson	28,887
38		21	(a)	Bournemouth	L 1-2	Rees	16,158
39		28	(h)	Oldham A	W 4-1	Kirby 3, Newton	23,516
40		30	(a)	Port Vale	D 1-1	Wilson (og)	17,567
41		31	(h)	Port Vale	D 1-1	Kirby	29,541
42	Apr	4	(a)	Bristol R	W 1-0	Hale	12,006
43		11	(h)	Queen's Park R	W 4-2	Kirby, Rees, Humphries, Farmer (pen)	27,384
44		18	(a)	Millwall	D 0-0		22,443
45		20	(a)	Peterborough U	L 0-2		26,307
46		25	(h)	Colchester U	W 1-0	Hudson	36,901

FINAL LEAGUE POSITION: 1st in Division Three

Appearances
Goals

FA Cup

1	Nov	16	(a)	Trowbridge	W 6-1	Hudson 3, Rees, Kearns, Prosser (og)	6,524
2	Dec	7	(h)	Bristol R	L 1-2	Hale	26,248

Appearances
Goals

League Cup

1	Sep	25	(a)	Luton T	W 4-3	Rees, Machin, Hill, Sillett	3,821
2	Nov	4	(a)	Rotherham U	L 2-4	Hudson, Humphries	7,826

Appearances
Goals

Wesson	Sillett	Kearns	Hill	Curtis	Farmer	Humphries	Hale	Hudson	Machin	Rees	Kletzenbauer	Whitehouse	Mitten	Barr	Bruck	Gould	Newton	Meeson	Kirby	Smith	
1	2	3	4	5	6	7	8	9	10	11											1
1	2	3	4	5	6	7	8	9	10	11											2
1		3	4	5	6	7	8	9	10	11	2										3
1	2	3	4	5	6	7	8	9	10	11											4
1	2	3	4	5	6	7	8	9	10	11											5
1	2	3	4	5	6	7	8		10	11				9							6
1	2	3	4	5	6	7	8	9	10	11											7
1	2	3	4	5	6	7	8	9	10	11											8
1	2	3	4	5	6	7	8	9		11		10									9
1	2	3	4	5	6	7	8	9	10	11											10
1	2	3	4	5	6	7	8	9	10	11											11
1	2	3	4	5	6	7	8	9	10	11											12
1	2	3	4	5	6		8	9	10	7			11								13
1	2	3	4	5	6	7	8	9	10	11											14
1	2	3	4	5	6	7	8	9	10	11											15
1	2	3	4	5	6	7		9	10	11				8							16
1	2	3		5	6	7		9	10	11				8	4						17
1	2			5	6					7	3	10	11	8	4	9					18
1	2			5	6	7	10	9		11	3			8	4						19
1	2	3	4	5	6	7	10	9		11				8							20
1	2	3	4	5	6	7	10	9		11				8							21
1	2	3	4	5	6	7	10	9		11				8							22
1	2	3	4	5	6	7	10	9		11				8							23
1	2	3	4	5	6	7	10	9		11		8									24
1	2	3	4	5	6	7	10	9		11		8									25
1	2	3	4	5	6		8	9		7			11		10						26
1		3	4	5	6	7	10	9		11	2	8									27
1	2	6	4	5		7	10			11	3	8		9							28
1		2	4	5	6	7	10			11	3	8		9							29
1		3	4	5	6	7	10		8	11	2			9							30
1	2	3	4	5	6	7	10	9		11		8									31
1	2	3	4	5	6	7	10	9		11		8									32
1	2		4	5	6	7	10			11	3			9			8				33
	2	6	4	5	7		10			11	3					9	8	1			34
	2	3	4	5	6	7	10	9		11							8	1			35
	2	3	4	5	6	7	10	9		11							8	1			36
	2	3	4	5	6	7	10	9		11							8	1			37
	2	3	4	5	6		7	8		11								1	9	10	38
1	2		3	5	6	7				11					4		8		9	10	39
1		2	3	5	6	7	8			11					4				9	10	40
1	2	3		5	6					11			7		4		8		9	10	41
1	2	3		5	6	7	8			11					4				9	10	42
1	2	3		5	6	7	8			11					4				9	10	43
1	2	3	4	5	6	7	8			11									9	10	44
1	2	3	6	5		7				11					4		8		9	10	45
1	2	3	4	5	6	7		8		11									9	10	46
41	41	42	40	46	44	40	39	32	17	46	9	9	4	13	10	2	8	5	9	9	
			2		11	10	16	24	3	13	1	3		3			3		5		

4 own-goals

1	2	3	4	5	6	7	10	9		11				8							1
1	2	3	4	5	6	7	10	9		11				8							2
2	2	2	2	2	2	2	2	2		2				2							
		1					1	3		1											

1 own-goal

1	2	3	4	5		7	8	9	10	11					6						1
1	2			5	6	7	8	9		11	3	10			4						2
2	2	1	1	2	1	2	2	2	1	2	1	1			2						
	1		1			1		1	1	1											

1964-65

Manager: Jimmy Hill

1	Aug	22	(h)	Plymouth A	W	2-0	Farmer (pen), Smith	34,650
2		25	(a)	Ipswich T	W	3-1	Hale, Rees, Humphries	17,252
3		29	(a)	Bolton W	W	3-1	Kirby 2, Lee (og)	14,891
4	Sep	1	(h)	Ipswich T	W	5-3	Hale 2, Kirby 2, Hudson	37,782
5		5	(h)	Middlesbrough	W	3-0	Hudson, Kirby, Humphries	36,086
6		9	(a)	Derby C	L	1-2	Parry (og)	32,720
7		12	(a)	Newcastle U	L	0-2		37,481
8		15	(h)	Derby C	L	0-2		38,278
9		19	(h)	Northampton T	L	0-1		30,069
10		26	(a)	Southampton	L	1-4	Curtis	22,196
11		29	(a)	Swansea T	D	1-1	Rees	12,794
12	Oct	3	(h)	Huddersfield T	L	2-3	Hudson, Farmer (pen)	26,994
13		10	(h)	Swindon T	W	3-2	Hale, Machin, Hudson	25,216
14		17	(a)	Portsmouth	W	2-0	Rees, Gould	14,621
15		24	(h)	Manchester C	D	2-2	Hudson, Gould	28,693
16		31	(a)	Charlton A	L	0-3		16,418
17	Nov	7	(h)	Leyton O	D	1-1	Hale (pen)	24,416
18		13	(a)	Bury	L	0-5		6,366
19		21	(h)	Crystal P	D	0-0		24,145
20		28	(a)	Norwich C	L	0-1		18,098
21	Dec	5	(h)	Rotherham U	L	3-5	Hudson, Keyworth, Hale	20,029
22		12	(a)	Plymouth A	W	3-2	Machin, Keyworth, Bruck	13,892
23		19	(h)	Bolton W	D	0-0		23,387
24		26	(a)	Preston NE	L	2-3	Hudson 2	22,215
25		28	(h)	Preston NE	W	3-0	Hudson, Machin, Humphries	22,667
26	Jan	2	(a)	Middlesbrough	W	3-2	Hudson, Machin, Hale	15,714
27		16	(h)	Newcastle U	W	5-4	Hudson, Hale (pen), Rees, Gould, Marshall (og)	28,032
28		23	(a)	Northampton T	D	1-1	Clements	18,741
29	Feb	6	(h)	Southampton	D	1-1	Clements	25,298
30		13	(a)	Huddersfield T	L	1-2	Clements	13,042
31		20	(a)	Swindon T	L	1-4	Hudson	14,053
32		27	(h)	Portsmouth	L	1-2	Rees	22,181
33	Mar	6	(a)	Rotherham U	W	2-0	Hudson, Clements	7,741
34		13	(h)	Charlton A	W	2-0	Clements, Rees	21,621
35		27	(h)	Bury	W	2-1	Clements, Keyworth	18,777
36	Apr	3	(a)	Crystal P	D	2-2	Clements, Mitten	15,900
37		10	(h)	Norwich C	W	3-0	Clements, Hudson, Rees	22,552
38		17	(a)	Manchester C	D	1-1	Hale	10,804
39		19	(a)	Cardiff C	L	1-3	Farmer	11,330
40		20	(h)	Cardiff C	L	0-2		23,881
41		24	(h)	Swansea T	W	3-0	Hudson 2, Clements	23,683
42		28	(a)	Leyton O	W	3-1	Hudson 3	6,355

FINAL LEAGUE POSITION: 10th in Division Two

Appearances
Goals

FA Cup

3	Jan	9	(a)	Aston Villa	L	0-3		47,656

Appearances
Goals

League Cup

2	Sep	23	(h)	Ipswich T	W	4-1	Hudson 2, Rees, Mitten	14,778
3	Oct	14	(h)	Mansfield T	W	3-2	Hale, Rees, Gould	12,387
4	Nov	10	(h)	Sunderland	W	4-2	Hudson 2, Hale 2	19,227
5	Dec	1	(h)	Leicester C	L	1-8	Hudson	27,443

Appearances
Goals

Wesson	Hill	Kearns	Smith	Curtis	Farmer	Humphries	Hale	Hudson	Kirby	Rees	Tedds	Bruck	Meeson	Sillett	Machin	Mitten	Glazier	Gould	Burckitt	Harris	Keyworth	Clements	Turner	Newton	Barr	
1	2	3	4	5	6	7	8	9	10	11																1
1	2	3	4	5	6	7	8	9	10	11																2
1	2	3	4	5	6	7	8	9	10	11																3
1	2	3	4	5	6	7	8	9	10	11																4
1	2	3	4	5	6	7	8	9	10	11																5
1	2	3	4	5	6	7	8	9	10	11																6
1	2	3	4	5	6	7	8	9	10	11																7
1			4	5	6	7	8	9	10	11	2			3												8
1		3	10	5	6	7	8		9	11		4		2												9
		3		5	6		8	9		7		4	1	2	10	11										10
		3	8	5	6			9		7	2	4	1		10	11										11
		3	8	5	6	7		9			2	4	1		10	11										12
	3	4	6	5		7	8	9		11			1	2	10											13
	3	6	4	5		7	8	9		11				2			1	10								14
		6	4	5	2	7		9		11					8		1	10	3							15
		6	4	5	2	7		9		11					8		1	10	3							16
		3	6	5		7	8			11		4		2	10		1	9								17
		3	6	5	4		8	9		7				2	10	11	1									18
		2	6	5	4		8	9		7					10	11	1		3							19
		6	4	5		7	8	9		10						11	1		2	3						20
		5	6			7	8	9		11		4					1		2	3	10					21
		6		5		7		10		11		4		2	8		1			3	9					22
		6		5		7		10		11		4		2	8		1			3	9					23
	3	6		5		7	10	9		11		4		2	8		1									24
	3	6		5		7	10	9		11		4		2	8		1									25
	3	6		5		7	10	9		11		4		2	8		1									26
	2	6		5		7	10	9		11		4					1	8		3						27
1	2	6		5		7	8	9		11		4								3		10				28
	2	6		5		7	8	9		11		4					1			3		10				29
	2	6		5		7	8	9		11		4					1			3		10				30
	2	6		5			10	9		7		4					1	8		3		11				31
	2	6	8	5		7		9		11		4					1			3		10				32
	6			5	4		10	8		7				2			1			3	9	11				33
	6			5	4		10	8		7				2			1			3	9	11				34
	6	2		5	4		10			7							1	8		3	9	11				35
	6	2		5	4		8	9		7						11	1			3		10				36
	6	2		5	4		8	9		7						11	1			3		10				37
	6	2		5	4		8	9		7						11	1			3		10				38
1	6	2	8	5	4			9		7						11				3		10				39
1	6			5			10			7		4		2				9		3		11	8			40
1	6		10	5	4			8		7				2						3	9	11				41
1	6		10	5	4			9		7				2						3		11	8			42
14	28	36	24	41	25	27	32	38	9	41	3	18	4	17	14	10	24	8	5	20	7	15	2			
			1	1	3	3	9	19	5	7		1			4	1		3			3	9				

3 own-goals

	8	6		5		7		9		11		4		2	10					3						3
	1	1		1		1		1		1		1		1	1					1						

		3		5	6			9		7		4	1	2	10	11								8		2
	3	6	4	5		7	8	9		11			1	2				10								3
1		3	4	5			8	9		7		6		2	10	11										4
1		3	6	5		7	10	9		11	2								3						8	5
2	1	4	3	4	1	2	3	4		4	1	2	2	3	2	2		1	1					1	1	
							3	5		2						1		1								

1965-66

Manager: Jimmy Hill

1	Aug	21	(h)	Wolves	W 2-1	Hudson 2	36,722
2		24	(a)	Bury	D 1-1	Hudson	7,564
3		28	(a)	Rotherham U	D 1-1	Hudson	10,917
4		31	(h)	Bury	W 1-0	Clements	28,265
5	Sep	4	(h)	Manchester C	D 3-3	Hudson, Clements, Farmer (pen)	29,403
6		8	(a)	Southampton	L 0-1		19,870
7		11	(a)	Bristol C	D 1-1	Connor (og)	19,887
8		14	(h)	Southampton	W 5-1	Hudson, Clements, Machin, Bruck, Kearns (pen)	30,042
9		18	(h)	Crystal P	L 0-1		25,203
10		25	(h)	Carlisle U	W 3-2	Hudson, Gould, Farmer (pen)	20,672
11	Oct	6	(a)	Cardiff C	W 2-1	Rees, Curtis	12,639
12		9	(a)	Preston NE	D 0-0		19,672
13		16	(h)	Charlton A	W 3-1	Roberts 2, Hudson	25,357
14		23	(a)	Plymouth A	W 2-1	Hudson, Roberts	14,650
15		30	(h)	Portsmouth	W 3-2	Hudson, Roberts, Farmer (pen)	25,434
16	Nov	6	(a)	Bolton W	L 2-4	Rees, Curtis	13,343
17		13	(h)	Ipswich T	W 3-1	Roberts, Gould, Farmer (pen)	23,195
18		20	(a)	Birmingham C	W 1-0	Farmer (pen)	25,950
19		27	(h)	Leyton O	D 1-1	Hudson	20,086
20	Dec	4	(a)	Middlesbrough	D 1-1	Farmer	12,024
21		11	(h)	Huddersfield T	L 0-3		27,735
22		27	(a)	Norwich C	D 1-1	Pointer	27,765
23		28	(h)	Norwich C	W 2-0	Rees, Mitten	24,869
24	Jan	1	(h)	Preston NE	W 5-1	Pointer 3, Curtis, Hudson	26,818
25		8	(a)	Ipswich T	L 0-1		13,099
26		15	(h)	Plymouth A	W 5-1	Farmer 2 (1 pen), Rees, Bruck, Williams (og)	21,315
27		29	(a)	Wolves	W 1-0	Pointer	44,718
28	Feb	5	(h)	Rotherham U	D 2-2	Pointer, Mitten	24,867
29		19	(a)	Manchester C	L 0-1		40,190
30		26	(h)	Bristol C	D 2-2	Pointer, Hudson	30,062
31	Mar	12	(a)	Crystal P	W 1-0	Rees	15,717
32		18	(a)	Carlisle U	D 2-2	Gould, Pointer	13,167
33		26	(h)	Cardiff C	W 3-1	Machin, Denton, Farmer (pen)	20,246
34	Apr	2	(h)	Bolton W	D 2-2	Gould, Rees	19,440
35		9	(a)	Portsmouth	L 0-2		19,216
36		11	(a)	Derby C	L 0-1		21,745
37		12	(h)	Derby C	W 3-2	Machin, Kearns (pen), Curtis	25,332
38		16	(h)	Birmingham C	W 4-3	Rees, Pointer, Machin, Curtis	27,063
39		23	(a)	Leyton O	D 1-1	Mitten	5,800
40		26	(a)	Charlton A	L 0-2		15,329
41		30	(h)	Middlesbrough	W 2-1	Pointer, Roberts	19,704
42	May	7	(a)	Huddersfield T	W 2-0	Gould, Pointer	24,997

FINAL LEAGUE POSITION: 3rd in Division Two

Appearances
Sub Appearances
Goals

FA Cup

3	Jan	22	(a)	Swindon T	W 2-1	Rees, Trollope (og)	20,200
4	Feb	12	(a)	Crewe A	D 1-1	Rees	10,040
R		14	(h)	Crewe A	W 4-1	Hudson 2, Farmer (pen), Mitten *	27,820
5	Mar	5	(a)	Everton	L 0-3		60,350

*Some sources credit Mailey (og)

Appearances
Goals

League Cup

2	Sep	22	(a)	Leyton O	W 3-0	Hudson, Machin, Harris	5,326
3	Oct	13	(a)	Manchester C	W 3-2	Hudson, Clements, Oakes (og)	18,213
4	Nov	3	(h)	West Brom A	D 1-1	Hale	38,476
R		10	(a)	West Brom A	L 1-6	Machin	31,956

Appearances
Goals

Wesson	Kearns	Harris	Farmer	Curtis	Hill	Rees	Hale	Hudson	Machin	Clements	Bruck	Turner	Smith	Gould	Mitten	Roberts	Denton	Sillett	Pointer	Glazier	
1	2	3	4	5	6	7	8	9	10	11											1
1	2	3	4	5	6	7	8	9	10	11											2
1	2	3	4	5	6	7	8	9	10	11											3
1	2	3	4	5	6	7	8	9	10	11											4
1	2	3	4*	5	6	7	8	9	10	11	12										5
1	2	3		5	6	7	8	9	10	11	4										6
1	2	3		5	6	7	8	9	10	11	4										7
1	2	3		5	6	7		9	10	11	4	8*	12								8
1	2	3		5	6	7		9	10	11	4		8								9
1	2	3	4	5	6	7		9	10					8	11						10
1	2	3	4	5	6	7		9	10					8	11						11
1	2	3	4	5	6	7		9	10*	11				12		8					12
1	2	3	4	5	6	7	8	9		11						10					13
1	2	3	4	5	6*	7	8	9	12	11						10					14
1	2	3	4	5	6	7	8	9		11						10					15
1	2	3	4	5	6	7	8	9	10	11											16
1	2	3	4	5	6	11	12		10					9		8*	7				17
1	2	3	4	5	6	11	8		10					9			7				18
1	2	3	4	5	6	11		8	10					9			7				19
1	2	3	4	5	6	11*		8	10					9			7	12			20
1	6	3	4	5		7*		9	10	11				12		8		2			21
1	6	3	4	5		7		9	10	11								2	8		22
1	3		6	5		7		9	10		4				11			2	8		23
1	3		6	5		7		9	10		4				11	2			8		24
1	2	3	6	5		7		9	10		4				11				8		25
1	2	3	6	5		7		9	10		4				11				8		26
1		3	6	5		7		9	10		4				11			2	8		27
1		3	6	5		7		9	10*		4				11	12		2	8		28
1	2	3	6	5		7		9		11	4					10			8		29
1	2	3	6	5		7		9	10	11	4								8		30
1	2	3	4	5	6	11			10					8			7		9		31
1	2	3	4	5	6	7			10	11				8					9		32
1	2	3	4	5		11			10		6			8			7		9		33
1	2	3	4	5		11			10		6			8			7		9		34
1	2	3	4	5		11			10	12	6			8			7		9*		35
	6	3	8	5		7			10	11	4			9				2		1	36
	6	3		5		7			10		4			8	11	9		2		1	37
	6	3		5		7			10		4			8	11			2	9	1	38
	6	3		5		7			10		4			8	11			2	9	1	39
	6	3	12	5		7			10		4			8*	11			2	9	1	40
	2	3	6	5					10	11	4					9	7		8	1	41
	2	3	6	5		7			8	11	4			9					10	1	42
35	40	40	34	42	22	41	12	28	38	22	22	1	1	17	12	10	9	10	19	7	
			1				1		1	1	1		1	2		1		1			
	2		9	5		7		13	4	3	2			5	3	6	1		11		

2 own-goals

Wesson	Kearns	Harris	Farmer	Curtis	Hill	Rees	Hale	Hudson	Machin	Clements	Bruck	Turner	Smith	Gould	Mitten	Roberts	Denton	Sillett	Pointer	Glazier	
1	2	3	6	5		7		9	10		4				11				8		3
1	2	3	10	5	6	7		9		11	4								8		4
1	2	3	10	5	6			9		11	4						7		8		R
1	2	3	8	5	6	11			7		4			10					9		5
4	4	4	4	4	3	3		3	2	2	4			1	1		1		4		
			1			2		2							1						

1 own-goal

Wesson	Kearns	Harris	Farmer	Curtis	Hill	Rees	Hale	Hudson	Machin	Clements	Bruck	Turner	Smith	Gould	Mitten	Roberts	Denton	Sillett	Pointer	Glazier	
1	2	3	4	5	6	7		9	10				8		11						2
1	2	3	4	5	6	7	8	9		11						10					3
1	2	3	4	5	6	11	8	9	7							10					4
1	2	3	4	5	6	7	8	9	11							10					R
4	4	4	4	4	4	4	3	4	3	1			1		1	3					
		1					1	2	2	1											

1 own-goal

1966-67

Manager: Jimmy Hill

1	Aug	20	(h)	Hull C	W	1-0	Bruck	27,740
2		24	(a)	Plymouth A	L	2-4	Gould, Pointer	16,061
3		27	(a)	Portsmouth	W	2-0	Gould, Clements	16,297
4		30	(h)	Plymouth A	W	1-0	Pointer	20,327
5	Sep	3	(h)	Birmingham C	D	1-1	Gould	36,400
6		5	(a)	Millwall	L	0-1		15,766
7		10	(a)	Norwich C	D	1-1	Gould	13,454
8		17	(h)	Bristol C	W	1-0	Kearns (pen)	21,082
9		24	(h)	Bury	W	3-0	Gould, Gibson, Clements	22,002
10	Oct	1	(a)	Preston NE	L	2-3	Tudor, Curtis	13,681
11		8	(a)	Carlisle U	L	1-2	Clements	10,885
12		15	(h)	Blackburn R	W	2-0	Gould, Tudor	21,016
13		22	(a)	Bolton W	D	1-1	Machin	14,569
14		29	(h)	Charlton A	W	1-0	Gould	19,868
15	Nov	5	(a)	Derby C	W	2-1	Tudor, Machin	22,949
16		12	(h)	Crystal P	L	1-2	Gould	23,035
17		19	(a)	Huddersfield T	L	1-3	Tudor	15,192
18		26	(h)	Cardiff C	W	3-2	Gibson 2, Tudor	19,680
19	Dec	3	(a)	Wolves	W	3-1	Gibson, Rees, Key	27,232
20		9	(h)	Ipswich T	W	5-0	Gould 3, Gibson, Key	25,715
21		17	(a)	Hull C	D	2-2	Tudor, Key	26,577
22		26	(h)	Rotherham U	W	4-2	Gould 2, Gibson, Farmer (pen)	31,689
23		27	(a)	Rotherham U	D	1-1	Clements	13,301
24		31	(h)	Portsmsouth	W	5-1	Gould, Tudor, Machin, Key, Mitten	24,981
25	Jan	7	(a)	Birmingham C	D	1-1	Machin	36,316
26		14	(h)	Norwich C	W	2-1	Machin, Farmer	27,724
27		21	(a)	Bristol C	D	2-2	Curtis, Bruck	21,600
28	Feb	4	(a)	Bury	W	1-0	Rees	9,871
29		11	(h)	Preston NE	W	2-1	Gould, Machin	29,031
30		18	(a)	Charlton A	W	2-1	Gould 2	17,914
31		25	(h)	Carlisle U	W	2-1	Gould, Machin	29,965
32	Mar	11	(a)	Northampton T	D	0-0		20,100
33		18	(h)	Bolton W	D	1-1	Gould	28,580
34		25	(a)	Blackburn R	W	1-0	Gould	26,380
35		28	(h)	Northampton T	W	2-0	Gould, Machin	38,560
36	Apr	1	(h)	Derby C	D	2-2	Gould, Machin	32,041
37		8	(a)	Crystal P	D	1-1	Gould	23,247
38		15	(h)	Huddersfield T	W	1-0	Gould	29,698
39		22	(a)	Cardiff C	D	1-1	Key	19,592
40		29	(h)	Wolves	W	3-1	Machin, Gibson, Rees	51,455
41	May	6	(a)	Ipswich T	D	1-1	Gibson	18,916
42		13	(h)	Millwall	W	3-1	Tudor, Machin, Key	32,659

FINAL LEAGUE POSITION: 1st in Division Two

Appearances
Sub Appearances
Goals

FA Cup

3	Jan	28	(h)	Newcastle U	L	3-4	Gibson, Rees, McNamee (og)	35,569

Appearances
Sub Appearances
Goals

League Cup

2	Sep	13	(h)	Derby C	W	2-1	Clements, Farmer	14,804
3	Oct	5	(a)	Brighton & HA	D	1-1	Rees	13,007
R		11	(h)	Brighton & HA	L	1-3	Gould	13,437

Appearances
Sub Appearances
Goals

Glazier	Kearns	Bruck	Hill	Curtis	Farmer	Key	Gibson	Gould	Pointer	Rees	Clements	Mitten	Machin	Tudor	Coop	Thomas	Glover	Morrissey	Lewis	Lowes	Burckitt	Roberts	
1	2	3	4	5	6	7	8	9	10	11													1
1	2	3	4	5	6		8	9	10*	7	11	12											2
1	2	3	4	5	6		8	9	10	7	11												3
1	2	3	4	5	6		8	9	10	7	11												4
1	2	3	4	5	6		8	9		7	11		10										5
1	2	3	4	5	6		8	9	11	7			10										6
1	2	3	4	5	6		8	9		7	11		10										7
1	2	3	4	5	6*		8	9	10	7	11	12											8
1	2	3	4	5		7	10	9		11	6			8									9
1	2	3	4	5		7	10	9		11	6			8									10
1	2	3*	4	5		12	10	9	8	11	6		7										11
1	2		3	5	6	7		9			4	11	8	10									12
1	2		3	5	6			9		7	4	11	8	10									13
1	2		3*	5	6			9		7	4	11	8	10	12								14
1	2	3		5	4			9		7	6	11	10	8									15
1	2	3		5	4			9		7	6	11	10	8									16
1	2	3		5	4			9		7*	6	11	10	8	12								17
	2			5	4	7	8*	9		11	6			10	3	1	12						18
1	2	3		5	4	7	10	9		11	6		8										19
1	2	3		5	4	7	10	9		11	6		8*					12					20
1		2		5	4	7		9		11	6		8	10	3								21
1	2	3	12	5	4	7	10*	9		11	6		8										22
1	2	3	4	5	10	7		9		11	6		8										23
1	2	3		5	4	7		9			6	11	8	10									24
1	2	3		5	4	7		9			6	11	8	10									25
1	2	3		5	4	7	10	9		11	6		8										26
1	2	3		5	4	7	10	9		11	6		8										27
1	2	3		5	4	7*		12		11	6		8	9					10				28
1	2	3		5	4		10	9		11	6		8						7				29
1	2	3		5	4		10	9		11	6		8						7				30
1	2	3		5	12	7*	10	9		11	6		8						4				31
1	2	3		5	4		10	9		11	6		8							7			32
1	2	3		5	4		10	9		11	6		8							7			33
1	2	3		5	4		10	9		11	6		8						7				34
1	2	3		5	4		10	9		11	6		8						7				35
1	2	3		5	4		10	9		11	6		8						7				36
1	2	3		5			10	9		11	6		8						4	7			37
1	2	3		5		7	10	9		11	6		8						4				38
1	2	3		5	12	7	10	9		11*	6		8						4				39
1	2	3		5		7	10			11	6		8	9					4				40
1	2	3		5		7	10			11	6		8	9					4				41
1	2	3		5		7	10			11	6		8	9					4				42
41	41	38	15	42	32	21	31	38	7	39	40	8	34	16	2	1			13	3			
			1		2	1		1				2			2		1	1					
	1	2		2	2	6	8	24	2	3	4	1	11	8									

1	2	3		5	4	7	10*	9		11	6		8					12					3
1	1	1		1	1	1	1	1		1	1		1										
																		1					
							1			1													

1 own-goal

1	2	6		5			8	9	10	7	11										3		2
1	2	3	4	5		7	10	9		11	6			8									3
1	3			5	6			9	10	7*	11	12	8		2							4	R
3	3	2	1	3	1	1	2	3	2	3	3		1	1	1						1	1	
												1											
					1			1		1	1												

1967-68

Manager: Jimmy Hill to 12 October 1967, then Noel Cantwell

1	Aug	19	(a)	Burnley	L	1-2	Merrington (og)	21,483
2		22	(a)	Nottingham F	D	3-3	Gould 2, Machin	44,950
3		26	(h)	Sheffield U	D	2-2	Key, Bruck	33,328
4		29	(h)	Nottingham F	L	1-3	Rees	41,212
5	Sep	2	(a)	Arsenal	D	1-1	Gould	30,404
6		5	(h)	Southampton	W	2-1	Tudor, Rees	32,986
7		9	(h)	Manchester C	L	0-3		34,578
8		16	(a)	Newcastle U	L	2-3	Rees, Gould	28,890
9		23	(h)	West Brom A	W	4-2	Lewis, Rees 2, Machin	31,258
10		30	(a)	Chelsea	D	1-1	Clements	29,800
11	Oct	7	(a)	Sheffield W	L	0-4		33,360
12		14	(h)	Tottenham H	L	2-3	Rees 2	38,008
13		25	(a)	Manchester U	L	0-4		54,253
14		28	(h)	Sunderland	D	2-2	Tudor, Lewis (pen)	30,005
15	Nov	4	(a)	Wolves	L	0-2		38,695
16		11	(h)	Fulham	L	0-3		32,231
17		18	(a)	Leeds U	D	1-1	Hannigan	32,465
18		25	(h)	Everton	L	0-2		32,300
19	Dec	2	(a)	Leicester C	D	0-0		30,102
20		8	(h)	West Ham U	D	1-1	Baker	28,393
21		16	(h)	Burnley	W	5-1	Rees, Gould 3, Machin	28,559
22		23	(a)	Sheffield U	L	0-2		17,631
23		26	(h)	Liverpool	D	1-1	Baker	42,207
24		30	(a)	Liverpool	L	0-1		48,866
25	Jan	6	(h)	Arsenal	D	1-1	Gould	32,839
26		20	(h)	Newcastle U	L	1-4	Baker	33,760
27	Feb	3	(a)	West Brom A	W	1-0	Hannigan	29,000
28		10	(h)	Chelsea	W	2-1	Baker, Hannigan	36,542
29		24	(h)	Sheffield W	W	3-0	Martin 3 (1pen)	28,528
30	Mar	2	(a)	Everton	L	1-3	Hannigan	38,802
31		9	(a)	Manchester C	L	1-3	Tudor	33,310
32		16	(h)	Manchester U	W	2-0	Machin, Setters	47,111
33		23	(a)	Sunderland	D	1-1	Hunt	26,286
34		30	(h)	Wolves	W	1-0	Martin	36,242
35	Apr	6	(a)	Fulham	D	1-1	Hill	20,869
36		13	(h)	Leeds U	L	0-1		37,678
37		15	(h)	Stoke C	W	2-0	Martin, Tudor	31,353
38		16	(a)	Stoke C	D	3-3	Hannigan, Carr, Tudor	20,142
39		20	(a)	Tottenham H	L	2-4	Martin 2	36,175
40		27	(h)	Leicester C	L	0-1		39,888
41	May	4	(a)	West Ham U	D	0-0		30,180
42		11	(a)	Southampton	D	0-0		25,617

FINAL LEAGUE POSITION: 20th in Division One

Appearances
Sub Appearances
Goals

FA Cup

3	Jan	27	(h)	Charlton A	W	3-0	Baker, Hannigan, Carr	25,297
4	Feb	17	(h)	Tranmere R	D	1-1	Rees	32,831
R		21	(a)	Tranmere R	L	0-2		20,996

Appearances
Sub Appearances
Goals

League Cup

2	Sep	12	(h)	Arsenal	L	1-2	Machin	22,605

Appearances
Sub Appearances
Goals

Glazier	Kearns	Bruck	Farmer	Curtis	Clements	Key	Machin	Tudor	Lewis	Rees	Dickie	Gould	Knapp	Morrissey	Denton	Carr	Coop	Gibson	Hill	Roberts	Shepherd	Hannigan	Baker	Setters	Martin	Cattlin	Hunt	
1	2	3	4	5	6	7	8	9	10	11																		1
	2	3	4	5*	6	7	8	9	10	11	1	12																2
1	2	3			6	7*	8	10	4	11		9	5	12														3
1	2	3			6		8	10	7	11		9			4		5											4
1	2	3	4		6		8	10	7*	11		9	5			12												5
1	2	3			6		8	10	4	11*		9	5	12		7												6
1	2	3			6	7		10	4	11		9	5			8												7
1		3	12		6		8		4	11		9	5			7	2	10*										8
1		3			11		10	12	4	7		9*	5	8			2		6									9
1	2	3			11		8	9	10	7			5	4					6									10
1	3				11		8		10	7			5	4			2		6	9								11
1					6		8	9	7*	11			5	4		12	2	10	3									12
1	4				6		8	9	7	11			5	12			2	10	3*									13
1	3				6	7	10	9	4	11			5				2				8							14
1	3				5	7	10	9		11				6		8	2		4									15
1		3			5		10	9		11				6			2		4			7	8					16
1		3			6		10	9	4	11									2			7	8	5				17
1		3			6		4	9		11							2	8				7	10	5				18
1	2	3			6		10	12		11							4	8*				7	9	5				19
1	2	3			6		10			11							4	8				7	9	5				20
1	2	3			6		4			11		9						10				7	8	5				21
1	2	3			6		4		7	11		9						10					8	5				22
1	2	3			6		8		4	11		9					12	10					7*	5				23
1		3			2		4	6		11*		9				12	7	10					8	5				24
1		3			2		4	6		11		9						10				7	8	5				25
1		3					4	6		11		9						10	2			7	8	5				26
1		2			3		4	5		11						8		10	6			7	9					27
1		3			12		4	6								11		10	2			7	8*	5	9			28
		2			3		4	6		11	1					10						7	8	5	9			29
1		2			3		4	6		11						10		12				7	8*	5	9			30
1		2			3		4	6	12	11						10						7	8*	5	9			31
1		2			6		4	10								11						7		5	9	3	8	32
1		2			6		4	10								11						7		5	9	3	8	33
1		2			6			10	4							11	12					7*		5	9	3	8	34
1		2			6		4	10								11			12			7*		5	9	3	8	35
1		2			6		4	10								11			12				7	5	9	3	8*	36
1				12	6		4	10	8							11			2			7		5	9*	3		37
1				8*	6		4	10								11			2			7	12	5	9	3		38
1					6		4	10	12							11			2			7	8*	5	9	3		39
1		12			6		4	10								11			2			7		5	9	3	8*	40
1		2			6		8	10								11			4			7		5	9	3		41
1		2			6		8	10	4							11*						7		5	9	3	12	42
40	17	33	3	3	40	6	40	34	20	30	2	13	11	6	1	20	13	14	16	1	1	23	18	25	15	11	6	
		1	1	1	1			2	2			1		3		3	2	1	2				1				1	
		1			1	1	4	4	2	8		8				1			1			5	4	1	8		1	

1 own-goal

Glazier	Kearns	Bruck	Farmer	Curtis	Clements	Key	Machin	Tudor	Lewis	Rees	Dickie	Gould	Knapp	Morrissey	Denton	Carr	Coop	Gibson	Hill	Roberts	Shepherd	Hannigan	Baker	Setters	Martin	Cattlin	Hunt	
1	2	3					10	6	4							11		8	12			7	9	5*				3
1	2	3					4	5		11						10	12	8*	6			7	9					4
		3					4	6		11	1			8		10			2			7	9	5				R
2	2	3					3	3	1	2	1			1		3		2	2			3	3	2				
																	1		1									
										1						1						1	1					

Glazier	Kearns	Bruck	Farmer	Curtis	Clements	Key	Machin	Tudor	Lewis	Rees	Dickie	Gould	Knapp	Morrissey	Denton	Carr	Coop	Gibson	Hill	Roberts	Shepherd	Hannigan	Baker	Setters	Martin	Cattlin	Hunt	
1		3*			6	7	8		4	11		9	5			12	2	10										2
1		1			1	1	1		1	1		1	1				1	1										
																1												
							1																					

1968-69

Manager: Noel Cantwell

1	Aug	17	(a)	Sheffield W	L 0-3		26,235
2		21	(a)	Manchester U	L 0-1		51,201
3		24	(h)	West Ham U	L 1-2	Setters	33,575
4		27	(h)	West Brom A	W 4-2	Hunt 3 (1 pen), Machin	36,678
5		31	(a)	Burnley	D 1-1	Gibson	12,936
6	Sep	7	(h)	Newcastle U	W 2-1	Baker, Gibson	33,361
7		10	(h)	Chelsea	L 0-1		36,217
8		14	(a)	Nottingham F	D 0-0		22,260
9		17	(h)	Tottenham H	L 1-2	Tudor	40,950
10		21	(h)	Everton	D 2-2	Setters, Gibson	37,846
11		28	(a)	Leicester C	D 1-1	Hunt	32,122
12	Oct	5	(h)	Wolves	L 0-1		39,271
13		9	(a)	West Brom A	L 1-6	Hunt	29,926
14		12	(a)	Arsenal	L 1-2	Hunt	35,240
15		19	(h)	Manchester C	D 1-1	Hateley	30,670
16		26	(a)	Sunderland	L 0-3		21,981
17	Nov	2	(h)	Southampton	D 1-1	Machin	24,126
18		9	(a)	Stoke C	W 3-0	Hateley 2, Martin	16,117
19		16	(h)	Leeds U	L 0-1		33,224
20		23	(a)	Liverpool	L 0-2		44,820
21		30	(h)	Ipswich T	L 0-2		26,760
22	Dec	7	(a)	Queen's Park R	W 1-0	Carr	17,921
23		14	(h)	Arsenal	L 0-1		27,333
24		21	(a)	Manchester C	L 2-4	Shepherd, Hateley	27,700
25	Jan	11	(a)	Southampton	L 0-1		19,616
26	Feb	1	(a)	Leeds U	L 0-3		32,590
27		25	(h)	Queen's Park R	W 5-0	Machin, Hunt, Martin, Clements 2	26,399
28	Mar	4	(h)	Sunderland	W 3-1	Martin 2 (1 pen), Carr*	29,549
29		8	(h)	Sheffield W	W 3-0	Curtis, Hunt, Martin	30,131
30		10	(a)	Chelsea	L 1-2	Martin	17,630
31		14	(a)	West Ham U	L 2-5	Machin, Hunt	29,310
32		18	(h)	Stoke C	D 1-1	Carr	25,097
33		22	(h)	Burnley	W 4-1	Clements, Martin, Hunt, Machin	26,585
34		25	(a)	Ipswich T	D 0-0		20,525
35		29	(a)	Newcastle U	L 0-2		27,500
36	Apr	1	(h)	Leicester C	W 1-0	Martin	41,846
37		4	(a)	Tottenham H	L 0-2		35,024
38		8	(h)	Manchester U	W 2-1	Curtis, Martin	45,402
39		12	(a)	Everton	L 0-3		36,146
40		15	(a)	Wolves	D 1-1	Hunt	32,535
41		19	(h)	Nottingham F	D 1-1	Hannigan	37,772
42		22	(h)	Liverpool	D 0-0		35,106

FINAL LEAGUE POSITION: 20th in Division One

Appearances
Sub Appearances
Goals

* Some sources credit this goal to Montgomery of Sunderland.

FA Cup

3	Jan	4	(h)	Blackpool	W 3-1	Machin, Curtis, Shepherd	28,223
4		25	(a)	Everton	L 0-2		53,289

Appearances
Sub Appearances
Goals

League Cup

2	Sep	3	(h)	Portsmouth	W 2-0	Gibson, Hunt	20,946
3		25	(a)	West Ham U	D 0-0		27,598
R	Oct	1	(h)	West Ham U	W 3-2	Hunt, Tudor, Clements	25,988
4		16	(h)	Swindon T	D 2-2	Tudor, Hateley	23,588
R		21	(a)	Swindon T	L 0-3		23,828

Appearances
Sub Appearances
Goals

Glazier	Bruck	Cattlin	Machin	Setters	Clements	Hannigan	Hunt	Curtis	Tudor	Carr	Baker	Hill	Gibson	Coop	Hateley	Martin	Shepherd	Blockley	Paddon	
1	2*	3	4	5	6	7	8	9	10	11	12									1
1	2	3	10	5	6	7	8		9	11		4*	12							2
1	2	3	4	5	11	7			8		9	6	10							3
1	2	3	4	5	11		7		10		9	6	8							4
1		3	4	5	11		7	12	8		9*	6	10	2						5
1		3	4	5	11		7		8		9*	6	10	2			12			6
1		3	4	5	11		7		8	12	9*	6	10	2						7
1		3	4	5	11		7		9	8		6	10	2						8
1		3	4	5	11		7		8	12	9*	6	10	2						9
1		3	4	5	11		7		8	12		6	10*	2	9					10
1		3	4		11		7	5	8	10		6		2	9					11
1	3		4		11		7	5	8			6	10	2	9					12
1	3		8	6	11		7	5	12	10		4*		2	9					13
1	3		4	5	10		7		12	8		6	11*	2	9					14
1	2	3	4*	5	11		7		10			6	8	12	9					15
1	2	3	4				8	5	12	7		6	11		9	10*				16
1			4		3		7	5		11		6	8	2	9	10				17
1			4		3		7*	5	12	11		6	8	2	9	10				18
1			4		3		7	5		11		6	8	2	9	10				19
1		12	4		3	7	10	5		11		6	8	2*	9					20
1			4		3		7	5		11	12	6	8*	2	9	10				21
1		3	4		6	7	8	5		11				2	9	10				22
1		3	4		6	7*	8	5		11				2	9	10	12			23
1		3	4		6		8	5		11				2	9	10	7			24
1		3	4		11	7		5		8		6		2	9		10*	12		25
1		3	4		11	7	8	5		10		6		2		9				26
1		3	4		11		8	5		10		6		2		9	7*		12	27
1		3	4		11	12	8	5		10		6*		2		9	7			28
1		3	4		11		8	5		10		6		2		9	7			29
1	12	3	4		11		8	5		10		6*		2		9	7			30
1		3	4		11	7	8	5		10				2		9		6		31
1		3	4		11		8	5		10				2		9	7	6		32
1		3	4		11		8*	5		10	12			2		9	7	6		33
1		3	4		11	7		5		10		8		2		9		6		34
1			4		11	7	8	5		10		3		2		9		6		35
1		3	4		11		8	5		10		6		2		9	7			36
1		3	4		11*		8	5		10		6		2		9	7	12		37
1		3	4			12	8	5		10	7*	11		2		9		6		38
1		3	4	11			8	5		10	7			2		9		6		39
1	6	3	4	5		7	8			10				2		9		11		40
1	3		4	5	11*	12	8			10				2		9	7	6		41
1	4	3*		5		7	8	12		11				2	10	9		6		42
42	12	32	41	17	37	13	39	28	13	33	8	31	17	36	17	25	11	10		
	1	1				3		2	4	3	3		1	1			2	2	1	
			5	2	3	1	11	2	1	3	1		3		4	9	1			

1		3	4		11		7	5		8		6		2	9	10*	12			3
1		3	4		11	12	8	5		10		6		2		9	7*			4
2		2	2		2		2	2		2		2		2	1	2	1			
						1											1			
			1					1									1			

1		3	4	5	11		7		8			6	10	2		9				2
1		3	8	5	11	7	9	4		10		6		2						3
1	3		4		11	12	7	5	9	8		6	10*	2						R
1	3		4	5			7		12	11		6	8	2	9	10*				4
1	12	3		5	2	7*	10	4	8			6	11		9					R
5	2	3	4	4	4	2	5	3	3	3		5	4	4	2	2				
	1					1			1											
					1		2		2				1		1					

1969-70

Manager: Noel Cantwell

1	Aug	9	(a)	Sunderland	D	0-0		20,974
2		12	(h)	West Brom A	W	3-1	Carr 3	37,025
3		16	(h)	Derby C	D	1-1	Martin	41,036
4		20	(a)	West Brom A	W	1-0	Blockley	34,815
5		23	(a)	Ipswich T	W	1-0	Carr	18,274
6		27	(a)	Stoke C	L	0-2		25,507
7		30	(h)	Wolves	W	1-0	Hunt	38,336
8	Sep	6	(a)	Liverpool	L	1-2	Gibson	48,337
9		13	(h)	Crystal P	D	2-2	Martin 2 (2 pens)	29,314
10		16	(h)	Notts F	W	3-2	Martin, Clements, Paddon	26,038
11		20	(a)	Manchester C	L	1-3	Hunt	34,230
12		27	(h)	Leeds U	L	1-2	Hunt	36,091
13	Oct	4	(a)	Arsenal	W	1-0	Hunt	28,977
14		8	(a)	Derby C	W	3-1	Martin, McFarland (og), Blockley	39,880
15		11	(h)	West Ham U	D	2-2	Joicey, Clements	34,277
16		18	(a)	Southampton	D	0-0		20,238
17		25	(h)	Everton	L	0-1		37,862
18	Nov	1	(a)	Chelsea	L	0-1		38,899
19		8	(h)	Manchester U	L	1-2	Hunt	43,648
20		15	(a)	Burnley	D	0-0		11,328
21		22	(h)	Newcastle U	W	1-0	Hunt (pen)	31,825
22	Dec	6	(h)	Tottenham H	W	3-2	Machin, O'Rourke, Gibson	28,372
23		13	(a)	Crystal P	W	3-0	Hunt, Joicey 2	16,763
24		26	(h)	Ipswich T	W	3-1	Hunt, Harper (og), Martin (pen)	32,755
25	Jan	10	(h)	Manchester C	W	3-0	Martin, O'Rourke 2	29,386
26		17	(a)	Leeds U	L	1-3	Madeley (og)	34,295
27		28	(a)	Sheffield W	W	1-0	O'Rourke	18,149
28		31	(h)	Arsenal	W	2-0	Martin, O'Rourke	31,661
29	Feb	11	(a)	West Ham U	W	2-1	Martin 2	22,723
30		21	(a)	Everton	D	0-0		45,934
31		28	(h)	Chelsea	L	0-3		37,448
32	Mar	3	(h)	Liverpool	L	2-3	Hunt, O'Rourke	29,497
33		14	(h)	Sheffield W	D	1-1	Blockley	25,586
34		21	(a)	Tottenham H	W	2-1	Martin, O'Rourke	34,492
35		24	(h)	Sunderland	D	1-1	Clements	24,597
36		28	(h)	Burnley	D	1-1	Martin (pen)	24,713
37		30	(a)	Manchester U	D	1-1	Martin	41,335
38		31	(h)	Southampton	W	4-0	Joicey 2, Martin, O'Rourke	25,431
39	Apr	4	(h)	Stoke C	L	0-3		27,754
40		7	(a)	Nottingham F	W	4-1	O'Rourke 3, Joicey	15,569
41		10	(a)	Wolves	W	1-0	Joicey	23,395
42		14	(a)	Newcastle U	L	0-4		32,840

FINAL LEAGUE POSITION: 6th in Division One

Appearances
Sub Appearances
Goals

FA Cup

3	Jan	7	(h)	Liverpool	D	1-1	Martin	33,688
R		12	(a)	Liverpool	L	0-3		51,261

Appearances
Sub Appearances
Goals

League Cup

2	Sep	2	(h)	Chelsea	L	0-1		24,790

Appearances
Sub Appearances
Goals

Glazier	Coop	Cattlin	Hill	Curtis	Blockley	Hannigan	Gibson	Martin	Carr	Clements	Gould T	Bruck	Machin	Hunt	Baker	Paddon	Setters	Joicey	Mortimer	Barry	O'Rourke	McManus	Parker	Rafferty	
1	2	3	4	5	6	7	8	9	10	11															1
1	2	3	4	5	6		8	9	10	11	7														2
1	2	3	4	5	6		8	9	10	11	7														3
1	2	3	4	5	6		8	9	10	11	7														4
1	2*	3	4	5	6		8	9	10	11	7	12													5
1		3		5	6		8	9	10	11	7*	2	4	12											6
1	2	3		5	6		8	9	10	11			4	7											7
1	2	3	10	5	6		8	9		11			4	7*		12									8
1	2	3		5	6	12	8	9		11		4			7*	10									9
1	2			5	6		8	9		3		4		7		11	10								10
1	2			5	6		8	9		3		4	10	7		11									11
1	2	3		5	6		8*	9	10	11		12	4	7											12
1	2			5	6		8	9	10	11		3		7			4								13
1	2			5	6		8	9	10*	11		3		7			4	12							14
1	2			5	6			9	10	11		3		7			4*	8	12						15
1	2			5	6			9	10	11		3	12	7			4*	8							16
1	2			5	6		8	9	10	11		3	4*	7				12							17
1	2	3		5	6		8*	9	10	11			4	7						12					18
1	2	3		5	6		12	9	10	11			4	7				8*							19
1	2	3		12	6			9	8	11			4	7			10			5					20
1	2				6		11		8	3			4	7			9			5	10				21
1	2				6		11	9	8*	3			4	7			12			5	10				22
1	2	12			6				8	3			4	7*			11	9		5	10				23
	2	3			6		11*	9	8	4				7					12	5	10	1			24
1	2	3			6			9	8	11			4	7						5	10				25
1	2	3						9	8	6			4	7				11		5	10				26
1	2	3			6			9	8	4				7				11		5	10				27
1	2	3				7		9	8	6				4					11	5	10				28
1	2	3	12			7		9	8	6*				4					11	5	10				29
1	2	3	11		6	7		9	8					4						5	10				30
1	2	3			6	7*		9	8					4				12	11	5	10				31
1	2	3	11		6	7		9	8					4						5	10				32
1	2	3			6	7		9	8			12		4				10	11	5*					33
1	6	3			5		4*	9	8		7	2						12	11		10				34
1	2	3			5		11*	9	8	6	7	4						12			10				35
1	2	3			5		11	9	8		7							12	4*		10		6		36
1	4	3			5		7*	9	11		6	2						10			8		12		37
1	2	3			5		4	9	8			6		7				11			10				38
1	2	3			5		4*	9	8			6		7				11	12		10				39
1	2	3			5		4	9	8	6				7				11			10				40
1	2	3			5		4	9	8	6				7				11			10				41
	2	3			5		7	8	11	6			4					10				1		9	42
40	41	32	8	19	39	7	28	40	38	33	9	14	15	30	1	3	8	13	6	14	20	2	1	1	
		1	1	1		1	1					3	1	1		1	1	6	3	1			1		
					3		2	14	4	3			1	9		1		7			11				

3 own-goals

1	2				6			9	8	3			4	7			12		11*	5	10				3
1	2	3						9	8	11			4	7			6			5	10				R
2	2	1			1			2	2	2			2	2			1		1	2	2				
																	1								
								1																	

1	2	3		5	6		8	9	10	11			4	7											2
1	1	1		1	1		1	1	1	1			1	1											

1970-71

Manager: Noel Cantwell

1	Aug	15	(a)	Nottingham F	L 0-2		25,137
2		18	(a)	Ipswich T	W 2-0	Martin 2	21,188
3		22	(h)	Southampton	W 1-0	Hunt	26,238
4		25	(h)	Wolves	L 0-1		31,160
5		29	(a)	Tottenham H	L 0-1		27,103
6	Sep	1	(a)	Derby C	W 4-3	Martin 2, Clements, Carr	31,621
7		5	(h)	Huddersfield T	D 0-0		26,087
8		12	(a)	Manchester U	L 0-2		48,939
9		19	(h)	Chelsea	L 0-1		29,648
10		26	(a)	Newcastle U	D 0-0		32,050
11	Oct	3	(h)	Everton	W 3-1	Martin, Hunt 2	29,212
12		10	(a)	Burnley	D 0-0		12,505
13		17	(h)	Nottingham F	W 2-0	Martin, Hunt	25,418
14		24	(h)	Arsenal	L 1-3	Martin	29,975
15		31	(a)	Leeds U	L 0-2		31,670
16	Nov	7	(h)	Manchester C	W 2-1	Doyle (og), Carr	25,287
17		14	(a)	Liverpool	D 0-0		50,503
18		21	(h)	Crystal P	W 2-1	Martin, Clements	23,074
19		28	(a)	West Ham U	W 2-1	Clements, O'Rourke	22,300
20	Dec	5	(h)	Stoke C	W 1-0	O'Rourke	23,785
21		12	(a)	Blackpool	L 0-1		11,381
22		19	(a)	Southampton	L 0-3		17,569
23		26	(h)	West Brom A	D 1-1	Martin (pen)	27,527
24	Jan	9	(h)	Ipswich T	W 1-0	Joicey	19,938
25		16	(a)	Wolves	D 0-0		27,441
26	Feb	6	(a)	Stoke C	L 1-2	Alderson	17,208
27		9	(h)	West Ham U	L 0-1		25,090
28		13	(h)	Blackpool	W 2-0	O'Rourke, Carr	18,643
29		20	(a)	Crystal P	W 2-1	Carr 2	24,114
30		26	(h)	Leeds U	L 0-1		40,022
31	Mar	13	(h)	Liverpool	W 1-0	O'Rourke	27,731
32		20	(a)	Manchester C	D 1-1	O'Rourke	22,120
33		27	(a)	Huddersfield T	L 0-1		15,141
34	Apr	3	(h)	Tottenham H	D 0-0		22,947
35		6	(a)	Arsenal	L 0-1		37,029
36		10	(a)	West Brom A	D 0-0		18,759
37		12	(a)	Everton	L 0-3		24,371
38		13	(h)	Manchester U	W 2-1	Hunt 2	33,849
39		17	(h)	Burnley	W 3-0	Hunt 2, Rafferty	18,377
40		24	(a)	Chelsea	L 1-2	Hunt	27,517
41		27	(h)	Derby C	D 0-0		22,051
42	May	1	(h)	Newcastle U	W 2-0	Hunt, Blockley	20,781

FINAL LEAGUE POSITION: 10th in Division One

Appearances
Sub Appearances
Goals

FA Cup

3	Jan	11	(a)	Rochdale	L 1-2	Hunt	13,011

Appearances
Sub Appearances
Goals

League Cup

2	Sep	9	(a)	Tranmere R	D 1-1	Machin	11,079
R		22	(h)	Tranmere R	W 2-1	Hunt, Blockley	14,179
3	Oct	6	(h)	West Ham U	W 3-1	Martin (pen), O'Rourke, Carr	19,362
4		27	(h)	Derby C	W 1-0	Martin	26,141
5	Nov	18	(a)	Tottenham H	L 1-4	O'Rourke	31,864

Appearances
Sub Appearances
Goals

Glazier	Coop	Bruck	Carr	Blockley	Strong	Hunt	Joicey	Martin	O'Rourke	Clements	Goodwin	Machin	Mortimer	Cattlin	Parker	Smith	Alderson	McManus	Hill	Rafferty	Barry	
1	2	3	4	5	6	7	8	9	10	11												1
1	2		8	5	6	7		9	10	3	4	11										2
1	2		8	5	6	7	12	9	10	3	4	11*										3
1	2		8	5	6	7	10	9		3	4		11*	12								4
1	2		8	5	6	7		9	10*	11	4			3	12							5
1	2		8	5	6	12	7	9		11		10		3		4*						6
1	2		8	5	6	7	10*	9		11		4		3			12					7
1	2	12	8	5	6	7		9	10*	11		4				3						8
1		12	8*	5	6	7		9	10	3		4				2	11					9
1	2		8	5	6	7		9	10	3		4					11					10
1	2	3	8	5	6	7		9	10	4							11					11
1	2	3	8	5	6	7	12	9	10*	4							11					12
1	2		8	5	6	7		9	10	4				3			11					13
	2		8	5	6	7	10	9		11		4				3		1				14
1	2		8	5	6	7		9	10	4			11			3						15
1	2		8	5	6	7		9	10	11			4			3						16
1	2		8	5	6			9	10	11			4			3			7			17
1	2		8	5				9	10	11			4		6	3			7			18
1	2		8	5				9	10	11			4		6	3			7			19
1	2		8	5				9	10	11			4		6	3			7			20
1	2		8	5	6			9	10	11			4		7	3						21
1	2		8	5	6	4		9	10	11					7	3						22
1	2		8	5	6	7		9	10	11						3			4			23
				5	6	7	10	9		3		4	8			2	11	1				24
1			8	5			9		10	3		4	7		6	2	11					25
1			8	5		10	9			3		4	7		6	2	11					26
1	2		8	5		7	10	9					4		6	3	11					27
1			8	5	3			9	10	11		4	7		6	2						28
1			8	5	3		9		10	11		4	7		6	2						29
1			8	5	3		9		10	11		4*	7		6	2	12					30
1			8	5	3		9		10	11		4	7		6	2						31
1			8	5	3		9		10	11		4	7		6	2						32
1			8	5	3	12	9*		10	11		4	7	2	6							33
1			8	5	2	10				11		4	7	3	6*		12			9		34
1	2		8	5	6	10	11					4	7	3						9		35
1			8	5	6	4	9*		12	11			7	3		2				10		36
1	2		8	5	6	10			4	11			7	3						9		37
1			8	5	6	10				11		4	12	3		2	7*			9		38
1			8	5		10				11		4	12	3	6	2	7*			9		39
1			8	5		10				11		4	7	3	6	2				9		40
1			8	5		10				11		4	7	3	6	2				9		41
1			8	5		10				11		4	12	3		2	7			9*	6	42
40	25	3	41	42	32	29	16	26	27	40	4	24	24	14	18	28	12	2	5	9	1	
		2				2	2		1				3	1	1		3					
			5	1		10	1	9	5	3							1			1		

1 own-goal

Glazier	Coop	Bruck	Carr	Blockley	Strong	Hunt	Joicey	Martin	O'Rourke	Clements	Goodwin	Machin	Mortimer	Cattlin	Parker	Smith	Alderson	McManus	Hill	Rafferty	Barry	
1			8	5	6	7	10	9		3		4				2	11					3
1			1	1	1	1	1	1		1		1				1	1					
						1																

Glazier	Coop	Bruck	Carr	Blockley	Strong	Hunt	Joicey	Martin	O'Rourke	Clements	Goodwin	Machin	Mortimer	Cattlin	Parker	Smith	Alderson	McManus	Hill	Rafferty	Barry	
1	2	3	8	5	6	7	10	9		11		4										2
1	2		8	5	6	7		9	10	3			4				11					R
1	2	3	8	5	6	7		9	10	4							11					3
1	2		8	5	6	7		9	10	4						3	11					4
1	2		8	5			7	9	10	11			4			3			6			5
5	5	2	5	5	4	4	2	5	4	5		1	2			2	3		1			
			1	1		1		2	2			1										

1971-72

Manager: Noel Cantwell until 12 March 1972, then Bob Dennison (acting) until end of season.

1	Aug	14	(h)	Stoke C	D	1-1	Hunt	20,894
2		17	(a)	Ipswich T	L	1-3	Carr	18,921
3		21	(a)	West Brom A	D	1-1	Hunt	25,449
4		24	(h)	Derby C	D	2-2	Joicey, Hunt (pen)	27,759
5		28	(h)	Newcastle U	W	1-0	Blockley	22,788
6		30	(a)	West Ham U	L	0-4		28,176
7	Sep	4	(a)	Chelsea	D	3-3	Rafferty, O'Rourke, Mortimer	35,459
8		11	(h)	Nottingham F	D	1-1	Hunt	20,380
9		18	(a)	Southampton	L	1-3	Hunt	17,443
10		25	(h)	Tottenham H	W	1-0	Carr	26,517
11	Oct	2	(a)	Everton	W	2-1	Young, St John	36,867
12		9	(h)	Leeds U	W	3-1	Chilton, St John, Hunt	32,108
13		16	(a)	Stoke C	L	0-1		20,540
14		22	(h)	Crystal P	D	1-1	St John	20,811
15		30	(a)	Wolves	D	1-1	Carr	25,841
16	Nov	6	(h)	Huddersfield T	W	2-1	Hunt 2	16,309
17		13	(a)	Sheffield U	L	0-2		32,630
18		20	(h)	Liverpool	L	0-2		25,452
19		27	(a)	Manchester C	L	0-4		31,003
20	Dec	4	(h)	Leicester C	D	1-1	McGuire	26,300
21		11	(a)	Arsenal	L	0-2		28,597
22		17	(h)	Chelsea	D	1-1	Carr	21,875
23		27	(a)	Manchester U	D	2-2	Young, Carr	52,117
24	Jan	1	(h)	Southampton	W	1-0	Mortimer	17,934
25		8	(a)	Newcastle U	L	2-4	Rafferty, Mortimer	25,830
26		22	(h)	Ipswich T	D	1-1	Blockley (pen)	18,183
27		29	(a)	Derby C	L	0-1		29,385
28	Feb	12	(a)	Crystal P	D	2-2	Carr, Chilton	19,339
29		19	(h)	Wolves	D	0-0		22,298
30	Mar	11	(a)	Leeds U	L	0-1		43,154
31		17	(h)	West Brom A	L	0-2		22,887
32		21	(h)	West Ham U	D	1-1	Smith	18,703
33		25	(a)	Nottingham F	L	0-4		12,205
34		31	(a)	Tottenham H	L	0-1		32,542
35	Apr	1	(h)	Manchester U	L	2-3	Barry, Graham	37,798
36		4	(h)	Everton	W	4-1	Hunt 2 (1 pen), Carr, Chilton	22,129
37		8	(a)	Liverpool	L	1-3	Hunt	50,628
38		11	(a)	Huddersfield T	W	1-0	Hunt	11,782
39		15	(h)	Manchester C	D	1-1	Mortimer	34,302
40		18	(h)	Sheffield U	W	3-2	Graham, Carr, Machin	19,220
41		22	(a)	Leicester C	L	0-1		24,254
42	May	1	(h)	Arsenal	L	0-1		23,504

FINAL LEAGUE POSITION: 18th in Division One

Appearances
Sub Appearances
Goals

FA Cup

3	Jan	15	(a)	West Brom A	W	2-1	Rafferty, Chilton	26,472
4	Feb	5	(h)	Hull C	L	0-1		24,621

Appearances
Sub Appearances
Goals

League Cup

2	Sep	7	(h)	Burnley	L	0-1		15,362

Appearances
Sub Appearances
Goals

Glazier	Smith	Cattlin	Machin	Blockley	Barry	Mortimer	Carr	Rafferty	Hunt	Clements	Alderson	Coop	O'Rourke	Parker	McGuire	Joicey	Young	Chilton	St John	Strong	Holmes	McManus	Healey	Graham	Green	
1	2	3	4	5	6	7	8	9*	10	11	12															1
1	2	3	4*	5	6	7	8		10			12	9	11												2
1	2	3		5	6	4	8		10				9		7	11										3
1	2	3		5	6	4	8		10						11	9	7									4
1	2	3		5	6*	4	8		10		12		9		11		7									5
1	2	3		5	6	4	8		10				9		11		7									6
1	2			5		4	8	9	10			3	7	6	11											7
1	3			5		4	8		10		7	2	12	6	11			9*								8
1	3	11		5		4	8		10			2		6			7	9								9
1	4	3		5			8		10			2		6			7	9	11							10
1	4	3		5			8		10			2		6			7	9	11							11
1	4			5	3	12	8		10			2		6			7	9	11*							12
1	4			5	3		8		10		12	2		6			7*	9	11							13
1	4			5	3	10	8					2		6			7	9	11							14
1	4			5	3	10	8		12			2		6			7*	9	11							15
1	4			5	3		8		10		11*	2		6	12		7		9							16
1	4			5	3	12	8		10		11	2		6	9		7*									17
1	4			5	3		8		10			2		6			7	9	11							18
1	4			5			8	11	10			2		6	7			9		3						19
1	2			5		10	8	9			11*			6	12		7		4		3					20
	2			5		10	8	9			11	12		6			7		4*		3	1				21
	2		11	5		12	8	9*						6			7	10	4		3	1				22
	2	3	4*	5		12	8	9						6			7	10	11				1			23
	2	3		5		10	8	9						6			7	11	4				1			24
	2	3		5		4	8	10						6			7	9	11				1			25
1	2	3	4	5		11	8	10						6			7	9								26
1	2	3	4*	5		11	8	10						6	12		7	9								27
1	2	3		5	4	12	8	10						6	7			9	11*							28
1	2	3		5	6		8	9						4	7			10	11							29
1	2	3		5	6		8							4	7			9	11					10		30
1	2	3		5	6	12	8							4	7			9	11*					10		31
1	2	3	4*	5	6	12	8		11						7			9						10		32
1	2	3	4	5	6	12	8		11						7			9*						10		33
1	2	3	4	5	6	11	8								7			9						10		34
1	2	3		5	6	4	8		11						7			9						10		35
1	2	3		5	6	4	8		11						7			9						10		36
1	2	3	9	5	6	4	8		11						7									10		37
1	2	3	9	5	6	4	8		11						7									10		38
1	2	3	9	5	6	4	8		11						7									10		39
1	2	3	9	5	6	4	8		11*						7			12						10		40
1	2	3	9	5	6*	4	8								7			11						10	12	41
1	2	3	9	5		4	8		11					6	7									10		42
37	42	29	15	42	27	26	42	13	26	1	5	13	5	27	23	2	21	26	18	1	3	2	3	13		
						8			1		3	2	1		3			1							1	
	1		1	2	1	4	8	2	12				1		1	1	2	3	3					2		

Glazier	Smith	Cattlin	Machin	Blockley	Barry	Mortimer	Carr	Rafferty	Hunt	Clements	Alderson	Coop	O'Rourke	Parker	McGuire	Joicey	Young	Chilton	St John	Strong	Holmes	McManus	Healey	Graham	Green	
1	2	3	7		5	4	8	10	12					6				9	11*							3
1	4*	3		5		12	8		10			2		6			7	9	11							4
?	2	2	1	1	1	1	2	1	1			1		2			1	2	2							
						1			1																	
								1										1								

Glazier	Smith	Cattlin	Machin	Blockley	Barry	Mortimer	Carr	Rafferty	Hunt	Clements	Alderson	Coop	O'Rourke	Parker	McGuire	Joicey	Young	Chilton	St John	Strong	Holmes	McManus	Healey	Graham	Green	
1	2			5		4	8	9	10			3	7	6	11*		12									2
1	1			1		1	1	1	1			1	1	1	1											
																	1									

1972-73

Manager: Gordon Milne

1	Aug	12	(a)	Tottenham H	L	1-2	Hunt	33,884
2		14	(a)	West Ham U	L	0-1		27,435
3		19	(h)	Southampton	D	1-1	Hunt (pen)	18,544
4		22	(h)	Arsenal	D	1-1	Graham	24,670
5		26	(a)	Leicester C	D	0-0		25,894
6		29	(h)	Wolves	L	0-1		24,569
7	Sep	2	(h)	Stoke C	W	2-1	Carr 2	16,391
8		9	(a)	Manchester U	W	1-0	Carr	37,073
9		16	(h)	Newcastle U	L	0-3		17,634
10		23	(a)	West Brom A	L	0-1		15,571
11		30	(h)	Chelsea	L	1-3	Alderson	20,295
12	Oct	7	(a)	Crystal P	W	1-0	Mortimer	22,229
13		14	(h)	Manchester C	W	3-2	Carr, Stein, Alderson	24,541
14		21	(a)	Leeds U	D	1-1	Carr	36,240
15		28	(h)	Birmingham C	D	0-0		35,304
16	Nov	4	(a)	Arsenal	W	2-0	Alderson, Hutchison	33,699
17		11	(h)	West Ham U	W	3-1	Hutchison, Stein, Alderson	27,172
18		18	(h)	Sheffield U	W	3-0	Alderson 2, Mackenzie (og)	22,079
19	Dec	2	(h)	Everton	W	1-0	Alderson	22,774
20		5	(a)	Ipswich T	L	0-2		17,809
21		9	(a)	Derby C	L	0-1		31,002
22		16	(h)	Norwich C	W	3-1	Stein 2, Alderson	19,873
23		23	(a)	Liverpool	L	0-2		41,550
24		26	(h)	West Brom A	D	0-0		31,545
25		30	(a)	Southampton	L	1-2	Alderson	15,261
26	Jan	6	(h)	Leicester C	W	3-2	Stein, Woollett (og), Carr	25,076
27		27	(h)	Manchester U	D	1-1	Alderson	42,911
28	Feb	10	(a)	Newcastle U	D	1-1	Stein	22,940
29		17	(h)	Tottenham H	L	0-1		26,854
30	Mar	2	(h)	Crystal P	W	2-0	Stein, Alderson	25,194
31		7	(a)	Norwich C	D	1-1	Carr	29,173
32		10	(a)	Manchester C	W	2-1	Carr, Stein	30,448
33		24	(a)	Birmingham C	L	0-3		34,775
34		26	(a)	Stoke C	L	1-2	Stein	20,218
35		31	(h)	Ipswich T	W	2-1	Alderson, Stein	17,130
36	Apr	2	(h)	Leeds U	L	0-1		24,435
37		7	(a)	Everton	L	0-2		27,474
38		14	(h)	Derby C	L	0-2		22,762
39		17	(h)	Liverpool	L	1-2	Alderson	27,334
40		21	(a)	Sheffield U	L	1-3	Barry	19,992
41		23	(a)	Chelsea	L	0-2		18,279
42		28	(a)	Wolves	L	0-3		21,520

FINAL LEAGUE POSITION: 19th in Division One

Appearances
Sub Appearances
Goals

FA Cup

3	Jan	13	(a)	Orient	W	4-1	Alderson 2, Carr, Hutchison	12,272
4	Feb	3	(h)	Grimsby T	W	1-0	Coop (pen)	38,814
5		24	(h)	Hull C	W	3-0	Alderson, Stein 2	31,724
6	Mar	17	(a)	Wolves	L	0-2		50,106

Appearances
Sub Appearances
Goals

League Cup

2	Sep	5	(h)	Hartlepool	W	1-0	Carr (pen)	8,687
3	Oct	3	(a)	Birmingham C	L	1-2	Alderson	27,803

Appearances
Sub Appearances
Goals

Glazier	Coop	Cattlin	Machin	Blockley	Barry	Mortimer	Graham	Hunt	Carr	Green	Smith	McGuire	Young	Rafferty	Alderson	Dugdale	Parker	Stein	Hutchison	Ramsbottom	Holmes	
1	2	3	4	5	6	7	8	9	10	11												1
1	2	3	4	5	6	7	8	9	10		11											2
1	2	3	4	5	6	7	8	9	10		11											3
1	2	3	4	5	6	7	8	9	10		11											4
1	2	3	4	5	6	7	8	9	10		11											5
1	2	3	4	5	6	7	8*	9	10		11		12									6
1	2	3	4	5	6	7		9*	10		11	12	8									7
1	2	3	4	5	6	7			10		11		8	9								8
1	2	3	4	5	6	7			10		11*		8	9	12							9
1	2	3	4*	5	6	7			10			12	8	9	11							10
1	2			5	6	7			10	8	12	4		9	11	3*						11
1	2	3	4		5	7			10		8				11		6	9				12
1	2	3			5	7			10		4				8		6	9	11			13
1	2	3			5	7			10		4				8		6	9	11			14
	2	3			5	7			10		4				8		6	9	11	1		15
1	2	3			5	7			10		4				8		6	9	11			16
1	2	3			5	7			10*		4	12			8		6	9	11			17
1	2	3			5	7			10		4				8		6	9	11			18
	2	3			5	7			10		4				8		6	9	11	1		19
	2	3			5*	7			10		4				8	12	6	9	11	1		20
	2	3				7			10		4				8	5	6	9	11	1		21
	2	3				7			10		4				8	5	6	9	11	1		22
	2	3			5	7			10		4*	12			8		6	9	11	1		23
1	2	3			5	7			10		4				8		6	9	11			24
1	2	3			5	7			10		4				8		6	9	11			25
1	2				5	7			10		4				8	3	6	9	11			26
1	2				5	7					4	10			8	3	6	9	11			27
1	2	10			5	7						4			8	3	6	9	11			28
1	4	3			5	7						10			8	2	6	9	11			29
1	2	3			5	7			10		4				8		6	9	11			30
1	2	3			5				10		4	7			8*	12	6	9	11			31
1	2	3			5	7			10	8	4						6	9	11			32
1	2	3			5	7			10			4			8	12	6*	9	11			33
1	2	3			5	7			10			4			8	6		9	11			34
	2	3			5	7			10		12	4*			8	6		9	11	1		35
	2	3			5				10	7		4			8	6		9	11	1		36
	2	3			5				10	7		4			8	6		9	11	1		37
	2	3			5	7			10		4				8	6		9	11	1		38
	2	3			5	7			10*	12	4				8	6		9	11	1		39
	2				5	7					4	10			8	3	6	9	11	1		40
	2				5	7				12	4	10*			8	3	6	9	11	1		41
	2				5*	7				12	4	10			8	6		9	11	1	3	42
28	42	36	11	11	40	39	6	7	36	5	32	13	4	4	32	16	24	31	30	14	1	
										3	2	4	1		1	3						
					1	1	1	2	8						13			10	2			

2 own-goals

1	2				5	7			10		4				8	3	6	9	11			3
1	2				5	7				12	4	10			8*	3	6	9	11			4
1	2	3			5	7			10		4				8		6	9	11			5
1	2	3			5	7			10		4*	12			8		6	9	11			6
4	4	2			4	4			3		4	1			4	2	4	4	4			
										1		1										
	1								1						3			2	1			

1	2	3	4	5	6	7			10		11		8	9								2
1	2	3	4		5	7			10		8			9	11		6					3
2	2	2	2	1	2	2			2		2		1	2	1		1					
									1						1							

1973-74

Manager: Gordon Milne

1	Aug	25	(h)	Tottenham H	W 1-0	Coop	25,094
2		28	(h)	Liverpool	W 1-0	Hutchison	29,364
3	Sep	1	(a)	Burnley	D 2-2	Green 2	20,711
4		5	(a)	Manchester C	L 0-1		30,931
5		8	(h)	Southampton	W 2-0	Coop (pen), Green	19,416
6		11	(h)	Manchester C	W 2-1	Coop, Craven	27,491
7		15	(a)	Chelsea	L 0-1		30,593
8		18	(h)	Derby C	W 1-0	Stein	26,511
9		22	(h)	Newcastle U	D 2-2	Alderson, Stein	25,556
10		29	(a)	Leicester C	W 2-0	Alderson, Cartwright*	29,317
11	Oct	6	(h)	Everton	L 1-2	Green	26,834
12		13	(a)	Norwich C	D 0-0		22,841
13		20	(h)	West Ham U	L 0-1		21,141
14		27	(a)	Stoke C	L 0-3		17,421
15	Nov	3	(h)	Ipswich T	L 0-1		18,733
16		10	(a)	Queen's Park R	L 0-3		20,416
17		17	(a)	Leeds U	L 0-3		35,552
18		24	(h)	Sheffield U	W 3-1	Stein, Cross 2	17,918
19	Dec	1	(a)	Arsenal	D 2-2	Alderson, Cross	22,340
20		8	(h)	Wolves	W 1-0	Stein	20,770
21		15	(a)	Manchester U	W 3-2	Stein†, Alderson, Cross	28,589
22		22	(h)	Leicester C	L 1-2	Cartwright	23,413
23		26	(a)	Birmingham C	L 0-1		33,423
24		29	(a)	Southampton	D 1-1	Craven	18,345
25	Jan	1	(h)	Burnley	D 1-1	Cross	24,876
26		12	(h)	Chelsea	D 2-2	Coop 2 (2 pens)	20,920
27		19	(a)	Tottenham H	L 1-2	Alderson	20,985
28	Feb	2	(h)	Manchester U	W 1-0	Alderson	25,407
29		5	(a)	Liverpool	L 1-2	Holmes	21,656
30		9	(a)	Newcastle U	L 1-5	Alderson	27,376
31		23	(a)	Everton	L 0-1		34,624
32		26	(h)	Norwich C	W 1-0	Mortimer	16,457
33	Mar	2	(h)	Birmingham C	L 0-1		27,863
34		9	(h)	Stoke C	W 2-0	Hutchison, Cross	17,037
35		16	(a)	West Ham U	W 3-2	Cross, Alderson, Carr	26,502
36		23	(h)	Queen's Park R	L 0-1		18,825
37		30	(a)	Ipswich T	L 0-3		17,393
38	Apr	6	(a)	Sheffield U	W 1-0	Hutchison	16,568
39		13	(h)	Leeds U	D 0-0		35,182
40		15	(a)	Derby C	L 0-1		23,348
41		20	(a)	Wolves	D 1-1	Craven	24,902
42		27	(h)	Arsenal	D 3-3	Alderson, Stein, Cross	19,945

FINAL LEAGUE POSITION: 16th in Division One

* Some sources credit this goal to Alan Birchenall (og).

† Some sources credit this goal to Martin Buchan (og).

Appearances
Sub Appearances
Goals

FA Cup

3	Jan	5	(a)	Sheffield W	D 0-0		16,799
R		8	(h)	Sheffield W	W 3-1	Cross, Hutchison, Coop (pen)	13,824
4		27	(h)	Derby C	D 0-0		41,281
R		30	(a)	Derby C	W 1-0*	Cross	31,907
5	Feb	16	(h)	Queen's Park R	D 0-0		30,310
R		19	(a)	Queen's Park R	L 2-3	Cross 2	28,010

*After extra-time

Appearances
Sub Appearances
Goals

League Cup

2	Oct	8	(h)	Darlington	W 5-1	Stein 3, Coop, Green	8,805
3		30	(a)	Bristol C	D 2-2	Smith, Cartwright	19,129
R	Nov	6	(h)	Bristol C	W 2-1	Alderson 2	13,127
4		20	(h)	Stoke C	W 2-1	Green, Stein	17,434
5	Dec	19	(h)	Manchester C	D 2-2	Alderson 2	12,491
R	Jan	16	(a)	Manchester C	L 2-4	Alderson 2	25,409

Appearances
Sub Appearances
Goals

Glazier	Coop	Holmes	Mortimer	Craven	Dugdale	Smith	Alderson	Stein	Green	Hutchison	Hunt	Parker	McGuire	Cartwright	Philpotts	Cross	Ramsbottom	Cattlin	Carr	Hindley	
1	2	3	4	5	6	7	8	9	10	11											1
1	2	3	4	5	6	7	8	9	10*	11	12										2
1	2	3	4	5	6	7	8	9	10*	11		12									3
1	2	3	4	5	6	7	8	9	10	11											4
1	2	3	4	5	6	7	8	9	10	11											5
1	2	3	4	5	6	7	8	9	10	11											6
1	2	3	4	5	6	7	8	9	10	11											7
1		3	4	5	6	2	8	9		11	10		7								8
1	2	3	4	5	6	7	8	9*		11	10		12								9
1	2	3	4	5	6	7	8		10	11	9*			12							10
1	2	3	4	5	6	7	8	9	10	11											11
1	2	3	4	5	6	7	8	9	10	11											12
1	2	3	4	5*	6	7	8	9	10	11				12							13
1	2	3	4		6	7	8	9		11				10	5						14
1	2	3	4		6		8	9		11			10	7	5						15
1	2	3	4		6	12	8	9		11			10	7	5*						16
1	2	3	4*		6		8	9		11		5	10	12		7					17
1	2	3			5*		8	9	12	11		6	7	4		10					18
1	2	3			5		8	9		11		6	7	4		10					19
	2	3			5		8	9		11		6	7	4		10	1				20
1	2	3					8	9		11		6	4	7		10		5			21
1	2	3			5		8	9		11		6	4	7		10					22
1	2	3		5	6		8	9		11			4	7		10*			12		23
1	2	3		5	6		8	9	12				4	7*		10			11		24
1	2	3		5	6		8	9		11*			12	7		10			4		25
1	2	3		5	6			9	12	11			8*	7		10			4		26
1	2	3*	7	5	6		8	9		11						10		12	4		27
1	2	3	4	5	6		8			11				7		9		10			28
1	2	3	4	5	6		8			11			12	7		9		10*			29
1		3	4	5*	6		8			11			12	7		9			10	2	30
1		3	4	5	6		8			11				7		9			10	2	31
1	2	3	4	5	6		8		7*	11			12			9			10		32
1	2	3	4		6		8		7	11						9			10	5	33
1		3	4		6	2	8*		7	11				12		9		5	10		34
1		3	4	5	6	2	8			11			7			9			10		35
1		3	4	5	6	2	8			11			7			9			10		36
		3	4	5		2	8			11				7		9	1		10	6	37
1			4	5		2	8			11		7*	10	12		9		3		6	38
1		3	4	7	6	2	8			11			10			9				5	39
1		3	4	7	6	2	8			11			10*	12		9				5	40
1		3	4	7	6	2		9		11			8			10				5	41
1		3	4		6	2	8	9		11			7			10				5	42
40	30	41	33	30	39	23	40	28	14	41	3	7	19	17	3	26	2	5	12	9	
						1			3		1	1	5	6				1	1		
	5	1	1	3			9	6	4	3				2		8			1		

Glazier	Coop	Holmes	Mortimer	Craven	Dugdale	Smith	Alderson	Stein	Green	Hutchison	Hunt	Parker	McGuire	Cartwright	Philpotts	Cross	Ramsbottom	Cattlin	Carr	Hindley	
1	2	3		5	6		8	9		11*			7	12		10			4		3
1	2	3		5	6		8*	9		11			4	12		10			7		R
1	2	3		5	6		8			11			4	7		9			10		4
1	2	3	4	5	6		8			11				7		9		10			R
1		3	4	5	6	2	8			11				7		9			10		5
1		3	4	5	6	2	8			11				7		9			10		R
6	4	6	3	6	6	2	6	2		6			3	4		6		1	5		
														2							
	1									1						4					

Glazier	Coop	Holmes	Mortimer	Craven	Dugdale	Smith	Alderson	Stein	Green	Hutchison	Hunt	Parker	McGuire	Cartwright	Philpotts	Cross	Ramsbottom	Cattlin	Carr	Hindley	
1	2	3	4	5	6	7	8	9	10	11											2
1	2	3	4		6	7	8	9		11		5		10							3
1	2	3	4		6		8	9		11			10	7	5						R
1	2	3			6		8	9	10	11		5	4	7							4
1	2	3			5		8	9	10*	11		6	4	7				12			5
1	2	3		5	6		8	9		11			4	7					10		R
6	6	6	3	2	6	2	6	6	3	6		3	4	5	1				1		
																		1			
	1					1	6	4	2					1							

1974-75

Manager: Gordon Milne

1	Aug	17	(a)	Newcastle U	L 2-3	Alderson, Hutchison	35,938
2		21	(a)	Derby C	D 1-1	Mortimer	25,717
3		24	(h)	Chelsea	L 1-3	Cross	21,251
4		27	(h)	Derby C	D 1-1	Carr	18,586
5		31	(a)	Burnley	L 0-3		14,619
6	Sep	7	(h)	Manchester C	D 2-2	Alderson, Stein	15,440
7		14	(a)	Stoke C	L 0-2		22,842
8		21	(h)	Everton	D 1-1	Holmes (pen)	14,814
9		24	(h)	Luton T	W 2-1	Stein, Cross	15,617
10		28	(a)	Leicester C	W 1-0	Holmes	21,354
11	Oct	5	(a)	Birmingham C	W 2-1	Lloyd, Holmes	30,282
12		12	(h)	West Ham U	D 1-1	Hutchison	22,519
13		19	(a)	Middlesbrough	D 4-4	Stein, Cross, Holmes 2	25,499
14		26	(h)	Carlisle U	W 2-1	Lloyd 2	17,070
15	Nov	2	(a)	Queen's Park R	L 0-2		17,256
16		9	(h)	Leeds U	L 1-3	Cross	25,414
17		13	(a)	Chelsea	D 3-3	Cross, Craven, Hutchison	11,048
18		16	(a)	Ipswich T	L 0-4		21,172
19		23	(h)	Arsenal	W 3-0	Mortimer, Stein (pen), Carr (pen)	15,669
20		30	(h)	Liverpool	D 1-1	Stein (pen)	23,089
21	Dec	7	(a)	Wolves	L 0-2		20,002
22		14	(h)	Newcastle U	W 2-0	Cross, Lloyd	15,562
23		20	(a)	Sheffield U	L 0-1		14,694
24		26	(h)	Stoke C	W 2-0	Cross, Hutchison	22,345
25		28	(a)	Tottenham H	D 1-1	Stein	20,307
26	Jan	11	(h)	Wolves	W 2-1	Carr, Lloyd	20,249
27		18	(a)	Liverpool	L 1-2	Alderson	43,668
28	Feb	1	(a)	Leeds U	D 0-0		33,901
29		8	(h)	Queen's Park R	D 1-1	Green	18,807
30		15	(h)	Tottenham H	D 1-1	Alderson	15,227
31		22	(h)	Ipswich T	W 3-1	Ferguson, Green 2	16,980
32	Mar	1	(h)	Burnley	L 0-3		17,346
33		8	(a)	Luton T	W 3-1	Alderson 2, Green	14,423
34		15	(h)	Leicester C	D 2-2	Green, Ferguson	23,139
35		22	(a)	Manchester C	L 0-1		25,903
36		28	(h)	Sheffield U	D 2-2	Craven, Cross	18,839
37		31	(a)	Everton	L 0-1		40,070
38	Apr	5	(a)	Carlisle U	D 0-0		10,857
39		8	(a)	Arsenal	L 0-2		17,291
40		12	(h)	Birmingham C	W 1-0	Green	24,180
41		19	(a)	West Ham U	W 2-1	Green, Mortimer	27,431
42		26	(h)	Middlesbrough	L 0-2		17,970

FINAL LEAGUE POSITION: 13th in Division One

Appearances
Sub Appearances
Goals

FA Cup

3	Jan	4	(h)	Norwich C	W 2-0	Alderson, Lloyd	19,252
4		25	(h)	Arsenal	D 1-1	Alderson	31,165
R		29	(a)	Arsenal	L 0-3		30,867

Appearances
Sub Appearances
Goals

League Cup

2	Sep	10	(h)	Ipswich T	L 1-2	Stein	13,066

Appearances
Sub Appearances
Goals

Ramsbottom	Smith	Cattlin	Mortimer	Hindley	Dugdale	Coop	Alderson	Stein	Carr	Hutchison	Lloyd	Craven	Cross	McGuire	Glazier	Oakey	Holmes	Cartwright	Green	Ferguson	
1	2	3	4	5	6	7	8	9	10	11											1
1		3	4	2	6	12	8	9		11	5	7*	10								2
1		3	4	2	6		8	9		11	5		10	7							3
1		3	4	2	6		8	9	7	11	5			10							4
		3	4	2	6		8	9	10	11	5			7	1						5
		3	4		6		8	9	10	11	5			7	1	2					6
1		3	4	6			8			11	5		9	7		2	10				7
1		3	4	6			8			11	5		9			2	10	7			8
1		3	4	6			8	9		11	5		10			2	7				9
1		3	4	6			8	9		11	5		10			2	7				10
1		3	4	6			8	9		11	5		10			2	7				11
1		3	4	6			8	9		11	5		10			2	7				12
1		3	4	6			12	9*		11	5	8	10			2	7				13
1		3	4	6			12	9		11	5	8	10*			2	7				14
1		3	4	6					10	11	5	8*	9			2	7		12		15
1		3	4	6				9	8	11		5	10			2	7				16
		3	4	6				9	8	11		5	10		1	2*	7		12		17
	2	3	4	6				9	8	11	5		10		1		7				18
	2	3	4	6				9	8	11	5*		10		1			12	7		19
	2	3	4	6				9	8	11		5	10		1				7		20
		3	4	6				9	8	11		5	10		1	2			7		21
1		3	4	6				9	8	11	5	12	10			2*			7		22
1	2	3	4	6*				9	10	11	5						12	7	8		23
1	2	3	4		6		8	9	7	11	5		10								24
1	2	3			6		8	9	7	11	5	4*	10				12				25
1		3			6		8	9	7	11	5	4	10			2					26
1		3					8	9	7	11	5	4	10			2	6				27
1		3			6		8		7	11	5	4				2			10	9	28
1					6		8		7	11	5	4				2	3		10	9	29
1				5	6		8		7	11		4				2	3	12	10*	9	30
1		3			6		8		7	11	5					2		4	10	9	31
1		3			6		8		7	11		5				2		4	10	9	32
1		3			6*		8		7	11		5				2	12	4	10	9	33
1		3			6		8			11	5	4				2		7	10	9	34
1		3			6		8			11	5	4				2	12	7	10	9*	35
1		3			6	12	8			11	5	4	9			2*		7	10		36
1		3			6	12	8*			11	5	4	9			2		7	10		37
1		3	7		6	2				11	5	4	9			8			10		38
1		3	7		6		12			11	5	4				2*	8		10	9	39
1		3	7		6	12	8*			11	5	4				2			10	9	40
1		3	7		6					11	5	4				2	8		10	9	41
1		3	7		6		12			11	5	4				2	8*		10	9	42
35	7	40	29	23	24	2	27	24	23	42	34	25	25	5	7	31	18	9	20	12	
						4	4					1					4	2	2		
			3				6	6	3	4	5	2	8				5		7	2	

1		3			6		8*	9	7	11	5	4	10			2	12				3
1		3			6		8	9	7	11	5	4	10			2					4
1		3			6		8		7	11	5	4*	9			2	10	12			R
3		3			3		3	2	3	3	3	3	3			3	1				
																	1	1			
							2				1										

		3	4		6		8	9	10	11	5	12		7*	1	2					2
		1	1		1		1	1	1	1	1			1	1	1					
												1									
								1													

1975-76

Manager: Gordon Milne

1	Aug	16	(a)	Everton	W 4-1	Cross 3, Green	33,214
2		19	(h)	Derby C	D 1-1	Coop	24,161
3		23	(h)	Manchester C	W 2-0	Green 2	21,097
4		27	(a)	Manchester U	D 1-1	Green	52,169
5		30	(a)	Aston Villa	L 0-1		41,026
6	Sep	6	(h)	Ipswich T	D 0-0		17,622
7		13	(a)	Sheffield U	W 1-0	Ferguson	20,153
8		20	(h)	Stoke C	L 0-3		18,965
9		23	(h)	Middlesbrough	L 0-1		15,124
10		27	(a)	Leicester C	W 3-0	Craven, Cross 2	20,411
11	Oct	4	(h)	Burnley	L 1-2	Cross	15,471
12		11	(a)	Arsenal	L 0-5		19,234
13		18	(h)	Liverpool	D 0-0		20,919
14		25	(a)	Leeds U	L 0-2		25,956
15	Nov	1	(h)	Queen's Park R	D 1-1	Cross	18,047
16		8	(a)	West Ham U	D 1-1	Powell	29,501
17		15	(h)	Norwich C	W 1-0	Mortimer	14,897
18		22	(a)	Liverpool	D 1-1	Powell	36,929
19		29	(h)	Birmingham C	W 3-2	Powell, Cross, Murphy	21,687
20	Dec	6	(a)	Newcastle U	L 0-4		26,372
21		13	(a)	Manchester C	L 2-4	Cross, Ferguson	27,256
22		19	(h)	Everton	L 1-2	Coop (pen)	14,394
23		26	(a)	Wolves	W 1-0	Craven	21,224
24		27	(h)	Tottenham H	D 2-2	Cross, Hutchinson	21,094
25	Jan	10	(h)	Sheffield U	W 1-0	Green	13,796
26		17	(a)	Ipswich T	D 1-1	Murphy	23,516
27		31	(a)	Derby C	L 0-2		24,253
28	Feb	7	(h)	Manchester U	D 1-1	Cartwright	33,821
29		14	(h)	West Ham U	W 2-0	Powell, Coop	16,173
30		21	(a)	Norwich C	W 3-0	Ferguson, Craven, Cross	20,798
31		24	(a)	Middlesbrough	L 0-2		18,279
32		28	(h)	Leeds U	L 0-1		25,568
33	Mar	6	(a)	Queen's Park R	L 1-4	Powell	19,731
34		13	(h)	Arsenal	D 1-1	Green	13,938
35		20	(a)	Birmingham C	D 1-1	Powell	22,956
36		27	(h)	Newcastle U	D 1-1	Murphy	14,144
37	Apr	3	(h)	Leicester C	L 0-2		18,135
38		10	(a)	Stoke C	W 1-0	Powell	16,059
39		13	(h)	Aston Villa	D 1-1	Coop (pen)	27,586
40		17	(h)	Wolves	W 3-1	Green 3	18,678
41		19	(a)	Tottenham H	L 1-4	Murphy	21,107
42		24	(a)	Burnley	W 3-1	Cross 3	11,636

FINAL LEAGUE POSITION: 14th in Division One

Appearances
Sub Appearances
Goals

FA Cup

3	Jan	3	(h)	Bristol C	W 2-1	Cross, Merrick (og)	15,693
4		24	(h)	Newcastle U	D 1-1	Murphy	32,004
R		28	(a)	Newcastle U	L 0-5		44,676

Appearances
Sub Appearances
Goals

League Cup

2	Sep	10	(a)	Bolton W	W 3-1	Cross, Green, Ferguson	12,743
3	Oct	8	(a)	Mansfield T	L 0-2		10,027

Appearances
Sub Appearances
Goals

King	Oakey	Brogan	Craven	Holmes	Dugdale	Coop	Mortimer	Green	Cross	Hutchison	Ferguson	Lloyd	Powell	Murphy	Hindley	Blyth	Cartwright	Cattlin	Roberts	
1	2	3	4	5	6	7	8	9	10	11										1
1	2	3	4	6	5	7	8	10	9	11										2
1	2	3	4	6		7	8	10	9	11		5								3
1	2	3	4	6		7	8	10	9	11	12	5*								4
1	2	3	4	6	5	7	8	10	9	11										5
1	2	3	4	6	5	7	8	10	9	11										6
1		3	4	2	5	7	8		9	11	10		6							7
1		3	4	6	5	2	8	10	9	11	12		7*							8
1	2	3	4	6	5	7	8	10	9	11										9
1	2	3	4	6	5	7	8	10*	9	11			12							10
1	2	3	4	6	5	8	7		9	11	10									11
1		3	4	6		2	8	10	9	11		5	7							12
1		3		6	4	2	8	10	9	11		5	7							13
1		3		6	4	2	8	10	9	11		5	7							14
1		3		6	4	2	8	10	9	11		5	7							15
1		3		6	4	2	8		9	11		5	7	10						16
1		3		6	4	2	8		9	11		5	7	10						17
1		3		6	4	2	8		9	11		5	7	10						18
1		3		6	4	2	8		9	11		5	7	10						19
1		3		6	4*	2	8	10	9	11	12		7		5					20
1*		3	12	6	4	2	8		9	11	5		7	10						21
		3		6		2	4		9	11	10	5	7	8		1				22
1		3	4	6	5	2		12	9	11			8	10*			7			23
1		3	4	6	5	2		10	9	11			8				7			24
		3	4	6	5	2		8	9	11			12	10		1	7*			25
	12	3	4	6	5	2		8	9	11			7*	10		1				26
		3		6	5	2		8	9	11			4	10		1	7			27
		3*	4	6	5	2		8	9	11			7	10		1	12			28
	2		4		5	6			9	11			8	10		1	7	3		29
	2		4	12	5	6			9	11	10		8			1	7*	3		30
	2		4	7	5	6			9	11*	10		8	12		1		3		31
	2		4		5	6		12	9	11	10*		8	7		1		3		32
	2		4*		5	6		10		11	9		8	7		1	12	3		33
	2		4		5	6*		10		11	12		8	7		1	9	3		34
	2		4			6		10	5	11			8	7		1	9	3		35
	2				5	6		8		11	4		10	9		1	7	3		36
	2				5	6		8	12	11	9*		10	7		1	4	3		37
	2		4	5		6		8		11	9		10			1	7	3		38
	2		4	5		6		8	9	11			10			1	7	3		39
	2		4*	5		6		8	9	11			10	12		1	7	3		40
	2			4	5	6		8	9	11			10	12		1		3*	7	41
				4	5	6		8	9	11			10	7		1		3	2	42
23	22	28	27	34	34	42	22	29	37	42	11	11	32	19	1	19	13	14	2	
	1		1	1				2	1		4		2	3			2			
			3			4	1	9	14	1	3		7	4			1			

	12	3	4	6	5	2		8*	9	11				10		1	7			3
1		3	4*	6	5	2		8	9	11			12	10			7			4
1		3		6	5	2		8	9	11			4	10			7			R
2		3	2	3	3	3		3	3	3			1	3		1	3			
	1												1							
									1					1						

1 own-goal

1	2	3	4		5	7	8	10*	9	11	12		6							2
1	2*	3	4	6	5	7	8	10	9	11	12									3
2	2	2	2	1	2	2	2	2	2	2			1							
											2									
								1	1		1									

1 own-goal

1976-77

Manager: Gordon Milne

1	Aug	21	(a)	Middlesbrough	L 0-1		17,694
2		24	(h)	Manchester U	L 0-2		26,624
3		28	(h)	Leeds U	W 4-2	Beck, Ferguson, Murphy, Cartwright	18,227
4	Sep	4	(a)	Liverpool	L 1-3	Ferguson	40,371
5		11	(h)	Norwich C	W 2-0	Ferguson, Forbes (og)	13,492
6		17	(a)	West Brom A	D 1-1	Ferguson	24,323
7		25	(h)	Birmingham C	W 2-1	Green, Yorath	25,988
8	Oct	2	(h)	Leicester C	D 1-1	Ferguson	20,957
9		16	(h)	Newcastle U	D 1-1	Powell	18,083
10		23	(a)	Tottenham H	W 1-0	Murphy	21,877
11		30	(h)	Sunderland	L 1-2	Ferguson	17,184
12	Nov	6	(a)	Bristol C	D 0-0		17,172
13		9	(h)	Queen's Park R	W 2-0	Powell, Murphy	16,190
14		20	(a)	Aston Villa	D 2-2	Ferguson 2	40,047
15		27	(h)	Arsenal	L 1-2	McDonald	18,262
16	Dec	11	(h)	Everton	W 4-2	Beck, Coop (pen), Wallace, Murphy	18,970
17		18	(a)	Manchester C	L 0-2		32,527
18		27	(h)	Ipswich T	D 1-1	Green	28,269
19	Jan	3	(a)	Sunderland	W 1-0	Murphy	24,942
20		15	(a)	Manchester U	L 0-2		46,567
21		22	(h)	Middlesbrough	D 1-1	Green	12,970
22	Feb	5	(a)	Leeds U	W 2-1	Green, Murphy	26,058
23		16	(a)	Stoke C	L 0-2		12,255
24		19	(a)	Norwich C	L 0-3		17,900
25	Mar	5	(a)	Birmingham C	L 1-3	Powell	22,607
26		9	(a)	Derby C	D 1-1	Wallace	22,808
27		12	(a)	Leicester C	L 1-2	Ferguson	16,766
28		23	(a)	Newcastle U	L 0-1		23,287
29	Apr	2	(h)	Tottenham H	D 1-1	Wallace	16,275
30		5	(a)	Ipswich T	L 1-2	Ferguson	23,633
31		9	(h)	West Ham U	D 1-1	Ferguson	15,816
32		11	(a)	Queen's Park R	D 1-1	Wallace	15,445
33		16	(h)	Aston Villa	L 2-3	Wallace 2	31,158
34		19	(h)	West Brom A	D 1-1	Ferguson	18,999
35		23	(a)	Arsenal	L 0-2		22,790
36		25	(h)	Derby C	W 2-0	Coop (pen), Ferguson	15,783
37		30	(h)	Stoke C	W 5-2	Wallace 3, Beck, Powell	15,719
38	May	4	(a)	West Ham U	L 0-2		25,461
39		7	(a)	Everton	D 1-1	Hutchison	24,569
40		10	(h)	Liverpool	D 0-0		38,032
41		14	(h)	Manchester C	L 0-1		21,429
42		19	(h)	Bristol C	D 2-2	Hutchison 2	36,903

FINAL LEAGUE POSITION: 19th in Division One

Appearances
Sub Appearances
Goals

FA Cup

3	Jan	8	(h)	Millwall	W 1-0	McDonald	17,620
4		29	(a)	Arsenal	L 1-3	Hutchison	41,078

Appearances
Sub Appearances
Goals

League Cup

2	Aug	31	(a)	Bristol C	W 1-0	Ferguson	13,878
3	Sep	21	(a)	Nottingham F	W 3-0	Ferguson, Coop (pen), Cartwright	15,969
4	Oct	26	(a)	Everton	L 0-3		21,572

Appearances
Sub Appearances
Goals

Blyth	Coop	Holmes	Craven	Lloyd	Dugdale	Cartwright	Green	Cross	Beck	Powell	Murphy	Oakey	Ferguson	McDonald	Yorath	Hutchison	Wallace	Roberts	Gooding	Sealey	Holton	
1	2	3	4	5	6	7	8	9*	10	11	12											1
1	2	3	4	5	6		8		10	7	9	11										2
1	2	3	4		6	7			10	8	5	11	9									3
1	2	5			6	7	11		10			4	9	3	8							4
1	2	5			6	7	11		10	4			9	3	8							5
1	2	5	4		6	7		11	10				9	3	8							6
1	2	5			6		8*		7	10	12		9	3	4	11						7
1	2	5			6	7	8			10			9	3	4	11						8
1	2	6			5	7	8*		11	10	12		9	3	4							9
1	2	6			5	7			11	10	8		9	3	4							10
1	2	6*			5				7	10	8		9	3	4	11	12					11
1	2	6		5					7	10	8		9	3	4	11						12
1	2	6		5					7	10	8		9	3	4		11					13
1	2	6		5					7	10	8*		9	3	4	12	11					14
1	2	6			5				7	10	8*		9	3	4	12	11					15
1	2	6			5				7	10	12		9*	3	4	11	8					16
1	2	6			5				7	10	9			3	4	11	8					17
1	2	6			5	12	8		7*	10	9			3	4	11						18
1	2	6*	12		5		8		7	10	9			3	4	11						19
1	2	6			5		8		7	10	9			3	4	11						20
1	2	6			5	12	8		7*	10	9			3	4	11						21
1	2	6			5		8		7	10*	12			3	4	11		9				22
1	2	6			5*		8		7	10				3	4	11	12	9				23
1	2	12			5				7	10			9	3	4	11	8*	6				24
1		6			5	12				10		2*	9	3	4	11	8	7				25
1		6			5				7	10			9	3	4	11	8	2				26
1						12	7*		4	10		2	9	3	5	11	8	6				27
1	2								4	10			9	3	5	11	8	6	7			28
1	6								7	10			9	3	4	11	8	2	5			29
1	6								7	10			9	3	4	11	8	2	5			30
1*	6						12		4	10			9	3	5	11	8	2	7			31
	6				5*		12		7	10			9	3	4	11	8	2		1		32
	6				5				7	10			9	3	4	11	8	2		1		33
	6					12			7	10		2	9	3	4	11	8			1	5*	34
	6					12			7*	10		2	9	3	4	11	8			1	5	35
	6					5			7	10		2	9	3	4	11	8			1		36
	6					7			4	10		2	9	3		11	8			1	5	37
	6					2			7	10			9	3	4	11	8			1	5	38
	6						12		7	10		2		3	4	11	8		9*	1	5	39
	6					12			7*	10		2	9	3	4	11	8			1	5	40
	6					12			7	10		2	9	3	4	11	8			1	5*	41
	6								7	10		2	9	3	4	11	8			1	5	42
31	39	25	4	5	25	11	14	2	40	40	13	13	32	39	38	31	24	12	5	11	8	
		1	1			8	3				5					2	2					
	2					1	4		3	4	6		13	1	1	3	9					

1 own-goal

1	2		6*		5	10	8		7	12	9			3	4	11						3
1	2	6			5	10	8		7		9			3		11		4				4
2	2	1	1		2	2	2		2		2			2	1	2		1				
										1												
														1		1						

1	2	5	4		6				10	7	11		9	3	8							2
1	2	5	4		6		11	12	10	7*			9	3	8							3
1	2	6			5	10*	12		11	7	8		9	3	4							4
3	3	3	2		3	1	1		3	3	2		3	3	3							
							1	1														
	1									1			2									

1977-78

Manager: Gordon Milne

1	Aug	20	(h)	Derby C	W	3-1	Ferguson 2, Wallace	17,740
2		24	(a)	Manchester U	L	1-2	Wallace	55,726
3		27	(a)	Chelsea	W	2-1	Wallace 2*	25,432
4	Sep	3	(h)	Leeds U	D	2-2	Ferguson, Wallace	21,479
5		10	(a)	Liverpool	L	0-2		45,574
6		17	(h)	Middlesbrough	W	2-1	Graydon 2	13,947
7		24	(a)	Newcastle U	W	2-1	Wallace 2	21,708
8	Oct	1	(h)	West Brom A	L	1-2	Wile (og)	25,909
9		4	(h)	Manchester C	W	4-2	Ferguson 3, Wallace	19,586
10		8	(a)	Birmingham C	D	1-1	Ferguson	27,414
11		15	(a)	Leicester C	W	2-1	Coop 2 (2 pens)	20,205
12		22	(h)	Ipswich T	D	1-1	Hutchison	20,014
13		29	(a)	Wolves	W	3-1	Ferguson 3	23,796
14	Nov	5	(h)	West Ham U	W	1-0	Wallace	23,276
15		12	(a)	Arsenal	D	1-1	Green	31,653
16		19	(h)	Queen's Park R	W	4-1	Wallace 2, Yorath, Coop (pen)	20,411
17		26	(a)	Everton	L	0-6		43,279
18	Dec	3	(h)	Bristol C	D	1-1	Ferguson	22,111
19		10	(a)	Nottingham F	L	1-2	Wallace	29,823
20		17	(h)	Arsenal	L	1-2	Coop (pen)	21,006
21		26	(a)	Aston Villa	D	1-1	Wallace	43,571
22		27	(h)	Norwich C	W	5-4	Powell (pen), Wallace, Gooding, McDonald, Graydon	21,578
23		31	(h)	Manchester U	W	3-0	Ferguson, Wallace, Yorath	24,729
24	Jan	2	(a)	Derby C	L	2-4	Ferguson, Powell	25,929
25		14	(h)	Chelsea	W	5-1	McDonald, Wallace, Coop (pen), Graydon 2	21,155
26		21	(a)	Leeds U	L	0-2		27,062
27	Feb	4	(h)	Liverpool	W	1-0	Ferguson	28,965
28		25	(a)	West Brom A	D	3-3	Coop (pen), Wallace, Beck	25,300
29	Mar	4	(h)	Birmingham C	W	4-0	Ferguson 3, Beck	22,925
30		11	(h)	Leicester C	W	1-0	Nardiello	24,241
31		18	(a)	Ipswich T	D	1-1	Osgood	21,110
32		21	(h)	Aston Villa	L	2-3	McDonald 2	30,957
33		25	(a)	Norwich C	W	2-1	Powell (pen), Wallace	20,732
34		28	(h)	Wolves	W	4-0	Thompson, Hutchison 2, Wallace	25,661
35	Apr	1	(a)	West Ham U	L	1-2	McDonald	19,260
36		4	(h)	Newcastle U	D	0-0		22,135
37		8	(h)	Everton	W	3-2	Thompson, Wallace, Green	26,025
38		11	(a)	Middlesbrough	D	1-1	Green	14,184
39		15	(a)	Queen's Park R	L	1-2	Green	17,062
40		22	(h)	Nottingham F	D	0-0		36,881
41		25	(a)	Manchester C	L	1-3	Green	32,412
42		29	(a)	Bristol C	D	1-1	Wallace	21,045

FINAL LEAGUE POSITION: 7th in Division One

* Some sources credit the first goal to Powell

Appearances
Sub Appearances
Goals

FA Cup

3	Jan	7	(a)	Middlesbrough	L	0-3		18,505

Appearances
Sub Appearances
Goals

League Cup

2	Aug	30	(a)	Huddersfield T	W	2-0	Wallace, Holton	8,577
3	Oct	26	(a)	Tottenham H	W	3-2	Hutchison, Powell, Graydon	35,099
4	Nov	29	(a)	Liverpool	D	2-2	Wallace, Powell	33,817
R	Dec	20	(h)	Liverpool	L	0-2		36,105

Appearances
Sub Appearances
Goals

Blyth	Oakey	McDonald	Yorath	Holton	Coop	Graydon	Wallace	Ferguson	Powell	Hutchison	Beck	Sealey	Dugdale	Nardiello	Roberts	Green	Murphy	Gooding	Osgood	Thompson G	
1	2	3	4	5	6	7	8	9	10	11											1
1	2	3	4	5	6	7	8	9	10	11											2
1	2	3	4	5	6	7	8	9	10	11											3
1	2	3	4	5	6	7	8	9	10	11											4
1	2	3	4	5	6	7	8	9	10	11											5
1	2	3	4	5	6	7	8	9	10	11											6
1	2	3	4		6	7	8	9	10	11	5										7
1	2	3	4	5	6	7	8	9	10	11											8
	2	3	4	5	6		8	9	10	11	7	1									9
	2	3	4	5	6		8	9	10	11	7	1									10
1	2	3	4	5	6	7	8	9	10	11											11
1	2	3	4*		6	12	8	9	10	11			5	7							12
1	2	3	4		6		8	9	10	11	5			7							13
1	2	3	4		6	12	8	9*	10	11	5			7							14
1	2	3	4		6		8		10	11				7	5	9					15
1	2	3	4		6		8		10	11	12			7	5	9*					16
1	2	3	4		6	9*	8		10	11				7	5		12				17
1	2	3	4	5	6		8	9	10	11				7							18
1	2	3	4	5	6		8	9	10	11				7							19
1	2	3	4		6	12	8	9	10	11				7*	5						20
1	2*	3	4		6	7	8	9	10	11	12				5						21
1		3	4			7	8	9	10	11	2				5			6			22
1		3	4			7	8	9	10	11	2				5			6			23
1		3	4			7	8	9	10	11	2				5			6			24
1		3	4		6	7	8	9	10	11					2				5		25
1		3	4		6	7	8	9	10*	11	12				2				5		26
1		3			6	7	8	9	10	11				12	2*			4	5		27
1		3			6		8	9	10	11	12			7	2			4*	5		28
1		3	4	5	6		8	9	10	11	12				2	7*					29
1		3	4	5	6		8	9*	10	11	12			7	2						30
1		3	4	5	6		8		10	11	12			7*	2				9		31
1		3	4	5	6				10	11	7				2		8			9	32
1		3	4	5			8		10	11	7				2				6	9	33
1		3	4	5			8		10	11	7				2		12		6	9*	34
1		3	4	5	12		8		10	11	7				2				6	9*	35
1		3	4	5			8		10	11	7				2	9			6		36
1		3	4	5	6		8		10	11					2	7			12	9*	37
1		3	4	5	6		8		10	11					2	7			9		38
1		3	4	5	6		8		10	11					2	7			9		39
1		3	4	5	6		8	9	10		11				2	7					40
1		3	4	5*			8	9	10		11				2	7			6	12	41
1		3	4		6		8	9	10	11	12				2	7*			5		42
40	21	42	40	25	34	17	41	30	42	40	15	2	1	12	26	10	1	5	13	5	
					1	3					8			1			2			1	
		5	2		6	5	21	17	3	3	2			1		5		1	1	2	

1 own-goal

Blyth	Oakey	McDonald	Yorath	Holton	Coop	Graydon	Wallace	Ferguson	Powell	Hutchison	Beck	Sealey	Dugdale	Nardiello	Roberts	Green	Murphy	Gooding	Osgood	Thompson G	
		3	4		2	12	8	9	10	11	7*	1			5			6			3
		1	1		1		1	1	1	1	1	1			1			1			
						1															

Blyth	Oakey	McDonald	Yorath	Holton	Coop	Graydon	Wallace	Ferguson	Powell	Hutchison	Beck	Sealey	Dugdale	Nardiello	Roberts	Green	Murphy	Gooding	Osgood	Thompson G	
1	2	3	4	5	6	7	8	9	10	11											2
1	2	3		5*	6	12	8	9	10	11	4			7							3
1	2*	3	4	5	6		8	9	10	11				7	12						4
1	2	3	4		6	7	8	9	10	11					5						R
4	4	4	3	3	4	2	4	4	4	4	1			2	1						
						1									1						
				1		1	2		2	1											

1978-79

Manager: Gordon Milne

1	Aug	19	(a)	Middlesbrough	W 2-1	Powell, Ferguson	17,956
2		22	(h)	Nottingham F	D 0-0		28,622
3		26	(h)	Norwich C	W 4-1	Beck, Powell, Wallace, Ferguson	20,452
4	Sep	2	(a)	Derby C	W 2-0	Hunt, Wallace	21,435
5		9	(h)	Chelsea	W 3-2	Wallace, McDonald, Ferguson	24,920
6		16	(a)	Liverpool	L 0-1		51,130
7		23	(h)	Leeds U	D 0-0		27,365
8		30	(a)	Tottenham H	D 1-1	Ferguson	35,806
9	Oct	7	(h)	Ipswich T	D 2-2	Green, Thompson	21,859
10		14	(a)	Manchester C	L 0-2		36,723
11		21	(a)	West Brom A	L 1-7	Ferguson	27,381
12		28	(h)	Birmingham C	W 2-1	Hutchison 2	25,446
13	Nov	4	(a)	Bolton W	D 0-0		22,379
14		11	(h)	Middlesbrough	W 2-1	Wallace, Thompson	18,603
15		18	(a)	Norwich C	L 0-1		17,696
16		21	(h)	Derby C	W 4-2	Wallace 2, McDonald, Powell	20,654
17		25	(h)	Arsenal	D 1-1	Hunt	26,787
18	Dec	9	(h)	Queen's Park R	W 1-0	Thompson	18,717
19		16	(a)	Southampton	L 0-4		19,102
20		23	(h)	Everton	W 3-2	Wallace, Thompson, Hunt	22,834
21		26	(a)	Bristol C	L 0-5		22,324
22		30	(a)	Wolves	D 1-1	Hutchison	21,514
23	Feb	3	(a)	Leeds U	L 0-1		22,928
24		10	(h)	Tottenham H	L 1-3	McDonald	25,131
25		21	(a)	Chelsea	W 3-1	Wallace, Powell*, Ferguson	15,282
26		24	(h)	Manchester C	L 0-3		20,116
27	Mar	3	(h)	West Brom A	L 1-3	Thompson	25,795
28		6	(h)	Liverpool	D 0-0		26,629
29		10	(a)	Birmingham C	D 0-0		17,311
30		13	(a)	Ipswich T	D 1-1	Thompson	16,095
31		17	(h)	Bolton W	D 2-2	Wallace, Powell (pen)	15,231
32		20	(h)	Manchester U	W 4-3	Powell, Thompson, Hutchison, McDonald	26,308
33		24	(a)	Nottingham F	L 0-3		29,706
34		28	(a)	Aston Villa	D 1-1	Thompson	25,670
35	Apr	3	(a)	Arsenal	D 1-1	Hunt†	30,091
36		7	(h)	Aston Villa	D 1-1	Hutchison	23,690
37		10	(a)	Everton	D 3-3	Wallace 2, Hunt	25,302
38		14	(h)	Bristol C	W 3-2	Powell (pen), Hutchison, Hunt	17,812
39		16	(a)	Manchester U	D 0-0		43,075
40		21	(h)	Southampton	W 4-0	Wallace 3, Blair	17,750
41		28	(a)	Queen's Park R	L 1-5	Wallace	10,951
42	May	5	(h)	Wolves	W 3-0	Powell 2 (1 pen), Bannister	21,825

FINAL LEAGUE POSITION: 10th in Division One

*Some sources credit the second goal to Ferguson.

†Some sources credit this goal to Nelson (og).

Appearances
Sub Appearances
Goals

FA Cup

3	Jan	9	(h)	West Brom A	D 2-2	Blair, Green	38,046
R		15	(a)	West Brom A	L 0-4		36,262

Appearances
Sub Appearances
Goals

League Cup

2	Aug	30	(a)	Chester	L 1-2	Thompson	8,598

Appearances
Sub Appearances
Goals

Sealey	Osgood	McDonald	Yorath	Holton	Gillespie	Nardiello	Wallace	Ferguson	Powell	Hutchison	Green	Beck	Bannister	Roberts	Hunt	Coop	Hagan	Thompson G	Blair	Gooding	Dyson	Blyth	Hateley	
1	2	3	4*	5	6	7	8	9	10	11	12													1
1	2	3		5	6*	7	8	9	10	11	12	4												2
1	2	3		5	6	7*	8	9	10	11		4	12											3
1		3		5	6		8	9	10	7		4		2	11									4
1		3		5	6		8	9	10	7		4		2	11									5
1		3		5	6		8	9	10	7		4		2	11									6
1		3	4	5	6		8	9	10	7					11	2								7
1		3	4	5	6		8	9	10*	11		12			7	2								8
1		3	4	5			8		10*	7	12				11	2	6	9						9
1		3	4	5	6		8		10	7					11	2		9						10
1		3	4	5*	6		8	9	10	7	12				11	2								11
1	5	3					8	9		11	7			2		6			4	10				12
1	5	3			6		8	9	10	11	7					2			4					13
1	5	3			6		8		10	11	7					2		9	4					14
1	5	3			6		8		10	11			7			2		9	4					15
1	5	3					8		10	11			7*	2	12	6		9	4					16
1	5	3					8		10	11				2	7	6		9	4					17
1		3		5	6*		8	12	10	11					7	2		9	4					18
1		3		5	12		8*	6	10	11					7	2		9	4					19
1		3		5			8		10	11					7	2		9	4		6			20
1	6	3		5			8		10	11					7	2		9	4					21
	2	3		5		7	8	12	10	11						6		9*	4			1		22
		3	7	5			8	9	10*	11					12	2	6		4			1		23
		3	7	5*			8	9	10	11					12	2	6		4			1		24
		3	7	5			8	9	10	11						2	6		4			1		25
		3	7	5*			8	9	10	11						2	6	12	4			1		26
1		3		5			8		10	11	7					2	6	9	4					27
1		3	4	5			8		10	11	7					2	6	9						28
1		3	4	5			8			11	7					2	6	9	10					29
1		3*	4	5			8			11	12			7		2	6	9	10					30
1		3	4	5		7	8		10	11						2	6	9						31
1		3	4	5		7	8		10	11						2	6	9						32
1		3	4			7			10	11*				5	12	2	6	9	8					33
1		3	4	5		7	8		10	11				2		6		9						34
1		3	4	5		7			10	11				2	9	6			8					35
1		3	4	5		7	8		10	11				2	9	6								36
1		3	4	5		7*	8		10	11				2	9	6			12					37
1		3	4*	5		7			10	11				2	9	6	12		8					38
1		3		5		7	8		10	11				2	9	6			4					39
1		3		5		7	8			11				2	9	6			4	10				40
1		3		5		7*	8		10	11				2	9	6			4	12				41
		3				7*			10	11			8	2		6			4	12	5	1	9	42
36	11	42	21	34	14	16	38	16	38	42	6	5	3	17	20	36	12	19	25	2	2	6	1	
					1			2			5	1	1		4		1	1	1	2				
		4					15	6	9	6	1	1	1		6			8	1					

Sealey	Osgood	McDonald	Yorath	Holton	Gillespie	Nardiello	Wallace	Ferguson	Powell	Hutchison	Green	Beck	Bannister	Roberts	Hunt	Coop	Hagan	Thompson G	Blair	Gooding	Dyson	Blyth	Hateley	
		3		5		7*	10		8	11	12					6	2	9	4			1		3
		3		5		7*	10		8	11	12					6	2	9	4			1		R
		2		2		2	2		2	2						2	2	2	2			2		
											2													
											1								1					

Sealey	Osgood	McDonald	Yorath	Holton	Gillespie	Nardiello	Wallace	Ferguson	Powell	Hutchison	Green	Beck	Bannister	Roberts	Hunt	Coop	Hagan	Thompson G	Blair	Gooding	Dyson	Blyth	Hateley	
1	2	3	6	5			10	9	8	11		4*	7					12						2
1	1	1	1	1			1	1	1	1		1	1											
																		1						
																		1						

1979-80

Manager: Gordon Milne

1	Aug	18	(a)	Stoke C	L 2-3	Powell 2 (1 pen)	23,151
2		21	(h)	Bristol C	W 3-1	English, Powell (pen), Hutchison	19,293
3		25	(a)	Nottingham F	L 1-4	English	23,025
4	Sep	1	(h)	Norwich C	W 2-0	McDonald, Ferguson	18,181
5		8	(a)	Liverpool	L 0-4		39,926
6		15	(h)	Bolton W	W 3-1	Wallace 2, Powell (pen)	15,353
7		22	(a)	Manchester C	L 0-3		30,869
8		29	(h)	Tottenham H	D 1-1	Wallace	20,125
9	Oct	6	(h)	Everton	W 2-1	Wallace 2	17,250
10		9	(a)	Bristol C	L 0-1		14,853
11		13	(a)	Southampton	W 3-2	Wallace 2, Gooding	22,986
12		20	(h)	Brighton & HA	W 2-1	McDonald, English	17,328
13		27	(a)	West Brom A	L 1-4	Coop (pen)	22,721
14	Nov	3	(h)	Stoke C	L 1-3	McDonald	16,761
15		10	(h)	Leeds U	W 3-0	Ferguson 2, Wallace	19,402
16		17	(a)	Wolves	W 3-0	Wallace, Ferguson 2	22,805
17		24	(a)	Crystal P	D 0-0		26,209
18	Dec	1	(h)	Ipswich T	W 4-1	Ferguson 4	16,439
19		8	(a)	Arsenal	L 1-3	Gooding	27,563
20		15	(h)	Manchester U	L 1-2	Ferguson	25,563
21		19	(a)	Aston Villa	L 0-3		24,446
22		26	(a)	Derby C	W 2-1	McDonald, English	15,531
23		29	(h)	Nottingham F	L 0-3		24,737
24	Jan	1	(h)	Middlesbrough	W 2-0	Blair, Gillespie	17,096
25		12	(a)	Norwich C	L 0-1		16,467
26		19	(h)	Liverpool	W 1-0	Dyson	31,578
27	Feb	9	(h)	Manchester C	D 0-0		17,114
28		23	(h)	Southampton	W 3-0	Thompson 2, English	18,034
29		27	(a)	Tottenham H	L 3-4	Dyson, English 2	22,536
30	Mar	1	(a)	Brighton & HA	D 1-1	English	21,605
31		8	(h)	West Brom A	L 0-2		23,287
32		15	(a)	Everton	D 1-1	Thompson	25,966
33		22	(a)	Leeds U	D 0-0		14,967
34		29	(h)	Wolves	L 1-3	English	19,507
35	Apr	5	(a)	Middlesbrough	W 2-1	Wallace 2	15,398
36		7	(h)	Derby C	W 2-1	Wallace, Hunt	19,538
37		12	(a)	Ipswich T	L 0-3		20,502
38		15	(a)	Bolton W	D 1-1	Thompson	8,995
39		19	(h)	Crystal P	W 2-1	English, Thompson	14,401
40		26	(a)	Manchester U	L 1-2	Thompson	52,154
41		29	(h)	Aston Villa	L 1-2	Wallace	17,969
42	May	3	(h)	Arsenal	L 0-1		16,817

FINAL LEAGUE POSITION: 15th in Division One

Appearances
Sub Appearances
Goals

FA Cup

3	Jan	5	(a)	Oldham A	W 1-0	Hutchison	12,151
4		26	(a)	Blackburn R	L 0-1		20,785

Appearances
Sub Appearances
Goals

League Cup

2	Aug	29	(a)	Ipswich T	W 1-0	English	13,217
R	Sep	4	(h)	Ipswich T	D 0-0		16,705
3		26	(a)	West Brom A	L 1-2	English	18,069

Appearances
Sub Appearances
Goals

Blyth	Jones	McDonald	Gooding	Holton	Collier	Hutchison	English	Ferguson	Powell	Hunt	Blair	Gillespie	Hateley	Roberts	Murcott	Sealey	Wallace	Whitton	Thomas	Coop	Nardiello	Bannister	Dyson	Thompson G	Phillips	Van Gool	Barnes	Jacobs	
1	2	3	4	5	6	7	8	9	10	11																			1
1	2	3		5		7	8	9	10	11*	4	6	12																2
1	2*	3		5		7	8	9	10	11	4	6		12															3
		3		5		7	8*	9	10	11	4	6	12	2	1														4
		3		5	4	7	8	9*	10	11	12	6		2		1													5
		3		5		7		9	10	11	4	6		2		1	8												6
		3		5		7		9	10	11	4	6		2		1	8												7
		3		5		7	9		10	11		6		2		1	8	4*	12										8
		3	4	5		7	9*		10	11		6				1	8		12	2									9
		3	4	5		9			10	11		6				1	8			2	7								10
		3	4	5		7				11	10	6				1	8			2	9								11
	2	3	4	5		7	9			11	10					1	8			6									12
	2	3	4	5		7	9			11	10					1	8			6									13
	2*	3	4	5		7	9			11	10					1	8	12		6									14
		3	4	5		7		9*		11	10	6				1	8	12		2									15
		3	4	5		7		9		11	10	6				1	8			2									16
		3	4	5		7		9		11	10	6				1	8			2									17
		3	4	5		7		9		11	10	6				1	8			2									18
		3	4	5		7		9			10	6				1	8			2		11							19
		3	4	5		7		9		11	10	6				1	8	12		2*									20
		3	4	5		7		9*		11	10	6		2		1	8	12											21
		3	4	5		7	11	9			10	6		2		1	8												22
		3		5		7	8	9		11*	10	6		2		1		12		4									23
		3	4	5		11	8	9			10	6		2		1					7								24
1		3	4			11	8				10	6	9					12		2	7*		5						25
1		3	4			11	7*				10	6	9				8			2			5	12					26
1		3	4			11	7				10	6					8*			2		12	5	9					27
1		3	4			7	8			11	10	6								2			5	9					28
1		3	4*			7	8			11	10	6		12						2			5	9					29
1		3				7	8			11	10	6								2			5	9	4				30
1		3				11	8			12	10*	6								2			5	9	4	7			31
1		3					8				10	6								2		11	5	9	4	7			32
1		3				11	8			10		6		12						2		7*	5	9	4				33
1		3				4	8			10	12	6								2		11*	5	9		7			34
1		3				11	8			10	4	6					7			2			5	9					35
1		3				7	10			11	4*	6		12			8			2			5	9					36
1		3	12			11	8			10		6		4			7*			2			5	9					37
1			4			11	8			10		6								2			5	9		7	3		38
1						7	10			11		6					8			2			5	9	12	4*	3		39
1	3					11	8*			10	4	6								2		12	5	9		7			40
1						11	10*			4		6					8		12	2			5	9		7	3		41
1			10							4		6					8			2		11	5	9		7		3	42
21	7	37	23	24	2	40	30	17	10	34	30	38	2	10	1	20	25	1		31	4	5	18	16	4	8	3	1	
			1							1	2		2	4				6	3			2		1	1				
		4	2			1	10	10	4	1	1	1					13			1			2	6					

		3	4			11	8	9			10	6				1				2	7		5						3
1		3	4			11	7				10	6	9				8			2			5						4
1		2	2			2	2	1			2	2	1			1	1			2	1		2						
						1																							

1		3	10*	5		7	8	9		11	4	6		2						12									2
		3		5		7	8	9	10	11	4	6		2		1													R
		3		5		7	9		10	11		6		12		1	8		4*	2									3
1		3	1	3		3	3	2	2	3	2	3		2		2	1		1	1									
														1						1									
							2																						

1980-81

Manager: Gordon Milne

1	Aug	16	(a)	Birmingham C	L 1-3	Blair	21,907
2		19	(h)	Liverpool	D 0-0		22,807
3		23	(h)	Arsenal	W 3-1	Thompson, English, Gillespie	15,399
4		30	(a)	Aston Villa	L 0-1		26,050
5	Sep	6	(h)	Crystal P	W 3-1	Daly 2, Blair	13,091
6		13	(a)	Wolves	W 1-0	Bodak	18,150
7		20	(a)	Ipswich T	L 0-2		20,507
8		27	(h)	Everton	L 0-5		14,810
9	Oct	4	(h)	Brighton & HA	D 3-3	Dyson, Thompson, Hutchison	11,462
10		8	(a)	West Brom A	L 0-1		16,377
11		11	(a)	Leicester C	W 3-1	Dyson, Gooding, English	17,104
12		18	(h)	Norwich C	L 0-1		12,235
13		21	(h)	Sunderland	W 2-1	Hunt, Thompson	13,115
14		25	(a)	Tottenham H	L 1-4	Gooding	25,414
15	Nov	1	(h)	Leeds U	W 2-1	Hunt, Bodak	13,970
16		8	(a)	Manchester U	D 0-0		42,794
17		11	(a)	Liverpool	L 1-2	Thomas	26,744
18		15	(h)	Birmingham C	W 2-1	Blair, Hunt	18,758
19		22	(a)	Manchester C	L 0-3		30,047
20		29	(h)	Nottingham F	D 1-1	Daly (pen)	15,171
21	Dec	6	(a)	Southampton	L 0-1		18,824
22		13	(h)	West Brom A	W 3-0	Blair, Daly (pen), Hunt	16,027
23		20	(a)	Norwich C	L 0-2		12,630
24		26	(h)	Middlesbrough	W 1-0	Daly	16,066
25		27	(a)	Stoke C	D 2-2	Hateley, Thompson	17,675
26	Jan	10	(h)	Manchester C	D 1-1	Hunt	18,248
27		17	(h)	Aston Villa	L 1-2	Hateley	27,020
28		31	(a)	Arsenal	D 2-2	Bodak, Daly	24,876
29	Feb	7	(h)	Wolves	D 2-2	Hunt, Hateley	18,243
30		17	(a)	Crystal P	W 3-0	Bannister, English 2	12,868
31		21	(a)	Everton	L 0-3		26,731
32		28	(h)	Ipswich T	L 0-4		17,557
33	Mar	7	(a)	Brighton & HA	L 1-4	Bannister	14,063
34		14	(h)	Leicester C	W 4-1	English 3, Thompson	21,430
35		21	(a)	Sunderland	L 0-3		20,622
36		28	(h)	Tottenham H	L 0-1		18,666
37	Apr	4	(a)	Leeds U	L 0-3		15,882
38		11	(h)	Manchester U	L 0-2		20,175
39		18	(h)	Stoke C	D 2-2	Daly, Thompson	12,766
40		21	(a)	Middlesbrough	W 1-0	Daly	11,371
41		25	(h)	Southampton	W 1-0	Thompson	18,213
42	May	2	(a)	Nottingham F	D 1-1	Thompson	21,511

FINAL LEAGUE POSITION: 16th in Division One

Appearances
Sub Appearances
Goals

FA Cup

3	Jan	3	(a)	Leeds U	D 1-1	Thomas	24,523
R		6	(h)	Leeds U	W 1-0	Thompson	22,057
4		24	(h)	Birmingham C	W 3-2	Daly 2 (1 pen), Blair	29,500
5	Feb	14	(a)	Tottenham H	L 1-3	English	36,688

Appearances
Sub Appearances
Goals

League Cup

2	Aug	27	(a)	Manchester U	W 1-0	English	31,656
	Sep	2	(h)	Manchester U	W 1-0	Blair	18,705
3		23	(a)	Brighton & HA	W 2-1	English, Hutchison	14,426
4	Oct	28	(h)	Cambridge U	D 1-1	Thompson	17,049
R	Nov	4	(a)	Cambridge U	W 1-0	Hunt	10,171
5	Dec	2	(a)	Watford	D 2-2	Thompson 2	27,542
R		9	(h)	Watford	W 5-0	Bodak, Hateley 2, Thompson, Hunt	30,348
SF	Jan	27	(h)	West Ham U	W 3-2	Thompson 2, Daly	35,468
	Feb	10	(a)	West Ham U	L 0-2		36,551

Appearances
Sub Appearances
Goals

Blyth	Coop	McDonald	Blair	Dyson	Gillespie	Van Gool	English	Thompson G	Gooding	Hunt	Roberts	Jones	Daly	Thomas	Haywood	Hateley	Bodak	Jacobs	Sealey	Hutchison	Bannister	Ferguson	Whitton	
1	2	3	4	5	6	7*	8	9	10	11	12													1
1	2		4	5	6	7*	10	9		11	3	12	8											2
1	2		4	5	6	7	10	9		11	3		8											3
1	2		4	5	6*		10			11	3		8	12	7	9								4
1	2		4	5			10	9*		11	3	6	8			12	7							5
1	2		4	5			10			11	3		8			9	7	6						6
	2		4	5			12			11	3		8			9	7*	6	1	10				7
1	2		4	5			10			11	3		8			9	12	6		7*				8
	2		4	5				9		11	3		8			10		6	1	7				9
	2		4*	5	6		10	9		11	3		8					12	1	7				10
	2			5	6	7	10	9	4	11	3		8						1					11
	2			5	6	7	10	9	4*	11	3		8						1		12			12
	2			5	6	10*		9	4	11	3		8				7	12	1					13
	2		8	5	6		12	9	4	11	3						7		1		10*			14
	2		8	5	6	10			4*	11	3			12		9	7		1					15
	2		4	5	6	8*	12			11	3			10		9	7		1					16
	2		4	5	6	8*	12			11	3			10		9	7		1					17
	2		8	5	6			10		11	3			4		9	7		1					18
			4	5	6*			8		11	3		12	10		9	7	2	1					19
			4	5	6		10*	12		11	3		8	2			7		1			9		20
			4	5	6			9		11	3		8	2		10	7		1					21
			4	5	6			9		11	3		8	2		10	7		1					22
			4	5	6			9	8*	11	3	12		2		10	7		1					23
			4	5	6			9		11	3		8	2		10	7		1					24
			4	5	6			9		11	3		8	2		10			1		7			25
	2		4	5	6			9		11*	3		8	7			12		1			10		26
	2		4	5	6			9		11	3		8	7		12			1			10*		27
			4	5	6			9		11	3		8	2		10	7*	12	1					28
			4	5	6			9		11	3		8	2		10	7		1					29
			4		5		10	9		11	3		8	2				6	1		7			30
				5	6*		10	9		11	3	12	8	2				4	1		7			31
				5	6		10	9		11	3		8	2			7	4	1					32
			4	5	6		10	9			3		8	2			7		1		11			33
			4	5	6		10	9			3		8	2			7		1		11			34
			4	5	6		10	9		11	3		8	2					1		7			35
	7		4*	5	6		10	9		11	3		8	2					1				12	36
	2			5	6		10	9		11	3		8	4			7*		1		12			37
	2			5	6		10	9		11	3		8	4					1		7			38
	2		4	5	6		10	9		11	3		8						1		7			39
	2		4	5	6		10	9	7	11	3		8						1					40
	2		4	5	6		10	9	7	11	3		8						1					41
	2		4	5	6		10	9	7	11	3		8						1					42
7	27	1	35	41	37	9	24	34	10	40	41	1	34	23	1	17	21	8	35	4	9	3		
							4	1			1	3	1	2		2	2	3			2		1	
			4	2	1		7	8	2	6			8	1		3	3			1	2			

Blyth	Coop	McDonald	Blair	Dyson	Gillespie	Van Gool	English	Thompson G	Gooding	Hunt	Roberts	Jones	Daly	Thomas	Haywood	Hateley	Bodak	Jacobs	Sealey	Hutchison	Bannister	Ferguson	Whitton	
			4	5	6			9		11	3		8	2		10		12	1		7*			3
	2		4	5	6			9			3		8			10	7		1		11			R
	2		4	5	6			9		11	3		8	12			7*		1			10		4
			4	5*	6		10	9		11	3		8	2		12		7	1					5
	2		4	4	4		1	4		3	4		4	2		2	2	1	4		2	1		
														1		1		1						
			1				1	1					2	1										

Blyth	Coop	McDonald	Blair	Dyson	Gillespie	Van Gool	English	Thompson G	Gooding	Hunt	Roberts	Jones	Daly	Thomas	Haywood	Hateley	Bodak	Jacobs	Sealey	Hutchison	Bannister	Ferguson	Whitton	
1	2	12	4	5	6	7	10	9*		11	3		8											2
1	2		4	5			10	9*		11	3	6	8	12							7			
1	2		4	5			10			11	3		8			9		6		7				3
	2		8	5	6		10	9	4	11	3						7		1					4
	2		4	5	6	8				11	3			10		9	7		1					R
			4	5	6			9		11	3		8	2		10	7		1					5
			4	5	6			9		11	3		8*	2		10	7	12	1					R
			4	5	6			9		11	3		8*	2		10	7	12	1					SF
			4	5	6			9		11	3		8	2		10	7*	12	1					
3	5		9	9	7	2	4	7	1	9	9	1	7	5		6	6	1	6	1	1			
		1												1				3						
			1				2	6		2			1			2	1			1				

1981-82

Manager: David Sexton

1	Aug	29	(h)	Manchester U	W	2-1	Whitton, Bodak	20,050
2	Sep	2	(a)	Stoke C	L	0-4		13,914
3		5	(a)	Notts C	L	1-2	Daly	10,889
4		12	(h)	Leeds U	W	4-0	Kaiser, Thompson 2, Whitton	13,065
5		19	(a)	Brighton & HA	D	2-2	Kaiser, Hunt	15,262
6		22	(h)	Liverpool	L	1-2	Daly	16,731
7		26	(h)	Southampton	W	4-2	Hunt 2, Thompson 2	12,610
8	Oct	3	(a)	Sunderland	D	0-0		19,269
9		10	(h)	Aston Villa	D	1-1	Hateley	16,306
10		17	(a)	Nottingham F	L	1-2	Hunt	20,101
11		24	(h)	Swansea C	W	3-1	Hateley 2, Kaiser	14,050
12		31	(a)	Arsenal	L	0-1		23,102
13	Nov	7	(a)	Wolves	L	0-1		13,193
14		21	(a)	West Ham U	L	2-5	Hunt 2	26,065
15		24	(h)	Stoke C	W	3-0	Daly, Thompson, Bradford	10,250
16		28	(h)	Middlesbrough	D	1-1	Hateley	11,309
17	Dec	5	(a)	Tottenham H	W	2-1	Hunt, Gillespie	28,073
18		12	(h)	Manchester C	L	0-1		12,398
19		26	(h)	West Brom A	L	0-2		15,033
20		28	(a)	Everton	L	2-3	Thomas, Bodak	23,895
21	Jan	16	(h)	Ipswich T	L	2-4	Hunt, Daly	11,719
22		26	(a)	Birmingham C	D	3-3	Hunt, Hateley, Thompson	13,023
23		30	(h)	Brighton & HA	L	0-1		11,023
24	Feb	6	(a)	Leeds U	D	0-0		16,385
25		16	(h)	Notts C	L	1-5	Hateley	10,203
26		20	(a)	Liverpool	L	0-4		28,286
27		27	(a)	Aston Villa	L	1-2	Thompson	24,474
28	Mar	9	(h)	Nottingham F	L	0-1		9,720
29		13	(a)	Swansea C	D	0-0		16,425
30		17	(a)	Manchester U	W	1-0	Whitton	34,499
31		20	(h)	Arsenal	W	1-0	Hateley	11,965
32		27	(h)	Wolves	D	0-0		11,514
33	Apr	3	(a)	Ipswich T	L	0-1		20,411
34		10	(a)	West Brom A	W	2-1	Thompson, Whitton	12,718
35		13	(h)	Everton	W	1-0	Singleton	11,858
36		17	(h)	West Ham U	W	1-0	Hateley	13,398
37		24	(a)	Middlesbrough	D	0-0		10,968
38		27	(h)	Sunderland	W	6-1	Gillespie, Thompson 2, Francis, Hateley 2	11,227
39	May	1	(h)	Tottenham H	D	0-0		15,431
40		4	(a)	Southampton	D	5-5	Whitton 2, Hateley 3	18,522
41		8	(a)	Manchester C	W	3-1	Whitton 3	27,580
42		15	(h)	Birmingham C	L	0-1		15,905

FINAL LEAGUE POSITION: 14th in Division One

Appearances
Sub Appearances
Goals

FA Cup

3	Jan	2	(h)	Sheffield W	W	3-1	Hunt 2, Hateley	14,213
4		23	(a)	Manchester C	W	3-1	Hunt, Hateley, Bodak	31,276
5	Feb	13	(h)	Oxford U	W	4-0	Thompson 2, Hateley 2	20,251
6	Mar	6	(a)	West Brom A	L	0-2		27,825

Appearances
Sub Appearances
Goals

League Cup

2	Oct	6	(a)	Everton	D	1-1	Hateley	17,228
		27	(h)	Everton	L	0-1		13,770

Appearances
Sub Appearances
Goals

Blyth	Thomas	Roberts	Jacobs	Dyson	Gillespie	Bodak	Daly	Thompson G	Whitton	Hunt	Kaiser	Hateley	Gooding	Bradford	Hendrie	English	Barnes	Francis	Hormantschuk	Hagan	Sealey	Butterworth	Singleton	
1	2	3	4	5	6	7	8	9	10	11														1
1	2	3	4	5	6	7*	8	9	10	11	12													2
1	2	3	4	5	6		8	9	10	11	7													3
1	2	3	4	5	6		8	9	10	11	7													4
1	2	3	4	5	6		8	9	10	11	7													5
1	2	3	4	5	6		8	9	10*	11	7	12												6
1	2	3	4	5	6		8	9	10	11	7													7
1	2	3	4	5	6		8*	9	10	11	7	12												8
1	2	3	4	5	6			9	8	11	7	10												9
1	2	3	4	5	6			9	8	10	7	11												10
1	2	3	4	5	6			9	8	11	7	10												11
1	2	3	4	5	6			9		11	7	8	10											12
1	2	3	4	5	6		8	9	10	11	7													13
1	2	3	4	5	6		8	9		11		10		7										14
1	2	3	4	5	6		8	9		11		10		7										15
1	2	3	4	5	6		8	9		11	12	10		7*										16
1	2	3	4	5	6		8*	9		11	12	10			7									17
1	2	3*	4	5	6		8	9		11	12	10			7									18
1	2	3	4	5	6		8	9	12	11		10*			7									19
1	2	3	4	5	6	7	8	9		11	12					10*								20
1	2			5	6	7	8			11		9			10		3	4*	12					21
1	2		12	5	6	7	8*	10		11		9					3	4						22
1	2		12	5	6	7	8*	10		11		9					3	4						23
1	2		4		6	7		10		11		9		8			3			5				24
1	2			5	6	7		10		11		9		8			3	4						25
1	2	3	8	5				10		11		9		7				4		6				26
1	8	2			5	7		10		11		9					3	4		6				27
	2	3	4	5	6				12	11*		9			7	10		8			1			28
	2	3	4	5	6				11			9			7*	10		8			1	12		29
	2	3	4	5	6				7			9				10		8			1	11		30
	2	3	4	5	6				7			9				10		8			1	11		31
	2	3	4	5	6				7			9				10		8			1	11		32
	2*	3	4	5	6			12	7			9				10		8			1	11		33
		3	4	5	6			10	7	11		9						8			1	2		34
		3	4	5	6			10	7	11		9							12		1	2	8*	35
	2	3	8	5	6			10	7*	11		9							12		1	4		36
	2		3	5	6			10	7	11		9						8			1	4		37
	2		3	5	6			10	7	11		9						8			1	4		38
	2	12	3	5	6			10	7	11*		9						8			1	4		39
	2		3	5	6			10	7	11		9						8			1	4		40
		3	2	5	6			10	7	11		9*							12		1	4	8	41
	2	3	6	5				10	7							9		8	12		1	4*	11	42
27	39	33	37	40	40	9	19	35	26	36	11	31	1	6	6	8	6	18	0	3	15	13	3	
		1	2					1	2		5	2							5			1		
	1				2	2	4	10	9	9	3	13		1				1					1	

Blyth	Thomas	Roberts	Jacobs	Dyson	Gillespie	Bodak	Daly	Thompson G	Whitton	Hunt	Kaiser	Hateley	Gooding	Bradford	Hendrie	English	Barnes	Francis	Hormantschuk	Hagan	Sealey	Butterworth	Singleton	
1	2		4	5	6	7	8			11	10*	9					3		12					3
1	4*			5	6	7	8	9		11		10					3		2			12		4
1	2		12	5	6	7		10		11		9		8			3	4*						5
1	8	2			5	7		10		11		9					3	4		6				6
4	4	1	1	3	4	4	2	3		4	1	4		1			4	2	1	1				
			1																1			1		
						1		2		3		4												

Blyth	Thomas	Roberts	Jacobs	Dyson	Gillespie	Bodak	Daly	Thompson G	Whitton	Hunt	Kaiser	Hateley	Gooding	Bradford	Hendrie	English	Barnes	Francis	Hormantschuk	Hagan	Sealey	Butterworth	Singleton	
1	2	3	4	5	6			9	8		7	11	10											2
1	2	3	4	5	6			9	8	11	7	10												
2	2	2	2	2	2			2	2	1	2	2	1											
												1												

1982-83

Manager: David Sexton

1	Aug	28	(h)	Southampton	W 1-0	Whitton	10,356
2		31	(a)	Swansea C	L 1-2	Whitton	11,712
3	Sep	4	(a)	Ipswich T	D 1-1	Thomas	16,662
4		7	(h)	Sunderland	W 1-0	Thompson	8,190
5		11	(h)	Arsenal	L 0-1		10,245
6		18	(a)	Birmingham C	L 0-1		11,681
7		25	(h)	Everton	W 4-2	Melrose 3, Hunt	9,319
8	Oct	2	(a)	Manchester C	L 2-3	Melrose, Thompson	25,105
9		9	(a)	Tottenham H	L 0-4		25,188
10		16	(h)	Notts C	W 1-0	Francis	8,320
11		23	(a)	Watford	D 0-0		17,334
12		30	(h)	Norwich C	W 2-0	Hateley, Thompson	8,305
13	Nov	6	(h)	Aston Villa	D 0-0		12,076
14		13	(a)	Liverpool	L 0-4		27,870
15		20	(h)	Luton T	W 4-2	Dyson, Whitton 2, Thompson	9,644
16		23	(h)	Ipswich T	D 1-1	Thomas	9,550
17		27	(a)	West Brom A	L 0-2		12,115
18	Dec	4	(h)	Brighton & HA	W 2-0	Hunt, Whitton	8,054
19		11	(a)	West Ham U	W 3-0	Hateley, Roberts, Whitton	19,321
20		18	(h)	Stoke C	W 2-0	Hateley 2	10,065
21		27	(a)	Nottingham F	L 2-4	Whitton, Melrose	24,487
22		28	(h)	Manchester U	W 3-0	Hormantschuk, Hateley, Melrose	18,938
23	Jan	1	(a)	Luton T	W 2-1	Whitton, Melrose	13,072
24		15	(a)	Southampton	D 1-1	Hateley	17,145
25		22	(h)	Swansea C	D 0-0		9,946
26	Feb	5	(a)	Sunderland	L 1-2	Whitton	14,356
27		12	(h)	Manchester C	W 4-0	Melrose, Hateley, Gillespie, Hunt	9,527
28		26	(a)	Notts C	L 1-5	Gillespie	8,689
29	Mar	5	(h)	Watford	L 0-1		11,235
30		12	(h)	Tottenham H	D 1-1	Hunt (pen)	11,004
31		19	(a)	Aston Villa	L 0-4		20,509
32		23	(a)	Norwich C	D 1-1	Whitton	13,944
33	Apr	2	(a)	Manchester U	L 0-3		36,814
34		5	(h)	Nottingham F	L 1-2	Whitton	9,720
35		9	(a)	Arsenal	L 1-2	Hateley	19,152
36		12	(h)	Liverpool	D 0-0		14,821
37		16	(h)	Birmingham C	L 0-1		10,420
38		23	(a)	Brighton & HA	L 0-1		14,674
39		30	(h)	West Brom A	L 0-1		9,410
40	May	2	(a)	Everton	L 0-1		12,972
41		7	(a)	Stoke C	W 3-0	Hateley, Hendrie, Thomas	12,048
42		14	(h)	West Ham U	L 2-4	Hendrie, Whitton	10,919

FINAL LEAGUE POSITION: 19th in Division One

Appearances
Sub Appearances
Goals

FA Cup

3	Jan	8	(h)	Worcester C	W 3-1	Whitton 2 (1 pen), Hateley	11,843
4		29	(h)	Norwich C	D 2-2	Roberts, Thompson	13,073
R	Feb	2	(a)	Norwich C	L 1-2*	Hateley	18,625

*After extra-time

Appearances
Sub Appearances
Goals

League Cup

2	Oct	5	(a)	Fulham	D 2-2	Melrose 2	6,237
		26	(h)	Fulham	D 0-0†		8,217
3	Nov	9	(h)	Burnley	L 1-2	Hunt	7,559

†After extra-time. Coventry City won on away-goals rule.

Appearances
Sub Appearances
Goals

Suckling	Thomas	Roberts	Jacobs	Dyson	Gillespie	Singleton	Francis	Hateley	Thompson G	Whitton	Hormantschuk	Sealey	Thompson K	Daly	Melrose	Hall	Hunt	Butterworth	Hendrie	
1	2	3	4	5	6	7	8	9	10	11										1
1	2	3	4	5	6	7*	8	9	10	11	12									2
	2	3	4	5	6		8	9	10	11	7	1								3
	2	3	4	5	6	12	8	9*	10	11	7	1								4
	2	3	4	5	6	12	8		10	11	7	1		9*						5
		3	4	5	6		8			9	2	1	11		7	10				6
	2	3	4	5	6		8		10	7		1	12		9		11*			7
	2	3	4	5	6				10	7		1		8*	9		11	12		8
	2	3	8	5	6				10	7		1			9		11	4		9
	2	3	7	5	6		8		10			1			9		11	4		10
	2	3	7	5	6		8		10			1			9		11	4		11
	2	3	8	5	6			9	10	12		1					11	4	7*	12
	2	3	12	5	6		8*	9	10			1					11	4	7	13
1	2	3	8	5	6			9	10	7							11	4		14
	2	3	4	5	6		8*	9	10	7		1					11	12		15
	2	3	8	5	6			9	10	7		1					11	4		16
	2	3	8	5	6			9*	10	7		1			12		11	4		17
	2	3	8	5	6			9	10	7		1					11	4		18
	2	3	8	5	6			9		7		1			10		11	4		19
	2	3	4	5	6		8*	9		7		1			10		11	12		20
	2		3*	5	6		8	9		7		1			10		11	4	12	21
	2			5	6		8	9		7	3	1			10		11	4		22
	2			5	6		8	9		7	3	1			10		11	4		23
	2			5	6		8	9		7	3	1			10		11	4		24
	2	3		5	6		8	9	12	7		1			10*		11	4		25
	2	3		5	6		8	9	12	7		1			10*		11	4		26
	2	3	8	5	6			9*	10	7		1			12		11	4		27
	2	3		5	6		8	9		7*		1	12		10		11	4		28
	2	3	12	5	6		8	9		7		1			10		11*	4		29
	2	3		5	6		8	9				1	7		10		11	4		30
	2	3		5	6		8	9		7		1	12		10		11	4*		31
	2	3	4	5	6		8	9		7		1					10		11	32
	2	3	4	5	6		8	9		7*		1					10	12	11	33
	2	3	4	5	6		8	9		7		1			10		11			34
	2	3	4	5	6		8	9		7		1			10*		11		12	35
	2	3	4	5	6		8	9		10		1					11		7	36
	2	3	4	5	6		8	9		10		1					11		7	37
	2	3	10	5	6		8	9		7*		1					11	4	12	38
	2	3	10	5*	6		8	9		7		1			12		11	4		39
	2	3	6		5		8	9		7	10	1			11*			4	12	40
	2	3			6		8	9		7	4	1					11	5	10	41
	2	3			6	8		9		7	4	1					11	5	10	42
3	41	38	30	39	42	3	32	35	18	37	10	39	2	2	21	1	35	26	8	
			2			2			2	1	1		3		3			4	4	
	3	1		1	2		1	9	4	12	1				8		4		2	

1	2			5	6		8	9		7	3	1			10		11	4		3
	2	3		5	6		8	9	10	7	4	1					11			4
	2	3	8	5	6			9	10	7		1			12		11*	4		R
1	3	2	1	3	3		2	3	2	3	2	3			1		3	2		
															1					
		1						2	1	2										

	2		8	5	6				10	7	3	1			9		11	4		2
	2	3	7	5	6		8*		10	12		1			9		11	4		
1	2	3		5	6	8			10	12					9		11	4	7*	3
1	3	2	2	3	3	1	1		3	1	1	2			3		3	3	1	
										2										
															2		1			

1983-84

Manager: Bobby Gould

1	Aug	27	(a)	Watford	W	3-2	Bolton (og), Gibson, Rice (og)	15,533
2		29	(a)	Tottenham H	D	1-1	Withey	35,854
3	Sep	3	(h)	Everton	D	1-1	Adams	12,532
4		6	(h)	Notts C	W	2-1	Gibson, Platnauer	10,912
5		10	(a)	West Ham U	L	2-5	Peake, Platnauer	22,195
6		17	(h)	Leicester C	W	2-1	Platnauer, Gibson	12,377
7		24	(a)	Sunderland	L	0-1		11,612
8	Oct	1	(h)	Ipswich T	L	1-2	Gibson	10,492
9		15	(a)	Arsenal	W	1-0	Bamber	20,290
10		22	(h)	West Brom A	L	1-2	Withey	13,441
11		29	(a)	Stoke C	W	3-1	Bennett, Gibson, Bamber	11,836
12	Nov	5	(a)	Birmingham C	W	2-1	Gibson, Bennett	16,169
13		12	(h)	Queen's Park R	W	1-0	Bamber	11,755
14		19	(a)	Wolves	D	0-0		11,419
15		26	(h)	Southampton	D	0-0		11,579
16	Dec	3	(a)	Luton T	W	4-2	Gibson 2, Gynn, Bennett	10,698
17		10	(h)	Liverpool	W	4-0	Platnauer, Gibson 3	20,586
18		17	(a)	Norwich C	D	0-0		16,646
19		26	(h)	Manchester U	D	1-1	Gibson (pen)	21,453
20		28	(a)	Nottingham F	L	0-3		22,169
21		31	(a)	Everton	D	0-0		13,659
22	Jan	2	(h)	Sunderland	W	2-1	Withey, Daly	13,249
23		14	(h)	Watford	L	1-2	Peake	13,307
24		21	(a)	Leicester C	D	1-1	Daly	16,262
25	Feb	4	(a)	Ipswich T	L	1-3	Gibson	13,406
26		11	(h)	West Ham U	L	1-2	Hunt	13,271
27		18	(h)	Stoke C	L	2-3	Bennett, Gibson	9,752
28		25	(a)	West Brom A	D	1-1	Gibson	10,900
29	Mar	3	(h)	Birmingham C	L	0-1		13,705
30		10	(a)	Queen's Park R	L	1-2	Daly	10,284
31		13	(h)	Aston Villa	D	3-3	Daly, Allardyce, Gibson	11,098
32		17	(a)	Notts C	L	1-2	Peake	6,564
33		24	(h)	Tottenham H	L	2-4	Withey, Daly (pen)	12,803
34		31	(h)	Arsenal	L	1-4	Bennett	10,550
35	Apr	7	(a)	Aston Villa	L	0-2		15,318
36		14	(h)	Wolves	W	2-1	Daly (pen), Ferguson	8,246
37		17	(h)	Nottingham F	W	2-1	Ferguson, Platnauer	9,818
38		21	(a)	Manchester U	L	1-4	Daly	38,524
39		28	(a)	Southampton	L	2-8	Grimes, Gynn	16,746
40	May	5	(h)	Luton T	D	2-2	Platnauer, Gibson	9,391
41		7	(a)	Liverpool	L	0-5		33,393
42		12	(h)	Norwich C	W	2-1	Ferguson, Bennett	14,007

FINAL LEAGUE POSITION: 19th in Division One

Appearances
Sub Appearances
Goals

FA Cup

3	Jan	7	(h)	Wolves	D	1-1	Withey	15,817
R		10	(a)	Wolves	D	1-1*	Peake	19,204
2R		16	(h)	Wolves	W	3-0	Withey 2, Hunt	18,003
4		30	(a)	Sheffield W	L	2-3	Gibson 2	26,154

*After extra-time

Appearances
Sub Appearances
Goals

League Cup

2	Oct	4	(a)	Grimsby T	D	0-0		6,088
		25	(h)	Grimsby T	W	2-1	Bennett, Grimes	8,705
3	Nov	9	(a)	Everton	L	1-2	Bamber	9,080

Appearances
Sub Appearances
Goals

Suckling	Hormantschuk	Roberts	Grimes	Butterworth	Jacobs	Gynn	Daly	Bamber	Gibson	Thompson K	Platnauer	Singleton	Peake	Adams	Withey	Avramovic	Bennett	Allardyce	Hendrie	Hunt	Pearce	Langley	Ferguson	McGrath	Spring	
1	2	3	4	5	6	7*	8	9	10	11	12															1
1	2	3	7		6			9	10		8	4*	5	11	12											2
1	2	3	4		6		8		10		9	7*	5	11	12											3
1	2	3	4		6		8		10		9	7*	5	11	12											4
1	2*	3	4	7	6				10		9	12	5	11	8											5
	2	3		4	6		8		10	11*	9		5		7	1	12									6
	2	3		4			8		10	11*	9		5		7	1	12	6								7
	2*	3	4				8		10		9		5		7	1	11	6	12							8
		3	10	2				7	8		9	4	5		12	1	11	6*								9
		2	4	3		7		9	10		11	8*	5		12	1		6								10
		2	4			8		9	10		11	3	5			1	7	6								11
		2	11			8		9	10*		3	4	5			1	7	6		12						12
1		2	4			8		9			12		5				7	6	10*	11	3					13
1		2	4			8		9	10*		12		5				7	6		11	3					14
1		2	4			8		9	10*		12		5				7	6		11	3					15
1		2				8		9	10		4		5				7	6		11	3					16
		2				8	11	9*	10		4		5		12	1	7	6			3					17
		2				8	4	9	10		11		5			1	7	6			3					18
		2	12			8	11	9	10		4*		5			1	7	6			3					19
		2	10	12		8	4				11		5		9*	1	7	6			3					20
		2	10				4				11		5		9	1	7	6		8	3					21
		2	10*	5	6	12	8				4				9	1	7			11	3					22
		2		6		4	12		10*		9		5	11		1	7			8	3					23
		2		6			7				11		5	10	9	1	4			8	3					24
		2		6		4*		9	8		12		5	3		1	7			10	11					25
		2	11				4	9	10				5			1	7	6		8	3					26
		2	11			4			10	9			5		12	1	7	6		8	3*					27
1		2	7			4*			10			11	5	3	12		9	6		8						28
1		2	7	6				12	10			11*	5	3	4		9			8						29
1		2	7	6			4	8	10*			11	5	3	12		9									30
1			11		2		4	9	10	8*			5	3			7	6		12						31
1			8	12	2		4*	9	10	11			5	3			7	6								32
1			8*	11	2		4						5	12	9		7	6			3	10				33
1				2			4		10		9	8*	5	11	12		7	6			3					34
1			12	2	6		4		10		9	8	5*				7				3	11				35
1			8	2	6		4		10		11			7				5			3		9			36
1			7	2	6	12	4		10*		8			3			11	5					9			37
1			8	2	6	10	4		12		11			3*			7	5					9			38
1			8	2	6	10	4		7		11								12		3		9	5*		39
1			8*	2	6	12	4		10		11						7	5			3		9			40
1				2	5	11	4		10		8						7	6			3		9*		12	41
1			12	2	6	8	4*		10		11						7	5			3		9			42
24	8	30	29	22	18	20	27	18	35	6	29	12	33	16	10	18	32	28	1	13	23	2	7	1		
			3	2		3	1	1	1		5	1		1	10		2		2	2					1	
			1			2	7	3	17		6		3	1	4		6	1		1			3			

2 own-goals

		2*				12	4		10		11		5	3	9	1	7	6		8						3
		2		5		4	12		11		10		6	3	9*	1	7			8						R
		2		6		4	7			10	11		5	3	9	1				8						2R
		2		4			8	12	11		10		5	3	9*	1	7			8						4
		4		3		2	3		3	1	4		4	4	4	4	3	1		4						
						1	1	1																		
									2				1		3					1						

		3	9		6				10		7	4	5		8	1	11	2								2
		2	11			4		9	10		3	8	5			1	7	6								
1		2	10			4		9			3	12	5				7	6	11*	8						3
1		3	3		1	2		2	2		3	2	3		1	2	3	3	1	1						
												1														
			1					1									1									

1984-85

Manager: Bobby Gould until 28 December 1984, then Donald Mackay.

1	Aug	25	(a)	Aston Villa	L 0-1		20,970
2		28	(h)	Norwich C	D 0-0		10,632
3	Sep	1	(h)	Leicester C	W 2-0	Bennett, Latchford	13,510
4		4	(a)	West Ham U	L 1-3	Pearce	14,949
5		8	(a)	Everton	L 1-2	Gibson	20,013
6		15	(h)	Manchester U	L 0-3		18,482
7		22	(a)	Sunderland	D 0-0		16,308
8		29	(h)	Arsenal	L 1-2	Gibson	14,394
9	Oct	6	(a)	Watford	W 1-0	Gibson	15,184
10		13	(h)	Newcastle U	D 1-1	Hibbitt	14,091
11		20	(a)	Queen's Park R	L 1-2	Gynn	10,427
12		27	(h)	Sheffield W	W 1-0	Gibson	14,348
13	Nov	3	(a)	Chelsea	L 2-6	Gynn, Latchford	17,306
14		10	(h)	Ipswich T	W 1-0	Adams	8,790
15		17	(h)	Nottingham F	L 1-3	Gibson (pen)	9,894
16		24	(a)	West Brom A	L 2-5	Barnes, Regis	12,742
17	Dec	1	(h)	Tottenham H	D 1-1	Regis	14,518
18		4	(a)	Liverpool	L 1-3	Hansen (og)	27,237
19		15	(h)	Southampton	W 2-1	Peake, Shilton (og)	10,369
20		23	(a)	Leicester C	L 1-5	Gynn	18,016
21		26	(a)	Luton T	L 0-2		9,237
22		29	(h)	West Ham U	L 1-2	Stephens	10,775
23	Jan	1	(h)	Stoke C	W 4-0	Gibson 2, Hibbitt, Stephens	9,829
24		12	(a)	Manchester U	W 1-0	Gibson	35,992
25		19	(h)	Aston Villa	L 0-3		15,226
26	Feb	2	(a)	Arsenal	L 1-2	Pearce	21,791
27		23	(h)	Chelsea	W 1-0	Gibson	11,430
28	Mar	2	(a)	Sheffield W	L 0-1		20,422
29		9	(h)	Queen's Park R	W 3-0	Gibson 2, Kilcline	8,988
30		23	(h)	Watford	W 3-1	Adams, Gibson 2	9,794
31		30	(a)	Norwich C	L 1-2	Gynn	14,067
32	Apr	13	(h)	Sunderland	L 0-1		9,668
33		17	(a)	Newcastle U	W 1-0	Bennett	19,578
34		20	(a)	Nottingham F	L 0-2		12,990
35		27	(h)	West Brom A	W 2-1	Barnes, Hibbitt	10,356
36	May	4	(a)	Tottenham H	L 2-4	Gibson, Pearce (pen)	16,711
37		6	(h)	Liverpool	L 0-2		18,951
38		11	(a)	Southampton	L 1-2	Regis	15,735
39		14	(a)	Ipswich T	D 0-0		14,038
40		17	(a)	Stoke C	W 1-0	Pearce (pen)	6,930
41		23	(h)	Luton T	W 1-0	Kilcline	14,833
42		26	(h)	Everton	W 4-1	Adams, Gibson, Regis 2	21,224

FINAL LEAGUE POSITION: 18th in Division One

Appearances
Sub Appearances
Goals

FA Cup

3	Jan	5	(h)	Manchester C	W 2-1	Gibson 2	15,643
4		26	(a)	Manchester U	L 1-2	Gibson	38,039

Appearances
Sub Appearances
Goals

League Cup

2	Sep	25	(a)	Walsall	W 2-1	Singleton, Gibson	8,399
	Oct	9	(h)	Walsall	L 0-3		9,214

Appearances
Sub Appearances
Goals

Ogrizovic	Stephens	Pearce	Jol	Kilcline	Peake	Bennett	Platnauer	Withey	Gibson	Gynn	Butterworth	Spring	Adams	Singleton	Barnes	Regis	McGrath	Bowman	Hibbitt	Latchford	Thompson K	
1	2	3	4	5	6	7	8	9*	10	11									12			1
1	2	3	4	5	6	7	11		10	8										9		2
1	2*	3	4	5	6	7	11		10	8									12	9		3
1		3	4	5	6	7	11		10	2									8	9		4
1		3	4	5	6	7	8		10	2									11	9		5
1		3	4	5	6	7	11		10	2	12									9*	8	6
1				5	6	7	11		10	8	12	2	3						4*	9		7
1			9*		6		11	12	10	8	5	2	3	7					4			8
1					6	7	9		10	8	5	2	3		11				4			9
1	2				6	7			10	8	5		3		11	9			4			10
1	2		10		6	7				8	5		3		11	9			4			11
1	2				6	7			10	8			3		11	9	5		4			12
1	2		4		6				10	8		12	3		11	9*	5			7		13
1	2		11		6	7			10	8	5		3						4	9		14
1	2		7		6				10	8	5		3	11		9			4			15
1	2		7		6				10	8	5		3		11	9			4			16
1	2			5	6	7			10	8	12		3		11	9			4*			17
1	2			5	6	7	12		10	8	4*		3		11	9						18
1	2		4	5	6	10				7			3		11	9		8				19
1	2	6	4	5		10				7			3		11	9		8				20
1	2	6	4*	5		12			10	7			3		11	9		8				21
1	2	3		5					10	8*			12		11	9	6	4	7			22
1	2	3		5		12			10	8			11				6	4	7*	9		23
1	2	3		5	6	7			10				11			12	8	4		9*		24
1	2	3		5	6	7*			10				11			9	8	4		12		25
1	2	3		5	6				10	8					11	9	7		4			26
1	2	3		5	6	12			10*	8					11	9	7		4			27
1	2	3		5		12			10	8			11			9	6	7*	4			28
1	2	3		5		7			10	8			11			9	6		4			29
1	2	3		5		7			10	8			11			9	6		4			30
1	2	3		5	12	7			10	8			11			9*	6		4			31
1	2	3				7			10	8	5		11*			9	6	12	4			32
1	2	3			6	7			10	12	5				11	9	8		4*			33
1	2	3			6	7*				12	5				11	9	8		4	10		34
1	2	3			6				10	12	5				11	9	8	7*	4			35
1	2	3			6				10	12	5		7		11*	9	8		4			36
1	2	3			6	12			10	8	5		11			9	7*		4			37
1	2*	3			6	7			10	12	5		11			9	8		4			38
1		3		5	6	7			10	8	2		11			9	12		4*			39
1		3		5	6	7			10	12	2		11			9	8		4*			40
1		3		5	6	7			10	12	2		11			9	8		4*			41
1		3		5	6	7			10		2		11			9	8		4			42
42	32	29	15	26	33	29	9	1	38	32	19	3	30	2	18	30	22	9	31	11	1	
					1	5	1	1		7	3	1	1			1	1	1	2	1		
	2	4		2	1	2			15	4			3		2	5			3	2		

2 own-goals

1	2	3		5					10	8			11				6	4	7	9		3
1	2	3		5	6				10	8*			11			9	7		4	12		4
2	2	2		2	1				2	2			2			1	2	1	2	1		
																				1		
									3													

1				5	6	7*	11		10	8	4	2	3	9							12	2
1				12	6	7	9		10	8	5	2	3		11*				4			
2				1	2	2	2		2	2	2	2	2	1	1				1			
				1																	1	
									1					1								

1985-86

Manager: Donald Mackay until 12 April 1986, then George Curtis.

1	Aug	17	(h)	Manchester C	D 1-1	McNab (og)	14,550
2		20	(a)	Chelsea	L 0-1		15,679
3		24	(a)	Everton	D 1-1	Gibson	27,691
4		26	(h)	Newcastle U	L 1-2	Gibson	12,097
5		31	(a)	Watford	L 0-3		13,835
6	Sep	3	(h)	Oxford U	W 5-2	Bennett, Hibbitt, Kilcline, Briggs (og), Gynn	10,266
7		7	(h)	Arsenal	L 0-2		11,962
8		14	(a)	Aston Villa	D 1-1	Culpin	12,198
9		21	(a)	Southampton	D 1-1	Gibson	12,576
10		28	(h)	West Brom A	W 3-0	Adams (pen), Gibson, Peake	10,295
11	Oct	6	(h)	Leicester C	W 3-0	Bowman, Gibson, Regis	10,959
12		12	(a)	Sheffield W	D 2-2	Adams, Gibson	19,132
13		20	(h)	Tottenham H	L 2-3	Bennett, Kilcline (pen)	13,545
14		26	(a)	Birmingham C	W 1-0	Gibson	9,267
15	Nov	2	(a)	Manchester U	L 0-2		46,748
16		9	(h)	Liverpool	L 0-3		16,497
17		16	(a)	Luton T	W 1-0	Bowman	9,607
18		23	(h)	West Ham U	L 0-1		11,042
19		30	(a)	Queen's Park R	W 2-0	Gibson, Byrne (og)	11,101
20	Dec	7	(h)	Chelsea	D 1-1	Gibson	8,721
21		14	(a)	Manchester C	L 1-5	Gibson	20,075
22		21	(h)	Everton	L 1-3	Gibson	11,059
23		26	(h)	Ipswich T	L 0-1		9,356
24	Jan	1	(a)	Nottingham F	L 2-5	Regis, Adams	13,860
25		11	(h)	Aston Villa	D 3-3	Regis, Kilcline 2 (1 pen)	10,328
26		18	(h)	Watford	L 0-2		7,499
27		25	(a)	Oxford U	W 1-0	Turner	9,383
28	Feb	1	(a)	Newcastle U	L 2-3	Regis, Brazil	16,637
29		8	(a)	Tottenham H	W 1-0	Regis	13,135
30		16	(h)	Birmingham C	D 4-4	Bennett 2, Kilcline 2 (2 pens)	14,271
31		22	(h)	Southampton	W 3-2	Bennett, Pickering, Brazil	10,881
32	Mar	8	(a)	Leicester C	L 1-2	Pickering	10,744
33		15	(h)	Sheffield W	L 0-1		10,168
34		19	(a)	West Brom A	D 0-0		8,831
35		22	(a)	Arsenal	L 0-3		17,189
36		29	(h)	Nottingham F	D 0-0		9,500
37		31	(a)	Ipswich T	L 0-1		13,485
38	Apr	5	(h)	Manchester U	L 1-3	Pickering	17,160
39		12	(a)	Liverpool	L 0-5		42,729
40		19	(h)	Luton T	W 1-0	Pickering	10,146
41		26	(a)	West Ham U	L 0-1		27,251
42	May	3	(h)	Queen's Park R	W 2-1	Kilcline, Bennett	14,086

FINAL LEAGUE POSITION: 17th in Division One

Appearances
Sub Appearances
Goals

FA Cup

3	Jan	4	(h)	Watford	L 1-3	Kilcline	10,498

Appearances
Sub Appearances
Goals

League Cup

2	Sep	25	(a)	Chester C	W 2-1	Gibson, Bowman	4,836
	Oct	9	(h)	Chester C	W 7-2	Regis 5, Gibson, Kilcline	5,504
3		29	(h)	West Brom A	D 0-0		9,804
R	Nov	6	(a)	West Brom A	L 3-4	Evans, Bennett 2	8,987

Appearances
Sub Appearances
Goals

Ogrizovic	Borrows	Downs	Bowman	Kilcline	Peake	Bennett	Gynn	Regis	Gibson	Adams	Hibbitt	Turner	Culpin	McGrath	Stephens	Evans	Williams	Rodger	Pickering	Brazil	McInally	
1	2	3	4	5	6	7	8*	9	10	11	12											1
1	2	3	4	5	6	7	12	9	10	11	8*											2
1	2	3	4	5	6	7	12	9	10	11	8*											3
1	2	3	4*	5	6	7	12	9	10	11	8											4
1	2	3	4	5	6	7	12	9	10	11	8*											5
1	2	3		5	6	7	11	9	10*		8	4	12									6
1	2	3		5	6		11	9*	10	7	8	4	12									7
1	2	3	4	5	6	12	11*		10	7			9	8								8
1	2	3	4	5	6	12	11		10	7			9*	8								9
1	2	3	4		6	11		9	10	7*	12			8	5							10
1	2	3	4	5	6	11		9*	10	7				8	12							11
1	2	3	4	5	6	11		9	10	7				8								12
1	2	3	4*	5	6	11	12	9	10	7				8								13
1	2	3	4	5	6	11		9	10	7				8								14
1	2	3	4	5	6	11	12			7		10*		8		9						15
1	2	3*	4		6	11			10	7				8		9	12	5				16
1	2	12	4		6	11	7*		10	3				8		9		5				17
1	2	3	4		6	11			10	7		12		8		9*		5				18
1	2	3	4		6	11		9	10	7		8						5				19
1	2	3	4			11		9	10	7		8		6				5				20
1	2	3	4			11		9	10	7	12	8		6*				5				21
1	2	3	4	5		11		9	10	7		8						6				22
1	2	3	4	5		12		9	10	7		8*		11				6				23
1	2	3	4	5		11		9	10	7		8		6								24
1	2	3	12	5*	6			9	10		7	8		4			11					25
1	2	3			6	11		9			7	8		4		10*	12	5				26
1	2	3			6			9			7*	8	10	4		12	11	5				27
1	2	3	4		6	12		9				8		5			11*		7	10		28
1	2	3	4	5	6	7		9						8					11	10		29
1	2	3	4	5	6	7		9				8							11	10		30
1	2	3	4	5	6	7		9						8					11	10		31
1	2	3	4	5	6	7		9						8					11	10		32
1	2	3		5	6	7*		9		4				8			12		11	10		33
1	2	3		5	6			9		11				4			12		10	8	7*	34
1	2			5	6	7				4*			9	8			12		11	10	3	35
1	2	3		5	6	7					9		12	4					11	10	8*	36
1	2	3		5	6	12		9			11			4					10	8	7*	37
1		3*	4	5	6	7		9		12				8					11	10	2	38
1	2	3	4*	5	6	7		9		12				8					11	10		39
1	2	3		5	6	7		9		4				8					11	10		40
1	2	3		5	6	7		9		4				8					11	10		41
1	2	3		5	6	7		9		4				8					11	10		42
42	41	40	29	32	37	33	6	34	24	29	11	14	4	32	1	5	3	10	15	15	5	
		1	1			5	6			2	3	1	3		1	1	5					
			2	7	1	6	1	5	11	3	1	1	1						4	2		

3 own-goals

1	2		12	5	6	11		9	10	7		8		4				3*				3
1	1			1	1	1		1	1	1		1		1				1				
			1																			
				1																		

1	2	3	4	5*	6	9	11		10	7	12			8								2
1	2	3	4	5	6	11		9	10	7				8*	12							
1	2	3	4*	5	6	11	12	9	10	7				8								3
1	2	3	4	5*	6	11						10	7	8		9		12				R
4	4	4	4	4	4	4	1	2	3	3		1	1	4		1						
							1				1				1			1				
			1	1		2		5	2							1						

1986-87

Manager: George Curtis

1	Aug	23	(a)	West Ham U	L 0-1		21,368
2		26	(h)	Arsenal	W 2-1	Regis, Pickering	11,182
3		30	(h)	Everton	D 1-1	Pickering	13,504
4	Sep	2	(a)	Chelsea	D 0-0		11,839
5		6	(a)	Manchester C	W 1-0	Regis	18,320
6		13	(h)	Newcastle U	W 3-0	Kilcline, Bennett, Adams	11,370
7		20	(a)	Charlton A	D 1-1	Aizlewood (og)	5,527
8		27	(h)	Watford	W 1-0	Bennett	11,058
9	Oct	4	(h)	Aston Villa	L 0-1		18,562
10		11	(a)	Oxford U	L 0-2		9,530
11		19	(h)	Wimbledon	W 1-0	Bennett	11,099
12		25	(a)	Sheffield W	D 2-2	Regis, Ogrizovic	20,035
13	Nov	1	(a)	Manchester U	D 1-1	Phillips	36,946
14		8	(h)	Nottingham F	W 1-0	Pickering	16,089
15		15	(a)	Tottenham H	L 0-1		20,255
16		22	(h)	Norwich C	W 2-1	Phillips 2	10,993
17		29	(a)	Liverpool	L 0-2		31,614
18	Dec	6	(h)	Leicester C	W 1-0	Regis	12,320
19		21	(h)	Manchester C	D 2-2	Culpin, Adams	12,430
20		26	(a)	Queen's Park R	L 1-3	Gynn	10,053
21		27	(h)	Tottenham H	W 4-3	Houchen, Bennett 2, Regis	22,181
22	Jan	1	(h)	Luton T	L 0-1		16,656
23		3	(a)	Newcastle U	W 2-1	Bennett, Regis	22,366
24		18	(a)	Arsenal	D 0-0		17,561
25		24	(h)	West Ham U	L 1-3	Borrows (pen)	14,191
26	Feb	3	(a)	Southampton	L 0-2		11,508
27		7	(a)	Everton	L 1-3	Regis	30,402
28		14	(h)	Chelsea	W 3-0	Kilcline (pen), McGrath, Pickering	12,906
29		28	(h)	Charlton A	W 2-1	Downs, Regis	12,261
30	Mar	7	(h)	Sheffield W	W 1-0	McGrath	12,878
31		20	(h)	Oxford U	W 3-0	Bennett, Regis 2	23,917
32		24	(a)	Wimbledon	L 1-2	Gynn	4,370
33		28	(a)	Aston Villa	L 0-1		18,689
34	Apr	4	(a)	Nottingham F	D 0-0		13,507
35		18	(a)	Luton T	L 0-2		9,380
36		20	(h)	Queen's Park R	W 4-1	Gynn, Regis 2, Phillips	20,925
37		25	(a)	Norwich C	D 1-1	Butterworth (og)	14,610
38		30	(a)	Watford	W 3-2	Downs, Houchen, McGrath	11,590
39	May	2	(h)	Liverpool	W 1-0	Pickering	26,709
40		4	(a)	Leicester C	D 1-1	Gynn	14,903
41		6	(h)	Manchester U	D 1-1	Gynn	23,407
42		9	(h)	Southampton	D 1-1	Kilcline	22,619

FINAL LEAGUE POSITION: 10th in Division One

Appearances
Sub Appearances
Goals

FA Cup

3	Jan	10	(h)	Bolton W	W 3-0	Downs, Regis, Bennett	12,044
4		31	(a)	Manchester U	W 1-0	Houchen	49,082
5	Feb	21	(a)	Stoke C	W 1-0	Gynn	31,255
6	Mar	14	(a)	Sheffield W	W 3-1	Regis, Houchen 2	48,005
SF	Apr	12	(n†)	Leeds U	W 3-2*	Gynn, Houchen, Bennett	51,372
F	May	16	(n‡)	Tottenham H	W 3-2*	Bennett, Houchen, Mabbutt (og)	98,000

†Played at Hillsborough, Sheffield. *After extra-time. ‡Played at Wembley Stadium.

Appearances
Sub Appearances
Goals

League Cup

2	Sep	23	(h)	Rotherham U	W 3-2	Bennett, Adams, Regis	6,663
	Oct	7	(a)	Rotherham U	W 1-0	Kilcline	4,694
3		28	(h)	Oldham A	W 2-1	Regis, Sedgeley (pen)	8,575
4	Nov	19	(h)	Liverpool	D 0-0		26,385
R		26	(a)	Liverpool	L 1-3	Bennett	19,179

Appearances
Sub Appearances
Goals

Ogrizovic	Borrows	Downs	McGrath	Kilcline	Peake	Phillips	Bennett	Regis	Houchen	Pickering	Adams	Sedgley	Evans	Gynn	Williams	Rodger	Emerson	Painter	Culpin	Dobson	Livingstone	Lane	
1	2	3	4	5	6	7	8*	9	10	11	12												1
1	2	3	4	5	6	8		9	10	11		7											2
1	2	3	4	5	6	8		9	10	11		7											3
1	2	3	4	5	6	8	7	9		11		10											4
1	2	3	4	5	6	8	7	9		11		10											5
1	2	3	4	5	6		7	9		11	8	10											6
1	2	3	4	5		6*	7	9		11	8	10	12										7
1	2	3	4	5	6	8	7	9		11	10												8
1	2	3	4	5	6	8*	7	9		11	10			12									9
1	2				6	8	7	9		11	3	10		4*	12	5							10
1	2	3		5*	6	8	7	9		11	10						4	12					11
1	2	3			6	8	7	9		11	10					5*	4	12					12
1	2	3	4		6	8	7	9		11		5					10						13
1	2	3	4		6	8	7	9		11		5					10						14
1	2	3	4		6	8	7	9		11		5					10						15
1	2	3	4		6	8	7	9		11		5					10						16
1	2	3	4		6	8	7	9		11		5					10						17
1	2	3	4*		6	8	7	9		11		5					10		12				18
1	2	3			6	8	7	9			11	5					4		10				19
1	2	3			6	8	7	9			11	5		10			4						20
1		3*			6	2	7	9	8	12	11	5		10			4						21
1	2			6		8	7	9	11	3		5		10			4						22
1	2	3		5	6	8	7	9		11		10					4						23
1	2	3	7	5	6			9	8	11				10			4						24
1	2	3	7	5*	6	11		9	8					10			4	12					25
1	2*	3	7	5	6	8		9	10	11				12			4						26
1	2	3	7*	5	6	8		9	10	11				12			4						27
1	2	3	7	5	6	8		9	10	11							4						28
1	2	3		5	6	8		9	10	11		7		4									29
1	2	3	7	5	6	8		9	10	11				12			4*						30
1	2	3		5*	6	8	7	9	10	11		12		4									31
1	2	3			6	8	7	9	10*	11		5		4		12							32
1	2		4	5	6	8	7	9	10	11				12						3*			33
1	2	3	4	5	6	8	7	9	10	11													34
1	2	3*	4	5	6	8	7		9			11		10							12		35
1	2	3	4		6	8	7	9				11*		10		5					12		36
1	2*	3	4	5	6	8	7	9	10					11		12							37
1	2	3	4	5	6			9	10	11		7		8									38
1	2	3	4	5	6	8	7	9	10*	11				12									39
1	2	3		5		8	7	9		11		10		4		6							40
1	2	3	4	5	6	8	7	9		11				10									41
1	2	3	4	5	6	8				11*		7		10							9	12	42
42	41	39	30	29	39	39	31	40	20	35	10	25		16		4	19		1	1	1		
										1	1	1	1	6	1	2		3	1		2	1	
1	1	2	3	3		4	7	12	2	5	2			5					1				

2 own-goals

1	2	3	6	5		7	8	9		11				10			4						3
1	2	3	6	5	7	8		9	10	11							4						4
1	2	3	6	5		8	7*	9	10	11		12		4									5
1	2	3	6	5	4*	8	7	9	10	11		12											6
1	2	3	6	5	4	8	7	9	10	11*				12									SF
1		3	6	5*	4	2	7	9	10	11				8		12							F
6	5	6	6	6	4	6	5	6	5	6				3			2						
												2		1		1							
		1					3	1	5					2									

1 own-goal

1	2	3		5	4	8	7	9		11	6	10*		12									2
1	2	3	6	5	4*	8	7	9		11	10			12									
1	2	3	6		4	8	7	9		11	10*	5		12									3
1	2	3	6		4	8	7	9		11		5						10					4
1	2	3	6		4	8	7	9		11	10*	5						12					R
5	5	5	4	2	5	5	5	5		5	4	4						1					
														3				1					
				1			2	2			1	1											

1987-88

Manager: John Sillett

1	Aug	15	(h)	Tottenham H	W	2-1	Speedie, Downs	24,681
2		18	(a)	Luton T	W	1-0	Kilcline (pen)	7,506
3		22	(a)	Norwich C	L	1-3	Kilcline (pen)	13,726
4		29	(h)	Liverpool	L	1-4	Regis	27,637
5		31	(a)	Sheffield W	W	3-0	Speedie, Rodger, Sedgley	17,171
6	Sep	5	(h)	Manchester U	D	0-0		27,125
7		19	(h)	Nottingham F	L	0-3		17,519
8		26	(a)	Everton	W	2-1	Regis, Phillips	28,153
9	Oct	3	(h)	Watford	W	1-0	Houchen	16,111
10		17	(a)	Chelsea	L	0-1		16,699
11		20	(h)	Southampton	L	2-3	Bennett, Gynn	14,522
12		24	(h)	Newcastle U	L	1-3	Regis	18,585
13		31	(a)	Derby C	L	0-2		15,738
14	Nov	7	(a)	Oxford U	L	0-1		7,856
15		14	(h)	Wimbledon	D	3-3	Kilcline (pen), Speedie, Gynn	13,966
16		21	(a)	Charlton A	D	2-2	Downs, Gynn	4,936
17		28	(h)	West Ham U	D	0-0		16,450
18	Dec	5	(a)	Portsmouth	D	0-0		13,002
19		13	(h)	Arsenal	D	0-0		17,557
20		18	(a)	Queen's Park R	W	2-1	Regis, Houchen	7,299
21		28	(a)	Nottingham F	L	1-4	Regis	31,061
22	Jan	1	(a)	Liverpool	L	0-4		38,790
23		16	(a)	Tottenham H	D	2-2	Regis, Bennett	25,650
24	Feb	6	(a)	Manchester U	L	0-1		37,144
25		13	(h)	Sheffield W	W	3-0	Phillips, Bennett 2	14,382
26		20	(h)	Norwich C	D	0-0		15,577
27		27	(a)	Watford	W	1-0	Speedie	12,052
28	Mar	5	(h)	Chelsea	D	3-3	Kilcline, Speedie, D.Smith	16,816
29		12	(a)	Southampton	W	2-1	D.Smith, Kilcline	12,914
30		15	(h)	Luton T	W	4-0	Sedgley, Bannister, Kilcline (pen), Regis	13,723
31		19	(h)	Derby C	L	0-3		19,871
32		26	(a)	Newcastle U	D	2-2	Speedie, D.Smith	19,050
33	Apr	2	(h)	Oxford U	W	1-0	Regis	15,748
34		5	(a)	Wimbledon	W	2-1	Kilcline (pen), Houchen	5,920
35		9	(h)	Charlton A	D	0-0		14,313
36		19	(h)	Everton	L	1-2	Regis	15,641
37		23	(a)	West Ham U	D	1-1	Regis	17,733
38		30	(h)	Portsmouth	W	1-0	Kilcline (pen)	14,296
39	May	2	(a)	Arsenal	D	1-1	D.Smith	16,963
40		7	(h)	Queen's Park R	D	0-0		16,089

FINAL LEAGUE POSITION: 10th in Division One

Appearances
Sub Appearances
Goals

FA Cup

3	Jan	9	(h)	Torquay U	W	2-0	Kilcline (pen), Regis	16,815
4		30	(h)	Watford	L	0-1		22,479

Appearances
Sub Appearances
Goals

League Cup

2	Sep	22	(a)	Cambridge U	W	1-0	Gynn	5,166
	Oct	6	(h)	Cambridge U	W	2-1	Regis, Gynn	10,096
3		27	(n*)	Luton T	L	1-3	Pickering	8,113

*Played at Filbert Street, Leicester.

Appearances
Sub Appearances
Goals

Ogrizovic	Borrows	Downs	McGrath	Kilcline	Peake	Bennett	Gynn	Regis	Speedie	Pickering	Houchen	Phillips	Rodger	Sedgley	Dobson	Emerson	Lane	Smith K	Livingstone	Smith D	Bannister	Cook	
1	2	3	4	5	6	7	8	9	10*	11	12												1
1	2	3	4	5	6	7	8		10	11	9												2
1	2†	3	4	5	6	7	8	9*	10	11	12	14											3
1	2	3†	4	5	6	7	8*	9	10	11	12	14											4
1		3	4		6	7			10	11	9	2	5	8									5
1		3	4		6	7		12	10*	11	9	2	5	8									6
1	12	3*	4		6		14	9	7		10	2	5	8	11†								7
1	2		4		6	7	11	9	10*	3	12	8		5									8
1	2		4		6	7	11	9		3	10	8		5									9
1	2		4			7	11	9	12	3	10*	8	5	6									10
1	2		4			7	11		9	3	10	8	5	6									11
1	2	3	4			7	6	9	10	11		8	5*	12									12
1	2	3				7	6	9	10*		11	8	5			4	12						13
1	2	3		5		7	14	9	10		11*	8†		12		4		6					14
1	2	3	8*	5		7	14	9†	10	11		12				4		6					15
1	2	3				7	6		10	11		8				4	12	5	9*				16
1	2	3				7	6		10	11	9	8				4		5					17
1	2	3		5	6	7	12		10*	11	9	8				4							18
1	2	3		5	6	7	11	9				8				4			10				19
1	2	3		5	6	7*	11	9			12	8	14			4†			10				20
1	2	3	4	5	6	7	11	9	10			8											21
1	2	3	4	5		7*	11†	9	10			8	14					6	12				22
1	2	3	4	5	6	7	11	9				8		10									23
1	2	3	4	5	6		11	9	10			8*		7						12			24
1	2	3		5	6	7	9*		10		12	8		4						11			25
1	2	3		5	6†	7			10		12	8		4		9*		14		11			26
1	2	3		5	6	7		9	10	11		8		4									27
1		3		5	6	7		9	10	11*		8	2	4						12			28
1		3		5	6	7*		9	10			2		4		12				11	8		29
1		3		5*	6			9	10			2	12	4		7				11	8		30
1		3			6	12		9	10	14		2	5†	4*		7				11	8		31
1				5	6		12	9	10	3		2		4		7				11	8*		32
1	2			5	6		12	9	10	3		8		4		7				11*			33
1	2			5	6				10	3	9	8		4		7				11			34
1	2			5	6			9	10	3	7*	8		4						11	12		35
1	2			5	6			9	10	3		8		4		7				11			36
1	2			5	6			9	10	3		8		4		7				11			37
1	2			5	6			9	10	3				4		7				11	8		38
1	2			5	6			9	10	3	12			4		7				11	8*		39
1	2			5	6			9	10	3				4		7				11	8		40
40	32	27	17	28	31	27	19	30	35	26	13	32	9	25	1	19		5	3	14	7		
	1					1	6	1	1	1	8	3	3	2		1	2	1	1	2	1		
		2		8		4	3	10	6		3	2	1	2						4	1		

1	2	3	4	5		7	11	9	10			8						6					3
1	2	3	4	5	6	7	11	9	12			8		10*									4
2	2	2	2	2	1	2	2	2	1			2		1				1					
									1														
				1				1															

1	2	3	4		6	7	11	9	10			8	5										2
1	2	12	4		6*	7	11	9		3	10†	8		5					14				
1	2	3	4*			7	8		10	11	9		5	6								12	3
3	3	2	3		2	3	3	2	2	2	2	2	2	2									
		1																	1			1	
							2	1		1													

1988-89

Manager: John Sillett

1	Sep	3	(h)	Everton	L 0-1		18,625
2		10	(a)	Sheffield W	W 2-1	Regis, Speedie	15,635
3		17	(h)	Charlton A	W 3-0	Smith 2, Bannister	11,890
4		24	(a)	Wimbledon	W 1-0	Bannister	4,474
5	Oct	1	(h)	Middlesbrough	L 3-4	Speedie 3	14,527
6		8	(a)	Newcastle U	W 3-0	Regis, Speedie, Gynn	22,896
7		15	(h)	Millwall	D 0-0		19,369
8		22	(a)	Liverpool	D 0-0		38,742
9		29	(a)	Arsenal	L 0-2		31,273
10	Nov	5	(h)	West Ham U	D 1-1	Thompson	14,651
11		12	(h)	Luton T	W 1-0	Rodger	12,631
12		19	(a)	Nottingham F	D 0-0		17,250
13		23	(a)	Tottenham H	D 1-1	Houchen	21,961
14		26	(h)	Aston Villa	W 2-1	Regis, Houchen	20,104
15	Dec	3	(a)	Queen's Park R	L 1-2	Speedie	9,853
16		10	(h)	Manchester U	W 1-0	Regis	19,936
17		17	(h)	Derby C	L 0-2		17,229
18		26	(a)	Southampton	D 2-2	Phillips, Bannister	16,008
19		31	(a)	Everton	L 1-3	Bannister	30,790
20	Jan	2	(h)	Sheffield W	W 5-0	Sedgley, Speedie 3, Kilcline (pen)	15,191
21		14	(a)	Norwich C	W 2-1	Speedie 2	14,399
22		21	(h)	Wimbledon	W 2-1	Kilcline, Speedie	12,472
23	Feb	4	(a)	Middlesbrough	D 1-1	Regis	17,352
24		11	(h)	Newcastle U	L 1-2	Pingel (og)	16,577
25		21	(h)	Arsenal	W 1-0	Kilcline (pen)	21,390
26		25	(a)	Millwall	L 0-1		13,021
27	Mar	11	(a)	West Ham U	D 1-1	Kilcline (pen)	15,205
28		18	(h)	Tottenham H	D 1-1	Bannister	17,156
29		22	(h)	Liverpool	L 1-3	Bannister	23,807
30		25	(a)	Charlton A	D 0-0		6,728
31		27	(h)	Southampton	W 2-1	Borrows, Speedie	11,734
32	Apr	1	(a)	Derby C	L 0-1		15,175
33		8	(h)	Norwich C	W 2-1	Phillips, Speedie	12,740
34		15	(a)	Luton T	D 2-2	Regis, Smith	8,610
35		22	(h)	Queen's Park R	L 0-3		11,319
36		29	(a)	Manchester U	W 1-0	Bannister	29,799
37	May	13	(a)	Aston Villa	D 1-1	Bannister	29,906
38		15	(h)	Nottingham F	D 2-2	Clark, Regis	14,011

FINAL LEAGUE POSITION: 7th in Division One

Appearances
Sub Appearances
Goals

FA Cup

3	Jan	7	(a)	Sutton U	L 1-2	Phillips	8,000

Appearances
Sub Appearances
Goals

League Cup

2	Sep	27	(a)	Bournemouth	W 4-0	Downs, Gynn 2, Bannister	6,543
	Oct	11	(h)	Bournemouth	W 3-1	Speedie, Gynn, Sedgley	7,212
3	Nov	2	(a)	Nottingham F	L 2-3	Bannister, Kilcline (pen)	21,201

Appearances
Sub Appearances
Goals

Ogrizovic	Borrows	Downs	Sedgley	Kilcline	Peake	Gynn	Speedie	Regis	Bannister	Smith D	Phillips	Rodger	Houchen	Emerson	Thompson K	Clark	McGrath	Bennett	Dobson	Livingstone	
1	2	3	4	5	6	7*	8	9	10	11	12										1
1	2	3	4	5	6	7	8	9	10	11											2
1	2	3	4	5	6	7	8	9	10	11											3
1	2	3	4	5	6	7	8	9	10	11											4
1	2	3	4	5*	6	7	8	9	10	11	12										5
1	2	3	4	5	6	7	8	9	10	11											6
1	2	3	4	5	6	7	8	9	10	11											7
1	2	3	4		6	7*	8	9	10	11	12	5									8
1	2	3	4		6		8	9	10		7	5	11								9
1	2	3	4				8	9	10*	11		6	12	5†	14	7					10
1	2	3	4	5			8	9	10	11		6				7					11
1	2	3	4	5	6		8	9		11	12		10			7*					12
1	2	3	4	5	6		8	9		11	7		10								13
1	2	3	4	5	6		8	9*		11	7		10				12				14
1	2	3*	4	5	6		8	9			7	11	10				12				15
1	2	3	4	5	6		8	9		11	7		10								16
1	2	3	4	5*			8	9	12	11	7†	6	10		14						17
1	2	3	4	5			8		10		7		11	6	9						18
1	2	3*	4	5			8		10†	14	7		9	6	9			12			19
1	2		4	5	6		8	9		11	3						10	7			20
1	2		4	5	6		8	9		11	3			7		12	10*				21
1	2		4	5	6		8	9		11	3			7			10				22
1	2		4	5	6			9	8	11				7			10		3		23
1	2		4	5†	6			9	8	11				7	14		10*	12	3		24
1	2		4	5	6		8	9		11				7				10	3		25
1	2		4	5	6		8	9		11				7				10	3		26
1	2			5	6		8	9*	10	11	4					12		7	3		27
1	2			5	6		8		9	11	4					12	10*	7	3		28
1	2			5	6		8	9	10	11*	4†		12	7	14				3		29
1	2			5	6		8	9*	10	11	4†		12	7		14			3		30
1	2		4	5	6		8			11			9	7	12	10*			3		31
1	2		10	5	6		8	9		11*	7			4	12				3		32
1	2		10	5	6		8	9		11	7			4					3		33
1	2	6	10				8	9	12	11	7	5		4*					3		34
1	2	14	4†		6		8	9	10	11*	7	5			12				3		35
1	2			5	6		8	9	10	11	7			4					3		36
1	2			5	6		8	9	10	11	7			4					3		37
1	2	14		5	6†		8	9		11	7*			4		12			3	10	38
38	38	20	31	33	32	8	36	34	22	34	22	8	10	18	2	4	6	5	16	1	
		2							2	1	4		3		7	5	2	2			
	1		1	4		1	14	7	8	3	2	1	2		1	1					

1 own-goal

Ogrizovic	Borrows	Downs	Sedgley	Kilcline	Peake	Gynn	Speedie	Regis	Bannister	Smith D	Phillips	Rodger	Houchen	Emerson	Thompson K	Clark	McGrath	Bennett	Dobson	Livingstone	
1	2		4	5	6		8	9*		11	3		12				10	7			3
1	1		1	1	1		1	1		1	1						1	1			
													1								
											1										

Ogrizovic	Borrows	Downs	Sedgley	Kilcline	Peake	Gynn	Speedie	Regis	Bannister	Smith D	Phillips	Rodger	Houchen	Emerson	Thompson K	Clark	McGrath	Bennett	Dobson	Livingstone	
1	2	3	4	5	6	7	8	9	10	11											2
1	2	3*	4	5	6	7	8†	9	10	11					14				12		
1	2	3	4	5*			8	9	10	11	7†	6	12	14							3
3	3	3	3	3	2	2	3	3	3	3	1	1									
													1	1	1				1		
		1	1	1		3	1		2												

1989-90

Manager: John Sillett

1	Aug	19	(h)	Everton	W 2-0	Bannister, Speedie	17,981
2		22	(a)	Arsenal	L 0-2		33,886
3		26	(a)	Crystal P	W 1-0	Kilcline	11,122
4		30	(h)	Manchester C	W 2-1	Gynn, Smith	16,111
5	Sep	9	(a)	Millwall	L 1-4	Smith	12,062
6		16	(h)	Luton T	W 1-0	Bannister	11,152
7		23	(a)	Chelsea	L 0-1		18,247
8		30	(a)	Sheffield W	D 0-0		15,054
9	Oct	14	(h)	Nottingham F	L 0-2		15,722
10		21	(h)	Manchester U	L 1-4	Drinkell	19,605
11		28	(a)	Charlton A	D 1-1	Speedie	6,149
12	Nov	4	(a)	Liverpool	W 1-0	Regis	36,433
13		11	(h)	Southampton	W 1-0	Drinkell	12,151
14		18	(a)	Aston Villa	L 1-4	Gynn	22,803
15		25	(h)	Norwich C	W 1-0	Regis	11,999
16	Dec	2	(a)	Everton	L 0-2		21,171
17		9	(h)	Arsenal	L 0-1		16,255
18		16	(h)	Wimbledon	W 2-1	Borrows (pen), Curle (og)	8,308
19		26	(a)	Queen's Park R	D 1-1	Speedie	9,889
20		30	(a)	Derby C	L 1-4	Speedie	17,011
21	Jan	1	(h)	Tottenham H	D 0-0		19,559
22		13	(h)	Crystal P	W 1-0	Speedie	10,858
23		20	(a)	Manchester C	L 0-1		24,345
24	Feb	3	(h)	Chelsea	W 3-2	Livingstone, McAllister (og), Regis	15,243
25		17	(h)	Millwall	W 3-1	Livingstone 2, Smith	10,981
26	Mar	4	(h)	Aston Villa	W 2-0	Drinkell, Smith	17,891
27		7	(a)	Luton T	L 2-3	Drinkell, Regis	8,244
28		10	(a)	Nottingham F	W 4-2	Gallacher, Speedie 2, Drinkell	18,750
29		14	(a)	Norwich C	D 0-0		13,673
30		17	(h)	Sheffield W	L 1-4	Gynn	13,339
31		24	(h)	Charlton A	L 1-2	Gallacher	9,997
32		31	(a)	Manchester U	L 0-3		39,172
33	Apr	7	(h)	Derby C	W 1-0	Wright (og)	11,157
34		14	(a)	Tottenham H	L 2-3	Smith, Speedie	23,917
35		16	(h)	Queen's Park R	D 1-1	Smith	10,039
36		21	(a)	Wimbledon	D 0-0		4,086
37		28	(a)	Southampton	L 0-3		16,359
38	May	5	(h)	Liverpool	L 1-6	Gallacher	23,204

FINAL LEAGUE POSITION: 12th in Division One

Appearances
Sub Appearances
Goals

FA Cup

3	Jan	6	(a)	Northampton T	L 0-1		11,648

Appearances
Sub Appearances
Goals

League Cup

2	Sep	19	(a)	Grimsby T	L 1-3	Kilcline (pen)	10,150
	Oct	4	(h)	Grimsby T	W 3-0	Drinkell, Speedie, MacDonald	15,327
3		25	(a)	Queen's Park R	W 2-1	Downs, Drinkell	9,227
4	Nov	22	(a)	Manchester C	W 1-0	Regis	23,335
5	Jan	17	(a)	Sunderland	D 0-0		27,218
R		24	(h)	Sunderland	W 5-0	Livingstone 4, Gynn	21,219
SF	Feb	11	(a)	Nottingham F	L 1-2	Livingstone	26,153
		25	(h)	Nottingham F	D 0-0		25,618

Appearances
Sub Appearances
Goals

Ogrizovic	Borrows	Dobson	Emerson	Kilcline	Peake	Gynn	Speedie	Regis	Bannister	Smith D	McGuire	MacDonald	Waugh	Livingstone	Clark	Middleton L	Downs	McGrath	Thompson K	Drinkell	Billing	Gallacher	Edwards	Middleton C	Titterton	
1	2	3	4	5	6	7	8	9	10	11																1
1	2	3	4	5	6	7	8	9	10*	11	12															2
1	2	3	4	5	6	7	8	9	10	11																3
1	2	3	4	5	6	7	8	9	10	11																4
1†	2	3	4	5	6	7*	8	9	10	11	12	14														5
	2	3	4	5	6	7	8	9†	10		11*	12	1	14												6
1	2	3	4*		6	7	8		10	11		9			5	12										7
1	2	3			6	7†	8*		10	11		4		9		12	5		14							8
1	2	3†		5	6	12	8	9	10*	11		4					14	7								9
1	2			5	6	12	8	9		11†		4*			14		3	7		10						10
1	2				6	12	8	9		11		4*					3	7		10	5					11
1	2				6		8	9		11		4					3	7		10	5					12
1	2				6	7	8	9		11		4*			12		3			10	5					13
1	2	3			6	7	8	9*	12	11†		4		14						10	5					14
1	2				6	7	8	9		11		4					3			10	5					15
1	2		8	6		7		9		11†		4*		14			3	12		10	5					16
1	2	6	8					9		11		4					3	7		10	5					17
1	2	6	8			5		9		11		4					3	7		10						18
1	2	6	8			5	9			11		4					3	7		10						19
1	2	6	10*			5	8	12		11	14	4†					3	9		7						20
1	2				6	10	8	12		11		4					3	9		7*	5					21
1	2				6	7	8	9	10*	11					12		3	4			5					22
1	2	3			6	7	8	9		11				10	12			4*			5					23
1	2	12			6	8		9		11		4*		10			3				5	7				24
1	2	4		5	6	8		9		11				10			3					7				25
1	2	3		5	6	4	8	9		11				10*						12		7				26
1	2	5*			6	4	8	9		11							3			10	12	7				27
1	2	3			6	4	8	9		11										10	5	7				28
1	2	3			6	4	8	9		11										10	5	7				29
1	2	3*			6	4	8	9†		11				14						10	5	7	12			30
1	2	3*			6	4	8	9		11†				14						10	5	7	12			31
1	2	12			6	4	8	9		11				14						10†	5*	7	3			32
1	2	5			6	4	8	9		11				10								7	3			33
1	2	5			6	4*	8	9		11					10							7	3	12		34
1	2	5			6		8	9*		11		4		12	10							7	3			35
1	2	5			6			9		11		4			8					10		7	3			36
1	2	5			6	4	8			11		9								10	12	7	3*			37
1		3†			6	4	8	9		11		12			2			5		10*		7			14	38
37	37	28	12	11	33	31	32	32	10	37	1	19	1	6	5		16	12		21	16	15	6			
		2				3		2	1		3	3		7	4	2	1	1	1	1	2		2	1	1	
	1			1		3	8	4	2	6				3						5		3				

3 own-goals

1	2				6	10*	8	12		11		4					3	9		7	5					3
1	1				1	1	1			1		1					1	1		1	1					
								1																		

	2	3	4*	5	6	7†	8		10	11		9	1	12					14							2
1	2	3			6		8	9	10	11		4					5			7						
1	2			5*	6		8	9		11		4					3	7		10	12					3
1	2	3			6	7	8*	9		11		12			4					10	5					4
1	2	3			6	7	8	9		11				10				4			5					5
1	2	12			6	4	8	9		11		7		10			3				5*					R
1	2	4		5	6	8		9		11				10			3					7				SF
1	2	12		5*	6	8	4	9		11				10			3			14		7†				
7	8	5	1	4	8	6	7	7	2	8		4	1	4	1		5	2		3	3	2				
		2										1		1					1	1	1					
				1		1	1	1				1		5			1			2						

1990-91

Manager: John Sillett until 14 November 1990, then Terry Butcher.

1	Aug	25	(a)	Manchester U	L 0-2		46,715
2		29	(h)	Everton	W 3-1	Speedie, Gallacher, Dobson	13,036
3	Sep	1	(h)	Nottingham F	D 2-2	Kilcline (pen), Borrows (pen)	12,630
4		8	(a)	Aston Villa	L 1-2	Borrows	27,001
5		15	(h)	Wimbledon	D 0-0		8,925
6		22	(a)	Luton T	L 0-1		8,336
7		29	(h)	Queen's Park R	W 3-1	Livingstone 2, Gynn	9,890
8	Oct	6	(a)	Manchester C	L 0-2		26,198
9		20	(h)	Southampton	L 1-2	Borrows (pen)	10,040
10		27	(a)	Sheffield U	W 1-0	Borrows (pen)	17,978
11	Nov	3	(h)	Arsenal	L 0-2		15,336
12		10	(a)	Sunderland	D 0-0		20,101
13		17	(h)	Liverpool	L 0-1		22,571
14		24	(h)	Leeds U	D 1-1	Gallacher	16,183
15	Dec	1	(a)	Crystal P	L 1-2	Regis	16,562
16		8	(a)	Everton	L 0-1		17,472
17		15	(h)	Manchester U	D 2-2	Gallacher, Regis	17,106
18		22	(a)	Chelsea	L 1-2	Gallacher	16,317
19		26	(h)	Tottenham H	W 2-0	Gallacher, Gynn	22,731
20		29	(h)	Norwich C	W 2-0	Borrows (pen), Speedie	12,039
21	Jan	1	(a)	Derby C	D 1-1	Regis	15,741
22		12	(a)	Nottingham F	L 0-3		18,344
23		19	(h)	Aston Villa	W 2-1	Gynn, Speedie	15,751
24	Feb	2	(a)	Wimbledon	L 0-1		4,061
25		23	(h)	Sunderland	D 0-0		10,453
26	Mar	2	(h)	Crystal P	W 3-1	Peake, Kilcline 2	10,891
27		9	(a)	Leeds U	L 0-2		28,880
28		13	(h)	Luton T	W 2-1	Borrows (pen), Pearce	9,521
29		16	(a)	Queen's Park R	L 0-1		9,510
30		23	(h)	Manchester C	W 3-1	Regis, Gynn, Gallacher	13,198
31		30	(a)	Tottenham H	D 2-2	Smith, Gallacher	29,033
32	Apr	1	(h)	Chelsea	W 1-0	Gynn	14,272
33		6	(a)	Norwich C	D 2-2	Gallacher, Gynn	12,012
34		9	(a)	Liverpool	D 1-1	Gynn	31,063
35		13	(h)	Derby C	W 3-0	Gallacher 2, Woods	11,961
36		20	(a)	Southampton	L 1-2	Gynn	15,461
37	May	4	(h)	Sheffield U	D 0-0		17,312
38		11	(a)	Arsenal	L 1-6	Gallacher	41,039

FINAL LEAGUE POSITION: 16th in Division One

Appearances
Sub Appearances
Goals

FA Cup

3	Jan	5	(h)	Wigan A	D 1-1	Gynn	10,802
R		9	(a)	Wigan A	W 1-0	Gynn	7,429
4		26	(h)	Southampton	D 1-1	Kilcline	14,013
R		29	(a)	Southampton	L 0-2		17,001

Appearances
Sub Appearances
Goals

League Cup

2	Sep	26	(h)	Bolton W	W 4-2	Livingstone 2, Gynn, Gallacher	6,193
			(a)	Bolton W	W 3-2	Regis 2, Gallacher	5,222
3	Oct	31	(h)	Hull C	W 3-0	Speedie, Livingstone, Regis	7,708
4	Nov	28	(h)	Nottingham F	W 5-4	Gallacher 3, Livingstone 2	16,304
5	Jan	23	(h)	Sheffield W	L 0-1		20,712

Appearances
Sub Appearances
Goals

Ogrizovic	Borrows	Edwards	McGrath	Kilcline	Peake	Gallacher	Dobson	Speedie	Drinkell	Smith	Regis	MacDonald	Clark	Gynn	Thompson	Perdomo	Titterton	Livingstone	Billing	Butcher	Emerson	Hurst	Sutton	Fleming	Woods	Pearce	Robson	Sansom	Rosario	
1	2	3*	4	5	6	7	8†	9	10	11	12	14																		1
1	2	3	4	5	6	7	8	9	10	11*			12																	2
1	2	3	4†	5	6	7	11*	9	10		14			8	12															3
1	2	3	4†	5	6	7	14	9	10*		12			8		11														4
1	2	3		5	6	7		9	10	11†		12		8		11*		14												5
1	2	3*		5	6	7		9	10†	11		4		8			12	14												6
1	2	3		5	6	7				12	9	4		8		11*		10												7
1	2	3		5	6	7				12	9	8*		8		11†		10			14									8
1	2				6	7	3†	4		12	9	11*		8				10	5		14									9
1	2	3			6	7		8		11	9			4					5		10									10
1	2	3			6			10		11	9			8				7	5		4									11
1	2	3			6			10		11	9			8				7	5		4									12
1	2	3	7		6	11		8*		12	9			10					5	4										13
1	2	3	7*		6	11†		10		12	9			8				14	5	4										14
1	2	3	12		6	7		8		14	9			11*				10	5	4†										15
1	2	3	10		6	7		8	9	11									5		4									16
1	2	3	4*		6	7			9	11	9			8					5		12									17
1	2	3			6	7		10	12	11*	9			8					5		4									18
1	2	3			6	7		10		11	9			8						5	4									19
1	2	3			6	7		10*	12	11	9			8						5	4									20
1	2	3		5	6	7				11	9			8					4		10									21
1	2			5	6		3		7	11*	9			8				12	4		10									22
1	2	3	4		6			10		11	9	7		8						5										23
	2			5					11	10	9	7*		8					4		6	3	1	12						24
1	2	3		5	6				10†	11	9	7*		8					4			12		14						25
1	2			5	6	10*				11	9		12	8							4	3			7					26
1	2		12	5*		10				11	9†			8							4	3			7	6	14			27
1	2		3		6	10				11	9			8							4				7	5				28
1	2		3		6	10				11	9			8											7	5	4			29
1	2				6	10				11	9			8											7	5	4	3		30
1	2				6	10			14	11	9†			8							12				7	5	4*	3		31
1	2				6	10				11	9			8							4				7	5		3		32
1	2		7*		6	10			14	11	9†			8							4					5		3	12	33
1	2				6	10				11	9*			8							4				7	5		3	12	34
1	2				6	10				11	9			8							4				7	5		3		35
1	2				6	10				11	9			8					5		4				7			3		36
1	2				6	10				11	9			8							4				7	5		3		37
1	2	12			6	10				11	9			8							4				7	5		3*		38
37	38	22	12	14	36	32	5	18	11	30	31	7		35		4		6	15	6	20	3	1		12	11	3	9		
		1	2				1		4	6	3	2	2		1		1	4			4	1		2			1		2	
	6			3	1	11	1	3		1	4			8				2							1	1				

Ogrizovic	Borrows	Edwards	McGrath	Kilcline	Peake	Gallacher	Dobson	Speedie	Drinkell	Smith	Regis	MacDonald	Clark	Gynn	Thompson	Perdomo	Titterton	Livingstone	Billing	Butcher	Emerson	Hurst	Sutton	Fleming	Woods	Pearce	Robson	Sansom	Rosario	
1	2	3			6	7			10	11	9	12		8					5		4*									3
1	2	3†		5	6	7*			12	11	9	14		8					4		10									R
1	2		3	5					11	10	9	7		8					4		6									4
1	2		3*	5					11		9	7	14	8†	10				4		6	12								R
4	4	2	2	3	2	2			3	3	4	2		4	1				4		4									
									1			2	1									1								
				1										2																

Ogrizovic	Borrows	Edwards	McGrath	Kilcline	Peake	Gallacher	Dobson	Speedie	Drinkell	Smith	Regis	MacDonald	Clark	Gynn	Thompson	Perdomo	Titterton	Livingstone	Billing	Butcher	Emerson	Hurst	Sutton	Fleming	Woods	Pearce	Robson	Sansom	Rosario	
1	2			5	6	7				11	9	12		8		4	3*	10												2
1	2	3		5*	6	7				11	9	12		8		4†		10			14									
1	2	3			6			4	12		9	11†		8	14			10	5		7*									3
1	2	3			6	7		8		11	9			4				10	5											4
1	2	3†	4		6			10	14	11	9	7*		8						5	12									5
5	5	4	1	2	5	3		3		4	5	2		5		2	1	4	2	1	1									
									2			2			1						2									
						5		1			3			1				5												

Coventry in Other Competitions

Division Three South Cup

The Division Three South and North Cups were started in the 1933-4 season. All clubs were requested to field their strongest teams, but many of the results and line-ups indicate that they did not and City were as guilty as any in this regard. Matches were generally played on weekday afternoons except when blank FA Cup dates allowed some ties to be played on Saturday afternoons. Consequently, attendances were often numbered in the hundreds rather than thousands and the competition never really caught on. World War Two killed it off and, indeed, the Final of the 1938-9 competition, held over until September 1939, was never played. The final, telling comment from the Watford FC chairman, R.J.Kilbey, as he presented the Cup to the Reading captain in 1938 was that the 'competition was a total washout'. It was, in fact, a predecessor of the Leyland DAF Trophy, which began 45 years later as the Associate Members' Cup.

1933-34
Round 2
Jan 13 v Bristol Rovers (h) 2-2
Lake, Lauderdale
Pearson; Brown, Perry, Mason, Boileau, White, Lauderdale, Bacon, Lake, Richards.
Attendance: 9,500
Replay
Feb 1 v Bristol Rovers (h) 2-1
Lake, Bacon
Pearson; Brown, Bisby, Baker, Mason, Boileau, White, Lauderdale, Bacon, Lake, Crisp.
Attendance: 3,098
Round 3
Feb 22 v Southend United (h) 3-1
Frith, Lauderdale, Bacon
Pearson; Brown, Wilmot, Baker, Mason, Boileau, Bacon, Lauderdale, Bourton, Frith, Richards.
Attendance: 2,995
Semi-final
Mar 14 v Exeter City (a) 1-1
Bourton
Pearson; Brown, Bisby, Baker, Davison, Boileau, White, Lauderdale, Bourton, Lake, Richards.
Attendance: 1,000
Replay
Mar 22 v Exeter City (h) 0-1
Pearson; Brown, Bisby, Baker, Davison, Boileau, White, Lauderdale, Bourton, Lake, Richards.
Attendance: 2,296

1934-35
Round 2
Oct 17 v Bournemouth & BA (a) 5-2
Birtley 2, Bourton 2, Watson
Pearson; Brown, Elliott, Wilson, Mason, Frith, Birtley, Jones, Bourton, Jones, Liddle.
Attendance: 1,000
Round 3
Feb 7 v Crystal Palace (h) 5-1
Bourton 3, Lake, Watson
Pearson; Brook, Bisby, Baker, Mason, Frith, White, Wilson, Bourton, Lake, Watson.
Attendance: 2,500
Semi-final
Mar 28 v Watford (h) 0-0
Pearson; Brown, Bisby, Baker, Mason, Frith, Birtley, Lauderdale, Bourton, Lake, Watson.
Attendance: 2,500
Replay
Apr 3 v Watford (a) 1-2
Wilson
Pearson; Brown, Bisby, Grundy, Mason, Frith, White, Wilson, Bourton, Jones, Lake.
Attendance: 1,000

1935-36
Round 2
Oct 24 v Millwall (a) 1-0
Lake
Morgan; Bisby, Elliott, Hall, Mason, Boileau, McNestry, Bourton, Bacon, Lake, Liddle.
Attendance: 2,000
Round 3
Nov 7 v Bournemouth & BA (h) 3-2
Lager 2, McNestry
Morgan; Brook, Elliott, Frith, Webb, Curtis, McNestry, Watson, Lager, Lake, Fitton.
Attendance: 2,000
Semi-final
Jan 11 v Crystal Palace (a) 2-1
Lake, Bourton
Pearson; Webb, Smith, McCaughney, Mason, Boileau, McNestry, Jones, Bourton, Lake, Liddle.
Attendance: 10,500
Final (1st leg)
Mar 25 v Swindon Town (a) 2-0
Frith, Lauderdale
Morgan; Astley, Smith, McCaughney, Elliott, Frith, Pritchard, Lauderdale, Crawley, Jones, Liddle.
Attendance: 3,610
Final (2nd leg)
Apr 2 v Swindon Town (h) 3-2
Jones, Liddle, Lake
Morgan; Brook, Smith, McCaughney, Elliott, Boileau, McNestry, Jones, Crawley, Lake, Liddle.
Attendance: 2,077
Coventry City won 5-2 on aggregate

Full Members' Cup

This competition is a descendant of the Texaco Cup/Anglo-Scottish Cup but differed in that it is restricted to full League members (ie. Division One and Two teams). From 1987 it has had two sponsors, Simod, a relatively obscure sportswear company, and Zenith Data Systems, a similar obscure computer company. Several of the top clubs have shunned the competition despite the Final having taken place at Wembley since 1986. City's record in the competition has been poor. In 1985-6 the competition was run on a group basis with the winners of eight groups qualifying for regional semi-finals. City played two average Second Division teams and gained one point. Since then the competition has been run on a knock-out basis and apart from 1988 City have fallen at the first hurdle each time. In 1988 modest victories over Wimbledon and Ipswich left City needing a win over Reading, then bottom of the Second Division, to reach Wembley. For the first time in the history of the Sky Blues they were involved in a penalty competition and lost 4-3 to the eventual winners of the trophy in a match that did not finish until 10.30pm. The attendance of 1,086 for the Millwall match in 1985 is the lowest ever at Highfield Road for a competitive match.

1985-86
Sep 18 v Stoke City (a) 0-3
Ogrizovic; Borrows, Downs, Bowman, Kilcline, Peake(Evans), Bennett(Williams), McGrath, Culpin, Gibson, Adams.
Att: 3,516
Oct 15 v Millwall (h) 1-1
Gibson
Ogrizovic; Borrows, Adams, Bowman, Kilcline, Peake, Bennett, Gynn, Culpin, Gibson(Evans), Hibbitt.
Att: 1,086

1986-87
Round 1
Bye
Round 2
Nov 4 v Norwich City (a) 1-2
Phillips (pen)
Ogrizovic; Borrows, Downs, Emerson, Sedgley, Peake, Bennett, Phillips, Painter, Gynn(Houchen), Pickering.
Att: 6,236

1987-88 (Simod Cup)
Round 1
Bye
Round 2
Bye
Round 3
Jan 13 v Wimbledon (h) 2-1
Bennett 2
Ogrizovic; Borrows, Downs, McGrath, Kilcline, Peake, Bennett, Phillips, Regis, Sedgley, Gynn.
Att: 5,549
Quarter-final
Feb 9 v Ipswich (h) 2-0
Gynn, Phillips
Ogrizovic; Borrows, Downs, McGrath(Phillips), Kilcline, Peake, Bennett, D.Smith, Speedie, Sedgley, Gynn.
Att: 7,607
Semi-final
Mar 2 v Reading (a) 1-1 a.e.t.
Speedie
Ogrizovic; Borrows(Rodger), Downs, Sedgley, Kilcline, Peake, Bennett, Phillips, Regis, Speedie, Pickering(D.Smith).
Att: 15,348
Reading won 4-3 on penalties.

1988-89
Round 1
Bye
Round 2
Bye
Round 3
Jan 11 v Middlesbrough (a) 0-1
Ogrizovic; Borrows, Phillips, Sedgley, Kilcline, Peake, Bennett, Speedie, Houchen, McGrath, D.Smith.
Att: 9,938

1989-90 (Zenith Data Systems Cup)
Round 1
Nov 29 v Wimbledon (h) 1-3 a.e.t.
Gynn
Ogrizovic; Borrows, Downs, Kilcline(Dobson), Billing, Peake, Gynn, Emerson(Clark), Regis, Drinkell, D.Smith.
Att: 3,781

1990-91
Round 1
Dec 19 v Derby County (a) 0-1
Ogrizovic; Borrows, Edwards, Emerson, Billing, Peake, Gallacher, MacDonald, Regis, Drinkell (Livingstone), Smith.
Att: 7,270

FA Charity Shield

1987
Aug 1 v Everton (h) 0-1
Ogrizovic; Phillips, Downs, McGrath(Sedgley), Kilcline, Peake, Bennett, Gynn(Borrows), Speedie, Houchen, Pickering.
Att: 88,000

Two and a half months after the Wembley FA Cup Final triumph the Sky Blues took over 50,000 fans back to Wembley for the Charity Shield versus League Champions, Everton. In a match lacking a lot of competitiveness, a Wayne Clarke goal clinched the Toffees' victory.

Southern Professional Floodlight Cup

Something of a forerunner of the Football League Cup, this competition ran for five seasons before being phased out and replaced by the League Cup in 1960-61. Coventry City did not enter until the 1958-9 season and were the last holders in 1959-60.

1958-59
Round 1
Nov 3 v Millwall (a) 1-6
Satchwell
Spratt; Shepherd, Harvey, Nicholas, Curtis, Austin, P.Hill, Straw, Satchwell, R.Hill, B.Hill.
Attendance: 5,283

1959-60
Round 2
Oct 19 v Southend United (a) 0-0
Caine; Kirk, Austin, Nicholas, Ballard, Kearns, P.Hill, Straw, Satchwell, Farmer, Boxley.
Attendance: 6,692
Replay
Oct 26 v Southend United (h) 4-0
Simcoe 2, Daley, Nicholas
Lightening; Kirk, Austin, Nicholas, Ballard, Farmer, Boxley, Simcoe, Satchwell, Ryan, Daley.
Attendance: 6,813
Round 3
Jan 18 v Fulham (a) 1-1
Satchwell
Lightening; Kirk, Bennett, Nicholas, Curtis, Austin, P.Hill, Straw, Satchwell, B.Hill, Daley.
Attendance: 15,309
Replay
Feb 1 v Fulham (Griffin Park) 1-0
Satchwell
Lightening; Kirk, Bennett, Nicholas, Curtis, Kearns, Stephens, Straw, Satchwell, P.Hill, Daley.
Attendance: 4,800
Semi-final
Mar 28 v Southampton (h) 2-1
Straw 2
Lightening; Kletzenbauer, Austin, Kearns, Curtis, Farmer, P.Hill, Straw, Satchwell, Hewitt, Stephens.
Attendance: 11,773
Final
Apr 27 v West Ham United (h) 2-1
Hewitt 2
Lightening; Bennett, Kletzenbauer, Nicholas, Curtis, Austin, Stephens, Hewitt, Straw, Hill, Daley.
Attendance: 16,921

Texaco Cup

The Texaco Cup was introduced in 1970 and was one of the first sponsored competitions. It was originally intended to cater for those clubs in England and Scotland who had just missed out on a European place. Coventry's efforts in the competition were mediocre to say the least, winning only one tie out of eight. There was always more interest in the games north of the border and the Sky Blues were seen as a feather in the cap by Motherwell. The competition became the Anglo-Scottish Cup in 1975-6 and was restructured on a regional basis.

1971-72
Round 1 (1st leg)
Sep 14 v Falkirk (a) 0-1
Glazier; Coop, Smith, Mortimer, Blockley, Parker, O'Rourke, Carr, Chilton, Hunt(Barry), McGuire.
Att: 9,900
Round 1 (2nd leg)
Sep 28 v Falkirk (h) 3-0 (agg 3-1)
Chilton, Hunt, Mortimer
Glazier; Coop, Cattlin, Mortimer, Blockley, Parker, Young, Carr, Chilton, Hunt, Smith.
Att: 14,283
Round 2 (1st leg)
Oct 19 v Newcastle United (h) 1-1
Blockley
Glazier; Coop, Barry, Smith, Blockley, Parker, Young, Carr, Chilton, Hunt(Mortimer), St John.
Att: 12,311
Round 2 (2nd leg)
Nov 3 v Newcastle United (a) 1-5 (agg 2-6)
Blockley
Glazier; Coop, Barry, Smith, Blockley, Parker, Young, Carr, Chilton, Hunt, St John.
Att: 25,230
Derby County won the competition beating Airdrie 2-1 in a two legged Final.

1972-73
Round 1 (1st leg)
Sep 12 v Motherwell (h) 3-3
Rafferty 2, Mortimer
Glazier; Coop, Cattlin, Machin, Blockley, Barry, Mortimer, Young, Rafferty, Carr, Smith(Alderson).
Att: 7,370

Round 1 (2nd leg)
Sep 27 v Motherwell (a) 0-1 (agg 3-4)
Glazier; Coop, Dugdale, McGuire, Blockley, Barry, Mortimer, Green, Rafferty, Carr, Alderson.
Att: 9,812
Ipswich Town won the competition beating Norwich City 4-2 in a two legged Final.

1973-74
Round 1 (1st leg)
Sep 25 v Motherwell (h) 0-1
Glazier; Smith, Holmes, Mortimer, Craven, Dugdale, Cartwright, Alderson, Hunt, Green, McGuire.
Att: 9,714

Round 1 (2nd leg)
Oct 3 v Motherwell (a) 2-3 (agg 2-4)
Alderson, Cartwright
Ramsbottom; Coop, Holmes, Mortimer, Craven, Dugdale, Smith, Alderson, Green, Cartwright, McGuire.
Att: 13,000
Newcastle won the competition beating Burnley 2-1 in the Final.

Skol Festival Tournament Edinburgh

THE Sky Blues were invited to play in the pre-season Skol Festival tournament in 1979. Four teams took part and all the matches were played at one or other of the big Edinburgh grounds in double-headers. By winning their first two games quite convincingly, City were left needing only a draw in their final match against Hibs to lift the trophy. They duly achieved this and won a rare trophy for the Highfield Road boardroom.

The tournament saw the first public appearances of the much-vaunted close season signings, Gary Collier (£350,000 from Bristol City) and David Jones (£250,000 from Everton). Both played a part in the success but were to contribute little else at Highfield Road. Collier played in only three League games, whilst Jones made 12 appearances including three as substitute. They are generally considered to be amongst the worst ever signings made by City.

1979
Aug 4 v Manchester City (at Easter Road) 3-1
Ferguson, English 2
Blyth; Roberts, McDonald, Gooding, Holton, Gillespie, Hunt, English(Bannister), Ferguson, Powell, Hutchison(Yorath).
Att: 10,815
Aug 6 v Hearts (at Tynecastle) 3-1
Hateley, Hunt, Liddell (og)
Blyth; Jones, McDonald, Yorath, Holton, Collier, Hunt, English, Ferguson(Hateley), Powell, Hutchison.
Att: 4,000

Jim Blyth

Aug 8 v Hibernian (at Easter Road) 0-0
Blyth; Jones(Roberts), McDonald, Yorath, Holton, Collier, Hunt, English(Nardiello), Hateley, Powell, Hutchison.
Att: 6,812

Steve Hunt

Third Division South v Third Division North

THESE matches took place between 1954 and 1958 with one match played in the North and one in the South each season. On 8 November 1956, the Third Division South beat the North 2-1 at Highfield Road with goals from Stan Newsham (nine minutes) and Roy Hollis (42 minutes). Ken Johnson (65 minutes) replied for the Northern Section. A crowd of 14,156 saw the game.

Third Division South: Matthews (Coventry City); Jardine (Millwall), Langley (Brighton & Hove Albion), Belcher (Crystal Palace), Parker (Southampton), Elsworthy (Ipswich Town), Gavin (Norwich City), Newsham (Bournemouth & Boscombe Athletic), Hollis (Southend United), Mills (Torquay United), Flint (Aldershot). Cook (Watford) replaced Newsham after 82 minutes.

Third Division North: Newlands (Workington); Currie (Bradford City), Brownsword (Scunthorpe United), Mays (Derby County), Moore (Hartlepools United), Sneddon (Accrington Stanley), Burrell (Chesterfield), Hewitt (Wrexham), Johnson (Hartlepools United), Smith (Chesterfield), Simm (Bradford City).

Harry Warren, the Coventry City manager at the time, was the manager of the Third South team and George Raynor was their trainer. The North were managed by former Coventry boss, Harry Storer, who was then in charge at Derby County. Other Coventry players to appear for the Third Division South in this fixture were Martin McDonnell, who was at right-back in the game at Reading on 16 March 1955, and goalkeeper Reg Matthews and right-half Noel Simpson, both of whom appeared in the match at Accrington on 13 October 1955.

Third Division South (back row, left to right): McPherson (Walsall, reserve), Belcher (Crystal Palace), Elsworthy (Ipswich Town), Parker (Southampton), Matthews (Coventry City), Jardine (Millwall), Langley (Brighton & Hove Albion), Cook (Watford, reserve), Pickering (Northampton Town). Front: George Raynor (Coventry City, trainer), Gavin (Norwich City), Newsham (Bournemouth & Boscombe Athletic), Hollis (Southend United), Mills (Torquay United), Flint (Aldershot), Harry Warren (Coventry City, manager).

Coventry City in Europe

European Fairs Cup

COVENTRY CITY'S only season in European competition was certainly eventful. After a fairly easy victory over distant Trakia Plovdiv in the first round they were drawn against mighty Bayern Munich, who at that time boasted half a dozen current West German internationals (West Germany were semi-finalists in the 1970 World Cup). There was great expectancy in the city and the club immediately made the second leg all-ticket with a 48,000 limit on the crowd. The first leg, played in torrential rain, proved to be a disaster for Coventry. With first-choice goalkeeper Bill Glazier injured, substitute Erie McManus had the sort of match that can only inhabit a goalkeeper's nightmares and by half-time the tie was effectively over, although it must be said that Coventry had none of the luck going. The second leg proved to be a formality. Coventry thought they had qualified for the UEFA Cup in 1978, but a late Roger Osborne goal in the FA Cup Final scuppered their chances. The post-Heysel ban prevented them taking their place in the 1987-8 European Cup-winners' Cup.

1970-71
Round 1 (1st leg)
Sep 16 v Trakia Plovdiv (a) 4-1
O'Rourke 3, Martin
Glazier; Coop, Smith, Machin, Blockley, Strong, Hunt, Carr, Martin, O'Rourke, Clements.
Att: 20,000
Round 1 (2nd leg)
Sep 30 v Trakia Plovdiv (h) 2-0 (agg 6-1)
Joicey, Blockley
Glazier; Coop, Bruck, Clements, Blockley, Strong, Hunt, Carr, Joicey(Rafferty), O'Rourke, Alderson.
Att: 20,771
Round 2 (1st leg)
Oct 20 v Bayern Munich (a) 1-6
Hunt
McManus; Coop, Cattlin, Machin, Blockley, Strong, Hunt, Carr, Martin, O'Rourke, Clements.
Att: 12,548
Round 2 (2nd leg)
Nov 3 v Bayern Munich (h) 2-1 (agg 3-7)
Martin, O'Rourke
Glazier; Coop, Smith, Mortimer, Blockley, Hill, Hunt(Joicey), Carr, Martin, O'Rourke, Clements.
Att: 26,033

Neil Martin

Overseas Matches

MATCHES on foreign soil were relatively infrequent until international travel became easier in the 1960s. Until 1967, however, Coventry City restricted overseas matches to end-of-season trips to Europe. In 1966, for example, a fleet of sky-blue Rover cars shipped the team off for a tour of the Continent.

Exotic trips were undertaken to the West Indies in 1967 (as a reward for promotion) and 1969, followed by a three weeks tour of the USA in 1970. In the 1970s and the 1980s, four trips were made to the Far East; on the 1972 trip, the Sky Blues played the famous Brazilian side Santos, who included Pelé. In 1973, City played in the inaugural triangular Anchor Cup and, although winning only one match out of three, they lifted the trophy. No similar success was achieved in 1978 in the Japan Cup, City losing at the semi-final stage to Palmeiras of Brazil.

The purchase of Steve Hunt from New York Cosmos in 1978 resulted in an invitation to play the Cosmos at the Meadowlands Stadium the following year. In the same month, City were invited to celebrate the Faroe Islands FA's 75th anniversary and a full first team hammered the locals 6-0.

When Bobby Gould took over as manager in May 1982, he took a largely unhappy squad to Zimbabwe and the following year made an extensive tour to Scandinavia. This included a match against the Finnish national team, played on a small island in the Baltic Sea.

In 1987, following their Wembley victory, City were invited to play a 'crack' Uruguayan side, Liverpool, in Trinidad. Controversy arose when the Uruguayans pulled out with City on the way to the airport. In 1989, City visited Bermuda again to play matches against Middlesbrough and a local side.

1932
Apr 6 v Dutch XI (at Sparta Stadium, Rotterdam) 3-0
Cull, Lauderdale, Bourton
Allen; Baker, Elliott, Simpson, Mason, Heinneman, Cull, Lauderdale, Bourton, Lake, White.

1946 Tour of Denmark
May 21 v Aarhus 2-1
Barratt, Setchell
Wood; Tooze, Metcalf, Snape, G.Mason, Crawley, Warner(D.Simpson), Roberts, Barratt, Aldecoa, Setchell.
May 23 v Vejle Boldklub 6-0
Roberts 3, Barratt 2, Crawley
Wood; Tooze, Kelley, Snape, G.Mason, Crawley, D.Simpson, Barratt, Roberts, Aldecoa, Setchell.
May 26 v Jutland XI 2-2
Roberts, Scorer unknown
Wood; Tooze, Kelley, Snape, G.Mason, Crawley, D.Simpson, Barratt, Roberts, Aldecoa, Setchell.
Att: 6,000
May 27 v Randers Freja 3-0
Roberts 2, Setchell
Wood; Tooze, Metcalf, Snape, G.Mason, Crawley, D.Simpson, Barratt, Roberts, Aldecoa, Setchell.

1951 Tour of Holland
May 13 v Enschede 5-3
Roberts 2, Chisholm, Allen, Lockhart
May 14 v GVAV Groningen 4-2
Simpson, Hart, Lockhart, Roberts
May 18 v Limburgia (at Heerlen) 1-1
Briggs
May 20 v HVC Amersgoot 3-3
Roberts 2, Timmins

1962 Tour of West Germany
May 11 v Hanau 1893 FF 3-2
Farmer 2, Imlach (pen)
Lightening; Sillett, Kletzenbauer, Bruck, Curtis, B.Hill, Dwight, Farmer, Holder, McCann, Imlach.
Att: 3,000
May 13 v Hassfurt 1917 EV 2-0
Farmer, Imlach
Wesson; Sillett, Austin, Bruck, Curtis, B.Hill, Dwight, Farmer, Holder, McCann, Imlach
Att: 3,000
May 16 v Singen 1904 EV 3-0
B.Hill, Sillett 2
Lightening; Sillett, Austin, Bruck, Curtis, B.Hill, Dwight, Farmer, Holder(Kletzenbauer), McCann, Imlach.
Att: 3,200

1963 Tour of West Germany
Tour party: Wesson; Meeson, Sillett, Kearns, Kletzenbauer, B.Hill, Curtis, Farmer, Bruck, Dwight, Hale, Whitehouse, Barr, Hudson, Machin, Rees.
May 26 v Neumunster 3-1
Machin, Opp own-goal, Dwight
Att: 4,000
May 28 v Bad Neuenahr 6-1
Dwight 2, Hudson, Machin, Rees, Farmer (pen)
Att: 5,500
May 29 v Kaiserslautern 2-0
Hudson 2
Att: 1,000

1964
May 24 v Onteniente (Spain) 5-2
Hudson, Farmer, B.Hill, Humphries, Smith
Wesson; Sillett, Kearns, B.Hill, Curtis, Farmer, Humphries, Hudson, Kirby, Smith, Rees.
Att: 2,000
A subsequent game planned for May 28 v Gandia was cancelled by the Spanish FA at short notice.

1965 Tour of Iceland
Tour party: Wesson; Harris, Kearns, Sillett, Bruck, Farmer, Machin, Clements, Hale, Mitten, Smith, R.Gould, Hudson, Turner, Rees.
May 24 v KR Reykjavik 4-1
Hale 2, Hudson, Farmer
Att: 2,000
May 26 v Keflavik 4-1
Mitten, Turner, Clements, Smith
Att: 1,000
May 28 v Iceland XI 3-0
Turner, Hudson, R.Gould
Att: 2,500

1966 Tour of Europe
May 25 v Offenbach Kickers 0-0
Att: 3,000
(Rees sent off)
May 31 v FC Austria Vienna 1-4
Machin
Glazier; Sillett, Kearns, Bruck, Curtis(Roberts), Farmer, Key, Gould, Pointer, Machin, Rees.
Att: 3,500
June 3 v Young Fellows Zürich 2-3
Gould 2
Att: 1,500
Jun 6 v Union St Gilloise (Belgium) 3-1
Pointer, Rees, Gould
Att: 3,000

1967 Tour of West Indies
Jun 2 v Trinidad and Tobago XI 5-2
Lewis 2, Key, Tudor, Curtis
Att: 5,000
Jun 4 v South Trinidad XI (at Point Fortin) 4-3
Machin, Lewis, Gould, B.Hill
Att: 2,000
Jun 6 v Barbados XI (at Bridgetown) 3-2
Gould 2, Key
Att: 8,000
Jun 12 v Barbados XI (at Bridgetown) 2-0
Rees, Key
Att: 8,000
Jun 18 v Bermuda Police (at Hamilton) 8-0
Rees 2, Tudor, Machin, Lewis 2, Clements, Bruck
Att: 3,000

1968 Tour of Belgium
Aug 7 v Club Brugge KV (at Knokke) 1-3
Setters
Glazier; Bruck(Coop), Clements, Tudor, Setters, Curtis, Hannigan(Shepherd), Hunt, Baker, Gibson, Carr.
Att: 4,000
Aug 11 v KSV Waregem 1-3
Gibson
Glazier; Bruck, Clements, Machin, Setters, Tudor, Hannigan, Hunt, Curtis, Shepherd, Gibson.
Att: 8,000

1969 Tour of West Indies
Tour party: Glazier; Curtis, Machin, Clements, B.Hill, Coop, Cattlin, Carr, Blockley, Martin, Hunt, Bruck, Setters, Shepherd.
May 23 v New South Wales (Barbados) 5-0
Shepherd 2, Martin 2, Carr
May 25 v Combined Barbados XI 7-1
Hunt, Martin 3, Cantwell, Shepherd, Scorer unknown
Jun 4 v Somerset (Bermuda) 1-1
Shepherd

1970 Tour of United States
May 3 v St Louis Stars 1-2
Martin
Glazier; Coop, Cattlin, T.Gould, Blockley, Clements, Rafferty(Hunt), Carr, Martin, O'Rourke, Joicey(Machin).
Att: 3,700
May 5 v Kansas City Spurs 3-1
Hunt, Martin (pen), O'Rourke
Glazier; Bruck, Cattlin, Coop, Blockley, Clements, Hunt, Carr, Martin, O'Rourke, Machin.
Att: 3,225
May 8 v Dallas Tornadoes 3-1
Martin, Joicey 2
Glazier; Coop, Cattlin, Bruck, Blockley, Clements, Hunt, Carr, Martin, O'Rourke(Joicey), Machin.
Att: 3,084
May 12 v Atlanta Braves 2-1
Joicey 2
Glazier; Coop, Cattlin, Hunt, Blockley, Mortimer, T.Gould(Joicey), Carr, Martin, O'Rourke, Clements.
Att: 5,604
May 15 v Hertha Berlin (at Chicago) 1-0
Machin
Glazier; Coop, Cattlin, Machin, Blockley, Hunt, Joicey, Carr, Martin, O'Rourke, Clements.
Att: 3,508
May 17v Hertha Berlin (at Detroit) 0-2
Glazier; Coop, Cattlin, Machin, Blockley, Hunt, Joicey, Carr, Martin, O'Rourke, Clements.
Att: 7,690
May 22 v Washington Darts 4-2
O'Rourke, Martin, Joicey 2
Glazier; Bruck, Cattlin, Mortimer, Blockley, Hunt, Rafferty, Joicey, Martin, O'Rourke, Clements.
Att. 5,684
May 26 v Rochester Lancers 2-1
Mortimer, O'Rourke
Glazier; Saward, Cattlin, Mortimer, Blockley, Clements, Rafferty, Carr, Joicey, O'Rourke, T.Gould.
Att: 4,107

1971
May 12 v Tunisia XI (at Tunis) 2-2
Rafferty, Alderson
McManus; Smith, Cattlin, Coop, Machin, Blockley, Barry, Mortimer, Carr, Rafferty, Hunt, Alderson.

1972
Feb 29 v Olympiakos of Greece 1-0
Rafferty
Glazier; Smith, Cattlin, Parker, Barry, McGuire, Mortimer, Carr, Chilton, Rafferty, St John(Alderson).
Att: 10,000

Tour of Far East
Tour party; Glazier; Ramsbottom, Coop, Smith, Holmes, Dugdale, Barry, Parker, Randell, McGuire, Mortimer, Carr, Young, Chilton, Graham, Hunt, Green.
May 25 v South Korea XI (at Seoul) 2-0
Hunt 2
May 28 v South Korea XI (at Seoul) 3-0
Graham, Hunt, Mortimer
Jun 4 v Japan XI (at Nagoya) 3-0
Carr, Hunt, Chilton
Jun 6 v Japan XI (at Tōkyō) 0-1
Jun 10 v Japan Amateur XI (at Kōbe) 2-1
Hunt, Carr (pen)
Jun 13 v Santos of Brazil (at Bangkok) 2-2
Green, Young
(Pelé played and scored for Santos)

1973
May 22 v Norrköping of Sweden 3-2
Stein 2, Dugdale
Party: Glazier; Ramsbottom, Coop, Cattlin, Smith, Barry, Dugdale, Alderson, Stein, McGuire, Hutchison, Parker, Green, Craven, Philpotts.
May 26 v Capdepera of Majorca 5-0
Details unknown

1974 Anchor Cup in Far East
Toui Party: Glazier; Ramsbottom, Dugdale, Oakey, Cattlin, Craven, Dugdale, Hindley, Parker, McGuire, Mortimer, Carr, Alderson, Cross, Ferguson, Stein.
May 12 v Derby County (at Kuantan, Malaysia) 2-3
Alderson 2
Glazier; Dugdale, Oakey, Mortimer, Craven, Parker, McGuire(Cattlin), Alderson, Stein, Cross, Carr(Green).
Att: 20,000
May 15 v Everton (at Singapore) 2-1
Carr, Cross
Att: 35,000
May 22 v Derby County (at Singapore) 1-1
Craven
Att: 30,000
(City win Anchor Cup)

1975
May 20 v Nantes 0-2
Ramsbottom; Oakey, Cattlin, Craven, Lloyd, Dugdale, Mortimer, Green, Ferguson, Cross, Alderson.
Att: 5,000
(Bernard Blanchet Testimonial)

1976 Tour of Sweden
May 25 v Helsingborg 1-2
Cartwright
Blyth(King); Oakey, Powell, Craven, Dugdale, Coop, Cartwright, Green, Cross, Murphy, Hutchison.
Att: 759
May 27 v Malmö 0-1
Blyth; Oakey, Powell, Craven, Dugdale, Coop, Cartwright, Roberts, Cross, Murphy, Hutchison.
Att: 5,009
Dec 6 v Saudi Arabia XI (at Riyadh) 1-1
Wallace

1977
Nov 13 v Malta XI 1-0
Wallace
Att: 7,000

1978 Japan Cup
May 21 v Japan (at Tōkyō) 1-0
Thompson
Sealey; Roberts, McDonald, Beck, Holton, Coop, Nardiello(G.Thompson), Wallace, Ferguson, Powell, Hutchison.
May 23 v 1.FC Cologne (at Tōkyō) 1-1
Wallace
May 25 v Thailand (at Tōkyō) 1-0
Green
Semi-final
May 27 v Palmeiras of Brazil (at Ōsaka) 0-1
Sealey; Roberts, McDonald, Yorath, Holton, Coop, Green, Wallace, Feguson, Powell, Hutchison.
Dec 13 v Malta XI 6-1
Details unknown

1979
May 9 v Faroe Islands 6-0
Ferguson 3, Wallace 2, Powell
Att: 4,000
(Faroe Islands FA 75th Anniversary match)
May 16 v New York Cosmos (at Meadowlands) 1-3
Hunt
Sealey; Roberts, McDonald, Blair, Holton, Coop, Bannister, Powell, Ferguson, Hunt, Hutchison.
Att: 30,000

1980
Nov 19 v Nicosia XI 2-2
Jacobs, Thompson
Att: 6,000

1981 Tour of South East Asia
Tour party: Sealey; Blyth, Coop, Thomas, Roberts, Gillespie, Dyson, Gooding, Blair, Hunt, Bodak, Ferguson, Hateley, G.Thompson, Daly, English, Whitton, Bannister.
May 16 v Thailand XI (at Bangkok) 2-2
Details unknown
May 23 v Selangor XI (at Kuala Lumpur) 1-0
Details unknown
May 31 v Halleluja of South Korea (at Hong Kong) 4-3
Daly, English, Hunt, Hateley
Jun 4 v Indonesia Juniors (at Surabaya) 4-1
Details unknown
Jun 6 v Surabaya National XI 7-1
Details unknown
Jun 8 v Jakarta 3-0
Details unknown
Jun 10 v Pardedetex 6-0
Details unknown

Jun 12 v Local Medan XI 4-0
Bannister 3, Scorer unknown

1983 Tour of Zimbabwe
Jun 5 v Zimbabwe (at Harare) 5-2
Whitton 3, Mardenborough 2
Jun 10 v Zimbabwe Under-20 XI (at Gweru) 4-2
Whitton 3, Mardenborough
Jun 12 v Bulawayo Saints 2-4
Whitton, Hunt
Jun 14 v Presidents XI (at Harare) 5-1
Dyson, Gillespie, Mardenborough, Gould, Dalton
Jun 15 v Harare Dynamoes 5-1
Whitton 3, Singleton, Jacobs
Jun 17 v Caps United 2-4
Details unknown
Jul 31 v Benfica 2-2
Butterworth, Bamber
Att: 30,000

1984 Tour of Scandinavia
Jul 28 v Gimo IF of Sweden 4-2
Withey 3, Gynn
Att: 2,000
Jul 30 v Oviksalliansen of Sweden 2-0
Latchford, Bennett (pen)
Suckling; Stephens, Adams, Jol(Pearce), Kilcline (Peake), Butterworth, Platnauer, Hibbitt, Latchford(Gibson), Withey, K.Thompson(Bennett).
Jul 31 v Hudiksaval IK of Sweden 2-0
Latchford, Gynn
Suckling; Spring, Pearce, Gynn, Butterworth, Peake, Bennett, Hibbitt, Latchford, Gibson, Adams.
Aug 2 v Finland XI (at Aland Island) 0-1
Ogrizovic; Stephens, Pearce, Jol, Kilcline, Peake, Bennett, Gynn, Latchford, Withey, Platnauer.
Aug 5 v Junsele IFK of Sweden 6-1
Pearce 3, Gibson, Latchford, Bennett
Suckling(Ogrizovic); Spring, Adams, Gynn, Kilcline, Butterworth, Pearce, Hibbitt, Latchford, Gibson, Bennett.
Aug 6 v Kramfors of Sweden 4-0
Pearce, Gibson 2, Withey

1986
May 19 v Gibralter Select 3-1
Culpin 2, Brazil

1987
Sep 10 v Los Boliches of Spain 2-0
Gynn, Bennett
Ogrizovic; Borrows(K.Smith), Downs, McGrath, Rodger, Peake, Bennett, Gynn, Regis(Houchen), Speedie(Livingstone), Pickering.

1988
May 14 v Hong Kong XI 2-1
Speedie, Regis
Ogrizovic; Borrows, Pickering, Emerson, Kilcline, Peake, Bannister, Speedie(Houchen), Regis, Sedgley, D.Smith(Downs).
Att: 15,000
(Carlsberg Challenge Cup)

1989 Tour of Bermuda
Feb 28 v Boulevard 4-0
Bannister, Bennett, Emerson, Regis
Ogrizovic; Borrows, Dobson, Emerson(Phillips), Kilcline, Peake(L.Middleton), Livingstone, Clark(Downs), Regis, Bannister, Bennett.
Att: 1,000
Mar 3 v Middlesbrough (at Hamilton) 2.1
Regis, Clark
Ogrizovic; Borrows, Dobson, Emerson, Kilcline, Peake, Livingstone, A.N.Other, Regis, Bannister, Bennett. Subs: Phillips, McGrath, Clark.

1990 Tour of Zimbabwe
May 13 v Dynamoes FC 2-3
Borrows, Dobson
May 16 v Zimbabwe XI 2-1
Speedie, Borrows
May 20 v Highlanders FC 1-1
Gynn

Brian Borrows

Coventry City Reserves

APART from the early years when they took part in local regional leagues in the Birmingham area, Coventry City Reserves spent 35 seasons in the Football Combination up to 1968, since when they have had unbroken membership of the Central League. Although these days attendances at Reserve matches average less than 500, it has not always been so. During the 1930s, attendances of 3,000 to 5,000 were quite normal, rising to five-figure 'gates' for matches against mighty Arsenal's second string. This trend continued after the war but fell away as clubs fell on to harder times in the 1950s. The switch to midweek and the enthusiasm of the Jimmy Hill era put the clock back and when Coventry City finished runners-up in the Second Division of the Football Combination in 1964-5, attendances at Highfield Road rose to 11,000 by the end of the season. This level of interest continued into the first season of the transfer to the Central League, but gradually fell away again and by the mid-1970s attendances were down to the thousand mark as squads had decreased in size and reserve teams consisted of a mixture of squad players and YTS juniors.

	P	*W*	*D*	*L*	*F*	*A*	*Pts*	*Pos*
United League North								
1908-09	12	5	1	6	27	31	11	5th
South Eastern League								
1909-10	34	20	3	11	70	46	43	3rd
1910-11	36	13	5	18	53	67	31	15th
1911-12	38	17	12	9	58	49	46	5th
Birmingham and District League								
1912-13	34	19	6	9	62	41	44	2nd
1913-14	34	9	7	18	56	83	25	16th
1914-15	34	8	4	22	52	115	20	17th
Birmingham Suburban League Div 1								
1918-19	16	8	0	8	32	38	16	6th
Birmingham and District League								
1919-20	34	18	3	13	88	57	39	4th
1920-21	34	12	9	13	58	57	33	9th
1921-22	34	10	10	14	54	61	30	14th
Southern League								
1922-23	38	15	8	15	56	61	38	12th
Southern League Eastern Section								
1923-24	30	10	8	12	39	34	28	9th
1924-25	34	12	9	13	51	41	33	11th
1925-26	34	9	5	20	54	93	23	17th
London Combination								
1926-27	42	11	5	26	58	94	27	21st
1927-28	42	11	9	22	73	114	31	20th
1928-29	42	16	5	21	70	104	37	17th
1929-30	42	11	9	22	75	106	31	18th
1930-31	42	15	4	23	81	97	34	16th
1931-32	42	12	10	22	71	93	34	16th
1932-33	46	16	8	22	93	95	40	16th
1933-34	46	19	10	17	76	62	48	8th
1934-35	46	20	4	22	91	85	44	10th
1935-36	46	18	7	21	85	92	43	15th
1936-37	46	26	7	13	117	62	59	4th
1937-38	46	23	11	12	87	61	57	3rd
1938-39	46	26	7	13	115	57	60	3rd
Football Combination Section 'B'								
1946-47	30	16	5	9	80	55	37	5th
1947-48	30	10	8	12	35	54	28	9th
1948-49	30	10	3	17	37	62	23	13th
Football Combination Section 'A'								
1949-50	30	10	8	12	48	55	28	13th
1950-51	30	11	8	11	32	36	30	8th
1951-52	30	13	8	9	50	43	34	6th
Football Combination Division One								
1952-53	30	10	4	16	33	55	24	15th
Football Combination Division Two								
1953-54	30	16	6	8	67	35	38	2nd

	P	*W*	*D*	*L*	*F*	*A*	*Pts*	*Pos*
Football Combination Division One								
1954-55	30	8	8	14	35	64	24	13th
Football Combination								
1955-56	42	11	5	26	59	114	27	19th
1956-57	42	10	8	24	65	103	28	19th
1957-58	42	7	12	23	49	84	26	22nd
Football Combination Division Two								
1958-59	32	6	8	18	47	83	20	17th
1959-60	38	9	9	20	57	96	27	19th
1960-61	38	15	4	19	70	87	34	15th
Football Combination Midweek Section								
1961-62	34	13	7	14	66	62	33	11th
1962-63	34	13	10	11	57	52	36	7th
Football Combination Division Two								
1963-64	34	14	9	11	66	63	37	8th
1964-65	36	20	7	9	96	55	47	2nd
Football Combination Division One								
1965-66	34	16	5	13	77	61	37	8th
1966-67	32	13	6	13	56	64	32	9th
1967-68	28	11	6	11	44	48	28	8th
Central League								
1968-69	42	12	8	22	45	68	32	20th
1969-70	42	17	6	19	53	60	40	11th
1970-71	42	14	16	12	69	50	44	8th
1971-72	42	16	12	14	71	55	44	8th
1972-73	42	23	8	11	77	50	54	3rd
1973-74	42	20	13	9	62	47	53	2nd
1974-75	42	16	12	14	70	63	44	9th
1975-76	42	16	13	13	54	46	45	7th
1976-77	42	18	5	19	61	65	41	12th
1977-78	42	14	11	17	61	70	39	14th
1978-79	42	19	8	15	87	71	46	7th
1979-80	42	21	14	7	96	57	55	2nd
1980-81	42	16	10	16	75	74	42	10th
1981-82	42	15	11	16	49	59	41	13th
Central League Division One								
1982-83	30	7	5	18	34	63	19	13th
Central League Division Two								
1983-84	30	15	6	9	54	30	51	3rd
Central League Division One								
1984-85	34	10	4	20	45	61	34	15th
Central League Division Two								
1985-86	34	21	4	9	76	34	67	3rd
Central League Division One								
1986-87	34	12	8	14	61	61	44	11th
1987-88	34	11	13	10	51	37	46	11th
1988-89	34	17	6	11	66	52	52	6th
1989-90	34	12	5	17	50	64	41	13th
1990-91	34	10	13	11	46	48	43	11th

FA Youth Cup

THE FA Youth Cup began in 1953 to provide competition for clubs' younger players. Players under the age of 18 years on 1 September are eligible for that season's competition. Coventry City first entered in 1955-6 and had little success until the late 1960s when, with an exceptional crop of youngsters, they were beaten Finalists in both 1968 and 1970. The four-game Final against Spurs (Perryman and Souness included) provided thrilling matches for substantial crowds. It was 15 years before Coventry City made an impact again, when they were beaten semi-finalists in 1986. City eventually captured the FA Youth Cup in 1987 when, three days before the FA Cup Final triumph, they defeated Charlton Athletic 1-0 after extra-time at Highfield Road.

Many Youth-team players have graduated to the first team, including seven from the 1970 side. The best crop, however, was in 1979 when ten players, including Danny Thomas, Mark Hateley and Steve Whitton, made it to the first team. When one considers the talented youngsters to come through this route and the transfer fees saved — and in many cases later earned — over the years, it emphasises the importance of a strong youth policy to a club of Coventry City's status.

1955-56
Round 1
Sep 24 v Gloucester City (a) 4-0
Allen, Sheppard, Charley 2
Round 2
Oct 25 v Kidderminster Harriers (h) 4-0
Sheppard 2, Savage, Charley
Att: 1,973
Round 3
Dec 3 v Wolverhampton Wanderers (a) 1-3
Sheppard
Normal team: Brindley; Burton, Walters, Kearns, Curtis, E.Jones, Allen, Sheppard, Savage, Charley, Southall.

1956-57
Round 1
Sep 26 v Aston Villa (h) 0-0
Replay
Oct 6 v Aston Villa (a) 0-4
Normal team: Spratt; Lee, Alcock, Brain, Walker, Charley, Wyatt, Peake, Hill, Walters, O'Leary.

1957-58
Round 1
Oct 12 v Port Vale (a) 3-1
Hill 2, Jephcott
Round 2
Nov 2 v Peterborough United (h) 8-1
Hill 2, Walters 2, Shropsall 2, Charley, England
Round 3
Dec 20 v Leicester City (a) 0-1
Normal team: Jones; Walters, Cox, Nelson, Walker, K.McCarthy, Shropshall, Vickers, B.Hill, Charley, England.

1958-59
Round 1
Oct 11 v Gloucester City (a) 2-3
Hunter, J.Mason
Gascoigne; Dixon, Meffin, Morris, P.Mason, Jenkins, Hunter, J.Mason, Haley, Kirk, Pask.

1959-60
Preliminary Round
Sep 28 v Peterborough United (a) 3-4
Holder 2, McLean
Batchelor; Sheppard, Tedds, McLean, Jenkins, Kirk, Crump, Puddy, Holder, Clarke, Abercrombie.

1960-61
Round 1
Oct 8 v Heanor Town (a) 4-2
Crump, Walker 2, Abercrombie
Round 2
Nov 1 v West Bromwich Albion (a) 3-3
Clarke, Crump, Holder
Replay
Nov 14 v West Bromwich Albion (h) 3-1
Mason, Cowin, Millington (og)
Att: 1,439
Round 3
Dec 20 v Sheffield Wednesday (a) 1-3
Walker
Normal team: Batchelor; Tedds, Gilks, Bruck, Mason, McCarte, Crump, Walker, Holder, Clarke, Cowin.

1961-62
Round 1
Oct 3 v Aston Villa (h) 1-9
Cowin
Batchelor; Brookes, Gilkes, Bruck, Nutt, R.Gould, Wright, Colvin, Holder, Rees, Cowin.
Att: 1,425

1962-63
Round 1
Nov 12 v Port Vale (h) 0-5
Johnson; Saunders, Burckitt, Oakes, Temel, George, Denton, Mole, R.Gould, Lilley, Motterham.
Att: 1,245

1963-64
Round 1
Nov 12 v West Bromwich Albion (h) 4-6
Denton, Thompson, Chambers, Docker
Partridge; Cartwright, Burckitt, Oakes, Roberts, Morrissey, Denton, Chambers, R.Gould, Thompson, Docker.
Att: 1,978

1964-65
Round 1
Nov 9 v Notts County (a) 2-2
Busby 2
Replay
Nov 12 v Notts County (h) 2-1
Chambers, Docker
Att: 585

Round 2
Dec 7 v Aston Villa (a) 1-0
Chambers
Round 3
Jan 7 v Derby County (h) 1-1
Morrissey
Att: 1,567
Replay
Jan 14 v Derby County (a) 2-1
Chambers, Burckitt (pen)
Round 4
Feb 17 v Stoke City (a) 2-3
Chambers, Docker
Att: 2,000
Normal team: Clamp; Coop, Burckitt, Morrissey, Keley, Cartwright (or Glover), Cox, Chambers, Busby (or Mander), Docker, Matthews.

1965-66
Round 2
Dec 16 v Leicester City (h) 3-1
Carr, Peachey, Docker
Att: 2,055
Round 3
Jan 4 v Stoke City (h) 0-2
Att: 4,818
Normal team: Clamp; Coop, Knox, Bloodworth, Keley, Morrissey, T.Gould, Carr, Peachey, Docker, Warrington.

1966-67
Round 2
Dec 7 v Wolverhampton Wanderers (a) 2-0
Peachey 2
Round 3
Jan 4 v Swansea Town (a) 1-1
R.Gould
Att: 1,000
Replay
Jan 18 v Swansea Town (h) 2-1
Peachey 2
Att: 3,132
Round 4
Feb 1 v Port Vale (a) 1-3
James (og)
Att: 5,397
Normal team: Spiers; Hayward, Dobbing, Knox, Keley, Blockley, Bloodworth, Carr, Peachey, T.Gould, Paddon.

1967-68
Round 2
Dec 13 v Wolverhampton Wanderers (a) 5-2
Sinclair, Allen 3, Blockley
Att: 1,718
Round 3
Jan 16 v Leicester City (h) 4-1
Blockley, Peachey, Paddon, Allen
Att: 3,903
Round 4
Feb 19 v Oxford United (h) 2-0
Sinclair, Paddon
Att: 3,349
Round 5
Mar 11 v Cardiff City (a) 2-1
Carr, Paddon
Semi-final (1st leg)
Apr 3 v Crystal Palace (a) 1-1
Allen
Att: 2,018
Semi-final (2nd leg)
Apr 9 v Crystal Palace (h) 2-0
Paddon (pen), Sinclair
Att: 8,327
Final (1st leg)
Apr 23 v Burnley (h) 2-1
Paddon, Allen
Att: 14,836
Final (2nd leg)
May 6 v Burnley (a) 0-2
Att: 13,962
Normal team: Icke (or Dighton); Crossley, Joy, Peachey, Blockley, Wilks, Sinclair (or Farmer), Allen, T.Gould, Carr, Paddon.

1968-69
Round 2
Dec 3 v Cross Castle United (h) 1-0
Allen
Att: 1,170
Round 3
Jan 20 v Leicester City (a) 1-0
Allen
Round 4
Feb 25 v West Bromwich Albion (h) 0-3
Att: 667
Normal team: McManus; Crossley, Parker, Goodwin, Wilks, Dugdale, Stevenson, Allen, Rafferty, Mortimer, Randell.

1969-70
Round 2
Dec 6 v Northfield (a) 4-1
Randell 2, McGuire, T.Smith
Round 3
Dec 23 v Birmingham City (a) 2-0
Stevenson, T.Smith
Round 4
Jan 27 v Nottingham Forest (a) 2-2
Green 2
Replay
Feb 5 v Nottingham Forest (h) 3-0
Mortimer 2, T.Smith
Att: 1,655
Round 5
Feb 26 v Ipswich Town (h) 2-0
Cartwright, Randell
Att: 1,793
Semi-final (1st leg)
Mar 26 v Manchester United (h) 3-1
Mortimer, T.Smith, Cartwright
Att: 2,401
Semi-final (2nd leg)
Apr 2 v Manchester United (a) 1-0
T.Smith
Att: 5,037
Final 1st leg
Apr 18 v Tottenham Hotspur (a) 0-1
Att: 10,700
Final 2nd leg
Apr 21 v Tottenham Hotspur (h) 1-0 (a.e.t.)
Holmes (pen)
Att: 9,968

Final Replay
Apr 28 v Tottenham Hotspur (h) 2-2 (a.e.t.)
Green, Stevenson
Att: 14,926
Final Second Replay
May 1 v Tottenham Hotspur (a) 0-1
Att: 7,560
Final team: Icke; Crossley, Holmes, Mortimer, Dugdale, Parker, Cartwright, Green, Randell, McGuire, Stevenson.
T.Smith played instead of Cartwright in the first match

1970-71
Round 2
Dec 1 v Shrewsbury Town (h) 6-0
T.Smith 4, Green, Stevenson
Att: 2,994
Round 3
Dec 22 v Northampton Town (a) 6-0
Green, Randell, T.Smith 2, Stockley, Holmes
Att: 900
Round 4
Jan 27 v Arsenal (a) 0-1
Att: 965
Normal team: Goodbourn; Stockley, Holmes, Stevenson, Dugdale, Parker, Diamond (or Burdett), Green, Randell, McGuire, T.Smith.

1971-72
Round 2
Nov 29 v Derby County (a) 4-0
Green 2, T.Smith, Ferguson
Round 3
Dec 21 v Leicester City (h) 1-3
Holmes (pen)
Att: 2,976
Normal team: Poole; Oakey, Holmes, Moore, Philpotts, P.Cahill, D.Murphy, Green, Ferguson, Diamond, T.Smith.

1972-73
Round 2
Nov 22 v Liverpool (a) 2-0
Ferguson, Murphy
Att: 583
Round 3
Jan 23 v Ipswich Town (a) 0-1
Normal team: Blyth; Oakey, Diamond (or Luckett), A.Bannister, A.Cahill, P.Cahill, Cameron, Coulson, Ferguson, D.Murphy, R.Murphy (or Roberts).

1973-74
Round 2
Nov 27 v Hereford United (a) 3-0
Seymour (og), Nardiello, O'Brien
Round 3
Dec 17 v Plymouth Argyle (a) 1-1
O'Brien
Replay
Jan 21 v Plymouth Argyle (h) 2-1
Kilduff, R.Murphy
(At Ryton)
Round 4
Feb 21 v Ipswich Town (h) 0-2
Att: 353
Normal team: Sherlock; Stallard, Luckett, Coulson, Kilduff, P.Cahill, Nardiello, Roberts, Robinson, R.Murphy, O'Brien.

1974-75
Round 2
Nov 19 v Aston Villa (h) 0-2
Sealey; Loose, Moss, Potter, Banks, Wood, Nardiello, O'Brien, Wilson, A.James, V.Thomas.
Att: 650

1975-76
Round 2
Nov 19 v West Bromwich Albion (a) 0-3
Sealey; Irwin, Christie, Reeves, Ellis, Dyson, Harvey, Groves, G.Thompson, V.Thomas, Wilson.

1976-77
Round 1
Nov 11 v Leicester City (h) 1-3
D.Butterworth
Hughes; Walker, Duffy, Reeves, Dyson, P.Hunt, G.Bannister, McGrellis, G.Thompson, Gooding, Blair.
Sub: D.Butterworth.
Att: 214

1977-78
Round 1
Oct 29 v Northfield (h) 2-2
Haywood, Mead
Att: 254
Replay
Nov 12 v Northfield (a) 3-4
Haywood, Whitton, Bannister
Normal team: Murcott; D.Thomas (or Mead), Jacobs, Phillips, Dyson, Duffy, Bodak (or Whitton), Blair, G.Thompson, Haywood, Bannister.

1978-79
1st Qualifying Round
Sep 18 v Sutton Coldfield (h) 7-2
Whitton, Cooper, English 4, Haywood
2nd Qualifying Round
Oct 9 v Northampton Town (a) 5-1
Haywood 4, Bodak
Round 1
Nov 7 v Cheltenham Town (h) 2-2
Cooper, Russell
Att: 831
Replay
Nov 15 v Cheltenham Town (a) 3-0
Whitton, Hateley, English
Round 2
Dec 5 v Wolverhampton Wanderers (h) 3-3
Haywood, Phillips, English
Replay
Dec 12 v Wolverhampton Wanderers (a) 1-0
Cooper
Att: 696
Round 3
Jan 11 v Cardiff City (h) 3-0
Hateley, Whitton, English
Att: 289
Round 4
Mar 8 v Derby County (h) 1-1
English
Att: 459
Replay
Mar 28 v Derby County (a) 2-1
Whitton 2

Round 5
Apr 5 v Everton (h) 1-6
English
Att: 1,004
Normal team: Murcott; Whitton, Barnes, D.Thomas, Cooper, Jacobs, Bodak, English, Hateley, Phillips, Haywood.

1979-80
Round 1
Nov 8 v Walsall (a) 2-2
Hateley, English
Replay
Nov 13 v Walsall (h) 4-5
Hateley, English 2, Lynch
Att: 639
Normal team: Taylor; Hormantschuk, Lynch, Singleton, Buchanan, Barnes, Bodak, English, Hateley, D.Thomas, Kennedy.

1980-81
Round 1
Nov 8 v Sutton Coldfield (h) 5-0
O'Brien, Barnett, Singleton, I.Butterworth 2
Att: 278
Round 2
Dec 2 v Peterborough United (h) 2-2
O'Brien, Hendrie
Att: 188
Replay
Dec 8 v Peterborough United (a) 3-3 (a.e.t.)
McGinty, Linton, Howlett
Second Replay
Dec 16 v Peterborough United (h) 3-0
Willock, Linton 2
Att: 337
Round 3
Jan 13 v Wrexham (h) 4-1
Willock 2, Linton 2
Att: 412
Round 4
Jan 29 v Queen's Park Rangers (h) 2-2
Howlett (pen), Barnett
Att: 1,308
Replay
Feb 9 v Queen's Park Rangers (a) 1-5
Barnett
Normal team: Suckling; Abbott, Hormantschuk, Singleton, I.Butterworth, Gordon, Hendrie, Barnett, Linton, Howlett, Willock.

1981-82
Round 1
Nov 3 v Sutton Coldfield (h) 8-0
Gordon 3, Willock 2, Mardenborough 2, Finn (og)
Att: 486
Round 2
Dec 23 v Oldham Athletic (a) 4-0
Mardenborough, K.Thompson, Hendrie, Hall
Round 3
Jan 5 v Burnley (h) 0-0
Att: 577
Replay
Jan 26 v Burnley (a) 1-2
K.Thompson
Normal team: Suckling; Abbott, McGinty, McGrath, I.Butterworth, Singleton, Hendrie, K.Thompson, Mardenborough, R.Gordon, Willock.

1982-83
Round 2
Dec 9 v Sheffield United (h) 2-2
K.Thompson 2
Att: 149
Replay
Dec 20 v Sheffield United (a) 1-0
Conroy
Round 3
Dec 30 v Leicester City (a) 0-1
Normal team: Suckling; McGrath, Matthews, McDonald, Anderson, Bollard, Spring, Mardenborough, Conroy, Hall, K.Thompson.

1983-84
Round 2
Dec 8 v Derby County (a) 0-2
Team: Dalton; Gould, Spring, English, Anderson, Doyle, Gethfield, Stratford, Evans, Conroy, McDonald.

1984-85
Round 2
Dec 6 v Derby County (a) 4-1
D.Smith, Evans, Tucker (og), Gethfield
Round 3
Jan 23 v Oxford United (h) 4-1
Keates 3, Evans
Att: 205
Round 4
Feb 25 v Swindon Town (h) 1-1
Doyle (pen)
Att: 307
Replay
Feb 28 v Swindon Town (a) 4-0
Doyle 2 (pens), Evans, D.Smith
Round 5
Mar 13 v Newcastle United (a) 0-3
Normal team: Creedon; Gould, Sedgley, Doyle, Gethfield, Dobson, Merriman (or Mahan), Stratford, Evans, Keates, D.Smith.

1985-86
Round 2
Dec 7 v Wolverhampton Wanderers (h) 7-1
Livingstone 3, Hathaway 2, Sedgley (pen), Dandridge
Att: 147
Round 3
Jan 13 v Newcastle United (a) 4-1
Livingstone 2, Cook, Sedgley
Round 4
Jan 27 v Watford (h) 1-0
Hathaway
Att: 394
Round 5
Mar 11 v Tottenham Hotspur (h) 0-0
Att: 945
Replay
Mar 20 v Tottenham Hotspur (a) 2-1 (a.e.t.)
Hathaway, Sedgley
Semi-final (1st leg)
Apr 7 v Manchester United (h) 0-2
Att: 3,434
Semi-final (2nd leg)
Apr 11 v Manchester United (a) 1-1
Dobson
Att: 5,000

Normal team: Creedon; Clark, McGrory, Sedgley, Dobson, Merriman, Dandridge, Mahan, Livingstone, Hathaway, D.Smith.

1986-87
Round 2
Dec 1 v West Bromwich Albion (a) 0-0
Replay
Dec 8 v West Bromwich Albion (h) 3-0
Cook, Shepstone, Marshall
Att: 302
Round 3
Jan 31 v Southampton (a) 0-0
Replay
Feb 9 v Southampton (h) 3-2
Livingstone, Cook (pen), Jones
Round 4
Feb 23 v Oldham Athletic (a) 0-0
Att: 279
Replay
Mar 4 v Oldham Athletic (h) 1-1 (a.e.t.)
Livingstone
Att: 425
Second Replay
Mar 7 v Oldham Athletic (a) 2-1
Cook (pen), Clark
Round 5
Mar 11 v Watford (a) 2-0
Cook, Livingstone
Semi-final (1st leg)
Mar 25 v Manchester City (h) 1-0
Clark
Att: 1,753
Semi-final (2nd leg)
Apr 2 v Manchester City (a) 0-1 (a.e.t.)
Att: 4,000
Replay
Apr 10 v Manchester City (h) 3-0
Livingstone 2, Shepstone
Att: 4,500
Final (1st leg)
Apr 28 v Charlton Athletic (a) 1-1
C.Middleton
Att: 833
Final (2nd leg)
May 13 (h) 1-0 (a.e.t.)
Livingstone
Att: 12,142
Final team: Bastock; L.Middleton, A.Smith, Dobson, Gowens, Cook, R.Smith, Clark, Livingstone, Shepstone, Marshall. (C.Middleton played number-9 in 1st leg).

1987-88
Round 2
Dec 7 v Wolverhampton Wanderers (h) 3-2
Shepstone, C.Middleton 2
Att: 576
Round 3
Jan 11 v Liverpool (h) 1-3
Galley
Att: 1,097
Normal team: Bastock; Mapletoft, Titterton, L.Middleton, Seymour, A.Smith, Booty, Jones, Galley, Shepstone, C.Middleton.

1988-89
Round 2
Dec 5 v Derby County (a) 1-1
Galley
Replay
Dec 12 v Derby County (h) 3-1 (a.e.t.)
Bufton, L.Middleton, C.Middleton
Att: 510
Round 3
Jan 10 v Liverpool (h) 2-4
Booty, C.Middleton (pen)
Att: 1,253
Normal team: Kiely; Taylor, Titterton, C.Middleton, L.Middleton, Harwood, Booty, Shepstone, Galley (or Bufton), Hurst, Jenkins.

1989-90
Round 2
Dec 4 v Birmingham City (h) 2-0
Titterton (pen), Bufton
Att: 284
Round 3
Jan 10 v Manchester City (a) 0-0
Replay
Jan 15 v Manchester City (h) 1-6
Bufton
Att: 612
Normal team: Barefield; Young, Smith, French, Titterton, Bickley, Fleming, Shepherd, Bufton, Jenkins, Dickson.

1990-91
Round 2
Dec 3 v Leicester City (a) 3-2
Bickley, Fleming, Stephenson
Round 3
Jan 15 v Wimbledon (a) 0-2
Normal team: Dowis; Young, Smith, Bickley, Upton, French, Fleming, Stephenson, Bufton, Wilson, Dickson.

Abandoned & Void Games

IT is now nearly 20 years since a Coventry City match was abandoned, due in the main to the Clean Air Act eradicating the heavy smogs and fogs that used to engulf the industrial areas of the United Kingdom, as well as much improved drainage systems. Nowadays it is normally ice and snow that cause matches to be postponed due to unsafe terrace conditions. There was a period, however, between the two wars when matches were played to completion, footballers and referees more or less ignoring the conditions. Thankfully, those days are now long since passed.

1903-04
Birmingham League
Nov 28 v Halesowen (h) 3-1
Abandoned after 82 minutes – fog
Taylor; Parish, Hewitt, Hadley, Smith, Pugh, Taplin, Spence, Walker, Craythorne, Porter.
Att: Unknown

1905-06
Birmingham League
Dec 2 v Stafford Rangers (h) 1-1
Abandoned after 60 minutes – rain
Cramp
Whitehouse; Kearns, E.Smith, C.Smith, King, Walker, Such, Arrowsmith, Cramp, McIntyre, Wright.
Att: 1,000

1907-08
FA Cup
Oct 19 v Bilston (a) 2-1
Abandoned after 70 minutes – hailstorm
Smith, Lewis
Whitehouse; Juggins, Kifford, Jones, Gilbert, Chaplin, Layton, Smith, Warren, Lewis, Tooth.
Att: 4,000

1908-09
Southern League
Division One
Mar 6 v Reading (a) 0-1
Abandoned after 45 minutes – rain
Moult; Juggins, Hanson, Marvin, Chaplin, Dougherty, Tickle, Arnold, Turner, Warren, Buckle.
Att: Unknown

1910-11
Southern League
Division One
Oct 1 v Northampton Town (a) 0-0
Abandoned after 51 minutes – bad light
Evans; Saul, Gordon, Hickleton, Boston, Johnson, Parkes, Arnold, Powell, Warren, Lee.
Att: Unknown

1937-38
Division Two
Dec 4 v Southampton (h) 1-0
Abandoned after 45 minutes – snow
McDonald
Morgan; Astley, Metcalf, Frith, Mason, Archer, Taylor, McDonald, McPhee, Davidson, J.Brown.
Att: 10,000

1949-50
Division Two
Nov 19 v Sheffield Wednesday (h) 1-0
Abandoned after 63 minutes – fog
Roberts
Wood; McDonnell, R.Mason, Snape, G.Mason, N.Simpson, Warner, Dearson, Roberts, Marsh, Murphy.
Att: 17,541

1954-55
Division Three South
Mar 26 v Southend United (h) 3-1
Abandoned after 68 minutes – heavy rain
Hawkings, Collindridge, Lee
Matthews; K.Jones, Kirk, Jamieson, McDonnell, Austin, Moore, Hawkings, Lee, P.Hill, Collindridge.
Att: 4,100

1956-57
Division Three South
Dec 22 v Crystal Palace (h) 0-0
Abandoned after 51 minutes – floodlight failure
Bentley; Timmins, Curtis, Regan, Kirk, N.Simpson, Rogers, Uphill, McPherson, P.Hill, Boxley.
Att: 8,226

George Curtis

Dec 25 v Newport County (a) 0-0
Abandoned after 71 minutes – blizzard
Bentley; Timmins, Curtis, Regan, Kirk, N.Simpson, Rogers, Uphill, McPherson, P.Hill, Boxley.
Att: 7,500

1962-63
Division Three
Dec 22 v Colchester United (h) 2-0
Abandoned after 45 minutes – fog
Farmer (pen), Hale
Wesson; Sillett, Kearns, Hill, Curtis, Farmer, Humphries, Hale, Bly, Whitehouse, Rees.
Att: 11,803

1971-72
Division One
Mar 4 v Sheffield United (h) 0-2
Abandoned after 62 minutes – heavy rain
Glazier; Smith, Cattlin, Parker, Blockley, Barry, McGuire, Carr, Rafferty, Chilton, St John.
Att: 16,408

1972-73
Division One
Nov 25 v Ipswich Town (a) 1-0
Abandoned after 61 mins – floodlight failure
Stein
Ramsbottom; Coop, Cattlin, Smith, Barry, Parker, Mortimer, Alderson, Stein, Carr, Hutchison.
Att: 19,336

Tommy Hutchison

The following games were completed but were later declared void and expunged from league records.

1894-95
Birmingham League
Jan 19 v West Bromwich Albion Reserves (h) 0-1
Edge; Cashmore, Alldrick, Chatland, Roberts, Edmund, Hubberd, Bird, Newall, Cotterill, Law.
Game scheduled for West Brom's ground but switched by clubs. Birmingham FA refused to sanction result and replay ordered.

1899-1900
Birmingham League
Sep 2 v Wellington St George's (a) 3-1
Holmes 2, Crofts
A.Harris; Wareham, J.Harris, Whitehouse, Brampton, Lomas, Holmes, Walker, Ridout, Porter, Crofts.
Dec 30 v Wellington St George's (h) 2-2
Ridout, Crofts
A.Harris; Wareham, Smith, Whitehouse, Roberts, Lomas, Walker, Holmes, Ridout, Porter, Crofts.
Att: 700
Wellington disbanded and their record was expunged.

Sep 23 v Worcester Rovers (h) 4-1
Crofts 2, Walker, Ridout
A.Harris; Wareham, J.Harris, Whitehouse, Brampton, Lomas, Holmes, Walker, Ridout, Porter, Crofts.
Worcester Rovers dropped out of the League and their record was expunged.

1914-15
Southern League
Division Two
Oct 31 v Mardy (h) 6-0
Dobson 3, Enright, Harkins, Allan
Blake; Roberts, Meunier, Fulljames, Morris, Harkins, Alderson, Dobson, Allan, Enright, Turner.
Att: 4,000
Mardy withdrew from the Southern League and their record was expunged.
Dec 12 v Abertillery (h) 8-0
Allan 3, Craig, Dobson, Holmes, Enright, unknown
Blake; Barnacle, Meunier, Roberts, Morris, Craig, Holmes, Dobson, Allan, Enright, Turner.
Att: 1,000
Abertillery withdrew from the Southern League and their record was expunged.

Leagues and Games Played

Birmingham League

	P	W	D	L	F	A	W	D	L	F	A
Aston Villa Reserves	28	2	3	9	17	38	0	3	11	14	63
Birmingham Reserves	28	4	2	8	23	31	2	1	11	13	58
Brierley Hill Alliance	28	6	3	5	35	26	3	3	8	20	35
Bristol Rovers	6	0	0	3	3	7	0	0	3	10	23
Bristol St George's	4	1	1	0	3	2	1	0	1	6	6
Burslem Port Vale Res	6	3	0	0	13	1	0	1	2	4	6
Burton United	2	1	0	0	2	0	0	0	1	0	4
Crewe Alexandra	14	1	2	4	10	19	1	0	6	10	24
Dudley	20	7	1	2	23	10	1	1	8	15	24
Halesowen	26	11	1	1	31	13	5	1	7	25	34
Hereford Thistle	8	1	2	1	7	8	1	0	3	6	7
Ironbridge	6	2	1	0	12	0	0	2	1	2	12
Hereford Town	12	2	1	3	7	8	1	0	5	2	12
Kidderminster Harriers	28	9	2	3	31	17	4	2	8	10	26
Old Hill Wanderers	2	0	1	0	0	0	0	0	1	2	5
Oldbury Town	6	2	0	1	7	3	2	0	1	10	4
Redditch	6	3	0	0	9	1	0	0	3	4	13
Ruabon Druids	8	3	1	0	10	3	1	0	3	9	16
Shrewsbury Town	26	11	0	2	42	17	3	1	9	12	26
Smethwick CW	2	0	0	1	2	3	1	0	0	4	1
Stoke Reserves	16	6	0	2	24	13	0	3	5	8	22
Stafford Rangers	20	6	2	2	28	13	1	1	8	8	28
Stourbridge	28	8	2	4	36	6	4	1	9	23	33
Walsall	12	6	0	0	19	4	1	0	5	6	11
Wellington Town	12	2	2	2	13	9	1	1	4	4	19
Wellington St George's	2	1	0	0	4	0	0	0	1	2	5
WBA Reserves	28	4	1	9	32	37	0	1	13	8	47
Wolves Reserves	28	4	4	6	23	37	3	1	10	13	45
Worcester City	28	4	3	7	16	20	4	5	5	28	28
Worcester Rovers	10	3	0	2	11	7	1	2	2	10	12
Wrexham	6	1	2	0	8	4	1	0	2	4	7

Southern League

	P	W	D	L	F	A	W	D	L	F	A
Barry	2	1	0	0	3	0	0	0	1	0	2
Brentford	12	5	0	1	21	4	0	0	6	4	17
Brighton	12	3	2	1	9	6	0	2	4	6	18
Bristol Rovers	12	1	2	3	12	12	2	1	3	7	8
Cardiff City	2	0	1	0	2	2	0	0	1	1	2
Croydon Common	2	1	0	0	6	1	1	0	0	3	1
Crystal Palace	12	2	2	2	8	8	2	0	4	4	12
Ebbw Vale	2	1	0	0	6	0	1	0	0	3	1
Exeter City	12	1	1	4	9	8	2	2	2	6	8
Gillingham	12	3	0	3	16	14	3	1	2	8	8
Leyton	8	3	1	0	8	3	1	1	2	1	6
Llanelly	2	1	0	0	1	0	1	0	0	2	1
Luton Town	8	3	1	0	13	5	1	0	3	13	5
Merthyr Town	6	0	1	2	3	5	0	1	2	1	7
Mid Rhondda	2	1	0	0	3	0	0	0	1	1	2
Millwall	12	4	2	0	12	4	1	0	5	2	14
Newport County	2	1	0	0	10	1	1	0	0	1	0
Norwich City	12	5	0	1	14	4	2	2	2	8	9
Northampton Town	12	1	2	3	8	12	2	1	3	5	9
Plymouth Argyle	12	2	2	2	16	10	1	0	5	6	24
Pontypridd	2	1	0	0	5	0	1	0	0	3	2
Portsmouth	10	3	1	1	11	8	0	2	3	1	8
Queens Park Rangers	12	3	2	1	10	5	0	1	5	2	20
Reading	10	3	1	1	12	4	1	0	4	1	5
Southampton	12	3	3	0	11	6	1	1	4	6	11
Southend United	8	2	0	2	10	8	1	1	2	3	9
Stalybridge Celtic	2	1	0	0	3	0	0	0	1	0	2
Stoke	6	2	0	1	9	7	1	0	2	3	8
Swindon Town	12	1	4	1	7	8	0	1	5	5	16
Swansea Town	2	0	1	0	0	0	0	0	0	0	1
Ton Pentre	2	1	0	0	7	2	0	0	1	1	2
Watford	12	6	0	0	20	6	2	1	3	9	17
West Ham United	12	4	1	1	16	8	2	1	3	6	8

Coventry City Testimonial Matches At Highfield Road

BEFORE 1939, testimonial matches were almost unheard of and it was standard procedure for players with five or ten years' service with Football League clubs to be granted benefits of up to £500 or nominate a League match of their choice from which a certain amount of the receipts were allocated to their benefit fund. Joe Whitehouse and Billy Smith both had benefit friendlies in the early 1900s. Since World War Two it has been common practice to arrange testimonials for players with at least ten years' service. As well as a prestigious football match, this normally includes social events such as dances, celebrity dinners and cricket tournaments. Additionally, benefit matches can be arranged for players whose careers have been terminated by illness or injury or the dependents of long-serving club officials.

1946
George Taylor
Sep 30 v Notts County (h) 4-1
Roberts, Simpson, Gardner, Bett
Wood; Barratt, Elliott, Snape, Cox, R.Mason, Simpson, Bett, Roberts, Gardner, Ashall.
Notts County: Wright; Corkhill, Southwell, Hitchin, Smallwood, Ellma, Freeman, Squires, Whittaker, Richards, Hill.

1947
Dick Bayliss
May 8 v Combined Birmingham XI (h) 0-2
Wood; Dobbs, O'Brien, Barratt, R.Mason, Dearson, Aldecoa, Crawley, Roberts, Murphy, Setchell.
Birmingham XI: Wheeler; Jennings, Shaw, Edwards, Duckworth, Lowe, Houghton, McIntosh, Dougall, Dorsett, Smith.
Att: 8,777

1953
George Mason
Apr 30 v All Star XI (h) 5-8
Stamps 3, Johnson, Thomas
Matthews; Timmins, R.Mason, Harvey, McDonnell, Jamieson, Nutt, Stamps (Derby County), Thomas, Chisholm (Cardiff City), Johnson.
All Star XI: Merrick (Birmingham City); Mozley (Derby County), Green (Birmingham City), Boyd (Birmingham City), Lever (Leicester City), Ryan (West Brom A), Hancocks (Wolves), Murphy (Birmingham City), Allen (West Brom A), Rowley (Leicester City), Mullen (Wolves).
Att: 11,143

1958
Peter Hill
Oct 13 v Derby County (h) 0-1
Wood(Spratt); Kirk(Walters), Harvey, Nicholas, Curtis, Kearns, Satchwell(P.Hill), Straw, R.Hill, P.Hill(B.Hill), Boxley.
Derby County: Oxford; Barrowcliffe, Davies, Parry, Young, Upton, Powell, Swallow, Darwin(Newbury), Hunt, Cargill. *Scorer: Swallow.*
Att: 5,748

1966
George Curtis & Mick Kearns
May 10 v Northampton Town (h) 2-2
Denton, Pointer
Glazier; Kearns, Hill, Bruck, Curtis, Farmer, Denton (Roberts), Machin, Gould, Pointer, Clements.
Northampton Town: Harvey; Everitt, Cockcroft, Kurila, Branston, Kiernan, Best, Martin, Hudson, Hall, Walden. *Scorers: Best, Hall.*
Att: 13,576

1967
George Curtis & Mick Kearns
May 9 v Liverpool (h) 2-1
Machin, Rees
Glazier; Kearns, Bruck, Lewis, Curtis, Clements, Key, Machin, Tudor, Gibson, Rees.
Liverpool: Lawrence; Byrne, Hughes, Strong, Yeats, Milne, Callaghan, Hunt, St John(Wall), Wilson, Thompson. *Scorer: Hunt.*
Att: 25,040

1969
Brian Hill
Apr 28 v Derby County (h) 1-1
Martin
Glazier(McManus); Coop, Hill, Carr, Curtis, Blockley, Hannigan(Baker), Hateley, Martin, Hunt, Paddon.
Derby County: Green; Webster, Robson, Durban, McFarland, Jones, McGovern, Carlin, O'Hare, Hector, Hinton. *Scorer: Hector.*
Att: 10,190

1972
Dietmar Bruck
Apr 26 v Charlton Athletic (h) 3-4
Graham, Mortimer, Machin (pen)
Glazier; Smith, Cattlin, Mortimer, Blockley, Parker, McGuire, Green, Machin, Graham, Hunt. Subs: Philpotts, D.Murphy.
Charlton Athletic: Dunn; Bruck, Warman, Went, Shipperley, O'Kane, Bond, Treacy, Plumb, Rogers, Peacock. Sub: Flanagan. *Scorers: Peacock, Bruck (pen), Flanagan, Treacy.*
Att: 4,381

1973
Ernie Machin
May 1 v Aston Villa (h) 1-1
Machin
Ramsbottom; Coop, Holmes, Mortimer, Smith, Dugdale, Alderson, Green, Stein, Machin(McGuire), Hutchison.
Aston Villa: Cumbes(Hughes); Turnbull(N.Rioch), Robson, Brown, Nicholl, Ross, Graydon, Little, Evans, Vowden, Hamilton. *Scorer: Vowden.*
Att: 4,181

1974
Bill Glazier
Nov 26 v England 1966 World Cup XI (h) 6-6
Hutchison, Cross, Green, Ferguson, Glazier 2
Glazier; Smith, Cattlin, Mortimer, Craven, Hindley, Green, Carr, Stein, Cross, Hutchison. Subs: Cartwright, Dugdale, Ferguson, Holmes, Ramsbottom.
England XI: Banks; Cohen, Wilson, Armfield, J.Charlton, Moore, Ball, Hunt, Eastham, Hurst, Peters. Subs: R.Gould, D.Clements, G.Curtis, M.McGuire. *Scorers: Peters 2, McGuire 2, Ball, Gould*
Att: 15,205

1977
Mick Coop
Nov 22 Coventry City Great Britain XI 7 Scottish International XI 5
Sealey; Coop, Holmes (Tottenham Hotspur), Yorath, McFarland (Derby County), Todd (Derby County), Oakey, Powell, Ferguson, Cross (West Brom A), Channon (Manchester City). Sub: Milne. *Scorers: Channon 2, Cross 3, Powell, Yorath.*
Scottish XI: Blyth; McDonald, Donachie (Manchester City), Rioch (Derby County), Holton, Buchan (Manchester United), Hutchison, Carr (Wolves), Stein (Rangers), Wallace, W.Johnston (West Brom A). Sub: Wylie. *Scorers: Wallace 2, W.Johnston, McDonald, Stein*
Att: 7,883

1984
Brian Roberts
Sep 10 Coventry City Present 4 Coventry City Past 4
City Present: Ogrizovic; Gynn, Hormantschuk, Jol, Kilcline, Pearce, Bennett, Platnauer, Spring, Gibson, K.Thompson. Subs: Dalton, J.McDonald, McGrath, Butterworth. *Scorers: Spring 2, Singleton, Jol.*
City Past: Suckling; Coop, Roberts, Gooding, Holton, Gillespie, Whitton, Carr, G.Thompson, Hutchison, E.Hunt. Sub: R.Gould. *Scorers: E.Hunt, Roberts (pen), Carr, Gillespie.*
Att: 3,000

1989
Jake Findlay
Aug 12 v West Bromwich Albion (h) 0-1
Ogrizovic; Billing, Dobson(Downs), Emerson, Kilcline, Peake, Gynn(Clark), Speedie, Bannister (Livingstone), MacDonald(McGuire), K.Thompson.
West Bromwich Albion: Bradshaw; Bradley(Thomas), Parkin, Talbot, Whyte, North, Ford(Rogers), Goodman, West, Robson, Anderson. *Scorer: West*
Att: 3,596

Coventry City Internationals

Many players won additional caps with other clubs but the totals given here are solely for appearances made while Coventry City players. Before 1924 there was only one 'Ireland' team. In that year the Republic of Ireland began separate matches and that position is reflected here. The date given for each match is the actual year in which it was played.

ENGLAND

Matthews R.D. (5 apps) 1956 v Scotland, Brazil, Sweden, West Germany, Northern Ireland.
Regis C. (1 app) 1987 v Turkey (sub).
Thomas D.J. (2 apps) 1983 v Australia (1 & 1 sub).

SCOTLAND

Blyth J.A. (2 apps) 1978 v Bulgaria, Wales.
Carr W.M. (6 apps) 1970 v Northern Ireland, Wales, England, Denmark; 1972 v Peru, Denmark.
Gallacher K. (1 app) 1991 v Sanmarino.
Hutchison T. (17 apps) 1973 v Czechoslovakia (2), West Germany; 1974 v West Germany, Northern Ireland, Wales, Belgium (sub), Norway, Zaïre (sub), Yugoslavia (sub), East Germany, Spain; 1975 v Spain, Portugal, England (sub), Romania (sub), Denmark.
Speedie D.R. (5 apps) 1988 v Yugoslavia (sub), Italy (sub); 1989 v Cyprus (1 & 1 sub), Chile.
Stein C. (4 apps) 1973 v England (sub), Wales (sub), Northern Ireland, England (sub).
Wallace I.A. (3 apps, 1 goal) v Bulgaria (sub), Portugal (sub); 1979 v Wales.

WALES

Allen B.W. (2 apps) 1950 v Scotland, England.
Cartwright L. (5 apps) 1974 v England (sub), Scotland, Northern Ireland; 1976 v Scotland (sub), West Germany (sub).
Evans R.O. (5 apps) 1911 v Ireland, England; 1912 v Scotland, England, Ireland.
Jones L.J. (5 apps) 1935 v Northern Ireland, Scotland; 1936 v England, Scotland; 1937 v Northern Ireland.
Lowrie G. (3 apps, 2 goals) 1947 v England, Scotland; 1948 v Northern Ireland.
Nardiello D. (2 apps) 1977 v Czechoslovakia, West Germany (sub).
Phillips D.O. (9 apps, 1 goal) 1987 v Finland, Czechoslovakia (2), Denmark (2); 1988 v Yugoslavia, Sweden; 1989 v Sweden, West Germany.
Rees R.R. (21 apps, 2 goals) 1964 v Scotland, Denmark, England, Greece; 1965 v Northern Ireland, Italy, Greece, USSR, England, USSR, Scotland, Denmark; 1966 v Northern Ireland, Brazil (2), Chile, England; 1967 v Northern Ireland, England, Scotland; 1968 v Northern Ireland.
Yorath T.C. (20 apps) 1976 v West Germany, Scotland; 1977 v Czechoslovakia (2), Scotland (2), England, Northern Ireland, Kuwait (2), West Germany; 1978 v Iran, England, Scotland, Northern Ireland, Turkey; 1979 v West Germany, Scotland, England, Northern Ireland.

NORTHERN IRELAND (and Ireland before 1924)

Barr H.H. (2 apps, 1 goal) 1962 v Poland, England.
Brown J. (4 apps) 1936 v England; 1937 v Wales, Scotland; 1938 v Wales.
Clements D. (21 apps, 1 goal) 1965 v Holland, Wales; 1966 v Mexico, Scotland; 1967 v Wales, Scotland, England; 1968 v Turkey (2); 1969 v Wales, USSR (2); 1970 v Scotland, England, Wales, Spain; 1971 v Cyprus, England, Scotland, Wales.
Humphries W.M. (10 apps, 1 goal) 1962 v Holland, Poland, England, Scotland; 1963 v Scotland, Wales, Spain (2), England; 1964 v Scotland.
Lockhart N.H. (3 apps) 1950 v Wales; 1951 v Wales, 1952 v Wales.

REPUBLIC OF IRELAND

Brown J. (2 apps) 1937 v Switzerland, France.
Daly G.A. (15 apps, 5 goals) 1980 v Holland, Belgium, Cyprus; 1981 v Wales, Belgium, Czechoslovakia, Poland (sub); 1982 v Algeria, Chile, Brazil, Trinidad & Tobago, Holland; 1983 v Spain (sub), Malta; 1984 v Israel (sub).
Grimes A.A. (2 apps) 1984 v Israel, Poland.
Holmes J. (17 apps) 1971 v Austria (sub); 1972 v France; 1973 v USSR, Poland (2), France, Norway; 1974 v Brazil, USSR; 1975 v Switzerland, Turkey; 1976 v Norway, Poland, England, Turkey, France; 1977 v Spain.

UNITED STATES

Baker G.A. (4 apps, 2 goals) 1968 v Canada (2), Bermuda; 1969 v Haiti.

'B' Internationals

ENGLAND

Borrows B. (1 app) 1990 v Czechoslovakia.
Matthews R.D. (3 apps) 1955 v West Germany; 1956 v Scotland, Switzerland.

SCOTLAND

Gallacher K. (2 apps) 1990 v Yugoslavia, East Germany.

Wartime Internationals

ENGLAND

Mason G.W. (2 apps) 1942 v Scotland, Wales.

WALES

Edwards G. (1 app, 1 goal) 1945 v England.
Lowrie G. (8 apps, 3 goals) 1942 v England (2); 1943 v England (2); 1944 v England (2); 1945 v England, Scotland.

Under-23 Internationals

ENGLAND

Blockley J.P. (6 apps) 1971 v Switzerland; 1972 v Wales, Scotland, East Germany, Poland, USSR.

Cattlin C. (2 apps) 1968 v Wales, Holland.
Glazier W.J. (3 apps) 1964 v Romania; 1965 Scotland, Czechoslovakia.
Matthews R.D. (4 apps) 1955 v Italy, Scotland, Denmark; 1956 v Scotland.
Mortimer D.G. (6 apps, 2 goals) 1972 v Wales; 1973 v Holland (2), Scotland, Czechoslovakia (2).

SCOTLAND

Alderson B.R. (1 app) 1973 v England.
Carr W.M. (3 apps) 1969 v France; 1971 v Wales, 1972 v England.

WALES

Cartwright L. (4 apps) 1974 v Scotland; 1975 v England, Scotland; 1976 v Scotland.
Rees R.R. (7 apps, 3 goals) 1962 v Scotland; 1963 v Northern Ireland, England, Scotland; 1964 v Northern Ireland, England; 1965 v Northern Ireland.

NORTHERN IRELAND

Clements D. (3 apps, 1 goal) 1965 v Wales; 1967 v Wales*; 1968 v Wales.
*Game abandoned after 73 minutes.

REPUBLIC OF IRELAND

Holmes J. (1 app)
Morrissey P.J. (1 app)

Under-21 Internationals

ENGLAND

Butterworth I.S. (2 apps) 1984 v Turkey; 1985 v Romania.
Dyson P.I. (4 apps) 1980 v Norway, Romania, Switzerland; 1981 v Republic of Ireland.
Hateley M.W. (5 apps, 2 goals) 1982 v Poland, Scotland, Greece; 1983 v Greece, Hungary.
McGrath L.A. (1 app) 1986 v Denmark.
Pickering N. (2 apps, 1 goal) 1986 v Denmark, Italy.
Rodger G. (4 apps) 1987 v USSR, France, Portugal, West Germany.
Sedgley S.P. (10 apps, 1 goal) 1987 v USSR, France (sub), Portugal; 1988 v France, Denmark (sub), Sweden; 1989 v Greece, Albania (2), Poland.
Smith D. (8 apps) 1988 v Mexico, USSR (sub), Morocco, Denmark, Sweden; 1989 v Albainia (2), Poland.
Suckling P.J. (1 app) 1986 v Denmark.
Thomas D.J. (5 apps) 1981 v Republic of Ireland; 1982 v West Germany (2); 1983 v Greece, Hungary.
Thompson G.L. (6 apps, 3 goals) 1981 v Romania, Switzerland, Hungary (2), Norway; 1982 v Scotland.

SCOTLAND

Blair A. (5 apps, 2 goals) 1980 v England, Sweden; 1981 v Sweden, Denmark; 1982 v Italy.
Gillespie G.T. (8 apps, 1 goal) 1978 v USA; 1980 v England, Denmark; 1981 v Sweden, Denmark; 1982 v Italy (2), England.
Wallace I.A. (1 app, 2 goals) 1977 v Switzerland.

WALES

Nardiello D. (1 app) 1978 v Scotland.

Youth Internationals

ENGLAND

George Curtis 1956-58	Alan Green 1971-72*	Lloyd McGrath 1982-83
Keith McCarthy 1957-58	Trevor Smith 1972-73	Keith Thompson 1983-84
John Burckitt 1964-65	Paul Cahill 1973-74	Perry Suckling 1982-84
Trevor Gould 1969-70	David Barnes 1979-80*	Darren Anderson 1983-84
Bobby Parker 1970-71*	Mark Hateley 1979-80*	Tony English 1983-84
Mick McGuire 1970-71*	Tom English 1970-80*	Dean Kiely 1987-88
Alan Dugdale 1970-71*	Martin Singleton 1981-82	David Titterton 1989-90
	Alan Boorn 1970-71 (amateur)	

* Members of the successful England team in the European Youth Tournament.

SCOTLAND

Willie Carr 1967-68
John Hendrie 1981-82

WALES

Les Cartwright 1969-70
Colin Randell 1969-71

REPUBLIC OF IRELAND

Pat Morrisey 1964-65, Jimmy Holmes 1969-70, Donal Murphy 1971, Tommy O'Brien 1973-74.

Football League

Blockley J.P. (1 app) 1972 v Scottish League.
Glazier W.J. (1 app) 1970 v Scottish League (sub).
Matthews R.D. (2 apps) 1955 v Scottish League; 1956 v League of Ireland.
Ogrizovic S. (1 app) 1987 v Rest of World (sub).

Inter-League

In the past greater importance was placed on the annual inter-League matches. In particular the Football League teams were often treated as England Trials and many promising players were tried out in these matches ahead of the award of any full caps. George Ashall, then of Wolves, played for the Football League in October 1937, was selected by England for the home match against Czechoslovakia but injured his ankle the Saturday prior to the match and lost his one and only chance.

The following Coventry City players played in inter-League matches prior to or after playing for the club.

FOOTBALL LEAGUE

G.H.Ashall (1), J.P.Blockley (1), A.F.Campbell (5), R.Craythorne (1), A.Knapp (1), R.D.Latchford (1), R.Pointer (1), D.Shea (1).

SCOTTISH LEAGUE

J.A.Brogan (1), N.Martin (1), J.M.Melrose (1), I.St John (4), C.Stein (3).

IRISH LEAGUE

H.H.Barr (4), J.Brown (2), H.R.Buckle (4), J.Enright (2), W.S.Humphries (10).

LEAGUE OF IRELAND

J.Matthews (2), P.Thomas (10).

SOUTHERN LEAGUE

E.T.Hanney (1), E.H.Hendren (1), D.Shea (3).

The following are Coventry City managers or coaches who made international appearances:

England

Harry Storer (2) 1924-28
Joe Mercer (5) 1939
Gordon Milne (14) 1963-64
Terry Paine (19) 1963-66
Terry Butcher (77) 1980-90
Mick Mills (42) 1973-74
Wilf Copping (20) 1933-39
Dick Hill (1) 1926
Tony Waiters (5) 1964-65
Jesse Pennington (25) 1907-20

Scotland

J.T.Robertson (16) 1898-1905
Alexander Bell (1) 1912
Neil Dougall (1) 1947

Northern Ireland

Tom Casey (12) 1954-59

Republic of Ireland

Pat Saward (18) 1954-63
Noel Cantwell (36) 1954-67

Jesse Pennington made a number of appearances in 1918-19 and Neil Dougall played between 1944 and 1946 (he was the son of 1920s City favourite Jimmy Dougall).

Other Representative Honours

In October 1960 George Curtis played for the RAF against an FA XI in Manchester.

~ ~

Tony Hateley toured the Far East and USA with an FA party in 1969.

~ ~

In 1971 Dennis Mortimer toured Australia with an FA party.

~ ~

Colin Stein played for The Three against The Six in January 1973 at Wembley in the game to commemorate the UK joining the EEC. He scored a goal in the 2-0 victory in front of 36,500 spectators.

~ ~

In September 1980 Jim Holton played for a Pick of the North American Soccer League in a game against the NASL champions New York Cosmos.

~ ~

Cyrille Regis played for an England XI in the game commemorating the reopening of Valley Parade in December 1986.

~ ~

Steve Hunt played for an England XI in a Testimonial match for the late Bill Taylor at Maine Road in February 1982.

~ ~

Ken Chisholm played once for Scotland in a wartime international prior to joining Coventry City, he was playing for Queen's Park at the time.

Harry Buckle, Eli Bradley and Harry Parkes appeared for the Southern League in representative matches. Buckle against the Football League at Stamford Bridge in April 1910 and Bradley on three occasions in September and October 1911 against the Irish League at Windsor Park, the Football League at the Victoria Ground and the Scottish League at Shawfield Park. Parkes played against the Irish League in Dublin in October 1913 and March 1914.

~ ~

Ernie Boston and Patsy Hendren played for the South East Counties League against the Northern League at Newcastle in February 1911.

~ ~

W.Jacques and Ernie Boston played for Birmingham Juniors against Scotland Juniors at Highfield Road in March 1912 in front of 1,500 spectators.

~ ~

F.Marr played for Birmingham Juniors against Scotland Juniors at Firhill Park in April 1913.

~ ~

Jack Snape appeared for England Juniors against Scotland Juniors at Molineux in October 1937. (This was considered to be the forerunner to the England Under-23 team.)

~ ~

Reg Matthews appeared for Young England in the 5-0 defeat by England at Stamford Bridge on 5 May 1955. This was the Under-23 team (no caps were awarded).

~ ~

G.Dexter and H.Dobson played for Birmingham Juniors against Scotland Juniors at Highfield Road in April 1914.

~ ~

Alan Boorn played for the England Amateur Youth XI in 1970-71.

Coventry City Awards

IN 1958, Derek Henderson, who wrote under the pen name of 'Nemo' in the *Coventry Evening Telegraph* started to make an annual award to the Coventry City player who had contributed most to the club's success in the year.

In the 1971-2 season, the Supporters' Club started an award based on the fans' votes at the end of the season, the successful player winning an impressive trophy.

In 1977 the recently-formed Coventry City London Supporters' Club started an award based on votes cast by members for the Man of the Match each week throughout the season.

Coventry Evening Telegraph Player of the Year

1958 Brian Nicholas
1959 Arthur Lightening
1960 George Curtis
1961 George Curtis
1962 Willie Humphries
1963 Brian Hill
1964 Ronnie Rees
1965 Ronnie Farmer
1966 Bill Glazier
1967 Ernie Machin
1968 Maurice Setters
1969 Mick Coop

Coventry City Supporters' Club Player of the Season

1971-72 Ernie Hunt
1972-73 Willie Carr
1973-74 Bill Glazier
1974-75 Graham Oakey
1975-76 Tommy Hutchison
1976-77 Jim Blyth
1977-78 Ian Wallace
1978-79 Bobby McDonald
1979-80 Gary Gillespie
1980-81 Danny Thomas
1981-82 Danny Thomas
1982-83 Gary Gillespie
1983-84 Nicky Platnauer
1984-85 Terry Gibson
1985-86 Trevor Peake
1986-87 Steve Ogrizovic
1987-88 David Speedie
1988-89 David Speedie
1989-90 Brian Borrows
1990-91 Kevin Gallacher

London Supporters' Club Player of the Season

1977-78 Tommy Hutchison
1978-79 Tommy Hutchison
1979-80 Gary Gillespie
1980-81 Steve Hunt
1981-82 Danny Thomas
1982-83 Garry Gillespie
1983-84 Gerry Daly
1984-85 Stuart Pearce
1985-86 Trevor Peake
1986-87 Cyrille Regis
1987-88 David Speedie
1988-89 David Speedie
1989-90 Brian Borrows
1990-91 Kevin Gallacher

Amongst the other awards won by players or managers of the club are the following:
George Curtis, 1963-64 Midland Footballler of the Year
Noel Cantwell, February 1970 Bells First Division Manager of the Month
Joe Mercer, November 1972 Bells Manager of the Month
Gordon Milne, September 1973 Bells First Division Manager of the Month
Tommy Hutchison, 1973-4 Rothmans Golden Boot Award
Danny Thomas, October 1981 Midland Player of the Month
Danny Thomas, 1982-3 PFA's Division One Select Team
Terry Gibson, 1984-5 Midland Footballer of the Year
John Sillett, April 1987 Bells Manager of the Month.

Players Sent Off 1967-1991

1967-68
Dietmar Bruck v Manchester City (a)

1968-69
Maurice Setters v Liverpool (h)

1970-71
Ernie Machin v Newcastle (a)

1971-72
Chris Cattlin v Everton (a)
Ernie Hunt v Liverpool (h)

1973-74
Jimmy Holmes v Manchester City (h) League Cup

1974-75
Chris Cattlin v West Ham (a)

1975-76
Donal Murphy v Birmingham City (h)

1976-77
Larry Lloyd v Manchester United (h)
Alan Dugdale v Aston Villa (h)

1979-80
Ray Gooding v Derby County (a)
Ian Wallace v Crystal Palace (h)

1980-81
Ray Gooding v Birmingham City (a)

1981-82
Steve Jacobs v Everton (a)
Garry Thompson v Aston Villa (a)

1982-83
Danny Thomas v Ipswich (a)
Garry Thompson v Norwich City (a) FA Cup
Steve Jacobs v Brighton (a)

1983-84
Terry Gibson v Grimsby (h) Milk Cup
Steve Hunt v Southampton (h)

1984-85
Terry Gibson v West Bromwich Albion (a)
Biran Kilcline v Manchester United (h)

1987-88
Nick Pickering v Manchester United (h)

1988-89
Trevor Peake v Queen's Park Rangers (a)
Garry Bannister v Southampton (a)

1989-90
Lloyd McGrath v Charlton Athletic (a)
Peter Billing v Wimbledon (h) Zenith Data Systems Cup
David Speedie v Sunderland (a) Littlewoods Cup

1990-91
David Speedie v Crystal Palace (a)

Coventry's Footballing Cricketers

UNTIL the 1960s it was not uncommon for professional footballers to play first-class cricket during the summer months. The most famous Coventry City cricketer-footballer was Elias 'Patsy' Hendren.

Patsy Hendren played for Queen's Park Rangers and Brentford before joining Manchester City. He appeared in their first team at the age of 18 and his future at Hyde Road seemed assured but the Manchester club offered him only £3 10s a week, £1 less than the maximum wage at that time, and Hendren decided to give up football.

However, his older brother, Dennis, knew Harry Buckle, the Coventry City player-manager, and Hendren was persuaded to move to Highfield Road on a month's trial. He scored two goals in a 3-0 win at Watford in October 1909 and was duly signed on. Hendren never really lived up to his early promise. Although he was a regular in 1909-10, he sustained a knee injury at the beginning of the following campaign and his first-team appearances were restricted before he moved to Brentford in 1911.

In an interview published in the *Coventry Herald* in 1938, Hendren recalled with affection his days at Highfield Road. He remembered in particular the excitement of the FA Cup run in 1909-10, in which he played a big part. Reminiscing about Charlie Tickle, he thought that a now hackneyed football story originated with him. It went like this: As Charlie Tickle was going through, a spectator shouted, 'Shoot Tickle'. Replied another spectator, 'Why just shoot Tickle? Shoot the lot'.

Hendren's first love, however, was cricket. He was largely a self-taught cricketer and did not establish himself at county level with Middlesex until 1919. But for the next 18 years he was a dominant figure in the summer game, scoring over 57,000 first-class runs, including 17 centuries, and over 3,500 runs in Test Matches including seven centuries. Upon his retirement in 1937, he took up cricket coaching. He died in 1962.

Other county cricketers who have been associated with Coventry City include Harry Storer and Charlie Elliott (both Derbyshire), Freddie Gardner (Warwickshire), Arthur Jepson (Notts), Jack Lee (Leicestershire) and Don Bennett (Middlesex).

Patsy Hendren in Coventry City colours.

Coventry City Career Records
1908-1915

†Also played in the Birmingham League. *Also played in the English League (Midland Section).
‡Also played in the Football League Second Division.

Name	Birthplace	Year	Pos	From	Year	To	Year	S League Apps	S League Gls	FA Cup Apps	FA Cup Gls
Alden W.F.	Mardy	c.1889	W	Merthyr T	1911	Llanelly	1912	8	0	0	0
Alderson R.G.	Wellbourne	c.1891	OR	Wellbourne	1914		1915	15	3	0	0
Allan J.‡	Carlisle	c.1890	CF	Rochdale	1914	Walsall	1920	24	21	1	0
Archer A.	Atherstone		GK	Atherstone	1908		1909	14	0	3	0
Arnold T.†	Coventry		F	W Arsenal	1907		1911	49	15	5	3
Barnacle R.	Coventry		FB	Foleshill St Grge	1908	Newport Co	1915	129	3	8	0
Bennett S.			LH	Lord St Jun	1914		1915	2	0	0	0
Bivins A.†	Coventry		FB	Foleshill St Grge	1907	Worcester	1909	4	0	0	0
Blake S.*	Whitley Bay		GK	Newcastle U	1914	Retired	1919	19	0	1	0
Boston E.	Coventry	1888	CH	Lord St Jun	1908		1914	54	3	0	0
Bourne G.			HB	Foleshill Gt Heath	1909		1910	1	0	0	0
Bradley E.J.	Dudley	1882	CH	Luton T	1909	Hearts	1912	104	19	12	1
Brown I.	Derby	1888	F	Tottenham H	1911	Reading	1913	56	19	0	0
Buckle H.R.	Belfast	1882	OL	Bristol R	1908	Belfast Celtic	1911	112	43	13	3
Bunn T.	Middlesbrough		IL	Wolves	1913		1914	1	0	0	0
Camwell A.	Coventry		CF	Clifton Vics	1908	Rugby T	1909	1	0	0	0
Casey T.J.	Oswestry	c.1894	OL	Oswestry U	1914		1915	3	0	0	0
Chaplin A.†	Foleshill	1879	HB	W Arsenal	1905	Retired	1912	127	1	14	1
Craig R.*	Newcastle		HB/F	Huddersfield T	1913	Nuneaton T	1919	25	1	0	0
Crutchley J.C.			RH		1914	Halesowen	1915	11	0	0	0
Davies C.	Bangor		OL	Bangor Univ	1910		1912	2	0	0	0
Davison G.	Newcastle	c.1892	CF	Blyth Spartans	1913	Bristol R	1914	38	18	1	1
Dexter G	Hucknall	c.1896	FB	Bestwood Col	1912	Preston NE	1914	11	0	0	0
Dobson H.	Newcastle	c.1891	IR	North Shields	1913	Newport Co	1917	33	15	2	0
Dodd S.			CH	Stockport Co	1908		1909	11	0	3	0
Doran J.	Dublin	c.1894	IR	Newcastle Empire	1914	Norwich C	1915	1	2	0	0
Dougherty J.	New Brighton	1878	HB	Birmingham	1908		1909	14	0	3	0
Drennan T.A.	Long Eaton	1885	FB	Northampton	1908		1909	16	1	3	0
Enright J.	Dublin	c.1890	IL	Newport Co	1914		1915	21	8	1	1
Evans R.O.	Wrexham	1881	GK	Croydon Com	1909	Birmingham	1913	126	0	13	0
Farrant S.	Bristol	1885	F	Luton T	1908	Aberdare A	1909	14	3	0	0
Feebury A.	Hucknall	1891	HB/F	Nottingham F	1911	Crystal Palace	1914	66	5	3	0
Fisher F.	Wednesbury		RB	Wednesbury OA	1910	Wednesbury OA	1911	1	0	0	0
Fisher W.			IL	Bradford	1908	Merthyr T	1909	6	0	3	1
Fulljames W.*	Cleethorpes	1890	RH	Grimsby T	1914	Nuneaton T	1919	9	0	0	0
Gilbert H.†	Coventry	1885	CH	Herberts A	1905		1909	11	0	0	0
Gordon J.	Arbroath	c.1887	FB	Leith A	1910	Leith A	1911	11	0	0	0
Gretton H.	Basford	c.1894	OR	Bulwell WH St	1912	Grantham T	1914	19	0	0	0
Hall F.			OR	Foleshill A	1913		1914	1	0	0	0
Hanson W.	Rushall	1887	LB	Aston Villa	1909	Bradford	1910	48	0	5	0
Harkins J.	Musselbrough		LH	Darlington	1914	Killed WW1	1915	18	1	1	0
Harris G.A.	Halesowen	1878	HB/F	WBA	1912	Retired	1915	59	2	2	0
Hendren E.	London	1889	IL	Manchester C	1909	Brentford	1911	27	11	6	3
Hickleton W.R.	Newcastle	c.1884	RH	Northampton	1909	Brentford	1911	54	0	9	0
Hickman J.		c.1886	CF		1908		1909	3	2	0	0
Hill W.	Birmingham		F	BSA	1910		1911	3	0	0	0
Hodges W.			HB	Croydon Com	1908	Hastings&St L	1909	2	0	0	0
Holmes A.	Mansfield		F	Mansfield Mechs	1911	Portsmouth	1915	101	17	6	0
Hopkins E.			F	New Brompton	1908		1909	2	0	0	0
Jackson S.	Smethwick		LB	Hay Mills	1911	Killed WW1	1914	13	0	0	0
Jacques W.	Northfleet	1888	GK	Northfleet	1911	Tottenham H	1914	57	0	1	0
Jarvis J.	Kenilworth	c.1888	CF	Kenilworth T	1912		1914	1	0	0	0
Johnson S.	Colne	c.1885	HB	Exeter C	1909	Leeds C	1911	47	0	5	0
Jones F.	Bestwood	c.1889	IL	Notts Co	1911	Notts Co	1912	37	21	2	1
				Notts Co	1913	Southampton	1914	19	4	0	0
				Southampton	1919	Pembroke Dock	1920	0	0	0	0
Jones H.†			HB	Dudley T	1904		1909	6	0	0	0
Juggins E.†	Darlaston		FB	Wolves	1907	Retired	1914	68	2	4	0

Name	Birthplace	Year	Pos	From	Year	To	Year	S League Apps	S League Gls	FA Cup Apps	FA Cup Gls
Kimberley W.	Birmingham		HB/F	Aston Villa	1912	Walsall	1914	21	1	2	0
Lawrance W.	Bladon	*c.*1893	HB/FB	Sunderland RR	1913	Sunderland RR	1914	4	0	0	0
Lee T.	Bolton	*c.*1885	OL	West Ham U	1909	Colne	1911	6	0	0	0
Legge S.G.	Willenhall	1881	IL	West Brom A	1909		1911	9	1	0	0
Lowes T.‡	Newcastle	*c.*1891	IR	Newcastle U	1914	Nuneaton T	1920	7	2	0	0
McCulloch A.	Edinburgh	*c.*1885	F	Swindon T	1912	Raith R	1913	23	4	2	0
Marr A.	Newcastle	*c.*1892	OR	Ashington	1912	Wolves	1913	1	0	0	0
Marvin T.			HB	Derby Co	1908		1909	32	1	0	0
Meunier J.	Manchester	1885	LB	Lincoln C	1914	Hyde U	1915	10	0	1	0
Mitchell J.	Coventry		F	Lord St Jun	1912		1914	22	3	2	0
Morris T.H.	Grimsby	1884	CH	Scunthorpe & Lindsey U	1914	Killed WW1	1915	18	2	1	0
Moult J.†			GK	Aston Villa	1907	Walsall	1909	26	0	0	0
Newbigging A.	Lanark	1880	GK	Reading	1909		1910	8	0	0	0
Parkes H.A.	Halesowen	1888	OR/RH	West Brom A	1908	West Brom A	1914	161	35	9	3
Parton J.	Oxford		FB	Dudley	1911	Halifax T	1914	24	0	1	0
Poole H.	Hucknall	*c.*1895	F	Nottingham F	1912	Sutton T	1913	2	0	0	0
Powell H.	Nottingham	1887	F	New Brompton	1909	Birmingham	1911	26	13	1	0
Roberts R.E.‡	Rhyl	*c.*1890	RB	Leeds C	1914	Rhyl U	1920	20	1	1	0
Robinson A.C.†	Coventry	1878	GK	Chelsea	1910	Retired	1915	6	0	1	0
Rogers E.	Wiltshire		GK	Sunbeam	1913		1914	2	0	0	0
Saul P.	Rotherham	1881	FB	Liverpool	1909	Rotherham Co	1911	59	0	7	0
Shields T.	Co Durham	*c.*1895	RB	Choppington	1914	Fulham	1915	5	0	0	0
Smith J.	Tollcross		F	Millwall	1912	Millwall	1913	17	4	0	0
Smith W.†	Brierley Hill	1882	F	Birmingham	1909		1912	63	24	10	2
					1913	Retired	1914	15	0	0	0
Sparkes W.	Coventry		FB	R Warks Reg	1908	R Warks Reg	1909	1	0	0	0
Styles L.	Coventry		HB	St Michaels	1912		1914	3	0	0	0
Talbot W.	Coventry		HB	Foleshill Gt Heath	1908		1909	1	0	0	0
Thomson J.H.	Shetland	1884	RB	Portsmouth	1911	Bury	1913	69	0	4	0
Tickle C.H.	Birmingham	1884	OR	Birmingham	1908	Retired	1911	112	18	13	2
Tosswill J.	Eastbourne	1890	HB/F	Southend U	1913	Killed WW1	1914	17	1	0	0
Turnbull F.	Wallsend	1888	F	Ashington U	1911	Southampton	1913	38	12	2	1
Turner F.	Oldbury	1882	CF	Bristol R	1908	Dudley	1910	32	8	0	0
Turner R.	Leicester	1885	OL	Darlington	1914		1915	13	1	1	0
Wakinshaw J.	Cullercoats	*c.*1892	IL	Wallsend	1912		1913	2	0	0	0
Warren G.†	Hinckley		F	Nuneaton T	1907	Stockport Co	1911	73	31	7	3
Welch H.	Coventry		IL	Foleshill Gt Heath	1910	Retired	1915	44	9	6	0
Wilson W.	Inverness	1886	LB	Aston Villa	1909	Inverness	1910	4	0	0	0
Yates W.	Birmingham	1884	HB/FB	Portsmouth	1911	Retired	1914	106	1	5	0

Coventry City Career Records 1919-1991

Below are the career records of all Coventry City players in major competitions since the club's election to the Football League in 1919. Some players appeared in the Southern League prior to this date, but only post-1919 figures are included. The Europe section includes Full Members' Cup.

Player	Played	From	To	League App	League Gls	FA Cup App	FA Cup Gls	FL Cup App	FL Cup Gls	Europe App	Europe Gls	TOTAL App	TOTAL Gls
Adams M.R.	1983-87	Gillingham	Leeds U	85/5	9	7	0	9	1	2	0	103/5	10
Aldecoa E.G.	1945-47	Wolves	A Bilbao	29	0	2	0	0	0	0	0	31	0
Alderson B.R.	1970-75	Lochee Harps	Leicester C	116/11	29	14	5	11	7	1	0	142/11	41
Alderton J.H.	1947-53	Wolves	Darlaston	62	0	2	1	0	0	0	0	64	1
Allan J.	1919-20	Rochdale	Walsall	5	0	0	0	0	0	0	0	5	0
Allardyce S.	1983-84	Tampa Bay	Huddersfield T	28	1	1	0	3	0	0	0	32	1
Allen B.W.	1949-53	Reading	Hereford U	88	26	4	1	0	0	0	0	92	27
Allen R.	1959-63	Wolves		25	2	0	0	0	0	0	0	25	2
Allen T.	1928-32	Southampton	Accrington S	155	0	9	0	0	0	0	0	164	0
Allon T.G	1921-25	Usworth Col	Nuneaton T	74	2	4	0	0	0	0	0	78	2
Alsop G.A.	1929-32	Bath C	Walsall	16	4	0	0	0	0	0	0	16	4
Archer J.W.	1936-39	Everton	Plymouth Arg	78	0	4	0	0	0	0	0	82	0
Armeson L.R.	1936-45	Rotherham U	Retired 1945	7	0	0	0	0	0	0	0	7	0
Ashall G.H.	1938-48	Wolves	Retired cs 1948	62	10	3	1	0	0	0	0	65	11
Ashcroft C.T.	1957-58	Ipswich T	Chorley	19	0	0	0	0	0	0	0	19	0
Askew H.F.J.	1926-29	Warwick T	Morton	7	0	0	0	0	0	0	0	7	0
Astley J.	1935-44	Brentford	Retired 1944	140	0	5	0	0	0	0	0	145	0
Austin J.F.	1950-63	Toton	Torquay U	302	2	10	0	1	0	0	0	313	2
Avramovic R.	1983-84	Inter Montreal	Retired 1984	18	0	4	0	2	0	0	0	24	0
Bacon A.	1933-37	Chesterfield	Burton T	16	17	0	0	0	0	0	0	16	17
Baker G.A.	1967-70	Ipswich T	Margate U	27/4	5	3	1	0	0	0	0	30/4	6
Baker J.E.	1929-32	Wolves	Lovells A										
	1932-35	Lovells A	Bristol C	185	11	7	2	0	0	0	0	192	13
Ball C.G.	1926-29	Leek St Lukes	Colwyn Bay U	10	0	0	0	0	0	0	0	10	0
Ball J.	1930-31	West Ham U	Stourbridge	22	4	3	0	0	0	0	0	25	4
Bamber J.D.	1983-84	Blackpool	Walsall	18/1	3	0/1	0	2	1	0	0	20/2	4
Bannister G.	1978-81	Apprentice	Sheffield W										
	1987-90	Queen's Park R	West Brom A	56/9	14	2	0	7	2	0	0	65/9	16
Barnes D.	1979-82	Apprentice	Ipswich T	9	0	4	0	0	0	0	0	13	0
Barnes J.	1927-29	Atherstone T	Walsall	2	0	0	0	0	0	0	0	2	0
Barnes P.S.	1984-85	Leeds U	Manchester U	18	2	0	0	1	0	0	0	19	2
Barr H.	1962-65	Linfield	Cambridge U	47	15	9	2	2	0	0	0	58	17
Barratt H.	1934-52	Herberts A	Retired cs 1952	170	12	8	1	0	0	0	0	178	13
Barry R.A.	1969-73	Dunfermline A	Crystal P	82/1	2	7	0	2	0	0	0	91/1	2
Bassett G.R.	1961-62	Groundstaff	Worcester C	1	0	0	0	0	0	0	0	1	0
Beck J.A.	1976-79	Queen's Park R	Fulham	60/9	6	3	0	5	0	0	0	68/9	6
Bell J.	1949-52	Chesterfield		10	0	0	0	0	0	0	0	10	0
Bell W.	1927-31	Manchester C	Portsmouth	120	5	10	0	0	0	0	0	130	5
Bellas J.H.	1924-26	Mansfield T	Heanor T	34	0	0	0	0	0	0	0	34	0
Bennett D.A.	1983-89	Cardiff C	Sheffield W	157/15	25	12	3	17	5	1	2	192/15	35
Bennett D.	1959-62	Arsenal	Hereford U	73	0	2	0	2	0	0	0	77	0
Bennett J.	1932-33	Sheffield U	Northampton T	24	0	4	0	0	0	0	0	28	0
Bentley A.	1955-57	Snowdown Col	Margate U	29	0	0	0	0	0	0	0	29	0
Best J.	1920-26	Mickley CW	Halifax T	224	0	12	0	0	0	0	0	236	0
Bett F.	1946-48	Sunderland	Lincoln C	27	11	0	0	0	0	0	0	27	11
Betts E.	1947-48	Mansfield T	Nuneaton B	1	0	0	0	0	0	0	0	1	0
Billing P.	1989-91	Crewe Alex		31/2	0	5	0	5/1	0	2	0	43/3	0
Binks L.	1919-21	Tinsley Ams	Grimsby T	15	0	0	0	0	0	0	0	15	0
Bird W.	1926-28	Hinckley A	Hinckley A	40	11	4	1	0	0	0	0	44	12
Birtley R.J.	1934-35	Everton	Crystal P	30	6	3	3	0	0	0	0	33	9

				League		FA Cup		FL Cup		Europe		TOTAL	
Player	**Played**	**From**	**To**	**App**	**Gls**	**App**	**Gls**	**App**	**Gls**	**App**	**Gls**	**App**	**Gls**
Bisby C.C.	1932-36	Notts Co	Mansfield T	100	0	6	0	0	0	0	0	106	0
Blair A.	1978-81	Apprentice	Aston Villa	90/3	6	8	2	11	1	0	0	109/3	9
Blair J.	1919-21	Kilwinning Rgs	Caerphilly	10	0	0	0	0	0	0	0	10	0
Blockley J.P.	1968-73	Apprentice	Arsenal	144/2	6	3	0	8	1	4	1	159/3	8
Bly T.G.	1962-63	Peterborough U	Notts Co	32	26	8	3	2	1	0	0	42	30
Blyth J.A.	1972-82	Preston NE	Birmingham C	151	0	10	0	13	0	0	0	174	0
Bodak P.J.	1980-82	Apprentice	Manchester U	30/2	5	6	1	6	1	0	0	42/2	7
Boileau H.A.	1930-45	Bedworth T	Retired 1945	158	0	8	0	0	0	0	0	166	0
Borrows B.	1985-91	Bolton W		227/1	9	14	0	28	0	9	0	278/1	9
Bourton C.F.T.	1931-38	Blackburn R	Plymouth Arg	228	171	13	9	0	0	0	0	241	180
Bowden F.	1929-32	West Ham U	Kidderminster H	32	7	5	2	0	0	0	0	37	9
Bowen T.	1928-30	Wolves	Kidderminster H	17	4	0	0	0	0	0	0	17	4
Bowman D.	1984-86	Hearts	Dundee U	38/2	2	1/1	0	4	1	2	0	45/3	3
Boxley J.	1956-60	Bristol C	Bristol C	92	17	2	1	0	0	0	0	94	18
Bradbury	1919-20			1	0	0	0	0	0	0	0	1	0
Bradbury W.	1950-55	Mod Machines	Birmingham C	24	7	0	0	0	0	0	0	24	7
Bradford D.W.	1981-82	Washington Dip	Tulsa R'necks	6	1	1	0	0	0	0	0	7	1
Brazil A.B.	1985-86	Manchester U	Queen's Park R	15	2	0	0	0	0	0	0	15	2
Breslin T.G.	1925-27	Glasgow Shawfield		22	2	0	0	0	0	0	0	22	2
Briggs T.H.	1950-52	Grimsby T	Birmingham C	11	7	0	0	0	0	0	0	11	7
Brogan J.A.	1975-77	Glasgow Celtic	Ayr U	28	0	3	0	2	0	0	0	33	0
Brook R.	1932-36	Loughboro' Cor	Southend U	9	0	0	0	0	0	0	0	9	0
Brown E.	1951-55	Southampton	Birmingham C	85	50	4	1	0	0	0	0	89	51
Brown J.	1936-38	Wolves	Birmingham	69	26	4	3	0	0	0	0	73	29
Brown V.C.	1933-39	Leeds U	Chester	100	0	7	0	0	0	0	0	107	0
Brown W.	1925-28	Bellshill Ath	Wolves	55	0	3	0	0	0	0	0	58	0
Bruck D.J.	1960-71	Apprentice	Charlton Ath	181/8	7	13	1	13/1	0	1	0	208/9	8
Bull W.H.	1947-50			1	0	0	0	0	0	0	0	1	0
Burckitt J.D.	1964-68	Apprentice	Walsall	5	0	0	0	2	0	0	0	7	0
Butcher T.	1990-91	Glasgow Rgs		6	0	0	0	1	0	0	0	7	0
Butterworth I.	1981-85	Apprentice	Nottingham F	80/10	0	5/1	0	5	0	0	0	90/1	0
Bytheway G.	1933-34	West Brom A	Mansfield T	7	2	2	0	0	0	0	0	9	2
Caine B.	1959-61	Blackpool	Northampton T	1	0	0	0	0	0	0	0	1	0
Campbell J	1920-21	Leadgate Park	Leadgate Park	1	0	0	0	0	0	0	0	1	0
Campling A.H.	1922-25	Grimesthorpe Col		11	0	1	0	0	0	0	0	12	0
Capel T.A.	1954-56	Nottingham F	Halifax T	36	19	4	4	0	0	0	0	40	23
Carr W.M.	1967-75	Apprentice	Wolves	245/7	33	21	2	14/1	2	4	0	284/11	37
Cartwright L.	1971-77	Apprentice	Wrexham	50/18	4	7/4	0	8	2	0	0	65/22	6
Cattlin C.	1967-76	Huddersfield T	Brighton & HA	213/4	0	11	0	7/1	0	1	0	232/5	0
Chaplin G.D.	1919-23	Bradford C	Suspended *sine die* 1923	106	0	7	0	0	0	0	0	113	0
Chilton C.R.	1971-73	Hull C	Retired 1972	26/1	3	2	1	0	0	0	0	28/1	4
Chisholm K.M.	1949-52	Leicester C	Cardiff C	68	34	3	1	0	0	0	0	71	35
Churms D.J.	1956-57	Rotherham U	Exeter C	10	2	0	0	0	0	0	0	10	2
Clark H.	1988-91	Apprentice		9/11	1	0/1	0	1	0	0/1	0	10/13	1
Clark J.	1924-25	Birmingham	Boston U	6	0	1	0	0	0	0	0	7	0
Clarke G.	1927-28	Merthyr T	Torquay U	5	0	0	0	0	0	0	0	5	0
Clarke H.	1919-20	Grimsby T	Merthyr T	17	0	0	0	0	0	0	0	17	0
Clements D.	1964-72	Wolves	Sheffield W	228/2	26	8	1	15	3	4	0	255/2	30
Clews A.H.	1922-23	Stoke Dairymen		3	0	0	0	0	0	0	0	3	0
Coen R.W.L.	1938-48	West Brom A	Sth Liverpool	20	3	2	0	0	0	0	0	22	3
Collier G.B.	1979-80	Bristol C	Portland Timbers	2	0	0	0	0	0	0	0	2	0
Collindridge C.	1954-56	Nottingham F	Bath C	34	6	1	0	0	0	0	0	35	6
Conwell L.	1936-39	West Ham U	Retired 1939	2	0	0	0	0	0	0	0	2	0
Cook J.	1923-24	Wigan B	Bradford	3	0	0	0	0	0	0	0	3	0
Cook L.	1949-55	Blackburn R	Rugby T	88	0	6	0	0	0	0	0	94	0
Cook M.J.	1986-89	Apprentice	Cambridge U	0	0	0	0	0/1	0	0	0	0/1	0
Coop M.A.	1966-81	Apprentice	Derby Co	413/12	18	25/1	2	36/1	2	4	0	478/14	22
Copeland C.	1919-20	Leeds C	Merthyr T	33	0	0	0	0	0	0	0	33	0
Corbett F.J.	1931-32	West Brom A	Burton T	6	0	1	0	0	0	0	0	7	0
Cox R.B.	1946-52	Wyken Pippin FC	Atherstone T	29	0	1	0	0	0	0	0	30	0

Player	Played	From	To	League		FA Cup		FL Cup		Europe		TOTAL	
				App	Gls	App	Gls	App	Gls	App	Gls	App	Gls
Craven J.R.	1973-77	Crystal P	Plymouth Arg	86/3	8	12	0	6/1	0	0	0	104/4	8
Crawley T.	1935-47	Preston NE	Retired 1948	42	16	3	0	0	0	0	0	45	16
Cresswell P.	1950-55	Mod Machines	Guildford C	2	0	0	0	0	0	0	0	2	0
Crisp G.H.	1933-35	Llanelly	Bristol R	8	0	0	0	0	0	0	0	8	0
Crisp J.	1926-28	Blackburn R	Stourbridge	22	3	0	0	0	0	0	0	22	3
Cross C.H.	1919-22	Sidely Deasy	Crystal P	11	0	1	0	0	0	0	0	12	0
Cross D.	1973-77	Norwich C	West Brom A	90/1	30	12	5	2/1	1	0	0	104/2	36
Crowe F.R.	1919-20	Birmingham	Merthyr T	2	0	0	0	0	0	0	0	2	0
Crown L.	1928-31	Bury	Retired 1931	112	0	5	0	0	0	0	0	117	0
Cull J.E.	1931-32	Stoke C	Shrewsbury T	17	4	0	0	0	0	0	0	17	4
Culpin P.	1985-88	Nuneaton B	Northampton T	5/4	2	0	0	1	0	2	0	8/4	2
Curtis E.R.	1934-37	Cardiff C	Hartlepools U	21	2	1	0	0	0	0	0	22	2
Curtis G.W.	1955-70	Snowdown Col	Aston Villa	483/4	11	29	2	22	0	0	0	534/4	13
Dailey W.S.	1926-27	Bradford		5	1	0	0	0	0	0	0	5	1
Dailey A.J.	1958-61	Crewe Alex	Cambridge U	56	10	3	1	1	0	0	0	60	11
Dalton R.	1919-24	Edgewick FC	Halifax T	54	4	0	0	0	0	0	0	54	4
Daly G.	1980-84	Derby Co	Birmingham C	82/2	19	9/1	2	7	1	0	0	98/3	22
Davidson J.C.	1922-23	Solway Star	Kilmarnock	4	0	0	0	0	0	0	0	4	0
Davidson R.T.	1937-48	Arsenal	Hinckley A	47	9	2	0	0	0	0	0	49	9
Davison T.R.	1932-35	Sheffield W	Rhyl A	100	5	8	1	0	0	0	0	108	6
Dearson D.J.	1946-50	Birmingham C	Walsall	84	10	4	1	0	0	0	0	88	11
Deeming H.	1924-25	Exhall Col	Nuneaton T	1	0	0	0	0	0	0	0	1	0
Dennison J.S.	1922-23	Amble FC	Retired 1924	2	0	1	0	0	0	0	0	3	0
Denton P.R.	1964-68	Gorleston FC	Luton T	10	1	1	0	0	0	0	0	11	1
Devlin W.	1920-22	Belfast Celtic	Exeter C	9	0	1	0	0	0	0	0	10	0
Dickie A.L.	1966-68	West Ham U	Aldershot	2	0	1	0	0	0	0	0	3	0
Dinsdale N.	1927-30	Notts Co	Bristol R	88	10	5	1	0	0	0	0	93	11
Dixon M.	1961-62	Luton T	Cambridge U	18	12	1	0	1	0	0	0	20	12
Dobbs E.	1946-48		Bristol R	5	0	0	0	0	0	0	0	5	0
Dobson A.J.	1986-91	Apprentice	Blackburn R	51/3	1	0	0	5/3	0	0/1	0	56/7	1
Dorman D.	1951-55	Birmingham C	Walsall	90	29	4	2	0	0	0	0	94	31
Dougall J.H.	1919-26	Motherwell	Reading	226	14	11	0	0	0	0	0	237	14
Downs G.	1985-90	Norwich C	Birmingham C	142/4	4	9	1	19/1	2	6	0	176/5	7
Drinkell K.S.	1989-91	Glasgow Rgs		32/5	5	4/1	0	3/3	2	2	0	41/9	7
Dugdale A.	1969-78	Apprentice	Charlton A	139/3	0	16	0	12	0	0	0	167/3	0
Dunne J.	1926-28	Wigan B	Kings Park	29	4	3	1	0	0	0	0	32	5
Dutton C.A.	1952-56	Derby Co	Northampton T	27	8	1	0	0	0	0	0	28	8
Dwight R.	1961-64	Gravesend	Millwall	31	8	2	0	0	0	0	0	33	8
Dyke G.	1920-21	Stafford Rgs	Blackpool	3	0	0	0	0	0	0	0	3	0
Dyson P.I.	1978-83	Apprentice	Stoke C	140	5	12	0	14	0	0	0	166	5
Edwards P.	1989-91	Crewe Alex		28/3	0	2	0	4	0	1	0	35/3	0
Elliott C.S.	1931-48	Chesterfield	Retired 1948	95	2	6	0	0	0	0	0	101	2
Emerson D.	1986-91	Rotherham U		88/5	0	6	0	2/3	0	3	0	99/8	0
English T.S.	1979-83	Apprentice	Leicester C	62/4	17	3	1	7	4	0	0	72/4	22
Evans G.J.	1984-87	Apprentice	Rotherham U	5/2	0	0	0	1	1	0/2	0	6/4	1
Evans J.J.	1946-52	Mod Machines	Nuneaton B	8	1	0	0	0	0	0	0	8	1
Farmer R.J.	1958-68	Nottingham F	Notts Co	281/4	48	18	4	12	1	0	0	311/4	53
Fenwick A.R.	1919-21	West Ham U	Craghead U	50	1	3	0	0	0	0	0	53	1
Fergus A.	1926-28	Burnley		30	0	1	0	0	0	0	0	31	0
Ferguson D.	1956-57	Alloa A		4	0	1	0	0	0	0	0	5	0
Ferguson M.J.	1974-81	Apprentice	Everton										
	1983-84	Birmingham (L)	Birmingham (L)	128/6	54	3	0	10/2	3	0	0	140/9	57
Ferguson R.L.	1926-28	Fulham	Fulham	40	3	3	0	0	0	0	0	43	3
Findlay N.	1921-26	Walker Celtic		9	0	0	0	0	0	0	0	9	0
Fitton G.A.	1935-38	Preston NE	Kidderminster H	55	22	4	0	0	0	0	0	59	22
Fleming T.	1990-91	Apprentice		0/2	0	0	0	0	0	0	0	0/2	0
Foster S.B.	1920-21	Mansfield T	Mansfield T	10	4	0	0	0	0	0	0	10	4
Francis G.C.J.	1981-83	Queen's Park R	Exeter C	50	2	4	0	1	0	0	0	55	2
Frith W.	1932-47	Chesterfield	Port Vale										
		Port Vale	Retired 1047	169	4	8	0	0	0	0	0	177	4
Gaffney P.	1926-27	New Brighton	Ashington	2	0	1	1	0	0	0	0	3	1
Gallacher K.	1989-91	Dundee U		47	14	2	0	5	5	1	0	55	19

Player	Played	From	To	League App	Gls	FA Cup App	Gls	FL Cup App	Gls	Europe App	Gls	TOTAL App	Gls
Gallagher T.H.	1919-20	Oldbury T		1	0	0	0	0	0	0	0	1	0
Galloway R.	1927-28	Luton T	Tottenham H	4	1	0	0	0	0	0	0	4	1
Gardiner J.	1926-28	Motherwell	Wolves	51	0	3	0	0	0	0	0	54	0
Gardner F.C.	1946-49	Birmingham C	Newport Co	13	3	0	0	0	0	0	0	13	3
Gay J.	1926-28	Rhyl A	Clapton Orient	29	0	2	0	0	0	0	0	31	0
Gibson F.T.B.	1919-22	Hearts	Nuneaton T	53	6	0	0	0	0	0	0	53	6
Gibson I.S.	1966-70	Middlesbrough	Cardiff C	90/3	13	3	1	8	1	0	0	101/3	15
Gibson T.B.	1983-86	Tottenham H	Manchester U	97/1	43	6	5	7	3	2	1	112/1	52
Gilbert W.A.	1948-53	Murton CW	Snowdown Col	14	0	0	0	0	0	0	0	14	0
Gillespie G.T.	1977-83	Falkirk	Liverpool	171/1	6	13	0	16	0	0	0	200/1	6
Gittos J.E.	1923-24	Scunthorpe U	Frickley Col	5	1	0	0	0	0	0	0	5	1
Glazier W.J.	1964-75	Crystal P	Brentford	346	0	21	0	25	0	3	0	395	0
Glover B.D.	1966-67			0/1	0	0	0	0	0	0	0	0/1	0
Godfrey J.	1919-20	Birmingham	Manchester C	6	0	0	0	0	0	0	0	6	0
Gooding R.	1976-82	Apprentice	Plymouth Arg	46/3	5	3	0	3	0	0	0	52/3	5
Goodwin I.A.	1969-71	Oldham A	Brighton & HA	4	0	0	0	0	0	0	0	4	0
Gough C.W.M.	1921-22	Swansea T	Swansea T	15	1	3	1	0	0	0	0	18	2
Gould R.A.	1963-68	Apprentice	Arsenal	78/4	40	2	0	5	2	0	0	85/4	42
Gould T.R.	1967-71	Apprentice	Northampton T	9	0	0	0	0	0	0	0	9	0
Graham R.	1971-74	Liverpool	Motherwell	19	3	0	0	0	0	0	0	19	3
Gray W.M.	1948-52	Mod Machines		2	0	0	0	0	0	0	0	2	0
Graydon R.J.	1977-78	Aston Villa	Washington Dip	17/3	5	0/1	0	2/1	1	0	0	19/5	6
Green A.P.	1971-79	Apprentice	Washington Dip	98/19	30	5/3	1	6/1	3	0	0	109/23	34
Green T.	1938-39	West Ham U	Worcester C	9	2	0	0	0	0	0	0	9	2
Grice M.J.	1961-62	West Ham U	Colchester U	37	6	1	0	0	0	0	0	38	6
Griffiths V.	1954-59	Sheldon T	Rugby T	15	1	2	0	0	0	0	0	17	1
Grimes A.A.	1983-84	Manchester U	Luton T	29/3	1	0	0	3	1	0	0	32/3	2
Grundy W.	1933-35	Annesley CW	Mansfield T	1	0	0	0	0	0	0	0	1	0
Gynn M.	1983-91	Peterborough U		167/31	27	14/2	4	21/4	7	5	2	207/37	40
Hackett E.	1931-32	Wolves	Newport Co	4	0	1	0	0	0	0	0	5	0
Hadley G.	1920-23	Aston Villa		72	3	5	0	0	0	0	0	77	3
Hagan J.	1978-79	Larne	Washington Dips										
	1981-82	Washington Dips	Birmingham C	15/1	0	3	0	0	0	0	0	18/1	0
Hale K.O.	1962-66	Newcastle U	Oxford U	98/1	27	4	2	8	4	0	0	110/1	33
Hall D.	1982-84	Apprentice	Torquay U	1	0	0	0	0	0	0	0	1	0
Hall T.I.	1931-34	Crawcrook Alb		2	0	0	0	0	0	0	0	2	0
Hann J.	1920-21	Birtley	Leadgate Park	1	0	0	0	0	0	0	0	1	0
Hanney E.T.	1919-21	Manchester C	Reading	32	0	4	1	0	0	0	0	36	1
Hannigan E.	1967-70	Preston NE	Morton	43/4	6	3/1	1	2/1	0	0	0	48/6	7
Harris A.J.	1964-66	Chelsea	Chelsea	60	0	5	0	4	1	0	0	69	1
Harrison J.C.	1951-53	Aston Villa	Corby T	20	2	3	0	0	0	0	0	23	2
Hart H.	1950-53	Rotherham U	Grimsby T	10	1	0	0	0	0	0	0	10	1
Harvey L.	1951-61	Mod Machines	Retired 1961	140	1	8	1	0	0	0	0	148	2
Hateley A.	1968-69	Liverpool	Birmingham C	17	4	1	0	2	1	0	0	20	5
Hateley M.W.	1978-83	Apprentice	Portsmouth	86/6	25	10/1	6	8	3	0	0	104/7	34
Hawkings B.	1949-56	Mod Machines	Lincoln C	34	12	0	0	0	0	0	0	34	12
Hawley F.	1919-20	Sheffield U	Birmingham	14	0	0	0	0	0	0	0	14	0
Haywood C.	1978-81	Apprentice	Washington Dip	1	0	0	0	0	0	0	0	1	0
Healey R.	1971-72	Manchester C (L)	Manchester C (L)	3	0	0	0	0	0	0	0	3	0
Heathcote J.	1926-28	Mansfield T	Accrington S	60	37	5	0	0	0	0	0	65	37
Heigh R.	1926-28	Tranent Jns	Arbroath	7	0	0	0	0	0	0	0	7	0
Heinmann G.H.	1931-34	Manchester C	Crystal P	52	1	6	0	0	0	0	0	58	1
Henderson W.J.	1928-29	Southampton	Carlisle U	15	1	0	0	0	0	0	0	15	1
Hendrie J.G.	1980-84	Apprentice	Bradford C	15/6	2	0	0	2	0	0	0	17/6	2
Herbert F.	1922-29	Exhall Col	Brierley Hill A	188	84	12	4	0	0	0	0	200	88
Hewett J.T.	1931-32	Watford		4	0	0	0	0	0	0	0	4	0
Hewitt R.	1959-62	Wrexham	Chester	59	23	3	1	1	0	0	0	63	24
Hibbitt K.	1984-86	Wolves	Bristol R	42/5	4	2	0	1/1	0	1	0	46/6	4
Hickman W.	1927-29	Burton T		9	2	0	0	0	0	0	0	9	2
Higham F.	1928-30	Wolves	Lincoln C	36	2	1	0	0	0	0	0	37	2
Hill B.W.	1957-72	Apprentice	Torquay U	240/4	7	22/1	0	16	1	1	0	279/5	8

Player	Played	From	To	League App	League Gls	FA Cup App	FA Cup Gls	FL Cup App	FL Cup Gls	Europe App	Europe Gls	TOTAL App	TOTAL Gls
Hill J.	1948-56	Mod Machines	Millwall	66	8	1	0	0	0	0	0	67	8
Hill P.	1948-62	Rutland U	Retired 1962	285	73	18	4	0	0	0	0	303	77
Hill R.W.	1957-59	Redditch T	Rugby T	14	5	0	0	0	0	0	0	14	5
Hindley P.	1973-76	Nottingham F	Peterborough U	33	0	0	0	0	0	0	0	33	0
Holder C.W.	1959-63	Junior	Chelmsford C	9	4	0	0	0	0	0	0	9	4
Holmes H.	1931-33	Heanor T	Heanor T	22	12	0	0	0	0	0	0	22	12
Holmes J.P.	1970-77	St John Bosco	Tottenham H	122/6	6	11/1	0	10	0	0	0	143/7	6
Holton J.A.	1976-81	Sunderland	Sheffield W	91	0	2	0	7	1	0	0	100	1
Hopper M.	1926-27	Sittingbourne	Ashington	15	1	2	0	0	0	0	0	17	1
Hormantschuk P.	1980-85	Apprentice	Nuneaton B	18/6	1	3/1	0	1	0	0	0	22/7	1
Houchen K.M	1986-89	Scunthorpe U	Hibernian	43/11	7	5/1	5	2/1	0	1/1	0	51/14	12
Houldey C.A.	1925-29	Harbourne L	Walsall	61	2	1	0	0	0	0	0	62	2
Howe F.	1919-20	KimberworthOB	Brentford	5	0	0	0	0	0	0	0	5	0
Howell H.	1920-21	Hednesford T	Jarrow	4	1	0	0	0	0	0	0	4	1
Hudson G.A.	1962-66	Peterborough U	Northampton T	113	62	6	5	10	8	0	0	129	75
Humphries W.M.	1961-65	Ards	Swansea T	109	23	12	0	5	1	0	0	126	24
Hunt R.P.(Ernie)	1967-74	Everton	Bristol C	140/6	45	6/1	1	11	3	4	1	161/7	50
Hunt S.K.	1978-84	NY Cosmos	West Brom A	178/7	27	14	4	17	3	0	0	209/7	34
Hunter W.	1927-29	Grimsby T	Walsall	31	1	2	0	0	0	0	0	33	1
Hurst L.	1990-91	Apprentice		3/1	0	0/1	0	0	0	0	0	3/2	0
Hutchison T.	1972-81	Blackpool	Manchester C	312/2	24	23	4	18	2	0	0	353/2	30
Imlach J.J.S.	1960-62	Luton T	Crystal P	73	11	5	0	1	0	0	0	79	11
Jacobs S.D.	1978-84	Apprentice	Brighton & HA	94/7	0	3/2	0	6/3	0	0	0	103/12	0
Jamieson I.W.	1948-59	Aberdeen	Rugby T	181	6	3	0	0	0	0	0	184	6
Jarvis A.W.	1919-20	Edgewick	Nuneaton T	3	0	0	0	0	0	0	0	3	0
Jenkins W.	1928-29	Staveley T	Staveley T	6	0	0	0	0	0	0	0	6	0
Johnson A.	1931-32	Bristol C		5	1	0	0	0	0	0	0	5	1
Johnson E.	1952-57	Winsford U	Torquay U	91	7	10	1	0	0	0	0	101	8
Johnson E.H.	1919-20	The Army		2	0	0	0	0	0	0	0	2	0
Johnson G.H.	1927-28	Newport Co		13	0	0	0	0	0	0	0	13	0
Johnstone W.	1927-29	Glasgow Shawfield	Walsall	30	14	2	0	0	0	0	0	32	14
Joicey B.	1969-72	North Shields	Sheffield W	31/8	9	1	0	2	0	1/1	1	35/9	10
Jol M.C.	1984-85	West Brom A	Den Haag	15	0	0	0	0	0	0	0	15	0
Jones D.R.	1979-82	Everton	Seiko	8/3	0	0	0	1	0	0	0	9/3	0
Jones E.J.	1955-62	Snowdown Col	Nuneaton B	14	0	1	0	1	0	0	0	16	0
Jones F.	1919-20	Southampton	Pembroke Dock	1	0	2	1	0	0	0	0	3	1
Jones J.T.	1922-24	Crystal P	Crewe Alex	50	1	3	0	0	0	0	0	53	1
Jones L.J.	1933-38	Cardiff C	Arsenal	138	70	6	4	0	0	0	0	144	74
Jones R.	1925-26	Celtic	Stourbridge	6	0	0	0	0	0	0	0	6	0
Jones R.K.	1949-56	Llanelly	Lockheed L	83	0	5	0	0	0	0	0	88	0
Kaiser R.	1981-82	Royal Antwerp	Nice	11/5	3	1	0	2	0	0	0	15/5	3
Kearns M.D.	1955-68	Stockingford V	Retired 1968	344	14	24	1	14	1	0	0	382	16
Kelley S.R.	1946-48	Herberts A		4	0	0	0	0	0	0	0	4	0
Kemp G.	1919-20	Bradford C	Grimsby T	3	2	0	0	0	0	0	0	3	2
Key J.P.	1966-68	Fulham	Orient	27/1	7	1	0	2	0	0	0	30/1	7
Keyworth K.	1964-65	Leicester C	Swindon T	7	3	0	0	0	0	0	0	7	3
Kilcar S.P.	1932-33	Bradford	Mansfield T	4	0	0	0	0	0	0	0	4	0
Kilcline B.	1984-91	Notts Co	Oldham A	173	28	15	3	16/1	4	7	0	211/1	35
King M.B.	1975-77	Millwall	Retired 1977	23	0	2	0	2	0	0	0	27	0
Kirby G.A.	1963-65	Southampton	Swansea T	18	10	0	0	0	0	0	0	18	10
Kirk R.	1951-60	Leeds U	Cambridge U	330	6	15	1	0	0	0	0	345	7
Kirton W.J.	1928-30	Aston Villa	Kidderminster H	16	0	1	0	0	0	0	0	17	0
Kletzenbauer C.F.	1952-64	Municipal Sp	Walsall	122	3	4	0	6	0	0	0	132	3
Knapp A.	1967-68	Southampton	Los Angeles W	11	0	0	0	1	0	0	0	12	0
Knox J.	1957-59	Raith R	Rugby T	2	0	0	0	0	0	0	0	2	0
Lager E.W.	1934-39	Sutton Junction	Retired 1943	51	25	0	0	0	0	0	0	51	25
Lake W.H.	1928-39	Walsall	Retired 1939	226	113	19	10	0	0	0	0	245	123
Lane M.J.	1986-89	Chester	Chester C	0/3	0	0	0	0	0	0	0	0/3	0
Langley T.W.	1983-84	AEK Athens (L)	Wolves	2	0	0	0	0	0	0	0	2	0
Latchford R.D.	1984-85	NAC Breda	Lincoln C	11/1	2	1/1	0	0	0	0	0	12/2	2
Latham L.	1946-49	Aston Villa	Banbury Spencer	1	0	0	0	0	0	0	0	1	0

Player	Played	From	To	League App	League Gls	FA Cup App	FA Cup Gls	FL Cup App	FL Cup Gls	Europe App	Europe Gls	TOTAL App	TOTAL Gls
Lauderdale J.H.	1931-37	Blackpool	Northampton T	171	60	11	3	0	0	0	0	182	63
Lavender H.A.	1926-28	Dudley T		9	1	0	0	0	0	0	0	9	1
Laverick R.M.	1962-63	Brighton & HA	Corby T	4	0	0	0	1	1	0	0	5	1
Lawrence J.	1920-25	Aston Villa	Retired 1925	130	2	6	0	0	0	0	0	136	2
Lee F.	1930-32	Yardley W Star	Walsall	7	0	0	0	0	0	0	0	7	0
Lee J.	1954-55	Derby Co	Retired 1955	15	8	3	2	0	0	0	0	18	10
Leitch W.	1920-23	Partick Thistle	Bournemouth	27	2	1	0	0	0	0	0	28	2
Lewis B.	1966-68	Portsmouth	Luton T	33/2	2	1	0	1	0	0	0	35/2	2
Lewis I.S.	1938-39	Langford St Thomas		1	0	0	0	0	0	0	0	1	0
Lewis T.	1947-53	Redditch T	Gillingham	11	0	0	0	0	0	0	0	11	0
Liddle J.F.	1934-37	Gillingham	Exeter C	62	13	4	1	0	0	0	0	66	14
Lightening A.D.	1958-63	Nottingham F	Middlesbrough	150	0	7	0	3	0	0	0	160	0
Lindley R.	1921-22	Bradford C		15	1	0	0	0	0	0	0	15	1
Lindon A.E.	1919-20	Barnsley	Merthyr T	26	0	2	0	0	0	0	0	28	0
Livingstone S.	1986-91	Apprentice	Blackburn R	17/14	5	0	0	8/2	10	0/1	0	25/17	15
Lloyd L.V.	1974-77	Liverpool	Nottingham F	50	5	3	1	1	0	0	0	54	6
Lockhart N.H.	1947-53	Swansea T	Aston Villa	182	41	7	3	0	0	0	0	189	44
Loughlin J.	1928-31	West Ham U	Dolphins FC	61	33	4	6	0	0	0	0	65	39
Lovering J.	1946-49	Holbrooks OB	Bedworth T	6	0	0	0	0	0	0	0	6	0
Lowes B.T.	1966-67	Bury	Swindon T	3	0	0	0	0	0	0	0	3	0
Lowes T.	1919-20	Newcastle U	Nuneaton T	9	2	0	0	0	0	0	0	9	2
Lowrie G.	1946-48	Preston NE	Newcastle U	83	56	2	3	0	0	0	0	85	59
	1952-53	Bristol C	Lovells A										
McCaig A.	1921-22	Stenhousemuir	Reading	10	2	0	0	0	0	0	0	10	2
McCann A.	1961-63	Luton T	Portsmouth	22	3	0	0	0	0	0	0	22	3
McCaughey C.	1935-37	Blackburn R	Cardiff C	35	0	0	0	0	0	0	0	35	0
McClure A.	1926-28	Stoke C	Walsall	49	7	2	0	0	0	0	0	51	7
MacDonald K.D.	1989-91	Liverpool	Walsall	26/5	0	3/2	0	6/3	1	1	0	36/10	1
McDonald R.W.	1976-81	Aston Villa	Manchester C	161	14	7	1	11/1	0	0	0	179/1	15
McDonald W.	1936-39	Tranmere R	Plymouth Arg	87	23	5	0	0	0	0	0	92	23
McDonnell M.	1949-55	Birmingham C	Derby Co	232	0	13	0	0	0	0	0	245	0
McGrath L.A.	1983-91	Apprentice		132/6	3	13	0	15	0	4	0	164/6	3
McGregor W.	1925-27	Duntocher Hibs	Burton T	8	1	0	0	0	0	0	0	8	1
McGuire D.	1989-91	Glasgow Celtic	Clyde	1/3	0	0	0	0	0	0	0	1/3	0
McGuire M.J.	1969-75	Apprentice	Norwich C	60/12	1	4/1	0	6	0	0	0	70/13	1
Machin E.T.	1961-73	Nelson	Plymouth Arg	255/2	33	13	1	16	5	2	0	282/2	39
McIlvanney M.	1925-27	Broxburn U	Thames FC	24	2	1	0	0	0	0	0	25	2
McInally J.E.	1985-86	Nottingham F	Dundee U	5	0	0	0	0	0	0	0	5	0
McIntosh A.	1947-49	Birmingham C	Kidderminster H	20	3	0	0	0	0	0	0	20	3
Mackay J.W.	1920-22	Newburn Col	Carlisle U	12	0	0	0	0	0	0	0	12	0
Mackrill P.	1919-20	Rotherham Co	Halifax T	1	0	0	0	0	0	0	0	1	0
MacLachlan F.	1923-26	Maidstone U	Grimsby T	67	0	5	0	0	0	0	0	72	0
McManus C.E.	1968-72	Coleraine	Notts Co	6	0	0	0	0	0	1	0	7	0
McNab D.	1930-31	Fulham	Llanelly	9	0	0	0	0	0	0	0	9	0
McNestry G.	1935-37	Bristol R	Retired 1937	46	20	2	0	0	0	0	0	48	20
MacPhee M.G.	1937-38	Bradford	Reading	12	6	1	0	0	0	0	0	13	6
McPherson K.	1955-58	Middlesbrough	Newport Co	89	38	2	2	0	0	0	0	91	40
McSevich P.	1932-33	Bournemouth	Walsall	34	0	4	0	0	0	0	0	38	0
Marsh J.K.	1948-50	Notts Co	Leicester C	20	7	0	0	0	0	0	0	20	7
Martin N.	1967-71	Sunderland	Nottingham F	106	40	5	1	8	2	3	2	122	45
Maskill T.	1923-26	York C	Caernarfon T										
	1928-29	Rhyl A	Scarborough	68	1	1	0	0	0	0	0	69	1
Mason G.W.	1931-52	Redhill Ams	Nuneaton B	330	6	20	2	0	0	0	0	350	8
Mason R.J.	1946-55	Nuneaton B	Bedworth T	253	2	10	0	0	0	0	0	263	2
Matthews H.	1945-46			0	0	2	0	0	0	0	0	2	0
Matthews R.D.	1950-57	Mod Machines	Chelsea	111	0	5	0	0	0	0	0	116	0
Meadows F.	1956-57	Rotherham U	Bath C	8	0	0	0	0	0	0	0	8	0
Meeson D.J.	1962-65	Reading	Wisbech	24	0	0	0	4	0	0	0	28	0
Melrose J.M.	1982-83	Leicester C	Glasgow Celtic	21/3	8	1/1	0	3	2	0	0	25/4	10
Mercer A.	1919-23	Bury	Suspended 1923	102	18	4	1	0	0	0	0	106	19
Metcalf W.F.	1937-46	Brentford	Retired 1946	76	1	4	0	0	0	0	0	80	1

Player	Played	From	To	League App	League Gls	FA Cup App	FA Cup Gls	FL Cup App	FL Cup Gls	Europe App	Europe Gls	TOTAL App	TOTAL Gls
Middleton C.D.	1989-90	Apprentice		0/1	0	0	0	0	0	0	0	0/1	0
Middleton L.W.	1989-90	Apprentice		0/2	0	0	0	0	0	0	0	0	0
Millard E.B.	1920-22	Birmingham	Crystal P	63	8	5	1	0	0	0	0	68	9
Miller J.	1919-20	Everton	Preston NE	7	1	0	0	0	0	0	0	7	1
Mitchell J.T.	1919-21	South Shields	Chesterfield	32	0	0	0	0	0	0	0	32	0
Mite R.	1919-20	Rotherham Co	Rotherham T	7	0	0	0	0	0	0	0	7	0
Mitten J.	1963-67	Manchester U	Plymouth Arg	34/2	5	1	0	3/1	1	0	0	38/3	6
Mokone S.V.	1956-57	Pretoria	PSV Eindhoven	4	1	0	0	0	0	0	0	4	1
Moore A.	1954-57	Nottingham F	Swindon T	57	13	3	1	0	0	0	0	60	14
Morgan W.A.	1931-43	Chopwell Inst	Retired 1944	150	0	6	0	0	0	0	0	156	0
Morgan W.A.	1920-22	Birmingham	Crystal P	53	13	4	0	0	0	0	0	57	13
Morris F.	1924-25	West Brom A	Oakengates T	24	8	2	1	0	0	0	0	26	9
Morrissey P.J.	1965-68	Apprentice	Torquay U	6/4	0	1/1	0	0	0	0	0	7/5	0
Mortimer D.G.	1969-76	Apprentice	Aston Villa	179/14	10	9/1	0	11	0	1	0	200/15	10
Murcott S.	1978-81	Apprentice	Worcester C	1	0	0	0	0	0	0	0	1	0
Murphy D.P.	1972-78	Apprentice	Torquay U	33/10	10	5	1	2	1	0	0	40/10	12
Murphy P.	1946-50	Dunlop	Tottenham H	114	37	5	0	0	0	0	0	119	37
Myerscough W.I.	1960-62	Rotherham U	Chester	58	16	3	3	3	1	0	0	64	20
Nardiello D.	1974-80	Apprentice	Detroit Express	32/1	1	3	0	2	0	0	0	37/1	1
Nash H.E.	1920-21	Aston Villa	Cardiff C	16	2	2	0	0	0	0	0	18	2
Nelson A.	1919-20	Foleshill Albs	Foleshill Albs	2	0	0	0	0	0	0	0	2	0
Newman R.	1955-57	Northampton T	Torquay U	13	2	0	0	0	0	0	0	13	2
Newsome R.	1947-48	West Brom A	Hereford U	7	2	0	0	0	0	0	0	7	2
Newton G.W.	1963-65	Walsall	Bournemouth	8	3	0	0	1	0	0	0	9	3
Newton J.	1926-29	Halifax T	Brighton & HA	70	0	5	0	0	0	0	0	75	0
Nicholas C.B.	1957-62	Chelsea	Rugby T	113	0	6	0	2	0	0	0	121	0
Nutt G.E.	1949-55	Sheldon T	Cardiff C	76	12	6	0	0	0	0	0	82	12
Oakey G.	1972-81	Apprentice	Retired 1980	87/1	0	3/1	0	7	0	0	0	97/1	0
O'Brien R.V.	1930-34	Morris Motors	Watford	57	2	1	0	0	0	0	0	58	2
Ogrizovic S.	1984-91	Shrewsbury T		278	1	17	0	29	0	9	0	333	1
Ormston A.	1922-23	Durham C	Barrow	3	0	0	0	0	0	0	0	3	0
O'Rourke J.	1969-72	Ipswich T	Queen's Park R	52/2	17	2	0	5	2	4	4	63/2	23
Osgood K.	1977-80	Tottenham H	Derby Co	24	1	0	0	1	0	0	0	25	1
Owen W.	1930-31	Fulham	Nuneaton T	5	0	0	0	0	0	0	0	5	0
Paddon G.C.	1968-70	Apprentice	Norwich C	3/2	1	0	0	0	0	0	0	3/2	1
Painter I.J.	1986-87	Stoke C	Retired 1987	0/3	0	0	0	1/1	0	1	0	1/4	0
Parker R.	1919-21	Sunderland	South Shields	26	11	0	0	0	0	0	0	26	11
Parker R.	1969-74	Apprentice	Carlisle U	77/3	0	6	0	5	0	0	0	88/3	0
Parkes	1919-20			1	0	0	0	0	0	0	0	1	0
Parkin T.	1924-26	Preston Col	Durham C	20	2	1	0	0	0	0	0	21	2
Paterson W.	1925-26	Cowdenbeath	Springfield USA	40	25	1	0	0	0	0	0	41	25
Patrick W.C.G.	1954-58	Snowdown Col	Gillingham	44	6	2	0	0	0	0	0	46	6
Peake T.	1983-91	Lincoln C		274/1	6	17	1	30	0	9	0	330/1	7
Pearce A.	1990-91	Halesowen		11	1	0	0	0	0	0	0	11	1
Pearce S.	1983-85	Wealdstone	Nottingham F	52	4	2	0	0	0	0	0	54	4
Pearson 'Harry'	1936-38	Northwich V	Queen's Park R	3	0	0	0	0	0	0	0	3	0
Pearson 'Herbert'	1924-25	Southampton	Nuneaton T	3	1	0	0	0	0	0	0	3	1
Pearson 'Horace'	1933-37	Oldham A	Newport Co	108	0	6	0	0	0	0	0	114	0
Perdomo J.T.	1990-91	Genoa (L)	Betis Seville (L)	4	0	0	0	2	0	0	0	6	0
Perry E.	1932-34	West Brom A	Dudley T	40	4	3	0	0	0	0	0	43	4
Phillips D.O.	1986-89	Manchester C	Norwich C	93/7	8	9	1	8	0	4/1	2	114/8	11
Phillips J.	1930-31	Bristol R	Merthyr T	25	17	3	1	0	0	0	0	28	18
Phillips N.	1978-81	Apprentice	Hong Kong	4/1	0	0	0	0	0	0	0	4/1	0
Philpotts D.R.	1971-75	Apprentice	Tranmere R	3	0	0	0	1	0	0	0	4	0
Pick W.E.	1928-31	Newport Co	Watford	74	25	4	1	0	0	0	0	78	26
Pickering N.	1985-88	Sunderland	Derby Co	76/2	9	6	0	7	1	2	0	91/2	10
Platnauer N.	1983-85	Bristol R	Birmingham C	38/6	6	4	0	5	0	0	0	47/6	6
Plummer A.	1929-32	Bath C	Bath C	25	0	0	0	0	0	0	0	25	0
Plunkett A.	1928-29	Walsall	Crystal P	23	0	1	0	0	0	0	0	24	0
Pointer R.	1965-67	Bury	Portsmouth	26	13	4	0	2	0	0	0	32	13
Pointon B.	1920-21	Nuneaton T	Redditch	2	0	0	0	0	0	0	0	2	0

Player	Played	From	To	League App	League Gls	FA Cup App	FA Cup Gls	FL Cup App	FL Cup Gls	Europe App	Europe Gls	TOTAL App	TOTAL Gls
Poole W.A.	1925-26	Watford	Kidderminster H	17	6	0	0	0	0	0	0	17	6
Pounder J.A.	1957-58	Luton T	Yeovil T	6	1	0	0	0	0	0	0	6	1
Powell B.I.	1975-80	Wolves	Derby Co	162/2	27	6/1	0	9	2	0	0	177/3	29
Pritchard H.J.	1935-37	Exhall Col	Crystal P	5	2	0	0	0	0	0	0	5	2
Proverbs R.J.	1956-57	Stratford T	Bournemouth	10	0	1	0	0	0	0	0	11	0
Pynegar A.	1923-25	Leicester C	Oldham A	54	25	3	0	0	0	0	0	57	25
Quinn P.	1919-20	Bradford C		15	2	0	0	0	0	0	0	15	2
Quinney J.	1949-54	Mod Machines	Cheltenham T	3	0	0	0	0	0	0	0	3	0
Rafferty W.H.	1969-73	Port Glasgow R	Blackpool	27	3	1	1	3	0	0	0	31	4
Ramage J.	1926-28	Hearts	Luton T	11	1	4	1	0	0	0	0	15	2
Ramage P.	1927-28	Newton G Star	Derby Co	26	6	2	1	0	0	0	0	28	7
Ramsbottom N.	1971-75	Blackpool	Sheffield W	51	0	3	0	0	0	0	0	54	0
Randle J.	1923-28	Exhall Col	Bournemouth	149	0	7	0	0	0	0	0	156	0
Raynor H.A.	1926-29	Halifax T	Colwyn Bay U	14	0	0	0	0	0	0	0	14	0
Reay G.T.	1930-31	Bristol R	Burton T	12	3	3	0	0	0	0	0	15	3
Rees R.R.	1962-68	Apprentice	West Brom A	230	42	17	5	15	5	0	0	262	52
Reeve F.D.	1927-28	Rugby T	Walsall	2	0	0	0	0	0	0	0	2	0
Regan J.	1955-57	Bristol C	Yeovil T	26	0	0	0	0	0	0	0	26	0
Regis C.	1984-91	West Brom A	Aston Villa	231/7	47	15/1	3	24	12	4	0	274/8	62
Richards C.S.	1925-26	Ruskin Social		9	0	0	0	0	0	0	0	9	0
Richards P.	1932-34	Leicester C	Bath C	46	7	0	0	0	0	0	0	46	7
Richards W.E.	1928-31	Wolves	Fulham	76	11	4	1	0	0	0	0	80	12
Richmond H.	1922-25	Leicester C	Queen's Park R	64	16	2	3	0	0	0	0	66	19
Robbins A.	1928-29	Aberstsswg FC	Hereford U	2	0	0	0	0	0	0	0	2	0
Roberts B.L.F.	1975-84	Apprentice	Birmingham	209/6	1	13	1	19/2	0	0	0	241/8	2
Roberts C.	1924-26	Birm Jun Football		1	0	0	0	0	0	0	0	1	0
Roberts D.E.	1963-68	Apprentice	Mansfield T	11/1	6	0	0	4	0	0	0	15/1	6
Roberts E.	1936-52	Derby Co	King's Lynn	212	85	11	2	0	0	0	0	223	87
Roberts R.E.	1919-20	Leeds C	Rhyl Ath	17	0	2	0	0	0	0	0	19	0
Robinson B.	1919-22	Swinburn FC	Nuneaton T	25	0	2	0	0	0	0	0	27	0
Robinson F.	1922-23	Nuneaton T	Bournemouth	9	0	1	0	0	0	0	0	10	0
Robson G.	1929-30	Walsall	Ashington	4	0	0	0	0	0	0	0	4	0
Robson S	1990-91	West Ham U		3/1	0	0	0	0	0	0	0	3/1	0
Rodger G.	1985-89	Wolves	Luton T	31/5	2	1/1	0	3/1	0	0/1	0	35/8	2
Roe T.W.	1930-31	Walsall		4	0	0	0	0	0	0	0	4	0
Rogers J.R.	1956-59	Bristol C	Bristol C	77	27	3	0	0	0	0	0	80	27
Rosario R.	1990-91	Norwich C		0/2	0	0	0	0	0	0	0	0/2	0
Ross R.	1924-25		Workington	20	0	1	0	0	0	0	0	21	0
Rowley J.	1922-26	Oakengates	Bristol R	148	2	6	0	0	0	0	0	154	2
Rowley K.F.	1954-55	Birmingham C		3	0	0	0	0	0	0	0	3	0
Russell	1932-33			1	0	0	0	0	0	0	0	1	0
Ryan R.A.	1958-61	Derby Co	Retired 1961	65	9	3	0	1	0	0	0	69	9
St John I.	1971-72	Hellenic FC	Tranmere R	18	3	2	0	0	0	0	0	20	3
Sambrook R.	1953-58	Wednesfield	Manchester C	96	25	3	0	0	0	0	0	99	25
Sambrooke C.L.	1919-20	Oldbury T	Nuneaton T	6	0	0	0	0	0	0	0	6	0
Sanders J.A.	1958-59	West Brom A	Hinckley A	10	0	0	0	0	0	0	0	10	0
Sansom K.	1990-91	Queen's Park R		9	0	0	0	0	0	0	0	9	0
Satchwell K.R.	1958-63	US Carburettors	Nuneaton B	68	21	4	1	3	2	0	0	75	24
Sealey L.J.	1975-83	Apprentice	Luton T	158	0	9	0	11	0	0	0	178	0
Sedgley S.P.	1986-89	Apprentice	Tottenham H	81/3	3	2/2	0	9	2	5	0	97/5	5
Setters M.E.	1967-70	Stoke C	Charlton A	50/1	3	3/1	0	4	0	0	0	57/2	3
Shankly J.	1925-26	Nuneaton T	Carlisle U	9	2	0	0	0	0	0	0	9	2
Shanks A.V.	1926-27	Leamington T	Leamington T	1	0	0	0	0	0	0	0	1	0
Shea D.	1923-25	Fulham	Clapton Orient	62	11	4	1	0	0	0	0	66	12
Sheldon A.	1919-20	Birmingham	Wellington T	12	1	2	0	0	0	0	0	14	1
Sheldon L.	1919-22	Notts Co	Mansfield T	6	0	0	0	0	0	0	0	6	0
Shepherd B.A.	1956-60	Hinckley A		29	0	0	0	0	0	0	0	29	0
Shepherd T.	1966-69	Nottingham F	Plymouth Arg	12/2	1	1/1	1	0/1	0	0	0	13/3	2
Sheppard W.	1931-32	Queen's Park R	Walsall	21	7	0	0	0	0	0	0	21	7
Shone D.	1928-29	West Ham U		9	1	0	0	0	0	0	0	9	1
Shore G.	1948-51	Port Vale	Hinckley A	2	0	0	0	0	0	0	0	2	0

Player	Played	From	To	League App	League Gls	FA Cup App	FA Cup Gls	FL Cup App	FL Cup Gls	Europe App	Europe Gls	TOTAL App	TOTAL Gls
Sillett J.C.	1961-66	Chelsea	Plymouth Arg	108/1	1	12	0	7	1	0	0	127/1	1
Simcoe K.E.	1959-60	Nottingham F	Notts Co	8	1	0	0	0	0	0	0	8	1
Simms G.H.	1957-58	Flavels FC	Notts Co	1	0	0	0	0	0	0	0	1	0
Simpson D.E.	1945-50	Salem Baptist	Reading	67	5	2	1	0	0	0	0	69	6
Simpson F.H.	1930-33	Marsden CW	Retired 1934	14	0	3	0	0	0	0	0	17	0
Simpson N.H.	1948-57	Nottingham F	Exeter C	258	7	12	0	0	0	0	0	270	7
Singleton M.D.	1980-84	Apprentice	Bradford C	20/3	1	0	0	4/1	1	0	0	24/4	2
Smailes M.	1930-31	West Ham U	Ashington	11	0	0	0	0	0	0	0	11	0
Smith A.	1919-20	Birmingham		1	0	0	0	0	0	0	0	1	0
Smith B.	1935-39	Birmingham	Retired 1940	54	0	3	0	0	0	0	0	57	0
Smith C.H.	1919-21	Northampton T		8	2	1	0	0	0	0	0	9	2
Smith D.	1987-91	YTS		115/9	14	5	0	15	0	3/1	0	138/10	14
Smith F.D.	1957-59	Derby Co	Kidderminster H	28	2	0	0	0	0	0	0	28	2
Smith G.	1926-27	Tranmere R	Runcorn	5	0	0	0	0	0	0	0	5	0
Smith H.	1930-31	Stourbridge	Merthyr T	5	0	0	0	0	0	0	0	5	0
Smith J.	1963-66	Tottenham H	Leyton Orient	34/1	1	0	0	4	0	0	0	38/1	1
Smith K.	1986-88	Rotherham U	York C	5/1	0	1	0	0	0	0	0	6/1	0
Smith N.L.	1938-48	Standard App	Millwall	13	0	2	0	0	0	0	0	15	0
Smith S.W.	1946-51	Nuffield Mech	Swansea T	29	0	2	0	0	0	0	0	31	0
Smith W.S.	1970-75	Sheffield W	Bristol R	132/3	1	9	0	7	1	2	0	150/3	2
Snape J.	1936-50	Solihull T	Bedworth T	106	2	4	0	0	0	0	0	110	2
Soden W.J.	1947-49	Boldmere St Mls	Hednesford T	2	0	0	0	0	0	0	0	2	0
Speedie D.R.	1987-91	Chelsea	Liverpool	121/1	31	3/1	0	15	3	3	1	142/2	35
Spencer D.	1951-54	Lockheed L	Lockheed L	20	0	3	0	0	0	0	0	23	0
Spratt G.W.	1956-59	Oadby T	Rugby T	28	0	2	0	0	0	0	0	30	0
Spring A.J.	1983-95	Apprentice	Bristol R	3/2	0	0	0	2	0	0	0	5/2	0
Springthorpe T.A.	1950-51	Wolves	USA	12	0	1	0	0	0	0	0	13	0
Stanford H.	1927-28	Brierley Hill A		11	0	0	0	0	0	0	0	11	0
Starsmore J.G.	1928-30	Kettering T	Kettering T	51	16	1	1	0	0	0	0	52	17
Stein C.	1972-75	Glasgow Rgs	Glasgow Rgs	83	22	8	2	7	5	0	0	98	29
Stephens K.W.	1984-86	Luton T	Rctired 1982	33/1	2	2	0	0/1	0	0	0	35/2	2
Stephens W.J.	1959-60	Swindon T		14	0	0	0	0	0	0	0	14	0
Stevens S.	1920-23	Notts Co	Dudley Bean	59	26	3	0	0	0	0	0	62	26
Stewart G.T.S.	1958-60	Accrington S	Carlisle U	40	23	0	0	0	0	0	0	40	23
Stiffle N.E.	1960-61	Exeter C	Banks T (NSW)	15	2	2	0	1	0	0	0	18	2
Stirling J.	1919-20	Stoke C	Alloa A	5	0	0	0	0	0	0	0	5	0
Stoddart W.H.	1927-28	Manchester U	Southampton	6	1	0	0	0	0	0	0	6	1
Stokes A.	1929-31	Notts Co	Watford	45	0	7	0	0	0	0	0	52	0
Stone J.	1919-20	Wolves		2	0	0	0	0	0	0	0	2	0
Storey T.	1922-25	Crystal P		60	3	4	0	0	0	0	0	64	3
Straw R.	1957-61	Derby Co	Mansfield T	142	79	8	6	1	0	0	0	151	85
Strong G.A.	1970-72	Liverpool	Retired 1972	33	0	1	0	4	0	3	0	41	0
Suckling P.J.	1982-86	Apprentice	Manchester C	27	0	0	0	2	0	0	0	29	0
Sutton S.	1990-91	Nottingham F (L)	Nottingham F (L)	1	0	0	0	0	0	0	0	1	0
Swindale L.	1921-22	Blyth Spartans	Shildon	4	0	0	0	0	0	0	0	4	0
Taylor G.T.	1937-39	Bolton W	Retired 1943	66	11	2	0	0	0	0	0	68	11
Taylor P.T.	1946-55	Nottingham F	Middlesbrough	86	0	4	0	0	0	0	0	90	0
Tedds W.H.	1960-65	Junior	Cambridge U	8	0	0	0	1	0	0	0	9	0
Thomas B.	1950-54	Longford R	Banbury Spencer	12	1	0	0	0	0	0	0	12	1
Thomas D.J.	1978-83	Apprentice	Tottenham H	103/5	5	9/1	1	11/1	0	0	0	123/7	6
Thomas P.J.	1966-67	GEC	Waterford	1	0	0	0	0	0	0	0	1	0
Thompson G.L.	1977-83	Apprentice	West Brom A	127/7	38	11	4	12/1	7	0	0	150/8	49
Thompson G.W.	1924-25	Reading	Nuneaton T	2	0	0	0	0	0	0	0	2	0
Thompson J.W.	1923-24	Millwall	Clapton Orient	2	0	0	0	0	0	0	0	2	0
Thompson K.	1982-85	Apprentice	Real Oviedo										
	1988-91	Real Oviedo		11/12	1	2	0	0/4	0	0/1	0	13/17	1
Thomson A.	1932-33	Southend U	Tranmere R	1	0	0	0	0	0	0	0	1	0
Thomson J.	1927-28	Plymouth Arg	NY Nationals	3	0	0	0	0	0	0	0	3	0
Tilford A.	1929-32	Blackpool	Fulham	57	0	5	0	0	0	0	0	62	0
Timmins C.	1946-58	Jack Moulds A	Lockheed L	161	5	4	0	0	0	0	0	165	5
Tinning G.E.	1925-29	Clydebank Jun		25	0	1	0	0	0	0	0	26	0

Player	Played	From	To	League App	League Gls	FA Cup App	FA Cup Gls	FL Cup App	FL Cup Gls	Europe App	Europe Gls	TOTAL App	TOTAL Gls
Titterton D.S.J.	1989-91	Apprentice		0/2	0	0	0	1	0	0	0	1/2	0
Toms W.	1922-23	Oldham A	Stockport Co	30	18	1	0	0	0	0	0	31	18
Tooze D.G.	1937-49	Redditch T	Retired 1949	36	0	0	0	0	0	0	0	36	0
Toseland E.	1925-29	Higham T	Manchester C	22	11	1	0	0	0	0	0	23	11
Townsend J.S.	1927-29	Nuneaton T	Nuneaton T	37	5	1	0	0	0	0	0	38	5
Tudor J.A.	1964-69	Ilkeston T	Sheffield U	63/6	13	3	0	4/1	2	0	0	70/7	15
Turner A.	1961-66	Scunthorpe U	Shrewsbury T	4	0	0	0	0	0	0	0	4	0
Turner H.L	1924-26	Merthyr T	Brierley Hill A	29	7	1	0	0	0	0	0	30	7
Turner W.L.	1985-87	Luton T	Brentford	14/1	1	1	0	1	0	0	0	16/1	0
Underwood B.R.	1931-34	Leeds U	Retired 1934	20	0	1	0	0	0	0	0	21	0
Uphill D.E.	1955-57	Reading	Mansfield T	49	17	1	0	0	0	0	0	50	17
Van Gool R.	1979-81	1.FC Cologne	Royal Antwerp	17	0	0	0	2	0	0	0	19	0
Waldock R.	1949-54	Loscoe YC	Sheffield U	27	8	2	1	0	0	0	0	29	9
Walker J.	1925-26	Broxburn U		16	1	1	0	0	0	0	0	17	1
Walker W.B.	1919-20	Birmingham	Merthyr T	20	7	2	1	0	0	0	0	22	8
Wallace I.A.	1976-80	Dumbarton	Nottingham F	128/2	58	4	0	6	2	0	0	138/2	60
Walters M.	1956-59	Junior	Rugby T	3	0	1	0	0	0	0	0	4	0
Walton J.A.	1956-58	Burnley	Kettering T	13	0	0	0	0	0	0	0	14	0
Ward D.	1927-29	Barry T	Newport Co	11	2	0	0	0	0	0	0	11	2
Ward R.A.	1945-46			0	0	1	0	0	0	0	0	1	0
Warner L.H.	1937-54	Jack Moulds A	Retired 1954	197	19	8	3	0	0	0	0	205	22
Warren C.E.	1921-23	Herberts A	Yeovil T	18	3	0	0	0	0	0	0	18	3
Wassall J.C.	1951-57	Mod Machines	Southport	17	0	0	0	0	0	0	0	17	0
Watson E.G.	1928-33	Wolves	Oakengates T	84	0	8	0	0	0	0	0	92	0
Watson J.G.	1934-36	Everton	Crystal P	16	1	0	0	0	0	0	0	16	1
Watson W.	1925-26	Vale of Leven		31	1	1	0	0	0	0	0	33	1
Waugh K.	1989-91	Bristol C	Watford	1	0	0	0	1	0	0	0	2	0
Webb H.	1935-36	Exeter C	Newport Co	3	0	0	0	0	0	0	0	3	0
Wesson R.W.	1958-67	Thornaby BB	Walsall	133	0	15	0	8	0	0	0	156	0
White F.	1931-35	West Brom A	Newport Co	119	26	8	0	0	0	0	0	127	26
Whitehouse J.A.	1962-64	Reading	Millwall	46	12	9	6	3	1	0	0	58	19
Whitton S.P.	1978-83	Apprentice	West Ham U	64/10	21	3	2	3/2	0	0	0	70/12	23
Widdowson A.	1927-31	Notts Co	Newark T	69	16	4	2	0	0	0	0	73	18
Williams A.	1985-87	Solihull T	Rotherham U	3/6	0	0	0	0	0	0/1	0	3/7	0
Wilmot K.	1932-33	Hinckley U	Nuneaton T	12	0	0	0	0	0	0	0	12	0
Wilson C.	1934-35	Aston Villa	Kidderminster H	10	4	2	0	0	0	0	0	12	4
Winship E.	1922-25	Prudhoe Celtic	Kidderminster H	79	0	6	0	0	0	0	0	85	0
Withey G.A.	1983-85	Bristol R	Cardiff C	11/11	4	4	3	1	0	0	0	16/11	7
Wolfe T.H.	1923-24	Sheffield W	Scotland	10	1	0	0	0	0	0	0	10	1
Wood A.	1922-26	Crystal P	Willenhall	83	17	3	0	0	0	0	0	86	17
Wood A.R.	1935-52	Nuneaton T	Northampton T										
	1955-59	Northampton T	Retired 1959	234	0	12	0	0	0	0	0	246	0
Woods R.	1990-91	Wigan A		12	1	0	0	0	0	0	0	12	1
Woolhouse R.	1932-33	Bradford C	Walsall	7	1	4	1	0	0	0	0	11	2
Wright H.D.	1919-20	Mansfield Mech	Exeter C	10	0	0	0	0	0	0	0	10	0
Wyer P.W.	1955-56	Junior	Derby Co										
	1958-59	Derby Co		5	0	0	0	0	0	0	0	5	0
Wynn G.A.	1919-21	Manchester C	Llandudno T	25	3	2	0	0	0	0	0	27	3
Yorath T.C.	1976-79	Leeds U	Tottenham H	99	3	2	0	6	0	0	0	107	3
Yorke A.	1923-25	Sunderland	Northampton T	16	0	1	0	0	0	0	0	17	0
Young C.W.	1938-48	Margate		1	0	0	0	0	0	0	0	1	0
Young Q.	1971-73	Ayr U	Glasgow Rgs	25/1	2	1	0	1/1	0	0	0	27/2	2

SUBSCRIBERS

Presentation Copies
1 Coventry City Football Club
2 The Football League • 3 The Football Association

4 Rod Dean
5 David Brassington
6 Jim Brown
7 Don Chalk
8 David Coulson
9 Alan Jones
10 J A Harris
11 Chris Lamb
12 Mike McCarthy
13 Brian & Maureen Stamper
14 A T Hastings
15 Alfred James Ward
16 Peter M Bow
17 David Marriott
18 John A Kinnie
19 Colin R Goodyer
20 Garry Thompson
21 Aaron James Kelly
22 Alan Sherwin
23 Tony Smith
24 Christopher Twigger
25 Warren Floyer
26 Leroy Brownson
27 Anthony B Jones
28 Graham Merriman
29 Trevor Ankers
30 Kevin Turley
31 Henry Darling
32 Clare Carter
33 Adrian Jackson
34 Barry M Greener
35 Ronald Morton
36 John Collins
37 Christopher Kenneth Savage
38 Paul Barton
39 Paul T Wattling
40 Alex Unsworth
41 M O'Halloran
42 Peter Farr
43 Richard Farr
44 Dave Jones
45 Gerald Hawthorne
46 Lee Davis
47 Andrew Barnsdale
48 David A Eaton
49 Karl John Kerr
50 Stephen Berrisford
51 Paul Jessup
52 Mr M A Smith
53 Adrian E Newbury
54 Kelly Davis
55 Andrew Miles
56 Paul Hawkeswood
57 John Colledge
58 Mr R W S Paine
59 Daryl Cashmore
60 Mr Pete Clarke
61 David Mobley
62 Matthew Gadsby
63 Stuart Lawrence Iley
64 Donald G Trelford
65 Allan Bull
66 David Edward Walsh
67 David Snape
68 John Bettles
69 Stuart Peter Holt
70 Simon Clements
71 Leonard Hornsby
72 Stephen Hornsby
73 Damien Smith
74 Michael R Styles
75 Carl Hurley
76 John Oughton
77 Robert M Sanders
78 Derrick Gough
79 Robert Judd
80 Derek Craig
81 Derek P Hunt
82 P M Wilkinson
83 A W Wilkinson
84 Martyn Harris
85 Alan Mynard
86 Glyn A Davies
87 L R Birchall
88 Mark Grocott
89 Geoff Clee
90 Robert H Sprake
91 Anne Kay
92 Stephen Millington
93 Stephen Millington
94 Philip A Coling
95 S A Keogh
96 Roy Evans
97 D G Panther
98 Michael V Wilson
99 Dick Tomlins
100 William Shipton
101 Martin L Walker
102 Mark Oxley
103 Steven McGladrigan
104 Derek Steven Harper
105 Jaime McIlroy
106 Len King
107 Terry Yates
108 P S Grace
109 Trevor Godwin
110 Martin Noble
111 Anthony Patrick Carroll
112 Douglas Andrews
113 Andrew Turrall
114 Mick Holland
115 Richard Bateman
116 Thomas Lawlor
117 M Woodford
118 Phillip Bond
119 Phillip Bond
120 Edward Smith
121 J Hepworth

122 S Hepworth
123 Stephen J Lawlor
124 Ronald W Allen
125 Robin M Suddens
126 Robert J D Lawrence
127 Phil Burton
128 Alan Mockford
129 Frederick Evans
130 Simon Miller
131 David Shakespeare
132 Gary Hodgson
133 Andrew McIntosh
134 R D Eyres
135 Steven Stokes
136 Adrian Shelswell
137 R D McKay
138 William Peter Brown
139 Barry Griffin
140 David Lindsley
141 Pauline Fisher
142 Jon Slade
143 E P Baker
144 Richard Cumberlidge
145 Syd & Joan Smith
146 John Smith
147 John Leekey
148 Quentin Carruthers
149 David V Skilling
150 J P Gallagher
151 A R Lang
152 Ian James Gutteridge
153 Angus Paton
154 Allan Timms
155 Neil Timms
156 Mr R E Weeks
157 Barry Jarvis
158 Adrian McIntosh
159 Steve Coyne
160 Geoffrey John Mitchell
161 Keith White
162 J E Owen
163 J E Owen
164 Paul Wildsmith
165 Richard Clay
166 Jon Tizick
167 Anthony Proctor
168 Ian Philip Gardner
169 Kevan Brown
170 Pete Wooding
171 Jim Farrell
172 John Twigger
173 Peter Beauchamp
174 M Cosgrove
175 Errick Peterson
176 Cheryl Lane
177 Russell Pugh
178 Jonathan Strange
179 Chris Fowler
180 Edwin W Lynch
181 Ian Mackey
182 David Ryan
183 Mr A Woolfenden
184 Michael Davies
185 Peter Farrelly
186 Simon Pitcher
187 B H Standish
188 Brian Spridgens
189 Brian H Hobbs
190 Raymond Shaw
191 John Motson
192 D E Womble
193 Albert A Heath
194 S L Gallemore
195 George H Rowland
196 David B Davis
197 Michael H Field
198 Martin Gallemore
199 Roger Sinclair
200 Derek Keith Ives
201 D B David
202 Richard D C Davis
203 Calvin Burton
204 R P Bennett
205 Philip Walker
206 Mr D Martin
207 Nick Dowell
208 Frederick C Burns
209 Colin W G Eden
210 Jeffrey Eden
211 Reginald Charles Hill
212 Robert E Leahy
213 John Mayne
214 Paul Timothy Roberts
215 Cyril Roberts
216 S A Gardiner
217 Gary Thomas Ball
218 R Hudson
219 M J Turbott
220 Peter Jardine
221 David Sullivan
222 K P Wood
223 Mike Young
224 Bruce Young
225 Harry Kay
226 Duncan Watt
227 Graham Edlington
228 Robert, Michael & Andrew Ainsbury
229 John Sowerby
230 Clifford Thomas
231 Peter J Race
232 John Seabourn
233 Andrew John Powling
234 Simon J Puddifoot
235 Ian P Puddifoot
236 Tony Perkins
237 Colin Heys
238 Paul J Midwood
239 Stephen Houghton
240 Mr M F Oakes
241 Sean Ryan
242 Iain Dale
243 R A Jacques
244 Mark Stockil
245 Steven Elliott
246 Gary R Leeson
247 Roy K Shoesmith
248 David Earnshaw
249 D T Bryant
250 Ian Willott
251 Clive A Rees
252 Tony Hagan
253 John W Wills
254 Gary Clifford
255 Geoff Wilkinson
256 Graham Watkins
257 John Joseph O'Donnell
258 A K Williams
259 David Wood
260 Alan Rattigan
261 Arthur J Wakefield
262 M Horner
263 Tony Chattaway
264 Michael Briggs

265 Peter Graham
266 J T Muir
267 M J Morrissey
268 Lars-Olof Wendler
269 John Treleven
270 John Clancy
271 David Keats
272 P J Cooke
273 David Cresswell
274 Kenny Sewell
275 Colin Swann
276 Daniel C Nutt
277 S C Bond
278 Paul Whitehead
279 Stephen Whitehead
280 Lyndon Vyse
281 Anthony Jones
282 Simon Smith
283 M G Sollis
284 S D Kinlan
285 J D Brash
286 Stuart A Wyer
287 Alar Aug
288 Ants K Aug
289 W D Walker
290 Mr F Barry Hiscox
291 W D Phillips
292 David Downs
293 Michael Holtom
294 Mr Mark Hopkins
295 Jim Duggins
296 Mr John Monks
297 Robert Hubert
298 Isobel Brown
299 K M Barker
300 Phillip Olorenshaw
301 Gareth Knight
302 Gary Perkins
303 R A B Payne
304 P Clifton
305 Peter Elliott
306 Tony Langford
307 Steve Bone
308 Jonny Stokkeland
309 C Williams
310 Roy West
311 Mr Frank Hunt
312 Barry Braithwaite
313 Paul Edward Smith
314 Colin Bartlem
315 Darren Rawlinson
316 John Keith Rawlinson
317 Michael J Sallabank
318 Michael J Sallabank
319 Michael J Sallabank
320 P H Whitehead
321 Alan Wheatley
322 Moira & Frederick Furness
323 Douglas Lamming
324 J M Moore
325 Graham G Paine
326 A N Davis
327 R H Roe
328 S D Haley
329 Colin Jose
330 Dave Hillam
331 John Harrison
332 Keith Sydney Reay
333 Derek Palmer
334 Frank Conway
335 John Conway
336 Gary Wynne
337 John Lathan
338 Mr R A Moore
339 P J Egan
340 S M Egan
341 A & J A Waterman
342 Dave Harrison
343 Alastair James Henry Brown
344 Vernon May
345 John Brocklehurst
346 Michael May
347 Christine Skinner
348 George 'Hammers' Brand
349 Richard Bellis
350 Pete Cowley
351 Brian L Swain
352 Sports Marketing
353 J Ringrose
354 Fred Beale
355 Fred Lee
356 Lee John Lawton
357 C J Morton
358 David J Godfrey
359 Gordon Small
360 Andrew Roberts
361 John Heffernan
362 Terry Potts
363 Derek Riley
364 Martin J Riley
365 Geoff S Bache
366 Mr J C Robinson
367 Garth I Dykes
368 Richard D N Wells
369 Donald Noble
370 Douglas Bidgood
371 Marcel Jones
372 Doug Kemp
373 Cyril & Brenda Peach
374 Roy Selby
375 William Grier
376 E F Dean
377 P J Morris
378 John Woodfield
379 Bert Woodfield
380 Richard Woodfield
381 Göran Schönhult
382 Wolf J Flywheel
383 Phillip Hart
384 Bruce William Jarvis
385 Lillian Aldred
386 Norman L Clarke
387 Terry Frost
388 Malc Hartley
389 Paul Stephens
390 Mike Rees
391 Robin Paul Ogleby
392 Mark Page
393 Roger Hulbert
394 Eamonn Kelly
395 Peter Moore
396 Maurice Curtin
397 Mark Styles
398 Peter J Morgan
399 Geoffrey Wright
400 Trond Isaksen
401 W Erle Shanks
402 Peter Moseley
403 J Musgrove
404 M P Waters
405 P J Blakemore
406 Graham H Coombs

407 P R Howard
408 Michael Cullinane
409 L A Zammit
410 Christopher Paul Weir
411 J S Pyke
412 Filippo Rossi
413 Christer Svensson
414 Geir Juva
415 Alan John
416 Hannu Solanne
417 Tony Smith
418 William Wilson
419 Norman Hendry
420 D J Nelson
421 Denise Knight
422 Nicholas Brown
423 Stephane Daugan
424 N G King
425 Peter Pickup
426 David Gregg
427 Mark Kowalik
428 Rampton Hospital Library
429 Michael Brett
430 Praveen Subhra
431 Mr Brian Haydon
432 A J Moore
433 Marshall Stewart
434 Kathleen Stewart
435 Robert McDonough
436 Andrew Pittam
437 C Austin
438 Chris Fleming
439 Roger Carvell
440 J A Hall
441 Mr Brian Kean
442 Ian Berry
443 Jonathan C Brown
444 Terry Osmond
445 Sean Osmond
446 Mark Georgevic
447 Steve Gillam
448 Robert Dewbery
449 Freddie Cross Jnr
450 J Sanders
451 Gordon Evans
452 Paul Seddon
453 Graham Nicholls
454 Anthony Goldie
455 George Ling
456 Jonathan Ling
457 Andy Millar
458 Robin Morden
459 Roy Sproule
460 Paul Naughton
461 John Latham
462 Peter Tarver
463 Graham Law
464 Paul Blenkinsopp
465 M R Fullwood
466 Alastair Laurie
467 Patrick Kelly
468 Frank A Aiers
469 Daniel Lloyd
470 R M Rowland
471 Stephen Parry
472 S R Pittam
473 W A Morrall
474 James A Asbridge
475 J A Furlong
476 David Kilcoyne
477 David Ronald Kilcoyne
478 J Gardiner
479 Martin Winter
480 David Winter
481 Blain Parsons
482 E C Brown
483 Mr L Thomas
484 Steven Welland
485 Dennis Hubbard
486 Ian Devoy
487 G Coleman
488 W B Prince
489 Terry Howard Paxton
490 Keith Hookham
491 Terry Allcott
492 Antony Allcott
493 Alex Field
494 John Haddon
495 John Haddon
496 John Sills
497 Dave Cure
498 Jonathan Edwards
499 Norman J Styles
500 Barrie Carvell
501 J D M Whitaker
502 Douglas Corbett
503 Anthony Perkin
504 Kevin McKeown
505 Janet Chamberlain
506 Keith B Ducker
507 Johnny Martin
508 Gogger Brown
509 T D Culshaw
510 P Marks
511 Paul H Bannister
512 M E Holder
513 Jim Walker
514 Edward Brown
515 Stephen Coton
516 Kishore Carpenter
517 Wayne Ratcliffe
518 Stephen Crowe
519 Bernard Wilson
520 Steve Carroll
521 Derek Wheatcroft
522 Mike Purkiss
523 Clive A Mosley
524 S B Lynch
525 Declan Ryan Harte
526 David Casson
527 Alex Johnston
528 T A Stradling
529 Terry Barnett
530 Margaret Barnett
531 Angus W Rodger
532 Eric N Hayton
533 John van den Elsen
534 Derek Hyde
535 Ingemar Stromberg
536 G D Painter
537 A Young
538 Souris Lamplighters FC PEI
539 Colin Cameron
540 David Lumb
541 Martin Simons
542 Q C M Olsthoorn
543 M Swart
544 S P Tomlin
545 Mario Sirianni
546 Christopher Minchin
547 Rudolf Iseli
548 Harry Thompson

549 Harald Lohr
550 Anders Johansson
551 Kåre M Torgrimsen
552 Andrew Tweddell
553 A H Atkins
554 R G Woolman
555 Richard Lane
556 Ake Axelsson
557 David Helliwell
558 John Knibbs
559 A P J M Otten
560 Michael Camill
561 Mr Paul Moore
562 Edward Murphy
563 M R Pearce
564 Paul Vibert
565 Brian Tabner
566 Derry Good
567 D J Williams
568 J Bradfield
569 Gerardo Mamalyga
570 Michael Joyce
571 David Richer
572 Mr Simon R Moston
573 Mr Peter Green
574 James O'Gorman
575 Paul Jerome
576 Ivan Ponting
577 D Hutt
578 Rune Nyland
579 Margaret Setter
580 James Gale
581 John Reeder
582 E Kautonen
583 Diamant Yozef
584 Mike Jackman
585 Gerald Hill
586 Dave Smith
587 Stanley A Robinson
588 Roger Wash
589 Dave Long
590 Mr Richard J Kelly
591 Mr Brian M Kelly
592 Mr Stephen Clohessy
593 Mr Tomas Racocha
594 Christopher M Lambert
595 James Walton
596 David Wheeler
597 Natalie Barlow
598 Philip Barlow
599 Gilbert Monnereau
600 Juergen Hohmann
601 Ian Griffiths
602 Alan Hindley
603 David Crawford
604 Michael McConkey
605 W H Rose
606 Harry Tranter
607 Mr Neil Smith
608 Theodoros Mantzouranis
609 Jon Tyler
610 James Abelson
611 Norman Green
612 P Baxter
613 David Pease
614 Dave Green
615 Tim Wilding
616 Michael Bradshaw
617 Dave Windross
618 Surapot Saengchote
619 Eric Heesom
620 Ian Greaves
621 Gary Tomlins
622 Stan Hefford
623 Stephen Hefford
624 David John Clark
625 T W Stevenson
626 M J Melvin
627 W D Graham
628 W J Edwards
629 W J Edwards
630 W J Edwards
631 W J Edwards
632 W J Edwards
633 W J Edwards
634 W J Edwards
635 W J Edwards
636 Stuart Fox
637 Roy Gardner
638 Pearl Freeman
639 Duncan Pierce
640 Andrew Anderson
641 Richard Stocken
642 J B Stevens
643 John T Diston
644 Michael Baldwin
645 J G McEwan
646 Ian Harraden
647 Frank Grande
648 John Irvine
649 R H Bubb
650 Christopher E C Hooker (Canada)
651 Robert Thomson
652 Roger Hudson
653 S Simpson
654 Joanne Louise Ward